Land of Sunshine, State of Dreams

The Florida History and Culture Series
USF Libraries' Florida Studies Center

UNIVERSITY OF
SOUTH FLORIDA

UNIVERSITY PRESS OF FLORIDA · STATE UNIVERSITY SYSTEM

Florida A&M University, Tallahassee
Florida Atlantic University, Boca Raton
Florida Gulf Coast University, Ft. Myers
Florida International University, Miami
Florida State University, Tallahassee
University of Central Florida, Orlando
University of Florida, Gainesville
University of North Florida, Jacksonville
University of South Florida, Tampa
University of West Florida, Pensacola

Gary R. Mormino

Foreword by Raymond Arsenault

LAND OF SUNSHINE,

University Press of Florida
GAINESVILLE
TALLAHASSEE
TAMPA
BOCA RATON
PENSACOLA
ORLANDO
MIAMI
JACKSONVILLE
FT. MYERS

STATE OF DREAMS

A Social History of Modern Florida

UNIVERSITY OF
SOUTH FLORIDA

Published in cooperation with USF Libraries' Florida Studies Center

Copyright 2005 by Gary R. Mormino
Printed in the United States of America on acid-free paper
All rights reserved

10 09 08 07 06 05   6 5 4 3 2 1

A record of cataloging-in-publication data is available from the Library of Congress.

ISBN 0-8130-2818-3

The University Press of Florida is the scholarly publishing agency for the State
University System of Florida, comprising Florida A&M University, Florida Atlantic
University, Florida Gulf Coast University, Florida International University, Florida
State University, University of Central Florida, University of Florida, University
of North Florida, University of South Florida, and University of West Florida

University Press of Florida
15 Northwest 15th Street
Gainesville, FL 32611-2079
http://www.upf.com

For Lynne,
First love, best love

Contents

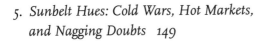

Foreword

Land of Sunshine, State of Dreams: A Social History of Modern Florida is the latest volume of a series devoted to the study of Florida history and culture. During the past half century, the burgeoning population and increased national and international visibility of Florida have sparked a great deal of popular interest in the state's past, present, and future. As the favorite destination of countless tourists and as the new home for millions of retirees and other migrants, modern Florida has become a demographic, political, and cultural bellwether. Unfortunately, the quantity and quality of the literature on Florida's distinctive heritage and character have not kept pace with the Sunshine State's enhanced status. In an effort to remedy this situation—to provide an accessible and attractive format for the publication of Florida-related books—the University Press of Florida has established the Florida History and Culture series.

The University Press of Florida is committed to the creation of an eclectic but carefully crafted set of books that will provide the field of Florida studies with a new focus and that will encourage Florida researchers and writers to consider the broader implications and context of their work. The series includes standard academic monographs, works of synthesis, memoirs, and anthologies. And, while the series features books of historical interest, authors researching Florida's environment, politics, literature, and popular or material culture are encouraged to submit their manuscripts as well. Each book offers a distinct personality and voice, but the ultimate goal of the series is to foster a broad sense of community and collaboration among Florida scholars.

The long-awaited publication of *Land of Sunshine, State of Dreams* is a major milestone in the historiography of modern Florida. Destined to be a classic, this insightful and illuminating book represents the culmination of more than twenty years of research and inquiry. In an introduction, nine thematic chapters, and an epilogue, Gary Mormino ranges across the entire spectrum of modern Florida's social and cultural history, from real estate booms and tourist empires to technological overlays and demographic revolutions. Along the way, he recaptures the feel and texture of a regional society experiencing the stresses and dislocations of unprecedented change. The story of Florida's evolution from Dixie to "dreamland"—from a state of fewer than 3 million inhabitants in 1950 to a superstate of nearly 16 million in 2000—is a unique and compelling historical saga. Indeed, as Mormino demonstrates, it is a complex tale of enterprise and folly, of growth and adaptation, of historical agency and unintended consequences.

Written with verve and more than a touch of whimsy, *Land of Sunshine, State of Dreams* is as entertaining as it is instructive. Time and again, the author comes up with an apt phrase or a telling anecdote, taking us on a historical joyride that no theme park can match. This is social history at its best, populated by flesh-and-blood human beings and punctuated by analysis that recognizes the interplay between text and context, history and memory, and time and space. Like the society that it seeks to explain, this remarkable book presents a range of experience and meaning that defies easy categorization or casual understanding. Read it in the shade or sunshine, but read it carefully—with an appreciation for what the historian's craft can render.

Raymond Arsenault,
University of South Florida, St. Petersburg,
Series Co-editor

Acknowledgments

"Give me a condor's quill! Give me Vesuvius' crater for an ink-well! Friends, hold my arms!" commands Ishmael as he contemplates the leviathan in *Moby Dick*. This historian, embarking upon a journey across the bayous and interstate highways of Florida, took heed of the advice of Herman Melville's Ishmael: "To produce a mighty book, you must choose a mighty theme."

"Wish you were here."
Florida postcard

Like Ahab, I, too, have been taken captive by my subject. This book has been part of my life for many years. To appreciate the canvas of Florida, I have tried my best to grasp it: searching for herons in Rookery Bay, crawling through Wakulla County in search of abandoned cemeteries, and walking through the alleys of Little Havana and Ybor City. I have also researched and written about Florida in Chicago's Newberry Library, California's Huntington Library, New York's FDR Library, and the Rockefeller Center's Bellagio Center in Italy.

To write a big book, Ishmael might have added, it helps to have good friends. Thankfully, family, friends, and colleagues helped soften the harsh edges of research and writing. John Belohlavek, over more café lattes than I dare admit, has listened, counseled, and, most important, led the good and honorable life. His heart attack reminded everyone of the preciousness of life and how important his life was to his friends.

Ray Arsenault, more than anybody I know, epitomizes the university professor and the ideals of the university. I look forward to sharing offices and experiences with him at the stately Snell House. A new generation of students will benefit from this collaboration. With grace, gentility, and wit, Kathleen Arsenault has read and improved this manuscript. Jim Schnur, Chris Meindl, Dave Carr, Darryl Paulson, and Mark Walters have also helped immensely. The newly created Florida Studies Program at the University of South Florida, St. Petersburg, offers a wonderful opportunity to enrich old friendships and create new relationships. Greta Scheid-Wells, Ralph Wilcox, Bill Heller, Karen White, and Mark Durand have helped make this career shift possible and exciting.

Other colleagues at the University of South Florida have supported this study. Ward Stavig's rare combination of temperament and intellect always improved my disposition and occasionally elevated my writing. For a quarter century, I have admired Georg Kleine's uncompromising professionalism; only in the last few years have I realized what a perceptive critic and passionate Floridian he is.

Much of my research has centered around the Special Collections at the Library of the University of South Florida. Thank you Paul Camp, Gayle Penner, and Pat Tuttle. I know the Florida Studies Center's Andy Huse, Yael Greenberg, and Mark Greenberg understand my deep love for this book. They cajoled and nursed me in a scary transition from my comfortable world of yellow legal pads to e-mail and computers. Andy was never too busy to help with an arcane request.

For more than a decade, Carole Rennick has been my indispensable link between the murky and often indecipherable world of my first (and tenth!) drafts and the alchemy of word processing. She has patiently and cheerfully managed to turn ink scratchings into readable prose. Marianne Bell heroically assisted in the last drafts of this manuscript. Bless you! In the Department of History, Gail Smith, Sharon Johnson-Hamilton, and Sylvia Wood have guided me through the labyrinths of the university bureaucracy and patiently—and sometimes with furrowed brows—typed note cards and letters of recommendations and processed endless paperwork. You were very kind.

In 1997, the Frank E. Duckwall Foundation expressed interest and showed faith in my passion for Florida history. Frank "Sandy" Rief has played an instrumental and inspirational role in the Duckwall Foundation and making Tampa Bay a more livable and interesting place. The Duckwall professorship in Florida history has permitted me to focus on studying and writing, preaching and teaching about the state.

More than three decades ago, Roger Lotchin began to guide my academic career as a graduate student at the University of North Carolina at Chapel Hill. In stellar roles as Millikin alumnus and UNC adviser, critic, correspondent, and friend, he has fully and enthusiastically supported my efforts. I would not be writing these words without his timely counsel and help.

The UNC connection enriched my career and life in other ways. There I befriended David Colburn and George Pozzetta. Character is destiny. In fateful turns, Dave and George found their calling at the University of Florida, where they helped pave my path to the Sunshine State. More important, they became friends and role models. The loss of George Pozzetta in 1994 robbed the profession of a great historian and took away a treasured *paesano*, colleague, and collaborator.

Colleagues around the state have generously helped shape this study. Paul George, a pillar of Miami history, has remained a trusted friend. Breaking Cuban bread in Little Havana will always be associated with don Pablo. Archivists Rebecca Smith and Dawn Hugh at the Historical Association of Southern Florida have for many years helped me find documents. Across the plaza, Sam Bolderick pointed me toward some archival gems at the Miami-Dade Public Library. The Historical Society of Palm Beach County's Debi Murray rescued me many times. Bob Beatty and Tana Porter of the Orange County Regional History Center kindly answered many inquiries. Gordon Patterson's keen intellect and wit often stirred my curiosity. He helped me refine the idea of the Big Bang as a metaphor for modern Florida. Tallahassee's Joe Knetsch has saved me from many embarrassing errors. His command of Florida sources is incomparable. Pam Gibson has helped me immensely in understanding Bradenton and Manatee County. James Crooks has kindly read several chapters and provided information about his beloved Jacksonville. Stuart McIver, a gentleman scholar and Tarheel, has always responded with generosity. From my first days in Tampa, Glenn Westfall has shared his files and life. Bob Kerstein kindly read chapters and offered encouragement and advice. Peggy Wilson helped me understand Florida's modern labor movement, while Patsy West answered questions about Seminoles. Ray Mohl's pioneering work on the Sunbelt provided a model of scholarship. Spencer Downing and Harvey Oyer III graciously critiqued the study.

Colleagues at the University of Florida have supported this project for several decades. Michael Gannon, a towering figure in Florida history, richly deserves his reputation as the "dean of Florida studies." He is the noblest Gator of them all. Bob Zieger, a scholar's scholar, is a good friend and a brilliant critic. Julian Peasants is the last of the southern gentlemen, a trusted confidante, a fellow Tarheel, and heir to Sam Proctor's legacy. Jack Davis, a multitalented scholar, has shared his thoughts and his critical eye, helping improve this manuscript. The university's P. K. Yonge Library is peerless.

Leland Hawes has shown faith in my career and provided great companionship over many lunches. Over countless bowls of seafood gumbo, he has listened carefully to the vicissitudes of career and writing, but always the conversation returns to Tampa history. We appreciate the legacy left by Tampa historians D. B. McKay, Tony Pizzo, and Hampton Dunn.

Meredith Morris-Babb and Ken Scott at the University Press of Florida have steadfastly supported the study of Florida and this book project for many years. I hope the many detours and drafts were worth the wait. Susan Brady and Susan Albury ably edited this manuscript. I deeply appreciate the friendship of Dr. Ferdie Pacheco.

The Florida Humanities Council (FHC) richly deserves its reputation as the state's most respected and beloved nonprofit institution. Janine Farver, Susan Lockwood, Laurie Berlin, Ann Schoenacher, Patricia Putnam, and Rene Reno —divas all!—have helped make the FHC the most meaningful cultural organization in the state. They always provided good cheer and contagious enthusiasm. *Forum* magazine allowed me to reach a larger audience and float several important ideas. I also appreciate the generosity of USF's Publication Council.

A generation of students has made me a better teacher and has made me proud of their professional accomplishments. Many, such as Chris Warren, Jack Davis, Rodney Kite-Powell, Evan Bennett, Rick Brunson, and Lee Irby, helped frame this study. I thank Tom Ankersen, David Shedden, Levi Gardner, Joe Mannard, Robert Taylor, Gary Garrett, Heather McClenahan, Stephen Andrews, Ellen Babb, Ruthmary Baur, Ana Varela-Lago, Sheila Cohen, Scott Rohrer, Gary Henkel, Gordon Mantler, Pam Iorio and many, many others. I should also offer thanks to the students and faculty of Dowdell School in Tampa, where I spent time as an NEH scholar. A special thanks to the Florida Studies Program inaugural class of 2003: Monica Rowland, Lucy Jones, Meeghan Kane, Suzanne St. John, Stephen Davis-Thompson, Sheila Stewart, Stephanie Cain, Nevin Sitler, Albert Vogt, Edward Woodward, and Merle Allshouse. They represent the future of Florida history.

I owe a huge debt to the many groups who invited me to discuss my research. Your questions, comments, and kindness shown toward me made me a better person and *Land of Sunshine, State of Dreams* a better book.

My family nurtured and inspired me to write a special book about an extraordinary place. When I began taking notes for this project, Amy and Rebecca were junior high students. They are now young women, accomplished and living far away. I am proud to be their father. I am proud to be Ross Anthony Mormino's son. As a Navy Seabee, refinery worker, and father of six children, he has lived quite a life.

My wife, Lynne, has accompanied and sustained me during the last thirty-five years. We first met at Millikin University—I was still a teenager!—and she has been at my side (and generally out front) ever since. She, too, waded through the Fakahatchee Strand in search of ghost orchids; she, too, encouraged me to write more than a monograph. She read every line; she shared her dreams and her love. The dedication of this book seems so right but also inadequate: First love, best love.

Introduction

THE nineteenth-century intellectual Stendhal described the modern novel as a mirror passing along the roadway, suggesting that the writer's vision depends upon the ability to aim the reflecting glass. In *Land of Sunshine, State of Dreams*, I have aimed the mirror toward Florida's people and places. More precisely, I have chosen to orient this study *away* from Tallahassee and the Capitol and *toward* Little Havana and the Big Scrub, Paradise Key and the Devil's Millhopper. This study places Floridians, the land, and the vast forces swirling around them at its center. In this book, senior citizens, construction workers, fruit hogs, orange groves, shopping malls, amusement parks, and interstate highways receive far more attention than governors or politics. Until the late 1960s, the Florida legislature met every other year for sixty days—wags suggested legislators should have gathered every sixty years for two days—but ordinary Floridians struggled every day to comprehend the powerful forces—immigration, migration, leisure, technology, growth, civil rights, environmental and economic change—whiplashing Florida.

To department store clerks and cattle ranchers, land salesmen and orchid thieves, Tallahassee and Washington were distant places, largely indifferent to their lives, loves, and travails. What changed the Sunshine State in profound and subtle ways was not legislation, but expressways and freezes; not bills and speeches, but revolutions in time and space; not senate chap-

The state with the prettiest name, the state that floats in brackish water . . . palm trees clatter like the bills of pelicans . . . the mosquitoes go hunting to the tune of their ferocious obbligatos.

"Florida," by Elizabeth Bishop (1946)

lains, but land booms. Historians searching for clues as to what changed Florida would be better served spending time atop the Clermont Citrus Tower or the Lake Okeechobee Levee. *Land of Sunshine, State of Dreams* is a social history of Florida, not a political history; it is organized around social, cultural, and economic themes, not gubernatorial eras. To be fair, Governors LeRoy Collins, Reubin Askew, Bob Graham, and Lawton Chiles were good men who fought for a better Florida. And they made a difference. But to understand modern Florida, one must appreciate the contributions of Kemmons Wilson, Brownie Wise, Sydney Adler, Mary McLeod Bethune, James McLamore, "Doc" Phillips, Polita Grau, Caridad Márquez, Ben Hill Griffin, C. D. Atkins, Marjory Stoneman Douglas, Marjorie Kinnan Rawlings, Marjorie Harris Carr, Willis Carrier, James Billie, the Mackle brothers, Leonard Rosen, John S. Knight, H. Irwin Levy, "Totch" Brown, Nathaniel Reed, Jim Walter, Eula Mae Johnson, Newton Perry, Robert Davis, and Jimmy Buffett.

The decades following 1940 changed Florida more than the previous four centuries, altering boundaries, reconfiguring landscapes, and casting new relationships. The march to and across Florida was irresistible and irrepressible, as orange groves became gated communities, small towns were transformed into cities, and big cities sprawled into metropolises and boomburbs. The reasons are ancient and modern. Dreams of better lives in exotic climes exercised a powerful hold on Americans and the world. The Florida dream reemerged more resonant and resounding than ever.

Florida's Big Bang, 1950–2000, is a story of astonishing growth, a state swelling from 2.7 to 15.9 million inhabitants. Wordsmiths coined new terms to understand paradigm shifts and the firestorm of change: jet age, space age, climate control, growth management, retirement community, theme park, the I-4 corridor, impact fee, edge city, boomburb, time-share condominium, suburban sprawl, shopping mall, snowbird, white flight, Sunbelt, Interstate, and Internet.

From its founding as an imperial outpost to its modern identity as a tourist empire, Florida has evoked contrasting and compelling images of the sacred and profane: a Fountain of Youth and a Garden of Earthly Delights, a miasmic hellhole and scuzzy wasteland. Florida's dreamscape stirred the imagination of Walt Disney and Dick Pope, Morris Lapidus and Elizabeth Bishop, Carl Hiaasen and John D. MacDonald. A powerful symbol of renewal and regeneration, Florida's dreamscape constantly shifts. Where once the land and climate were sufficiently inspiring to bewitch artists and travelers, now gated condominiums, age-restricted communities, and theme parks constitute that firmament.[1]

Florida remains a state of enchanted reality and shattered dreams, of second chances and the trifecta at Gulfstream. It was here that Elias Disney lost his orange grove, voted for Socialist Eugene Debs, and uprooted his family to the Midwest. His son Walt reclaimed the family dream, transforming Central Florida groves and ranches into a capitalist paradise. Lake County, the home of Elias and Flora Disney, has paid a heavy price for their son's success.

Florida imported dreamers and exported oranges. Here, too, the spiritual and mundane intersected. To an America unaccustomed to exotic fruit, the orange served as a signature template to Mediterranean dreams. A 5-acre orange grove combined Jeffersonian republicanism with democratic romanticism. On countless pine and cedar crates, under artwork depicting pink flamingoes and rolling groves, the place-names Frostproof, Indian River, and Clermont touched a shivering public. Realities shattered the myth of yeoman farmers. Increasing economic concentration transferred power from farmers to corporations. Behind the veneer of oranges, winter vegetables, and sugar existed the reality of a degraded and ill-treated labor force.

Florida held no monopoly on American dreamstates, but unlike in sunny rivals Hawaii and California, fantasies could be validated in Florida on the cheap. The developers of Port St. Lucie, Spring Hill, and Lehigh Acres marketed Florida dreams not to the fabulously rich, but to veterans, retirees, and middling folk. The strategy worked. Consider that every single day since 1950, about a thousand new persons have become new Florida residents. Of course, several hundred have also fled the state, repulsed or disillusioned by what they found.

Here the line between realities and illusions is easily blurred. A state of lottery sweepstakes and tropical resorts, Florida has attracted more than its timeshare of bunko artists who sold land by the gallon and dreams for ten dollars down, ten dollars a month. In Florida, quipped William Jennings Bryan, a lie told at breakfast could become the truth by lunch. A state of enchanted Februarys and cursed Septembers, Florida brokered the fantasies of Americans who lived vicariously through the exploits of the Brooklyn Dodgers, Philadelphia Athletics, and St. Louis Cardinals. Each spring, the sandy diamonds of St. Petersburg, Fort Myers, and West Palm Beach beckoned rookies and veterans. In crackerjack parks and wooden grandstands, fans shared a collective past and waited for a better future. Spring training and spring football encouraged fantasies; major league baseball and college football packaged those dreams into associations.

Sun cities and fresh starts coincide with old age and second chances in the Sunshine State. Old age, as much as spring break, defined modern Florida. Florida's vaunted climate, embellished by public relations, provided a siren's song to the elderly. One carload at a time, millions of retired postal clerks and insurance salesmen began new lives in places that did not even exist when they were young: Port Charlotte, Cape Coral, and Palm Beach Gardens. Few contemporaries realized the portents. Never in human history would so many people live so long, so well, in places so far from where they were born. The figures numbed even the boldest soothsayer. In 1900, about one in forty Floridians had celebrated a sixty-fifth birthday; by the end of the century, the proportion had grown to one in five. Floridians aged seventy and older at the end of the century outnumbered the total inhabitants of the Sunshine State on the eve of World War II. As late as 1950, Floridians' median age (28.8) was still younger than the rest of America. By 2000, Florida's median age (39.3) was four years older than that of the average American. Americans were in the process of reinventing retirement and the meaning of old age.[2]

Senior citizens became part of one of the greatest mass movements in American history. Every retiree, tourist, and air-conditioner mechanic needed housing, roads, food, and amenities. Business satisfied needs and created new wants. Not merely a consequence of a population expanding eightfold in sixty years, growth became theme, mantra, and creed.

Growth and development have exacted a grievous toll upon Florida's wildlife and natural habitat. Reconciling that growth with environmental responsibility poses a daunting challenge to Floridians, who have witnessed the straightening of rivers; the decline of the manatee population; the near-extinction of the Florida panther, crocodile, and Key deer; and the extinction of the dusky sparrow. The demise of the Everglades marks only the most glaring of Florida'a environmental tragedies.

The story is told of how medieval courtiers, wishing to flatter King Canute, assured the monarch that he alone held the power to command the waters to retreat. King Canute, unlike modern developers, realized that even the most powerful man in Denmark could not impose his will upon nature. Floridians want to "improve" Florida. In its natural state, Florida may appear poorly designed: meandering rivers, shifting coastlines, and shore-hugging mangroves.

Malleable, accessible, and seemingly inexhaustible, the Florida landscape can become anything that humans want it to be. Hot was made cool, and wet became dry. What private enterprise would not finance or could not fathom, the federal government audaciously attempted. Monuments of futility, the "new" Kissimmee River and the old cross-state barge canal were born of Florida fantasies and Washington realities.

The landscape yielded to ax, machete, plow, steam shovel, dragline, and construction crane. Wildly confident of their capacity to tame the land, farmers, developers, and engineers left their imprint upon the state. Like an avenging angel, however, nature has exacted a cruel price for human hubris. Hurricanes Donna, Andrew, and Charley, a series of devastating freezes, and a combination of wildfires and droughts have cost Floridians billions while also exposing human flaws and arrogance. Such natural calamities, however, have been magnified by the insistence on developing barrier islands, the compulsion to build on beaches and flood-prone coastal areas, and the practice of suppressing wildfire. Beach "renourishment" programs and generous flood-insurance policies subsidized at taxpayer expense for some of Florida's wealthiest citizens pose further challenges to the fragile ecosystems.

Twentieth-century Florida witnessed a firestorm of change, much of it technologically driven. The automobile helped to conquer the "tyranny of distance" and "democratize" tourism. Technology and greed made possible the straightening of the Kissimmee River, the drainage of the Everglades, and the very existence of Deltona and Golden Gate Estates. Liberal application of the pesticide DDT and the introduction of air conditioning allowed Floridians to domesticate nature. Ironically, the rage against nature has produced climate-controlled malls, housing developments, and golf courses with dissociated names like Eagle Lake, Sawgrass Mills, and The Groves.

Civic, mechanical, and social engineers perfected an imperfect Florida. Air conditioning lowered the temperature, DDT banished the mosquito, and the bulldozer eliminated the mangrove. Floridians, more than most Americans, are hooked on technology. In a state where distances isolated people socially and physically, the automobile and truck, the airport and interstate highway provided critical transportation links. In the case of instant cities, the shopping mall made people forget the missing downtown link. In a society in flux, the mobile home and portable classroom seem at home in Florida.

Reinventing Florida is a cottage industry. Shifting images and associations cast and recast Florida as a haven for the elderly, the fruit and winter vegetable basket for North America, a citadel and arsenal, and the crossroads for the Americas. No identity, however, conveys Florida's meaning to Americans and citizens of the world more than its association as a vacation paradise.

Florida's identity as a tourist center was well established by 1950. The names Cypress Gardens, Weeki Wachee, and Miami Beach conjured up magical allusions and illusions. But there was nothing inevitable about marshland in Winter Haven, a natural spring on the Gulf coast, and a barrier island on Biscayne Bay becoming vacation destinations. Tourism is not destiny. Beach resorts and alligator farms, no less than paper mills and power plants, involve human decisions. Investors in Winter Haven might just as easily have drained Lake Eloise and planted sweet corn, as happened at Lake Apopka and Zellwood. Instead, Dick Pope converted wetlands and hammocks into Cypress Gardens.

The process of reinventing Florida was complex. No single individual, no solitary corporation possessed a blueprint to sell Florida as a vacationland. Travel writers, chambers of commerce, advertising agencies, gasoline stations, poets, grove owners, businesses, and state and local governments all promoted Florida's image. The net effect was irresistible.

Between 1950 and 2000, millions of tourists visited the Sunshine State. Such a stunning accomplishment was made possible because of the convergence of myriad cultural, political, and economic developments. America's postwar affluence lifted millions of families into the middle classes and generated vast new sums of disposable income. The two-week paid vacation and the Ford station wagon symbolized the American way of life. Air conditioning allowed Floridians to have its sunshine and cool it, too, transforming a seasonal business into a 365-day-a-year enterprise. Millions of Floridians (and the state's tax structure) depend upon tourism.

Every tourist knows the way to Florida: when you hit the East coast, turn south. Imagine a map of the continental United States without the Florida peninsula. The mainland assumes the shape of a rough-edged box. But consider again a map of the Caribbean basin and the southeastern United States. It becomes incomplete without the flying foot of peninsular Florida. Just where *does* Florida belong?

On the eve of the Big Bang, Florida's place seemed well understood. "Politically and socially, Florida has its own North and South," observed the authors of the WPA guide to Florida (1939), cautioning, "its northern area is strictly southern and its southern area definitely northern." Such distinctions may have been clear in places like St. Petersburg and Sarasota, Palm Beach and Miami Beach, but vast sections of South Florida—imprecisely defined as what lies south of an imaginary line drawn from Cedar Key through Gainesville to Daytona Beach, or the later I-4 corridor, or the Suwannee River—conform to no such neat categories. Environmentally, both Panhandle and peninsula are southern but distinctively Floridian. Sociologist John Shelton Reed deftly divined: "Florida is not unique in the United States. It's just unique in the South."[3]

If the South were defined solely by race relations, Florida in 1950 would not have appeared very different from Georgia or Tennessee. The state's lynching rate between 1890 and 1930 was the highest in the South. Other watermarks of the New South—Jim Crow customs, strict adherence to segregation, a poll tax, and a white primary—had been staunchly defended or were still present. In 1950, not a single Florida school was integrated; a decade later, the statement still held true, except for a single school in Dade County. Even Florida's vaunted beaches were shaped by the racial mores of the time. Blacks called a handful of beaches their own; the rest were maintained strictly and exclusively for whites.

What is most striking about Florida is how quickly things changed. So much of Florida and southern culture—NASCAR, football, pop music, wrestling, reverence for the military, foodstuffs, fashion, and politics—has transcended the state and region to become mainstream.[4]

Regional change was only one of the most recognized—and most studied—aspects of the newly emerging Florida. Demography is destiny. Daily, scores—even hundreds—of retirees and transplants from New York and Ohio settled in Florida. Consequences came quickly: Since the 1960s, Florida has clearly and distinctly separated from its southern neighbors. Florida was more climate controlled, technologically inclined, and also older, more ethnic, more religiously and racially diverse, wealthier, whiter, and less agrarian than the rest of the South.

Florida represents both the southernmost outcropping of North America and the northernmost edge of the Caribbean. Culturally and geographically, Miami and Key West share closer ties with Havana and Nassau than with Tallahassee and Pensacola. The peninsula has served as a bridge since Hernando de Soto, setting out from Cuba in 1539, declared Spanish dominion over *La Florida*. The Florida-Caribbean connection has ebbed and flowed, sending trade goods and travelers in times of peace, warriors and refugees in times of turmoil. As historian Michael Gannon reminds us, not until 2055 will an American flag have flown over Florida as long as did the Spanish banner.[5]

Florida's Caribbean connection did not end when Spain withdrew in 1821 nor begin anew in 1959. Fidel Castro frequently lectured Cubans and hectored Americans that "the republic of Cuba is the daughter of the cigarmakers of Florida."[6] A reading of Florida's past suggests that the present-day embargo of Cuba represents a historical aberration. Florida's ever-growing social and economic connections to the Caribbean and the Americas have resulted in a multicultural, fabulously diverse state.

Streams of Hispanic immigrants have dramatically altered the demographic complexion of Florida. Cubans dominated the immigration debate, flooding South Florida in unprecedented numbers. Beginning in the 1970s, large numbers of non-Cuban Hispanics and Caribbeans began to make their homes in Florida. During the decades of the 1980s and 1990s, Florida's Hispanic population soared, increasing 83 percent and 63 percent respectively. The 2000 census confirmed the stunning changes wrought by four decades of intense immigration. Such dynamics changed Osceola and Hardee counties, now ethnic hothouses for Puerto Ricans and Mexicans.

From colonial St. Augustine to modern Jacksonville to postmodern Miami, Florida's cities have displayed a remarkable vitality, creating new visions of urban life on the edge. Since World War II, the process of urbanization and suburbanization has relentlessly covered the state. Cities in Florida have attracted an amazing diversity of migrants. When anthropologist Franz Boas asked Zora Neale Hurston where she wanted to study, she looked homeward. "Florida is a place that draws people," she explained simply.[7]

Urbanization in Florida also distinguished the Sunshine State from the Deep South. At a time (1950) when one out of two southerners resided in a city, two of three Floridians did so. Florida lacks an Atlanta or New Orleans, cities that dominate their respective states. Jacksonville, Pensacola, and Tampa exercise important regional influence, but only Miami and Orlando—one because of immigrants and economics, the other due to tourism and consumption—transcend Florida and the South as global cities. No other Florida cities have received the acclaim or the criticism accorded Miami and Orlando.

Shaped by the automobile and Main Street and reshaped by the interstate highway and suburbs, downtown Florida has experienced the trajectory of boom, decline, and renaissance. Midcentury photographs of Jacksonville, Tallahassee, Tampa, Sarasota, and Fort Lauderdale skylines are unrecognizable a half century later. Urban critics decry the blandness and conformity of modern urban architecture: the glass-paneled towers, parking garages, and chain stores. In a "wish you were here" state, postcards freeze time and place. "Welcome to Orlando," gushed one such card, the greeting bracketed by a gleaming downtown. Except the skyline wasn't Orlando's! When the *Orlando Sentinel* invited readers to identify the elusive place, the responses confirmed critics' worst suspicions—there is no here, here. Halifax, Nova Scotia, it seems, looks a lot like Orlando. The City Beautiful had become the City Indistinguishable.[8]

Modern Florida is simply irresistible to writers and cultural critics. "In the 60's and 70's if you were listening to the national tuning fork, there was a sense that California was the state that was defining America," writes Michael Paterniti. "Right now the tuning fork points to Florida." From retirement in St. Petersburg to alien exotics in the Everglades, from the Elián González controversy in Miami to ballot-chasing lawyers, Florida is a trendsetter. Cultural styles and bizarre sightings that once rolled to or began on the West Coast now germinate in Florida. Modern Florida incorporates Margaritaville and Future Shock.[9]

Florida's excesses and surreal synchronicities have inspired a distinctive reporting and literary genre. What do late-twentieth-century literature and journalism suggest about the nature of Florida? Typically, modern novelists depict Florida as a lost utopia—a dystopian, overdeveloped land overrun by corporate theme parks, rapacious developers, and crazed drug lords.

The history of modern Florida compresses massive social change in an astonishingly brief span of time. In 1950, Florida's 2.7 million inhabitants were predominantly white, Protestant, and southern-born. Florida's scant number of immigrants were more likely to come from Great Britain and Canada than Honduras and Mexico. The portrait of Florida emerging from the 2000 census revealed a state more ethnically, racially, and religiously diverse than the South and the nation. Florida has joined Texas and California as melting-pot states of the Sunbelt. For at least a generation, Florida has grappled with the complexities of multiculturalism, immigration, aging, and development—salient issues facing all Americans in the next century. The last decades of the century encompassed motion, migration, and mobility—a movement of capital, technology, culture, and, most of all, people. The Florida of today is the America of tomorrow. If so, speculates Carl Hiaasen, the future will be "almost Toffleresque in its chaos." To paraphrase John Locke, "In the end, all the world will be Florida."[10]

Astrophysicist Fred Hoyle coined the expression *Big Bang* in 1948, ironically, to deride theorists who believed that the universe began in a cosmic, explosive instant and evolved from that point. Today the debate by leading thinkers like Stephen Hawking involves not the beginning but the *mass* of the universe, and questions of its limits. Will the universe expand forever, implode, or remain constant? The answer depends upon how one gauges the matter density of the universe. So it is with modern Florida, a state threatened not so much by gravity—the force drawing objects to the center of the earth—as by gravitas, the weight of character. Here, too, the debate rages.[11]

Can Florida continue to add unlimited numbers of new residents and tourists, condominiums and superhighways? How can Florida instill and inspire magic and passion while maintaining a sense of moderation and balance? Or will Florida collapse from the demands upon the land and infrastructure? Perhaps the issue for Floridians parallels the astrophysicists' debate. How *should* the proper balance, ratio, and limitations of growth and environment, population and land, freedom and community be defined in the Sunshine State?

Look Away Dixieland

The Contours of Sunbelt Florida

EVERAL generations of Americans helped fulfill the modern Florida dream. Scarred and shaped by the Great War and the Good War, the Roaring Twenties and the Great Depression, these citizens brought to Florida a deeply held system of values enshrining freedom, individualism, and the pursuit of happiness. While this doctrine was less than egalitarian, it formed the cornerstone for history's greatest experiment in economic democracy. Between the 1920s and the 1950s, millions of Americans—many with memories of czarist pogroms, 40-acre farms, and speeded-up assembly lines—were lifted from the working classes to the middle classes. For these Americans, Florida held the promise of dignified endings and new beginnings. If Americans were identified by what they thought, they were also defined by what they bought. A 1950 dream list included a house, a car, and a vacation. The Sunshine State thus intersected with the American dream.

For a country constantly on the move, a nation symbolized by the Conestoga wagon, Model T, and moving van, Florida holds a special place for the modern migrant and immigrant. "The great travel story of our time," writes David Rieff, "is called migration."[1] The history of modern Florida can be reduced to millions of individual and collective migrations: young Cubans; old Jews; Italians from the Upper East Side; autoworkers fleeing Detroit, Toledo, and Akron; Rustbelt re-

"You've come back different. You've taken a punishment. You ain't a yearling no longer."

Penny Baxter to Jody, in Marjorie Kinnan Rawlings, *The Yearling*

tirees; Canadians trekking south; Colombians headed north; Jamaican cane cutters; African Americans who had left the New South only to return to the Sunbelt; businessmen bringing Holiday Inns and McDonalds to new markets; millionaire athletes and bankruptcy lawyers, risk takers and fortune makers.

Demographically, Florida's transformation was nothing short of revolutionary. Florida, however, was not alone. Between 1950 and 2000, Florida participated in one of the great population shifts in history. Millions of workers, retirees, and families in the North and Midwest migrated to the South and West. Millions of emigrants from the Caribbean, the Americas, and Asia also flocked to California, Texas, Florida, and surrounding states. The Sunbelt was born of this demographic explosion.

Coined in 1969 by the political partisan Kevin Phillips, the term *Sunbelt* loosely identified the expanding regions of the South, Southwest, and West into a super-region defined by its moderate climate, reliance upon air conditioning, support of the military and defense programs, dynamic economy, favorable business climate, modern transportation advantages, and drift toward conservatism and Republicanism. "The persons most drawn to the new sun culture," stated Phillips, "are the pleasure seekers, the bored, the ambitious, the space-age technicians and the retired—a super slice of the rootless, socially mobile group known as the American middle class." Columnist Kirkpatrick Sale dubbed this phenomenon the "Southern Rim."[2]

Since 1950, Florida's population has confounded demographers, exasperated planners, and exhausted interstate movers. Only Texas and California exceed Florida's absolute gains, and those states are, respectively, four and two and one-half times physically larger than Florida. In the last half century, while California and Texas had tripled in population, Florida's advance was sixfold.

The 1950s triggered Florida's Big Bang. Postwar prosperity and Social Security made the Florida dream affordable, attainable, and acceptable to millions of Americans. With Geiger-counter intensity, the state's population nearly doubled, from 2.7 million to nearly 5 million, an increase of 78.7 percent. In contrast, Pennsylvania, the Keystone State and the nation's third largest, grew by only 6.9 percent. No other state matched Florida's velocity, and only California attracted more new residents during the 1950s. Florida fever became a pandemic during the "I like Ike" years. A newspaper headline trumpeted the news, "1,000 Residents Each Week Move into Florida." During that decade, upstart Florida vaulted over Kentucky, Minnesota, Alabama, Tennessee, Virginia, Wisconsin, Georgia, Indiana, Missouri, and North Carolina. Massachusetts stood

TABLE I. State Populations (in millions), 1950–2000

State	1950	1970	1990	2000
California	10.5	19.9	30	34
Florida	2.7	6.7	13	16
Texas	7.7	11.1	17	21

Source: U.S. Census Bureau, Census 2000 <http://www.census.gov/statab/www/part6.html>.

next in line. Symbolic of the growing significance of the Sunbelt, Florida supplanted Massachusetts as the nation's ninth-most-populous state during the presidency of Bay State native John Kennedy. With a steady influx of migrants and immigrants, Florida gained 1,721,538 new residents in the 1960s, a growth clip of 35 percent. The twentieth-most-populous state in 1950, Florida edged past New Jersey in late 1972 to take its impermanent place as the nation's eighth-most-populous state, overtaking recession-wracked Michigan later in the decade. Metaphors seemed inadequate to describe the rate of change. "If one colored a map of the United States and used the brightest hues for those areas that were growing the fastest," explained the *New York Times,* "Florida would light up like the nose of a circus clown." Aptly, Florida was red-hot in the 1970s, gaining almost 3 million more residents. The *New York Times'* Jon Nordheimer chose Interstate 95 near Richmond, Virginia, as his 1976 vantage point. "All day and through the lonely night," he wrote, "the moving vans push southward, 14-wheeled boxcars of the highway changing the demographic face of America." The *Wall Street Journal* utilized the hurricane metaphor to describe Florida's sudden population explosion, noting the "gale-force growth" during the 1980s that made the state home to nine of the nation's fastest-growing cities. During the dizzying decade and a half following 1980, Florida registered a net population increase of almost 4 million persons, outpacing California and Texas. At some moment during 1985, a transplanted retiree or Cuban refugee boosted Florida's population past that of Illinois, making Florida the nation's fifth-most-populous state. The least populous southern state in 1940, Florida became America's fourth-most-populous state in 1998, passing Pennsylvania and the 15 million plateau during the 1990s. The thirst for Florida neither slacked nor slackened during the 1990s, a decade that attracted almost 3 million more residents, a growth spurt equivalent to the population of Iowa. To place our pace of growth into some perspective, consider that every single day since 1950, about seven hundred new persons have become Florida residents.

Overall, immigrants and migrants found Florida irresistible, but the torrent of newcomers ebbed and flowed according to national confidence, international instability, and domestic peace. The last two decades of the twentieth century saw the number of daily newcomers jumping to over a thousand; however, four hundred residents were leaving, in large part because of the growth. In the 1990s, according to the Census Bureau, Florida was the number-one destination for interstate movers: over 1 million persons migrated here from other states. Sometime in the early twenty-first century, Florida will likely surpass New York, becoming the nation's third-most-populous state.[3]

"Everyone, it seems, is from someplace else." The phrase, quoted so often, might qualify as the state motto. Perception is reality. Florida is a transient state and a state of transience. The character and composition of Florida changed profoundly after 1950, the result of two powerful forces: migration and immigration.

In modern Florida, contended the *South Florida Sun-Sentinel*, "natives have seen so much change that they might as well be [from somewhere else]." The migration of millions of Americans perceptibly changed the pace of life and tone of Florida. In Florida, a Bronx cheer might fairly be considered to be as native as a southern drawl: Florida is the place Yankees have long come to die and work, play, and invest. By 1980, every third Floridian was a native; two-thirds were transplants. Even Alaska contained a greater percentage of natives than did Florida. In contrast, eight of ten Pennsylvanians and seven of ten Georgians were native born. Frostbelt migrants shaped and reshaped the Sunbelt, bringing their attitudes, as well as their investments, cuisine, and automobiles, with them. In Plantation and Sebring, reunions allowed ex–New Jersey residents to reconnect.[4]

In "a nation of strangers," the American propensity to uproot and move was never more evident than in the mobile decades during and after World War II. Prosperity, longevity, and leisure tempted and allowed the middle classes to spend long periods of time in Florida but also to maintain their residences back home. In 1980, the U.S. Census Bureau clumsily attempted to measure the phenomenon of seasonal migration. The *Wall Street Journal* scoffed at the bureau's imprecision, suggesting that a census taker stand on I-95 Thanksgiving weekend and count out-of-state license plates headed south. The "snowbird" had settled in. In 1980, about a half million Americans lived away from home for more than a few months a year, most of them preferring Florida. Fully one in ten snowbirds flocked from New York. Florida was "home" to almost a million temporary residents in 2003.[5]

New South to Sunbelt

In the 1950s, vestiges and symbols of the Old South lingered everywhere: schools named after Generals Kirby Smith, Robert E. Lee, and Stonewall Jackson; county courthouse squares and town cemeteries adorned with statues honoring Johnny Reb; Confederate Memorial Day observed by shrinking numbers. Florida's last Confederate veteran, William A. "Uncle Bill" Lundy, died at Crestview in 1957 at the age of 109. At the time, only one Florida school was integrated, Jim Crow laws seemed impregnable, and the state legislature was so malapportioned that the so-called Pork Choppers (rural politicians) ruled. But

FIGURE 1. To celebrate his 107th birthday, "Uncle Bill" Lundy, Florida's last surviving Confederate veteran, climbs aboard an F-100 at Eglin Air Field, 1955. William A. Lundy died in 1957. State of Florida Photographic Archives, Tallahassee.

for all of the symbols and geographic realities, Florida was fast becoming the first southern state to become by dint of population distinctively nonsouthern. Wave after successive wave of city-dwelling New Yorkers, Ohioans, Cubans, Colombians, and retirees reconfigured Florida. The result was that by 2000, surveys indicated that Floridians, more so than other southern residents, rejected the label *southerner*. Oklahoma ranked slightly above Florida in number of residents claiming southern identity.[6]

Like shifting tectonic plates, the modern movement of people has rearranged the United States in ways not seen since the Great Migration. Economically depressed and racially intolerant, the American South exported 9 million people to the urban North between 1910 and 1950. Beginning in the 1970s, the South—becoming more Sunbelt than Cotton Belt—reversed course and began attracting large numbers of Rustbelt refugees and returning African Americans. Between 1970 and 1990, as America's population grew by 21 percent, the South surged by 40 percent, while Florida soared by 76 percent.[7]

The Great Migration left its mark upon the South in abandoned sharecropper shacks and blues music. Florida, however, represented the South's great aberration. In 1910, Florida's population was less than half of Mississippi's, a third of Alabama's, and about a quarter of Georgia's. During the next four decades, Florida's population gains equaled the combined increases of Georgia, Alabama, and Mississippi. During this period, Florida's new white residents dwarfed the stream of black migrants. In 1910, Florida's whites outnumbered black residents by only 134,649; by 1950, the racial gap was 1.56 million, a margin increasing by 1970 to 4.65 million, and accelerating to 10.6 million by 2000. Pointedly, Florida's widening racial-demographic gap was *not* the result of African Americans fleeing the state; rather, burgeoning numbers of white retirees and Hispanic immigrants simply overshadowed black population gains. Southern blues music typically laments the loss of culture and neighbors headed northward on the Illinois Central or Greyhound bus. Conversely, "The Orange Blossom Special" lyricizes the coming of tourists and settlers to Florida. For years, pundits insisted that Florida served as an asylum for Georgia's poor. A reporter once asked a governor of Georgia about the consequences of so many sons and daughters of the Peach State having moved to the Sunshine State. "It will improve the IQs of both states!" he quipped. In modern Florida, the faint Georgia drawl is lost in the din of a Tower of Babel. By 1980, Florida's hold on the North was so pronounced that four of every ten Yankees living in the South called Florida home. By 2000, two of every three Jews and one of every two Italians living in the South called Florida home. More extraordinary, Florida became the first southern state where a majority of whites were born outside of the South. For good reason, historian James C. Cobb called Florida the "cornerstone of the Sunbelt South."[8]

If the Sunshine State was emblematic of the Sunbelt South, not everyone was happy with the new identity. Change came unevenly. Heavy population growth in South and Central Florida distanced those areas from slow-paced North Florida. Some North Florida counties had been in decline for more than a half century. Hamilton, Lafayette, Madison, Holmes, Jefferson, Liberty, and Washington counties all had greater populations in 1910 than in 1970. Jefferson and Gadsden—the last remaining counties with African American majorities—lost seven thousand inhabitants during the 1960s and 1970s. Coastal counties—even in Northwest Florida—registered greater population gains than did interior counties. Nor did all of South Florida embrace the Sunbelt mantle. Glades, Hardee, DeSoto, and Hendry counties largely maintained their southern heritage and rural lifestyle.[9]

A portrait of midcentury Florida would show a state in repose before an avalanche of immigrants. In 1950, Florida's ethnic diversity was impressive only when measured by the demographic bar of the Deep South. In 1950, the numbers of Florida's foreign born (122,731) dwarfed those of neighboring Alabama (13,813) and Georgia (16,730), but immigrants still comprised only 4.5 percent of the Sunshine State's population (compared to .5 percent of the Peach State). The most numerous immigrant groups were, in numerical order, Canadians, Russians (principally Jewish), Britons, and Germans. Cubans (the term *Hispanic* was not yet used in 1950) comprised only 10 percent of the state's immigrants, and less than 1 percent of the foreign born. Tampa and Key West may have held the historic claims to *cubanidad,* but already in 1950, Miami was the Cuban city of the future, even though no identifiable Cuban neighborhood or colony yet had taken hold in Miami. If immigration is historically associated with youth, Florida's midcentury immigrants were atypical. Pockets of aging Greeks in Tarpon Springs, Finns in Lake Worth, Canadians in St. Petersburg, Russian Jews in Miami Beach, and Cubans, Spaniards, and Italians in Tampa characterized 1950 Florida.[10]

A youthful rebel altered the course of history. Fidel Castro's seizure of power in 1959 unleashed revolutionary forces in Cuba, the reverberations of which convulsed the Americas and Florida. Forty years later, the consequences of the Cuban revolution can be seen and heard throughout Florida. Statistics drama-

FIGURE 2. Florida's other Great Migration. In 1940, a young family leaves Florida for promises of a better life in the North. Library of Congress, Washington, D.C.

tize the new relationship between Florida and the Americas: almost as many Hispanics resided in Florida in 2000 as there were Floridians in 1950. Fully one in six Floridians was born abroad; almost 2.5 million state residents spoke Spanish at home. The 2000 census revealed several interesting nuances and significant trends. Florida's Hispanic population (2.7 million) outnumbered the state's African Americans (2.3 million).[11]

Demographers point out that the surging numbers of new immigrants have fractured the Sunbelt into megastates (California, Texas, and Florida) with huge Hispanic and Asian populations, and that the New South–Sunbelt states (Virginia to Georgia and across to Arkansas) are attracting large numbers of blacks returning home and whites fleeing the Rustbelt. In recent decades, Florida has been less successful in luring African Americans back to the "southernmost state." During the period 1995–2000, almost 170,000 blacks moved to Florida; however, 118,000 left the state. In contrast, Georgia and North Carolina registered much greater gains among African Americans.[12]

Florida's connection to the South, long a tenuous relationship, cracked and loosened visibly after 1950. A southern culture created and sustained by one-crop agriculture, rural folkways, and small-town life seemed irrelevant and incomprehensible to Floridians living in Miami, Palm Beach, and St. Petersburg. To be sure, the South's tenacious hold on biracialism and Jim Crow practices pervaded 1950s Florida. But Florida was also the most urbanized state in the South. In 1950, almost two-thirds of Floridians lived in cities, a level considerably higher than the South's (48.6 percent). The process of urbanization quickened. By 1960, three of every four Floridians were city dwellers.[13]

Metropolitanization

The variety and vitality of urban life defined and shaped modern Florida as much as did theme parks and interstate highways. Shaped by the automobile and real estate developer more than by streetcar or industry, cities in Florida tended to be characterized by low-density development, horizontal sprawl, and small urban centers. Post-1950s growth spilled across city, county, and even state boundaries, resulting in metropolitan communities. Geographers called the phenomenon of cities and counties growing and blending together "conurbation."

In 1950, only Miami, Tampa–St. Petersburg, Jacksonville, and Orlando qualified as Florida's metropolitan areas, and ranked respectively fifth, eighth, thirteenth, and thirty-fifth in the South. Rapid growth in the 1960s created six new Standard Metropolitan Statistical Areas (SMSA): Lakeland–Winter Haven, Daytona Beach, Sarasota-Bradenton, Fort Myers, Gainesville, and Tallahassee. Florida's urban growth quickly overwhelmed that of its southern neighbors in the coming decades. By 1970, the Miami–Fort Lauderdale metro area had become the South's most populous urban center, a rank it held for three decades. Tampa Bay grew to become the South's third-largest metro area in 1970. From 1.1 million inhabitants in 1970, the Tampa Bay region (Hillsborough, Pinellas, Pasco, and Hernando counties) doubled in thirty years. The Orlando metropolitan area (Orange, Lake, Osceola, and Sumter counties) exceeded 1.5 million residents by 2000, surpassing the metro populations of New Orleans, San Antonio, and Richmond.[14]

Nationally, Florida has dominated the list of fastest-growing Metropolitan Statistical Areas (MSA). The MSA designation signified the social and economic links between urban cores and the hinterlands. During the 1970s, ten of

TABLE 2. Florida Cities, 1950 and 2000

	1950	2000
Jacksonville	204,517	735,617
Miami	249,276	362,470
Tampa	124,681	303,447
St. Petersburg	96,738	248,232
Hialeah	19,676	226,419
Orlando	52,367	185,951
Fort Lauderdale	36,328	152,397
Tallahassee	27,237	150,624
Hollywood	14,351	139,357
Pembroke Pines	—	137,427

Sources: U.S. Bureau of the Census, Census of Population: 1950, vol. 1,
Number of Inhabitants, Florida, table 7; U.S. Bureau of the Census, Census 2000 Summary File.

America's top twenty-five metro areas were located in Florida, a record topped in the 1980s with nine of the nation's twelve fastest-growing places. Florida's torrid growth continued in the 1990s. Four Florida metro areas, Naples, Ocala, Orlando, and Punta Gorda—all relatively insignificant until the 1970s—ranked among the fastest-growing areas in the United States. The metropolitanization of Florida, once confined to Miami, Jacksonville, Tampa Bay, and Orlando, has spread statewide. By the 1990s, Fort Walton Beach, Fort Myers–Cape Coral, Melbourne–Titusville–Palm Bay, Naples, Ocala, Panama City, Pensacola, Punta Gorda, and West Palm Beach–Boca Raton also qualified as metropolitan units. Indeed, only a few hundred thousand of Florida's 15 million residents reside outside a metropolitan area, so complete and pervasive has urban and suburban growth been. To appreciate these changes, consider that in 1950, the cities of Punta Gorda, Naples, and Melbourne had a _combined_ population of 7,605.[15]

Expansion and development into new locales represent a significant dimension of Florida's growth. Who could have imagined that in the 1980s and 1990s, the nation's fastest-growing cities would have names such as Pembroke Pines, Coral Springs, Cape Coral, Plantation, Palm Bay, Coconut Creek, Sunrise, Davie, Deltona, Celebration, Tamarac, Spring Hill, and Lauderhill? Most of these communities did not even exist in 1950.[16]

The Urban Landscape

The dynamism of Jacksonville, Miami, and Orlando epitomizes the vitality and reality of Sunbelt Florida. The cities (and sprawling hinterlands) represent the hopes and dreams of new generations of Floridians. In 1950, Jacksonville struck visitors as a city of contrasts: an imposing skyline and solid business community surrounded by flophouses, bars, and deteriorating buildings; prosperous neighborhoods graced with elegant mansions and terraced lawns in the shadows of slums more reminiscent of the Third World. Each morning at 7 o'clock, "Big Jim," the waterworks whistle, awakened residents. Jacksonville may have had Florida's most imposing skyline, but it also had the state's worst poverty. Neighborhoods on the periphery of the business district still awaited modern sewers. The riverfront was a cluttered collection of aging wharves and warehouses.

For three-quarters of a century, the stately Windsor Hotel had stood on Hemming Park, the historic center of Jacksonville. When it closed its doors in 1950, one chapter of the city's history ended, and a new chapter, in which Jacksonville would become known as the "Insurance Center of the Southeast," began. In the 1950s and 1960s, Jacksonville fortified its claim to being the "Hartford of the South" as the Prudential Company of America, the State Farm Group, and other insurance firms expanded their operations. Downtown Jacksonville saw the completion of the Prudential Building, a new Duval County Courthouse, the Atlantic Coast Line Railroad Building, the Gulf Life Building, and the Independent Life Building. The Korean and Vietnam wars also reestablished Jacksonville's prowess as a military town; new docks, runways, and hangars appeared. Jacksonville, throughout the 1950s, continued as a center of retail trade, drawing residents from hundreds of miles away to shop at its premier stores.[17]

Throughout the 1950s and 1960s, as bankers and insurance executives made their daily commute downtown, the growing skyline masked grave urban and civic problems. Perhaps no city in Florida confronted more troubling crises than Jacksonville. Urban sprawl was feeding the suburbs and cutting off the downtown. Between 1950 and 1965, the city's population actually fell from 204,500 to 196,000, while Duval County added 150,000 new residents. Suburban office parks and the opening of the first shopping malls—Regency Square, Gateway Mall, and Roosevelt Mall—siphoned off shoppers and workers. Interstate 95 facilitated the movement of workers, shoppers, and new residents, but left behind in the lengthening shadows of its overpasses were deteriorating black neighborhoods such as LaVilla and Brooklyn. Jacksonville's reputation as a military town with a gritty edge turned away tourists and retirees. A bitter racial divide and a failing educational system threatened Jacksonville and Duval County. In 1964, the Southern Association of Colleges and Schools disaccredited Duval County's high schools, citing "inadequate financial support." Between 1964 and 1968, Duval County leaders doubled the school budget in an effort to reform the system and rebuild public confidence. Led by Mayor W. Haydon Burns, city leaders and businessmen rebuilt the riverfront, revitalized downtown, and constructed many new civic and cultural buildings. The culmination of and the creative solution to serious problems afflicting Jacksonville and Duval County residents, the 1968 consolidation of city and county governments marked a pivotal moment in the area's history. Remarkably, by a vote of nearly two to one, Duval County residents endorsed metropolitan consolidation. City-county consolidation and civic leadership forged a new Jacksonville.[18]

The salvation of downtown Jacksonville hung precariously upon the 1968 consolidation vote; indeed, the district's subsequent revival is even more remarkable knowing that leaders had to convince far-flung voters spread across 840 square miles that a reenergized downtown was in everyone's interest. A succession of talented mayors held steadfast to the proposition that a prosperous, well-rounded Duval County depended upon the renaissance of the downtown. City, state, and federal leaders have invested billions of dollars to advance that dream.

The transformation of downtown Jacksonville did not emerge from a single blueprint but rather through convoluted negotiations, opportunities, and politicking. Beginning in the late 1970s, residents and visitors observed the beginnings of an urban renaissance. Private enterprise underwrote the construction of new office buildings and towers, while the city and state financed the Prime Osborne Convention Center, the Jacksonville Landing, Metropolitan Park, and the Southbank Riverwalk. In the late 1980s, the city tore down the blighted Blodgett Homes, a public housing complex on the edge of downtown. New government buildings appeared. In the 1990s, Mayor Ed Austin proposed a $220 million River City Renaissance program. The ambitious project involved the demolition of deteriorating structures in the LaVilla neighborhood, the renovation of the Times-Union Center for the Performing Arts, the restoration of the St. James Building as the new city hall, and the conversion of the venerable Gator Bowl into the sleek Alltel Stadium.[19]

By 2000, Jacksonville–Duval County had swollen to 778,879 residents. The urban gamble worked. Only Miami outnumbers Jacksonville's downtown employment. Once known for its navy, shipping, and insurance, Jacksonville has carved a niche as a regional medical center, attracting the prestigious Mayo Clinic to open its first complex outside Minnesota there. The city has survived the 1990s financial raids on its homegrown banks and has adjusted to the loss of its beloved Cecil Field, turning the base closure into an asset.[20]

Since 1950, the Gold Coast counties of Palm Beach, Broward, and Dade have encapsulated all of Florida's urban dreams and nightmares: Arthur "Come on down!" Godfrey strumming his ukulele from Miami Beach; the transformation of agricultural communities into gated developments; the march of development from the Atlantic Ocean toward the Everglades; the popularity of walled compounds for the super-rich; the persistence of the desperately poor; the "invasion" of the Cubans; the migration of retirees and Jews from the Northeast; the business of professional sports; urban sprawl; race riots; and balkanization. Palm Beach, Broward, and Dade constitute an immense landmass (5,160 square miles), an area greater than Connecticut. Appreciate that in 1950, Dade, Broward, and Palm Beach accounted for about 700,000 residents, up from 388,000 a decade earlier. The 1950s riveted attention on the breakneck growth of the Gold Coast. Astonishingly, the population of the counties doubled during the fifties. Demographers and the press noticed. In 1973, the *New York Times* called the 100-mile stretch of coastal communities from Jupiter Inlet to Key Biscayne the "nation's newest megalopolis." Between 1960 and 1990, the metro population of Dade, Broward, and Palm Beach counties doubled again, surpassing 3 million. Topping 5 million inhabitants in 2000, the Gold Coast remained among the twenty fastest-growing, large metro areas in the United States. To put these facts into perspective, consider that New York's metro population is 20 million, followed by Los Angeles with 16 million.[21]

At the start of the 1950s, Broward, a huge county sprawling over 1,200 miles, held but few residents (83,933). Places such as Deerfield Beach, Pompano Beach, Dania, and Hallandale still had one foot in their rural past, with the other striding toward a dynamic future. Broward County's transformation from small towns and agricultural communities to densely populated retirement centers and suburban developments is stunning in its size, scale, and scope. The county's population quadrupled during the decade, nearly doubling again in the 1960s. In 1980, Broward County had reached 1 million residents, in-

creasing to 1.6 million by 2000. During the 1990s, Broward grew by an as-
tounding 22.3 percent, making it the nation's third-fastest-growing county
among counties of more than 1 million people.[22]

Governor Lawton Chiles once compared Broward County's political fiefdoms
to the Balkans. Broward's growth aptly identifies what urbanologists call "suburbs without cities." Urban geographer Peter Muller suggested the term _urban
realms_. Commentator John Dorschner describes Broward County's "formless,
trackless present" as a "Blob." In 2000, Broward's largest city, Fort Lauderdale,
had only 152,397 inhabitants. County commissioners confront twenty-nine
separate cities, including Lazy Lake Village (population 35 in 1998) and Sea
Ranch Lakes (population 619). When compared to Broward, Palm Beach
County is even more fragmented, listing thirty-seven municipalities ranging
from Orchid (population 10) to West Palm Beach (population 67,000). Low-
density settlement has devoured much of Broward's seemingly inexhaustible
landscape.[23]

Broward County also illustrates the dynamic nature of urban change in late-
twentieth-century Florida. A refuge from the racial, urban, and ethnic turbulence buffeting Dade County, Broward County attracted young and old white
ethnics and many upwardly mobile Hispanics and African Americans anxious
to flee Opa-locka and Hialeah. During the 1980s, the county's black and Hispanic population grew by 150,000. Jews once regarded Broward County as pro-
vincial, preferring the urbanity of Miami and Miami Beach. In 1950, only about
two thousand Jews resided in Broward County; today, a quarter million have
chosen this area as home, a figure that climbs dramatically during the winter
season. Italian Americans, a negligible presence in Fort Lauderdale and South
Florida before the 1950s, have settled in huge numbers, sparking interest in
Sons of Italy clubs and ethnic _feste_. Interestingly, six of the 9-11 terrorists lived
and worked in Broward County, perhaps preferring the anonymity one could
find in such a fast-changing place.[24]

Once I-95 and the Florida Turnpike served as Broward's distant western
boundaries, but frenzied development has pushed the suburbs inexorably westward so that today more people live west of the turnpike than east of it. The
Everglades retreats and recedes each day. Pembroke Pines typifies this rapid
suburban spread. Numbering a scant 1,429 in 1960, Pembroke Pines has become a sprawling city of 112,000 inhabitants. Broward County's demographic
boundaries shifted perceptibly during the 1990s. Fully seven in ten new residents were immigrants, which caused the county's non-Hispanic white popula-

tion to decline. Many whites fled the older neighborhoods—Fort Lauderdale lost nearly one in ten white inhabitants—and settled in fast-growing communities like Weston, Miramar, and Davie. Not long ago, Davie was best known for its horse ranches and stables. Now Davie touts its "country way of life." Developers fret that Broward is running out of cheap land.[25]

Dade County grew furiously in the 1950s, nearly doubling its population from 495,084 to 935,047. Miami-Dade County, Florida's largest, also became the first to reach a 1 million population. Dade's population doubled again between 1960 and 1990, nudging the 2-million milestone. Since the 1960s, the wellspring for Dade County's spectacular growth has been Cuba, Nicaragua, Haiti, and the Dominican Republic. If it were not for the recurrent waves of new immigrants, the population of Dade County would be stagnant.[26]

In 1950, Miami reveled in its reputation as the most recognizable and most exotic city of a dream state. Miami and Miami Beach were synonymous with the Orange Bowl and Parrot Jungle, Jackie Gleason and Arthur Godfrey, the Latin Quarter and Hialeah Race Track, Key Biscayne and Collins Avenue. Miami attracted more tourists than any other place in Florida. In 1950, the Magic City claimed 250,000 inhabitants, making Miami Florida's largest city. By 1960, Miami required two telephone directories.[27]

While Miami was a fascinating city in the 1950s, few regarded it as a leading American city. The future changed Miami's image and reputation. A speeded-up newsreel concentrates the energy and fury of Miami and Miami Beach's four decades of change: Little Havana, Marielitos, boat people, race riots, Liberty City, _Miami Vice_, Arquitectonica, the Dolphins, Versace, South Beach, and Miami Sound. _Miami Herald_ columnist Al Burt observed in 1980, "Miami boils and bubbles, making history faster than even South Florida ever saw before. This is an urban frontier." Miami has emerged as one of America's great cities, a hemispheric capital of immigrants, banking, and capital. By 2000, Miami's significance was as unquestioned as it was compelling. The magnitude and speed of change strain the word _metropolis_. Miami is the capital of Florida's first megalopolis.

If geography is destiny, Miami's destiny was well placed. Situated on the end of a subtropical peninsula, Miami was buffered from destructive freezes and extreme heat by Key Biscayne, the Gulf Stream, and the Atlantic Ocean. The Everglades, Dade County pine, and coral rock provided room to grow and natural resources. Human agency enhanced Miami's advantages. The Florida East Coast Railroad, Dixie Highway, the Tamiami Trail, and aggressive salesmen

and city leaders made Miami accessible and special. By 1950, Miami had cultivated a special relationship with New York and Cuba. Miami was a winter playground for New Yorkers and a summer escape for Cubans. When the boys of
summer played for the Brooklyn Dodgers and Fidel Castro was plotting a revolution in the Oriente Mountains, Miami had already become an important
colony for Jewish retirees and Cuban expatriates—a mixture of the Catskills
and Casablanca. Miami's early relationships with Jews, retirees, and Cubans
channeled millions of future residents, refugees, and tourists into South Florida.

Miami's raw energy dazzles and confounds. A city of contrasts, Miami pre-
cariously balances Coconut Grove and Liberty City, Calle Ocho and Biscayne
Boulevard, Third World poverty and First World luxury. Miami's capacity to re-
invent itself reflects reality and packaging within and outside the community.
Miami, more than any other city in Florida, intrigues and repulses outsiders.
Most Floridians insist they would never, under any circumstances, live in Mi-
ami. Most of the rest of the world, however, would risk life and limb to live in
Miami.

If Miami is one of the world's most important cities, an international crossroads of travel, finance, and intrigue, Orlando is Florida's most influential city,
a place synonymous with tourism, high-tech business, and urban sprawl. Like
New York and Chicago, Miami and Orlando are antipodes. Miami functions in
Florida as Ellis Island did in New York City—as a gateway. Orlando cannot escape Walt Disney's shadow. In a 1991 cover story in _Time_ magazine, Priscilla
Painton observed: "Orlando, the boomtown of the South, is growing at a staggering pace on the model of Disney World; it is a community that imitates an
imitation of a community."[28]

Orlando, too, is a product of its geography. Nature endowed Central Florida
with the world's most perfect combination of sandy soil, eternal sunshine, and
spring water for the cultivation of oranges. Orlando's status as capital of the
citrus belt, like its reputation as a tourist center, had less to do with geography
than with human agency. Sanford, Winter Garden, and Leesburg rivaled Orlando, but farsighted leaders in that city ensured that all roads leading into
Central Florida funneled into Orlando. The arrival of Mississippi-born Martin
Andersen in 1931 may have been the most important event next to the coming
of Disney World four decades later. Andersen's meteoric rise through the ranks
of the _Orlando Morning Sentinel_ and _Orlando Evening Star,_ and his single-

FIGURE 3. Train service, once considered the most elegant way to travel, declined perceptibly after World War II. In 1952, passengers at Orlando's Mediterranean-inspired Atlantic Coast Line Station board the Orange Blossom Special. Orange County Regional History Center, Orlando.

minded determination to bring business and travelers to his beloved "orange-scented" hometown, altered the future of Central Florida. A city of 52,367 in 1950, Orlando expanded its economic base and boundaries substantially before Disney World opened. The population of Orlando doubled by 1970. More remarkably, Orange County's population trebled between 1950 and 1970, rising to 345,000. The rise of the Space Coast, aggressive recruitment of industry (Martin-Marietta), and corporations (Tupperware) placed Orlando in the ranks of Florida's most dynamic places. In 1966, the Greater Orlando Chamber of Commerce placed an ad in *Time* magazine touting Orlando as the "Action Center of Florida." Orlando's promise was lockset in 1970: the city prospered amidst a flourishing agricultural empire; new industries and businesses generated a diverse economic base; Interstate 4, the Florida Turnpike, and Orlando International Airport made the city accessible to travelers. Economically progressive, Orlando was culturally and politically conservative. Central Florida was not South Florida. Prior to 1971, Orlando offered visitors fishing, golfing, and especially Gatorland, the area's premier tourist attraction.[29]

Events of singular power and intensity altered the trajectories of Orlando and Miami, transforming cities, a state, and lifestyles. Castro's revolutionary triumph in 1959 and the opening of Walt Disney World in 1971 signify Genesis chapters for chroniclers of Miami and Orlando. Historical causation is almost always complex and multilayered, but in the cases of Miami and Orlando, Cuban émigrés and Walt Disney World lend a certain birth-myth quality to the history of Florida. When Carl T. Langford, the mayor of Orlando, exclaimed that the coming of Disney World was "the greatest thing that's happened since the city got its charter," he wasn't exaggerating. "Ask children at a northern airport where they're heading," observed writer Richard Corliss, "and they don't say Orlando; they say, with an almost desperate glow, 'Disney.'" Orlando has been branded. The presence of a Cuban exile community and the establishment of an extraordinarily successful amusement park triggered new explosions: the arrival of succeeding waves of expatriates, right-wing politics, and ethnic and racial tensions; land speculation and investment, the construction of new theme parks and hotels, and massive urban sprawl. Cubans in Miami and Disney World in Orlando transcended reality and became *the* images of their respective cities. If Miami's kinetic energy and too-close-to-the-edge ethnic velocity frightened many Americans, Orlando's theme parks energized visitors with antiseptic, simulated fright and over-the-edge illusions.[30]

Walt Disney World may specialize in illusion and fantasy, but Central Florida has had to confront the real urban consequences of hosting millions of tourists. In 1950, Metro Orlando (Orange, Seminole, Osceola, and Lake counties) comprised a combined population 185,579. On the eve of the opening of Disney World in 1971, the metro population had grown to 522,575. By 2000, Metro Orlando had surpassed 1.6 million inhabitants. Since the 1980s, Lake, Seminole, Osceola, and Orange counties combined added over 150 new residents every day. In 1950, the area teemed with orange groves, cattle ranches, and truck farms; Metro Orlando had become a hothouse for service and factory jobs, adding nearly 2,500 jobs a year. If Metro Orlando were a nation-state, its 2000 economy (with nearly $60 billion in goods and services) would have ranked eighty-sixth in the world, only slightly behind that of Puerto Rico. The census skips over the 40 million tourists who come annually. Their impact— strip malls, congested highways, and hotels—can be seen everywhere. Kissimmee once proclaimed itself the "Cow Capital of Florida"; today, it might be the motel and fast-food capital of the world. Langford, the former mayor of Orlando who proclaimed that the coming of Disney World was a seminal event, has retired and moved to North Carolina: "I spent 30 years of my life trying to get people to move down there [Orlando], and then they all did."[31]

Downtowns, Sprawl, and Edge Cities

Poets and novelists, anthropologists and demographers have all taken the measure of modern Florida. Consider as a signpost the following 1950 reminiscences: "If you stuck a pin in the map at the center of Five Points [Sarasota], within a mile of that pin could be found everything to satisfy your religious, recreational, political, medical and shopping needs. Then in 1955, the Ringling Shopping Center opened. . . . Maas Brothers opened in 1956 and Southgate Shopping Center opened in 1957." Fort Myers, according to a veteran reporter, was in 1950 "a small river town where the birth of the first baby of the year stirred local merchants into giving free gifts." Cortez was a quaint Gulf community where, "for hundreds of years, the people of this small, unincorporated fishing village . . . lived a quiet life." In 1950, every vacationer who visited Orlando's downtown tourist office got his or her name in the paper. Visitors found Orlando a charming place, more small town than big city. Shoppers flocked downtown to patronize department stores and a half-dozen car dealers. By 1980, nearly a decade after the opening of Disney World brought gale-force changes, the last downtown department and grocery stores had closed. In February 1967, Disney officials held a celebratory press conference at Winter Park's elegant Park West Theatre. Ironically, downtown Orlando had lost its last movie theater. The year 1967 also saw desperate acts undertaken to save downtown St. Petersburg, once considered one of the state's friendliest places. As private enterprise tore down ornate downtown buildings that year, the city council ordered the removal of the beloved green benches. Then they came: migrants, retirees, developers, access roads, strip malls, private walls, and shopping malls. Sarasota, Fort Myers, and St. Petersburg serve as archetypes of urban pride, suburban sprawl, declension, and renaissance.[32]

In 1950, Florida cities reached their apex. Revealing remarkable capacity for change, cities had incorporated new technologies (electrification, the internal combustion engine, mass communications) and created and adapted urban forms (department stores, skyscrapers, and movie theaters). Miami, Pensacola, Jacksonville, and Tampa spilled over with workers and shoppers competing for parking places. At midcentury, Florida's richest banks, most luxurious movie palaces, most prestigious churches, and most fashionable department stores were all located downtown. Civic boosters saw the future in shades of the past. Businessmen dreaded a postwar recession, but few feared prosperity. Nothing, warned economist Joseph Schumpeter decades earlier, was so revolutionary and unsettling as unbridled capitalism.

Fundamental changes in the relationships between Floridians and cities occurred in the decades after 1960. In 1950, most Americans lived and worked in cities. By the 1990s, about two-thirds of Americans worked and lived in the suburbs. Florida's Big Bang occurred largely outside the old central business districts.[33]

Downtowns that were so vital and magical in 1950 seemed like dinosaurs in 1980. Fort Lauderdale illustrates the urban roller coaster. When Burdines opened a department store on Andrews Avenue in 1947, Broward residents cheered. Shoppers no longer had to drive to Palm Beach or Miami to acquire the latest fashions. While 750 new families moved to the Fort Lauderdale area each week in the 1950s, its downtown was clearly reeling. By 1963, over 125 stores in downtown Fort Lauderdale stood vacant. By 1980, Burdines departed for the suburban mall. The city's reputation for revelry and hi-jinx during spring break proved a mixed blessing; while it brought hundreds of thousands of young students for a few weeks, it alienated many older residents year-round.[34]

The reorganization of government known as Metro Miami-Dade has done little to revitalize Hialeah or Opa-locka. Best known as 1920s boomtowns, Hialeah and Opa-locka began with optimism. Florida's first modern race track, Hialeah Park opened in 1924. Beginning in the 1940s, Hialeah's fortunes waned. Politicians adopted a laissez-faire attitude, imposing *no* rules on land development and growth. Recreational space in the two cities is precious and rare. By the late 1990s, Hialeah had become Florida's fourth-largest city, with over 207,000 residents, 90 percent of them Hispanic. Factories and sweat-shops were attracted to Hialeah because of the absence of zoning laws and cheap wages. After the U.S. Navy abandoned Opa-locka following World War II, the "Baghdad of the South" declined. Only 4 square miles in size, today's Opa-locka remains one of Florida's poorest cities, with forty junkyards, thirty churches, and a falling tax base.[35]

In Orlando, the prosperity generated by Martin-Marietta and Disney World could not lure new residents downtown nor stop businesses from leaving. In 1965, the beloved Dickson and Ives Department Store closed. By 1975,

Orlando's Downtown Motor Inn, Morrison's Cafeteria, the Kress store, the Beachem Theatre, Ivy's Department Store, Sears-Roebuck, and the venerable San Juan Hotel were all gone. A seeming paradox confounded Orlando's leaders determined to revive downtown.[36]

Buried in the U.S. Census of 1990 was an alarming statistic, resonant with meaning: More Floridians resided in unincorporated areas than in incorporated municipalities. The statistic underscored several significant trends. First, more and more Floridians rejected emphatically the long-held belief that cities, invested with public trust and resources, can maximize human potential and best solve problems of the present while planning for the future. But Florida cities, unlike older cities in the North and Midwest, came of age *after* mass transit; they were shaped not by streetcars and elevated subways but by the automobile. Consequently, Florida cities tend to be decentralized with relatively low levels of density.[37]

County commissioners and state legislators had already begun to consider the necessity of some kind of planning to meet the future crunch of new development. Florida's 1972 legislature courageously tackled the issue of growth by passing the Florida Environmental Land and Water Management Act (ELMS Act), and the State Comprehensive Planning Act, the latter undertaken to "provide long-range guidance of the orderly social, economic, and physical growth of the state." Moreover, the legislature authorized the Land Conservation Act, which allowed the state to purchase environmentally threatened lands. The voters of Florida overwhelmingly approved the Land Conservation Act in November 1972. Bolstered by Supreme Court decisions that reapportioned the legislature, a new generation of urban, moderately liberal legislators took control in Tallahassee.

In 1985, the Florida legislature passed the Growth Management Act, applauded as a blueprint for enlightened land use regulations. The legislation included a key component, a "concurrency" provision that required that local government pay for infrastructure (schools, sewers, roads) simultaneously with new growth, the so-called pay-as-you-build doctrine. In practice, however, Floridians have found it nearly impossible to effectively regulate growth, and mandates from Tallahassee intended to achieve that end have melted like snowballs in July. When lobbyists' push came to developers' shove, county commissioners almost always ignored the jeremiads of planners and environmentalists, listening instead to the progrowth choir. Developers earnestly believed that, as in the miracle of the loaves and fishes, unencumbered growth (low impact fees with minimal regulation) would pay for the new streets and sewers. At workshops and rezoning hearings, property owners invoked the ghosts of Jefferson and Locke, pleading that the right to develop one's property was inherently American and Floridian. Investigating the issue, the Sierra Club's Florida office could not find one comprehensive plan that had not been amended within two years. Politically, unincorporated sprawl has thrust more and more responsibility upon Florida's county commissions, an institution better designed to govern rural areas than rapidly urbanizing ones. If census figures, road construction, and building permits trumpeted the successes of sprawl, congested access roads and septic tanks symbolized the failures of growth management.[38]

Commuters and county commissioners may not have been able to define it, but they understood it all too well. "Sprawl," according to the Sierra Club, "is low-density development that separates where people live from where they shop, work, recreate, and educate—thus requiring cars to move between zones." A 1999 study by the Sierra Club found that Florida led the nation in "edgeless" urban sprawl. Among the metro areas most affected by low-density development, Fort Lauderdale, Tampa, Miami, Daytona, and Pensacola ranked high on the sprawl meter, and Orlando held the dubious honor of being America's sprawl leader.[39]

Among critics of urban gridlock, civic fragmentation, and suburban life—such as the proponents of the new urbanism promoted by Miami architect Andres Duany—"sprawl" has become the buzzword that signifies what has gone wrong with modern development. Pointing to the erosion of the quality of life, cultural conformity, and the price tag (psychic and fiscal) of building twelve-lane freeways on which one-way traffic heads toward the suburbs at 5 o'clock, new urbanists blame sprawl for the deterioration of central cities, for the loss of fertile farmland, and even for road rage. In Florida, suburbs and private communities sprout like toadstools, without any relationship to cities. Instead of liberating residents, the choices have pulled communities apart, or at least reconfigured them, disintegrating urban life.

But sprawl has its defenders, chiefly those millions of citizens who made the choice to live in the suburbs and unincorporated areas. Urban sprawl may be messy and tweak our urbane sensibilities, but it also represents the free enterprise outcome of the most propertied and affluent society in history. Sprawl has allowed the working classes to become homeowners, a powerful tenet of the American dream.

Kendall provides an alarming tale of sprawl's transforming powers. Bordering the eastern edge of the Everglades, its lands historically wet and seasonally inaccessible, Kendall's natural resources attracted modern investors. Henry Flagler drew Kendall and south Dade County into his empire, building a rail station, cutting the tall pines, and planting citrus groves. Albert Baxter Hurst erected a coontie mill, processing the native cycads into starch. By 1950, Kendall was known for its Rare Bird Farm, a tourist attraction along Dixie Highway, as well as its horse ranches, which sponsored rodeos and horse shows. In the early 1950s, aluminum magnate Arthur Vining Davis began purchasing large tracts of rural Kendall, paying about three hundred dollars an acre. Davis's Arvida Corporation began platting several large housing developments in the Kendall area. In the 1960s, the Janis brothers, Ernest and Bernard, bought a large tract of land in Kendall from Davis for $5,300 an acre, convinced that development would follow modern roads. In rapid succession, the Janises constructed the Village of Kendale, Kendale South, and Kendale Lakes. In the sprawling subdivision Kendale Lakes, the Janises added 15-foot-high "hills" to the flat Kendall landscape. The construction of the Palmetto Expressway and Interstate 95 in the early 1960s allowed easy access. In 1962, the Dadeland Shopping Center opened on Kendall Drive. Critics scoffed at the idea of a megamall located so far from Miami, but the crowds and new residents adored the attraction.

By the 1990s, the sprawling, unincorporated suburb encompassed almost 250,000 residents. Square miles of urban congestion exist without semblance of towns. Kendall's success came largely by offering South Floridians, especially Cubans, Nicaraguans, and Costa Ricans, a place to achieve the American dream. Writers called Kendall the "Queens of Florida," a reference to New York's magnet borough for the upwardly mobile working classes. Kendall may be Florida's most-integrated "city," home to Anglos, first- and second-generation Latin Americans, and blacks. "Progressive" planners, backed by county commissioners with vision and backbone, would never have allowed a Kendall to develop pell-mell, insisting instead that Dade County impose an aesthetic greenbelt (the Portland model) on the edge of major cities, forcing high-density living by promoting multifamily housing, creating row housing, and shrinking home lots. Thousands of working-class families, of course, could never have become homeowners in this system. But one must ask, how many more Kendalls can Florida afford? Nothing, however, eviscerates the quality of life more than poverty and lack of freedom. Clearly and emphatically, most Floridians want the freedom to choose low-density, single-family homes, *and* the independence gained by their automobiles.[40]

In the 1990s, commentators introduced still another term to define America's shifting urban patterns: *edge city*. Journalist Joel Garreau originated the term to identify the growing number of automobile-oriented, self-sufficient, new-age "cities" that had emerged in the 1980s. Garreau identified 125 such edge cities. Qualifications included at least 5 million square feet of leaseable office space and 600,000 square feet of retail space; a place with more jobs than bedrooms; a population that appears at 9:00 a.m. every Monday on a site that has only recently emerged as urban; and linkage to a major transportation network. In Florida, Kendall, Miami's airport corridor, Tampa's Westshore, and Maitland (Orlando) function as edge cities. Threshold edge cities include Fort Lauderdale's Cypress Creek, Coral Gables, Orlando's airport district, St. Petersburg's Gateway, Tampa's I-75 Parkway, and Brandon.[41]

Along with "edge city," demographers also coined "boomburb" to describe recent growth patterns. Distinct from traditional cities, boomburbs have populations of at least 100,000, retain a suburban feel, and lack a downtown or business core. Florida boomburbs included Cape Coral, Hialeah, Coral Springs, and Pembroke Pines. The automobile is king.[42]

Precisely at the moment the public seemed to be dismissing downtowns as anachronisms, some urban centers sprang back to life in the 1980s and 1990s. In Fort Lauderdale, the Downtown Development Authority, private enterprise, and a vast infusion of public funds have endowed the city with cultural complexes, a riverwalk, Beach Place, and the Las Olas Riverfront. Fort Lauderdale has attracted workers, tourists, and crowds to its city roots on the New River. West Palm Beach, which had experienced similar urban decay in the 1970s and 1980s, has also revitalized its downtown.[43]

Delray Beach provides a model case study of urban demise and renaissance. Incorporated in 1911, the Palm Beach County community resembled its quaint, neighboring towns along the Atlantic coastal ridge. While there had always existed divisions among wealthy beach residents, downtown merchants, and African Americans, the growth west of Interstate 95 threatened the very relevance of Delray Beach. Vegetable farms turned into condominiums. Businesses lining Atlantic Avenue moved to outlying shopping malls. "Delray Beach always had a sense of place," remembered civic activist Frances Bourque, but "somewhere between the 1960s and 1980s, it kept its place and lost its sense." At a critical crossroads in the community's history, leaders encouraged dialogue and sought common ground. The community fought Florida Department of Transportation's plans to widen Atlantic Avenue; instead, a local task force insisted that the thoroughfare be narrowed. Citizens also rejected the idea of a "big fix," a festival marketplace or a designer developer. Instead, the downtown was transformed one building and one block at a time. Construction crews buried overhead utility wires, planted shrubbery, and created an art district. The *Palm Beach Post* considers the refurbished Delray Beach "as close to ideal as it gets."[44]

In 1950, Stuart, Martin County's largest city, typified the seaside communities clustered along u.s. 1, its economy balanced by agriculture, fishing, and tourism. Stuart's downtown functionally and aesthetically blended feed stores, docks for deep-sea fishing boats, and an elegant 1920s arcade. In 1959, in a harbinger of urban decline, the post office moved from the arcade. By the late 1980s, only a handful of stores remained in the once-thriving downtown. Martin County rekindled its love affair with downtown Stuart in the 1990s. By 2000, as part of an overall successful restoration of the downtown, a feed store housed the local historical society, and trendy bars along Haney Circle attracted large numbers of patrons—an ironic turn of events considering that Cynthia Burnett Haney was a stalwart prohibitionist.[45]

Beginning in the 1980s and most emphatically in the 1990s, downtown Orlando reemerged in stainless-steel and glass-paneled skyscrapers. New monuments appeared: the $110 million arena and scores of new banks and buildings. Tourists initially flocked to Church Street Station; young people discovered and rejuvenated Orange Avenue. But for all of the successes of downtown Orlando, the pulse of Central Florida can be felt not on Orange Avenue or in the high-rise office buildings but in places like Alafaya Trail, Oviedo, Clermont, Celebration, DeBary, and Kissimmee, where the population surge remains intense. Orlando braces for a wave of downtown condominiums.

In 2000, Jacksonville stood on the threshold of still another transformation. Modeled after Charlotte, North Carolina, the Better Jacksonville Plan proposes to invest another $435 million for construction of a new courthouse, arena, library, and baseball park. A new $155 million Adams Mark hotel and $86 million federal courthouse complement the first new housing built in the downtown area in decades. Mayor John Delaney orchestrated the plan, helped by political alliances with fellow Republican and Senate Majority Leader John Thrasher of

Urban Florida

Orange Park. In addition, the plan calls for massive expenditures in LaVilla and Brooklyn, two downtown communities long afflicted by urban blight.[46]

Some Florida cities and downtowns rebounded dramatically in the 1980s. Explaining how and why downtowns experienced an urban renaissance is easier than sorting out the consequences of high-rise office buildings and public monuments. How does one explain why Floridians invested staggering sums of capital (moral, political, and economic) to save their imperiled central business districts? First, political will and leverage motivated city councils, county commissioners, and congressional leaders to invest in downtowns. An astonishing number of public monuments (libraries, performing arts centers, sports arenas, and government buildings) stand as testaments to the newfound economic resources and political vanity.

Second, the urban renaissance of the 1980s and 1990s coincided with a period of stupendous economic prosperity. Florida real estate developers, bankers, financiers, and lawyers made billions of dollars, significant amounts of which were reinvested in glass-paneled monuments. The decision to invite out-of-state banks into Florida introduced powerful institutions, more than a few adorning skyscrapers with their corporate logo. New models of public/private partnerships underwrote the construction of new buildings during this era. Sports moguls and corporations shrewdly played city against city, threatening to move franchises or companies if municipalities or states did not award them new stadiums or tax advantages.

Third, cities appealed to the aesthetic sensibilities of residents, making themselves relevant again to people's lives. Americans, perhaps weary of the commercial homogeneity of suburban shopping malls, rediscovered the vitality of cities. Jacksonville's renaissance, aided by powerful politicians, involved massive economic-cultural investments downtown and along the waterfront. St. Petersburg's expansive public waterfront and charming sense of scale have drawn many residents to the city. In other communities, cities have added modern amenities to old settings: Pensacola's Seville Square, Miami's CoCoWalk, Tampa's Old Hyde Park, Jacksonville's Riverwalk, and Orlando's Church Street Station.[47]

Fourth, the rise of so many downtown private and public monuments in the late twentieth century underscores an encouraging theme: philanthropy. For much of its history, Florida was a place to make money, not to endow universities, museums, or foundations. If Florida was a "mistress state," the mistress rarely received an inheritance. One searches for a nineteenth-century Florida counterpart to Leland Stanford, Collis P. Huntington, James B. Duke, Asa Candler, or Andrew Carnegie. A state of fabulous wealth, yet one without many Fortune 500 corporate headquarters, Florida has only just begun to reap the fruits of prosperity. South Florida has led the charge. The Greater Miami Jewish Foundation has contributed much to the region's betterment. Miami's Mount Sinai Hospital embodies Jewish charity. In 1950, the University of Florida's and University of Miami's combined endowment totaled a few million dollars; a half century later, the result of aggressive fund-raising and generous alumni and citizens, the schools' endowments surpassed $1 billion dollars. The 1990s may be remembered as the golden decade of gift giving. The number of philanthropic foundations doubled during the decade, while total assets rocketed from $3.2 billion to over $10 billion. Still, as of 2000, Florida had only eleven of the nation's four hundred largest nonprofit charities/philanthropic institutions. In contrast, Atlanta alone boasts eleven such organizations.[48]

Aesthetically, private philanthropists, public taxpayers, city/counties, and the state legislature have endowed Florida with an impressive repertoire of cultural facilities. In 1950, few Florida cities enjoyed a first-class museum or a modern symphony hall. The period since the 1980s has ushered in more than a dozen state-of-the-art facilities: the Saenger Theatre (Pensacola), Florida Theater Performing Arts Center (Jacksonville), Daytona Beach Museum of Arts and Sciences, Maxwell King Performing Arts Center (Melbourne), Raymond F. Kravis Center for the Performing Arts (West Palm Beach), Broward Performing Arts Center (Fort Lauderdale), Tennessee Williams Fine Arts Center (Key West), Philharmonic Performing Arts Center (Naples), Barbara B. Mann Performing Arts Hall (Fort Myers), Van Wezel Performing Arts Hall (Sarasota), Tampa Bay Performing Arts Center (Tampa), Ruth Eckerd Hall (Clearwater), and Gusman Center for the Performing Arts (Miami). In addition, Cummer Gallery of Art (Jacksonville), the Jacksonville Museum of Modern Art, the Appleton Museum of Art (Ocala), Florida State Museum (Tallahassee), the Salvador Dali Museum (St. Petersburg), the Harn Museum of Art (Gainesville), the Norton Museum of Art (West Palm Beach), the A. F. "Bean" Backus Gallery (Fort Pierce), the Wolfsonian and Historical Museum of Southern Florida (Miami), and Sanford Ziff Museum (Miami Beach) have contributed immensely to raising the cultural bar. Critics suggest that Florida's fine arts explosion tells one more about urban-civic boosterism, legislative largesse, and class elitism than a democratic outpouring of culture. Sarasota, a city of only 52,000, boasts its own ballet, opera company, botanical garden, and renowned art museum. Unquestionably, "cultural tourism" has become a powerful economic engine, generating in 2000 over 28,000 jobs, $2 billion in revenues, and drawing 400 million attendees.[49]

The wave of public and private construction between 1980 and 2000 left a new and unrecognizable urban Florida in its wake, as dramatic as the skyline endowed by the Florida boom of the 1920s. If quality of life is defined by the presence of fine libraries, colleges, museums, theaters, and professional sports, Florida is a much better place today than in 1950. If the quality of life includes consideration of sterile architecture and urban sprawl, Florida suffers.

A society is defined by the vitality and harmony of its new architecture as well as by its preservation of its old. On the eve of 1950, Florida cities boasted a remarkable body of architecture: 1920s boom-era mansions and movie palaces, 1930s art deco hotels, and a variety of vernacular buildings. In the postwar rush,

FIGURE 4. Beginning with the arrival of emigrants from the Dodecanese Islands, Tarpon Springs became the most famous Greek community in America. The Tarpon Springs Sponge Exchange—a colorful collection of cells where merchants and fishermen cleaned and auctioned their valuable wares—stood for decades along the Anclote River, until it was radically remodeled in 1981. Tampa-Hillsborough County Public Library, Tampa.

the wrecking ball took a toll on Florida's historic architecture: St. Petersburg's La Plaza Theatre, Tampa's Hillsborough County Courthouse, Fernandina's Egmont Hotel, the Hotel Ormond, the Tarpon Springs Sponge Exchange, Sarasota's John Ringling Towers, the Everglades Hotel in Miami, the Hotel Floridian in Tallahassee, and Sam W. Wolfson Baseball Park in Jacksonville. When Hollywood's Sportatorium was torn down in 1993 and replaced by a subdivision, the fans of "Loser Leaves Florida" wrestling matches, Elvis concerts, and Grateful Dead reunions wept. In 1978, wrecking crews dismantled the august Welaka's Sportman's Lodge overlooking the St. Johns River. The creation of the Bureau of Historic Preservation by the Florida legislature in 1983 was a timely stroke of genius. Between its inception in 1983 and 2000, the State Bureau of Historic Preservation awarded $178 million in grants to over 2,400 projects in all of Florida's sixty-seven counties. National, state, and local preservation laws and guidelines have recognized the historic significance of hundreds of structures in Florida, shielding them from the maw of development. At the same time, tax incentives and a rising consciousness have persuaded businessmen and citizens as to the profitability of historic preservation. The successful battle to preserve the Old State Capitol—the juxtaposition of the Old Capitol and New Capitol speaks volumes as to the sterility of modern architecture—awakened many Floridians to look to their own communities for architectural gems.[50]

Some of the most lovingly preserved and picturesque downtowns are found in Florida's small towns. For sheer harmony and grace, DeFuniak Springs may be the state's most unspoiled city. Laid out around an oval spring-fed lake in the 1880s, DeFuniak Springs became winter home to Florida's Chautauqua Circuit. The Chautauqua movement, which began in New York in the 1870s, brought speakers and winter travelers to Florida. North Florida boasts a cluster of charming small towns. Quincy's fame as a shade-tobacco center and home to the state's largest concentration of Coca-Cola stock owners is reflected in the town's courthouse square, Victorian homes, and stately churches. Like bangles on a Highway 90 necklace, the courthouse squares of Monticello, Madison, Quincy, Marianna, Bonifay, Chipley, and DeFuniak Springs exude a sense of place and price. Other communities have managed to preserve their brick-street, small-town charm. Havana, Fernandina, Palatka, Green Cove Springs, New Smyrna Beach, Mount Dora, Gulfport, Dunedin, Dunnellon, Floral City, Sanford, Lake Wales, DeLand, White Springs, Venice, Winter Park, Cedar Key, and Sebring have capitalized on and preserved their distinctive assortment of historic neighborhoods and main streets.[51]

Critics ponder the meaning of Florida's urban fabric. William H. Whyte, appalled at the bland and dreary towers looming over American cities, stated, "The Blank Wall is on the way to becoming the dominant feature of many U.S. downtowns." "Why can't Miami be Miami?" asked the acerbic Frank Lloyd Wright in a 1955 visit to the Magic City. "Nature must be ashamed of these hotels that you're building down here." Of downtown Miami's new buildings, Wright had an opinion: "They have no feeling, no richness, no sense of that region. Why don't you do something here that belongs? You have something in Miami that belongs to Miami. It has character. It has charm." Wright knew Florida all too well. In 1938, Ludd Myrl Spivey—a man with dreams but little money—sent Wright, a visionary desperately needing rich clients, a fateful telegram inviting the master to build a "great educational temple in Florida." With more bravado than cash, the Methodist minister and president of Florida Southern College collaborated with the briary architect to design and build a stunning collection of campus structures. They survive today overlooking Lake Hollingsworth in Lakeland.[52]

The architectural style known as Arquitectonica left its imprint upon late-twentieth-century Miami. The daring design burst upon Brickell Avenue in the late 1970s, the work of Laurinda Spear, Bernardo Fort-Brescia, Andres Duany, and Elizabeth Plater-Zyberk. Critics branded the work "Beach Blanket Bauhaus," but locals liked the brash, florid, cantilevered balconies and pyramid shapes of the Babylon, Helmsley Palace, and Atlantis. Critic Vincent Scully believed that "Miami embraces the [urban] world in a way no city in the U.S. has ever done before." Some Miamians lament the transformation of Brickell Avenue as "Mondo Condo." The architect and founder Spear, responding to critics who contend her buildings look better on film, agreed that they are best seen at fifty-five miles per hour.[53]

Tampa's Ybor City offers a case study in the turbulent world of urban renewal, architectural splendor, and bureaucratic blunders. In 1950, Ybor City represented many things to many people. Depending upon one's perspective, it was the proud remnant of a community that once boasted the largest concentration of skilled laborers in Florida; it was a neighborhood in transition, as poor blacks replaced Cubans, Spaniards, and Italians, who took advantage of the GI Bill and moved away, leaving behind substandard wooden homes and mom-and-pop grocery stores.[54]

In the 1960s, Ybor City lost thousands of residents and homes, as bulldozers cleared the way for urban renewal and Interstate 4. Lyndon Johnson's Great

Society had arrived. In spite of grievous assaults upon the community, Seventh Avenue and most of its picturesque buildings survived. Throughout the 1970s and 1980s, special committees, preservation boards, and think tanks pondered Ybor City's future, but little happened. For three decades, little stirred in Ybor City besides the shuffling of planning reports and development schemes. If any one episode befitted Ybor's quixotic past, it was the 1967 idea to transform the decaying community into a medieval "Walled City," drawing tourists into the Spanish oasis with the attraction of "bloodless bullfighting." Tampa tycoon Jim Walter pledged to bankroll Florida's newest theme park. After convincing state legislators to legalize the "sport" of bullfighting, developers staged a star-crossed exhibition. A stampeding bull spoiled the spectacle, suddenly gone sober when a state trooper shot the berserk animal with a high-powered rifle. The Walled City died with the hapless bull. Dramatically and unexpectedly, a new Ybor City emerged in the 1990s: raucous, irreverent, and marketable. Real estate developers and financiers invested millions of dollars to cater to the surging crowds. Ybor City became Tampa's greatest public space, where huge crowds abandoned their middle-class sensibilities to revel in ritual and ceremony: Guavaween, Tropical Heat Wave, and the Krewe of Santiago Night Parade.[55]

Florida's future points inexorably toward development of more open spaces as investors search for cheap land, low impact fees, and minimal zoning restrictions. Development has crept into the crevices of every county; indeed, Florida was one of only ten states to register growth in almost every county. Only a handful of municipalities registered population losses in the 1990s. Places like Jay, Jasper, and Chattahoochee—North Florida towns—lost population during the decade. In a boom-time state, such places were freaky exceptions. In the 1980s and 1990s, Flagler, Wakulla, and Sumter counties fit those criteria. Between 1920 and 1970, Flagler grew slowly, from 2,442 residents to 4,454. Over 50,000 resided in Flagler County in 2000, living in new communities like Palm Coast. Planned by International Telephone and Telegraph (ITT), Palm Coast is designed for hundreds of thousands of homesteaders along the multiconglomerate's vast holdings between the Atlantic Ocean and the St. Johns River, communities connected by an intricate network of canals and lagoons. Often criticized for its environmental damage, once envisioned as a home for senior citizens seeking modest residences, Palm Coast is recruiting upper-income transplants interested in active lifestyles.[56]

Unrelenting growth (retirees and transplants) and the ease of mobility (geographic and economic) have also disrupted small-town Florida. Interstate highways and Internet technology have closed the distance between small towns and big cities. New developments have altered the character of Apopka, Live Oak, and Jupiter, among others. Small settlements along the Peace, the Homosassa, the Withlacoochee, the Crystal, and the Suwannee rivers have received steady numbers of new settlers seeking solace and bargains. The fastest-growing cities in Central Florida are places like Ocoee, Sanford, and Winter Garden. Combining elements of urban, suburban, and small-town America, these communities exemplify a familiar pattern in Florida and the Sunbelt.

At the dawn of a new millennium, critics may decry Florida for being overdeveloped and overhyped, but few can deny that it is an urban megastate.

Florida on the Installment Plan

The Third Great Land Boom

I N 1986, tourism officials unveiled a new marketing campaign aimed at luring young and middle-aged adults who perceived Florida as a retirement home for their parents, an insipid stretch of fuddy-duddy theme parks and alligator farms. In the most memorable advertisement, a scantily clad female promises, "When you got it bad, Florida's got it good." Critics found the product both grammatically and morally incorrect. New advertisements appeared. The most infamous poster features a young woman explaining, "Come to Florida. The Rules Are Different Here."

Florida has always straddled the line between respectability and scandal, between honest toil and an easy buck, between strict adherence to the Protestant work ethic and games of luck and chance. For all of the Bible-thumping and sermonizing that Florida was going to hell in a Ford Edsel, the rules *were* different here. In romantic and scandalous hues, illegal slavers, Key West wreckers, blockade runners, bird plumers, binder boys, and confidence men shaped Florida history. Whether it concerned taxes, building codes, or environmental regulations, Floridians take a brazen delight in flouting the law, or at least show a well-worn indifference in ignoring it. Self-reliance, free enterprise, and a distaste for tax collectors and politicians bound Floridians philosophically in ways the state's long coastline and hinterland could never unite them geographically. In such an environment, booms and busts rewarded and punished sinners and saints. In

"I just got wonderful news from my real estate agent in Florida. They found land on my property."

Milton Berle

a state where the sun was enshrined in optimism, the line between speculation and investment is very thin. To be a Floridian was to gamble on the future.

Historically, land in Florida represented both place and vision: To Americans and Europeans, a grove or homestead in Florida involved an exchange of capital, but it also involved a spiritual investment, with the hopes that a tropical climate and sea breezes might rehabilitate weakened bodies and rejuvenate dreams. Three great land booms stand as testament to the powerful hold of Florida real estate.

Florida's first great land boom occurred from 1782 to 1784, when Loyalist British families fled the Patriot army in eastern seaboard cities and settled in St. Augustine and along the upper St. Johns River, boosting the population of British East Florida from about 6,000 to 17,000.

The second great land boom, from 1920 to 1925, resulted in a dramatic shifting of the state's population centers and the identification of Florida as a place of speed, glamour, fashion, and celebrities. As late as the 1880s, most residents still resided in Middle Florida, the cluster of towns and farms lying between the Suwannee and the Apalachicola rivers. As late as 1920, Florida's population stood at 968,470 (in contrast, Georgia, Alabama, and Mississippi had populations of 2.9 million, 2.4 million, and 1.8 million respectively). During the 1920s—a period of serious demographic decline in most southern states—Florida exploded, adding a half million new inhabitants, an increase of 51.6 percent. At its core, the 1920s boom involved furious speculation and investment in property, especially in South and Central Florida. Miami and Fort Lauderdale, St. Petersburg and Sarasota came of age in the 1920s. Across the state, abandoned subdivisions also became graveyards of dreams.

The third Florida boom resulted from complex interrelated forces and factors. Breathtaking shifts in technology, rising levels of affluence, the emergence of large numbers of senior citizens and retirees, new freedoms and old customs, political and leisure revolutions, a Great Society and a Cold War, cul-de-sacs and coast-to-coast expressways all shaped the development of modern Florida. Florida's future was shaped not only in Havana, Florida, but in Havana, Cuba, Washington, D.C., Wall Street, the Sunbelt South, and the Rustbelt North.

The nation's media fell in love with the Sunshine State in the 1950s and 1960s. Americans discovered Florida while reading cover stories entitled "Expanding Florida: A State of Mind, A State of Frolic," "A Playboy Grows Up," "Florida: A Place in the Sun," "The New Florida Land Rush: $10 Down for a

FIGURE 5. Florida's LeRoy Collins, considered by many to have been Florida's greatest governor (1955–61), graced the cover of the 19 December 1955 *Time* magazine. Courtesy, Stephen Whitfield, Time Life Pictures/Getty Images.

Dream," "Big Rush to the Sun: Taking an Amazing 250-Mile Journey in Florida," "The Boom That Space Built," "Fast-Growing Florida," "The Moon Boom," and "Big Rush to the Sun." What the stodgy print media would not or could not publish, developers and boosters printed, televised, and dispensed by reel and truckload.[1]

The state's media had, by 1950, been well versed in the promotion of Florida. Few publicists promoted the Sunshine State, or more precisely Central Florida, with more gusto and grandiosity than Martin Andersen, the publisher-owner of the *Orlando Sentinel*. He was not the first newspaperman to boost his city. "Major" Lew B. Brown, the editor of the *St. Petersburg Evening Independent*, capitalized upon the image of the Sunshine City by promising to give away papers "every day the sun doesn't shine on St. Petersburg." For years, many Florida newspapers refused to report on approaching hurricanes, lest the bad news drive away tourists. To heighten the sensory pleasure of the *Orlando Sentinel*'s annual citrus edition, Andersen demanded gallons of cheap orange perfume be dumped into the press's ink wells. "Newspapers build cities," he insisted.[2]

In Sunday newspaper supplements, on the radio, and through crude black-and-white televised images, the selling of Florida became big business. In 1950, an officer of the Florida East Coast Railroad addressed the membership of the Florida Advertising Club. Salesmanship, promotion, and public relations, he declared, contributed more to the history of Florida than had Spanish corsairs or legislative debates. "Had one of our modern high-pressure publicity organizations been in existence at the time," he postulated, "we might have capitalized on the Fountain of Youth story more extensively." Mythic figures—part John Gruden, part Willy Loman—the salesmen and ad forces played indispensable roles in defining, packaging, and redeeming the Florida dream. In the annals of salesmanship, there are few purer examples of optimism than the endlessly repeated mantra of the Second Great Land Boom: "$10 Down and $10 a Month. See how easy it is to own a bit of Florida Sunshine." Writes California chronicler Kevin Starr, "Land sales involved flamboyance, gross exaggeration occasionally, and sometimes deliberate deception." But in Florida, like California, real communities emerged from converted pastureland, scrub palmetto, and mangrove shore. Places with exotic names—Cape Coral, Port Malabar, and Indian Lakes Estates—seemingly appeared overnight, like Athena springing from the head of Zeus. Retired bus drivers, schoolteachers, and accountants could afford this Florida dream—on the installment plan. But first, salesmen had to sell Florida. "From this perspective," writes Starr, "the real estate salesmen, for all their brass bands, aviation stunts, and other exaggerated claims, were not hucksters at all but were rather like shamans of a new, and it was hoped, better identity and circumstances."[3]

The future belonged to an eclectic collection of hucksters and boosters, risk takers and fortune makers who saw retirement communities and instant cities where others saw sand and swamp. Sand merchants and swamp salesmen succeeded a colorful cast of characters drawn to the state for similar reasons. "Something in Florida's humid, languorous air," observed *Fortune*'s Lawrence Lessing at midcentury, "has attracted pirates, derelicts, remittance men, thieves, madams, gamblers, blue-sky promoters, moneybags, exhausted noblemen, black-market operators, profiteers, all the infections of Western life." Realtors, contractors, and developers may have disregarded rules, but they built Florida. Air conditioning, DDT, and interstate highways helped modernize Florida, but someone still had to sell and build Florida. The 2000 census suggests the scale of salesmanship and construction. Only 6 percent of the state's dwellings at the end of the twentieth century were standing in 1950, and only 3 percent of those constructed prior to 1940 remained by 2000. What is Florida? It is a state of dreams, but it is also a place of construction and reconstruction.[4]

There may be no second acts in life, but Florida provided an alluring stage for the newly rich, the repeatedly failed, and the always ambitious. Lee Ratner—he of the perfect trade name—made his first million dollars by manufacturing D-Con rat poison. He parlayed his fortune into the Lucky Lee Cattle Ranch, a 62,000-acre tract of land in eastern Lee County. In 1954, Ratner and fellow Miamian Gerald Gould turned the ranch land into Lehigh Acres, a sprawling complex fourteen miles east of Fort Myers, the first of Florida's massive planned, postwar developments. "At first, this [Lehigh Acres] was frankly a $10 down, $10 a month lot selling snow job," chuckled veteran Florida realtor Walter Fuller. At some point, "Ratner suddenly realized there was a national mood that made the pitch" sellable. Improbably, Lehigh Acres became a city in spite of the fact that it was distant from a main highway, downtown, or a body of water. By 1959, Ratner and his sales team had sold 40,000 lots in Lehigh Acres. On the east coast, the community of Miramar sprang into existence in 1955. Abraham L. Mailman, the successful manufacturer of Persona razor blades, purchased one square mile of Broward County dairy land. Determined to create an "inexpensive, bedroom, blue-collar" community, Mailman and his son-in-law founded Miramar. Appropriately, Miramar's slogan was "a city sprints to life." By the 1960s, Miramar was welcoming two families a day, becoming Broward's fastest-growing suburb. In 2000, Miramar's population exceeded 70,000.[5]

Developers converted goat farms, garbage dumps, and lemon groves into low-cost, middle-class homes in the sun. Palm Bay, Sun City, and Miramar invited retired teachers, mechanics, and accountants to purchase the Florida dream on the installment plan. Dreams, however, came in different sizes. Hoping to achieve an economy of scale, financiers, corporations, and gamblers purchased huge tracts of raw Florida, creating instant cities for Americans eager to escape northern winters or society's turmoils. By the 1960s, at least four hundred projects of one hundred or more acres had already been completed. In Zora Neale Hurston's novel *Their Eyes Were Watching God*, Tea Cake might have been philosophizing about the future of South Florida when he muses: "This ain't no game for pennies. Po' man ain't got no business at the show." Just a short drive away from Belle Glade stand the imposing mansions of Palm Beach

FIGURE 6. Lehigh Acres emerges from Charlotte County ranch land in the 1950s. State of Florida Photographic Archives, Tallahassee.

and Boca Raton. But as late as the 1950s, Palm Beach County was invitingly undeveloped. West Palm Beach stretched only one mile. But land that could grow winter green beans could easily sprout subdivisions and cities. This was no game for pennies, however. Much of spacious Palm Beach County was then managed by the West Palm Beach Water Co., which was still owned by the Flagler interests. In 1955, the City of West Palm Beach bought the water company and 27 square miles of land.

Enter Lou Perini. A native of Massachusetts, Perini grew up around his father's construction business. Upon his father's death in 1925, he took over the business at age twenty-one. His firm prospered during the New Deal and World War II. In 1941, he purchased the Boston Braves of baseball's National League. His greatest coup, however, was not moving the team to Milwaukee or even signing Henry Aaron but purchasing 5,500 acres of Palm Beach County for $4.35 million. Engineers attacked the Herculean challenge of moving 30 million cubic yards of earth to fill in wetlands and deepen lakes. Obligingly, Interstate 95 directed motorists and customers past his property. Perini developed the Villages of Palm Beach Lakes, part of an explosion of new developments. In the 1950s alone, sixteen new cities appeared in Palm Beach County.[6]

For Arthur Vining Davis and John D. MacArthur, Florida dreams evoked images of King Midas and Hamilton Disston. The son of a minister, the founder and chairman of the American Aluminum Company, Davis was one of the wealthiest men in America when he settled in Miami in the late 1940s. Recognizing opportunities beneath his feet, the octogenarian embarked on a land-buying spree. Davis envisioned a great future for tomato fields in a place called Kendall in Dade County. In 1956, at age eighty-eight, he purchased 1,500 acres of land, including one mile of oceanfront property and the Boca Raton Hotel and Club, for $22.5 million, then the biggest real estate deal in Florida history. Davis turned to south Palm Beach County, where he acquired several mammoth farms and ranches for seventy-five dollars an acre. He proceeded to build some of the county's most lavish and successful developments: Royal Palm Yacht and Country Club and Boca West. *Look* magazine labeled him the "World's Fastest Spender." By 1957, he retired from Alcoa to pursue his Florida investments full time, founding the Arvida Corporation (he took the first two letters of his full name to come up with Arvida). In the late 1950s, Arvida invested heavily in Sarasota, purchasing large tracts of undeveloped land on Lido and Longboat keys. So influential was he that the *Miami Herald* once speculated, "What Happens to Dade's Economy When Arthur Vining Davis Goes?" Ultimately, Davis's Arvida Corporation became Florida's second-biggest land company, owning 125,000 acres of Florida real estate, and another 200,000 acres in Cuba. In 1984, Disney purchased Arvida for $214 million, selling it three years later for $400 million.[7]

Not even Davis's lofty accomplishments approached the fortune accumulated by John D. MacArthur. The son of a preacher and a grammar school dropout who sold one-dollar-a-month insurance policies, he conducted business from the coffee shop located in the Colonnades Beach Hotel on Singer Island, where he drank twenty cups of coffee a day. Philosophically, the rags-to-riches MacArthur understood Americans' yearning for security, selling policies during the Great Depression for "the dollar a man had in his pocket," a concept land developers borrowed. MacArthur invested shrewdly. When he died in 1978, he belonged to the world's most exclusive fraternity: a brotherhood of billionaires. His modest lifestyle belied his portfolio, which included the Bankers Life and Casualty Corp., and 200,000 acres of Florida property. America's wealthiest man also laid claim to the title of Florida's largest private landowner.

Holdings included the 33,000-acre Ringling tract in Sarasota, 10,000 acres at Rocket City near Orlando, and 41 square miles of Palm Beach County. The eccentric billionaire was a hands-on landlord, taking pride in the development of Lake Park and Palm Beach Gardens. More than anyone else, he built and sculpted northern Palm Beach County. Resisting any effort to regulate growth and unwilling to contemplate limits—the defiant billionaire announced he was leaving the state in 1973, tired of battling tree huggers—MacArthur's philosophy might well be the motto of the Sunshine State: "You just can't tell another American he can't move to Florida."[8]

In John Ford's *The Man Who Shot Liberty Valence* (1960), the origins of the mythology of the West are succinctly expressed: "When fact becomes legend, print the legend." In Florida, when truth interfered with hyperbole, developers embellished the hype. The name *Lehigh Acres* improved upon the settlement's flat terrain. Sam J. Kellner marketed his rolling Citrus County development as the "Alps of Florida." In Florida, borrow pits become lakes, landfills are anointed hills, and hurricanes are euphemized as zephyrs. "The Beaches at Pembroke Pines" are in reality west of I-75, spoofs Carl Hiaasen, "meaning the closest real beach is either Hollywood or Naples, depending upon traffic." Hollywood Hills may be flat as a pancake, but bus drivers ferrying prospective residents to a sales picnic were instructed to downshift when the tour guide announced, "We are now entering Hollywood Hills." Developers are especially fond of naming new subdivisions after the thing they cleared away: Cypress Pointe, Clear Lake, and Panther Run.[9]

Nor does a close connection to place guarantee sensitivity or truth in advertising. In 1950, the Plantation Golf Course opened in Broward County. Laid out amid hammocks and pastureland where Seminoles once lived, the golf course incorporated its Native American heritage. Construction workers uncovered an Indian burial mound on the fourteenth hole, which the developers tastelessly named "Funnee-Okko-Pokko" (Bone Heap Burial Mound). In the 1970s, developers must have been whistling "Song of the South" when they named their elegant Nassau County creation Amelia Island Plantation. Only a sand dune away stood American Beach, Florida's historic "black beach."[10]

Salesmen Leonard and Julius Rosen established legendary reputations as pitchmen and barkers on the streets of Baltimore, trades polished on the Atlantic City boardwalk and later perfected in the appliance business. Early in their careers, the brothers realized the importance of installment sales as a key to their business. On one particularly slow day, contemplating a warehouse of

FIGURE 7. In 1950, Cape Coral was an uninhabited spit of land at the mouth of the Caloosahatchee River known as Redfish Point; by 2000, it had become Southwest Florida's largest city. State of Florida Photographic Archives, Tallahassee.

unsold televisions, an epiphany struck Leonard: "Why should we sell TVs when we might be able to sell things *on* TV?" The Rosens vowed to master this new medium. Leonard's most famous idea involved a lanolin hair conditioner—dubbed Charles Antell—with Formula Number Nine. The ad featured an announcer and a lamb, both graced with magnificent manes. After explaining the magical link between lanolin and wool, the host asked, "Have you ever seen a bald sheep?"[11]

In 1957, Leonard Rosen, newly rich but a medical wreck, sought the curing waters of the Charlotte Harbor Spa in Punta Gorda. His eye caught the roadside signs hawking Florida real estate. Writes author John Rothchild, "It was as if everything in his life had prepared him for the meaning of this." Selling Florida real estate, concluded Rosen, combined salesmanship, blanket advertising, and faith in the American dream. Ably advised by Milton M. Mendelson, who brilliantly understood Florida's possibilities, the Rosens purchased 1,724 acres in Lee County. Situated at the mouth of the Caloosahatchee River, Redfish Point was an elevated and well-drained peninsula. For $678,000, the Rosens gambled on a plot of land devoid of human habitation. The developers dropped the name Redfish Point for the more exotic-sounding Cape Coral. In the spring of 1957, the first national ads for Cape Coral offered shivering northerners the opportunity to buy into the Florida dream on the installment plan.[12]

The risks were enormous. Before the first down payments arrived, developers invested in national advertising, colorful sales brochures, recruitment, offices, salesmen, and a fleet of planes, cars, and buses. Financing had to be arranged; model homes had to be built; builders and contractors had to be in place. Creating the Gulf American Land Corporation, the Rosens recruited an aggressive, commission-driven sales force and unleashed an advertising blitz blanketing Sunday tabloids and vacation spots. Gulf American gave away homes on the popular daytime TV shows *Queen for a Day* and *The Price Is Right*. The latest version of the Great American Land Rush involved free steak dinners and air tickets to Southwest Florida, followed always by hard-sell, tag-team, boiler-room tactics. At its peak, Gulf American Land Corporation owned a fleet of airplanes plus a national travel agency. For all of the new sophistication—the autotype machine, the WATS line, the television ads—Cape Coral ultimately relied on old-fashioned salesmanship to clinch the deal. In a brilliant public relations stroke of luck, the Rosens befriended Connie Mack Jr., son of the baseball legend and Fort Myers hero. Mack went on to play an important role in the selling of Cape Coral, which was incorporated as a city in 1970. By 1959, the new community consisted of thousands of lots (sales of which had already reached $19 million) but only eighty standing houses. Public relations officers pointed out that it had more miles of canals than Venice. Its developers were fined what was then a record $19 million in 1977 to correct "an environmental tragedy," the obliteration of thousands of acres of mangrove habitat. "If man had created the earth," a disgruntled Fort Myers resident uttered, "it would look like Cape Coral." According to the 2000 census, 102,000 persons resided in Cape Coral, the largest city in Southwest Florida. Moreover, it has attracted the largest percentage of Korean War veterans of any U.S. city.[13]

Few families have changed the face of Florida land sales—indeed, the very face of Florida—as much as the Mackles. The family dynasty began in 1908

Jacksonville when Frank Mackle, a twenty-five-year-old emigrant from Great Britain, formed the Mackle Construction Company. He taught the construction business to his three sons, Frank Jr., Robert, and Elliot. Their collaboration began with the building of 125 low-cost homes in Delray Beach, the first of 30,000 Mackle houses constructed in Florida. The Mackle family gambled everything on its first great project, Key Biscayne. In the late 1940s, they purchased 227 acres of land for $870,000, on a site buffered by the ocean on its east, Biscayne Bay to the west, and Crandon Park to the north. A *Miami Herald* reporter described the early stages of the development as a "giant residential grouping in a palm-covered setting so beautiful it defies description." The first homes sold for $11,500.

"When we talked about building on Key Biscayne, people said we were crazy," reminisced Frank Mackle. "Who in the world would pay a dime to cross a toll bridge to look at a model of a home?" The mosquitoes, remembered Robert, were so thick that some laborers simply walked off the job. In 1953, a newlywed couple arrived to become the first guests at the Key Biscayne Hotel and Villas. As they walked to the new hotel, a raccoon bolted from the brush. The frightened bride locked herself in the car and refused to leave. Not until 1954 were Miami's untreated sewers, which emptied into Biscayne Bay, capped. Sun-worshipping on Key Biscayne in 1955, essayist and *New York Times* columnist Arthur Krock commented favorably on the changes he had witnessed: "In the winter of 1952 this part of Key Biscayne was an open stretch of palm trees and wild grass." Within a decade, Richard Nixon listed Key Biscayne as his address.[14]

The Mackles' early success had not prepared them for the wild ride that followed. A slim black-and-white advertisement in a 1955 *Life* magazine demonstrated the early Mackle approach: "Own Your Own Home in Florida for $350 down. Total price $4,950 includes house and lot. It's Pompano Beach Highlands on the famed Florida east coast!" Eighteen thousand people requested more information about the Florida homes, but only 127 persons purchased homes immediately. "We've got to sell them *something!*" thought Frank Mackle Jr. The Mackles would change the nature of Florida real estate by selling the customers the lot—at ten dollars down. The buyer paid the final installment upon retirement. The Mackles would only then build a home upon lots owned free and clear. "With one stroke," writes a journalist, "it shifted the Mackle Brothers Inc., out of the house sales business and into the land sales business." The Mackles understood the power of promotion, purchasing ads in *Saturday*

Evening Post and *Look*. "We've got millions of customers," an optimistic Frank Mackle said in 1959. Rarely has an American businessman understood so well his place and product amid rapid change: "Everything works toward helping us. We've got the doctors trying to get people to live longer. We've got the unions trying to get people to retire quicker. We've got a tremendous growth of pension funds; social security is getting stronger. There's a shorter work week."[15]

In 1954, the developers paid $2.5 million for 80,000 high-and-dry acres on the border of u.s. 41 and the Myakka River in undeveloped Charlotte County. They transformed the Frizzell ranch and hinterland into Port Charlotte, a proto-type community that attracted thousands of retirees and families thankful to purchase a modest slice of paradise. In 1957, the Mackle brothers combined their construction expertise with a Canadian firm to form the giant General Development Corporation (GDC). The chairman of the GDC board published *Look* magazine. The company erected a Florida tract home inside Mandel Brothers' department store in Chicago and New York City's Grand Central Station, bringing bathing beauties to pass out brochures and orange juice. GDC spent an astounding $2 million for publicity. Houses started at $6,960, with $210 down. So many "young" retired servicemen fell in love with Port Charlotte that its average age was only forty-two in 1960. In 1959, Frank Mackle predicted Port Charlotte would become Florida's fourth-largest city, this at a time when Port Charlotte consisted of 65,000 already sold lots, but only 1,600 homes. Already, Port Charlotte (148 square miles) was bigger than Detroit. Hundreds of separate developments transformed Charlotte County, which in 1950 numbered 4,286 residents. Sudden, unplanned development overwhelmed officials. In the late 1950s, the closest hospital for retirees in Port Charlotte was the thirty-four-bed Charlotte Hospital, on the edge of Punta Gorda. Soon Port Charlotte's population surpassed Punta Gorda's. In 1958, GDC sold $45 million worth of homes, most priced from $7,000 to $17,000. Sales in 1959 jumped another 40 percent.[16]

The Mackle-GDC empire expanded. New colonies would appear at Port St. Lucie, Port Malabar, Marion Oaks, Citrus Springs, Sunny Hills, Tierra Verde, Pine Ridge Country Estates, and St. Augustine Shores. In 1958, GDC platted Port St. Lucie, 80,000 lots on 80 square miles of swamp and forest. Aggressively advertising in national magazines, Port St. Lucie salesmen sold lots of homesites, but few people arrived before the 1980s. Originally intended as a retirement community, Port St. Lucie became a popular and affordable alternative to Stuart and Jupiter. Port St. Lucie had exploded to almost 90,000 residents by 2000, becoming the largest city between Orlando and Broward County. In the 1980s, the New York Mets left their historic spring training site in St. Petersburg for St. Lucie West, a 4,600-acre "new town." Throughout the 1990s, St. Lucie County had one of the state's healthiest economies, largely because of booming home construction that brought the population to 192,000.[17]

In 1962, the Mackles sold their interests in GDC, launching a new company, Deltona. Purchasing large tracts of land in undeveloped Bay, Volusia, St. Johns, Citrus, Hernando, Marion, and Collier counties, the Mackles created a home and lifestyle for every consumer. The brothers eventually acquired more than 300,000 acres of Florida real estate. In Volusia County, the Mackles dredged and expanded a chain of lakes to create the town of Deltona. The company hired popular ABC radio host Don McNeill to tout the gentle rolling hills that reminded him of Wisconsin. The town grew slowly until Central Florida exploded in the 1970s. By 2000, Deltona had a population of 60,000 residents. Company officials misrepresented Deltona's serious problems relating to drainage and dredge-and-fill mistakes. "It's just the most messed-up place to build a city you've ever seen," confessed a Deltona city manager. Because company officials designed Deltona without a sewer system, most of the homes came with septic tanks. Typical of many such developments, Deltona lacks a downtown. On 30 square miles of rolling sand hills and hammock in Hernando County, the Mackles carved out 33,000 lots and called the development Spring Hill. A brick and concrete waterfall on u.s. 19 greeted motorists, while sales teams flew in five hundred northerners every weekend for a "free" look around. Sales topped $16 million the first year. Spring Hill appealed to frugal retirees: the first lot/homes sold for ten thousand dollars. Unincorporated Spring Hill (no mayor or police department) has grown enormously, with somewhere between 70,000 and 80,000 inhabitants in 2000.[18]

Flush with the success of selling dreams to bus drivers and drill instructors, the Mackles envisioned Marco Island as a place for CEOs. Six miles long and four miles wide, it was the largest jewel of the Ten Thousand Islands. Some time in the 1950s, the Collier family had offered land to the State of Florida for $1 million, but officials showed little interest.[1] Instead of becoming a nature reserve, Marco Island was "improved," divided into 11,000 homesites, carved into 91 miles of canals, and dredged and diked for mosquito control and landfill. Construction began in 1964. An early 1960s brochure advertised Marco

FIGURE 8. For centuries, Marco Island was Florida's grandest barrier island, home to glorious dunes and Calusa artifacts. Beginning in the 1960s, the Mackle brothers transformed Marco into one of the world's most exclusive places. State of Florida Photographic Archives, Tallahassee.

Island homes, ranging from the Samoa ($19,900) to the Martinique ($41,500). The Mackles employed celebrities to endorse the Marco Island lifestyle. "Come to Marco Island—Florida's Primitive Paradise," implored Joe Garagiola, sports broadcaster and television host. Not everyone approved of the concept. "Primitive Paradise?" asked Mary S. Lundstrom, hearing the advertisement for the first time. "Oh no, Joe, you're more than thirty years too late for that description." Lundstrom offered a rare perspective. She had first set eyes upon the Ten Thousand Islands as a nineteen-year-old, arriving to become principal of a three-room schoolhouse at Marco Village. She asked pointedly, "What's primitive about the bulldozer-flattened land cut into regular strips by concrete walks and streets; monotonous rows of attractive-enough houses on their city-sized lots; the neat regulation-landscaping that's seen all the way down the East Coast and across the state and back up the Gulf Coast?" Nor was the Department of Interior pleased at the Mackles' plans for Marco Island. In September 1968, the Department of Interior denied Deltona's request for what was then considered a routine dredge-and-fill operation. Lawsuits, fines, and delays haunted the project. Environmentally unsound but a stupendous economic success, Marco Island eventually lured Americans and Europeans to its dunes and waters.[19]

Collier County's hinterlands also awakened to sounds of bulldozers and hammers in the 1960s. What Naples and Marco Island achieved for the wealthy, Golden Gate Estates attempted to duplicate for the middling classes. The Rosen brothers' Gulf American Corporation eyed the fabled Fakahatchee Strand, purchasing a tract of ancient cypress and royal palms the size of Manhattan. The fact that cypress thrive in standing water never discouraged the Rosens. Their formula was unerring: Build a model subdivision, market aggressively, and sell, sell, sell. While crews paved 880 miles of road and dug 183 miles of canal, Gulf American Corporation salesmen convinced thousands of vacationers and visitors that this could be home. Most customers arrived during the winter, the dry season. If customers sitting in carrels bugged by listening devices dragged their feet because they had not brought their checkbook, the sales office maintained a library of blank checks from out-of-state banks. A 1960s brochure urged customers to "Buy Now! Yes, our down payment and monthly payment structure is set so amazingly low you can start today—toward the day you no longer have to work." This Florida dream turned nightmarish. The Rosens sold Golden Gate Estates to General Acceptance Corporation, which declared bankruptcy. Congressional investigators damned Gulf American in the Interstate Land Sales Full Disclosure Act of 1968. Few buyers ever moved to the development because of persistent flooding. The environmental degradation threatened the fabled Fakahatchee and Corkscrew Swamp Sanctuary, causing a drastic drop in the water table. From the sky, Golden Gate Estates now resembles a "ghost town without the town," a modern Machu Pichu. In the 1970s, Everglades Boulevard became a favorite landing strip for DC-3s loaded with South American drugs. Today, the sprawling city that never was sits abandoned as environmentalists, bureaucrats, lawyers, and a handful of homesteaders sort out the future. Most of the 22,000 lots have been repurchased by authorities under federal and state Everglades-restoration programs.[20]

Volusia City, wrote *Miami Herald* columnist Stephen Trumbull in 1956, was "a true turkey among turkeys in the mail order real estate business." In the early 1950s, land-scam artists printed 25,000 slick brochures. The prospective Volusia City lay 14 miles west of u.s. 1; however, artists' conception of the tract depicted surf and sailboats within an easy walk. In his investigative series, Trumbull also found inaccessible "on the waterfront" Everglades swamp lots for sale at $450.[21]

Golden Gates Estates and Volusia City represent only the most spectacular cases of Florida dreams and common sense submerged in land scams. Letters complaining of misleading salesmen and fraudulent ads filled warehouses; the letters described brochures touting "nearby shopping centers" that turned out to be rural grocery stores and "waterfront property" where the water consisted of a murky canal. Future archaeologists may stumble upon the platted markers of Poinciana, Lindfields, Cape Atlantic, Palm Beach Heights, Cape Orlando Estates, Flagler Estates, Columbia Acres, Imperial Acres, Larre-Al, Sun Valley, Orlando Highland Park West, University Highlands, Space City, and River Ranch Acres—projects launched with bravado and a wink but destined to become ghost subdivisions. Pelican Island promised to be Florida's next Venice. Developers purchased a 102-acre "island" off Miami Beach in 1945 for thirty-five thousand dollars. Like the original Venice, much of Pelican Island was underwater and more than a mile from terra firma. Schemes to develop Pelican Island as a "fairyland" for children and a water sports complex also failed. Today, Pelican Island remains three feet underwater. Rocket City seemed destined to be Florida's city of the future. Conceived during JFK's New Frontier, the name fit the optimism of the early 1960s. Rocket City's dreams were big: 10,000 acres on land 26 miles east of Orlando. Alas, Rocket City exploded on the launch pad. Intended to supply housing to employees at Cape Canaveral, the All State Development Company never envisioned the Kennedy Space Center or President Johnson moving thousands of highly paid engineers and technicians to Texas. Today, the Wedgefield development occupies the site, but a Rocket City curse haunts the development. A string of lawsuits has followed the project. *Orlando Sentinel* reporter Joe Newman writes, "Florida officials estimate there are 2.1 million unbuilt, platted lots in every part of the state, many of them in 'ghost' subdivisions that exist only on paper." If one thinks that modern consumers are too sophisticated for the boiler-room scams, think again. The electronic highway allows Web sites and the Internet to lure new customers to eBay, where sellers offer promises of "ocean views and prime waterfront land" and virtual reality tours.[22]

Not even the specter of Florida Busts Past could spook investors bent on profiting from America's greatest land rush. In spite of pell-mell planning, land fraud, and modern prophets warning of the sins of excess, Florida experienced in the half century after 1950 a period of growth so spectacular, so searing, that it dulled the glitter of the 1920s. The lure of retirement villages, beachfront condominiums, and trailer parks brought millions of new residents to the state,

Florida's Great Land Boom

causing a chain reaction that resulted in new construction, landscaping, utilities, schools, highways, hospitals, and strip malls. To the question, what does Florida do for a living? Modern history seemed to answer, Florida grows!

As consumers and dreamers, African Americans also wished to improve their lives. The state's black newspapers and the "News about Negroes" supplements published in urban dailies promoted new postwar subdivisions. "Colored veterans," a 1954 advertisement began, "Lincoln Gardens is your finest development." Homes in this new Tampa subdivision began at $8,150. In 1950, Washington Park opened in Fort Lauderdale at NW Sixth Street and Twenty-first Avenue. One of the most successful postwar projects, Richmond Heights, opened in 1949 and quickly became a refuge for Dade County's black veterans and middle-class professionals. In the 1950s, writes Marvin Dunn, "living in the Heights was a status symbol"; a local paper called it "the Negro's Shangri-la." Developers opened the 320-acre Bunche Park in Opa-locka, as well as Magnolia, "a colored subdivision." Homes sold for $5,500 each. In Palm Beach County, Roosevelt Estates, a middle-class neighborhood, received high praise. When Panama City's first black subdivision opened in 1947, Lincoln Park was an immediate success. Featuring street names such as Willie Mays, King Cole, and Belafonte, Washington Shores offered Orlando's African American middle class an escape from decaying neighborhoods. By the 1950s, a shopping center, funeral home, service station, and schools served the area. Booker Park, located on the edge of the Everglades near Indiantown, attracted upwardly mobile agricultural workers and store owners.[23]

Many Floridians either could not afford a traditional home or did not wish to live in a trailer. Jim Walter offered an alternative. Returning to Tampa after the war, the young veteran and his wife (who outranked him) resided with his parents. In 1946, an ad in the newspaper caught Walter's eye: "Nice little unfurnished house to be moved. $895." He purchased the semi-finished home, loaded it onto a flatbed truck, and moved it to a hundred-dollar lot. He then went into business with the carpenter, Lou Davenport, buying him out in 1948. The early Jim Walter "shell" homes specialized in offering inexpensive housing to homeowners willing to move them and finish the interiors. In 1955, Tallahasseans purchased Walter's "Lakeshore" one-bedroom homes for $995: terms included no money down, a four-year mortgage, and the buyer's lot as collateral. In 1960, *Life* magazine named the builder one of the "100 Most Important Americans under Age 40." By the mid-1950s, the Jim Walter Corporation diversified into manufacturing and mining and climbed the ranks of the Fortune 500. Lawsuits followed. The name Jim Walter—many customers believed it was a fictitious name, like Betty Crocker—adorned 330,000 homes constructed in Florida and the Southeast. Upon his death in 2000, obituaries called him a "home- building tycoon" and "believer in do-it-yourself homes."[24]

Jim Walter had many counterparts throughout the state, but only Leonard Miller built more homes. Miller and Walter were homebuilders, not developers. Arriving in Miami in 1954, the Harvard-educated Miller launched F & R Builders with ten thousand dollars in capital. That modest investment grew into Lennar Homes, which first specialized in low-priced homes for young families. In a half century, Lennar built a record half million Florida homes. Miller's ten-thousand-dollar investment grew to a billion dollars. Hurricane Andrew besmirched Miller's reputation, as large numbers of Lennar-built homes were destroyed in the 1992 storm.[25]

Homebuilding necessitated building materials, and enterprising Floridians created fortunes supplying concrete, roofing tile, and shrubbery. In 1925, Jacob E. Rinker left Indiana to test his talents in Florida. Borrowing a thousand dollars, he purchased a truck and formed Rinker Rock & Sand Co., in Delray Beach. He soon moved the company to West Palm Beach. Ironically, the devastating hurricane of 1928 boosted his business because of the demand for building materials. Rinker Materials Corp. was well situated to take advantage of the construction boom after World War II. His specialty was concrete materials. Disney World, Patrick Air Force Base, and innumerable shopping malls are built upon foundations poured by Rinker's crews. In 1985, Rinker sold his company for $515 million.[26]

Rich and poor, blacks and whites, all wanted a slice of the Florida dream, which happened to be the state's greatest export. Dreams were seemingly immune from recession and pessimism. Nothing could deflate Florida optimism in the 1950s and 1960s. In a land of perpetual hope, reality can disillusion, but it can also strengthen dreams. Not even the national recessions of 1973–74, 1981, 1991–92, and 2000 dashed Florida dreams on the rocks of unemployment and failure. The first severe test of Florida's overexuberance came in the early 1970s. The hawks of Vietnam came home to roost, as the American economy stalled in the quagmire of an unpopular war, a disgraced president, and years of a wartime economy without the pain.

The opening of Disney World in 1971 had created, in the minds of many leaders and businessmen, a sense of invulnerability. Capital and people poured into Florida. Basking in its reputation as the country's fastest-growing state, Florida welcomed nearly a million new residents between 1970 and 1973. Then a series of cataclysmic and catalytic events seemed to unloose the furies upon the world, exposing Florida's vulnerabilities. For a nation and state accustomed to optimism and progress, the year 1973 brought pessimism and dislocation writ large.

Nationally, Vietnam and Watergate hung like a funeral pall. Watergate tracks led back to offices in Tampa and Jacksonville, Orlando call girls, and CIA agents in Miami. In March 1973, the first wave of American POWs returned home to a forest of yellow ribbons. Florida's most famous prisoner-of-war, future U.S. Senator John McCain, reunited with his family in Jacksonville.

The year's most destabilizing event occurred in the Middle East on 6 October 1973. Egyptian and Syrian forces attacked Israel. The Yom Kippur War quickly reverberated far beyond the Sinai Peninsula. The United States and

Soviet Union supplied the combatants with F-4 Phantoms and MIG-21 Inter-
ceptors, but Arab leaders unsheathed an even more powerful weapon: oil. Angry at American support of Israel, OPEC (the oil-producing export countries)
sharply cut the supply of oil to the United States.[27]

Floridians awoke on Sunday, 1 December 1973, to an eerie quiet. In the affluent postwar decades, Americans had fallen in love with their big automobiles.
Big Oil had ensured and sustained a drive-in civilization. In a "wish you were
here" state, getting here and getting around depended upon four-wheel gas-
guzzlers and foreign oil tankers. Who cared if the automobile generated low-
density suburban sprawl and gridlock traffic? Cheap, plentiful gas was part of
an American way of life. Not since World War II had American citizens faced a
"gasless Sunday." Panic gripped the state. Headlines sounded like funeral
dirges: "Fuel Pinch—State Facing Drastic Shortages" and "Gas Shortage Hits
Tourist Business."[28]

Orlando was the epicenter of the great gas crisis. Since its opening, Walt
Disney World had galvanized and redirected Central Florida's economy and
future. But fuel shortages and gas lines threatened the Magic Kingdom and
hinterland. Bible World, a planned, $11 million "full-scale Palestinian village,"
fell victim to the economic crisis. Headlines, unthinkable six months earlier,
announced: "Disney: Trouble in Dreamland," "Disney World Triggers Trouble
for Orlando," "Orlando's Hotel Boom Faces Bust," and "Florida: Biggest Fraud
Yet?" These headlines appeared not in *Mother Jones* or *National Enquirer* but in
Duns, Business Week, Miami Herald, and *Newsweek.* "To tell you the truth," confessed the president of the Orlando Area Innkeepers association, "I'm scared
out of my wits."[29]

Floridians adjusted to reduced highway speed limits (55 mph), inflated
prices (fifty-cents-a-gallon gasoline), and lifestyle changes (Jacksonville City
Hall's thermostat, for example, was set at 80 degrees in the summer). In Key
West, city officials encouraged employees to wear hot pants and shorts to work.

In 1974, Florida experienced its most serious real estate crash since the
1920s. What the Arab oil embargo did not wreck, the Federal Reserve derailed
with a huge raise in the prime lending rate. Florida insiders also pointed fingers
at abuses in the Real Estate Investment Trust (REIT). Massive overbuilding and
overspeculation resulted in a real estate collapse. New construction plunged
from $7 billion in 1974 to $2.8 billion in 1975. Worse, thousands of empty condos and office buildings went begging. Half of Metro Orlando's six thousand
condominiums stood empty, a rate matched in Miami. The *Orlando Sentinel*

questioned the timing and wisdom of the 100,000-acre Palm Coast development.[30]

Coping with explosive growth, Floridians reconciled years of living dangerously with a future pockmarked by the realities of urban gridlock and environmental calamity. Dade County became a poster child for antigrowth advocates. In one seven-day span in 1973, residents gasped as a typhoid epidemic scoured a migrant labor camp, contaminated water caused a massive fish kill in Biscayne Bay, and brownouts paralyzed downtown Miami.

In the short run, the Florida boom simply ran out of steam. Steel skeletons of abandoned skyscrapers silhouetted Gold Coast cities for years. Between 1974 and 1976, more than a thousand projects worth more than a quarter of a million dollars each failed in Dade and Broward counties alone. "People got drunk on Florida," confessed a candid chairman of a Savings and Loan. "People who didn't know Fort Lauderdale from Pumpkin Gardens were building or financing projects there. They produced row on row of junk. Bulldozers should go in and tear them down."[31]

The age of perpetual shortages seemed permanently at hand. However, Cassandras predicting doom and gloom underestimated Florida's resourcefulness and Americans' love affair with sunshine and beaches. Pointing to rows of vacant buildings, a developer explained, "Florida is not overbuilt; it's undersold." While cheap gas never returned, tourists and investors did, in even greater numbers than before. Speculating that Americans needed a vacation and a retirement home more than ever, smart investors made huge profits.

The stunning success of Disney World seemingly laid the cornerstone for a recession-proof economy. Walt Disney had bequeathed more than a world of fantasy; he had created a perpetual-growth machine. The Sunshine State had become Lotusland. Prosperity returned. Developers' wildest fantasies could barely keep pace with clicking turnstiles, new construction, and demographers' calculators. The 1970s added 3 million new residents. Over 100 million tourists descended upon Florida by air and ground, sparking the greatest construction boom in state history. When asked about the location of a proposed housing development or motel, salesmen now responded, "It's close to Disney World."[32]

Mickey Mouse not only defined Florida tourism, he also defied critics and defined the state of the Florida economy. In 1976, when a University of Florida environmentalist warned Floridians that the boom had crested, he was widely denounced as a Rasputin. Professor Howard Odum is "crazy, crazy," pronounced a Fort Myers resident. "How could there be an end to a boom in a town that added ten thousand new residents every year for the last five years?" A collective smirk appeared on Floridians' faces when a resurgent economy lifted the state into a period of even greater growth. So powerful was the appeal of Florida that the state largely avoided the national recession of 1981–82.[33]

Portents of bad economic times appeared in the late 1980s, but Floridians confidently believed that Florida was recession-proof. The *New York Times*, in a page-one 1990 story, reported, "Economists Predict Florida Can Keep Recession at Bay." Many factors seemed to cushion Florida from the aftershocks of a national recession: the sustained migration of out-of-state retirees, a robust housing market, and steady streams of tourists.[34]

To be a Floridian is to be confident. But in the early 1990s, Florida's luck ran out. A devastating recession rocked America, the result of massive S & L failures, bad investments, and overconfidence. Bad times even drove President George Bush, the hero of the Gulf War, from office, but his son Jeb prospered in South Florida. Florida's role in the 1990s recession, however, was not merely that of an innocent or passive victim; rather, Florida contributed to the economic crisis, worsening its effects. "Our industry contributed mightily to the nation's economic and financial woes," observed Lewis M. Godkin, economist. "We were not victims, we were perpetrators."[35]

The Florida Bubble burst, or seemed to. Weekly, Floridians read about scandal-tainted S & Ls and corrupt practices. "The most evocative image of the economy in 1991," writes *Florida Trend*'s Philip Longman, "was not the idle steel mill, but the boarded-up strip mall, the empty office park, the faded S & L." The statistical toll was painful for a state used to straining upward. During one eighteen-month period in 1990–91, more than 200,000 Floridians lost their jobs. Between 1988 and 1993, Florida's unemployment rate exceeded the national average. At its nadir, the state's unemployment rate hovered around 9 percent, second only to Rustbelt Michigan. *U.S. News & World Report* diagnosed Florida's economy as "Beached Like a Whale." Cranes and scaffolding seemed to freeze; the value of new construction fell 14 percent in 1991 and another 4.3 percent in 1992. Even the rate of migration slowed. Some metropolitan areas even experienced a net out-migration, unheard of in modern Florida. Eastern and Pan American airlines declared bankruptcy, a severe blow to South Florida. Across Florida, overbuilt skyscrapers and strip malls stood empty. Office vacancy rates averaged almost 22 percent in Florida's leading cities.[36]

Bankruptcy became an almost fashionable feature of the 1990s recession. Florida acquired such a notorious reputation for bankruptcy that *Forbes* magazine branded it the "Deadbeat State." Florida bankruptcy law reinforced a popular image at the time that was reflected in a tourist ad beckoning, "Come to Florida. The Rules Are Different Here." Florida's bankruptcy law—like its constitutional amendments prohibiting a state income tax and allowing for a homestead exemption—provided a legal incentive for the propertied classes to move to Florida. The generous laws allow creditors to shield expensive houses and all wages, annuities, pension plans, and property owned jointly with a spouse. In the midst of the worst economic downturn since the Great Depression, Florida welcomed new migrant-millionaires seeking shelter. Florida law allowed corporate raider Paul A. Bilzerian to keep his $5 million, 36,000-square-foot estate, in spite of his declared debts of $140 million. Former baseball commissioner Bowie Kuhn purchased a $1 million home on Ponte Vedra Beach before his New York law firm went under. Marvin Warner, an Ohio banker sentenced to prison for securities fraud, purchased a $2.25 million Ocala horse farm. The bankruptcy boom prompted one developer to declare, "You can't be bankrupt in America without a lot of cash." If Florida's laws were intended to help the yeoman farmer or poor worker, they failed. As Rosalind Resnick noted in *Forbes,* "The law protects precisely the kinds of assets poor people are unlikely to possess."[37]

In 1992, Hurricane Andrew seemed to add an exclamation point to the nightmare. Yet in spite of—some economists suggest because of—Andrew, Florida rebounded. Hurricane Andrew may have been a physical and environmental disaster, but it was an economic godsend. The catastrophe jump-started the economy by creating a massive source of investment from insurance claims and government assistance.[38]

Prosperity returned to Florida, again. A sign of genuine optimism occurred in 1991. In spite of the worst crisis since the Great Depression, almost one-quarter million new residents moved to Florida. Dampened but not discouraged, the Florida dream endured. Looking back from the vantage point of the 1930s, journalist Mark Sullivan observed, "All of America's gold rushes, all her oil booms, and her free-land stampedes dwindle by comparison . . . with the torrent of migration pouring into 1920s Florida." The same might be said of the decade of the 1990s. Not since America's Gilded Age had so much wealth and ostentation been amassed in such a short period of time and with such intensity. The 1990s endowed Florida with more barrel-tile-roofed homes and strip malls, but the most lasting memory may be the stunning new wealth invested in Florida and apparent in new levels of luxury. Florida has always been associated with wealth, but the extravagances associated with the 1990s are truly eye-popping. Owning multiple luxury homes became a rage in the fast-paced decade of the 1990s. A phenomenal increase in the number of house-holds owning three or more residential properties—from fewer than one in a hundred in 1990 to almost one in five a decade later—suggested that many Americans sought comfort, refuge, and even identity in prestigious mansions. An astonishing 482,994 dwellings in Florida served as second-home pur-chases in 2000. The fact that so many of those wealthy homeowners chose Florida had as much to do with the state's generous benefits, most notably a 1990s constitutional amendment putting a brake on rising home assessments, as it did with location, location, location. Creativity characterized Florida's housing market.[39]

Originating in ancient Rome, the condominium has become an integral fea-ture of modern Florida's housing market. By 2000, Florida was home to an astonishing 1 million condominium units, half of America's estimated inven-tory. Cooperative apartments—the word *condominium* was not commonplace until the 1970s—date to turn-of-the-twentieth-century New York and arrived in Florida in 1946. The Cloisters in Pompano Beach advertised itself as a coopera-tive apartment. Retirees from the Northeast popularized the concept, and until the 1960s, 95 percent of all such units stood along the Gold Coast, especially Broward County.

In 1970, *Florida Trend* first introduced the term *condominium* to its readers. "A new life-style is evolving in Florida and with it, a new habitat, the condo-minium," began the article. Soon, the terms *condo craze* and *condomania* were commonplace, as the custom spread across Florida.[40]

In a state of extravagance and hyperbole, Florida's most celebrated addresses (Palm Beach, Mountain Lake, and Miami Beach) and dysfunctional celebrities (the Pulitzers, Kennedys, and Johnsons) are regulars in and on America's tab-loid media. Landed families and the newly rich have amassed fortunes, display-ing their status in places that exude exclusivity: Golden Beach, Fisher Island, and Osprey. Bound together by zip codes and consumption, Florida's most prestigious communities exude luxury and privilege but also signal disturbing signs of vulgarity laced with antisocial overtones. Journalists called such greed a bad case of "affluenza." The rich and famous have always validated their dreams in Florida, but recently the "stuff of dreams" has moved beyond sun, beach, and mansion to gated compounds, private jetports, and restricted access. California and Florida lead the nation in gated addresses. In an earlier era, cough drop barons and Old World dowagers erected palaces of pleasure, but the public (albeit white) was invited to gawk and walk along Brickell Avenue, Riverside Drive, and Bayshore Boulevard to admire their neighbors' success. Wealthy Floridians increasingly seek sanctuary in gated communities whose walled compounds and security guards keep the public—even census takers—out. The cult of celebrity, however, invades the privacy of the most protected Floridians. Whimsically and appropriately, *National Enquirer* and *Vanity Fair* have found permanent homes in Florida; hauntingly and understandably, the kidnapping of Barbara Mackle and the death of Gianni Versace reminded celebrities that fame can carry a terrible price.[41]

A state of conspicuous consumption, Florida's passion for lists—"The 100 Best Places to Live"—fits hand-in-Gucci-glove. Tabloids lavish attention on the lifestyles of the rich. Consumer/lifestyle magazines introduce envious readers to the "other" Florida: *Millionaire, Ocean Drive, Robb Report for Luxury Lifestyle, Distinctive Homes of South Florida, Latitudes and Attitudes, Florida Architecture, Florida International Style, Islands, Coastal Living,* and *Spa Finder.* Cities, too, flaunt the beautiful people: *Ponte Vedra Lifestyle, Biscayne, Boca Raton.* In a nation where citizens spend $3 billion a year on cosmetic surgery, South Florida is its capital, as is evident in pages of advertisements for eye lifts and liposuction. No city/area has refined modern public relations and sybaritic living more than Southwest Florida and its seductive magazines: *Naples Illustrated: The Magazine of Gracious Living, Naples: The Magazine of Living,* and *Gulfshore Life.*[42]

For more than a century, Palm Beach has retained its rarefied luster. Each winter, more multimillionaires congregate along the shores of Lake Worth, the Intracoastal Waterway, and the Atlantic than any place in the world. Palm Beach County ranks third in U.S. per-capita income in 2000: $110,000. The total value of Palm Beach County property exceeds that of forty other Florida counties combined. Boca Raton, Palm Beach's elegant neighbor, has also carved out a reputation for the good life. The 1950s revived Addison Mizner's other dream place. With fewer than 1,000 residents in 1950, the city grew to nearly 7,000 by 1960, about the time leaders touted the place named for a rat's mouth as "Utopia on Earth." For many of Boca's 1960 residents, life was indeed utopian: one of every eighty inhabitants was a millionaire. Alarmed at the galloping growth—Boca Raton's population quadrupled in the 1960s—its citizens approved a 1972 referendum that put limits on the city's growth. "Boca Raton," wrote Jon Nordheimer in 1973, "has more Polo fields (four) than it has bowling alleys (one), [and] a cost-of-living index higher than New York City." In the 1980s, Boca became Florida's "Silicon Beach," as it attracted high-tech industries. Boca has kept its civic promise to limit growth; the 2000 population rested at 75,000. The city's median household income of $54,163 is one of Florida's highest.[43]

At the close of the twentieth century, South and Central Florida held no lock on consumption. Destin and Fort Walton Beach may have been on Eglin Field's radar, but the Gulf beaches of Okaloosa and Walton counties were largely ignored until the 1980s and 1990s. The virgin forests of yellow pine had long been gone, but the Panhandle possessed something far more valuable: hundreds of miles of stunning white sand and magnificent dunes. Beginning in the 1980s, Range Rovers and SUVs suddenly crowded u.s. 98. The stampede to places like Sopchoppy, Carrabelle, and St. Joseph Sound was part of a massive movement to the waterfront. Construction cranes and high-rises have transformed some of the last vestiges of Old Florida. The success of Seaside and Destin, located in what was once some of Florida's poorest areas, has spiked the price of real estate. Condominiums in 2004 start at $300,000 and climb toward $3 million. Peering at the new skyline of "concrete condominiums," writer Rick Bragg pondered "why it took so long."[44]

Exclusion and exclusiveness bring a steep price tag. Million-dollar homes used to be as rare in Florida as a turtle crossing Alligator Alley with shell intact. Not until 1990 did a Coconut Grove home sell for $1 million; within a decade, the average sale price had surpassed $650,000. In 2000, Broward County realtors sold 174 homes worth $1 million or more. The Census Bureau confirmed what Rolls Royce dealerships on Las Olas Boulevard know too well— living even modestly in Fort Lauderdale is expensive. Among cities of 100,000 and more, Fort Lauderdale ranks as fifth in the nation in the percentage of homesteads worth at least $1 million. Almost one in every twenty-five homes qualifies. Prior to the 1990s, almost all of Broward County's luxury homes lay east of the Florida Turnpike. That Rubicon was crossed by developers constructing subdivisions with names like Hawk's Landing. In Palm Beach County, over 3,000 homes are assessed at $1 million, prompting one realtor to wonder if the Census Bureau's threshold of $1 million did not seem a bit dated. "For one million dollars, you're going to get an old house that needs to be redone or bulldozed." In 2000, $1 million would buy a four-bedroom, 3,467-square-foot home in Palm Beach. Sniffed an architect, "Some clients may spend one million dollars just for decorative hardware." In 2004, a seven-acre estate sold for $70 million.[45]

For sheer exclusivity, Jupiter Island has vaulted from a place once damned by shipwrecked Jonathan Dickinson and disillusioned British planters to the "richest city" in the nation. A 1959 story noted that Jupiter is "so exclusive that residents consider Palm Beach a little gaudy." Median-priced homes in this Martin County refuge cost $2 million (doubling in price since 1996), leaving swanky Aspen, Colorado, and trendy Malibu, California, in Jupiter's BMW exhaust. Personal income averages $200,000. Since Mary Duke Biddle and her siblings invested in Jupiter Island in the 1920s, the 17-mile island has offered the wealthy a luxurious retreat. Eleven other Florida cities earned exclusive places in *Worth* magazine's millennial list of America's 250 "richest towns:" Palm Beach (#31), Highland Beach (#37), Boca Grande (#77), Golden Beach (#93), Sea Ranch Lakes (#126), Bal Harbour (#129), Indian River Shores (#155), Captiva (#160), Key Biscayne (#173), and Ocean Ridge (#208). Fisher Island, a magic carpet-ride away from Miami, ranks as America's richest community.[46]

For a long time, luxury seemed synonymous with beaches and oceanfront living. Orlando's Isleworth broke the saltwater hold. An agricultural paradise in the 1890s, boosters dubbed the rich Central Florida grove lands surrounded by cypress lakes the Isle of Worth. The Chase family owned the 560-acre property for over a century. Florida Ranchlands of Orlando persuaded the Chases to sell the prized acreage, plus 400 acres of Lake Butler frontage, for $30 million. Arnold Palmer, one of the partners, promised to build one of America's great golf courses along the watery paradise. Isleworth opened in 1987. Ironically, the development's modestly priced homes and golf club memberships flagged, victim of a recession and a wrongful death lawsuit. Eccentric British billionaire Joe Lewis rescued Isleworth from bankruptcy court. Revamped as an exclusive retreat, Isleworth became Florida's hottest property in the 1990s. A who's who of celebrities called Isleworth home: actor Wesley Snipes; Michael Jackson; athletes Shaquille O'Neal, Grant Hill, Vince Carter, Tracy McGrady, Dennis Scott, Ken Griffey Jr., Orel Hershiser, and Tiger Woods; and business executives Robert Earl and Bob Vander Weide. The 1999 *Robb Report* named Isleworth America's best country-club community.[47]

Marion County, known for Silver Springs, The Villages, and thoroughbreds, is also home to one of the state's most exclusive estates: Jumbolair. The 550-acre gated development contains only 125 homes but features crocodiles and other exotic animals. Most famously, the actor John Travolta has not only a mansion there but, like other homeowners, a private runway for his jet.[48]

Interstate 75 once cleaved Southwest Florida like a Berlin Wall. Luxurious developments concentrated population and power along the west Gulf Coast; agricultural and service workers lived east of the highway. Beginning in the late 1980s, however, expensive and extensive subdivisions crossed the interstate. The *Bradenton Herald,* responding to demography, now publishes daily the *East Manatee Herald.* In the words of longtime resident Pam Gibson, "It's the '50s all over again down here, but at supersized prices."

In 1958, the producers of *Wind across the Everglades* searched for a community resembling turn-of-the-century Miami. They discovered Everglades City. Miami had its Flagler; Everglades City had its Collier. Too big for a canvas, Barron G. Collier cast big shadows. In the 1910s and 1920s, he purchased one million acres of land in Southwest Florida and then proceeded to create his own county and name it after himself. His influence diverted the route of the Tamiami Trail. But for all of Collier's will, his county slumbered. In 1950, with a landmass rivaling that of Delaware, Collier County's population stood at 6,448.[49]

In 1950, Naples was a modest town of 1,465 residents. Founded in the 1880s, Naples-by-the-Sea served as a winter resort for Kentucky colonels and northern invalids. As late as 1949, Naples did not have a single bank. Wealthy Americans fell in love with Naples in the 1950s, so much so that *Florida Trend* crowed in 1959 that the place claimed "more important industrialists per capita . . . than any American city." Naples was well poised for spectacular growth. Hurricane Donna in 1960 wiped away many of the older homes. Developers such as the Collier family and John Glen Sample had plenty of prime land for sale. Sample, a radio advertising pioneer, arrived in Naples in 1938. By 1950, he had purchased two square miles of property in the heart of Naples. He began Naple's most luxurious development, Port Royal. By 1970, Naples was the fastest-growing city in the fastest-growing county in America's fastest-growing state. The city has been compared to Long Island's Southampton, home to two five-star Ritz-Carltons, the Naples Philharmonic Center, and the Naples Museum of Art.[50]

In 2000, Naples became America's highest-ranked metropolitan area in percapita income (over $43,000), in spite of the fact that only 40 percent of its residents work for weekly wages. Throughout the gilded decade of the 1990s, it was not unusual for the *Naples Daily News* to print a half-dozen or more real estate sections in its Sunday edition. Astonishingly, the ten most expensive homes purchased in Collier County in 2000 totaled $130 million; the exclusive Port Royal neighborhood accounted for four such sales. Jaguar and Aston-Martin dealerships thrive. In the summer of 2004, the median sales price for Collier County homes soared past $430,000.[51]

For decades, Bonita Springs had languished as a village south of Fort Myers along the Tamiami Trail. Tourists enjoyed the picturesque Imperial River and the landmark Shell Factory, which burned in 1952. The 1990s transformed the village as wealth and capital infused the place with luxurious new developments. Bonita Springs led Florida in the number of wealthy new arrivals. Between 1990 and 1999, transplants with incomes greater than $150,000 increased by 6,273 percent. A $3 million art center graces the community. New wealth also widens the gap between old poverty. At Bonita Bay, where median income exceeds $136,000 per household, life is good; at Dunbar, a black neighborhood near downtown Fort Myers, where median household income is slightly more than $14,000, life is bleak. The places represent the richest and poorest neighborhoods in Lee County, where 11 percent of the population resided in poverty. The real story is certainly bleaker because of the number of illegal aliens working and living on the bottom tier.[52]

Not only are mansions getting more expensive, they are also getting bigger. Beginning in the 1980s, investors and speculators began purchasing homes in desirable locations, then tearing them down to build "McMansions," "Megamansions," or "trophy" homes. The practice is hardly new. In the early 1980s, a Colombian purchased President Nixon's celebrated Key Biscayne five-bedroom house for $455,000, only to level the structure and replace it with a palace. Only the helicopter pad survived the wrecking ball. Such practices accelerated in the last decades of the century. In Hillsborough County, the five largest homes are in Avila, a gated community. In Sarasota, "Mansionization" has changed the texture and landscape of neighborhoods such as Siesta Key and Country Club Shores as the new, bigger homes dominate the more intimate, older structures. Only in a few places in America could a 2004 real estate advertisement list a Largo "waterfront handyman special" for $1,095,000![53]

In John Sayles's film *Sunshine State*, the director selects a trio of wisecracking Yankees to comment on manners and morals, a 2002 equivalent of an ancient Greek chorus. The chorus laments and exalts Florida's virtues and flaws, not in an ancient amphitheater but on a sculpted golf course flanked by cypress and live oak. Before shopping malls and golf courses, asks Murray Silver, a chorus member and developer, what did Florida have? "Poor people who ate catfish!" And how did developers tame cypress swamps to become housing tracts? By putting "nature on a leash."

The golf course, perhaps as much as the modern beach, perfectly encapsulates modern Florida. Sporting names like Addison Reserve, Saddlebrook, Alaqua Lakes, John's Island Club, and Mediterra, "master-planned communities" have sprung up across the state, with golf courses as centerpieces. Golf courses have become bigger, more luxurious, and more popular than ever. In 2000, Florida boasted over a thousand such facilities. That year developers built 41 new golf courses. Jupiter is home to the National Golf Foundation. Collier and Lee counties claim more than 140 eighteen-hole courses, a greater concentration of fairways and sand traps than any other place outside Myrtle Beach, South Carolina. In 1950, Collier County boasted a single golf course. Consider Golf Village, Palm Beach County, with a 2000 population of 230 and average income of $145,000. The Concession, a $600 million, Jack Nicklaus–designed golf community is planned for Manatee County. One need not have a titanium driver to appreciate golf's lifestyle. On Fisher Island, residents spend as much as $20,000 on golf carts/cars detailed to resemble a Rolls-Royce or Jaguar. Environmentalists question the wisdom of devoting so many resources to create amenities for the few. "Golf courses," writes commentator Diane Roberts, "are an assault on Florida's fragile ecosystems. . . . [they] wreck habitat, suck up vast amounts of water, and spit out poisons." A typical golf course demands up to a million gallons of water per day. Few forms of idealized nature impose as much upon the natural habitat as a golf course. Appropriately, *Caddy Shack*, arguably the most famous golfing movie ever made, was filmed in Davie at the Rolling Hills Golf and Country Club.[54]

Generations of Americans, Europeans, and Asians have invested in the Florida dream. Unlike the esoteric utopias described by Plato, Thomas More, and Karl Marx, the Florida Dream is accessible and obtainable. In his essay on utopian visions in literature, Edward Rothstein notes, "It is astonishing how few [utopias] one would feel comfortable living in." Walt Disney Americanized the concept of utopia. His Tomorrowland interpreted a future limited only by our dreams and the creativity of artists, engineers, and scientists. Optimism, technology, and corporate America came together at Disney World's Carousel of Progress. Alas, even Disney's Tomorrowland is subject to revision. In 1998, the Walt Disney Company redesigned its signature exhibit. The old Tomorrowland, according to James Sterngold, "has effectively been abandoned in favor of a more guarded, even pessimistic view of the limits of planning and, to some degree, of the human imagination." Florida's vision of Paradise—a tract home in Lehigh Acres, a beach cottage in Bokeelia, or a lakefront mansion at Isleworth—allows multiple meanings and a modest down payment. If, in this age of moral relativism, the idea of utopia no longer excites, the idea of Paradise by the gated golf course or trailer park still does.[55]

What will high-brow critics and plain folk in the twenty-second century think of the homes Floridians built and lived in during the latter years of the twentieth century? Will surviving ranch-style homes be exalted and appreciated in the same ways that Americans rediscovered the once-ordinary bungalow and beach cottage?

What would Floridians living in the early twentieth century think of the homes built by their compatriots living at the end of the century? The sheer size of the modern home, especially when the size of the shrinking family is calculated, would flabbergast an earlier generation. Space devoted to modern amenities—walk-in closets, three-car garages, and entertainment centers—would no doubt impress. The changing meaning of the words *landscape* and *landscaping* suggests the cultural distance between Victorian America and post-modern Florida. In 1880, front yards consisted of swept sand and pine straw. Today's elaborately manicured, green-grass lawns are the result of scientific triumphs, the democratization of home ownership, and class distinctions. In 1950, Floridians paid the next door neighbor fifty cents to mow the lawn; in 2003, Floridians spent a billion dollars on professional landscaping.[56]

Almost certainly, however, old carpenters would shake their heads at the quality of wood used in hundreds of thousands of homes built after 1950. Soaked in arsenic and pressure treated, modern hardwood (especially pine) compares poorly with previous building materials. Once longleaf pine forests blanketed vast stretches of Florida and the Southeast. When Europeans first touched the continent, as many as 85 million acres covered the South's coastal plains. Longleaf pine forests stretched across the Florida Panhandle. By the 1930s, most of the virgin pine (*Pinus palustris*) had been felled and milled, replaced—if at all—by slash pines and inferior species. The forests may have vanished, but the venerable frame homes milled from heart of yellow pine have not. In Florida, another species (*Pinus elliottii*) popularly known as Dade County pine grew atop a long ridge stretching between Stuart and Homestead.

Homes fashioned of Dade County pine acquired a legendary status, breaking power saws, repulsing termites, and mellowing to a burnished gray.[57]

Buildings crafted from virgin pine resisted insects and time. Twentieth-century archaeologists marveled at the charred remains of the Mission San Luis de Apalachee, located near present-day Tallahassee. Begun in 1656, the mission was burned by early-eighteenth-century marauders, but remnants of the yellow pine, with its high resin content, endured. When preservationists wished to re-create San Luis in the 1980s, builders brushed new pine with a preservative. Within a decade, termites and wood-eating fungus were ravaging the new structures.[58]

Tourist Empires and the Invention of Florida

B.D. (Before Disney) to A.D. (After Disney)

O n the killing floor of a turn-of-the-century Philadelphia meat factory, two young immigrants conversed
in Serbo-Croatian while pointing to a newspaper
clipping depicting a fashionably dressed family boarding a Pullman parlor car headed for Florida.

"We stopped picking oranges and started picking tourists."

An Orlando banker, 1979

"What's Florida?" asked the Croat.

"That's a place that's warm in the winter," responded the
Serb.

"Who goes there?"

"You can see who goes, only bosses."[1]

Stjepan Mesaros had not read Karl Marx or Thorstein Veblen,
but the Croatian meat cutter understood their message. To
Marx, the Philadelphia slaughterhouse epitomized the class war
between parasitical owners who wintered in Florida and the exploited workers who were becoming more militant and desperate by the day. Worker solidarity brought together historic Balkan enemies. In *The Theory of the Leisure Class* (1899), Veblen
coined the term *conspicuous consumption* to explain the elite's
fondness for fashionable resorts, and even more, for being seen
at such places. To Veblen, such behavior did not quicken class
warfare; rather, workers strove to sample the fruits of capitalism. Consumption and culture, not merely production and
power, identified industrial America and its hopeful workers.
Material things mattered. By purchasing homes and clothes,
workers could enhance their status. At the turn of the century,

few Americans could imagine, let alone afford, a week in Florida, but they might indulge in a day at Coney Island or Atlantic City. Marx disapproved of such proletarian frivolities, believing that display and play served as mere opiates for the masses. Marx was not alone in his concerns about leisure. Still struggling with Puritan notions of amusement and sin, many American ministers warned of the dangers of wanton pleasure.[2]

Neither Marx nor Veblen lived long enough to witness the social and economic transformation that swept the United States in the decades after World War II. In history's most spectacular burst of economic expansion and upward mobility, millions of European immigrants and their children, industrial laborers, and displaced farmers acquired middle-class status and comforts unimaginable a generation earlier. World War II, the GI Bill, a resurgent labor movement, technological advances, a buoyant economy lifted by housing, automobiles, and durable goods purchases, a Cold War, and an activist federal government salvaged and redeemed capitalism. A vacation in Florida signified both a democratic right and a republican virtue. The transformation of leisure into consumption signaled the rise of modern Florida tourism.

Tourism at Midcentury

Between the hot war and the cold front of 1950, a George Gallup poll confirmed what every Detroit autoworker or New York stockbroker already knew: Americans were in love with California and Florida. Identified by what they thought, and defined by what they bought, Americans' postwar dream list included a house, a car, and a vacation. Buoyed by a booming economy and pressured by unions, most American employers provided workers two weeks of paid vacation a year. In America, unlike Europe, the impetus for paid vacations came from private enterprise and enlightened corporate interest, not from government. The formula worked. In 1950, two of every three families took a vacation. If, as the writer Wallace Stegner insisted, the West represented "the geography of hope," places like Tiki Gardens and Bonita Springs expressed dreams of individual happiness amid tropical splendor.[3]

Since 1950, a staggering 1 billion tourists have sought sun and fun in Florida. The names Silver Springs, Cypress Gardens, and Weeki Wachee; the Magic Kingdom, SeaWorld, and Busch Gardens read like a roll call of American leisure. Tourism has also drawn hordes of writers and commentators interested in the meaning of leisure and recreation in modern America. The Florida vacation allows social critics and travel writers to peer into an American—and, increasingly, a global—way of life. Questions abound. How, why, and when did the Florida vacation come to be a defining signature of American life? How has the vacation changed between 1950, when about 4.5 million tourists sought comfort in Florida, and the 1990s, when over 50 million travelers packed mega-theme parks in greater Orlando alone? What does it mean when the most popular tourist attractions in the world are controlled by one multiconglomerate, which also happens to be one of the most powerful media empires in history? What are the social and economic implications for the fourth-largest state in the nation when its economy and image are built upon and dependent upon tourism?[4]

Contrary to popular myth, theme parks dotted the state *before* Disney. The theme was purely and unapologetically Florida. Abundantly endowed with sugar-white beaches, emerald water, and eternal sunshine, Florida converted nature into dream vacations. As charming and understated as it was later brash and universal, tourism sanctioned fun and profit in an era when consumption was replacing production as a national template. Postwar affluence, gleaming new cars, and paved roads made Florida vacations attainable for large numbers of Americans. To a public all too familiar with Great Depression scarcities and wartime rationing, a vacation underscored the American way of life and served as a marker of middle-class status.

Dixie Highway's dual routes diverted Michiganders and Ohioans to Florida's west coast and New Yorkers and Jerseyites down the east coast. Like swallows, select sons and daughters of prairie cities and the Great Plains returned each winter. Dixie Highway's western route originated in Sault Sainte Marie, Michigan, funneling through the Midwest and South, ending in Miami. u.s. 41 began at Cooper Harbor, Michigan, and arrived in Tampa, where it became the Tamiami Trail. The famed road hugged the Gulf coast from Tampa to Naples, offering travelers oases of comfort. Identified by their black socks with sandals and Wally Byam Airstreams, midwesterners adored Fort Myers and Lake Apopka. Tourists displayed unquenchable curiosity, crowding Tampa's banana docks to witness "plodding Negro stevedores" and pulling off to the side of roadways to walk through groves and pick Parson Brown oranges. Gulf Coast mobile home parks abounded with flat accents and arching rectitude, as seasonal residents tossed horseshoes and exchanged stories of frontier Florida, how before 1949 livestock routinely crowded the highways, ruining many vacations. Many families planned their vacations around spring training. Lakeland,

PLATE 1. Published in 1939, *Florida: A Guide to the Southernmost State* represented a significant literary and cultural achievement. Stetson Kennedy, Zora Neale Hurston, and many others worked on the New Deal project. In Florida, the *Guide* noted, to travel to the South you must head north. An original jacket cover. Author's collection.

PLATE 2. The 23 January 1926 cover of *Liberty* magazine romanticized Americans' fascination with Florida. With their Ford Flivver and dreams of winter sunshine and beaches, a young couple heads south on Dixie Highway for Miami. Author's collection.

PLATE 3. In the period following World War I, ballyhoo, tourism, and old-fashioned salesmanship created and sustained the Florida boom. As depicted by *Judge*, a popular 1923 magazine, women played an indispensable role in shaping Florida's image. Author's collection.

PLATE 4. An orange-crate label glorified Dixie Highway, one of the major north-south arteries in the 1920s and 1930s. Author's collection.

Pensacola Beach, Florida, "On the Gulf of Mexico"

PACKARD
IN FLORIDA

Visit us this season
ship us your car by
boat or rail. We take
care of freight and
adjustments. Have
car ready on your
arrival.
    Leave car with
us when you return
We attend to all
details for re-shipping
    Packard service
in South Florida.

CARY-CRANE MOTORS, Inc.
TAMPA   ST. PETERSBURG

PLATE 5. Summer crowds flocked to popular Pensacola Beach in the 1950s. Author's collection.

PLATE 6. Since the first cars raced across the sands of Ormond Beach in 1904, Floridians have been captivated by the speed and sensuality of the automobile. This 1920s advertisement in *Suniland* glamorized life in boom-time Florida. Author's collection.

home of the Detroit Tigers since 1934, developed a special relationship with Wolverine State autoworkers and cherry growers.

Florida's west coast offered winter visitors an extraordinary range of festivals and sites to visit. Since 1906, Greek immigrants at Tarpon Springs observed Epiphany with the ceremonial tossing of a cross into Big Bayou. By 1921, so many tourists were attending the pageant that the archbishop ordered young divers to wear bathing suits! Tampa's Gasparilla Festival, begun in 1904 to celebrate the mythical pirate José Gaspar, a purely invented tradition, drew crowds of a half million throughout the 1950s. Each winter throngs of motorists converged upon Bradenton for its DeSoto Pageant and Tin Can Tourists' convention. Sarasota served as the winter headquarters for the "Greatest Show on Earth," the Ringling Bros. Barnum and Bailey Circus, and as the home of the Sara-De-Soto Pageant. In October 1950, the Naples Swamp Buggy Races attracted 5,000 enthusiasts, twice as many persons as lived in the sleepy community.[5]

Flush with ruddy-faced tourists, St. Petersburg radiated a midcentury confidence born of decades of winter relationships. Many Heartland tourists became residents, bringing to the Pinellas peninsula their deep-felt values (moral campaigns aimed at liquor and gambling) and convictions (that the sacred waterfront must remain public space). Perhaps no other city in Florida has or had so perfected and refined the importance of image in selling itself. The sole industry of St. Petersburg—a city devoid of manufacturing and isolated on a peninsula of a peninsula—involved manufacturing its friendly image as the "Sunshine City." The first city to hire a public relations director, St. Petersburg was also one of the first to cultivate the elderly. Period postcards document tourists and winter residents clustered on green benches, reading a newspaper, playing checkers, or enjoying a dipper of water from the Fountain of Youth. The spring training home to two fabled sport franchises, the New York Yankees and the St. Louis Cardinals, St. Petersburg also was home to the Festival of States Parade. Annually, sunburned midwestern and northern expatriates and winter transplants participated in the spectacle. Resembling Grand Army of the Republic conventioneers, residents of Kalamazoo, Kokomo, and Kankakee marched behind their city and state placards.[6]

Land of Lincoln and Dairy State license plates adorned Gulf Coast–bound Fords and Chevys; on the packed-sand beaches of Hollywood and in the parking lots of Miami Beach, one encountered Empire State and Garden State plates. Dixie Highway's (U.S. 1) eastern terminus stretched from Fort Kent,

Maine, to Miami. After the terrible Labor Day hurricane of 1935 washed away Flagler's Impossible Railway, the railbed became highway, extending U.S. 1 to Key West. Before the completion of the interstate highway system in the 1960s and 1970s, U.S. 1 was the busiest vacation thoroughfare in America. Paralleling U.S. 1 and hugging the Intracoastal Waterway and Atlantic Ocean, Highway A1A navigated barrier islands and beach towns. Bolstered by its identity as the "oldest city in America," St. Augustine combined antiquity and modernity. The call letters of the city's then lone radio station, WFOY, stood for Wonderful Fountain of Youth. Confident that a massive makeover would provide the ancient city with an economic lift equivalent to the restoration of Williamsburg, Virginia, St. Augustine began reconstruction and restoration in 1959. If tourists fell in love with St. Augustine's narrow streets and seventeenth-century charm, they also knew which cities to avoid. For all of its economic assets—its wharves, paper mill, and banks—Jacksonville acquired a reputation as a gritty city well worth avoiding. Indicative of the city's plight, Robert L. Ripley spurned Jacksonville, his home for twenty years, to locate his Ripley's Believe It or Not Museum of Oddities and Curiosities in St. Augustine's Castle Warden Hotel. Motorists and families developed special affinities for the small towns and cities strung out along Dixie Highway and A1A: Fernandina Beach, Jacksonville Beach, Ormond Beach, Daytona Beach, New Smyrna Beach, Rockledge, Melbourne, Fort Pierce, Stuart, Boynton Beach, Delray Beach, Boca Raton, Pompano Beach, Fort Lauderdale, Dania, Hollywood, Hallandale, and Miami. In January 1951, newspaperman Ben Funk traveled to Miami down U.S. 1. "We were struck," he remembered, "by the sight of seaside towns spread out in pastel colors over white sands." Towns developed niches. Stuart was renowned for sailfishing, Daytona because of its auto races, and Dania for its tomato-tossing festival. Weathered clapboard cottages shared the roadways with gleaming new gasoline stations and motels.[7]

To both casual observers and highway patrolmen, the steady stream of Studebaker Land Cruisers, Hudson Hornets, and Nash Ambassadors was heady stuff. Never had one seen so many automobiles traveling southward as in 1950. Numbers of travelers ebbed and flowed in seasonal rhythms: swelling in the winter and spring, trickling in the summer and fall. In Buick Roadmasters and Willys station wagons—but also in Pan American Clippers, Pullman berths, and Greyhound buses—Americans trekked and trafficked to the Sunshine State. The fabled Orange Blossom Special still sped rail passengers from New York to Miami—and achieved immortality because of Ervin Thomas Rouse's fiddling melody and homage—but for the most part, tourists arrived by car. Motorists ventured down roads with magical names and mystical associations: the Jackson-Lee Highway, the St. Johns River Trail, Dixie Highway, the Buccaneer Trail, the Gulf Coast Scenic Highway, the Old Spanish Trail, the Scenic Highlands Highway, the Highway of Southern Hospitality, the Orange Blossom Trail, the Sugarland Highway, and the Tamiami Trail.

At the most remote crossroads and isolated archipelagos, the automobile had conquered Florida. Signs and symbols of an automobile culture pervaded the state's thoroughfares. Florida's roadside landscape radiated the business of tourism and travel: gasoline stations, five-seat diners, and tourist courts. In the 1950s, fourteen national/international petroleum companies sold gasoline in Florida, and each attempted to package its product with a distinctive signature. Motorists identified Pure Oil stations by their high-pitched sloping roofs and shaded canopies. Mediterranean revival– and art deco–styled gasoline stations blended into the built landscape, while others leapt out at the motorist in the jarring but whimsical forms of dinosaurs or lighthouses. Service stations dispensed more than gasoline. Standard Oil, Gulf, and Phillips distributed millions of free travel maps. Glove compartments documented vacations past, with routes carefully mapped out in pencil and pen. Commercial artists festooned these road maps with festive images of tarpon springing from the water, lush golf courses, and trees laden with Spanish moss and oranges.[8]

Travelers instantly recognized the familiar corporate logos of Standard Oil and Sinclair. Such was not the case with other roadside establishments. Motorists discovered 1950s Florida largely devoid of national franchised motels and restaurants. Families bedded down and ate at an astonishing variety of locally owned establishments. Patrons could choose between motor courts—some posting "summer rates" as low as $1.50 a night—and genteel hotels, such as the Vinoy and the Breakers with their stiff tariffs. Establishments vied for attention with eye-catching billboards and striking architecture. "There are signs that turn like windmills," wrote one observer describing the Dixie Highway, "startling signs that resemble crashed airplanes; signs with glass lettering that blaze forth at night when automobile headlight beams strike them; flashing neon signs; signs painted with a professional touch; signs crudely lettered and misspelled." On Sunny Isles in Dade County, a sphinx, mermaids, and Tahitian decor adorned hotels with whimsical names: the Suez, the Blue Mist, the Castaways Beach Resort. Visitors to Rainbow Springs and Wakulla Springs stayed at rustic lodges built of wood and stone. Dinosaurs once roamed the Florida roadsides, concrete and stucco creations that stunned many motorists. In Orlando, Wigwam Village featured Depression-era cabins designed in the shape of tee-pees. Motels, motor courts, and auto camps offered economy-minded tourists an alternative to stuffy downtown hotels and expectant bellhops. Brochures promised "all the comforts of the best hotels at much less cost." Concrete block was fast replacing wood as the favored building material. On beaches, pastel-painted concrete walls were becoming the rage. *Fortune* magazine reported in 1951 that owning a motel in Florida had become the new American dream. Between 1942 and 1952, the number of motel courts in Pinellas County in-creased tenfold. Florida's roadside was part American Gothic, part honky-tonk, and part tropical paradise. Not everyone appreciated the assorted vagaries of hotels, motels, and service. During a 1951 family vacation, one guest was so upset with his shabby accommodations that he conceived of his own motel chain so future guests would encounter no surprises. Kemmons Wilson launched Holiday Inn the following year.[9]

Visitors extolled the virtues of local foodstuffs and cooks. Combining ele-ments of a Cuban fiesta, a New England seafood boil, and a southern harvest, Florida cuisine was a glorious feast of imported traditions and local delicacies. Refreshingly free of franchised uniformity and frozen portions, Florida menus tempted diners with the pride of quality and quantity, and with no shame ac-companying turtleburgers, swamp cabbage, and larded piecrust.

With little effort, a motorist could discover an old-fashioned fish fry in Crest-view, an oyster roast in Apalachicola, baked gopher (land tortoise) in Vernon, rice pilau (pronounced *perloo*) in St. Augustine, heart-of-palm salad topped with pistachio ice cream in Cedar Key, Hoppin' John in Quincy, fried mullet and grunts near the docks of Cortez, bread baked in banana leaves at No Name Key, side table condiments of Old Sour (a prized bottled condiment made from Key limes and local Scotch bonnet peppers) at Marathon, and "snarly conchs" roast-ing on hot coals on Chokoloskee Island. Tourist guides and gas station atten-dants identified legendary eateries: Bartels of Pensacola, famous for its chicken and homemade wine; the Valley Café in Blountstown, with its ample portions of fried catfish; any place in Apalachicola that served oysters; Littlefield's Fish-ing Camp in Fernandina, the city where modern shrimping began, proud of its fried shrimp platters; the Pig 'n' Whistle, one of Jacksonville's many barbecue establishments; Gene Johnson's fish camp on the Intracoastal Waterway near Matanzas Inlet, renowned for its steamed oysters and clam fritters; the Dolphin Restaurant, operated by Marine Studios on A1A, with its celebrated baked pompano in a brown paper bag, and its celebrity diners Ernest Hemingway and Marjorie Kinnan Rawlings; the beloved Bucky's Five O'clock Club in Port Orange, which served a half-chicken on toast; the Coffee Cup, located on u.s. 41 in Ruskin, which offered patrons platters of homemade biscuits and ethereally light meringue pies; the colonnaded Clewiston Inn, where deep-fried Lake Okeechobee catfish was an everyday staple; Louis Pappas Riverside Café in Tarpon Springs, home of the "original" Greek salad; Tampa's Columbia, the "Gem of Spanish Restaurants," with its original Snapper Alicante; St. Petersburg's Wedgewood, where Duncan Hines proclaimed the "world's best apple pie"; Gary's Duck Inn of Orlando, "where good food predominates"; Fisher's Restaurant in Sebring and its advertised sour orange pie; the Everglades Rod and Gun Club in Everglades City, where the chef obligingly prepared the patrons' catch of the day; Joe's Stone Crab of Miami Beach, purportedly the establishment that first served the prized crustacean; Lake Worth's La Conga Restaurant, proud of its frog legs; the A & B Lobster House of Key West, with its specialty of Florida lobster; and the Green Turtle Inn at Islamorada with its turtle steak.[10]

In 1950, the pollster George Gallup asked Americans, "If you had your choice of going anywhere you wanted in the world on a vacation this summer— and cost didn't matter—where would you most like to go?" Florida finished third, ahead of Europe, but behind California and Hawaii. The increasing popularity of air conditioning made languid nights in June, July, and August more tolerable. The Atlantic Coast Line's Palm City and Seaboard Air Line's Orange Blossom Special boasted air-conditioned railcars. In the 1940s, Miami Beach calendars contained only three pages: "January, February, and March." Hotel owners invested in air conditioning in the 1950s. By 1955, every Miami Beach hotel had air conditioning. Delta Airlines' "Millionaire Dream Vacations" popularized summer travel to Miami Beach. White southerners invaded Florida's largely undeveloped beaches from Santa Rosa to Destin to Panama City Beach's Miracle Strip Park in numbers that earned their vacation spots the affectionate nicknames—"L.A." (Lower Alabama) and "Redneck Riviera." Historically, June, July, and August drew about five times as many visitors to Pensacola Beach than did January, February, and March. Cypress Gardens attempted to entice summer visitors by offering a special summer admission fee of thirty-five cents. Admission included a free gardenia blossom "to every lady."[11]

Pre–Magic Kingdom Orlando was a mouse that barely roared. Although Orlando considered 50,000 visitors a good season, the "City Beautiful" prided itself in being a wholesome place where visitors might enjoy a free band concert

FIGURE 9. A 1940s tourist brochure touts Orlando as the "City Beautiful." University of South Florida Special Collections, Tampa.

on Lake Eola, lawn bowling and shuffleboard at Sunshine Park, a stroll through Orchid Gardens, a swim at nearby Sanlando Springs, or a drive to Big Tree Park in Longwood to gaze at the "Senator," a 127-foot-high cypress tree that measured 47 feet around. Still others might trek to Winter Haven, where each December city fathers crowned a Tangerine Queen at Cypress Gardens. Travelers who wished to find the Wild West in Central Florida could attend the Silver Springs Rodeo, held in Kissimmee each winter. A tourist brochure highlighted

Orlando's recreational facilities: "golf, tennis, bridle paths, bathing, a municipal solarium, park games, etc." Locals and tourists mingled at Kemp's Coliseum on Orange Avenue, where they danced and attended big band concerts and wrestling matches. Each March, residents anxiously awaited the arrival of the woeful Washington Senators, who strained and trained at Tinker Field. Even if the Senators were awful, Orange County's bountiful groves rewarded travelers with free bouquets of orange blossoms. Journalist James Clark, surveying Orlando promotional literature from the 1880s to the 1960s, described it as "a journey through hyperbole and desperation."[12]

On the eve of the Mouse, alligators still reigned as Central Florida's cultural icon. In 1940, Owen Godwin bought 15 acres south of Orlando on u.s. 441. A third-generation Cracker, Godwin genuinely wished to share his love of natural Florida. Filling a pit with water and reptiles, he called his slice of paradise

FIGURE 10. Kitschy but compelling, Gatorland's signature sculpture defined pre-Disney tourism. State of Florida Photographic Archives, Tallahassee.

Gatorland. Admission fee was voluntary. When the tourists returned home, Godwin toured the East Coast with a hand-fashioned cypress trailer and his favorite gator, a 12-foot specimen named "Cannibal Jake."[13]

Midcentury tourism combined pluckish capitalism and puckish fun. Sunken Gardens and McKee Jungle Gardens exuded Florida wholesomeness and tropical exotica. Opened near Vero Beach in 1932, McKee Jungle Gardens offered Depression-weary Americans pure splendorous nature. The star attractions were gru gru palms, Madagascar screw pines, Amazonian lily pads large enough to cradle a baby, and the greatest concentration of orchids in North America. Designed by William Lyman Phillips, an associate of the renowned Olmsted Brothers firm, the park's 80 acres dazzled visitors who strolled under the Cathedral of Palms (three hundred royal palms) and navigated the bougainvillea glade hugging the Indian River. Many gushed that they could not believe they were "still in America"; others contemplated that the experience made them "closer to God."[14]

At the turn of the century, George Turner purchased an unusual tract of land a short distance from downtown St. Petersburg. A plumber by trade and an avid horticulturist, Turner transformed this four-and-one-half-acre sinkhole into a Florida dreamscape, installing a maze of drainage tiles and planting guavas and banana trees. Turner grew tropical fruits and orchids but discovered his most lucrative crop was Yankees, who wished to stroll along the paths and gawk at the tropical foliage and rock formations 15 feet below street level. Each winter, Sunshine City tourist hotels and boarding houses filled with midwesterners and northerners enjoying the site's eccentricities while drinking cups of papaya juice. In time, the family-run facility added gift shops and bird shows.[15]

If Sunken Gardens maximized upon nature's oddities, Silver Springs and Weeki Wachee ranked as two of the natural wonders of the world. One of the state's earliest destinations for travelers, Silver Springs first gained fame after the Civil War when glass-bottomed boats began gliding across its crystal waters. After his celebrated 1880 tour of Central Florida, ex-president Ulysses S. Grant exclaimed, "This is the greatest wonder I have ever seen." An Ocala businessman purchased 80 acres surrounding the springs for a few thousand dollars in 1909. But the decline of steamboating and the area's inaccessibility limited the appeal of Silver Springs; in 1920, fewer than 10,000 visitors a year made their way to the site. Aggressive advertising and highway construction made Silver Springs a popular destination, and by the early 1950s it was annually attracting

FIGURE 11. In the late 1940s, the impresario-showman Newton Perry introduced the mermaid to tourists at Weeki Wachee, combining beauty, sex, the awesome wonder of natural springs, and Barnumesque promotion. State of Florida Photographic Archives, Tallahassee.

a million visitors. Promoters added a Jungle Cruise and speedboat ride, the Ross Allen Reptile Institute, and a Seminole Indian Village. By 1952, gift shops, restaurants, and concessions alone grossed over $1 million. Since 1916, filmmakers have found the crystal waters irresistible. Monkeys—extras from six Tarzan movies filmed at the locale—thrived and multiplied. In the late 1950s, Lloyd Bridges starred in the successful TV series *Seahunt* filmed on site.[16]

The flood of postwar tourists spawned a commercial creativity that survives to this day. In the 1890s, the artist Winslow Homer marveled at the watery wilderness between the Homosassa and the Chassahowitzka rivers, but few tourists visited the isolated area. Newton Perry possessed a vision to change the nature of tourism. Florida's natural springs had long been a favorite destination for visitors, but tourism was confined to glass-bottomed boats and swimming. As a youth, Perry had worked as a lifeguard at Silver Springs, but it was his experience as a physical education instructor with navy frogmen during World War II that prepared Perry for his greatest innovation. On 1 June 1947, Perry resigned his position as manager of the Wakulla Springs Lodge. He explained to Ed Ball, the flinty banker and owner of the lodge, that he was going to manage a new tourist facility in Hernando County. "The Springs are called Weeki Wachee and is located just north of Tarpon Springs on a well traveled highway, U.S. 19. . . . We will not be going into competition with Wakulla Springs as we are going to have an underwater Photo Gallery that will seat fifty people and will have aquatic shows put on." In a Barnumesque moment, Perry introduced live "mermaids," local bathing beauties with air hoses. The mermaid show became an instant hit. By the 1960s, so popular was the mermaid show that women from five continents auditioned for the privilege of wearing sequins and spending forty-five minutes in 72-degree water. When Elvis Presley was filming *Follow That Dream* in 1961, he visited Weeki Wachee, seeking out the mermaids for a photo opportunity. In 1959, American Broadcasting Co. purchased the attraction and began an ambitious expansion program.[17]

Arguably the best-known Florida attraction between the 1950s and the opening of Disney World in 1971, Cypress Gardens possessed none of the advantages of Weeki Wachee or Jungle Gardens. Located on Lake Eloise in Polk County, Cypress Gardens lacked a spectacular natural setting or a busy highway funneling tourists north and south.

But countless birdhouses, bumper stickers, and weekly magazines urged Americans to "See Cypress Gardens," where they encountered a place and dream lovingly fashioned by one of Florida's greatest promoters. Born in Iowa in 1900, Dick Pope accompanied his father to Florida during the 1920s land boom. He never left. In the early 1930s, he raised $2,800 to purchase a 16-acre site on Lake Eloise. Vowing to "make a real Venice out of the place," Pope first had to drain and clear the marshlands bordering the cypress groves. He then carved out canals to connect the lakes. Pope claimed the park's inspiration derived from a story about a cash-strapped South Carolina aristocrat who charged visitors money to tour his plantation. With optimism and fanfare, he opened his park on 2 January 1936. The first day 136 customers paid twenty-five cents each for a grand total of thirty-four dollars.[18]

The Popes were consummate image makers. One morning after a storm, Julia discovered that the garden's floral entrance had been damaged. Undaunted, she dressed up several secretaries and cashiers in antebellum hoop skirts, gardenias, and bonnets, creating an instant tradition. On another occasion, visiting military officers wished to know when the "show" started. Under pressure, the Pope family produced the first of the now-famous water ski shows. Necessity begat the aquamaids and barefoot skiing. Pope himself cut quite a figure with his trademark pastel plaids and checkered wardrobe. "I'm not a funeral director," he explained, "I'm a salesman of sunny Florida."[19]

No single feature identified Cypress Gardens; rather, Pope's perpetual promotion connected the public and place. The irrepressible Pope assigned employees to plaster Cypress Gardens decals on the auto bumpers of guests' cars. He insisted that local meteorologists describe overcast days as "partly sunny" rather than "partly cloudy." When asked in 1963 to name their favorite tourist spot in the United States, travel editors chose Cypress Gardens in a first-place tie with the Grand Canyon. Indicative of Cypress Gardens' devotion to detail, Pope elevated the common camera to new heights. He employed eight full-time photographers simply to help guests load and shoot film. In the 1950s, the gift shop sold more Kodak film than any place in America. Pope reduced his formula for success to a simple formula: "OPM Squared, or Our Photographic Materials Times Other People's Money." Throughout the 1950s, publicity about the park saturated the media; photographs appeared in hundreds of newspapers each day. The founder kept a million and a half negatives in his office safe. Hollywood also shot films in Winter Haven. Swimming champion–turned–Hollywood actress Esther Williams starred in two romantic, travelogue MGM musicals there, *On an Island with You* (1948) and *Easy to Love* (1953). Twentieth-Century Fox's *Moon over Miami* (1941), featuring Betty Grable as a gold digger, also took advantage of Cypress Gardens.[20]

Cypress Gardens succeeded because it offered something for everyone. To sober and taciturn midwesterners, it supplied clean-cut family entertainment; to the middle classes who could not afford Paris or would not tolerate French waiters, it was America's Versailles Garden; to a public not yet saturated by cable television and cynical about packaged entertainment, Dick Pope created something beautiful and entertained crowds with thrilling water sports and pure corniness (such as playing a piano on skis).

Silver Springs, Cypress Gardens, and Weeki Wachee thrived as tourist attractions because of Mother Nature and Madison Avenue. Nature supplied the stage setting, but shrewd advertising and contrived gimmickry (alligator wrestling, barefoot skiing, and mermaids) brought customers to the parking lots. Tourists had choices. Florida's springs, rivers, and lakes simply spilleth over. Humans improved upon nature. Like New York's Saratoga Springs and Coney Island, Florida's Silver Springs, Marineland, and Cypress Gardens were as much deliberate human constructions as they were natural phenomena. There was nothing inevitable about the invention or success of Sunken Gardens or Weeki Wachee. Neither tourism nor nature is destiny. In the end, tourism relies upon manufactured images, carefully crafted and packaged.

The tourists who arrived in 1950 Florida came for many of the same reasons that visitors were first attracted to the state a century earlier. Tourism has always involved escape and fantasy, satisfaction through commodification. What had changed dramatically was the audience. In the Gilded Age, a vacation was emblematic of the privileged classes. To restore nerves shattered by the pressures of modernity, the "best men" and their families enjoyed the waters of Saratoga Springs or spent the season at the Breakers or the Alcazar, assiduously avoiding the great unwashed masses. American society, however, was changing from an economy and culture geared to production and work to one increasingly organized around consumption and leisure. The 1920s ushered in middle-class tourism. The same technologies and economies that invented Betty Crocker and created Rand McNally road maps could, with equal flair and precision, package, commodify, and market aquamaids in Central Florida or concrete pools filled with water and dolphins. Islands of wealth and resort architecture radiated new tastes. Tourism reflected such cultural and class tensions.[21]

Marineland illustrated the connection between nature and spectacle. One of Florida's most popular tourist attractions, Marineland enjoyed success built upon location, promotion, and dolphins. Begun in 1938 as a remarkable partnership between Cornelius Vanderbilt Whitney (the commodore's grandson)

FIGURE 12. Marineland made nature spectacular, entertaining crowds with leaping dolphins and barking sea lions. State of Florida Photographic Archives, Tallahassee.

and Ilya Tolstoy (the count's grandson), by the early 1950s Marine Studios and its acclaimed oceanarium were drawing a half million customers annually. Whitney and Tolstoy possessed strong naturalist credentials: the former served as a trustee of the American Museum of Natural History; the latter was a pioneer in the production of underwater films. They originally conceived of Marine Studios as a motion picture facility for studying and filming sea specimens in an enclosed, oceanlike environment. But when the partners discovered that blue bottlenose dolphins (also called porpoises) could be trained to perform tricks above water, the oceanarium became primarily a tourist attraction. The public oohed and aahed over leaping dolphins, a porpoise pulling a poodle on a surfboard, and sea lions barking at clowns. Marineland attracted huge crowds, in part because of the novelty of "spectacular nature"; in part because of its location on AIA between St. Augustine and Daytona Beach, perfectly situated to snag Miami-bound travelers.[22]

In the half century between the Florida boom of the 1920s and the beginning of Disney World in the 1970s, no other Florida destinations so captivated and tempted Americans as Miami and Miami Beach. So many travelers poured into Greater Miami in the early 1950s that tourism fostered a $300 million economy. Old-fashioned attractions awaited crowds converging upon Dade County in the 1950s: Fairchild Tropical Garden, Coppinger's Tropical Paradise, Anirama, Famous Trees, Lost Lake and Caverns, Seaquarium, the Rare Bird Farm, Riviera Tropical Gardens, Musa Isle, the Serpentarium, Monkey Jungle, and Parrot Jungle. The annual Orange Bowl Parade, held on New Year's Eve, typically drew a half million spectators. But another world also awaited tourists, a world of pleasures distant from the innocent charms of Key Biscayne or the Coral Castle.[23]

What made 1950s Miami and Miami Beach so alluring was not resplendent Biscayne Bay or tropical foliage but the arresting combination of sun, sand, and sea; of sex, sport, and sin. Part Monte Carlo and part Babylon, Miami and Miami Beach seemed bold and risqué, at least by the relative standards of the Eisenhower years. Elsewhere, tourist attractions packaged wholesomeness; on Flagler Street and Collins Avenue revelers expected and accepted a brush with mischief and even naughtiness. Families vacationed at Cypress Gardens; couples reveled in Miami. From poolside bookies and beach bikinis to all-girl revues and risque comedians, Miami was awash in temptation. Notorious and venerable establishments—the Colonial Inn, Chez Paree, Club Jewel Box, Club 36, Ball & Chain, the Paddock, the Blue Sales Club, and the Bouché—featured "girls, girls, girls," "female impersonators," and "bronze beauties." To be sure, Miami held no monopoly on the seven deadly sins, but the city allowed tourists and conventioneers anonymity and socially sanctioned escape. "Full undress was the rule," observed journalist Helen Muir, "enough so that the Miami Beach Council even passed a law to ban scantily clad tourists strolling along Lincoln Road." Perfectly respectable citizens of Buffalo and Toledo arrived eager to indulge by night at Ciro's and the Latin Quarter or by day at Hialeah, Gulfstream, or Tropical Park racetracks. Miami was simply the epitome of Gold Coast sophistication.[24]

Revelers who complained that Miami's gaming parlors and dance shows were too tame could with ease hop to Havana, an overnight cruise or a forty-minute flight away. With the blessings of the Cuban government, American mobsters—including Floridians Meyer Lansky and Santo Trafficante Jr.—built and operated sumptuous casinos and hotels. Havana's Club Montmarte advertised "craps-roulette-baccarat"; Club Hollywood promised "nights of pleasure." If 1950s Miami was a springboard to Havana, Batista's Cuba was a bridge to

Miami. Cuba's middle classes flocked to South Florida during the "low season" summer months. In the short run, Fidel's revolution and the subsequent Cuban embargo and travel ban only accentuated Miami's exotic status and accessibility.[25]

More than any other place in Florida, Miami and Miami Beach mirrored popular culture. The cities' five hundred hotels and clubs offered an extraordinary range of variety and cultural tastes. Miami Beach pioneered the American Plan, one price that covered breakfast and dinner. The city's expensive prices simply reinforced its exclusive status. At a time when one dollar covered a complete seafood dinner in Pensacola, the Beach Comber charged five dollars for dinner, a cocktail, and a floor show. Miami, the home to corporate giants Eastern and Pan American, was a trendsetter in air travel, allowing the rich and famous to jet in and out. Millions of Americans romanticized South Florida after watching 1950s films such as *The Miami Story* and *Miami Exposé*, associating the magical place in Irving Berlin songs, or hearing Walter Winchell broadcast his radio show from the Roney Plaza's Bamboo Room. Later, Miami Beach served as backdrop and locale for Arthur Godfrey's radio and television shows. In the words of the ukulele-stroking Godfrey, "Come on down!" They did. In 1950, about 2 million tourists visited the area, a figure nearly doubling by 1964 when television audiences first heard the words, "From the sun and fun capital of the world, Miami Beach, it's the *Jackie Gleason Show.*" The locale became a popular venue for a series of hit films: Jerry Lewis's *The Bellboy* (1960), Sean Connery's *Goldfinger* (1964) and *Thunderball* (1965), and Frank Sinatra's *Tony Rome* (1967).

Tourism also solidified Miami Beach's reputation as a haven for Jews. "A vacation in Miami Beach," proclaimed the writer Isaac Bashevis Singer, "was a chance to be among my own people." Jewish delicatessens, kosher restaurants, synagogues, temples, and bakeries specializing in bagels, kugel, and "New York cheesecake" satisfied Jewish tourists' needs and wants. Miami Beach first competed and then replaced the Catskills as a must-stop for Jewish entertainers. Shecky Greene, Buddy Hackett, Joey Bishop, and Sophie Tucker played to adoring crowds.[26]

In the early 1950s, "America's Playground" underwent a dramatic facelift. The dedication of the Morris Lapidus–inspired Fontainebleau (1954) signaled a new era for Miami Beach and triggered the architectural equivalent of an arms race. The Fontainebleau's main lobby, with its black-and-white marbled columns and pastel colors, awed visitors; its ballroom was spacious enough for

FIGURE 13. On the eve of the tumultuous 1968 election, Key Biscayne resident and presidential candidate Richard Nixon plays golf with Miami Beach's most famous ambassador, Jackie Gleason. Historical Association of Southern Florida, Miami.

3,000 guests. Gaudy but glamorous, comedians mocked the Fontainebleau as "Miami Beach French," a "palace of kitsch." Architectural critic Louise Huxtable ridiculed Lapidus-designed bellhop uniforms as "an exploding gilded eggplant," but visitors adored his designs. Lapidus dismissed critics as taking his designs far too seriously. "You want to have fun," he explained. "You are in my hotel. You're having fun . . . this is the greatest experience of your life." The art deco–styled hotels of the 1930s and 1940s had stood three to four stories, but the new hotels zoomed to ten and fifteen stories, stacked, in the words of Norman Mailer, "like sugar cubes and ice-cube trays on edge." The Eden Roc, Americana, Shelbourne, and Doral Beach stamped their showy signature on a changing Miami Beach. In contrast to the lavishly decorated facades of the art deco buildings, the 1950s hotels expressed extravagant tastes in interior lobbies and ballrooms while baring stark exteriors. Later, critics labeled these new designs

MiMo, short for Miami modern. Designed for the motoring public, the new generation of hotels featured prominent driveways. Earlier beach hotels—the Senator, Tiffany, and Berkeley—hugged the street. Miami Beach trafficked in glamour and style. It was, according to one writer, "probably the only place in the country where you may see a lady dawdle down to the beach for a dip with an eighteen-carat diamond on her finger, drop on the sand for a sunning, and put a $1,000 bet on the second at Hialeah without moving an eyelash."[27]

Buoyed by the affluence of the 1950s and the popularity of travel, Florida's tourist trade doubled during the decade, rising from 4.5 million in 1950 to 9 million in 1959, and doubling again by 1967. In 1956, almost three-quarters of travelers arrived by automobile, spending an average of $5.95 per day and staying an average of eleven days. In 1957, a journalist predicted that "Florida is on the threshold of the jet age and its tourist business may see great change." By the 1960s, air travel was no longer a privilege for the wealthy, but most tourists continued to travel by car. By decade's end, tourists were spending $1 billion a year in the Sunshine State. Almost one-quarter of visitors to the state steered toward Miami and Miami Beach, followed by St. Petersburg, Daytona, Fort Lau-

FIGURE 14. Decadent but so moderne, the Hotel Fontainebleau defined 1950s Miami Beach elegance and extravagance. Historical Association of Southern Florida, Miami.

derdale, and Key West. When asked to indicate why they had selected Florida as a destination, visitors overwhelmingly selected beaches, sunshine, and natural scenery, followed distantly by commercial attractions. On the eve of the opening of Disney World in 1971, Florida attracted 23 million tourists. Pinellas, Dade, Broward, and Volusia counties were the most popular destinations.[28]

Beach resorts, amusement parks, and even alligator farms were not so much an escape from modern life as a reflection or reconstruction of it. In Florida, race, class, age, religion, and ethnicity segregated tourists. In the 1950s and 1960s, vacation destinations often reinforced one's identity: working-class Heartlanders to Ocala, Gulfport, and Lakeland; wealthy midwesterners to Clearwater, Naples, and Captiva; prosperous New York Jews to North Miami Beach, middle-class Jews to South Beach; southern whites to Destin and Panama City; southern blacks to American Beach; old money to Palm Beach; old folks to St. Petersburg; Finns to Lake Worth; Canadians to Broward and Pinellas counties; and college students to Daytona Beach and Fort Lauderdale.

A 1950 brochure depicted Volusia County's Ellinor Village as an exotic dreamplace, where spacious beaches and charming cabanas beckoned tourists. The brochure, however, carried a discreet warning: "Restricted Clientele," a genteel code for gentile discrimination. Cultural markers, as much as highway signs, steered and deflected families toward their destinations. For some, vacation choices validated their hard-won status; for others, the choice of lodging or restaurant reminded them of their unshakable identity. A vacation in Florida may have confirmed the American way of life, but it was a world of prescribed and proscribed barriers. Signs subtly and not so subtly defined one's place: "Restricted Clientele," "Gentiles Only," "Exclusive," "For Whites Only," "No Latins Allowed," and "We reserve the right to refuse service to anyone."[29]

Jews had long faced anti-Semitism in Florida, most notably in Miami and Miami Beach in the 1920s and 1930s. In 1953, Florida's B'nai B'rith Anti-Defamation League surveyed the state's tourist accommodations and declared "marked success" in combating the most blatant policies. Delray Beach and Fort Lauderdale were singled out, however, as "intractable in their discriminatory attitudes." Over 80 percent of Fort Lauderdale resorts still displayed "restricted clientele" signs. By 1960, B'nai B'rith noted improvement, although Fort Lauderdale and Delray Beach remained the "sore spots of Florida." Fully 60 percent of Fort Lauderdale hotels still maintained odious discriminatory policies. In 1953, one in five Miami Beach hotels continued to bar Jews; by 1960, the number had plunged to four out of 155. Such customs continued, in spite of the fact that the Florida legislature passed a law in 1955 prohibiting discriminatory advertising based on religion.[30]

Racism, however, pervaded 1950s Florida tourism. In St. Augustine, brochures advertised "Horse-drawn surreys, driven by top-hatted Negroes." If one doubted whether Florida ever belonged to the South, signs pointed to St. Augustine's Old Slave Market. In Winter Haven, a place not even incorporated until 1925, hoop-skirted southern belles strolled to the musical accompaniment of "Old Folks at Home." Travelers wishing to find an unapologetic slice of the Old and New South could stop at Brooksville and visit the Lewis Plantation and Turpentine Still. A 1950s brochure depicted "pickaninnies," "care-free darkies," and "mammies." A 1946 story lamented the passing of the "quaint little carts wheeled by negro drivers, in which visitors are ridden around about the streets of Palm Beach at the rate of $2 an hour." Called "Afro-mobiles" by an earlier generation, rickshaws graphically defined the place of blacks in Palm Beach. At Palm Beach resorts, but also elsewhere, race distinguished high-paying guests from low-paid help. Blacks—as well as white service workers—at exclusive Miami Beach and Palm Beach needed IDs, lest they be confused with trespassers. Blacks dominated the ranks of dishwashers, cooks, busboys, bellhops, maids, and Pullman porters. Along rural highways and city streets, middle-class blacks felt the sting of humiliation from routinely denied restrooms and accommodations.[31]

Although many whites imagined African American lives as confined solely to service work, blacks also participated as tourists and consumers of leisure. Legendary jazz and blues establishments—Orlando's Ever Ready Club, St. Petersburg's Manhattan Casino, the Two Spot and Club Harlem in Jacksonville—attracted big-name bands and enthusiastic crowds. The double-domed Strand in Jacksonville may have been the state's most elegant theater. For customers who demanded tablecloths and waitresses with crisply ironed uniforms, places like Rogers Dining Room on Central Avenue in Tampa and Hayes Luncheonette on Ashley Street in Jacksonville awaited diners. The Florida State Fair sponsored a popular Negro Day. Each February, black students, businessmen, and rural folk rode trains, autos, and buses to Tampa's Plant Field. Many schools declared Negro Day at the fair a holiday.[32]

By the 1950s, a handful of exclusive (and exclusively) Negro beaches and black resorts had been created. Opened on Emancipation Day 1949, Paradise Springs allowed African Americans to enjoy Silver Springs on their own terms (or the least objectionable terms within the framework of a Jim Crow society *and* the dignity of race pride). Black tourists glided across the waters in separate glass-bottomed boats. Vacationers who preferred their spring water with bourbon patronized Buddy B's jook joint in west Ocala, or the VIP Quarterback Club in the Parramore section of Orlando. Florida's most popular and renowned black tourist spot, however, was American Beach, on Amelia Island in Northeast Florida. In the 1930s, executives from the Afro-American Life Insurance Company purchased large tracts of American Beach, erecting facilities for black patrons. American Beach drew African American vacationers from forty-eight states. Cab Calloway, Ray Charles, Paul Robeson, and Joe Louis highlighted the marquees. If the local Rendezvous Club was too crowded, visitors could easily drive to Duval County and frequent Black Cat Hall and the Waiters Club, located in Jacksonville Beach's black district. Local singers and comedians such as Happy Reid, Billy Daniels, and "Buddy" Austin entertained tourists and natives. Ray Charles began his singing career in LaVilla, the center of Jacksonville's black culture. Saturday night crowds on Jacksonville's Ashley Street could visit five black movie theaters, plus scores of black-owned barber/beauty shops, cafes, pharmacies, music stores, and service stations. Miami's Overtown was a popular stopover for African American entertainers on their way to Cuba. Count Basie, Sammie Davis Jr., Sam Cooke, Lena Horn, Jackie Wilson, and Ella Fitzgerald performed at Overtown's Zebra Room, Lyric Theater, and Harlem Square Club, often after playing the segregated nightclubs on the beach. Each December, Overtown hosted the Orange Blossom Festival (originally the Coconut Festival), which culminated with a parade down NW Second Avenue, the crowning of a queen, and the playing of the Classic, a football game that determined America's black collegiate champion.[33]

While Jim Crow tourism separated and marginalized black Floridians, popular culture and capitalism first demonized, then romanticized, and finally enriched Florida's Seminoles. Early in the twentieth century, Florida's Seminoles, numbering only a few thousand, lived in a handful of isolated settlements in the Everglades. Even there, capitalism was shaping a global culture. Indians bolstered their subsistence economy by trading pelts, plumes, and hides in Miami and Fort Lauderdale. After navigating the Miami and the New rivers, they negotiated Musa Isle and Coppinger's Landing. Occasionally Seminoles encountered parties of tourists brought up the Miami River by steamboat. Kodak-toting tourists, however, discovered something far more exotic than banyan trees and the Miami River Falls: the descendants of Osceola and Micanopy. Attraction operators quickly realized that Yankees adored the spectacle of "wild" Indians dressed in their colorful patchwork garb. The Seminoles also under-

FIGURE 15. An invented tradition, alligator wrestling introduced tourists to Seminole culture while emphasizing the pride and heritage of Florida's Native Americans. State of Florida Photographic Archives, Tallahassee.

stood their value as a commodity. An industry was born. By the 1920s, Seminole Indian villages had become commonplace along Florida's tourist highways.[34]

The opening of the Tamiami Trail (Tampa to Miami) in 1928 changed the ecological and economic dynamics of the Seminoles. The new highway cut across the heart of the Everglades, bringing motorists and tourists into the world of the Seminoles and Miccosukees. Though such traffic also brought hunters and automobiles that decimated wild game, it encouraged new businesses. Family clans accepted the rush of strangers, organizing and sponsoring airboat rides, the sales of handcrafted artifacts, and alligator wrestling. Access to markets and consumers allowed control of the product and message. Seminoles carefully and forcefully articulated the theme of the unconquered people, reminding the audience as well as reservation dwellers that the tribe had valiantly defied presidents and armies.[35]

Alligator wrestling may have been a novelty to tourists, but the animal had long represented a vital component in the lives of Indians of the American

Southeast. The spectacle of man and beast in a pit appealed to Americans' love of "sport." Alligator wrestling—and other enterprises, such as the Dania Seminole Rodeo—helped refine a new image of the Seminoles, one that Floridians and Americans applauded and accepted. The invented custom of alligator wrestling allowed Florida's Seminole Indians, who only a century earlier had been hunted down by bloodhounds and cursed as bloodthirsty savages, an opportunity to earn a living within and outside the reservation and to do so largely on their terms.[36]

For all of the charm and quaintness of pre-Disney Florida, not everyone adored spring break hi-jinks, motels shaped like wigwams, and alligator farms. In a state where billboards hyped rattlesnake milkings and two-headed calves, fantasy mixed freely with business. Humorist Lewis Grizzard declared that anyone dumb enough to think that a few reptiles in a ditch qualified as an alligator farm deserved to be robbed. "After all," Grizzard deadpanned, "how many Southerners have you ever seen paying money to visit a reptile farm?" As visitors wound their way across the peninsula, they encountered enterprising pitchmen eager to separate Yankees from their dollars. Just how many Fountains of Youth had Ponce de León discovered? Tourists interested in illegal games of chance found ample opportunities to play bolita, feed slot machines, and bet book. Exposés in the 1940s and 1950s uncovered the existence of gambling and "white slavery" in South Florida. Fleeced and humiliated, some visitors complained of "roadside zoos," "gyp joints," and "tourist traps." Even FBI Director J. Edgar Hoover weighed in on the subject of tourist camps, writing in 1940 that such "camps of crime" served as "dens of vice and corruption."[37]

The Mouse That Roared

Walt Disney understood Americans' distrust of geegaws, honky-tonk shows, and the carnival. Critics frequently label Disney creations as sterile and antiseptic, but he sincerely wished to fashion a world of entertainment beyond the tawdry netherland of grifters and boardwalk barkers, sideshow freaks and burlesque queens. In 1950, Walt Disney's brother visited Florida. He ignored the roadside traps and instead headed toward Winter Haven. Following a burst of populist creativity and financial success in the 1930s, the Disney mystique seemed spent. The business manager of Walt Disney Studio, Roy, called upon Dick Pope, the master of Cypress Gardens. Roy knew all too well that Disney Studio lost money in 1949. Disney peppered Pope with questions about attendance figures and overhead costs. Satisfied, he then asked if he could telephone California. "Walt," he began, "I'm down here with a guy named Dick Pope back in the woods of central Florida and all he has is some flowers and girls and he is drawing 2,500 to 4,000 people a day."[38]

But for the curmudgeonly Ed Ball, Disney World might have transformed Florida's Big Bend, making Port St. Joe the bridesmaid who would be Orlando. The irascible Ball received a telephone call from Walt Disney in the early 1960s. The latter wished to know about available property; the former controlled the du Pont family fortune and the St. Joe Land Company, the largest landowner in Florida. Ball did not recognize Disney's name and assigned the task of checking out the inquiry to a junior clerk. When Disney called back, Ball abruptly dismissed him. "We don't deal with carnival people," he explained.[39]

Nor apparently did Walt Disney. A genius at packaging and producing popular culture, Disney helped sanitize amusement, creating wholesome alternatives for a middle-class suspicious of carnies and games of chance. If the carnival epitomized the netherworld of tawdry excitement, Disneyland inaugurated a world of pious predictability and staged amusement. The marriage of Walt Disney to Florida culminated with the opening of Walt Disney World in 1971. In the history of tourism, Disney World represents the Biggest Bang. The Disney empire imposed its will upon the Sunshine State, promoting a commercial vision and corporate model that redefined tourism: managed fun, dazzling technology, simulated reality, and total control.

Born in 1901, Walter Elias Disney grew up in midwestern cities and farms. His father, Elias, failed at farming in Florida and Missouri, railing against economic injustice and voting for Socialist Eugene Debs. Walt's earliest works drew upon his populist sympathies and his nostalgic memories of rural life in Marceline, Missouri. *Snow White, Pinocchio,* and *Dumbo* celebrate, in the words of Steven Watts, "the triumph of the underdog, the value of hard work, and the virtues of community among common people."[40]

In 1955, banking upon the success of movies, cartoons, and a new television series, the West Coast businessman launched Disneyland, a $17 million gamble. Located on 80 acres in Anaheim, California, Disneyland caused a sensation, becoming such a part of American culture that when Soviet premier Nikita Khrushchev visited the United States in 1960, he asked to tour the park. Rebuffed, Khrushchev threw a tantrum, threatening to erect Miracle Land, a Soviet vision of play and leisure. Perfected in southern California, Disneyland orchestrated tourists' movement around a central hub, drawing them out of the humdrum world of today and into the world of yesterday, tomorrow, and fantasy—an experience originally conceived and implemented without a single thrill ride. Visitors stroll down Main Street USA, Disney's nostalgic re-creation of turn-of-the-century Marceline, Missouri. Evoking a sense of childlike belonging, Disney designed Main Street buildings at five-eighths scale. "This cost more," Walt explained, "but made the street a toy, and the imagination can play more freely with a toy." The idea, contend critics, was also a brilliant marketing idea, forcing tourists to go through profitable Main Street shops before the crowd can arrive at the sought-after rides.[41]

Disneyland encapsulated the dynamic quality of American managerial capitalism; its wholesome and nostalgic views of the past dovetailed with the founder's fascination with cutting-edge technology and compulsive control. His obsession with details, his zeal for profit, and the opportunity to correct mistakes made at Anaheim brought him eastward in the 1960s. California was too remote for many Americans residing east of the Mississippi. Preliminary research identified St. Louis, Niagara Falls, Baltimore, and Florida as potential sites. The possibility of Disney World located at Port St. Joe—a town fittingly more at home with Mike Fink and the keelboat men than modern Orlando—was not as farfetched as it may seem. The great hunt demanded rigid moral, economic, and demographic criteria that few locales could meet. Prudish and imperious, Disney walked away from St. Louis because August Busch Jr. ridiculed his insistence that alcohol not be sold on park grounds. Philosophically, Walt spurned east coast and Gulf Coast beach resorts because of their associations with boardwalk manners and seasonal audiences. Ultimately, Ocala and Orlando possessed the right stuff. Ocala, Walt's sentimental choice because of childhood associations—his father and mother, in 1886, became the first couple to be married in Lake County—could not match Orlando's winning combination of climate, cheap land with plenty of room for expansion, and a large nonunion workforce to meet the park's needs.[42]

Upon Disney's first flight over Central Florida's landscape—the fateful date was 22 November 1963—the maestro became animated as he envisioned a network of turnpikes, interstate highways, and airports funneling millions of visitors to the gates of Disneyland East. "This is it!" he exclaimed. Identifying "it" was easy, but implementing "Project X" involved clandestine real estate agents and five dummy corporations. Disney managed to purchase 27,443 acres (43 square miles) of Central Florida ranch land, groves, and swamp—an area twice the size of Manhattan. Several Disney operatives had actually served in the

Office of Special Services (OSS) during World War II, among them "Wild Bill" Donovan. Their skills served Disney's clandestine efforts to disguise the purpose and identity of the operations. Had his motive been discovered, Disney's task of assembling large tracts of contiguous land would have been far more difficult—and expensive. As it was, Disney paid an average of $180 an acre. Purchases ranged from the acquisition of Ira Bronson's 8,380-acre ranch to 5-acre parcels. For months, rumors ran rampant about who or what was buying up Central Florida. In October 1965, the headline of the *Orlando Sentinel* read: "We Say 'Mystery' Industry Is Disney." A year later, at a press conference held at Orlando's Cherry Plaza Hotel, Walt officially announced plans for a "bigger and better" version of Disneyland. The Associated Press called Disney "the most celebrated visitor since Ponce de Leon." The announcement signaled a land grab, as investors speculated from Altamonte Springs to Kissimmee. Unlike the 1920s Florida land boom, national corporations and chains acquired many of the choicest sites.[43]

Disney's grandest accomplishment may not have been his bold vision but his political shrewdness. A Florida legislature bent upon growth and development awarded extraordinary powers to the Disney corporation without debate. The legislature granted the Reedy Creek Improvement District, a quasi-governmental body controlled by Disney World, sweeping powers to regulate the environment, to police, tax, seek federally subsidized municipal bonds, and zone with immunity from state and local land-use law. In effect, the corporation was granted its own government. "Never before or since," writes Carl Hiaasen, "has such outlandish dominion been given to a private corporation." Disney World essentially acts as a county within a county, a private corporation with the power and autonomy to construct and manage an amusement park. It became, in scholar Richard Foglesong's words, "a sort of Vatican with Mouse ears: a city-state within the larger state of Florida."[44]

In 1969, three years after the founder's death, Walt Disney World began to take form—150 times larger than Disneyland with a price tag of $400 million, more than double the original estimate. To appreciate the construction complexities, consider that the foreman of the construction company had previously served as a major general in the U.S. Army Corps of Engineers and as governor of the Panama Canal Zone. Cinderella's Castle, an eighteen-story, 185-foot creation, came equipped with air conditioning and elevators. Overall, Disney crews dredged, blasted, constructed, and raised 40 miles of canals, 18 miles of levees, more than a dozen flood-control structures, and 8 million cubic yards of earth. Resort hotels, pavilions, and more theme parks followed. Curiously, for all of the investment and planning, Disney World is *in* Florida but offers visitors precious little *of* Florida. It epitomizes what Susan G. Davis, author of *Spectacular Nature,* calls "corporately produced public space."[45]

In one of Disney's last speeches, the founder proclaimed that here in Florida "we have something we never enjoyed at Disneyland . . . the blessing of size." Little did anyone appreciate how true that statement was. Walt Disney World's success begat complementary and complimentary enterprises. The opening of the Magic Kingdom instantly changed the dynamics of Florida and American tourism. Never in the history of the Sunshine State had the opening of a single business so altered the course of an industry. In its first year alone, 11 million visitors walked through Disney's turnstiles; Disney hotels enjoyed 100 percent occupancy. Lake Buena Vista became the improbable setting for the world's grandest tourist empire. EPCOT (the Experimental Prototype Community of Tomorrow) opened in October 1982. When the Disney Company unveiled plans for Epcot Center in 1975, then Secretary of State Henry Kissinger predicted that the bold experiment would do more for world peace than "all my shuttle diplomacy." Originally envisioned by Walt Disney as an experimental city for 20,000 dwellers, Epcot became instead a paean to the corporate world, offering customers a taste of ethnic cuisine and high technology. By the 1990s, Epcot was attracting as many as 10 million visitors annually. The opening of Disney/MGM Studios (1989) and Disney's Animal Kingdom (1998) brought more visitors to Lake Buena Vista. A brash challenge to Busch Gardens in Tampa, Disney's Animal Kingdom drew nearly 9 million visitors in its first full year. Altogether, Disney's Florida consists of four theme parks, seventeen resorts, three water parks, two nightlife zones, a sports complex/stadium, and the community of Celebration. In 2000, Walt Disney World parks drew almost 43 million tourists.[46]

Profits drive and prophets decry Florida's successes. Orlando serves as the big tent in the mega–theme park universe. SeaWorld opened in 1973, a 125-acre, $20 million attraction starring acrobatic dolphins and killer whales. In the late 1990s, it drew about 5 million visitors annually. In 2000, SeaWorld unveiled a swim-with-the-dolphins park called Discovery Cove. Universal Studios Florida opened its $600 million East Coast attraction in Orlando in the late 1980s; it drew 9 million visitors in 1997. Remarkably, five of America's top seven mega–theme parks are located in Orlando, annually bringing crowds who purchase nearly 50 million tickets and spend $17 billion. To put such numbers in perspective, consider that on the eve of the Magic Kingdom's opening in 1971 about 3.5 million tourists visited Central Florida annually.[47]

Orlando represents more than a modern entertainment mecca. Disney's empire reveals a dynamic capitalism that has transformed society and the so-cial-economic basis of wealth. Historically, manufacturing, trade, and property defined wealth. Today, argues economist Jeremy Rifkin, "The Age of Access is about, above all else, the commodification of play . . . in the form of paid-for personal entertainment."[48]

Customers pay dearly for the experiences of posing with Goofy, touring a simulated Universal or MGM Studio, or being splashed by Shamu. Deter-mined to keep the undesirable classes out of Disneyland, Walt Disney set the gold standard. Crowds came, and profits soared. By 1982, admission to the Magic Kingdom averaged $13.50, inflating to $28 in 1988. In 2005, the price of riding teacups and standing in line rose to $60 a day. Universal Studios, Sea-World, and Busch Gardens follow the leader. The opening of Orlando's Dol-phin Key in 2000 tested consumers' financial threshold. For an eye-popping admission fee of $179, Anheuser-Busch promises to limit guests to one thou-sand a day, enabling them to snorkel and swim among tropical fish and dol-phins.[49]

Consequences

The opening of Walt Disney World was the equivalent of a ten-point earth-quake; the aftershock still reverberates today. In the 1920s, the number of American amusement parks peaked. Almost two thousand attractions oper-ated, chiefly in the heavily populated Northeast and Midwest. On the eve of World War II, the number had fallen to below 250. The success of Disneyland, spurred by new investors who saw dollar signs in the growing numbers of baby boomers, dramatically reversed the decline in amusement parks. Rising from four hundred in 1954 to a new peak of almost a thousand in 1963, the new attractions also generated stunning revenues.[50]

When Dick Pope first heard that Walt Disney was going to build a theme park in Central Florida, he remarked, "Anyone who is going to spend $100 million near is good, and a good thing." Pope and others would later regret Disney's fateful arrival. Only soothsayers could have understood that events in and around Orlando would trigger massive dislocation and disintegration in the tourist industry. The new era of the mega–theme park doomed the old world of roadside attractions. In truth, many smaller establishments—Ani-rama, Eagles Nest, Floridaland, Idylwyld Gardens, Lost Lake and Caverns, and Wonder House—had already closed. Future archaeologists will someday discover lost worlds of Florida tourism. When they opened in the 1960s, Six Gun Territory in Ocala, Pirate's World at Dania Beach, and Pioneer City in Davie blazed promising trails, hoping to cash in on Americans' seeming obsession with cowboys, pirates, and nostalgia. Off Interstate 4 in Haines City, first Circus World and then later Boardwalk and Baseball offered visitors a roller coaster ride and sports fantasies. Competitors, however, unable to match Disney's star qualities and technological wizardry, paid dearly. Undercapitalized and overwhelmed, most of the newly launched attractions failed.[51]

Family-run businesses located along once-busy thoroughfares became anachronisms. Ironically, while the Florida Turnpike and interstate highways introduced millions of new motorists to Florida, the new roadways bypassed the old tourist attractions. The energy crises of the 1970s encouraged visitors to fly to Florida, thereby speeding the demise of longtime favorite destinations like Rainbow Springs and Sanlando Springs. Dog Land in Chiefland, Everglades Tropical Gardens in Clewiston, Florida Reptile Land of Lawtey, and the Waite Bird Farm of Boynton Beach also failed to survive the 1970s. Who remembers Frog City (Tamiami Trail), Sunshine Springs and Gardens (Sarasota), Atomic Tunnel (Allendale), the Rare Bird Farm (Kendall), Shark World (St. Petersburg Beach), Midget City (Sanford), and Bongoland (South Daytona)? McKee Jungle Gardens, considered by many the most stunning of Florida's tropical wonderlands, closed in 1976. The owners refused to compromise founder Arthur McKee's mission. "I could not in good faith . . . put monorails or Snow White or mechanical monkeys or a high-dive tiger act on these precious grounds," explained Arthur McKee Latta, the founder's grandson. "People no longer want to feel like Thoreau," he lamented. "They don't want to walk the Appalachian Trail, they want to ride it." Even tradition-rich Cypress Gardens ultimately succumbed to its location and failure to attract new generations of visitors. Nature no longer was enough. As late as 1983, the park still attracted a million visitors a year, but attendance plummeted in the 1990s. During the venerable park's last few years, over 90 percent of its customers were retirees.[52]

Challenging Cinderella and Shamu was foolhardy; instead, businesses hoped to profit from the tourist traffic they created. If Disney and SeaWorld dominated the entertainment market by day, investors attempted to capture the visitors at night. Ambitious, corporate-financed, second-tier attractions appeared in the 1980s and 1990s. King Henry's Feast, Medieval Times, American Gladiators Orlando Live, Arabian Nights, Pirate's Dinner Adventure, Capone's Dinner and Show, and Wild Bill's Wild West Dinner offered customers dinner and theater with a theme setting. While dining on boiled potatoes and Sherwood Forest roast chicken, patrons watched streams of acrobats, wenches, jesters, cowboys, Native American dancers, and Andalusian stallions. But competition for nighttime crowds proved fierce. The entertainment giants Disney and Universal opened ritzy leisure complexes and built lavish hotels to isolate guests from competitors. By 2000, King Henry's Feast, American Gladiators Orlando Live, and Wild Bill's Wild West Dinner had closed.[53]

The Magic Kingdom and SeaWorld not only threatened Orlando competitors and honky-tonk Florida, but they also displaced Miami and Miami Beach as the state's most alluring places. Covering the opening of Disney World in 1971, the *New York Times*' Paul Friedlander asked, "What will this vast Disney-promoted amusement park-resort-tourist center do to Florida's major industry, tourism, and especially to that part of it situated south of Orlando?" Five years later, a headline projected, "Hotel Owners See Hard Times Ahead in Miami Tourism." Fifteen years later, no Miami attraction made the list of the state's top forty amusement parks. The nightclub, so perfectly matched for Miami Beach in the 1950s, seemed passé in the 1980s. Miami, which seemed so deliciously naughty in the 1950s, now scared Americans. The Caribbean, which in the 1950s seemed too remote, now offered to millions of Americans all of the exotica of Miami Beach plus affordability. The negative press stemming from the Mariel boatlift debacle, race riots, geriatric South Beach, and the 1983 film *Scarface* dampened enthusiasm for the beleaguered city. An aging Orange Bowl languished in Little Havana. Damning press coverage signified Miami's fall. *New York Times Magazine*'s July 1987 cover story asked the question, "Can Miami Save Itself?" But remarkably and unpredictably, Miami rallied and reinvented its image once again in the 1990s. The popularity of the television show *Miami Vice,* cheap airfares, celebrity residents, a booming cruise-ship industry, and surging numbers of Latin tourists and investment (drugs and money) made South Florida and SoBe (South Beach) very chic.[54]

Today, an oligopoly rules the tourist industry, as a few megacorporations dominate the business. Universal Studios revealed the high costs of theme park membership when it invested $600 million to open its attraction in 1990. Mergers and takeovers document the perilous industry: American Broadcasting Corporation (ABC), ESPN, the Fox Family Channel, and the Walt Disney Company joined hands in the 1990s. By 2001, the Walt Disney Company included ten theme parks located in California, Florida, France, and Japan. If the parks' $6 billion in revenues had been listed on the Fortune 500, they would have ranked 265th. SeaWorld, Busch Gardens, and Discovery Cove represent part of the Anheuser-Busch entertainment empire of ten theme parks, including four SeaWorlds. In 1999, Anheuser Busch–run theme parks in Florida generated $750 million in revenues. Six Flags was purchased by Time-Warner, while Harcourt Brace Jovanovich and the Busch Entertainment Corporation briefly owned Cypress Gardens. Universal Studios Tours is owned by MCA, a media conglomerate once owned by Matsushita electronics. At one time, ABC owned Silver Springs and Weeki Wachee. In the 1960s, Holiday Inn and S & H Green Stamps acquired Rainbow Springs. Ogden Corporation, with massive holdings in energy, aviation, and entertainment, purchased Silver Springs from Florida Leisure Acquisition in 1996.[55]

Public ownership of fading and failed nature parks has marked a new chapter in the history of Florida tourism. Reacting to political pressures from environmentalists and local business interests, state and local governments have rescued several prominent attractions. In the early 1980s, Homosassa Springs Nature World closed. Citrus County purchased the grounds for $3.4 million to prevent private development. Between 1987 and 1993, the state also purchased or acquired Silver Springs, Wakulla Springs, and Rainbow Springs, in some cases allowing the previous owners to operate the parks. When Sunken Gardens closed in 1999, the City of St. Petersburg purchased the site, converting it into an educational center. McKee Botanical Gardens emerged from McKee Jungle Gardens after the Indian River Land Trust purchased a small parcel of the original park, which had closed in 1976. Cypress Gardens shut its historic gates in 2003, but the Trust for Public Land, the State of Florida, and Polk County purchased part of the property. Critics have complained that unlike the natural springs, Cypress Gardens is an artificial landscape. Weeki Wachee represents the latest of the once-grand parks in peril of closing. "The situation cannot be good when mermaids are joining manatees as endangered species," quipped one writer.[56]

The history of Busch Gardens literally and figuratively illustrates the roller-coaster nature of the modern theme park. In 1957, the Anheuser-Busch Corporation purchased 130 acres of land that had only recently served as a site for a World War II air base. August Busch Jr. was steering his family's business through a remarkable decade of expansion and diversification. Long familiar with the Tampa Bay area because of his ties with the St. Louis Cardinals and their spring training facility in St. Petersburg, Busch enthusiastically dedicated a brewery, soon to be overshadowed by its beer garden. Set in a live oak hammock, Busch Gardens opened in June 1959, intended originally as a refuge for brewery tourists and home to a growing population of parrots and macaws. So many visitors packed the gardens—3 million during the first three years—that in 1962 officials transformed 70 acres of palmetto scrubland into a Serengeti Plain. A mile-long, high-tech monorail whisked guests above the savanna, while elephants, zebras, and antelope grazed below. Two concepts clicked in popularizing Busch Gardens: uncaged animals running free and the lure of free admission. In 1966, almost 3 million visitors flocked to the sprawling complex. Free enterprise inevitably overcame free rides. In 1970, Busch Gardens first charged guests $1.25.[57]

Park officials, ever mindful of the cutthroat entertainment business, expanded and diversified at a frantic pace. What began as a beer garden was reinvented in the 1970s as the "Dark Continent." Visitors could experience an African safari only a giraffe's gallop from bustling Busch Boulevard. Billboards reminded Americans, "If you can't afford to go to Kenya next year, it's waiting for you just outside Tampa." Stage sets followed. Moroccan Village opened in 1975, followed by Timbuktu, Congo River Rapids, and the Edge of Africa. As tourists floated above and walked by imported African lions and hippos, they saw few Africans. After criticism from African American groups over the inference of racism in the name *Dark Continent*, Busch Gardens dropped the marketing concept in 1983.[58]

To lure youth and young families, Busch Gardens invested heavily in cutting-edge thrills. Almost as soon as workers finished the last track of the Scorpion, officials unveiled the Python, an even bigger and better roller coaster. The 1990s introduced Kumba, touted as the fastest, largest steel-rail ride in the South, as well as Montu and Gwzai, death-defying roller contraptions. Visitors pay dearly. Tickets have escalated from $5.25 in 1975 to $50 in 2000. Still they come, although the numbers leveled off in the 1990s. The state's most popular tourist attraction in the 1960s and the third-most popular in 1985, Busch Gardens was the seventh-most-visited place in Florida in 2000, drawing 4 million visitors. In 2005, Busch Gardens unveiled its latest thrill ride: Sheikra, a 200-foot straight-drop roller coaster.[59]

Busch Gardens and SeaWorld share common ownership but also face a challenge confronting rivals: how to package and deliver new stimuli. Thrill rides dominate theme parks, each attempting to take crowds to new sensory thresholds. Walt Disney World first debuted Thunder Mountain Railroad, followed by Splash Mountain in the early 1990s. Universal Studios Park boasts Dueling Dragons and the Incredible Hulk roller coasters, Jaws and Back to the Future rides, and the Amazing Adventures of Spider-Man, the latter a dazzling 3-D experience. In 1999, Disney–MGM Studios unleashed its Rock 'n' Roller Coaster, while DisneyQuest debuted a 100,000-square-foot arcade of video games, motion simulators, and virtual-reality experiences. For almost three decades, SeaWorld resisted flashy technological gimmickry, but in 1997 it added a combination roller coaster/flume ride called Journey to Atlantis. In 2000, SeaWorld unveiled Kraken, described by a publicist as the "dominator of all coasters in the region." Even Epcot Center, considered the tamest park on the visceral shock scale, has introduced Proving Ground, where visitors can get behind the wheel of General Motors vehicles. In 2004, Panama City Beach's beloved Miracle Strip Amusement Park closed. Generations of southerners fondly remember Goofy Golf and the 2,403-foot "Starliner" roller coaster, the "fastest in the world."[60]

Tourists demand new exotica. The old roadside alligator farm holds little fascination to new generations of information-hyped travelers. One by one the attractions that had delighted previous generations with creepy snakes and chicken-eating crocodiles vanished: Boca Raton's Africa U.S.A., Casper's Ostrich and Alligator Farm in St. Augustine, Florida Reptile Institute in Silver Springs, the World of Miniature Horses in Pompano Beach, Florida Wild Animal Farm in Callahan, Lion Farm in Fort Lauderdale, Jungle Land in Kissimmee, the Sarasota Reptile Farm, the Miami Serpentarium (with a giant cobra head inviting visitors), and Snake-A-Torium in Panama City. Parks featuring lions, tigers, and wild beasts replaced reptile farms. In 1967, Lion Country Safari opened in West Palm Beach. A zoo designed for the automobile age, the facility housed ferocious and friendly animals, seen from the safety and comfort of one's automobile. Since 1954, Caribbean Gardens had dazzled visitors with its rare collection of plants and trees. But the establishment needed a boost, provided by a safari theme makeover in the early 1970s, when Jungle Larry and Safari Jane brought their fifty-five big cats to Naples. Recognized by the kitschy concrete gator jaws at its entrance, the venerable Gatorland—itself located in the jaws of the theme-park beast of Central Florida—survives by giving crowds what they want: a feeding-frenzy called Jumparoo, where several dozen 13-foot alligators and crocodiles leap in the air to snatch dangling chickens. Parrot Jungle, which opened in south Dade County in 1936 with twenty-five birds and one hundred paid admissions, moved to tony Watson Island in 2003.[61]

In a delicious reversal of fortune, Florida's Native Americans came to master and apply the new economies of politics and entertainment. Desperately poor in 1950, Seminole and Miccosukees endured harsh poverty; by 2000, the Seminole and Miccosukee Nations spawned tourist empires, including plush gambling casinos, hotels, and museums. Their names and logos adorn businesses and athletic teams. Such successes resulted, in part, from massive lobbying by the Seminole and Miccosukee tribes to politicians. Since 1979, Florida's Seminoles have amassed five casinos that by 2003 were bringing in $300 million annually in gambling profits, enough to support 3,000 tribal members with an annual dividend of $36,000. Ironically, the tribes now have difficulty finding young Native Americans interested in wrestling alligators. In 2000, the Seminole Tribe placed advertisements recruiting alligator wrestlers: Pay: twelve dollars an hour.[62]

Writers, critics, and students of popular culture have found mass tourism both repellent and irresistible. In Carl Hiaasen's novel *Tourist Season*, the protagonist, Skip Wiley, resorts to serial murder in order to save Florida. Disgusted that South Florida has become "Newark with palm trees," Wiley feeds one tourist to the crocodiles and kills a vacationing Shriner by stuffing a toy gator down his throat. Only his fez is found in the surf. Wiley's recipe for redemption is simple: "Scare away the tourists and pretty soon you scare away the developers. No more developers, no more bankers. No more bankers, no more lawyers. . . . Now, tell me I'm crazy." Writer P. J. O'Rourke has observed that Epcot "has accomplished something I didn't think possible in today's world. They have created a land of make-believe that's worse than regular life. Unvarnished reality would be preferable. In fact, it might be fun." In his searing indictment of Central Florida theme parks, writer John Rothchild describes "tourists . . . more dutiful than overjoyed; the whole Orlando migration has the feel of a pilgrimage site." But the Italian philosopher Umberto Eco is especially attracted to Disney's enchanting mix of schlock and shock. "Consumers want to be thrilled," he writes, "not only by the guarantee of the Good but also by the shudder of the Bad. And so [there], along with Mickey Mouse and the kindly Bears, there must also be, in tactile evidence, Metaphysical Evil (the Haunted Mansion) and Historical Evil (the Pirates)." The urban scholar Mike Davis describes

Orlando's theme parks as "tourist bubbles" and "hyperreality" that exist separate from real cities and reality. "Thus, in Orlando," he writes, "Disney created a stunning Art Deco mirage of MGM's golden age, and arch-competitor MCA countered with its own idealized versions of Hollywood Boulevard and Rodeo Drive at Universal Studios Florida." In *The Image,* Daniel Boorstin coined the term *pseudo-event* to describe the "synthetic novelty which has flooded our experience." A pseudo-event aptly defines modern American culture, where hype often overwhelms genuine significance. Travel, contends Boorstin, "has become diluted, contrived, prefabricated." Tourist attractions, he argues, represent "artificial products to be consumed in the very places where the real thing is as free as air." Florida's amusement of the billions now occurs in insulated, air-conditioned, passive capsules, rarely requiring face-to-place relationships. Florida seems incidental. In a world of "total experiences," Florida is becoming a backdrop against which tourists create digital postcards of themselves being hugged by a robot.[63]

The New Tourist Landscape

Modern highways, motels, and restaurants do not encourage public interaction among travelers and guests. Victorian-era hotels invited dialogue and interaction as guests mingled in dining rooms, on dance floors, and in billiard or whist parlors. Expensive suites at the Windsor, Royal Palm, and Breakers were surprisingly small and modest when compared with the extravagant display of public space seen in the era's dining rooms, salons, and gardens. Every modestly sized town boasted at least one downtown hotel. Ironically, modern travel —with its emphasis upon the automobile and the location of theme parks near superhighways—speeded the demise of the downtown hotel. Public space has shifted from the hotel to the theme park. Main Street, Magic Kingdom, has replaced Main Street, U.S.A. Tightly scripted and technologically driven, such "public" places as SeaWorld and the Magic Kingdom present facades of the real world.[64]

A Florida vacation, once a luxury reserved for the conspicuous few, has become commonplace for millions of working- and middle-class Americans, Europeans, and Asians, a triumph of free enterprise and democratic freedoms. "In sightseeing," writes Dean MacCannell, "all men are equal before the sight." But the vacation landscape is highly fragmented and stratified. Seemingly every profession, age and ethnic group, race and lifestyle has claimed its niche in Florida's vacation calendar. The cruise-ship industry has perfected specialty marketing, offering voyages for singles, seniors, families, gays, the handicapped, the athletic, and even nudists. Florida leads the nation in the number of nude resorts and clubs (thirty). Drawing more than 100,000 visitors annually, Pasco County has existed as an unlikely center for nudists since the 1940s. Sporting names such as Caliente, Lake Como, and Paradise Lakes, five nudist resorts now call Land O' Lakes home. Naturalists adore Cape Canaveral's Playalinda Beach and Miami's Haulover Park, two of the state's "legal" nude beaches. The Miami Beach Ritz-Carlton has adopted a Mediterranean-style topless swimsuit policy. The Gay Trolley Tour of Key West now whisks visitors past the homes of Truman Capote and Tennessee Williams, pointing out a Fleming Street locale locally known as "gay guest house row." Disney World—in spite of its founder's staunch conservatism and the protests of Southern Baptists—hosts "Gay Days," a gathering held every June. Fort Lauderdale also serves as a major resort destination for homosexuals. The Fort Lauderdale Convention and Visitors Bureau claimed that in 2003, about 830,000 gays and lesbians sought the area's beaches and nightclubs, spending $760 million. Gay or straight, the Magic Kingdom offers lovers dream weddings, although only the straight wedding comes with an actual marriage license. Since 1991, Walt Disney World has offered "destination" weddings for couples willing to pay thousands of dollars for a glass carriage ride, blaring trumpets, and cartoon creatures as attendants.[65]

If lovers fantasize Cinderella's Castle as a bridal threshold, the desperately ill and religious faithful envision the Magic Kingdom, in one scholar's words, "as an antechamber to heaven." *Time* magazine has noted, "So many terminally ill children have made a trip to Disney World that a foundation has established a permanent village nearby to accommodate them." Orlando, according to one wag, presently functions as America's Burned-Over District, referring to the area of upstate New York that was a center of religious revivalism in the nineteenth century. Wycliffe's WellSpring Discovery Center, a Christian organization that translates the Bible into foreign languages, as well as the Campus Crusade for Christ, offer tours at their Orlando headquarters. Orlando's Holy Land Experience theme park depicts and re-creates biblical stories. Religion can be profitable. Fort Lauderdale has cultivated a huge market for Jews who wish to enjoy Passover at luxury hotels.[66]

Ironically, civil rights and free-market revolutions may have doomed many of Florida's most historic and celebrated black tourist establishments. American Beach, depicted in filmmaker John Sayles's *Sunshine State* (2002) as Lincoln Beach, struggles to retain its historic identity amid galloping real estate prices. MaVynee Betsch has witnessed the steep decline of American Beach. To the self-proclaimed "beach lady," the greatest loss is a sense of race pride and economic self-determination: "Now you [blacks] go to the motel. You don't own it. You eat at the restaurant. You don't own it." The success of the neighboring resort, Amelia Island Plantation—an interesting choice of names considering Fernandina's notorious role in the slave trade—and the world's unquenched thirst for beachfront property make American Beach's future as a haven for blacks uncertain at best. The identity of Bethune Beach (in New Smyrna Beach) began to fade in the 1960s, as speculators began to purchase black-owned lots. Today's visitors would never know that Bethune Beach was once a black vacationland. Census takers in 2000 found few black households in this now-prestigious place.[67]

Prior to jet travel and charter tours, foreign voices were rare in tourist communities, aside from American ethnic accents. American cultural hegemony, jet travel, and global prosperity have made Florida a convenient destination for the planet's affluent travelers. Orlando theme parks alone host over 5 million foreigners annually. Cities and counties have developed special ties with foreign tourists: Germans and Fort Myers, Britons and Pinellas County, French-Canadians and Hollywood, Finns and Lake Worth, Brazilians and Miami. Since the 1970s, a million or more Canadians have spent winters in the Sunshine State, so many that commentators wryly refer to Le Florida as the "eleventh province." Many Gulf Coast hotels fly the Canadian Maple Leaf and carry the *Toronto Globe and Mail*. So many French-Canadians flock to Hollywood and the Gold Coast that a new term, *Floribec*, describes their status. Tourism officials admit they have neglected America's burgeoning Hispanic population, a lucrative market. Osceola County has begun aggressive advertising to lure Hispanics, including nationwide commercials in Spanish.[68]

Touted as a kinder, gentler kind of business, ecotourism offers visitors a "more authentic" Florida experience. The numbers of tourists exploring state parks and historical sites are increasing rapidly, as are the commercial attractions catering to environmentally sensitive travelers. The big theme parks have established high-priced, environmentally friendly zones for tourists. Carl Hiaasen spoofs such efforts in his novel *Native Tongue,* where an adventuresome tourist is thrashed to death by an amorous dolphin. In Key Largo, guests wishing to stay at Jules' Undersea Lodge must dive more than three fathoms to enter the facility. Pointing to the hordes of tourists descending upon Yosemite and Yellowstone National Parks, critics caution that so many visitors wishing to appreciate the grandeur of the wilderness parks threaten their fragility. Curiously, for all of the optimistic signs suggesting ecotourism's possibilities, Florida's premier environmental wonder, the Everglades, has failed to capture the public's affection. "Most people think it is a yucky, mucky place," acknowledges an Everglades tour guide. The Everglades has never captivated the public like Yosemite or Yellowstone. Since 1972, the numbers of visitors to Everglades National Park have plunged. Throughout the 1990s, about a million people toured the South Florida site annually, about one-tenth of the number who visited the Great Smoky Mountains Park. Nonprofit and for-profit associations offer a wide range of excursions and classes involving the Everglades and the Florida state parks. Elderhostel has tapped into the huge market of senior citizens interested in personal enrichment. The Disney Institute's self-improvement seminars include canoeing and hiking.[69]

At the dawn of the new millennium, Florida's identification with travel is so entrenched that the Sunshine State is synonymous with tourism. In free-spending, class-bending, nation-mixing sprees of consumption, hordes of visitors descend upon Florida to fantasize and maximize leisure experiences. Can one billion tourists be wrong? Contrast the democratized tourism of today with the tourism of nineteenth-century Victorian America, when only the wealthy could realize their dreams of winter paradise.

What hath tourism wrought? The answer, as Shakespeare's Henry V understood, depends upon the questions. On the eve of the battle of Agincourt, a diplomat warned the English king that the French army was only a few leagues away. "How hath thou measured the ground?" replied Henry. An accounting of tourism's impact requires a seismograph as much as a calculator. Florida tourism richly deserves its companion noun, industry. Not until the end of the 1950s did tourism produce $1 billion in revenues. By the end of the century, tourism generated 663,000 jobs and $50 billion in revenues, accounting for $17 billion or 12 percent of the gross state product. In just a half century, Florida's tourist trade rocketed from 4.5 million visitors in 1950 to over 70 million in 2000.[70]

In an example of the tail wagging the dog, Florida has become utterly dependent upon tourism and revenues generated by visitors. The Trojan Horse of Florida politics, tourism dominates any discussion of economics and politics. In some counties, special hotel/tourist taxes generate staggering sums of revenue, but such funds are often restricted to promoting tourism. With its excessive reliance upon a sales tax, Florida's treasury depends necessarily upon out-of-state tourists who pay-for-play. Democrats and Republicans may disagree upon the regressive nature of a sales tax, but all politicians have promoted expensive projects to boost tourism. Billions in public funds have been earmarked for convention centers, luxury hotels, cruise-ship terminals, sports stadiums, museums, and aquariums. The success of developer James Rouse in revitalizing Baltimore's waterfront in the 1980s spurred scores of Florida cities to invest heavily in festive marketplaces, downtown cultural facilities, and refurbished harbors. Panama City Beach is no longer known for its mom-and-pop motels and all-you-can-eat fish fries. It now claims the most meeting space of any Gulf city between New Orleans and Tampa. Orlando's success in attracting conventioneers has been especially dramatic. In 1981, Orlando ranked twenty-seventh in the nation in the number of conventions and attendees. By 1992, the city had vaulted to second place, an astonishing tribute to the drawing power of theme parks, aggressive marketing, and a public-financed, 2-million-square-foot convention center.[71]

Any discussion of tourism must focus upon the transformation of Orlando and Central Florida. In 1970, the population of pre–Magic Kingdom Orange County was 344,311; in 2000, it surpassed 800,000. The impact upon neighboring counties has been even more momentous. In 1970, the combined population of Lake, Osceola, and Seminole counties barely exceeded 150,000; in 2000, it topped 750,000. Disney World functioned as a rocket booster. A census, of course, captures only the number of permanent residents on one day every ten years. Between 1990 and 2000, as any Central Florida commuter can testify, about a half billion tourists converged upon Orlando alone, each staying, dining, and clogging the roads for a few nights or a few weeks.[72]

The impact of the Magic Kingdom has been so forceful, so profound, that one is tempted to append "A.D." (After Disney) to the years following 1971. Disney World transformed tourism. In its first year of operation, park officials counted 11 million visitors (the entire state attracted only 9 million additional tourists), surpassing the most sanguine predictions. Originally employing

13,000 persons, Disney's weekly payroll exceeded $1 million. Three decades later, the Disney empire employs 40,000 workers (55,000 during its peak). In its brief history, 300 million customers have made the pilgrimage to the Magic Kingdom. Disney World has transformed tourism into a 365-days-a-year enterprise, a place that knows no "off" season. From an insignificant regional facility in the 1950s, Orlando International Airport has been transformed into one of America's busiest places, drawing 30.8 million passengers in 2000.[73]

Since its opening, Disney World has become the world's most successful commercial attraction. As a tourist shrine, Disney World is rivaled only by Kyoto, Mecca, and the Vatican. Each year more customers wait in line to see the Pirates of the Caribbean than to visit Britain; since 1971, more tourists have made pilgrimages to Orlando and Anaheim than there are Chinese.[74]

Orlando and Central Florida have profited mightily by offering shelter to their secular pilgrims. On the eve of the park's dedication in 1971, the metropolitan region mustered 5,900 hotel rooms; Orange County claimed only 2,200. By the dawn of the millennium, the region had become the nation's bedroom, amassing the second largest concentration of hotel rooms in the country, over 100,000, surpassing even the Big Apple. In 2000, the state's eleven largest hotels and resorts, and thirty-five of Florida's top-fifty largest facilities, are located in the Orlando area. Notably, only five of Orlando's thirty largest hotels are locally owned. Known in the 1950s for cattle and pastureland, Osceola County has become Orlando's innkeeper. Motels and automobiles have replaced longhorns and alfalfa, while thousands of residents work in the region's theme parks. Most recently, the Villas of Grand Cypress, Gaylord Palms Resort, Portafino Bay Hotel, Westin Grand Bohemian, and the Ritz-Carlton offer the Orlando area five-star extravagance amid high-tech, high-expectation settings. Highlighted by soaring atriums and a temperature-controlled biosphere (which could hold Chicago's Wrigley Field!), Kissimmee's Gaylord Palms Resort offers guests glimpses of old St. Augustine, Key West, and the Everglades.[75]

Metropolitan Orlando, perhaps more so than any place in America, has been reinvented by Disney World and tourism. A modestly important agricultural city in 1950, Orlando now enjoys a global identity as an international destination, a place/region/shrine synonymous with mouse ears and theme parks. "What is clear is this," concluded the *Orlando Sentinel*, "The nation's 27th-largest metropolitan area [Orlando] excels at little beyond being one of the world's top tourist destinations, and it lags behind most comparably sized U.S. cities in virtually every category." In salaries, the number of Fortune 500 companies headquartered locally, home-ownership, per-capita income, and school spending, the Orlando Metropolitan area ranks near the bottom when compared with like-sized areas. When the criteria measured are the percentage of service jobs, overcrowded schools, crime rates, and commuting times, Orlando ranks near the top. Sadly, the quality of life in Orlando and other tourist-dominated centers is eroding and falling behind other locales. Orlando may function as an economic and demographic magnet, a capital of mobility, but many newcomers leave Central Florida disillusioned. Disney World, Universal Studios, and SeaWorld are the chief reasons Central Florida employs 150,000 people in tourism and hospitality services. Yet regrettably, Orlando's best-known attractions and service industries pay beginning workers paltry salaries, barely above minimum wage and clearly less than a living wage. Significantly, more than a third of Disney's employees work part-time and receive no health or retirement benefits. "It is the paradox of Orlando's transformation," contends scholar Richard Foglesong, "low wages amidst rampant job growth."[76]

Critics have taken on Florida's sacred rodent. Tourism is blamed for crowded highways; creating low-skill, low-wage service jobs that tax the infrastructure; encouraging a plastic, throwaway society; and spreading visual blight. Getting travelers *to* Orlando has been accomplished with remarkable efficiency and progress; getting them *around* Central Florida has confounded planners and experts. Curiously, for all of the technological wizardry displayed inside the Magic Kingdom, park officials have shown little interest lending their expertise outside the company gates; indeed, Disney officials threaten to scuttle a voter-approved, high-speed rail project if the train stopped at rival parks or the Orlando Convention Center. In the 2004 election, Floridians voted to repeal the high speed rail project they had previously approved. Anyone who has navigated Orlando's International Drive or Tampa's Busch Boulevard understands the social costs of tourism. Ironically, Disney's dream to avoid the commercial blight that surrounded Anaheim haunts Greater Orlando. "The entire [Orlando] region has the look of a freeway exchange," complains John Rothchild. "The sprawl, gridlock and malling that accompanied Disney World is a mess, aesthetically and environmentally," writes *Miami Herald* columnist Carl Hiaasen, a mordant critic of Disney and author of *Team Rodent* (1998).[77]

In tourism, all roads lead to Lake Buena Vista. Built on the edge of the ecologically sensitive Green Swamp, Walt Disney World received high marks from environmentalists for its early efforts at managing water resources and waste disposal. Engineers buried all power lines underground to present a clean, crisp look. But lately, critics have savaged Disney's bullying tactics and environmental indifference. Mark Derr charges that Disney "has run afoul of its own astonishing growth and corporate negligence."[78]

Tourism, so synonymous with leisure and consumption, may also signify profligacy and indulgence. A vacation is the antithesis of conservation. Why recycle? Why take a modest shower? Why turn the light off? Why take public transportation? The consequences document a state and society living beyond their capacities. The fact that most tourists arrive in the winter and spring, Florida's driest seasons, only amplifies the problems. To feed, house, water, and dispose of the wastes of 70 million tourists imposes a "super-size" burden upon the state's beleaguered environment.

Tourism has inflicted a cruel and ironic dialectic upon Florida: the more people that come to enjoy lakes, river, and beaches, the less appealing and natural the places become. The same is true with places deemed charming by travel writers. Not long ago, Apalachicola, Fernandina, Cortez, and Tarpon Springs resembled quaint fishing villages. Still-intact Gilded Age gabled cottages and storefronts survive, largely because no one had the money to tear them down. Prosperity brought change. "We have to settle for nostalgia because there is so little else left," wrote the critic Beth Dunlop. "The irony is that festivals such as Cedar Key's end up celebrating more what is already gone than what is still there."[79]

The public adored places like Cypress Gardens because they seemed slices of pure, unspoiled nature. Scholars distinguish between first nature (Central Florida's chain of lakes before alterations) and second nature (an ecosystem that replaced the original). Dick Pope's Cypress Gardens may have seemed natural, but it represented a sophisticated patchwork of drainage canals and imported flora and fauna. But at least the trees and macaws were real. Walt Disney World proved a triumph over nature, luring the masses with high-tech, theme-park experiences. Who needs Santa Rosa Island when Disney World offers Blizzard Beach, with its assemblage of slides, sandcastle building pits, and white concrete snow? Who needs a real banyan tree to appreciate the Swiss Family Robinson experience when engineers can fabricate flora and fantasies? At Disney World, the "natural" can be deceiving. The story is told of how Walt Disney reacted upon his first glimpse of a glorious setting of ancient cypress trees towering over a black lagoon. Disney was not pleased. "Can you change it?" he asked his engineer, hinting strongly that water in Florida should be blue, not black. "I can if you have the money," came the reply. Disney had the money. His engineers would uproot the cypress trees and dredge the ancient tea-colored lakes, replacing them with imported white sand and lagoons of blue-tinted water—all more suitable for image.[80]

Technology and creativity allow millions of tourists to experience cherished Florida sites without visiting them. The ultimate pseudo-event may have been the now-closed Key West at SeaWorld exhibit. Tourists could meander down Duval Street while never leaving Orange County. The Gaylord Palms biosphere in Kissimmee invites guests to munch on conch fritters while dining aboard a sailboat in a simulated Key West lagoon (complete with a wave machine and salt-air mist). The real-life, overstimulated Key West seems an unlikely candidate for a theme-park simulation.

Tourism has tested the limits and limitations of the Keys archipelago. In 1950, only 190,000 tourists visited Key West. As late as 1970, fewer than 44,000 passengers arrived at Key West's postage-stamp-sized airport. Thirty years later, over a quarter million people use the facility. Even more remarkably, almost 1 million passengers boarded or disembarked from cruise ships at the Port of Key West in 2002, part of an even greater migration of 3 million tourists to the Florida Keys. Factor in automobiles and motorcycles and one begins to understand the crush of traffic on the Keys. In the 1970s, Parrotheads, artists, and gays discovered Key West's laid-back atmosphere and cheap, wooden-framed cigar-makers' cottages. The world seemed to follow, drawn by Jimmy Buffet's anthems and the locals' tolerance. Key West now faces big-city problems: homelessness, traffic gridlock, rocketing housing costs, and environmental calamities. Overloaded services trigger fecal bacteria alerts. Key West officials have attempted to regulate "transient renting"—condominium and homeowners who sublease their dwellings to vacationers—but any effort to slow the Keys' growth roils the waters. Frightening to the residents of the Upper Keys, the impact of tourism has spread to once isolated and serene places like Islamorada, Marathon, and Big Pine Keys. Environmentalists blame out-of-control tourism for damage to the Keys barrier reef, the third largest in the world. Massive die-offs of endangered coral alarm officials.[81]

An underground movement to discourage tourism surfaced in the late 1980s and 1990s, partly in response to progrowth tourist jingles: "Florida—The rules are different here," and "Florida. When you want it bad, we got it good." In 1987, The Florida Conservation Foundation inaugurated its "Calamity Calendar," reminding natives and visitors that the Sunshine State "leads [the nation] in injuries, and deaths from lightning," that high mercury levels endanger the Everglades, and that March 26 commemorates the date strollers found a human brain on St. Augustine Beach. New Age, bad-taste bumper stickers warned: "Welcome to Florida, Now Go Home," "When I Grow Old, I'm Going North and Driving Slow," "If It's Tourist Season, Why Can't We Kill Em?" and "Happiness is 100,000 Canadians Heading Home with a New Yorker under Each Arm." What manifestos failed to achieve, real-life disasters accomplished. Events in the 1990s cast Florida in new and threatening images: race riots, boat people, Versace, ram-n-rob murders, hurricanes, red tide, cocaine cowboys, and wildfires. Even the sun turned against Florida, as beach worshippers confronted a new threat: melanoma.[82]

Nothing lasts forever, most certainly not leisure trends. Theme parks have carefully cultivated three generations of Americans, but tourism remained flat throughout the 1990s, despite massive investments and hype. Industry officials, engineers, and futurologists feverishly tweak and reinvent attractions to create and fulfill each generation's needs and wants. The new century presents a particularly challenging problem: how to capture the affections of Generation X-ers, those citizens born between 1965 and 1976. Will dazzling new rides and childhood traditions be sufficient to bring them back to Florida? Most distressing, many young adults bring a different frame of reference toward work, leisure, and family, than their parental baby boomers.[83]

From the vantage point of a new century and millennium, the history of tourism in Florida represents a story of stunning accomplishments and enormous costs. Few aspects of Florida have been more scrutinized and critiqued than its tourism. What would Marx, Veblen, and the two Serbo-Croation immigrants whose exchange began this chapter have thought of these changes? Almost certainly, today's immigrant workers and their children understand Florida's pull. And yet for all of the democratization of tourism, relatively few working-class immigrants and children can afford the stiff price tag of a week at the Magic Kingdom. Marx would be shocked—and perhaps awed—at the pace and degree of collective change and the improvements in American workers' lives. In the United States, workers became consumers; unions accepted capitalism, and labor leaders sat on company boards. Middle-class workers—and the middle classes grew enormously—expressed less and less interest in class conflict while investing more and more interest in consumption. A Florida vacation served purposes of getting away from the "rat race." More than ever, the rich validated Veblen's notions of conspicuous consumption, while amusement parks and resort hotels both provide a leveling arena for classes and accentuate the gap between the rich and the middle classes. "We live on sweet potatoes and consumptive Yankees," bragged William "Pig Iron" Kelly more than a century ago. "But mostly we sell atmosphere."[84] Today, Florida sells experiences.

Old Folks at Home

The Graying of Florida

I N lyrical song and soulful meditation, the idea of Florida as a place of youth and renewal persists as a powerful metaphor. For many Floridians, their real-life Odyssey ends at home, albeit a new one; the fruits of war and work guarantee not only tribute and laurels but a condominium in Lauderdale-by-the-Sea. Ponce de Léon's quest for the Fountain of Youth incorporates Florida's birth myth, a perfect symbol for a state obsessed with second chances and eternal exuberance.

Florida's dual identification took hold long before the writers of the *Seinfeld* television show created Del Boca Vista as a retirement home for Jerry's neurotic parents. Florida's state song, "Old Folks at Home," depicts a tale of a homesick slave longing for the place that composer Stephen Foster never visited. Late-nineteenth-century travel writers extolled Florida's restorative powers. "Consumptives are said to flourish in this climate," reported a hopeful Sidney Lanier. Hired by a railroad company to write a guidebook, Lanier rhapsodized Florida's recuperative powers, describing "cadaverous persons coming here and turning out successful huntsmen and fisherman, of ruddy face and portentous appetite, after a few weeks." Alas, the dashing poet and musician of the Old and New South soon died of tuberculosis. Abbie Brooks—she of the delicious nom de plume Silvia Sunshine—cautioned readers, "Too many invalids before coming to Florida, wait until they have already felt the downy flappings from the wings of the unrelenting destroyer"[1]

For all of the ballyhooed fountains of youth miracles wrought by sunshine and salt air, Florida's isolation and desolation initially imposed barriers to settlement by America's elderly. In 1880, Florida's median age was eighteen, decidedly younger than the national average. Births far outnumbered deaths. As late as the 1940s, Florida's median age was younger than America's.[2]

If an earlier America venerated the elderly because of their piety and exceptionalism, Cold War America lionized baby boomers because of their narcissism and volume. Never in American history had society lavished upon youth so many resources and so much attention as in the decades after 1950. Florida's most identifiable generation, however, was not the pampered teenager or twenty-something, but that of his or her grandparents.

Popular culture drew inspiration from Florida's intergenerational tensions. *Where the Boys Are* (1960) introduced millions of prepubescent moviegoers to Fort Lauderdale and the cult of spring break. Florida may have been where the boys were, but it was also where the sunshine boys of vaudeville retired. Prune juice and beach music did not mix. In February 1964, more than 7,000 shrieking teenagers crashed police lines when the Beatles landed at Miami International Airport. Not everyone approved. While Beatlemania gripped the young, Bob Hope and Kate Smith quietly entertained silver-rinsed rooms at the Hotel Fontainebleau. Keith Richards wrote the lyrics to "Satisfaction" at the Fort Harrison Hotel in Clearwater, but raucous behavior at a 1965 Rolling Stones concert prompted the Clearwater City Council to ban rock concerts. The Stones exacted revenge. "What a drag it is getting old," begins "Mother's Little Helper." Jim Morrison, poet-philosopher of youthful rebellion, was born in Melbourne in 1943, the son of a navy pilot and future admiral. Morrison's grandparents lived in retirement-heaven Clearwater, where Jim spent much of his youth. In 1969, while touring with the Doors, Morrison was arrested in Miami for lewd and lascivious behavior. Concerned for the morality of America's youth, officials organized a "decency" rally at the Orange Bowl that was headlined by Jackie Gleason and Anita Bryant. That same year, rocker Janis Joplin was arrested at a Tampa concert for using obscene language, and Jack Kerouac, the symbol of youthful rebellion for the Beat Generation, met his road's end after an alcoholic binge in St. Petersburg.[3]

A refuge and dream, a trap and a time warp, Florida became a favorite setting for artists invoking the theme of growing old. In *Travels with Charley,* John Steinbeck wrote: "The very name Florida carried the message of warmth and ease and comfort. It was irresistible." The author, then approaching sixty, understood Florida's lure but cautioned readers that eternal sunshine came with a price. "I'd like to see how long an Aroostook County man can stand Florida. . . . For how can one know color in perpetual green, and what good is warmth without cold to give it sweetness?" Steinbeck resisted "irresistible" Florida, turning west before reaching the state boundary. Others would not or could not turn away. Florida, writes cultural historian Stephen Whitfield, "is the home stretch for 'Ratso' Rizzo in *Midnight Cowboy,* Seymour Glass in J. D. Salinger's 'A Perfect Day for Bananafish,' [and] 'Rabbit' Angstrom at rest. . . ." In *Follow That Dream* (1962), Elvis Presley homesteads a Gulf beach with his hillbilly family. In *Godfather II* (1974), mob boss Hyman Roth welcomes Michael Corleone to his Miami home, with its easy access to Mount Sinai Hospital and Cuban casinos. Octogenarians discover, in *Cocoon* (1985), a modern Fountain of Youth in a St. Petersburg pool. A 1980s sit-com, *The Golden Girls,* depicted the humor of sexually frustrated, naive, and cynical retirees in South Florida.[4]

Not only metaphors for Florida, old age and death have become big business. So many expatriate midwesterners and expired Floridians requested that their bodies be shipped "back home" for burial or cremation that transporting coffins and cadavers became a busy freight operation. Delta Airlines and Daytona Beach International Airport once awarded funeral directors 500 frequent-flier miles for every air-freighted body. The payoff was considerable: during the 1990s, 1.5 million people died in Florida. Ironically, the deaths of so many Floridians delayed the demise of Eastern Airlines, so profitable was its "coffin run" from Florida. In a case of life imitating the art of advertising, Delta was ready when they were. Politicians have seized upon Florida's coffin-shipping trade as a metaphor for the state's lack of community and connectedness, decrying the so-called Cincinnati factor. The term, coined by U.S. Senator Bob Graham, referred to Floridians who moved to Florida physically, but emotionally never left Ohio. "Florida," observes the writer John Rothchild, "has not become a true home of those residents, but merely their penultimate resting place, a warm way station in which to relax and play golf, the blessed limbo between Cleveland and the Pearly Gates."[5]

Behind the metaphors of funeral parlors and air-freight coffins lie some compelling questions: How and when did Florida become a magnet for the nation's elderly? How, in the blink of the historical eye, did Florida evolve from a state numbering fewer than 2 million residents in 1940, to more than 2 million inhabitants over the age of seventy in 2000? How have the meanings of "retirement" and "old age" changed in modern Florida?

Before Florida convinced the nation's elderly to migrate south for their golden years—more significantly, before senior citizens took seriously Florida's siren's call—there had to be a seismic shift in the way Americans thought about growing old. In an older world steeped in the Protestant work ethic, a society where church and neighbors revered elders, the notion of "retirement" in Florida was as socially unimaginable as it was morally abhorrent. Growing old in twentieth-century Florida represented a social and regional aberration, as well as a demographic frontier. For the first time in American history—probably the first time in history—society faced the presence of an unusually large concentration of "old" citizens. Above all, Florida allowed millions of elderly Americans to test their new freedoms (social, cultural, economic, medical, and demographic).[6]

In her classic study *The Coming of Age,* Simone de Beauvoir wrote that retirement was "the most loathsome word in the language." Traditionally, one worked until death. No society had ever confronted or even conceived a future in which a large part of its population lived for two or more decades after they stopped working. As the United States became an industrial power, and as more Americans worked for corporations, mandatory retirement became commonplace. The decades after World War II witnessed a dramatic decline in the percentage of seniors in America's labor force. In 1950, more than half of all sixty-five-year-old men were working. As late as 1970, seniors comprised only a quarter of the workforce, declining to 16 percent in 1985, and 8 percent at the end of the century. Exemplars of sacrifice and deferred gratification existed, such as Floridians Robert Carter, age ninety-five, who lived in Sarasota and "hoped" to quit work before he reached the century mark. At age 115, ex-slave Charlie Smith was still picking Polk County citrus.[7]

Certainly the notion that grandparents should move away from their families and hometowns cut across the ethical and ethnic grain of history. Old age, as much as adolescence, is socially constructed; in other words, aging is not merely a biological process but involves cultural, economic, and political meanings. Wordsmiths coined new terms to understand old age in modern America: active-adult retirement community, age-restricted community, caregivers, in-home elder care, assisted living, Meals on Wheels, and ageism. For much of human history, life was, in the words of Thomas Hobbes, "nasty, brutish, and short." The aged were respected because there were so few of them. Beginning in the nineteenth century, life expectancy rates climbed steadily as science, government, and capitalism redefined the meaning of "progress." Living longer befitted the American century; between 1900 and 2000, life expectancy increased by more than thirty years.[8]

At the turn of the twentieth century, one in twenty-five Americans had attained the age of sixty-five. The population of Florida was perceptibly younger than that of the United States. In 1900, only one in forty Floridians had reached age sixty-five. On the eve of World War II, the median age of the U.S. population (twenty-nine) and the percentage of residents age sixty-five years and older (6.8) mirrored the state of Florida perfectly. Compared to her Dixie neighbors, however, Florida had become the oldest state south of the Mason-Dixon Line. By midcentury, Florida's birth rate was lower than, its death rate higher than, and its median age decidedly above those of other southern states.[9]

Old age distinguished Florida from the Deep South. Bent on attracting newcomers to people the state's vast spaces, salesmen had long promoted Florida as a modern Fountain of Youth. Scores of communities actually claimed the "original" wellspring of youth. The communities of St. Cloud and Lynn Haven committed what would have been regarded as apostasy in Georgia or South Carolina by erecting statues of Billy Yank and urging Union Civil War veterans to move to Florida. In Osceola County, the Grand Army of the Republic purchased 35,000 acres, making St. Cloud the retirement home for thousands of old soldiers. To encourage the aging heroes of the Civil War to move to the southernmost point of the Pinellas peninsula, developers changed the name of Disston City to Veteran City. When few veterans purchased lots, developers changed the city's name once again, this time to Gulfport.[10]

By the 1930s, Florida was fast acquiring a reputation as a winter refuge for America's elderly. Displaying the impulse for organizing voluntary associations that had impressed Alexis de Tocqueville a century earlier, seniors organized Townsend Clubs, Three-Score-and-Ten Clubs, and Old-Age Revolving Pension Associations. In Miami, even ex-slaves had their own society. Old-age relief was a hot-button organizing issue in the 1930s. On elegant stationery and on penny postcards, hundreds of Floridians wrote Eleanor Roosevelt, encouraging her to lobby her husband and Congress to pass some legislation easing the worries of seniors. "I am appealing to you to use your influence with the President for some substantial relief for the aged poor," wrote Rena A. Briggs of Orlando. From Miami's El Comodora Hotel, Harriette E. Stoddard penned a poem for the cause.[11]

"This state, long a haven for tourists," observed a prescient reporter in 1947, "also could easily become a Shangri-La for the rest of the nation's elderly relief recipients." To appreciate the boldness of the reporter's notion, one should understand that in 1945 census takers counted a total of 156,021 seniors in Florida. Beginning in the 1940s, accelerating in the 1950s and 1960s, and cresting in the 1980s, the graying of Florida created enormous wrinkles in the Sunshine State. The silver migrations resulted from a number of interrelated factors. Americans lived significantly longer by the 1950s, and seniors were measurably healthier during their latter years. Work became a means to an end: security and comfort in retirement. A new notion of retirement transcended merely quitting work; by the 1990s, one could expect to live 7,000 days between retirement and death. Retirement was becoming a process, a season rather than an event. The generations arriving after 1950 capitalized upon political, medical, and technological revolutions. Scientific advancements, most notably affordable air conditioning, made Florida tolerable during the summer months, opening up the state to year-round living.[12]

Corporate America and the federal government underwrote the massive demographic and population shift to Florida. The passage of the landmark Social Security Act in 1935 paralleled an effort by private enterprise to offer employees pension plans. Working-class Americans benefited most from the twentieth century's greatest piece of legislation. Without the monthly check, millions of retirees would never have considered Florida as a place to live. More programs followed. The Veterans Administration and the Federal Housing Administration enabled millions of Americans to purchase modest homes at affordable rates. World War II and the Cold War created a vast educational-medical-military bureaucracy; by the 1990s, nearly 2 million veterans lived in Florida. This generation also profited from a robust economy, guaranteed pensions, and generous and rising real estate markets in the North, taking advantage of Florida's inexpensive housing and tax advantages.

Florida's gray wave—part of a series of connected and unconnected migrations—occurred in a blink of time. No single event or date signaled this demographic stampede, but one of its starting places was Miami Beach. In 1943, Wolfie Cohen opened his fabled sandwich shop on Collins Avenue in Miami Beach. A stranger patronizing Wolfie's, the Concord Cafeteria, or the kosher Lincoln Manor Restaurant in 1950 was struck by two phenomena: the thickly accented sounds of Yiddish and the age of the patrons. Miami Beach was fast becoming the last stop of elderly Jews.

Miami, distant and exotic, exerted a special attraction to millions of Eastern European immigrants and their children. For Jews, postwar America's freedom, tolerance, and acceptance made New York's congested quarters, expensive housing, and brutal winters as much a relic of the past as six-story walkups and the *Daily Forward*. Florida beckoned. About 5,000 Jews had settled in the Magic City by the early 1930s. Anti-Semitism expressed in the covenants and restrictions invoked by hotels and realtors tempered their optimism. On Miami Beach, "Restricted" and "For Gentiles Only" signs expressed blatant anti-Semitism. The real estate crash in the late 1920s dampened discrimination against Jewish travelers and residents. Many young Jews saw Miami Beach for the first time during the war, when the U.S. Army Air Corps took over the hotels. By 1950, 50,000 Jews resided in Dade County. Many more came in the winter months. Neighborhoods such as Riverside and Shenandoah quickly became identified as Jewish.[13]

For American Jews, the 1950s signaled the beginning of a great new diaspora. Miami beckoned. Between 1945 and 1960, Miami's Jewish population grew by a startling eight hundred persons each month. By the 1970s, so many Jews had moved to Miami that the area boasted the fifth-largest Jewish population in America, trailing only New York, Chicago, Philadelphia, and Los Angeles. In Miami Beach, one out of six voters listed Russia as place of birth. Even more startling than the rush of new residents was their age. The median age of Miami Beach's Jewish residents escalated from forty-three in 1950 to fifty-four a decade later. Miami Beach had once again reinvented itself; by 1960, over one-third of the city's inhabitants were sixty-five and older. A transplanted Jewish culture took hold in the thin sand of South Florida. Jews brought to Florida a heritage of and a commitment to voluntary associations and institution building. When South Florida hospitals discriminated against the newcomers, Jewish philanthropists opened Mount Sinai Hospital. The Greater Miami Jewish Federation, the *Jewish Floridian*, and scores of synagogues stand as testaments to such efforts.[14]

Overt evidence of anti-Semitism waned. When, in 1947, Miami Beach banned "Restricted Clientele" signs, Mitchell Wolfson, the city's first Jewish mayor, signed the order. The elections of Richard Stone to the U.S. Senate and Robert Shevin as attorney general in the 1970s confirmed Jewish influence and statewide acceptance. The 2000 vice-presidential candidate, Joseph Lieberman, raised money and consciousness in the vote-rich, heavily Jewish precincts of Broward and Palm Beach counties. In Tamarac, an adoring voter—she of silver hair and red lipstick—told Senator Lieberman that kissing his hand was "like kissing the Torah."[15]

TABLE 3. Median Age of the Population, 1880–2000

Year	Florida	U.S.
1880	18.0	20.9
1900	20.4	22.9
1930	25.8	26.5
1940	28.9	29.0
1950	30.9	30.2
1960	31.2	29.5
1970	32.3	28.1
1980	34.7	30.0
1990	36.3	32.9
2000	38.7	35.3

Sources: Historical Statistics of the United States: Colonial Times to 1970, 19; *The Florida Almanac 1983–84*, 106; Donald Bogue, *The Population of the United States*, 95, 109–16; *Statistical Abstract of the United States, 1942*, 25; *Statistical Abstract of the United States, 1962*, 27; *Statistical Abstract of the United States, 1982–83*, 25, 28–29; U.S. Bureau of the Census, *1970 Census of Population*, vol. 1, *Characteristics of the Population*, pt. 1, sec. 1, table 63; U.S. Census Bureau, *Census 2000*, "Profile of General Characteristics for Florida: 2000," table DP-1.

The 2000 presidential election thrust Florida and its senior citizens in the media spotlight. Comedians poked fun at addled, aged voters confused by chads and butterfly ballots. The Jewish presence along the Gold Coast, a critical factor in Al Gore's bid to win Florida, also signified a marked shift in migration patterns of the elderly. The turbulence and tribulations whiplashing Miami-Dade County in the 1980s and 1990s, coupled with the death of many of the early settlers, resulted in a white flight and a diminution of Jews in Miami and Miami Beach. Simultaneously, large numbers of elderly Jews continued to stream to Florida, but they were choosing new places like Delray Beach, Coral Springs, and Boynton Beach. New streams of Jews are bolstering Miami-Dade's declining Jewish population, but the newcomers are typically young, foreign-born émigrés who live in places such as Aventura. By the 2000 election, Jews in Broward and Palm Beach counties outnumbered their religious cohorts in Miami-Dade by more than three to one. Revealingly, the 2000 census reported that for the first time since the 1890s, the Jewish population of New York City dipped below 1 million—as recently as 1957 it had stood at 2 million. The number of Jews in Florida was estimated at 628,000, greater than the combined Jewish populations of New Jersey and Ohio.[16]

Old age was not confined to Jews or Southeast Florida; indeed, Southwest Florida had aggressively courted seniors for decades. Soon almost every county

TABLE 4. Percentage of Population 65 Years Old and Over, 1880–2000

Year	Florida	U.S.
1880	2.3	3.4
1900	2.6	4.1
1920	4.2	4.7
1930	4.8	5.4
1940	6.9	6.8
1950	8.5	8.2
1960	11.2	9.1
1970	14.6	9.9
1980	17.3	11.4
1990	18.3	12.6
2000	18.4	12.4

Sources: Irene and Conrad Taeuber, *People of the United States in the Twentieth Century*, 142, 975; *Florida Statistical Abstract, 1983*, 21, 30; Donald Bogue, *The Population of the United States*, 96, 112–13; *Statistical Abstract of the United States, 1993*, 38; *Statistical Abstract of the United States, 1942*, 5, 15; *Statistical Abstract of the United States, 1962*, 19; *Twelfth Census of the United States: 1900*, vol. 2, *Population*, pt. 2; U.S. Bureau of the Census, *Thirteenth Census of the United States: 1910*, vol. 1, *Population*, 331; U.S. Bureau of the Census, *1950 Census of Population*, vol. 2, pt. 10, *Florida*, table 16; *U.S. Bureau of the Census, 1970 Census of the Population*, vol. 1, *Characteristics of the Population*, pt. 1, sec. 1, table 59; *Florida Trend* 41 (April 2000): 50.

in the state targeted this group as potential residents. By the 1950s, more than half of Englewood's (Sarasota County) 2,000 residents lived off retirement incomes. By the early 1960s, retirees were flocking to Florida at a rate of 1,000 per week. In the decades following, almost one-quarter of all new arrivals were aged sixty and older, equaling the number of newcomers under the age of twenty. These migrants poured into new communities across South and Central Florida. The Sunshine State had become a Sunbelt magnet, snaring more seniors than any other state during the period 1950–2000. Florida attracted three times more elderly migrants than its closest competitor, California. In the last half of the twentieth century, Florida attracted one of every four seniors moving across state boundaries. By the 1990s, ten of eleven of America's most senior counties, and fifteen of the top nineteen, belonged in Florida. The long line of moving vans headed southward reinforced Florida's hold as the number-one destination of seniors in 1995–2000. During that period, another 149,440 seniors migrated to the Sunshine State.[17]

Growing old in Florida depended largely on being sold on Florida. There was nothing inevitable about St. Petersburg or Miami Beach becoming retirement destinations. Private enterprise perfected the sale. Sunday supplements and promotions promised "retirement in Florida at $35 a month." The mantra of ten dollars down and ten dollars a month was repeated endlessly. Hundreds, perhaps even thousands of books addressed the hot issue of aging and retirement. *How to Retire to Florida*, first printed in 1947, became a primer for those seeking a slice of the Florida dream. In *The Truth about Florida* (1956), a retiree exclaimed that a Florida couple "can live comfortably, have a whale of a good time and save money on an income of about $40 per week." Conventional wisdom held that seniors hated to be cut off from their traditional communities and families. Aging parents depended upon their children, neighbors, and friends for emotional support. Socioeconomic change, however, swept away tradition. The aging of Florida resembled earlier transoceanic migrations, with their chain linkages, immigrant letters, and word-of-mouth propaganda. But selling Florida was always a business, and developers learned that promoting a slice of paradise could be a lucrative industry.[18]

In 1959, Del E. Webb built America's first Sun City, a self-contained community of 46,000 seniors located near Phoenix, Arizona. Flush with success—he also owned the New York Yankees—Webb purchased 12,000 acres of land 25 miles southeast of Tampa. Sun City Center, an age-restricted, leisure-oriented community, appealed to America's moderately successful seniors who wished to enjoy comfort and security. "We love our grandchildren, but we simply don't want them as neighbors," became the residents' unofficial motto. Webb employed forty-five full-time salesmen. The first residents moved into this new community in 1962. Webb sold the project to investors in 1972, and by 1980 Sun City Center grew to 5,605 residents. The population included 1,870 transplants from New York, Michigan, and Illinois, but only 18 native Floridians. Only 62 families fell below the poverty line. For decades, billboards depicting mustachioed Cesar Romero proclaimed, "Sun City Center, The Town Too Busy to Retire." The concept worked. By 2000, Sun City Center had grown to about 16,000 residents, a self-sufficient community attracting banks, medical clinics, and golf cart repair shops. Eerily absent in this "Silver City" was a cemetery, in spite of the fact that the community's median age was seventy-five. In 1998, 60 percent of new homes purchased in Sun City Center were bought with cash, the highest such percentage in the United States.[19]

If Webb's "City on a Hill" was affordable only to America's affluent, others catered to the middle and working classes. Few succeeded as wildly as H. Irwin Levy. As a young lawyer in West Palm Beach, he quickly realized that selling real estate was more lucrative than litigating deeds. In 1968, he boldly launched the

FIGURE 16. Acclaimed Farm Security Administration photographer Marion Post Wolcott's depiction of a retiree enjoying *Life* magazine at a 1941 Sarasota trailer camp. Library of Congress, Washington, D.C.

prototype senior citizen community, Century Village. Located on 685 acres in West Palm Beach, the first condominiums—then called "apartments"—sold for $9,000. Levy's genius was tapping a vast new market. Retirement hotels had existed in St. Petersburg and Miami Beach for decades, but Levy was the first to create a modestly priced retirement complex. Century Village offered buyers concrete boxes but allowed them access to upscale golf courses, clubhouses, and swimming pools. Levy sold his condos cheaply and instead made money by charging for the use of recreational facilities. He built lakes so residents could boast to friends back home that they lived on the waterfront. The Century Village philosophy was modest: Keep it simple and unadorned. Levy created a leisure-club atmosphere but avoided unnecessary expenses. Rejecting elevators, he built instead outside stairs and small apartments. Social life flourished at these centers: Yiddish-language folktales, swimming classes, and widowed persons support groups. The "condominium belt" stretching from Fort Lauderdale to Miami served as a last stage for Jewish comedians such as Myron

Cohen and Jan Murray, who had begun their careers in the Catskills, the so-called Yiddish Alps.[20]

Levy lured vacationers by offering free lunches, transportation, and lodging to preview his model development. "We give years to your life and life to your years," brochures promised. High-pressure salesmen sealed the deal, selling hundreds of apartments in a day. Levy shrewdly employed comedian Red Buttons to promote Century Village. Born Aaron Chwatt on New York's Lower East Side, Buttons served as a popular spokesman to Century Village's principal audience: New York Jews. The nation's leading exporter of senior citizens, New York became the richest source for Florida's retirement communities.[21]

Levy's success in West Palm Beach begat Century Village spin-offs at Deerfield Beach, Boca Raton, and Pembroke Pines. In total, Levy constructed 30,000 condominium units in Southeast Florida. Century Village became the blueprint for rival developments: Kings Point, Sunrise Lake, Hollybrook, and Hawaiian Gardens.

Initially, the early migrations of seniors into Florida were restricted to the most urbanized counties. But successive waves of new residents lapped over Pinellas, Sarasota, Dade, and Broward counties, pushing into new areas in search of cheaper, safer, and less crowded areas. In 1945, Citrus, Hernando, and Charlotte counties were sleepy entities, none exceeding 5,700 residents. The *combined* 1945 senior population for the three counties was 1,407. The counties' median age dipped under thirty-three. Mass migration has "gray-rinsed" these Gulf Coast counties; astonishingly, the median age fifty-five years later pushed past fifty-two. Charlotte County's metamorphosis began in the 1950s with the launching of Port Charlotte, a sprawling "city" especially attractive to retired members of the military and law enforcement. According to the 2000 census, Charlotte County has the second-highest median age (54.3) of any county in America (the oldest is a leper colony in Hawaii). Similar patterns occurred in Pasco, Sarasota, Lee, and Collier counties. The composition of the lower Gulf Coast resembles a Twilight Zone populated by extraordinary numbers of old people and precious few children, an inverted pyramid. In a demographic warp that once seemed impossible even to imagine, residents sixty-five and older in the year 2000 outnumbered Floridians fourteen and younger in over one-third of the state's counties. In seven counties (Charlotte, Highlands, Sarasota, Hernando, Pasco, Flagler, and Citrus), the ratio of seniors to juniors was two to one. The eighty-five-and-over population of Southwest Florida grew by 53 percent in the 1990s; in Charlotte County, that age bracket nearly doubled.[22]

FIGURE 17. In 1959, the opening of S. S. Kresge's in Bradenton drew an enthusiastic crowd of seniors. The dinette's special was turkey dinner, pumpkin pie, and coffee for seventy-seven cents. Eaton Florida History Room, Manatee County Public Library, Bradenton.

Many Florida communities stretch the demographic limits of clustered longevity. Between 1950 and 1980, Miami Beach and St. Petersburg grappled for the title of America's "oldest" city. That distinction in 2000 was shared by several Florida places. Clearwater boasted the highest percentage of residents sixty-five and older (21.5) and was home to the largest percentage of World War II veterans (5.4). Cape Coral ranked second. Venice, however, claimed the county's highest median age (68.8). In Venice, one in ten residents had celebrated an eighty-fifth birthday.[23]

North Florida has remained relatively youthful. Its population more resembles South Georgia and Alabama than peninsular Florida. Increasing numbers of "young" retirees are flocking to North Central Florida, especially Tallahassee and Gainesville, towns that lure wealthy alumni to places of lost youth. Such communities also offer residents a rich cultural life. "When you live in a college town," promised an advertisement for SouthWood, "life is your major." But increasing numbers of seniors are discovering places like Madison and Monticello. "We have people moving in here—we call them 'South Florida Yankees,'" sighed Tommy Greene, publisher of the *Madison Enterprise Recorder.* "They come from the North and they go south, and then they get fed up with that down there and they move up here. We're the ham between two pieces of bread."[24]

To some Florida leaders, the presence of so many senior citizens stigmatized the state as a vast gerontopolis, a barrier to more dynamic growth. Nowhere was both the mutual affection and the tension between seniors and boosters more expressed and exposed than in St. Petersburg. A 1950 visit by Dr. Francis E. Townsend, who had organized a popular movement in the 1930s to promote federal aid to senior citizens, "created a mild sensation," as admirers flocked to the local Townsend Club. St. Petersburg, more than any other place in America's imagination, was inseparable from old people. The green bench bonded city and citizen. First appearing in 1916, pedestrian green benches lorded over downtown sidewalks and parks. At any one time, gushed publicists, 20,000 tourists and residents lounged on the benches. Period postcards and photographs document the Sunshine City awash in a sea of elderly white pedestrians seated along Central Avenue or in Williams Park. Under the shade of palm trees and eaves, "devotees" and "visitors"—the city never used the word "retirees"—sensed here the possibility of Ring Lardner's "golden honeymoon."[25]

The golden honeymoon turned brassy. The media began poking fun at St. Petersburg, satirizing it as "God's Waiting Room" and the "City of the Unburied." St. Petersburg richly deserved the title "capital of aging," thought *Fortune's* Lawrence Lessing, who described "a bustling, cheery, thoroughly American sort of death." Writer Benedict Thielen lampooned, "The old people sit like passengers in a motionless streetcar, without a destination." He added, "The grayness of age lies over them like a fine dust." Mocking the softball team Kids and Kubs (whose members must be at least seventy-five) and the Mirror Lake Shuffleboard Center (which boasted stadium seating), the author concluded cruelly, "Old age has its wry amusing aspects but to see it concentrated as it is here is to see human frailty become magnified by numbers." A prominent business leader piled on, declaring that the elderly "sit on them [green benches] and buy nothing in the stores. They just sit." The *St. Petersburg Times* identified one census tract as "Gerontoville," a place populated by more eighty-five-year-olds and older residents than those forty-five and younger.[26]

City leaders reacted with consternation and denial. Local publicists maintained St. Petersburg was getting younger, but the 1960 census confirmed what gerontologists knew firsthand: St. Petersburg's median age (47.3) and its per-

Favorite Out Door Pastime, St. Petersburg, Fla.—11   1923

FIGURE 18. A sea of straw hats and bonnets along St. Petersburg's renowned green benches in 1923. Heritage Park, Largo.

centage of senior citizens were rising, not falling. Downtown St. Petersburg, where half of the residents were over sixty-six years old, and where median per-capita income in 1960 was only $1,200, served as an inviting target. In America's New Frontier, the city's green benches, along with its shuffleboard and roque courts, seemed quaint anachronisms. If the lifestyles of downtown residents bothered city leaders, the actions of other newly arrived retirees alarmed planners. St. Petersburg was also becoming a magnet for trailer parks. The breaking point may have come when Swift's Premium Meats pulled an ad in the *St. Petersburg Times* because they thought local readers were too old to chew bacon! Politicians sought a new image. If the problem was too many old people, the solution was to repackage and restyle the city as "Funderful St. Pete." Frustrated and impatient, the St. Petersburg City Council ordered the benches painted pastel colors, and removed them entirely in 1967.[27]

Life in Florida can be mercurial. A population built upon elderly residents cannot stand (indefinitely). For decades, many Florida counties registered more deaths than birth. The character and composition of neighborhoods and communities can change swiftly. In the decade after 1990, the median age of Coconut Creek dropped from fifty to forty-one, as retirees died and young couples moved in. As late as the 1980s, Miami Beach was synonymous with aging Jews.

A one-mile section of South Beach contained 37,000 "old people living on fixed incomes." A reporter noted that for many of Miami Beach's impoverished seniors, "the bright spot of the day is a 50-cent meal" at a local church. In 1984, the *Miami Herald* asserted that "the most intensely populated Jewish area in the world is the four-square-mile section of North Miami Beach, with approximately 85,000 Jews." Dramatically, Miami Beach was reinvented in the 1990s, becoming synonymous with wealth, glamour, sensuality, and beautiful youth. Synagogues, all-kosher hotels, and *mikvahs* were replaced by chic boutiques, Floribbean bistros, and cigar bars. Places like the Hebrew Home for the Aged, built in 1954 for low-income Jewish retirees, now house Hispanic seniors. For decades, tummlers and yentas enlivened Century Village in Pembroke Pines. But Jewish residents are being replaced by a new wave of retirees, chiefly Hispanic and French Canadians.[28]

Stereotypes die hard. An Atlanta journalist covering the 1999 Super Bowl ripped, "Southerners—especially Atlantans—love Miami. What's not to like about the city where so many Yankees go to die?" In the 1970s and 1980s, comedians nightly poked fun at St. Petersburg and its elderly citizens, "the newly arrived and the nearly dead," maneuvering walkers along Central Avenue. But St. Petersburg's demographics shifted. Shuffleboard courts once deserted now attract skateboarders; sushi bars replaced cafeterias once famous for early-bird specials. The landmarks that once associated the Sunshine City with retirees—Aunt Hattie's, Webb's City, and the inexpensive residential hotels—are largely gone. The city council has even debated the propriety of mosh pits![29]

The boldest and most controversial experiment in modern senior living involved The Villages. Sprawling across Lake, Marion, and Sumter counties, The Villages' 30,000 residents point with pride to their sixteen golf courses and four hundred social clubs. Defenders describe The Villages as a Disney World for adults, "Florida's Friendliest Hometown"; critics decry it as Sun City on steroids. Founder Harold Schwartz—whose statue sits in the Lady Lake Villages' town square—envisioned instant communities where residents could enjoy and find a good life on a golf cart. It was as if Schwartz's life had prepared him for his moment in the Sunshine State: he had sold Florida swampland out of his mail-order Chicago office; he helped launch the career of Wolfman Jack at a Mexican radio station. In 1982, he had a vision. He purchased Orange Blossom Gardens, a mobile home park on Highway 27/441, converting it to The Villages. The Villages provided its 36,000 middle-class retirees with everything from polo fields, bowling alleys, and a microbrewery to a developer-run TV station and daily newspaper. Highly stratified by income and ethnicity, The Villages is also wildly successful. Scholar Stephen Golant believes that The Villages' success stems from its success at instilling a sense of certainty. "The land uses are under control. The people in the neighborhoods are under control." The Villages may enshrine the values of small-town America, but its leaders can play hardball, bulldozing political opponents when challenged. Following a bruising fight, Sumter County recently authorized The Villages to build 21,000 new homes.[30]

When the first retirees poured across Florida borders in the 1950s, society tended to define them as part of a monolithic and undifferentiated bloc of old people. Old is relative. In 1950 America, to have survived to collect Social Security benefits was an accomplishment, but life expectancy and the expectations of life confounded actuarial tables and aging experts. New terms emerged: the aged and the super-aged. In 1970, Florida's eighty-year-old-and-older population comprised 154,467 residents; by 1990, it had soared past the half-million mark. To put these numbers in perspective, consider that in 1900, census takers counted only 123,000 persons over the age of eighty-five in the entire country. This age cohort is the fastest-growing segment of the state's population. U.S. Senator Bob Graham liked to tell the story of a picnic planned for forty-five centenarians in Tallahassee. The event had to be postponed because so many hundred-somethings were on vacation! When the Kings Point retirement community opened its doors near Delray Beach in the 1970s, most of its residents were "young" retirees, northern transplants anxious to exchange New York winters for the "active retirement lifestyle." Surrounded by swimming pools and golf courses, few of the cost-conscious pioneers objected to the fact that developers neglected to build elevators. In 2000, Kings Point was part of Florida's new frontier: almost half of its residents were eighty and older. Blood-pressure kiosks and golf carts signify the new order.[31]

Florida's gray wave has resulted in a more diverse state. Profound distinctions in ethnicity, race, education, and class characterize the elderly population. That Jews and other ethnic groups seemed so much a part of Florida's modern landscape was remarkable because so few of them had been part of it prior to recent times. Italians dramatically illustrate this point. In 1940, when the United States hosted 4.5 million Italian immigrants and children, Florida accounted for only about 10,000 such immigrants, mostly in Tampa. St. Petersburg, Fort Lauderdale, Hollywood, Palm Beach, and Miami possessed neither classic Italian colonies nor substantial numbers of immigrants. If Italian immigrants preferred the Bronx and Hoboken, their children fell in love with Spring Hill and Lake Worth. By 2000, over 1 million Floridians identified themselves as Italian Americans, a third of them residing along the Gold Coast. Florida now boasts hundreds of Sons of Italy and social lodges (including the Italian Angels Motorcycle Brotherhood of Palm Harbor), populated largely by senior citizens and the result of massive postwar migrations. Winter Park seemed an unlikely setting to find a colony of elderly Central Europeans. Slovak Gardens originated in 1952, when leaders of the National Slovak Society purchased grove land for the purpose of establishing retirement cottages and a winter retreat for Pennsylvania miners and mill workers. Huge numbers of elderly Canadians—including first- and second-generation Asians and Europeans (especially Finns)—also sought warmth and group solidarity in wintertime Florida. The profile of Hispanics, however, contrasts sharply with other newcomers. A quarter of Florida's Hispanics are under eighteen, making them one of the state's youngest groups. Florida's Cuban population, however, is aging. The 2000 census identified 147,143 Cubans sixty-five and older. Three-quarters of all Cuban-born Americans older than sixty reside in Florida.[32]

Overall, the selling of Florida to senior citizens has been a whitewash, with only a tincture of black. During the silver decades of the 1960s and 1970s, when St. Petersburg was the best-known city for old people in the world, fully one in three white residents was sixty-five years old and older (a percentage rising during the winter months). Black Americans, however, rarely participated in this rite of passage. White Americans born at the turn of the century could expect to live fifteen more years than black Americans. Only one in twenty-five black St. Petersburgers was a senior citizen. Custom had long dictated that green benches and golden sand were reserved exclusively for whites. Citrus County, one of Florida's oldest, is also the state's whitest county. For reasons of health and wealth, perception and deception, African Americans are far less likely to retire to Florida.[33]

Senior citizens also mirror America's class tensions. With the force of a sledgehammer, the 1962 publication of Michael Harrington's *The Other America* pricked society's smugness, shattering the myth of affluence absent class divisions. The 1960s also linked in the public mind senior citizens and poverty. For much of American history, old age exposed the elderly to the dreaded old folks' home or the poor farm. A 1959 *Life* magazine shocked readers with an exposé on aging, noting, "The income of three-fifths of all the aged is under

$1,000 a year." Harrington identified 8 million senior citizens living in poverty. Swept into the vortex of Lyndon Johnson's Great Society, the plight of the elderly became an emotionally charged and politically popular cause. The 1965 passage of Medicare and Medicaid depended upon a harmonic convergence of an irresistible cause, perfect timing, and adept leadership. President Johnson wanted medical care for the elderly to be a cornerstone of his domestic program. Floridians who opposed Johnson's civil rights initiatives helped pass Medicare and Medicaid. The short- and long-term consequences were dramatic. In 1965, fully one-half of senior citizens had *no* health insurance. Although flawed—the legislation never anticipated the sheer number of participants or explosive drug and health costs—Medicare and Medicaid proved immensely popular and helped alleviate the specter of senior poverty. Social Security reforms have also helped, most notably COLAs (cost-of-living adjustments). Long-term health care, in particular, has perplexed philosophers, families, and governors. In 1970, for example, Florida paid less than $200 million for Medicaid. By 2004, the Medicaid budget had soared to $14 billion. By percentage of the population, Florida had the highest Medicare enrollment in the country (17.8 percent). Whether credit should be given to dynamic capitalism or an activist state, millions of Americans have realized levels of comfort and security unimaginable to earlier generations. Consequently, the poverty rate has fallen from one in three seniors living in poverty in the 1950s to one in ten in 2000. Still, as an authority on aging remarked, "It's hell to be old in Florida if you're poor."[34]

Once depicted as the most impoverished and ignored group in American society, senior citizens now constitute one of the more comfortable and most powerful classes in the United States. Since its founding in 1958, the American Association of Retired Persons (AARP) has evolved into one of the most feared and effective lobbies in Washington and state capitols. From a membership in 1969 of just 1.5 million, AARP has grown into an organizational behemoth, numbering 35 million members in 2004 (including 2.6 million card-carrying Floridians). Politicians, however, frequently overestimate the clout of the AARP, since the organization rarely speaks with a single voice for its diverse membership. Aware that many aging baby boomers reject the notion of growing old and snicker at retirement publications such as *Modern Maturity,* the AARP has revised its magazine to focus more on money and sex.[35]

Senior citizens became acutely adept at wielding political power, staking a third rail that no politician dares touch. The political odyssey of Claude Pepper embodied the new political clout of America's senior citizens. Bursting upon the political scene in 1936 as a U.S. senator, Pepper embodied youthful energy and New Deal optimism. Devastated by his humiliating defeat in 1950, Pepper retired to Tallahassee before joining a law firm in Miami. In 1962, Pepper returned to Washington, elected to the U.S. House of Representatives from a safe Miami district. If act 1 had cast Pepper as the youthful darling of the New Deal, FDR's weathercock in depression and war, Pepper in act 2 patterned the role of an elderly statesman, hectoring conservatives from Johnson's Great Society to the Reagan revolution. An active participant in shaping the Great Society, Pepper articulated the concerns for the elderly in the 1970s and 1980s, arguably becoming America's most beloved figure. He championed a law that raised the mandatory retirement age from sixty-five to seventy. He became known as "Mr. Social Security." As chairman of the House Select Committee on Aging, he spoke out and publicized long-term health care, housing for the elderly, and age discrimination. In the 1980s, Pepper was receiving eight hundred letters a week. In 1981, he launched a national "Dear Claude" column. One of his last legislative accomplishments involved a successful fight to abolish mandatory retirement based on age. The *New York Times* eulogized him in 1989 with a front-page headline, "Claude Pepper, Fiery Fighter for Elderly Rights, Dies at 88."[36]

The hurly-burly of the 1960s and 1970s did not go unnoticed by America's elderly. African Americans, women, environmentalists, and students triumphed in protest and protested triumphantly. To be heard, one mobilized. A prescient Barbara Isenberg observed in 1973: "And when old people become aware that there is power in their numbers, something is going to give. 'Senior power' has become a political force to be reckoned with." By the end of the decade, America's formerly inchoate senior citizen lobby had emerged in full force. Old people became a distinct interest group with special needs and interests. The fact that American society allocated a disproportionate amount of its resources to senior citizens—a 1999 congressional study indicated that the United States spent seven times as much on the elderly as on children—exposed children's inability to deliver the vote on election day.[37]

Gender and class divide young Americans and isolate senior citizens. Elderly women, far more than men, associate old age with loneliness. Many feel the worst quality of old age is uselessness. The 2000 census found nearly 1.6 million Florida women sixty-five and older and about 1.2 million such men. In 2000, two-thirds of Florida seniors living alone were women, many of them widows, prompting a journalist to compile a list of the "ten loneliest places in Florida." The ten places include Century Village (Palm Beach) and Ocean Breeze Park (a mobile home park on the Indian River in Martin County), where two-thirds of the residents are live-alones. Elderly widowers reap a windfall of eligible, interested widows. Octogenarians and nonagenarians residing at a Lantana retirement complex posed for a beefcake calendar.[38]

Northeastern retirees living in fading downtown hotels and trailer parks are likely to vote and think very differently from their midwestern counterparts at Sun City Center and Marco Island. Wealth, along with health, matters greatly. Lifelong associations with work and purpose need not be severed at retirement. Labor unions envisioned Florida as a place to reward members and invest pension funds. Leaders planned communities for retired railroaders and policemen (including a Policemen's Hall of Fame), as well as for members of the Upholsterers International Union, United Steelworkers of America, and the Brotherhood of Locomotive Engineers. In 1956, the Teamsters announced Sun Valley, a model retirement community. Polk County's Fedhaven became a home for retired federal workers. Its Polk County neighbor is Nalcrest, a dogless place in the sun named for the National Association of Letter Carriers Retirement Education Security Training Foundation. Penney Farms, a French Norman village set down in Clay County, has served as a progressive-care center for Christian missionaries and pastors since its founding in 1926 by chainstore magnate J. C. Penney. About the same time as the founding of Penney Farms, the Loyal Order of the Moose, a national voluntary association, purchased acreage in Orange Park, south of Jacksonville. Since the 1920s, Moosehaven has served as a retirement center for longtime members of Moose lodges. Clermont is home to City of Legends, a place for former and aging athletes, and Gibsonton takes pride in its reputation as a safety net for retired carnival workers.[39]

In a place of second and third chances, Florida's dynamic economy has allowed—or the state's failed promises have forced—many retirees to return to work. A critical shortage of teenage workers and a persistent need for minimum-wage employees have motivated grocery stores and fast-food chains to recruit senior citizens. School districts actively search for retirees to drive buses. Seventy-year-old ticket takers and ushers have become familiar sights at tollbooths and athletic events. But seniors are not restricted to minimum-wage jobs. Large numbers have resumed careers in Florida or sought new challenges. In 1950, Walter Berrman moved to Lakeland, leaving his job at General

Motors. He became a real estate broker and worked until his death in 2001 at age 107.[40]

Large numbers of Florida seniors retain residences—and allegiances—in the North, living lives of the proverbial swallow. The "snowbird" has been around since the 1950s, but the Census Bureau did not even collect data on the subject until the 1980s. Of America's half million "non-permanent residents" in 1980, half spent portions of winter and spring in Florida. So many more followed that by 2000, a million people enjoyed winter in Florida and summer elsewhere. Thousands of New Yorkers living in Florida voted in *both* places in the 2000 election. Many more followed. Canadians have carved out special relationships and niches in Florida, especially along the Gulf Coast. Fully one-quarter of Charlotte County's residents and 22 percent of Manatee County's inhabitants remain only during the winter and spring. Cable connections, newspaper subscriptions, church attendance, and traffic jams spike upward each November and shrink in the late spring. The population of Zephyrhills in Pasco County fluctuates from 25,000 to more than 90,000 in the winter. Among the retirees who live in Florida but consider Ohio home, there are many who use their golden years to volunteer and share time and resources. "They [seasonal residents] are tour guides, airport greeters, hospital helpers, and fund raisers," noted a Fort Myers reporter. "The arts scene without them would be bleak."[41]

The mobile home and trailer park have become especially popular among elderly residents in Florida. Of the 1.2 million persons who lived in mobile homes at the end of the century, half were senior citizens. Many held long-term leases so as to foster a sense of familiarity and belonging; many retained homes in the North and took advantage of mobile homes' affordability and mobility. Recreational vehicle (RV) parks also shelter pilgrims who prefer a more upscale lifestyle. Florida's Silver Coast, the area between Cedar Key and Naples, has attracted attention because of the concentration of RV and trailer parks. The *Zephyrhills News* recently published a directory listing 145 such facilities. "This is a great place for older folks and Canadians," said an enthusiastic tenant of a Bradenton trailer park. "It's an inexpensive way to live," he boasted. Others are less blessed. The fear of being evicted from one's mobile home park—or blown away in a storm—is especially worrisome to seniors. Some of Florida's oldest trailer parks—Tradewinds in Citrus County, Gulfstream in Marathon, and Pinehurst in Gainesville—have closed because of rising land values.[42]

Mobile-home dwellers face the same problems as country club residents and suburbanites: getting around. Florida's woeful lack of public transit forces many seniors to take to the road, in spite of the fact that many should not be driving. In 2000, Florida had more than 1.2 million drivers older than seventy-five and almost 400,000 older than eighty. Florida also led the nation in the number of elderly drivers—and young bicyclists—killed in traffic accidents.[43]

Senior economic power crested in the 1990s. Annually, pension and Social Security checks, supplemented by dividends, portfolios, and other earnings, brought to Florida $55 billion—exceeding the amounts generated by agriculture, tourism, or construction. Florida's retirees alone contribute $3 billion a year in military benefits. Largely because of this "gray in gold" pipeline of investment into the Sunbelt, Florida led the nation (21 percent) in the percentage of new-home buyers who paid for their purchase in cash. Over 2 million Florida residents in 2000 received a check from Social Security; such monthly checks provided over 7 percent of all personal income in the state. The presence of 1.7 million military retirees residing in Florida amounted to a massive government investment. Florida enjoyed a vast, invisible economy, reaping the rewards of decades of work and savings as many retirees transfer their wealth to Florida. Between 1985 and 1990, seniors transferred over $8 billion of assets to Florida, while transferring only $1.8 billion *out* of Florida. Senior citizens in Pinellas County (almost a quarter million) accounted for $3 billion in economic assets in 1998 alone. Sarasota County's residents derived more income from entitlements and investments than wages, a stunning fact. Seniors represent a new frontier for marketing, consumption, and work.[44]

Senior citizens bring a smile to investment planners, but they make politicians tremble. Voting early and often, retirees have established themselves as a force to be reckoned with and listened to. The rise of Florida's Republican Party can be partly understood by migration streams from the Midwest to the Gulf Coast of Florida. By the early 1950s, transplanted midwesterners had energized a dormant GOP, electing St. Petersburg's William Cramer—"Mr. Republican"—to Congress. The success of the GOP followed the pattern of retirees down the Gulf Coast and across Central Florida.[45]

Woe to the politician who assumes all senior citizens vote a straight Republican ticket. The condominiums lining the Gold Coast constituted a fertile crescent for liberal Democrats, greatly boosting the campaigns of Bob Graham, Richard Stone, Lawton Chiles, Bill Clinton, and Al Gore. Retirees from New York and New Jersey brought a tradition of New Deal zealousness and Democratic loyalty. Dade, Broward, and Palm Beach counties produced nearly a third of the state's Democratic votes in the 1980s. Condominium leaders like Century Village's Amadeo "Trinchi" Trinchitella became legends because of their ability to deliver votes. Elderly women, transplants from the urban Northeast, bolstered and buoyed the Democratic Party. Many such women recalled the struggle to win the franchise in 1920 and faithfully rewarded the party of Roosevelt and Pepper with their votes. But recent trends suggest that the retirees who faithfully voted for Vito Marcantonio and Bella Abzug in New York and Claude Pepper in Florida are dying out. As Republican-voting Cubans replace staunch Democratic Jews, political wars have scarred retirement enclaves.[46]

Whether Democrat, Republican, or Independent, senior citizens vote so faithfully as to demand the supplications of every Florida office seeker. "In the 1998 election cycle," wrote political scientist Susan MacManus, "people aged sixty-five and over comprised eighteen percent of the state's overall population, twenty-four percent of the voting age population, and twenty-seven percent of registered voters. Exit surveys in the 1998 gubernatorial election reported that nearly one-third of the voters were sixty-five and older (forty-two percent were sixty and older). Retirees are twice as likely to vote as Floridians aged eighteen to twenty-four."[47]

Not all seniors pulled the lever on election day; many simply left the state. Florida is not the dreamstate imagined by all retirees. The summer heat, crime, noise, congestion, and lack of municipal services have dulled Florida's luster as a retirement heaven or even haven. In the last several decades, for every three retirees arriving in Florida, one left. Aggressive marketing by new rivals—Hattiesburg, Mississippi; Fairhope, Alabama; Bainbridge, Georgia; Branson, Missouri; and McCormick, South Carolina—promises southern amenities without Florida's excesses. Alabama and Mississippi entice retirees with an assortment of property and income-tax breaks. The Carolinas lured many disenchanted Florida transplants, called "halfbacks" because they have returned halfway back home. Decades earlier, Brother Dave Gardner—a better comedian than prophet—claimed he had never heard of anyone retiring to New Jersey.[48]

The aging of Florida from 1950 to 2000 has forced America to examine anew the meaning of retirement, new life stages, and senior-care living. Florida serves as a bellwether, a sort of gray dawn. The Florida of today is the America of tomorrow. But the America of today—a multicultural nation with a large mass of aging baby boomers who have brashly announced that they do not intend to age quietly—will shape tomorrow's Florida. Business has taken heed. The antiaging industry is booming. Americans spend $6 billion a year on metabolic and cosmetic curatives. The term *retirement communities* is out; *active adult communities* is in. In 1999, a developer unveiled Florida's first senior center for gays, a 270-unit high-rise in downtown Fort Lauderdale. The haven will not come cheap—two bedroom units begin at $235,000. The *Wall Street Journal,* charting senior trends, noted recently: "A slow game of shuffleboard in the sun is losing its appeal for a new generation of older Americans, who see the traditional retirement spots as dull and socially isolating. Worse yet, Florida and Arizona are places their parents went to retire, and these new retirees see themselves as far too young to be hanging out with that crowd of geezers."[49]

Indeed, Florida's powerful hold on older Americans slipped in the decade of the 1990s. Where once the Sunshine State snared a full quarter of America's seniors who moved, that figure dropped to one in five in the 1990s. Still, Florida attracted three times more Americans age sixty and older than its nearest rival, Arizona. To one group of Americans, military retirees, Florida is and has always been a promised land.[50]

In death as in life, the military casts a long shadow across Florida. The somber rites of duty and honor are played out dozens of times each day as veterans are buried. Many are part of the World War II generation, of whom 1,000 veterans a day have been dying since the 1990s. Nowhere is the fact seen with more urgency than in the small community of Bushnell, south of Ocala. The National Military Cemetery at Bushnell is Florida's largest veterans' burial ground. Opened in 1988, the 400-acre complex is the third most-active veterans' cemetery in the United States, daily averaging twenty-seven interments—with as many as thirty-four. Presently, 43,000 servicemen and women rest at the handsomely groomed facility.[51]

In a nation struggling to redefine family values and meanings of community, retirement in Florida may become as unfashionable as it was once stylish. One generation's golden years can be another's economic burden. Coping with the explosive costs of senior entitlements and the rising expectations of baby boomers, society faces class and generational wars. The economist Robert J. Samuelson calculated that the costs of Social Security, Medicare, and Medicaid approached nearly half of all federal spending in 2000. "Even if these costs were easily affordable," he argued, "they are increasingly socially unjust." Floridians' unwillingness to invest in its youth is not encouraging. Almost twice as many children as older Floridians live in poverty. The most pressing needs of elderly (long-term health care, Meals on Wheels, medical costs) often clash with the budgetary imperatives of children (school construction, day care, and recreation). The generational chasm is deepened by the socioeconomic reality that minority groups tend to be poorer, younger, and have a disproportional number of children on welfare and in school. Historically, retirees have not supported educational bond referenda. Among indicators of child health and care, Florida ranks near the bottom. Defenders laud compassion shown the elderly; critics charge that such priorities are tantamount to one generation eating the seed corn of the next. The future points to a poorer workforce that is more multiracial and multicultural. Will young, twenty-first-century Floridians accept the covenant of Social Security and Medicare, where one generation helps another, when senior lifestyles include golf courses and age-restricted gated communities? The portents are numbing. In 1940, forty-two workers were paying benefits for every Social Security recipient; by 2030, the ratio will be two to one. "By 2030, the [baby] boomers, who begin retiring in 2008," wrote George Will, "will have made America's population older than Florida's is today." Florida will grow even older. Today, almost one in five residents is older than sixty-five; by 2020, that figure will be one in four. The crisis is hardly restricted to Florida or the United States. Italy, Spain, Germany, and Greece are peopled today by more inhabitants over sixty than under twenty.[52]

The public perception of old age depends not only upon the sheer number of senior citizens but also upon the relative number of young people. Since 1950, Florida's population explosion was fueled largely by steady streams of retirees. For forty years, Florida lured one out of every four American retirees migrating out of their home state. At some moment in the early 1990s, two demographic trends converged: the number and proportion of seniors migrating to Florida slowed, while the number and proportion of young Floridians swelled. The 2000 census revealed that Floridians age five to nineteen slightly exceed those age sixty-five and older.[53]

The image of Florida as a senior-citizen haven remains firmly embedded in the popular psyche. Neither economic calamity (stock market collapse) nor dour signs (South Florida is running out of cemeteries) nor ultimate reality (every single hour fourteen Floridians die) can sour the marriage of Florida and America's elderly. The moving van and Social Security check remain vital signs of Florida's modern profile—400,000 "new" seniors moved to the Sunshine State in the 1990s. "The future," the philosopher Yogi Berra once pronounced, "ain't what it used to be." But the future of the state as a welcome wagon and Fountain of Youth situated between work and death will depend upon Florida's image. It has always been so.[54]

Sunbelt Hues

Cold Wars, Hot Markets, and Nagging Doubts

5

I F Rip Van Winkle had fallen into his long slumber in Florida as the twentieth century dawned, he would have been astonished to awaken in the present day. Florida farmers were harvesting more with fewer workers; Sunbelt cities glistened with skyscrapers crowned by logos of powerful corporations; suburbs, boomburbs, and edge cities had sprung from citrus groves and forests. Timber and fishing, cigars and phosphate, once powerful industries, had been reduced to economic sideshows. An endless stream of entitlements, programs, and regulations emanated from Washington and Tallahassee. But upon closer inspection, one finds dissonance and uneasiness. Florida is a fabulously wealthy state with large pockets of poverty. If Florida were a nation-state, its gross national product would surpass that of Argentina, yet Florida often finds itself an economic pawn in a multiconglomerate, multinational world. Appallingly few corporations call Florida home, while too many Floridians still work in minimum-wage service jobs. A half century ago, Florida was one of the South's least-developed states; it is now one of the most developed. But Florida's dilemma is like that of Disney's sorcerer's apprentice—it must keep growing to avoid disaster.

In 1950, Florida's economy rested uneasily upon a tripod of agriculture, extractive industries, and tourism. As many Floridians worked in agriculture and forestry as were employed in manufacturing and services. In 1950, Florida was an economic

Florida, the fabled location of a 16th-century Fountain of Youth, would become the actual location of a 20th-century Fountain of Wealth.

Daniel Boorstin,
The Democratic Experience

frontier, a state eager and willing to accommodate Americans willing to invest in its future. Witness an enterprise widely touted as a popular path to success: the smoked food shack. Florida readers learned that in 1950, "a new money harvest has sprouted along Florida roadsides where a man with $150 [in] capital can go into business for himself." Northern tourists, it was said, were acquiring a taste for smoked mullet. In 1947, Ted Peters began his now-legendary open-air, smoked-fish shack at Blind Pass on St. Petersburg Beach. Florida's postwar boom, however, had more to do with Cold War defense spending, manufacturing, real estate sales, and new construction.[1]

In 1956, Governor LeRoy Collins received a confidential phone call from Del Webb. A man of many talents and careers—owner of the New York Yankees, creator of Sun City, and savvy investor—Webb was calling on behalf of his client, the enigmatic and powerful industrialist Howard Hughes. Contemplating a major investment—an aircraft factory in Florida—Hughes wished to meet personally with the governor. During the secret meeting held at the Beverly Hilton Hotel in California, Hughes proposed to finance and build the world's largest medical research center on an island off the Florida Gold Coast. Alas, Howard Hughes's schemes became entangled in a convoluted disagreement with the government. Undaunted, Collins set a style for future Florida governors: the chief executive as promoter. LeRoy Collins, swore Hughes, was "just about the best salesman any state ever had." In 1955, Collins appeared on the cover of *Time*. On several occasions, he toured northern states, glad-handing the "fat cats" who vacationed in Florida but invested their money in the Rustbelt. To lure northern factories and tourists, Collins encouraged the legislature to establish the Florida Development Commission. Outfitted with two Greyhound buses to tour the United States and Europe as "Traveling Showcases," the governor's caravan sold Florida. Collins's greatest achievement, however, was not his recruitment of industry but rather his deft handling of racial crises. Compared to his reactionary contemporaries Orville Faubus of Arkansas, George Wallace of Alabama, and Ross Barnett of Mississippi, the moderate Collins managed to defuse several racial time bombs, outflanking the more conservative Florida legislature. Tourist attractions and manufacturers worried foremost about location, workforce, and profits, but race relations and image mattered too. Would Walt Disney have located his Magic Kingdom in Mississippi, a state that also boasted a mild climate, cheap land, low taxes, and a nonunionized labor force? In hindsight, Collins and his successors, however, might have better served Florida with the selective recruitment of responsible industries instead of with the growth-at-any-price mentality.[2]

A succession of Florida governors evangelized free enterprise and rugged individualism, cursing big government and federal control, all the while becoming dependent upon an array of Washington programs. In a conservative state resistant to taxation, the federal government played an ever-important role in fiscal affairs. Beginning with the New Deal, accelerating during World War II, and climaxing during Johnson's Great Society, Washington became a major partner in shaping Florida's fiscal future. In 1974, not yet a half century after the New Deal, the magnitude of Washington's largesse could be seen: the amount of federal aid had grown from $2.7 million in 1937 to $1.2 billion. By 1990, federal aid to Florida had soared to $4.5 billion. The number of federal employees rose accordingly, from 59,000 in 1939 to 440,500 in 1974. An editor once quipped that there are no boll weevils in Florida's tourist crop. He might have added another weevil-free Florida harvest—federal spending. By the 1950s, Uncle Sam not only subsidized research to combat boll weevils, but he paid farmers not to plant cotton. A flood of federal revenues rained upon Florida in the half century following 1950, the result of a Cold War, the Great Society, and changes in the meaning of poverty and social welfare. Commentators described federal aid as an "invisible economy," but in myriad forms it was ubiquitous, from military installations, campus dormitories, veterans' hospitals, interstate highways, public housing, Social Security offices, senior citizen communities, to the dike encircling Lake Okeechobee, the drainage of the Everglades, the creation of Everglades National Park, and the scientific expertise making possible DDT, frozen juice concentrate, and the space race.[3]

Fortress Florida

Like Banquo's ghost in *Macbeth*, the spirits of World War II lived well past their appointed hour. In matters social, cultural, and economic, World War II functioned as a turbo-charged jet engine, compressing and accelerating local, regional, national, and international forces whiplashing Florida.

Between 1941 and 1945, millions of young men and women, farm boys and cowgirls from New England and the Rocky Mountains, New York Jews and Georgia blacks, encountered this dreamy place called Florida for the first time. Their half-century relationship with the Sunshine State represents one of the

FIGURE 19. For over three centuries, St. Augustine's El Castillo de San Marcos has stood as citadel and arsenal. Coast Guardsmen march across the parapets during World War II. St. Augustine Historical Society.

compelling themes of Florida. World War II involved the grand movement of armies and navies, but the war was also intensely personal. "The whole setup is a Paradise beyond my fondest dreams," wrote John Armstrong to his parents in Virginia. He was referring to his "barracks," the Boca Raton Club. The list of impressionable veterans of field and factory included George Herbert Walker Bush (Fort Lauderdale Naval Air Station), Andy Rooney (Camp Blanding), and Robert Byrd (McCloskey Shipyard, Tampa). But most veterans became teachers, accountants, or truck drivers, not presidents, journalists, or U.S. senators. Florida remained high on their dream list.[4]

Veterans returned home to a grateful but nervous government: there were laurels for those who sacrificed, but there was also genuine fear over the prospects of 16 million homeless and jobless GIs. The Servicemen's Readjustment Act of 1944—better known as the GI Bill of Rights—was a brilliant stroke of legislation. The GI Bill's generous housing and education entitlements reaffirmed and emboldened the American dream, making it possible for millions to also realize the Florida dream. Between 1945 and 1965, fully one in five of all single-family homes was financed by the GI Bill. Communities supplemented the federal government's benefits. In Pahokee, Sanford, Clearwater, and St. Petersburg, cities awarded free lots to veterans. Tarpon Springs, DeLand, and other cities extended the offer to African American vets.[5]

The GI Bill, for all of its egalitarian elements and far-reaching features, reinforced deep-seated attitudes regarding race, gender, and housing. Female veterans, widows, and homosexuals battled the status quo. African Americans also felt the frustration of having fought a war against Nazism and totalitarianism only to return to a rigid Jim Crow social order. Housing represented only one pillar of a biracial Florida, but in 1945 the promise of the GI Bill of Rights collided with the bitter reality of entrenched housing patterns. The quantity and quality of housing available to black veterans was disappointing and disillusioning. "The overall housing picture in Jacksonville has become very acute," testi-

FIGURE 20. V-J Day, 14 August 1945, was collectively and spontaneously Florida's happiest day. Historical Association of Southern Florida, Miami.

fied T. L. Redding, a local NAACP leader. "Negroes are regimented generally in neighborhoods where there are located industrial plants . . . 91 percent of the houses occupied by Negroes are of frame construction, most of which are old." Concluding his 1947 testimony, he contended, "Colored veterans cannot beat the red tape required by local financing agents to qualify them for GI loans." Postwar housing policies reinforced historic residential segregation. A phalanx of Floridians—real estate agents, politicians, civic officials, homeowners, and the Ku Klux Klan—enforced the code of Jim Crow. In November 1945, Dade County deputies arrested two black couples in Brownsville for defying local legislation restricting the area to whites. A wave of bombings in 1951 sent a chilling message to black and white activists. Precisely at the moment when some opportunities were expanding—by the 1950s, blacks had been hired as policemen in larger cities, served on juries, and registered and voted as Democrats with relative ease—the quest for better housing lagged far behind need and demand. For too many African Americans, low-income public housing served as the bitter reality of Florida.[6]

On August 15, 1945, V-J Day (Victory over Japan) signaled the end of one epic struggle but also the beginning of a long and costly Cold War. Floridians worried that peace would spell the end of the federal pipeline were relieved to know that the United States would not dismantle its formidable defenses, as had occurred with previous wars.

From a handful of training bases and airfields, Florida became citadel and fortress during the years 1941–45. Not all of Florida's 175 military installations survived the end of World War II; the dismantling of obsolete and smaller military outposts had begun before V-J Day. Many communities fretted over the dreaded demobilization. "Crestview, like all other small towns around 2,500, will have to sink or swim after the war is finished," philosophized the editor of the *Okaloosa News Journal* in 1944. "What will we do after the war?" Crestview need not have worried. Powerful congressman Bob "He-Coon" Sikes vowed to protect his hometown and defenseless coons. "My concern now was to protect the economy in my district."[7]

Small towns lacking a "He-Coon" lamented base closings and reeled from the economic losses. Other communities found creative ways to utilize abandoned barracks and aircraft hangars. Sebring's Hendricks Field, which served as an early B-17 combat training school in the United States, became Sebring Airport. Others saw better use for the long, well-paved runways, and on December 31, 1950, the Sebring Grand Prix was born. Marianna Army Air Field, declared surplus property, became a state tuberculosis hospital. Florida's Indus-trial School for Girls, located near Ocala, replaced a facility treating women with social disease. Arcadia's Carlstrom and Door Fields, aviation training schools in both world wars, closed to reemerge as a mental hospital and prison. Talla-hassee's Dale Mabry Army Air Field housed the first males to attend the Florida State College for Women, which would soon become Florida State University. Colleges were later built upon former runways and bombing ranges in Tampa, Boca Raton, Palm Beach, Marianna, Miami, and Opa-locka. In Leesburg, a Ger-man prisoner-of-war compound was razed to build today's Lake Sumter Com-munity College. The Richmond Naval Air Station, located 12 miles south of Miami, exchanged seaplanes for tigers, lions, and the Miami Metro Zoo. Lake-land's Lodwick School of Aeronautics, the home of Stearman bi-planes, wel-comed the Detroit Tigers baseball team; the Vero Beach Naval Air Station be-came "Dodgertown," spring home for Brooklyn's famed baseball team. Not every city, however, wept at the final bugle call. In December 1945, the army announced it was leaving Miami Beach's Pancoast Hotel, the last such occupied facility.[8]

Panama City understood all too well the vicissitudes of war and depression. Energized by shipbuilding and Tyndall Army Air Field, the city better known for its bathing casinos and fried fish dinners boomed during the war. By Octo-ber 1945, shipyard workers received their final paycheck; within weeks, docks, laundries, and warehouses were declared surplus property. The University of Florida claimed many of the workers' homes, shipping them to Gainesville to be used as married housing. Shipyard administration buildings wound up years later as Gulf Coast Community College facilities. Only Congressman Sikes's influence saved Tyndall Air Field.[9]

By December 1945, 70 of the state's 175 military installations had survived demobilization. In 1942, communities could acquire an airfield or a WAC base simply by donating land, hosting a banquet, or befriending Eleanor Roosevelt. These were new times. Hanging onto a military jewel now required relentless lobbying and shrewd politicking. The ghosts of depressions past flashed before Pensacola businessmen at a 1945 gathering, when leaders passed out a 1911 *Journal* headline: "Local Navy Yard Officially Closed." Congressman Sikes and Congressman-elect George Smathers understood the game. The former en-sured Pensacola's future; the latter pleaded with President Harry Truman to save Dade County's Opa-locka Naval Air Station.[10]

An adoring and grateful public idolized scientists who helped win the war of technology. World War II marked the first time that scientific breakthroughs developed during a war actually helped win the war. As Floridians anxiously awaited the peacetime hammering of swords into plowshares, they eagerly and optimistically embraced new technologies. In August 1945, as Floridians cheered victory and worried about hurricanes, the Lee County Commission offered the U.S. government 7,500 acres "as a base for the atomic bombing of hurricanes." For years, Floridians continued to express hope that a well-placed atomic bomb might deflect hurricanes.[11]

The Cold War settled into some of Florida's most unlikely bayous and crevices. Renowned for its pristine beaches and Indian River citrus, Brevard County seemed serenely isolated from Berlin airlifts and Middle East conflict. Few soothsayers could have imagined Nazi rocket scientists huddling at an obscure outpost, described in 1946 as a wild and mysterious place. "Canaveral, a small community on the sparsely populated cape of a scrub-covered key . . . has no port, and no commerce, nothing but a battered pier." Cape Canaveral, one of the oldest place-names in North America, became one of the newest sites in the Cold War arsenal. Before Titusville became "Space City, U.S.A.," it was known for its high-quality citrus.[12]

It was precisely Cape Canaveral's isolation, as well as its geophysical position in the earth's rotation and its proximity to tracking stations in the Caribbean, that caught the attention of scientists and officers. In 1947, the Joint Chiefs of Staff eyed 15,000 acres in Brevard County as a site for the Joint Long-Range Proving Ground. The presence of the Banana River Naval Air Station and the promise of transportation improvements also secured the cape's destiny. A vanguard of scientists arrived in 1948. On July 24, 1950, Florida's space age began with the firing of a 56-foot, 14-ton missile consisting of a German-built V-2 rocket with an American-developed WAC-Bumper in its nose. The missile roared over Cocoa, reaching a speed of 2,700 mph. When asked what was happening to old Brevard County, a motel owner explained simply, "We've all got rocket fever here." The population also blasted off; Brevard increased tenfold between 1950 and 1970.[13]

The Soviet Union's successful launch of the orbiting spacecraft *Sputnik* in 1957 galvanized America, spurring massive investments in scientific education and new frontiers. The battle for "control" of outer space focused attention in this world on the obscure spit of land called Cape Canaveral. In 1958, the National Aeronautics and Space Administration (NASA) was created, the same year scientists launched *Explorer* I, the first U.S. satellite. By the end of the

1950s, the newly nicknamed "Space Coast" had attracted a veritable army of 75,000 scientists, engineers, technicians, and workers. Events in Washington, Berlin, and Havana swept away the old (the beloved Banana River Naval Air Station) and bolstered the new (Patrick Air Force Base) under the aegis of a scientific and holy crusade. Bolstered by President Kennedy's pledge to put a man on the moon, the Cape Canaveral annual payroll, $2 million in 1950, soared to $136 million by 1962. Local bars cashed in on the space race, inventing drinks called "moonshots" (rum and vodka topped with cream). The Mercury, Gemini, and Apollo projects beat the Russians to the moon; in the process, Brevard County fully grew into its new identity as the Space Coast. The slumber was over. In the decade following 1950, the county's population quadrupled, topping the 110,000 mark, making it America's fastest-growing county. In 1950, Brevard County claimed 434 manufacturing jobs; by 1970, it exceeded 17,000. Income rose dramatically. "On almost every hand," noted *U.S. News and World Report* in 1962, "from the launching pads of 'the cape' to Orlando, sixty miles inland, this once-quiet countryside is in upheaval. New factories, new subdivisions, new shopping centers are going up with startling speed." Brevard County scrambled to build schools, part of the costly invasion of engineers' sons and daughters to "Missile Land." Melbourne High and Cocoa's Satellite High soon led the state in National Merit Scholars. In 1958, scientists launched Brevard Engineering College, better known by its later name, Florida Institute of Technology. In 1965, as a capstone to the state's space program, the legislature authorized Florida Technological University to be built in Orlando to create a synergy between Central Florida and the Space Coast.[14]

If modern Cape Canaveral owed its success to the Gulf Stream and Cold War, Florida's failure to capitalize upon its spectacular successes was the result of hardball politics and human will. Florida's opportunity to become the uncontested center for all U.S. space activities may have been bargained away at a party in Washington, D.C. In spring of 1961, Democratic Texas congressman Albert Thomas, Vice President Lyndon Johnson, and newly appointed NASA director James E. Webb gathered to discuss America's space program. Webb quickly sized up his dinner companions. Johnson, a man of legendary cunning and charm, was also chairman of the National Aeronautical and Space Council. Thomas sat on the House Appropriations Committee, key to the purse strings of NASA. Bluntly and forcefully, Thomas and Johnson informed Webb that they wanted the manned space center to be placed in Houston, Texas. Snubbing Eglin Air Field, Jacksonville, and Tampa, Webb announced in September

1961 that NASA had selected Houston. Vice President Johnson promised NASA generous funding and predicted that Houston's Rice University would soon rival MIT and Cal Tech. As president, Johnson lavished even more spending on Texas facilities. While Cape Canaveral's space complex still contributed $1 billion annually to Florida's economy in the 1990s, questions persist. What if Florida's LeRoy Collins, not Lyndon Johnson, had been selected as vice president in 1960? Would Florida Technological University (now University of Central Florida) or Florida Institute of Technology have become the Cal Tech of the Southeast? In the fiscal year 1999, not a single Florida university ranked among the top ten schools awarded NASA contracts. Not only did politics move jobs from Florida to Texas, but the public grief surrounding the president's death in 1963 prompted Congress to change the place-name from Cape Canaveral to Cape Kennedy. The original name was restored in 1973.[15]

Ironically, America's greatest achievement in space—the successful mission to the moon—marked Cape Canaveral's rapid decline. The walk on the moon may have been "one giant step for mankind," but for NASA, it meant drastic budget cutbacks. By the early 1980s, NASA employed 14,000 workers with an annual payroll of $300 million, but the numbers declined through the 1990s.[16]

The Cold War spurred America to race the Soviet Union to the moon. The ideological conflict also tapped a rich wellspring of federal funds to maintain Florida's network of military installations and defense contractors. The Cold War guaranteed the survival of the state's leading military bases, while the military-industrial complex created and sustained a multitude of defense contractors. Economies triggered by defense spending became a major economic force in Florida, a source jealously guarded and protected by generations of legendary politicians: Claude Pepper, Spessard Holland, Bob Sikes, George Smathers, Charles Bennett, Earl Hutto, Dante Fascell, Sam Gibbons, William Cramer, and Bill Young. Their legacy was easily measured: In 1980, 1,111 square miles of Florida—an area equal to that of Rhode Island—was dedicated to the tactics of war. By the late 1990s, only California boasted more defense establishments, and only tourism brought in more dollars than defense, with revenues from tourism at $17 billion and from defense at $13 billion.[17]

In the history of Florida, few politicians perfected the art of pork-barrel politics like Robert Lee Fulton "He-Coon" Sikes. Representing Northwest Florida in Congress from 1940 to 1978, the Okaloosa County Democrat staunchly defended the military-economic interests of his district. First elected to Congress in 1940—his campaign slogan rang, "Every quail in the woods is calling

Bob Sikes, Bob Sikes"—he sat on the House Appropriations Committee and House Armed Services Committee through World War II, the Korean War, and Vietnam, carefully cultivating and improving installations at Whiting Field, Pensacola Naval Air Station, Eglin Air Force Base, and Tyndall Air Force Base. Considering that in the 1970s, fully one-quarter of the residents in the congressman's district received their incomes directly from the military, the meaning of Fortress Florida can be easily understood. In his autobiography, *He-Coon,* Sikes succinctly explained his success: "Throughout my career in Congress I worked for the establishment and expansion of military bases in West Florida. After my first few months in office, there was not a time that the bases were not the backbone of the economy of much of the district. . . . the 1960's brought a golden age for our bases. I had progressed to the point in congress where I could materially influence military construction programs." Friends and neighbors paid tribute to the self-styled He-Coon: Crestview's Robert Sikes Library, the Robert L. F. Sikes Elementary School in Crestview, the Robert Sikes Airport, and the Robert Sikes Chair at Okaloosa-Walton Community College.[18]

While journalists debated the meaning of the "New" South, few underestimated the importance of military defense in modern Dixie. Stewards of domestic largesse and hawks on defense, southerners dominated Capitol Hill committee rooms in the half century following World War II. From Mendel Rivers, Richard Russell, and John Stennis, to Trent Lott, Newt Gingrich, and Strom Thurmond, southern politicians have championed defense spending. Symbolizing the Republican ascendancy in the 1990s, Florida's C. W. Bill Young (R–Indian Rocks Beach) succeeded Sam Gibbons (D-Tampa) as chair of the powerful—the prefix "powerful" seems permanently attached—House Appropriations Committee. What Bob Sikes was to the Panhandle, Bill Young was to Tampa Bay. Championing defense and pork, the congressman has directed millions of dollars to area military establishments, defense plants, universities, and colleges.[19]

Fortress Florida survives. At its postwar peak in 1978, the Defense Department controlled 700,000 acres across Florida, exceeding the acreage devoted to citrus. Florida's Panhandle is setting for the greatest concentration of military installations in the state. Anchored by Eglin Air Force Base, aka the "largest air base in the Free World," the facility sprawls 380 miles across Okaloosa, Walton, and Santa Rosa counties, encompassing nearly a half million acres. No section of Florida is so dependent upon federal funds, and no county is so tied to military spending as Okaloosa. With a 1970 population of only 88,187, Okaloosa

County's 1973 base payroll included 56,099 military and civilian employees. Three-quarters of Okaloosa County's income is derived from Eglin. In the early 1990s, Pensacola and Eglin Field combined to bring in $1.2 billion in defense spending and a $1 billion payroll. The war on terrorism has created a plethora of opportunities for West Florida defense contractors.[20]

The Korean War introduced dramatic changes at Pensacola's Naval Air Basic Training Command Headquarters, as aviators and mechanics made the transition from propeller craft to jet planes. During the war, Pensacola graduated 6,000 aviators. Whiting Field in nearby Milton became the headquarters for advance flight and helicopter training. In 1968, Congress designated Eglin as the Air Proving Ground Center, later becoming the Armament Development and Test Center. In 1985, Pensacola's venerable Naval Air Station graduated its last aviators, the same year that the city acquired the Pensacola Naval Supply Center. In 1991, Eglin and Pensacola brought to Florida's northwest coast over $1 billion in appropriations, plus another $1 billion in payroll. Once home port to the USS *Lexington,* the 1994 decommissioning of the USS *Forrestal* left the Pensacola Naval Air Station without a training aircraft carrier for the first time since the 1920s, but Pensacola remains a major defense center. Eastward, at the elbow of Florida's Big Bend, lies Tyndall Field. Covering 32,000 acres, the World War II–era base survived base closings to become a weapons center for the Air Defense Command. The U.S. Mine Defense Laboratory also established an oceanographic research center at Panama City.[21]

During World War II, Orlando gained fame for its Army Air Force Tactical Air Command (AAFTAC). Between 1946 and 1947, Pinecastle test pilots conducted experiments in supersonic flight with x-1 "rocket planes." By 1950, however, the Defense Department had deactivated Orlando's air bases. But if the 1940s ended on a depressing note, the 1950s brought Orlando crescendos of optimism. The Korean War prompted the air force to reactivate Orlando and Pinecastle Air Fields. The defense build-up and linkages to Orlando military alumni brought to Central Florida aviation training schools and units. In 1954, the Strategic Air Command established a combat unit at Pinecastle Field, with Col. Michael Norman McCoy its commander. Orlando residents became accustomed to the sounds and sights of c-124 Globemasters and b-47 bombers. Orlando's McCoy Air Force Base was named in honor of Col. McCoy, who died in a b-47 crash in 1957. u-2s deployed at McCoy flew over Cuba during the 1962 missile crisis.[22]

But Orlando's reputation derived not only from its prowess as an aviation center. Remarkably for an inland city known for its lovely lakes, Orlando became a navy town. In 1966, the navy announced that Orlando had been selected as an advanced training center and boot camp for recruits. Acquiring the abandoned Orlando Air Force Base, the Naval Training Center commenced operations. The economic-military coup was made possible by adroit lobbying by Florida power brokers and by the political friendship between Orlando publisher Martin Andersen and President Lyndon Johnson. Congressman Bob Sikes was furious to lose a military base to upstart Orlando. At its peak in the 1970s and 1980s, the Orlando Naval Training Center, which trained raw recruits and officers for nuclear-powered submarines, functioned as a city within a city, a 1,100-acre complex, including 300 buildings and the beloved *Blue Jacket*, a full-sized, landlocked, metal-and-wood training ship. First opened in 1940 as part of Orlando Army Air Field, the base became a naval boot camp and training center in 1968, training more than 5,000 recruits at a time. The complex generated $575 million a year for Central Florida's economy. Deactivated by the Defense Department in 1993, the Orlando facility was reborn as Baldwin Park, an old-style, new-urbanist development.[23]

Central Florida and the Space Coast, bolstered by Martin-Marietta Aerospace and the Harris Corporation, have amassed huge government contracts, $2 billion in 1990, doubling to $4 billion in 2000. Since its arrival in Orlando in the 1950s, Martin-Marietta has dominated Florida's aerospace industry. Harris and Martin-Marietta employ more than 10,000 employees each.[24]

Northeast Florida remains a military dependent. The Cold War bolstered Jacksonville's military ties. While elite Blue Angel formations soared above, cranes and construction crews have rarely been idle. Congressman Charles Bennett first proposed a carrier base for Northeast Florida in the late 1940s, an idea brought to fruition at Mayport in the 1950s. Cecil Field and the Jacksonville Naval Air Station emerged as modern fortresses, brandishing jet bases, antisubmarine forces, and helicopter squadrons. Jacksonville's Mayport Naval Station proudly served as the home port for two carriers, the *Saratoga* and *Roosevelt*. By 1980, the navy's payroll was so vital to Jacksonville's economy that it employed as many workers as the city's top twenty-five private companies. In 1991, only Orlando received more dollars ($1.8 billion) from defense spending than Jacksonville ($1.4 billion), and no place in Florida relied upon more defense dollars for payroll ($1.2 billion). By 2000, the area's principal bases—

Mayport, Jacksonville Naval Air Station, Blount Island Marine Corps Base, and Kings Bay Trident Submarine Complex across the St. Marys River—dwarfed any other economic sector, employing 53,000 persons and pumping nearly $5 billion annually into the area. Winn-Dixie, the region's largest private company, employs 13,000 people. The federal government distributed more than $1.5 billion in salaries and wages in 2000 in Duval County, more than in any other Florida county.[25]

The end of the Cold War marked a milestone. How would a post–Cold War U.S. military affect Florida and its military-industrial complex? In 1993, the Department of Defense, with the rare cooperation of Congress, agreed to a massive cut of fifty-two military bases within and outside the United States. Compared to California, Florida's losses were light: the Orlando Navy Training Center and Jacksonville's Cecil Field. The announcement, however, rocked Northeast Florida. First opened in 1941, Cecil Field Naval Air Station trained dive-bomber pilots and crews for aviation combat in the South Pacific. Deactivated in 1949, Cecil Field reopened in 1950, shortly after the outbreak of the Korean War. In 1961, aircraft based at Cecil Field discovered evidence that Soviet missiles were being stockpiled in Cuba. Home to the S-3 Viking, ES-2 Shadow, and the FA-18 Hornet, Cecil Field survived until the Cold War's end. In an earlier era, the closure of Cecil Field with its 8,000 jobs might have been a calamity; in the boom economy of the 1990s, Jacksonville leaders coveted the possibilities of 19,000 acres of hangars, runways, buildings, and marshland. Cecil Field's legacy included four runways, one running 12,500 feet, the second-longest commercial tarmac in the state. Renamed Cecil Commerce Center, the site is envisioned as a business community, with the hope of aerospace partnerships.[26]

While Orlando and Jacksonville calculate the potential profit from base closures, Green Cove Springs still laments its lost military ties. In 1939, the U.S. Navy selected Green Cove Springs, situated on the St. Johns River, as a 1,407-acre site for its deepwater, well-protected harbor. At its peak in the 1940s, the Green Cove Springs Naval Base boasted eleven huge docks and two runways. Once a popular nineteenth-century resort community, the depressed town leapt to life with the coming of the navy, its population doubling in the 1940s from 1,752 to 3,921. Clay County, in one of Florida's poorest regions, also revived during the 1940s, largely because of the naval presence at Green Cove Springs but also due to the military spillover from nearby Jacksonville and Camp Blanding. In 1945, Green Cove Springs claimed the largest collection of ships in naval history, as over 600 ships anchored on the St. Johns, part of the navy's "mothball fleet." The Korean War breathed new life into Green Cove Springs, but the navy deactivated the base in 1962. Confident that it could market the complex, the City of Green Cove Springs acquired the base. Business leaders, however, have struggled to lure tenants and investors to the site. A variety of activities, ranging from a yarn plant to a firm manufacturing air-conditioning ducts, have resulted in meager returns. The city eventually sold the facility to J. Louis Reynolds, whose efforts to develop an industrial park have failed. By the 1970s, the wharves were crumbling into the river. In 2000, the population of Green Cove Springs hovered around 5,000, not many more than in the 1950s. Most of Clay County's labor force works in Jacksonville.[27]

World War II endowed Tampa Bay with a multidimensional arsenal: shipyards along Tampa's Hooker's Point, sophisticated aerial complexes at Drew, Henderson, and MacDill fields, and a Coast Guard base anchoring St. Petersburg's Bayboro Harbor. To survive postwar geopolitical-budgetary crises, military and civilian leaders adapted to the new order. The Coast Guard resumed its old duties of assisting disabled vessels and seizing contraband goods. Drew Field evolved into Tampa International Airport, Henderson Field became a county industrial park, and MacDill Field lived on the edge, thriving during Cold War crises and skirting base closing during lulls. The Korean War brought new weapons and urgency to MacDill's role. B-47 Stratojet bombers and Strategic Air Command bombers crisscrossed Tampa Bay skies in the 1950s. In November 1960, the Department of Defense announced that MacDill, deemed obsolete in the missile age, would be closed. A July 1961 pre-obituary headline read, "When the Base Closes." The Cuban Missile Crisis doomed Tampa's cigar industry, but the crisis saved MacDill Field. While 300 air force personnel checked into the Floridan Hotel, MacDill rented every available forklift to load and unload planes. The base became the headquarters for the U.S. STRIKE Command (an elite airborne unit) and later the home for the F-4 (and later F-16) 56th Fighter Tactical Wing. Since before the Gulf War, MacDill has maintained the Central Command. MacDill also maintains SOCOM (Special Operations Command Central), a commando force ready to strike anywhere in an area stretching from the Horn of Africa through the Arabian Gulf into Central Asia. In 1998, officials reported 72,000 retirees and dependents living within a 50-mile radius of MacDill. The Avon Park bombing range, 100 miles southeast of Tampa, sprawls across 106,000 acres in Polk and Highlands counties. The largest such site east of the Mississippi, the complex allows F-16s and F-4 Phantoms to practice aerial combat, drop bombs, and strobe targets with laser weapons. Several dozen defense contractors—most notably Sperry Rand and Honeywell Inc.—have established plants in Pinellas County.[28]

Florida's proximity to Cuba placed the state in the crosshairs of Cold War conflict. The presence of a Communist threat 90 miles from Florida sent American leaders into paroxysms of panic. When Soviet Premier Nikita Khrushchev rattled his saber, Conchs in Key West and Crackers in Crestview felt the reverberations. While Brevard Civil Defense officials handed out pamphlets labeled "Individual and Family Survival Requirements," schoolchildren practiced civil defense drills on how to survive a nuclear attack. The family bomb shelter became a status symbol. In 1960, the air force promised Homestead Air Base the addition of 1,900 new troops and 30 new aircraft. Following the Bay of Pigs debacle, authorities secretly trained 150,000 Cuban and American forces in Florida. To protect President Kennedy's family, the government constructed a fallout shelter on Peanut Island in Palm Beach County. During the thirteen days of October 1962, all of Florida became an armed camp and a staging base for invasion. Strategic Air Command Bases in Tampa, Orlando, and Satellite Beach clicked to high alert. MacDill dispatched RF-101 low-level reconnaissance planes. To prepare for a counterattack, the military rushed Hawk antiaircraft missiles to Key West. The Cold War touched the most familiar and remote areas in Florida. Deep in Everglades National Park lie the relics of the missiles of 1962. Someday an Everglades museum may showcase the 10,000-pound, 41-foot Nike Hercules missiles. Before Marco Island became a fashionable retreat, the Department of Defense established a missile tracking station along the dunes. A reporter described the Marco Island site in 1959 as "an electronic oasis in an area of nothing." Other missile tracking sites included Cudjoe Key, Anclote, Bonita, Temple Terrace, Fort Lonesome, Cape San Blas, and Santa Rosa Island.[29]

The twin pillars of military defense and retirement living have made the Sunshine State a center for almost 2 million military veterans plus retirees. Only California claimed more veterans. According to the 2000 census, 650,000 World War II and Korean veterans resided in Florida. By the late 1990s, retiree benefits were bringing $3 billion annually to Florida, up from $250 million in 1971. Retirees put a human face on Fortress Florida. Millions of Americans first encountered Florida as young men and women in the 1940s; many vowed to return, lured by the state's climate, cost of living, and military infrastructure. Florida's six veterans hospitals—in Lake City, Gainesville,

Tampa, St. Petersburg, West Palm Beach, and Miami—care for about a half million patients each year. The Veterans' Administration has not responded to shifting demographics, and veterans in Orlando, the Panhandle, and Southwest Florida complain about the lack of medical facilities. Tens of thousands of veterans have chosen to be interred at the Florida National Cemetery in Bushnell, home to 47,000 veterans buried there since its opening in 1988. Because of the shortage of space and Bushnell's accessibility, V.A. officials have planned for more cemeteries in the state. Consider the case of Porter Wassum. A twenty-one-year-old West Virginian, Wassum arrived in Central Florida in 1940, eager to serve his country at Orlando Army Air Base. "When you come out of places like Alabama, Tennessee, or West Virginia, and you come to Florida, you think you've come to heaven, and you want to stay there," explained Wassum. After a career spanning the army air corps, the air force, and three wars, Wassum moved his family to Orange County. He was not alone. Wassum joined about 80,000 military veterans living in Central Florida.[30]

At the dawn of the twenty-first century, Florida's defense establishment bristles with military bases and contractors. The twentieth century transformed the Sunshine State into the Citadel State. The Spanish navy had once posed the greatest threat, as recently as 1898. In 1900, the federal government maintained a negligible presence in Florida: a naval station in Key West, a crumbling brick fort on the Dry Tortugas, and gun batteries on Egmont Key. Two world wars, the Korean War, Vietnam, and the Cold War created hundreds of naval air stations, basic training facilities, air bases, and a military-industrial complex. By 2000, contracts to Florida's defense establishment topped $15 billion, ranking the state among the nation's leaders. From Palm Bay to Orlando to Milton to Jacksonville to Largo, the military-industrial complex thrives.[31]

Sunshine and Shadows

While technicians fueled Apollo rockets with liquid oxygen and Cold Warriors plotted Operations Mongoose and Distant Shore, the blessings of domestic peace and uninterrupted prosperity created what John Kenneth Galbraith called the "affluent society." Florida's economy was white-hot, producing a binge of spending, growth, and jobs for the world to envy. Yet for all the dreams that growth would bring high-paying, high-tech jobs, the reality has been a plethora of low-skill, minimum-wage service jobs. Fittingly, Florida's economy more resembles Space Mountain than Silicon Valley or the Mahoning Valley.

The number employed in services has climbed twentyfold in fifty years, from about 89,000 workers in 1950 to over 2.6 million persons in 2000. No other economic sector can match the service industry's dynamism. During that same period, the number of miners in Florida fell, construction workers increased about threefold, manufacturing workers more than doubled, wholesale and retail trade workers increased fivefold, and government employees saw their ranks swell fivefold.[32]

Florida has led the South in manufacturing growth since the 1950s. Overall, statewide employment doubled during the decade, income nearly tripled, and value added by manufacturing nearly quadrupled. Florida added over 2,000 new manufacturing plants and major expansions during the decade, a number that would double again in the 1960s. Manufacturing employment doubled alone in Greater Miami from 1950 to 1953. Hialeah emerged as an important center for distribution and manufacturing. The *Miami Herald*'s Ben Funk compared the rhetorical "ballyhoo" of the 1920s with this new era's "sterner stuff— of exploding population and rapidly increasing industrial payrolls." Florida's advantages were manifold: a mild, appealing climate; cheap, abundant land; modern transportation links; a compliant state government; low taxes; non-union labor in a right-to-work state; and a willingness of skilled workers to relocate to the state. Before the 1950s, Florida's manufacturing base was modest: cigar factories in Ybor City and Key West; shipyards in Panama City and Jacksonville; boatyards in Fort Myers, Stuart, and Destin; and plants processing Spanish moss in Gainesville and Apopka. New companies flooded Florida after World War II. Pratt and Whitney chose West Palm Beach to build a jet aircraft engine plant, and Honeywell established a semiconductor plant at Riviera Beach. Pinellas County was so ecstatic at the news of a General Electric plant in 1956 that a new county seal featured nuclear weapons components alongside golfers and fishermen. In 1958, Honeywell established a missile guidance systems facility in Pinellas County, also taking advantage of the business climate, location, and skilled labor. Titusville, Cocoa, and Melbourne boomed with high-tech workers. The 1952 announcement that the Tupperware Company was moving its headquarters to Kissimmee warranted banner headlines. In 1956, the Glenn L. Martin Company, builder of Matador and Pershing missiles, purchased 10 square miles of land near Orlando for a plant site. The new plant on Sand Lake Road, opined the *New York Times,* "most dramatically symbolizes the changes in the area." Cape Canaveral and Martin-Marietta helped spark Orlando's growth spurt *before* the arrival of Disney World. In the first ten months of 1957, Orlando registered a 69-percent increase in building permits. By the early 1960s, Martin-Marietta's Orlando facility, Florida's largest industrial plant, employed more than 10,000 workers. In 1953, West Floridians cheered the opening of Chemstrand, a huge plant manufacturing nylon north of Pensacola. At its peak in 1970, Chemstrand (later Monsanto) employed 6,000 persons, making it the region's largest employer. Other chemical factories established plants in Santa Rosa County along the bay: Escambia Chemical Corp., and American Cyanamid. Pensacola, Fernandina, and Jacksonville initially welcomed paper mills only later to reconsider the benefits of such plants.[33]

For all of the hoopla surrounding manufacturing, a service economy defined Florida. Some of Florida's most creative and best-known businesses emerged from this milieu. In a state dependent upon tourism, thousands of family-owned and -run cafes and restaurants served locals and visitors. As national chains invaded Florida in the 1950s, innovative businessmen took the lead in the fast-food revolution. Insta-Burger King opened its first store on Beach Boulevard in Jacksonville in 1953. David R. Edgerton Jr., the proprietor of the first establishment, opened Miami's first Insta-Burger King on Thirty-sixth Street. James W. McLamore, who had run several Miami diners and restaurants, went into business with Edgerton. Burger King was born. The headquarters of Burger King sits on an oceanfront campus in Miami. Florida has become an incubator for other home-grown fast-food chains. Hooters, Hops, Olive Garden, Outback, Bonefish Grill, Bahama Breeze, Pollo Tropical, Roadhouse Grill, Shells, Lee Roy Selmon's Smokey Bones Barbecue and Grill, Barnies Coffee, Arby's, and Checkers also began operations in the state or have their headquarters here.[34]

Motorists navigating big city streets and suburban parking lots may not realize that some of the most familiar corporate logos originated in Florida. Prior to the 1950s, most drugstores and groceries were small, family-owned businesses. The pharmacist and grocer typically owned the cramped establishments. Proprietors frequently advanced credit. Jack Eckerd and George Jenkins changed the formula. In 1952, Eckerd purchased three failing Tampa Bay drugstores for $150,000. The stores reopened under the Eckerd name using the discount, self-service, over-the-counter drugs California model. By 1960, the modern American drugstore had emerged. Eckerd pioneered senior-citizen discounts for prescriptions, two-for-one photo prints, and drugstores that sold more than drugs. In 1959, Eckerd and Publix Super Markets agreed to open new stores together as they expanded from shopping centers to plazas. Eckerd broke out of the Tampa Bay area and expanded to 600 stores across Florida by 2000. Expansion and profits made Eckerd vulnerable, and in 1997, J. C. Penney purchased the company. Seven years later the pharmacy giant CVS acquired Eckerd.[35]

Publix, Winn-Dixie, and Kash n' Karry also trace their origins to Florida. From a small grocery store in Miami, the roots of Winn-Dixie can be traced. Carl and W. M. Davis called the original store Table Supply, and by 1931 owned 31 stores from Tampa to Miami. After a series of expansions and acquisitions, the logo Winn-Dixie first appeared in 1955. By 1969, Winn-Dixie operated 715 stores in the South, expanding to 1,073 stores in 2003. In 1914, Salvatore Greco, an Italian immigrant, began peddling fruits and vegetables in the Latin quarters of Tampa. The family opened a grocery store in 1922. From this single store, Kash n' Karry emerged (1962), ultimately becoming the third-largest retail food business in Florida. In 2005, it was rebranded Sweetbay. George Jenkins started his first Publix in Winter Haven with $1,300 and quickly acquired a reputation for his clean, well-run, art deco stores. By the late 1990s, Publix boasted 564 stores in the Southeast with sales surpassing $10.4 billion.[36]

After franchising the state from Pensacola to Homestead, some of America's most successful businessmen invested their fortunes in Florida. Kemmons Wilson, the father of Holiday Inn, developed 357 acres 4 miles west of Disney World's main gate, calling the $100 million time-share resort "Orange Lake Country Club." In 1984, he launched Wilson World, a $10 million hotel complex. Jeno Paulucci, the flamboyant founder of Jeno's Pizza Rolls, Chun King, and Michelina's, purchased 2,000 acres of pineland in Seminole County, moved his corporate headquarters from Duluth, Minnesota, and developed the upscale Lake Mary–Heathrow community. Paulucci had first surveyed in Florida in 1945, when he purchased celery from Sanford growers to begin his Chun King operations.[37]

Mitchell Wolfson cut quite a swath in his remarkable life. Born in Key West in 1900, the son of Polish Jews, Mitchell exuded confidence. Following a brief stint at Columbia University, he returned to work at his family's wholesale dry goods business. He invested wisely and well in South Florida's real estate boom. In 1925, he purchased Miami's Capitol Theatre, the beginning of what would become a movie house empire, Wometco. Elected the first Jewish mayor of Miami Beach, he resigned the post to enlist in World War II. For the rest of his life, friends called Wolfson "the Colonel." In 1949, he gambled on a new venture, television. He owned Florida's first television station, WTVJ, an im-

FIGURE 21. In 1940, George Jenkins opened his first Publix in Winter Haven. The art moderne–inspired structure also boasted air conditioning, one of the first grocery stores to enjoy the new technology. State of Florida Photographic Archives, Tallahassee.

mensely profitable venture. He went on to acquire five additional TV stations, a soft-drink bottling division, and the Miami Seaquarium—all part of a $1 billion empire.[38]

While Mitchell Wolfson made a fortune selling movie tickets and bringing television to Floridians' homes, Wayne Huizinga reaped profits by encouraging Americans to skip the theater and watch rented movies at home. A venture capitalist, his first fortune was founded on trash; at thirty-one he established Waste Management Inc. His next venture also hit pay dirt; he steered Blockbuster Entertainment Corp. into the nation's largest renter of videocassettes, driving thousands of small operations out of business. Huizinga sold Blockbuster to Viacom. The Fort Lauderdale resident also invested heavily in Florida real estate, but he is best known for his ownership of the Miami Dolphins, the Florida Marlins, and Joe Robbie Stadium. After the Marlins' world championship in 1997, Huizinga dismantled the team, earning the scorn of baseball fans and public officials. He once proposed building a giant theme park in the Everglades, derisively called "Wayne's World." Throughout the 1990s, *Forbes* ranked Huizinga as one of America's and the state's wealthiest moguls. In 2000, his assets totaled $1.3 billion.[39]

Florida's most passionate, imaginative, and celebrated businessman was a woman, the incomparable Brownie Wise. A divorcée with a child, Wise moved to South Florida in 1949. In her first year in Plantation, she sold $200,000 worth of a product few Floridians had seen—a new type of plastic ware known as Tupperware. She, more than any other person, pioneered and perfected the Tupperware home party; indeed, so successful were her parties that Tupperware soon removed the polyethylene products from store shelves to specialize in home sales. Tupperware shrewdly hired Wise to direct sales. From a sales force of a few hundred dealers (mostly housewives), Wise quickly built an empire of 10,000 with sales of $100 million.[40]

Tupperware became an American institution, the burp became an icon, and the company became a Florida corporation, moving its headquarters to Kissimmee in 1952 (at Wise's urgings). Annually, Wise hosted a jubilee in Kissimmee, where she greeted thousands of party faithful, boosted morale, and gave away mink robes and new Cadillacs. In 1954, she became the first woman to grace the cover of *Business World*. Upon her death in 1992, a longtime friend and *Orlando Sentinel* reporter said simply, "What a lady."[41]

If pizzas, motels, video rental stores, and plastic bowls could be franchised nationally, why not banks? Florida bankers had long taken pride in local ownership and control, fiercely resisting outside threats. Following the disastrous loss of public faith during the economic panic of 1926–29, banks carefully rebuilt their confidence and reserves. Banks and bankers held extraordinary power and influence, in courthouse squares and corporate boardrooms, in small towns and metropolises.[42]

Ed Ball's emergence as a banker king and the single most powerful individual in Florida since Henry Flagler dates from a timely marriage. In 1922, Ball's sister Jessie married one of America's wealthiest men, Alfred I. du Pont. Distrusting Delaware tax collectors, du Pont moved his chemical-based fortune to Florida, trusting his brother-in-law to manage his Florida portfolio. Upon Alfred's death in 1935, Ball was responsible for running the Du Pont Trust, a task he accomplished with iron-fisted determination. Ball built the Wakulla Springs Lodge, providing legislators a fancy watering hole and a refuge from inquiring Capitol reporters. He headed the Florida National Bank in Jacksonville, once controlling the largest bank group south of Philadelphia. Ball expanded the Du Pont empire by rejecting the glitter of South Florida, preferring to acquire cheap property in North Florida. The Du Pont–Ball St. Joe Paper Company controlled a large swath of Florida's Big Bend, including 54,000 acres in Leon County plus a half million acres in Bay, Franklin, and Gulf counties. Land served as the du Pont–Ball family bedrock, a fortune encompassing citrus, lumbering, banking, communications, and transportation interests. Not everyone supported Ball's aggressive style. U.S. Senator and later Representative Claude Pepper challenged Ball's aggrandizement, sparking a bitter personal feud. In 1966, Congress defied Ball, ordering the tycoon to break up his banks and businesses. From the 1920s until his death in 1981, Ball wielded enormous influence over Florida affairs. At its peak, the du Pont–Ball empire was worth $2 billion.[43]

Ed Ball shrewdly understood the importance of banks as a centerpiece of his financial empire and the future of Florida. The collapse of the Florida land boom in 1926—a disaster punctuated by the failure of hundreds of banks—convinced Ball of the need for consolidation—and ruthlessness. Banks recovered, aided, ironically, by Franklin Roosevelt and the New Deal, Ball's nemeses. During the 1940s, Florida bank deposits grew fourfold. In 1950, Florida banks led southeastern rivals; investments and deposits increased dramatically each year. From twenty-two banks in 1950 to thirty-one in 1963, Ball's Florida National group had achieved impressive economic concentration. A growing population and thriving real estate market made Florida a lucrative banking center. By 1982, the *New York Times* observed: "Banking in Florida is brimming with cheap deposits, flush with Latin American flight money and narcotics cash. It thrives on the health of Orlando and the wealth of Palm Beach. Large and small, the Florida banks turn in profit margins that are the envy of the banking world." Florida's banking future was bright. Bedazzled by the prospects, the chairman of Boca Raton's Gulfstream Banking Corp. said Florida reminded him of California in 1948.[44]

For a century, Jacksonville served as the center for Florida's banks and insurance companies. The post–World War II decades were heady times for the state's banks. *Florida Trend* noted in 1961 that a contagion was sweeping Jacksonville. "There isn't a major bank in the city that hasn't started construction for new facilities, expanded its present quarters, or projected plans for the immediate future." In 1971, two of Florida's three largest banks (Atlantic National and Florida National) and three of the top six (Barnett) were located in Ed Ball's Jacksonville. The Independence Life Building, the tallest structure in the state in 1971, symbolized Jacksonville's reputation as an insurance center.[45]

In the 1920s, Ed Ball, against the grain of opinion, had avoided investing in Florida's hottest real estate market, Miami. By the 1970s, Miami engaged Jacksonville in a fierce struggle for banking supremacy. In 1971, Miami's First Atlantic led all state commercial banks in deposits ($872 million), doubling its closest rivals, Atlantic National and Florida National of Jacksonville. Miami runneth over with cash: real estate extravaganza, Cuban success stories, illicit drug traffic, and Latin American capital. So much money poured into Miami's banks that it aroused investigators at the Federal Reserve. For example, between 1975 and 1977 alone, over $5 billion flooded into the United States from Latin America, much of it diverted to Miami. An approving *Forbes* magazine wrote, "Those bolivars and pesos have already eaten up the heavy inventory of condominiums left sitting on the market in 1974." Miami had become the financial capital and unofficial Bank of the Americas. Scores of multinationals—Morgan Guaranty, Dow Chemical, Citibank, and Chase—opened Latin branches in Miami.[46]

In 1982, a *New York Times* headline announced, "Banks Grow Fat on Florida's Boom and Abundant Cash." The paper predicted ominously, "Now the big boys want a place in the sun." For decades, Florida's largest banks resisted interstate banking. But fierce lobbying and financial pressure began to erode Florida's protectionist barriers. Many Floridians welcomed the competition; operators of small banks realized that the bidding enhanced the value of their institutions. In 1980, the Florida legislature passed a measure barring out-of-state banks from establishing loan offices in the state. Governor Graham vetoed the bill. The president of Southeast Banking Corp. admitted, "We don't know if we'll be the acquirer or the acquired." The Branch Banking Act, passed by the legislature in 1984, answered the question. Ironically, legislators and financial officials justified the legislation on the grounds it would keep the northeastern banks out of the state. Instead, Florida—described by one powerful official as "banking heaven"—became prey to southeastern banks. By 1990, twelve of the top fifteen largest banks in Florida had national headquarters out of state. Miami's Southeast Bank became one of those "acquired." Once one of the most respected financial institutions in the South, Southeast Banking Corp. lost over $100 million in 1989, the most sensational of the area's sordid banking scandals. In succession, Sun Bank, Pan American Bank, and Landmark Bank were swallowed up by more aggressive out-of-state institutions. By the late 1990s, Florida officially became a banking colony for Charlotte, Atlanta, and Birmingham. In 1997, NationsBank bought out Jacksonville's Barnett for $15.5 billion. "Now I own Florida," gloated Hugh McColl the day his North Carolina corporation acquired Barnett Bank, along with one-third of Florida's banking deposits.

Florida, deadpanned an economist, "is now an important branch center." Amid the scramble, Florida counted only one black-owned banking institution.[47]

More romantic than Barnett Bank and more dashing than the *Miami Daily News,* Pan American and Eastern Airlines had deep Florida roots, but they suffered the same fate. When Pan American World Airways declared Chapter Eleven bankruptcy in 1991, it marked an inglorious ending to a remarkable story of flight. *Newsweek*'s John Schwartz eulogized, "It may be hard for today's all-too-frequent fliers to remember that once, air travel was an adventure; that airlines once had a soul." Starting in Miami in the 1920s, Pan American emerged as the largest airline in the world following World War II, controlling nearly all of the international air traffic. Juan Trippe—the company's co-founder (with C. V. "Sonny" Whitney) and leader from 1927 to 1968—perfected the role of the glamorous executive, personally negotiating landing rights with foreign dignitaries and consulting with Charles Lindbergh on new routes. Evoking the mystery of the tall ships, Trippe called his early planes "clippers," all the while investing in the most modern aircraft. He boasted that Pan American was the "chosen instrument" of the U.S. government in international aviation. Eastern Airlines, like Pan Am, was born in the 1920s with roots in Miami. Eastern also emerged from World War II eager to expand its domestic markets. Eastern's "air shuttles" helped popularize air travel in the 1950s and 1960s, taking an experience once reserved for the wealthy and adventurous and turning it into a mass industry: Eastern helped pioneer charter flights, which allowed millions of Americans to travel to Florida and other tourist destinations. By the late 1980s, Pan American and Eastern had invested heavily in Miami. The airlines were easily the region's largest private employer. Eastern had moved its executive headquarters from New York's Rockefeller Center in 1972, and by 1986 it employed 14,000 workers in South Florida. Eastern employees represented some of Florida's best-paid workers, representing an annual payroll of $400 million.[48]

The demise of Eastern and Pan American is a story of good intentions gone wrong, financial mismanagement, labor strife, and greed. Deregulation promised airlines the liberation from government interference, but few experts imagined it would help bring down some of the nation's largest carriers. Deregulation allowed millions of Americans to fly cheaply and encouraged the start-up of scores of new, aggressive airlines, but it also cut deeply into established companies with aggressive unions and high fixed costs. A shakeout and shake-up occurred. Tourism benefited from a dramatic increase in air passenger traffic, but the losses of Florida-based Pan American, Eastern, Braniff, and National caused great misery.

Florida's newspaper industry also witnessed sweeping changes. In 1950, few Floridians could have imagined the technological and structural changes about to sweep the newspaper industry. At midcentury, Florida's vast array of daily and weekly newspapers tended to be locally owned. The closest thing to a media chain belonged to John J. Perry, who owned four radio stations and twenty-five Florida newspapers, including the *Jacksonville Journal*, the *Ocala Star-Banner*, and the *Palm Beach Post*. Florida's growth made the state's newspapers attractive targets. By 1973, thirty-four of Florida's fifty-one dailies were owned or controlled by out-of-state interests. In 2004, only two major Florida newspapers, the *Daytona Beach News-Journal* and the *St. Petersburg Times*, remained independent and locally owned. Corporate raiders coveted and courted the growing Florida markets. The *New York Times* purchased the *Ocala Star-Banner*, the *Sarasota Herald*, the *Gainesville Sun*, and the *Lakeland Ledger*. The Chicago Tribune Company owns the *Orlando Sentinel*, the *South Florida Sun Sentinel*, and the *Osceola Sun*, while the Knight-Ridder Company controls the *Miami Herald*, the *Boca Raton News*, the *Bradenton Herald*, the *Florida Keys Keynoter*, *El Nuevo Herald*, and the *Tallahassee Democrat*. The *Tampa Tribune* is owned by Richmond, Virginia's Media General Corporation; the Gannet Company controls the *Pensacola News-Journal*, the *Fort Myers News-Press*, *Florida Today*, and *USA Today*. In 1982, Morris Communications purchased the *Key West Citizen* and the Jacksonville *Florida Times-Union* from CSX Corp. By the 1980s, all of the once-great Florida afternoon newspapers had folded or been swallowed by morning rivals: witness the fate of the *Miami Daily News*, the *Tampa Daily Times*, the *St. Petersburg Independent*, the *Orlando Star*, the *Pensacola News*, and the *Jacksonville Journal*.[49]

In Florida newspaper circles, the name Knight resonates with distinction. John S. Knight, born in 1894, the son of an Ohio newspaper editor, purchased the *Miami Herald* in 1937 for $2 million. Knight modernized the *Herald*, which at the time he purchased it still used carrier pigeons for delivery messages. He also expanded the paper's coverage, insisting that the paper cover the community's growing Jewish community. In 1949, the *Herald*'s exposé of gambling rackets won the paper its first Pulitzer Prize for investigative reporting. In 1961, several *Herald* reporters picked up conversations in Little Havana hinting of an imminent invasion of Cuba. Furious, CIA Director Allen Dulles persuaded

Knight to can the story. Considering the revolutions taking place in Miami, the *Herald* was strangely indifferent to the plight of the early Cuban exiles arriving daily. David Lawrence, future publisher of the *Herald*, explained simply, we "just did not get it."[50]

The *Miami Herald*, buoyed by a growing population, was immensely profitable. In 1972, the paper reported profits of $22 million. Two years later the Knight Co. became the Knight-Ridder group, acquiring nineteen additional papers, part of a media empire of thirty-five dailies with a circulation of 23 million. John Knight died in 1981. In the 1990s, Knight-Ridder moved its corporate headquarters from Miami to California. The *Miami Herald,* under the leadership of talented publishers, remains one of the country's leading papers, home to some of America's most respected writers (Dave Barry, Carl Hiaasen, Edwin Pope, Tom Fiedler, and Edna Buchanan).[51]

Media critics consistently praise the high standards of Florida's leading papers. Such praise is especially impressive considering the modest status occupied by three of the papers in 1950. The extraordinary commercial success and critical acclaim of the *St. Petersburg Times,* the *Orlando Sentinel,* and the *Fort Lauderdale Sun-Sentinel* represent three great success stories. In 1980, the daily circulations of the *Times* and the *Sun-Sentinel* stood at 110,000 and 68,000 respectively. To put these numbers into perspective, consider that the *Pensacola Journal* in 1964 boasted a daily circulation of 65,000. Both papers were overshadowed by their more powerful neighbors, the *Tampa Tribune* and the *Miami Herald.* The *Tampa Tribune* may have been the state's best newspaper in 1950, widely known and feared for its crusading style. The *Orlando Sentinel* was lightly regarded outside Central Florida, although its circulation ranged to the Space Coast and Lake County. In 2000, the *St. Petersburg Times,* the *Orlando Sentinel,* and the *South Florida Sun-Sentinel* ranked respectively first, third, and fourth in state circulation, combining daily for sales of 750,000 newspapers. Sweeping cultural, demographic, and technological changes, however, challenge the role and relevance of the traditional newspaper.[52]

Florida has become a hotly contested colony in the media wars of the 1980s and 1990s. Communication empires brought cable, choices, and confusion to Floridians accustomed to ABC, CBS, NBC, and PBS. Media moguls invaded Florida's rich markets, purchasing television and radio stations, raising the corporate logo of Turner, Fox, Paxson, and Viacom. Cable TV has revolutionized America's information culture. It has also liberated venture capitalists and innovative producers from the media axis of New York and Los Angeles. In the 1990s, Latin American entrepreneurs brought popular Spanish-language networks, Telemundo and Univision, to Miami. South Florida, a safe haven for Latin American banking and commerce, has also become a cable gateway. The popular Home Shopping Network began in St. Petersburg, but control has been wrested by a New York conglomerate.

In the post–Cold War world of borderless nation-states and revolutionary upheaval, Florida's role as a cultural magnet and financial center for the Americas is enormous. In the Darwinian world of business competition, Florida has proven wildly popular in luring regional centers and back-office phone-sales operations but sadly disappointing in recruiting (or growing) corporations to move their headquarters to the Sunshine State. Throughout the 1990s, a decade in which Florida strode the Sunbelt South like a Colossus, Florida claimed only a dozen corporations ranked among America's top 500 by *Fortune* magazine. Indeed, the individual cities of Seattle, Minneapolis, St. Louis, and Dallas/Fort Worth each claimed more powerful corporations than did Florida. Tampa, once home to one of the state's most dynamic economies, boasted few corporate headquarters during the 1990s. Houston claimed fifteen. In a state that champions tourism, none of the leading theme park owners has headquarters in the state. Sunbelt rival Texas claimed the headquarters of thirty-seven Fortune 500 firms. The 1990s and the new century represented an era of lost opportunities, as a number of prestigious Florida-based companies (Eckerd, Sound Advice, Maas Brothers, Burdines, Florida Power, Barnett Bank, GTE, American Bankers Insurance Group, W. R. Grace and Company, Knight-Ridder, Scotty's, and Pharmerica) either were acquired by out-of-state conglomerates went bankrupt, or simply moved to new headquarters.[53]

Florida's lackluster record of recruiting Fortune 500 companies is even more alarming when one understands the state's generous tax benefits. In 1971, after years of discussion, Floridians approved a constitutional amendment to authorize a corporate income tax. Governor Reubin Askew championed the measure, calling it a cornerstone in reforming Florida's regressive tax system. The measure marked the only significant reform of Florida's tax structure since the state enacted its first sales tax (three percent) in 1949. In 2000, the state collected far less corporate tax revenue than it did in 1975. Creative accounting and subsequent legislatures have diluted—or, as some charge, "virtually eliminated"—the tax. Carnival Corp., Florida's tenth-largest public company, recorded $1 billion in profit in 2001 yet paid no Florida corporate income taxes. Carnival, owned by Florida's wealthiest resident, is incorporated in Panama, although it sails from Miami.[54]

Corporations may reluctantly move from the Rustbelt, but their executives adore Florida. Jupiter Island glitters as a sanctuary for some of the most expensive housing in America. Median-priced homes in 2004 cost $4.5 million. Other Florida communities, such as Gulf Stream, Palm Beach, and Golden Beach, also ranked among the nation's most expensive housing. Three Florida metro areas also ranked high nationally in per-capita income: West Palm Beach–Boca Raton (third), Naples (seventh), and Sarasota (sixteenth). Florida must reconcile its heritage as a cheap state in which to do business with its future needs. Too many corporations move back-office operations to Florida to maximize profits; too many corporate executives and millionaires call Florida home to take advantage of the state's generous tax advantages.[55]

Florida has always been a state associated with winners and losers. Never was this truer than in the 1980s and 1990s, decades of eye-popping profits, accompanied by dislocation and pain. Poverty may be more concentrated and visible in Miami and Orlando, but the state's poorest counties remain in North Florida. Union County's 1998 per-capita income ($8,894) paled in comparison with that of Palm Beach ($35,690). In 2004, the disparity had only widened (Union County, $13,400, to Palm Beach County, $45,614). The closing of apparel factories has aggravated the systemic economic problems in Union County and neighbors Baker, Columbia, and Gilchrist counties, often called Florida's "prison belt" because of the number of corrections facilities. The "Other Florida" used to refer to the Panhandle; today, it defines the state's underclass.[56]

When asked about the new prosperity, a southern mayor replied, "There is a lot of shade in the Sun Belt." Writes historian David R. Goldfield, "Sun Belt sophistry has replaced the New South creed as the prevailing rhetorical ruse in the region and, like its philosophical predecessor, has obscured the region's economic and social problems." Marion County illustrates Goldfield's assertion. A rural county of 38,000 in 1950, Marion surpassed the quarter million benchmark in 2000. In the 1980s, a new resident arrived every thirty-nine minutes, many of them congregating in retirement communities. A Martin-Marietta plant at Silver Springs Shores manufacturing components for laser-guided missiles stood out because of its high-paying jobs. Ocala, reported the

New York Times in 1990, "is largely barren of the entrepreneurial-minded executives and professionals." Ocala's economy centers around minimum-wage, limited-benefits service positions at franchise restaurants or retail centers. In 1993, Ocala's median income fared poorly when compared to other locales—ranking 309 out of 315 metropolitan areas. Per capita income in 2004 ($24,982) was below the state average of $31,242. The biggest building in Ocala was a 36-acre Kmart distribution center, with a 1.5-million-square-feet warehouse. In the early 1990s, *Restaurants and Institutions* magazine ranked Ocala, with its proximity to I-75, as the best place in America to start a restaurant. Anyone attempting to navigate the roadways feeding the interstate understands all too well Ocala's attraction of franchises.[57]

Other counties appreciate the price of economic change. The coming of Disney World altered the rhythms and traffic patterns of Kissimmee, Osceola County's only incorporated city, described by a 1943 reporter as the "cow capital of the state." For decades, census takers counted far more cattle than people. Boasting 730,000 acres of pastureland, Osceola County seemed destined to be forever linked with its "cow capital" identity. A meager economy supplemented cattle and citrus: crate manufacturing, production of tropical fruit jellies, rattan furniture making, and leather goods, principally saddles and buggy whips. As late as 1960, Osceola County had only 19,000 residents. Then came Walt Disney World in 1971, with its main entrance only 10 miles from Kissimmee. Soon, Osceola County had 19,000 hotel rooms! The proliferation of motels and fast-food establishments, built to feed the maw of overflow tourist traffic, created a service economy employing thousands of maids, cashiers, and cooks, many of them Hispanic. Paid paltry salaries, many work without health insurance, struggling to maintain an automobile in an area that requires a car. In 2004, Osceola County's workers' average income of $21,227 trailed the state per-capita income of $31,242. Each year, the county lost about 5,000 acres of pasture. Traditions die hard. Osceola County recently authorized $68 million on a new rodeo center, even though only a few hundred residents still farm, an occupation comprising fewer than 1 percent of the county's jobs.[58]

Bordering the east and west banks of the Apalachicola River, Liberty and Calhoun counties exemplify the poverty that has frustrated residents and bedeviled officials throughout the twentieth century. One has to go back to the 1840s, when Apalachicola boomed as a cotton entrepôt, to find upriver prosperity. The Apalachicola River Valley may be a natural paradise, but it is largely devoid of people. In population, Liberty ranks sixty-seventh among the state's sixty-seven counties. Its principal city, Bristol, peaked in 1915 and has declined since. In 1950, Liberty and Calhoun counties claimed about 11,000 inhabitants; in 2000, the duo counted 20,000 residents. Historically, local inhabitants looked to the river and forests for principal employment, with meager salaries at sawmills and turpentine camps supplemented by moonshine, tupelo honey, and night crawlers (bait businesses). Most recently, corrections facilities have emerged as a source of employment. The Old Marianna and Blountstown Railroad ceased operations in 1977. At that time, Liberty County had no doctor. Isolation has contributed to the area's economic neglect, but even when outsiders discover West Florida, a patronizing demeanor often accompanies the encounter; witness the film *Vernon, Florida* (1981), directed by Errol Morris. Many African American residents would agree with a harsh assessment of the region. As late as 1963, Liberty County had no registered black voters. The elevation of Blountstown native son Fuller Warren to the governorship (1949–53) brought a sprinkling of patronage but little substantive change. In 1957, residents of Liberty and Calhoun counties earned yearly salaries averaging $800, considerably less than the state average of $1,500. Forty-seven years later, area workers still ranked near the bottom of Florida's income scale, earning an average of $17,800.[59]

Forests dominate Calhoun and Liberty counties' lifestyles and economies. Nothing—not the promise of tung trees, catfish farms, or deadhead logging—has helped. Together, the counties boast more than 800,000 acres of timberland, comprising more than 95 percent of the area's landmass. Slash pine and tupelo, hickory and magnolia, and thickly wooded bayous and creeks surround the small towns and mills. The gopher tree—mentioned in Genesis—grows only on the bluffs of the Apalachicola River. But timber also underscores the area's vulnerability. Logging once employed many of Liberty County's 2,000 workers, but international competition and new conservation policies at national forests have crippled lumber interests. The Du Pont interests also tie up much of the area's land. In 1998, the Florida Coast Paper Mill closed its doors in nearby Gulf County, eliminating many local jobs. Liberty County's greatest natural resource—its longleaf pine forests—is ironically the source of the economic depression. Because more than half of the county lies inside the Apalachicola National Forest, Liberty's tax base is restricted. To add environmental insult to economic injury, more endangered red-cockaded woodpeckers live in area forests than anywhere else in the world. To protect the woodpecker, officials have curtailed logging in the national forest. "Help a logger. Eat a woodpecker" reads a local bumper sticker.[60]

In a state of conspicuous consumption, some counties measure growth not in BMW dealerships or high-rise construction but in jobs. Environmental purity is sacrificed to economic necessity. Such is the case in Taylor County, one of Florida's poorest areas. Thus, in the early 1950s, when Procter and Gamble's Buckeye Cellulose Corporation came calling with a $20 million investment, the Big Bend listened. The arrival of the pulp plant seemed heaven-sent, considering that Perry's Brooks-Scanlon Lumber Co., the largest sawmill in the South, shut its doors in 1951. Residents knew from experience that a wood-cellulose plant was not a clean industry. In 1949, the Florida legislature, at the request of local leaders, designated the Fenholloway "an industrial river," permitting industry the right to "discharge and deposit sewage, industrial and chemical wastes and effluent . . . into the [river] waters and the Gulf of Mexico." The act turned the Fenholloway into Florida's most polluted river and fouled the air with the smell of rotten eggs. Daily the plant pumped 50 million gallons of water, processed it, and dumped it into the river. But Buckeye supplied steady work in a county suffering the worst unemployment rate in the state. In the 1970s, the mill employed 1,000 workers and delivered a $13 million company payroll. Buckeye also kept taxes low, paying the lion's share of Taylor County's bills and donating land for the golf course. At what cost? The U.S. Environmental Protection Agency has charged the mill with a litany of crimes, most notably the releasing of deadly dioxins at more than two hundred times the safe level.[61]

Not all Florida industries thrived in the postwar boom. To truckers, Tampa is still affectionately known as "Cigar City," but in reality the cigar industry has been more smoke than fire for a half century. Tampa was once home to 12,000 highly skilled cigar makers, but Tampa factories and personnel managers had to adjust to postwar tastes that no longer treasured the expensive, hand-rolled Tampa Girl and Antonio Céspedes cigars. The cedar cigar box emblazoned with elegant, chromolithographic labels was becoming as obsolete as the cigar store Indian and corner tobacco shop. As it desperately sought to win over cigarette devotees and retain loyal cigar smokers, the industry replaced skilled *tabaqueros* with nonunion female workers and machines. By the 1950s, thousands of elderly cigar rollers, selectors, and packers sat unemployed and unappreciated. Factories produced more cigars with fewer workers, but Americans' tastes were shifting. Millions of GIs had returned from service in World War II with lifelong addictions to cigarettes, which were practically given away to servicemen during the war. Young Americans, captivated by powerful advertising, preferred cigarettes to cigars, which reeked of stogies and grandfathers. Even the smell of Cuban tobacco would soon be a distant memory. In February 1962, President Kennedy ordered his press secretary, Pierre Salinger, to secure as many Havana cigars as possible, and promptly. Salinger delivered a cache of Cuban cigars, only then to watch the president sign the Cuban embargo, cutting off all supplies of Cuban cigars and tobacco. "We tried to exempt cigars," Kennedy confessed to Richard Goodwin, "but the cigar manufacturers in Tampa objected." The Cold War and a national antismoking campaign devastated an already crippled cigar industry. Tampa's thirty-five cigar manufacturers still employed 6,000 persons in 1962. The embargo marked a new chapter. The Fuente family, in the cigar manufacturing business since 1912, left Tampa for new operations in Honduras and the Dominican Republic. Miami briefly became the U.S. center of hand-rolled cigars, but even low-paid cigar makers could not compete against lower-paid foreign labor. Manufacturers scrambled for new sources of tobacco leaf, but their greatest problem remained finding new smokers. Sales plummeted. By 1965, fewer than 100 Tampa employees made cigars by hand. When this author talked to an elderly *tabaquera* in 1982 as she was leaving the Perfecto-Garcia factory for the last time, she sighed, "We're the last of the Mohicans!" Who could have imagined that a decade later, young Americans would fall in love with expensive hand-rolled cigars? The fabled cigar-mania of the 1990s, highlighted by the glossy cigar *Aficionado* magazine and the popularity of ten-dollar *Macanudos* and *Cohibas*, was short-lived. Tampa's role was principally as a distribution, not a manufacturing, center.[62]

Metro Orlando all too well illustrates the limitations and strains of a region utterly dependent upon tourism. While the cost of living in Greater Orlando approximated the national average in 2000, many of the area's workers, 40 percent of whom hold low-paying amusement park and hotel jobs, struggled to find affordable housing, medical benefits, and transportation. Fully one in eight workers had an extra job.[63]

Tourism continued to dominate the economy of Central Florida in the late 1990s. Nearly 5 percent of Metro Orlando workers were employed at Disney World, part of Disney's massive workforce of 55,500 employees. Universal Studios employed 11,800 workers, as many Florida employees as Wal-Mart. Tourism's impact upon Central Florida's service economy can be understood by the workforce of 11,000 employed in the area's McDonald's and Burger Kings. A vast service infrastructure makes the modern vacation and tourist economy possible: fast-food outlets, motels, linen suppliers, sanitation companies, T-shirt firms, gift shops, architectural firms, and lawn services. Masses of un-skilled, semi-skilled, and high-skilled workers supply a human face—but one rarely seen—by vacationers: laundresses, fast-food workers, trash haulers, deliverymen, cleaning staff, airport custodians, baggage handlers, customer-service representatives, cabbies, construction workers, landscapers, painters, truckers, waiters, sommeliers, concierges, managers, chocolatiers, ice sculp-tors, and architects. Tellingly, service jobs—maids, short-order cooks, busboys, and waitresses—made up 44 percent of Florida's work force in 2000.[64]

No section of Florida has experienced higher economic highs and lower lows than Miami. Southeast Florida has become an economic engine, hyperventil-ating jobs and opportunities, imports and exports. Miami is the only Florida city that has linked its economic health to international business. Few modern cities have achieved such status without a significant manufacturing base. De-spite some apparel factories in Hialeah and cigar making in Little Havana, Mi-ami never developed a solid manufacturing base. In the 1990s, only about one job in twenty in Miami-Dade County was manufacture related; fully one in three was service-oriented. In 1977, *Forbes,* a conservative business magazine, observed candidly, "All that refugee money is putting the glitter back in the Gold Coast." Billions of dollars, "flight capital" from the Americas, poured into Mi-ami. Reinforced by staggering profits from narcotics—estimated in 1982 at $10 billion a year—Miami's economy boomed. Latin American military generals and politicians discovered what Cuban officials learned in the 1940s and 1950s—Miami banks and property are safe hedges against a coup d'état or revo-lution. For Brazilians, but also for Nicaraguans, Colombians, and Dominicans, Miami is, in the words of a journalist, the "off-shore haven of choice." Miami is the geographic and economic gateway to the Americas, headquarters to three hundred multinational companies, the second-largest financial center in the United States, and the leading American airport for drugs and international cargo. In just six years, between 1977 and 1983, Miami went from having no foreign banks to having more than 130. South Brickell Avenue resembles a United Nations of international banking. Such synergy has created a $60 bil-lion economy, even greater if one calculates the underground economy. If Mi-ami were a nation-state, its economy would be greater than the economies of Colombia, Chile, Egypt, and the Philippines, as well as those of twenty-one states, an extraordinary point considering the city's weak manufacturing base.

TABLE 5. Florida in the 1990s: National Rankings

Category	Year	Rank	Year	Rank
Median household income	1990	33rd	1999	40th
Percentage living in poverty	1990	29th	1999	33rd
Income disparity between rich and poor	—	—	2000	7th
Florida teacher salaries	1989	26th	1999	29th
Per-student spending, K-12	—	—	2001	33rd
Per-capita spending on public education	—	—	2000	50th
Assets of commercial banks based in Florida	1990	6th	2000	21st
Crimes per 100,000 population	1990	1st	2000	2nd
Per-capita state Gross Domestic Product	1990	37th	1999	37th

Sources: "The Cheap State," *St. Petersburg Times*, 18 November 2001; "More People, More Problems," *Tampa Tribune*, 23 February 2003; Morris and Morris, *Florida Handbook*, 620; U.S. Bureau of the Census, *1990 Census of Population and Housing*; "Families Try to Get by on Low Wages," *Fort Myers News-Press*, 7 December 2003; "2000 State-by-State Crime Index," *St. Petersburg Times*.

In *The Nine Nations of North America,* Joel Garreau considered Miami as the cultural and economic capital of the Caribbean and Americas: "This is why the geographic reorientation that South Florida has undergone . . . has been the most sweeping of any not caused by war in North American history. The economy and culture have turned completely around, and are now facing the south." Downtown Miami throbs with the sounds and traffic generated by businessmen and middle classes from the Americas, here to purchase consumer goods from the myriad electronics/appliance and sporting goods shops. NAFTA may have been catastrophic for Carolina textiles, but the Free Trade Treaty has made Miami a "midwife" for the Americas. Numbingly, Miami also leads the United States with numbers living in poverty and violent crime.[65]

The beginning of a new century finds Florida at a familiar crossroads. A state of fabulous wealth and gaudy excess, Florida remains a state of great contrasts and broken promises, a place of First World luxury and Third World poverty. The mantra of growth—housing and construction, space and defense industries, the recruitment of national and international giants—failed to lift Florida from the bottom-tier state economies. For all of the rhetoric about high-tech corridors, cyberspace start-ups, and global convergence, Florida's economy drags along, overreliant upon tourism, service jobs, back-office salaries, a regressive tax structure, agriculture, and widening gaps in income and wealth. Florida's constitutionally mandated right-to-work law, coupled with a fierce antiunionism, has curbed union membership and especially hurt blue-collar workers. In 1998, about 7 percent of the state's workforce belonged to a union, ranking Florida forty-fourth nationally. Even more depressing, almost 10 percent of workers earned the minimum wage ($5.15 per hour in 1997) or less. In 2000, Florida's median income ($33,234) fell behind America's average ($37,779). In 2003, manufacturing amounted to only 5.9 percent of Florida's gross state product, compared to fully 26 percent for services. Experts branded Miami the poorest large city in America. Distressingly, Florida fell behind many other states in the 1990s. "This is a train wreck in slow-motion," confessed a state budget official in the 1990s. Shockingly, hourly wages adjusted for inflation actually *declined* during the prosperous decade of the 1990s, a telling sign of a state with too many workers mired in minimum-wage service and agriculture. Not until the 1970s did Florida replace Virginia as the southern state with the highest per-capita income, but Floridians' income still lagged and lags behind the North, West, and Midwest. Florida remains a rich state amid stark poverty. This paradox pervades the state. More than four of every ten children in Miami live in poverty. Children in Tampa, Hialeah, Fort Lauderdale, and Orlando also rank among the poorest in America. The 2000 census uncovered a quarter of the residents of Hardee, Hamilton, Gadsden, Holmes, and Dixie counties living in poverty. One in five Florida workers lacks health insurance. Among the fifty states, Florida ranked thirty-ninth in children living in poverty, forty-sixth in children living with single parents, and forty-seventh in state funding for education. In the 1990s, Florida's per-capita income had still not reached the national average; indeed, few counties exceeded the national average.[66]

Wondrous Fruit, Bountiful Land

From Farms to Agribusiness

6

O N New Year's Day 1950, Thomas William Sherley, described as a "cracker fellow with big town ideas," hosted a party for his Miami neighbors. A Bradford County native, Sherley had moved to South Florida in 1923. Homesick for the rural customs of his youth, he purchased five acres of country, described by the *Herald* as "where metropolitan Miami starts driving off into the Everglades." There he grew fruits and vegetables, but mostly he raised sugarcane. Every January, Miamians nostalgic for a taste of cane juice and the spectacle of cane grindin' congregated at the Sherley farm. Friends bemoaned that Dade County cane produced a weak "buck," the popular "likker" concocted in the skimming kettle. Fifty years later, Sherley's cane fields have been devoured by North Kendall's strip malls and suburban growth.[1]

Modern inhabitants of Delray Beach, Sanibel, St. Cloud, and Key Largo might be astonished to know that until recently, tomato fields and citrus groves thrived where tony residential developments now stand. In 1950, citizens of Orlando, Jacksonville, and St. Petersburg could leave the city limits and within minutes encounter grove, field, and forest. As more and more Floridians abandoned the land, living climate-controlled lives in insulated environments, residents have become detached from their rural roots.

The saga of modern Florida agriculture incorporates the most powerful themes propelling the state's growth: displace-

Things grow big around here. My old man planted sweet potatoes one year, and when it came 'tater-digging time, one of 'em was so big we had to make a sawmill job out of it . . . we all lived off potato pone made from the saw dust."

Folktale in
Stetson Kennedy,
Palmetto Country

FIGURE 22. For centuries, distinctive rituals signified the grinding of sugarcane. Note the mule, another symbol of a vanishing Florida. State of Florida Photographic Archives, Tallahassee.

ment and resettlement, increasing specialization and the concentration of capital, and new levels of consolidation and scale. Already under assault for decades from railroads, corporations, and big planters, small independent farmers became scarce. As cities and towns encroached upon grove and field, many farmers realized greater profits in land sales than in harvests. Fewer but larger farms now dot the landscape. Technological advancements have made possible dazzling new hybrids and spectacular harvests, but at the dawn of the twenty-first century citrus workers still picked oranges by hand, the same way they did at the end of the nineteenth century.

On New Year's Day 1950, several old-fashioned water-powered mills still operated in the Panhandle. In places called Bell's Mill on Hard Labor Creek, Shepherd's Mill, and Shore's Mill, residents enjoyed stone-ground corn meal and grits. But grist mills, like mules and small family farms, have gone the way of the open range and charcoal burners. Many of the great plantations that once made Leon and Jefferson counties the envy of city dwellers have been converted into hunting preserves, country estates, and weekend retreats. Media mogul Ted Turner, the nation's largest private landowner (nearly 2 million acres), epitomized Florida's country gentleman in 2000. His holdings included several large plantations in Jefferson County.[2]

Farming, more so than in any other section, has defined place and time for the inhabitants of North and West Florida. Autumn harvests melted into football season; farmers allowed their hogs to root in peanut fields; Saturdays meant a visit to town, a joyous journey to Chipley, Marianna, or Monticello. County fairs crowned queens of tobacco, peanuts, and watermelons. Fewer and fewer residents of the Panhandle and North Florida are now so tied to the soil. Residents in Liberty and Washington, Bradford and Union counties were more likely to work at a military base, corrections facility, or convenience store than on a family farm.

Modern farmers in Jackson, Gadsden, and Madison counties bring an efficiency to the craft that pioneers could not have imagined. In just three decades, corn yields in Jackson County jumped from eight bushels an acre in 1950 to over 150 by the 1980s. While Jefferson County watermelons, Gadsden County shade tobacco, and Santa Rosa County peanuts remain identifiable staples, the newest cash crops found in the region include hothouse tomatoes, honey, soybeans, mushrooms, catfish, ducks, blueberries, marijuana, and antiques.[3]

The complexion of the family farm has also changed. Isolated and impotent against an intimidating network of federal, state, and county agricultural bureaucracies, black farmers mustered few powerful allies. Powerful elites conspired against not only black agriculturalists but also poor white farmers. The black yeoman farmer, once a familiar sight across North Florida, is vanishing. In 1920, close to a million black-owned farms dotted America's land—principally in the South. Their numbers have plunged drastically. The arc of black yeomanry can be traced graphically in middle Florida, the historic area located between the Apalachicola and Suwannee rivers. Once Florida's richest and most heavily populated region, Jackson, Gadsden, Leon, Jefferson, and Madison counties recognized wealth by the number of cotton bales ginned, the number of slaves owned, and the size of the plantations. In 1860, slaves outnumbered whites two to one in Florida's "Black Belt." During Reconstruction, substantial numbers of freedmen came to own and operate their own farms. In 1945—after decades of economic intimidation, boll weevils, the Great Migration, and failing farms—census takers still identified over 6,000 black Florida farm owners, including 2,000 in the black-majority counties. In 2002, African American farm owners had shrunk to 1,068 statewide, including 302 in the old cotton belt. The number of Hispanic-owned farms now doubles African American farmsteads early in the new century.[4]

Nature and history have rerouted the agricultural promise of North Florida. Cotton dominated the rural economy until oversupply, foreign competition, and the boll weevil devastated planters and crops in the early decades of the twentieth century. Until the great freezes of 1886 and 1895, farmers in Northeast and North Central Florida courted citrus as a cash crop, albeit a risky one. Early in the century, Bradford County proclaimed itself the "Winter Strawberry Capital of the United States," an honor now belonging to Plant City. By World War II, North and West Florida's once-lavish yellow pine and cypress forests had been largely harvested, a monumental achievement chiefly benefiting out-of-state corporations. Hundreds of abandoned turpentine camps, sawmills, and even towns pay homage to Florida's once-thriving naval stores industry.

The promise of a lucrative cash crop has powered a series of booms and busts in North Florida: pear and pecan orchards, castor beans and shade tobacco, yellow pine and red cedar. The decline of Gadsden County shade tobacco is especially dramatic. A way of life associated with the once-lucrative crop is vanishing: the wooden curing barns, the muslin awnings, and the festivities surrounding the harvest. The tung tree also had its hour in the sun. First introduced into Tallahassee in 1906, the exotic import was more curiosity than crop until the Japanese occupation of China in the 1930s forced America to seek new sources of tung oil. Used in the manufacture of paint products and wood preservatives, the varnishlike oil extracted from tung nuts tantalized North Florida farmers with its possibilities. In 1940, the American Tung Oil Association held its convention in Tallahassee, the unofficial capital of the emerging industry. The *Tallahassee Democrat* reinforced conventioneers' optimism with its April 3, 1940 headline, "Million Acres Tung Trees Needed in U.S." By the end of World War II, Leon County boasted 25,000 acres of tung trees. Workers harvested orchards as far south as Alachua County, but the Big Bend was the center of the tung industry. Capps, an impoverished Jefferson County hamlet best known for turpentine, sprang to life as a company town, the headquarters for the St. Joe Paper Company's tung division. At its peak, St. Joe's employed 100 persons year-round and 300 during harvest. Company president Ed Ball reacted angrily when reporters questioned labor conditions at the Capps camp. At its peak in the 1950s, Florida maintained six processing plants and 40,000 acres of tung trees. Postwar demand for tung oil diminished quickly as synthetic substitutes made tung oil dispensable. By the 1970s, bulldozers were flattening tung orchards, replacing them with pine seedlings.[5]

Cattle State

If the tung nut experiment proved ephemeral, the story of cattle in Florida completes the full historic trajectory. First introduced in 1521 by the man who named this new land *La Florida,* Andalusian cattle accompanied Ponce de León on his pursuit of colonization and conquest. The Spanish cattle brought to La Florida—the ancestors of Texas and Florida longhorns—came from stock colored predominantly red or black. By 1737, a Spanish engineer noted, "The country seems to be well stocked with horned cattle and wild horses." Raised on haciendas and ranchos like La Chua in North Central Florida, the original cattle survived foreign invasion and imperial transfers, insects, and diseases. Genetically adapted to the hot, humid climate, parasitical threats, and poor grazing lands, a distinctive breed evolved—the legendary Florida scrub, or cracker, cattle. The scrubs, reminisced veteran cattleman J. H. Platt of Hardee County, "were not very big. Cows weighed about four hundred pounds. The bulls about six hundred pounds. Most of them had long horns. They were fairly wild cattle." Platt, whose family had worked the South Florida open range for more than a century, marveled at the pioneer cattle's resourcefulness. In the winter, the scrubs "browsed on oak leaves. They'd eat acorns and, of course, they ate the [Spanish] moss and air plants and things like that."[6]

Distinctive human lifestyles and work patterns also evolved. The introduction of the truck, slaughterhouses, and dipping vats "modernized" the cattle industry, but many of the techniques of raising and handling herds had not changed markedly in a century. Cattlemen learned to "mammy" (separate) calves from their mothers, perfect the use of a buckskin whip, and train cow dogs. They also applied the art of bare-knuckle political fighting at the Capitol. While cattlemen won costly battles against the Texas fever tick and the Texas screw worm, they lost the long campaign to preserve the open range. More symbolic than significant, the end of the open range in 1949 required cattlemen to fence their stock, a move already taken by most operators. Roadside collisions between automobile and bovine allowed owners of the animals to collect damages. Florida's open range ended as the Space Age began. The fence law quickened efforts to breed out the Florida cracker cattle because of the animals' size and ranginess. New and improved grasses and pastureland followed the introduction of Brahmas, Herefords, and Angus.

Midcentury Florida cattlemen were as diverse as their stock. New York investors mingled with fourth-generation ranchers; businessmen clad with camel-hair coats bid in auctions against sunburned men wearing Levis and boots. It was a business, but an enterprise embroidered whiplike with the legends of Ziba King and the Cow Cavalry. The owners of Florida's great ranches were as likely to sit on the board of—or even own—a bank as sit on a marsh pony for twelve hours a day. Through the 1950s and 1960s, elderly cowboys—"cow-hunters" in the local vernacular—still walked the streets of modern Arcadia, Fort Pierce, and Kissimmee, men who had fought the DeSoto County range wars of the 1890s and had ridden with Francis Asbury Hendry and Jacob Summerlin, men who kept sacks of gold doubloons on their front porches. Curiously, Florida has never embraced its cattlemen and ranchers with the historic reverence that Texas has shown its iconic cowboys.[7]

In 1950, Florida's 1.25 million cattle (beef and diary) ranked twelfth nationally. Almost 30,000 farms raised some cattle, while 21,600 farms reported dairy cows on the premises. Between 1950 and 1970, income from cattle grew fivefold, the result of new investments and the introduction of purebred stock. The Big B Ranch near Belle Glade typified the new ranching order. In 1963, Osceola Operating Co., a New York conglomerate, purchased a 42,000-acre ranch in Palm Beach County. The corporation also acquired Rainbow Springs. Big B Ranch obtained its breeding stock from the King Ranch in Texas, which introduced Santa Getrudis beef to the state. Alvaro Sánchez Jr., a Harvard graduate and a rancher in pre-Castro Cuba, managed Big B's massive operations, which included 60 miles of canals, 200 miles of ditches, and 115 miles of rock roads.[8]

Florida has retained its status as the most important beef cattle state east of the Mississippi River: over a million beef cattle, plus an additional 800,000 calves and cows populate Florida pens and pastures. Florida's beef cattle center remains Osceola, Highlands, Okeechobee, Polk, Hendry, Hardee, and DeSoto counties. The once vast cattle herds of Manatee and Hillsborough counties have declined in recent decades, although they still rank among the state's top-ten beef and dairy producers. Modern Florida beef producers specialize in selling their yearly stock to feeder lots, mainly on the Great Plains, before the cattle are slaughtered.[9]

Florida's great cattle ranches, some of the last vestiges of the open range, are being sold and subdivided. During the 1990s, one ranch in ten disappeared. For over a century, the name Platt has resonated through the ranks of Florida's great cattle families. Calvin Platt was one of Brevard County's great cattlemen, holding more than 100,000 acres of ranch land at midcentury. His son, Frank Lester "Judge" Platt, built upon the land and cattle empire in Brevard County. Before Calvin's death in 1997, Platt had sold substantial acreage to the Duda family and allowed huge amounts of wetlands to be acquired by local water management districts. In St. Lucie County, Alto "Bud" Adams presided over the Adams Ranch and 10,000 head of cattle in the 1990s. The Starkey Ranch was neither the biggest nor the most glamorous, but it exemplified the struggle and rewards of the calling. Early in the twentieth century, Jay B. Starkey Sr. began ranching with a modest purchase of 10 acres near Largo, in today's Pinellas County. In 1937, he amassed 16,000 acres of land in Pasco County for $1.30 an acre. Many of Florida's great landholders purchased large swaths of land by paying back taxes on the property, in accordance with the Murphy Act. The Starkey Ranch boasted several thousand head of beef cattle at its peak, but urban pressures and new regulations frustrated the family. Jay B. Starkey Jr. cursed developers, whom he called "fast-buck boys." By the 1990s, the Starkey family sold or gave away much of the ranch, retaining a small parcel that opened in 1999 as J. B. Starkey's Flatwoods Adventures.[10]

Since 1950, urban, economic, and familial pressures have diminished many of Florida's great cattle dynasties. Modern Florida's two greatest cattle ranches —and the largest "spreads" east of the Mississippi River—belong to a legendary family and a church. In 1926, the Lykes family purchased 274,000 acres in Glades County. The Lykes family maintains an agricommercial empire of meat-processing plants, orange groves, citrus packinghouses, and a 300,000-acre ranch, the 7-L, that wraps around the northwest shore of Lake Okeechobee. If the Lykes family has deep roots in Florida, the Mormons are relative newcomers. In 1950, the Church of Jesus Christ of Latter-Day Saints purchased large parcels of cheap land in Brevard, Osceola, and Orange counties (most notably the Graddick brothers' ranches in Brevard County). The Deseret Ranch emerged, now the largest ranch in Florida. The Mormons maintain citrus groves, timberland, and a herd of 50,000 cattle. The ranch spans 40 miles north to south, including 3,000 miles of fences. To guard against rustlers and poachers, ranchers patrol the property in airplanes and airboats. In 1968, the church considered selling the 300,000-acre tract for $84 million. Land-hungry, water-thirsty neighbors have driven up the value of the pristine lands. In 1991, the church sold 3,000 acres to Brevard County for $8 million.[11]

Few places in Florida summon deeper associations of cattle than Alachua County. By the mid-seventeenth century, Florida's largest cattle ranch was *la hacienda de la chua* (the ranch of the sinkhole), a far-flung enterprise managed by the Menéndez-Márquez family. Extending from the St. Johns River to the Gulf marshes, the ranch was centered in present-day Alachua County. Cattle raised on the Alachua prairie helped feed the workforce constructing El Castillo de San Marcos in St. Augustine. In 1702, British and Creek marauders destroyed the Spanish missions and ranches on the Santa Fé River, but the creole cattle survived on the range. On the eve of the American Revolution, southeastern Indians had filtered into British Florida and occupied the Alachua prairie. Seminole herdsmen and Hitchiti-speaking Oconees revived cattle raising. Chief Cowkeeper, the Oconee chief, welcomed the naturalist William Bartram at Payne's Prairie in 1774. Cowkeeper dubbed the thirty-five-year-old traveler "Puc Puggy" (Flower Hunter). To Bartram, this harmony of man and nature represented a "Peaceable Kingdom." Wrote Bartram: "The extensive Alachua is a level green plain, above fifteen miles over, fifty miles in circumference, and scarcely a tree or bush of any kind to be seen in it. Herds of sprightly deer, squadrons of the beautiful fleet Siminole [sic] horse, flocks of turkeys, civilized communities of the sonorous watchful crane, mix together." Periodic fire renourished the Alachua Savanna, and cattle flourished in this environment.[12]

In 1775, Bernard Romans surveyed the area, noting, "Herds of cattle in Alachua are so numerous that from seven-thousand to ten-thousand head can be seen grazing at once on Payne's Prairie." The First and Second Seminole Wars removed the Indians of Alachua, but southern herdsmen quickly filled the vacuum. Today, Payne's Prairie is more wetlands and sanctuary than ranch or hacienda, but Floridians can take pride in knowing that one of Alachua County's most historic ranches has been preserved. In 1978, the Boston family deeded to the University of Florida the 868-acre Santa Fé River Ranch. Located in northern Alachua County, the ranch complements a long-standing commitment to agriculture by the state's land grant institution.[13]

Generations of Seminole leaders and Indian agents dreamed of cattle ranches on the South Florida reservations. During the New Deal, leaders acquired the first herd of Angus cattle for the Dania reservation in Broward County. The first cattle arrived in the wake of the 1930s tick eradication program, which necessitated the killing of thousands of Everglades deer. In 1936, the government provided the Muskogee-speaking Cow Creek band of Seminoles with a herd of cattle on the Brighton Indian Reservation (Glades County). Seminoles residing on the Big Cypress Reservation in Hendry County obtained so-called Dust Bowl stock Herefords brought to South Florida.[14]

In 1950, over 2,400 farms provided Floridians with a rich variety of dairy products. Dairies sprawled across Florida, occupying pasture and barns where Winter Park High School, Tampa's Town 'N Country suburb, and the cities of Miramar and Briny Breezes today stand. From Pensacola to Key Largo, consumers enjoyed home delivery, glass bottles, and the luxury of locally produced milk and dairy products. Consumption and taste depended upon the varieties of Florida pastureland and the talents of the dairyfolk. Survivors of the lean decades of the 1920s and 1930s, Florida dairies capitalized upon cheap land, expanding urban markets and agricultural subsidies. No giant firms dominated the industry; indeed, many consumers knew the men and women who personally milked the cows: the Larsons and Raulersons of Okeechobee, the Guagliardos of Tampa, and the Bassetts of Monticello.[15]

In the decades following 1950, as the number of dairies declined and the surviving dairies grew in size, Florida began to lose control of the one industry that seemed so much part of its own heritage. The evolution of the Lee and Miller dairies are apt metaphors for this story. In 1925, Thomas Gilbert (T.G.) and Elizabeth Lee of Orlando entered the dairy business—with the purchase of one cow and a calf. The pasture occupied land where the Colonial Plaza stands today. In the 1930s, the Lees expanded their operations, purchasing 2,000 acres of land in south Orange County. The family paid sixteen dollars an acre for the land. Ultimately, the land and the name were worth far more than the dairy operations. The family created Lee Vista, a development located near Orlando International Airport, and sold T. G. Lee Dairies to Dean Foods of Illinois in 1980.[16]

Pastureland in Florida's growing urban counties proved far too valuable to be occupied by cows. In the 1950s, J. Neville McArthur operated one of Florida's largest dairies in Broward County. He sold the land to real estate developers, purchasing cheaper pasturelands in Dade and Okeechobee counties. By the late 1960s, McArthur Jersey Dairy Farms owned over 14,000 cows. The Graham dairy business provided the foundation for one of Florida's most influential families. Ernest Graham arrived in South Florida in the 1920s, a foreman with the Pennsylvania Sugar Company. Hurricanes and the Great Depression ruined the sugar business, but the departing company rewarded Graham with a 3,000-acre tract of pastureland in northwest Dade County. A dairy was born. By the 1950s, the family realized that developing land could be more profitable than pails of milk. Engineers transformed pastureland into finger lakes. The Graham dairy farm became Miami Lakes, an immensely successful development. The family's political ties and economic successes augmented their landed interests. Ernest Graham ran for governor and became a passionate advocate for urban Florida. A son, Phil, married Katharine Meyer, the daughter of Eugene Meyer, publisher and owner of the *Washington Post*. Another son, Bob, a dedicated and popular public servant, served in the state legislature and was elected governor in 1978 and U.S. senator in 1986.[17]

Cows and people do not coexist easily; more precisely, the ample pastures that once supported tens of thousands of milk cows in Orange, Broward, and Dade counties are more valuable as condominiums and shopping malls. In the 1940s, Orange County residents could patronize more than ninety separate dairies; Orange County's last dairy farm closed in 1989, its proprietor moving his operations to Hamilton County. Moreover, urban dairy farms face increasing environmental restrictions, regulations nonexistent a generation ago. The story is a familiar one across Florida. Today, Seminole and Osceola counties have no dairies. In 1990, Lake County had twenty-five dairies; by 1998, the number had fallen to five. Since the early 1990s, Okeechobee County has become the state's most important dairy center, with over 30,000 milk cows and fifty dairies. Florida's newest dairy belt is the Suwannee River basin. Even along the bucolic countryside of Columbia, Gilchrist, and Dixie counties, newcomers are frequently jolted to realize that dairy farms exude a country odor. A scientist has developed "a fixed-film anaerobic digester," fancy words for a machine removing the smell from cow dung.[18]

The Orange State

For reasons fair and foul, Texas and Wisconsin denigrated Florida longhorns and milk cows. The same cannot be said of the Florida orange. The lordly orange, above all other fruits and crops, held a divine place in the Florida dreamscape. In the 1950s, Orange County students sang joyfully:

I love the fresh air and sunshine
That's so good for us, you know

That's why I make my home in Florida,
Where the orange blossoms grow.

When Hillcrest students sang homage to their Orange County namesake, they were following a long line of poets and artists who praised the fruit of the gods, the golden apples of the Hesperides. Like sugarcane, the orange made a journey to the New World that was long and legendary. First mentioned in the *Five Classics* of Confucian China, the orange migrated from Asia to Malaysia, and then to India, Persia, Africa, Sicily, and southern Spain. In the garden of earthly delights, the orange held an honored spot. Columbus introduced citrus to the star-crossed Spanish colony at La Navidad; Dominicans and conquistadors carried seeds across the Straits of Florida. A dazzling variety of oranges took root in Florida. Hamlins and Temples, Parson Browns and Murcotts, Lue Gim Gongs and Sanford Bloods became so identified with the Florida dream, so synonymous with hyperbolic rhetoric and restored health, that America's love affair with Florida must, in part, be credited to the orange. Today, citrus labels may seem hopelessly old-fashioned and low-tech, but earlier generations' first taste and vision of "liquid sunshine" derived from wooden crates adorned with allegorical and fanciful labels: "Indian River Sweets," "Gem of the Hills," and "Flamingolds"; "Tropic Gold," "Gator Supreme," and "Sunny Florida." Endorsements by Hollywood stars, cartoon characters, and exotic animals helped make oranges Americans' favorite fruit, so much so that 1950 consumers purchased more oranges than all other fresh fruit combined.[19]

Generations of Floridians first encountered the Florida dream because of the iconography of the orange. Conferring health and vitality upon a nation, oranges also allowed thousands of Americans to become grove tenders. Beginning in the late nineteenth century, orange fever brought boatloads of citizens eager to purchase a five-acre tract and homestead. Entire cities—Temple Terrace, Howey-in-the-Hills, and Dunedin—were built upon the ideal of a symbiosis between town and grove. If not a grove, many new Floridians at least planted an orange tree in the backyard. So interwoven in the Florida dream was the orange tree that an agricultural commodity became a "natural" component of the Florida landscape.[20]

A midcentury traveler must have been awestruck at the sheer breadth of Florida grove land. Standing at strategic points along the fabled citrus belt—the Ridge, the Golden Triangle, Indian River, and the Peace River Valley—Floridians scanned unbroken rows in groves of orange and green. The concentration and ubiquity of orange trees pervaded the landscape and popular culture. Each spring, the aroma of billions of orange blossoms saturated the nostrils, wafting through every crevice and into windows of house and car. Emblazoned on billboards and brochures, the orange was the state's most pervasive symbol, bringing together visions of health, sunshine, and fertility. Oranges inspired the naming of towns and counties, bowl games, and fiddling tunes.

Florida's eclectic grove owners exhibited a curious blend of optimism and pessimism in 1950. The fecundity of Clermont, Leesburg, Mount Dora, Eustis, Tavares, Citra, Dunedin, Dade City, Winter Haven, Davenport, Frostproof, Sebring, Auburndale, Titusville, Vero Beach, Lucerne Park, Merritt Island, and Fort Pierce made Florida the world's greatest producer of oranges. As late as 1920, California claimed 75 percent of America's orange crop. The Sunshine State topped the Golden State during the 1943–44 season and never trailed its rival again. In 1950, Florida harvested a record 100 million boxes of citrus, including 55 percent of the country's oranges. Even as fruit hogs picked Navels and Valencias, new acreage in citrus was being planted. Orange fever was again infecting grove owners, but many farmers must have lamented more competition. The number-one problem was overproduction. In 1948, *Fortune* magazine described a citrus industry "sick with a sickness that mocks the malnutrition of the world . . . an unprofitable surplus." The *New York Times* concurred, describing Florida's citrus industry as one plagued by "overproduction, disorderly marketing and shipping." Historically, farmers are notoriously independent, and in Florida, farmers, cooperatives, and corporations struggled to enforce and maintain a byzantine system of citrus boards and regulations.[21]

The days of the gentleman farmer and the retiree tending to his five-acre grove were drawing to a close; the business of oranges was becoming a very big industry. Groveside packinghouses were vanishing; agribusiness was on the rise. In 1965, the author John McPhee scoured Florida's citrus belt in search of oranges and groves. To his astonishment, it was almost impossible to find a cup of freshly squeezed orange juice. Alas, even the "fresh orange juice" touted at Florida welcome stations was made from concentrate. In fact, so accustomed were they to the taste and texture of juice made from frozen concentrate that most Americans in 1965 actually preferred it to freshly squeezed. "Fresh oranges have become, in a way, old-fashioned," wrote McPhee in his magisterial book *Oranges*. "The frozen product . . . is pure and sweet, with a laboratory-controlled balance between its acids and sugars . . . a consumer opening the six-ounce can is confident that the drink he is about to reconstitute will taste almost

FIGURE 23. Once a familiar sight, the roadside fruit stand has become increasingly rare. In the 1940s, Lee County's Estero River Groves tempted customers with bags and bins of freshly picked Hamlins, Parson Browns, and Temples. Special Collections, University of South Florida Library.

exactly like the juice that he took out of the last can he bought." Fresh orange juice was simply too inconvenient and too inconsistent for modern consumers increasingly accustomed to national franchises and standardization.[22] But it was not always so.

Farmers have always pushed for and been pulled by technological innovation. "Uncle Jeff" Sligh, born near Ocala in 1863, reminisced how as a young man he had shipped oranges in wooden barrels, hauling them by mule cart onto steamboats plying the Oklawaha River. The Model T and the Waterloo Boy tractor, the truck and the refrigerated railcar, the mechanical sprayer and biotechnology, the fruit elevator and the lightning loader, all revolutionized farming. The citrus industry has particularly benefited from modern herbicides, fertilizers, and irrigation. Technological advancement maximized the natural advantages of California and Florida, making possible the democratization and globalization of fruit consumption. Two great challenges, however, eluded practical solutions: a machine that harvested citrus, eliminating the intensive labor required for harvest, and a process or formula to preserve juice during surpluses, eliminating the urgency of shipping fresh fruit to market. Grove owners still largely rely upon human labor to pick oranges, while scientists untied the Gordian knot of preservation in the 1940s.[23]

The most powerful symbol and salvation of the citrus industry was a small can of frozen orange concentrate. The simplicity of frozen concentrate belied the daunting task of putting orange flavor into a can. Orange growers had wrestled with the challenge for decades. The problem of perishability—how to get crates of luscious oranges to distant households before they rotted—had long frustrated growers. Later, refrigerated railcars sped the crop to markets, but wholesalers and distributors had little control over the fruit's three-week shelf life. For decades, in an effort to impose standards upon fiercely independent growers, the industry attempted to ban shipment of green fruit. In addition, consumers demanded oranges that looked, well, orange. Losses due to blemishes and late-ripening fruit cut into groves' profits. The first breakthrough came in the early 1930s. Dr. Philip Phillips urged researchers to come up with a better-tasting canned juice. At a citrus processing plant on Orlando's Princeton Street and Orange Avenue, his workers bottled the genie, or, in this case, canned the genie. Pasteurized canned juice had been available for decades, but consumers' palates did not appreciate its metallic taste. Finally, researchers perfected the process of "flash" pasteurization. Most important, consumers liked the product.[24]

Dr. Phillips, the man behind the can, left legendary footprints in the quest to build an orange empire. He, perhaps more than any other person, impressed upon the public the linkage between orange juice and good health. "Doc" Phillips—the origin of the medical title is obscure—was a highly successful entrepreneur, buying and selling 100 million oranges a year on the eve of Pearl Harbor. Generations of Floridians recall his irresistible jingle, "Drink Dr. Phillips' orange juice because the Doc says it's good for you." Dr. Phillips's contributions notwithstanding, canned juice was not the panacea the industry had hoped for. Canning helped salvage blemished and undersized fruit, but the problems of shipping and storage remained. Was there a way to recapture the taste of fresh orange juice without the orange or can?[25]

World War II provided government funding, a patriotic impetus, and economic motivation to solve the problem. A new crisis spurred scientists: How might we produce and transport a new orange juice product to troops and civilians starving for vitamin C? Chemists at Citrus Concentration, Inc., in Dunedin first developed a dehydrated juice that was tested in Great Britain. The reconstituted juice was preferable to Axis blood oranges from Sicily, but it tasted awful. Spurred by the possibilities of manufacturing powdered orange juice, Boston-based National Research Corporation established operations in Plymouth (Orange County) in 1945.[26]

Florida's equivalent of the Manhattan Project—the quest to find a good-tasting reconstituted orange juice—was conducted by the Florida Citrus Commission in USDA laboratories located at Dunedin, Lakeland, Winter Haven, and Lake Alfred. The concentration process, involving the evaporation of water from heated juice, was already well known. The juice, however, tasted, as John McPhee characterized it, "like a glass of water with two teaspoons of sugar and one aspirin dissolved in it." Three remarkable scientists, C. D. Atkins, Louis G. MacDowell, and Edwin Moore, solved the conundrum of flavor. Working at the Lake Alfred Experiment Station, the team perfected the "cutback process," adding freshly expressed, single-strength orange juice and citrus oils to the evaporated product, then canning and freezing it. Having removed the water and bulk, the product could be more easily and cheaply shipped.

Fabulous wealth eluded the revolutionaries. U.S. Patent number 2,543,109 belonged to the government, but Atkins, MacDowell, and Moore never complained. When Dr. MacDowell retired in 1968, the Florida Citrus Commission jokingly presented him a check made out thusly: "Several Million Dollars and No Cents." The National Research Corporation quickly dropped the idea of manufacturing powdered orange juice. Chemist Wallace Roy improved upon the idea of frozen concentrated juice. In 1945, Minute Maid purchased the National Research Corporation. The following year, Minute Maid began the first commercial production and sale of orange juice concentrate under the Snow Crop and Minute Maid labels.[27]

The results were astonishing. Frozen concentrate revolutionized the planting and processing of citrus, the distribution and marketing of Florida oranges, and changes in consumption and taste. The popularity of frozen concentrate was swift and dramatic, a phenomenon evident in grocery stores, family kitchens, citrus groves, and corporate boardrooms. Few sentences in the English language are more identifiable than the instructions for making orange juice: "Add three cans of water and mix." In 1940, there was literally no place for frozen foods in the typical American grocery store or family home. In many places refrigeration depended upon daily deliveries of blocks of ice for the ice box. The frozen-foods section of the grocery store was itself a postwar phenomenon, the result of national chain stores, American affluence, and new kitchen appliances. By 1991, Americans were purchasing 1 million home freezers annually. The acceptance of frozen orange juice may have been immediate, but the transition of oranges from the fruit bins to the freezer was not always smooth. A 1950 newspaper article catalogued the confusion surrounding the new product. One New York grocer sold the concentrate next to the cash register, straight from the box. When customers refroze the product, the cans exploded. Consumers, however, would not be denied. New consumer trends and lifestyle changes made Minute Maid and Birds Eye instant hits. A 1950 headline explained the new phenomenon in simple terms: "American Housewife Holds Answer to the Future of Florida Citrus Industry." Mothers rearing large families preferred the ease of adding three cups of water to the old-fashioned juicer. Seemingly overnight, frozen concentrate juice penetrated American markets. "The American housewife no longer squeezes nearly as much orange juice as she did a few years ago," understated the *New York Times* in 1954.[28]

The revolutionary product that captured consumers' taste buds also redistributed the orange crop. In an astonishingly fast turnaround, grove owners redirected the orange crop toward processing plants. Fresh fruit, the staple of the industry, became a secondary concern. Frozen orange juice concentrate production expanded from 226,000 gallons in the 1945–46 season to almost 10 million gallons in 1948–49. By 1999, the industry produced 158 million gallons of frozen concentrate. The revolution also brought profound changes in distribution. One tank car of concentrate replaced thirty railcars of fresh fruit.[29]

Researchers determined that certain varieties of Florida oranges resulted in the new taste that consumers preferred. The sweeter and pulpier Valencias and pineapple oranges largely replaced Hamlins, Temples, and Parson Browns. By the 1960s, Valencias—once known in Florida as Hart's Tardiff and Rivers Late, and imported into the United States not from Spain but England—constituted half of the state's orange crop. With its thin skin and juicy interior, Valencias became the dominant crop. As early as 1950, a Hillsborough County fertilizer executive announced that he was switching his Lake Magdalene grove from Hamlins to Valencias because of the market shift toward frozen concentrate. He hired veteran nurserymen to "hang bud" his twenty-acre grove at a cost of three dollars a tree. The process required pruning the original Hamlin limbs at the top and slipping a Valencia bud at the tree's base. Within a few months, Valencia buds appeared. Workers "buckhorned" the old Hamlin limbs.[30]

America's love affair with orange juice reenergized the Florida citrus business. The California orange, the Navel, is harvested for fresh-fruit markets; Florida's most popular orange, the Valencia, is used primarily for juice. Packinghouses registered dramatic increases in production. From 28.6 million boxes of oranges produced in the 1940–41 season, growers and workers sent 67.3 million boxes to plants and markets in 1950–51. Speaking at a gathering of the National Wholesale Frozen Food Distributors in 1950, the chairman of the Florida Citrus Commission predicted frozen concentrate's potential was "virtually unlimited." Even as he spoke, nurseries expanded and new groves appeared. The proportion of the orange crop destined for processing grew exponentially. From three-quarters of the 1960 orange crop to over 90 percent by 1980, more and more Florida oranges went to consumers in tank cars, not citrus crates. Where once packinghouses placed a premium upon color, size, and quality, technicians now measured enzymes and sugar content. Frozen concentrate also allowed processors to bank bountiful citrus harvests as a hedge against freezes. As the world developed a taste for orange juice—Americans alone drank a billion gallons of orange juice in 1980—Florida growers kept up the supply. By the 1970–71 season, Florida groves produced 142.3 million boxes of oranges. In 1990–91, the industry recorded a $1 billion harvest, 151.5 million boxes of oranges. By 1999–2000, the figure had peaked to over 225 million boxes.[31]

Florida citrus has evolved from family grove and small packinghouses offering free samples of orange juice to giant multinationals sprawling over counties and countries. Once fiercely competitive and decentralized, the citrus industry became an oligopoly. The frozen concentrate boom encouraged the largest processors to invest heavily in Florida grove land to ensure a supply of oranges. Between 1945 and 1950, the "Big Four" citrus powers took control of the concentrate business: Minute Maid, Snow Crop (Vacuum Foods, Inc.), Pasco Packing Company (Lykes Bros.), and Birds Eye (General Foods). Originating in Plymouth, Florida Foods, Inc., exemplified the new order. Swallowing up packinghouses and orange groves, Florida Foods grew rapidly in the 1940s, changing its name to Vacuum Foods. The company also exhibited a fierce anti-unionism. Incorporating the latest technology, the firm helped promote and perfect frozen concentrate, building the first concentrate plant in the country. In 1945, Minute Maid purchased Vacuum Foods. Minute Maid aggressively sought Florida grove land and packinghouses. In 1949, the firm purchased 4,700 acres of citrus lands for $5 million from the DiGiorgio Fruit Corp., a deal then considered the largest transaction in Florida citrus history. In 1954, Minute Maid made history again with the purchase of "Doc" Phillips's massive Central Florida groves. In a brilliant public relations stroke, Minute Maid hired America's most popular singer, Bing Crosby, to croon the merits of Florida orange juice. In 1960, Coca-Cola purchased Minute Maid and later acquired Snow Crop. "[Minute Maid] is the great orange dukedom now," wrote author John McPhee in the mid-1960s, noting the corporation's three concentrate plants, 30,000 acres of groves, and central headquarters in Orlando. When

McPhee interviewed Ben Hill Griffin, the legendary captain of industry philosophized, "No man on earth ought to have more than one concentrate plant."[32]

The ascendancy of the Tropicana company combines elements of Horatio Alger, Johnny Appleseed, and A. P. Giannini, the founder of Bank of America. A Sicilian emigrant, Antonio Rossi arrived in America in 1921. In the 1930s, he opened a cafeteria in Bradenton, where he also tended a small tomato farm. During World War II, he sold his café and began selling gift boxes of Florida fruit in a Palmetto building he purchased for $15,000. His Manatee River Packing Co. expanded as he specialized in selling chilled grapefruit and orange slices in glass jars. He also perfected a new way to bottle orange juice, and in 1954 he introduced Tropicana Pure Premium Orange Juice in cartons. Fleets of refrigerated trucks, trains, and ships rushed freshly squeezed juice from Bradenton plants to northern markets. In 1957, his company became Tropicana Products, Inc. In 1978, Rossi sold Tropicana to Chicago-based Beatrice Foods for $490 million in cash. In 1998, PepsiCo bought Tropicana for $3.3 billion, setting up a battle of the juice giants: Coca-Cola and Pepsi. An immense market rewards the biggest. In 1996–97, U.S. firms produced 804 million gallons of reconstituted orange juice, resulting in $3 billion in retail sales.[33]

The drive to control citrus production at the grove and plant levels produced some homespun, bigger-than-life figures. Ben Hill Griffin Jr. was to Florida's citrus what Henry Plant had been to railroads. Born at Tiger Bay and raised in Frostproof, Griffin cut short his University of Florida education in 1933. That year his father gave him a 10-acre orange grove as a wedding present. The grove became a cornerstone for a citrus empire. Taking a job in a fresh fruit packinghouse paying fifteen cents an hour, Griffin strove single-mindedly to make his fortune in citrus, learning every task and scrutinizing every detail of the business. At his death in 1990, he was one of the richest men in Florida, controlling a fortune worth more than $300 million. At one time, Griffin owned or controlled a string of processing plants, 200,000 acres of groves and ranch land, and 49 percent of Alico, an agribusiness giant.[34]

Griffin shared much with his great rival, James Emmett Evans. Born in 1900, Evans left Georgia when boll weevils destroyed successive cotton crops. He found fortune in Florida, first selling Fords to citrus workers in Polk County. Beginning with his first purchase of a twenty-acre grove in 1925, Evans's citrus empire grew steadily. By the 1990s, Evans controlled 33,000 acres of Florida grove lands, including principal interests in packinghouses and processing factories. When he died in 1996—still actively involved in the business—*Forbes* magazine listed him as one of America's four hundred richest persons.[35]

If Evans and Griffin personified the gritty individualism of the men who built citrus dynasties one grove at a time, Consolidated Citrus LP and Cutrale Juices U.S.A. signify a new corporate presence, more multiconglomerate and multinational than personal and local. Boasting 40,000 acres in citrus holdings, Consolidated Citrus LP became America's largest citrus operation when Collier Enterprises of Naples and King Ranch of Texas merged in 1998. In 1996, Sucocitrico Cutrale, a Brazilian agriconglomerate, purchased significant citrus holdings in Florida. Additionally, Cargill Citrus America controls huge groves in Florida and Brazil.[36]

Historic freezes, new hybrids, and the relentless development of grove land have pushed Florida's orange belt southward. In 1950, the orange belt buckled together the state's leading citrus counties: Orange, Polk, and Lake. Fifty years later, the belt drooped southward. St. Lucie, Indian River, DeSoto, Hardee, Highlands, Hendry, Collier, and Polk counties have emerged as leading citrus counties. Farmers had long praised the fertility of the lands banking the Caloosahatchee River. Citrus had been planted in the area since the first groves at Alva in 1877. In spite of the fact that the Caloosahatchee River Valley largely escaped the Great Freeze of 1895, the region was simply too isolated, too wet, and too ill-served by transportation to encourage attempts at large-scale farming. As late as 1965, Hendry and Lee counties totaled fewer than 3,000 acres of citrus, in contrast to 106,000 acres in Lake County. In the succeeding thirty-five years, investors have planted 100,000 new acres of citrus trees in Hendry County alone. The land between Naples and Lake Okeechobee has become Florida's newest groves. If Winter Haven and Clermont served as unofficial capitals of Florida's orange empire in 1950, Indiantown and LaBelle now claim that title. The scale of these new "groves" is massive.[37]

In December 1962, a severe freeze scoured the state, damaging a quarter of the state's citrus crop and hitting Central Florida especially hard. The temperature plunged to 12 degrees at Lake Alfred. Grove owner Jack Berry Sr. reconsidered establishing new groves in Central Florida. A risk taker, he startled his colleagues by purchasing and draining 6,000 acres of land and planting 600,000 trees in western Hendry County. Connecticut General Life Insurance Company financed the transaction. A half dozen freezes later, Berry's move anticipated a major shift in citrus production from Central to South Florida. In 1981, only Minute Maid owned more Florida grove land than Berry. The Duda family also joined the stampede toward Southwest Florida.[38]

During citrus's golden century, 1880–1980, no place in the world produced more oranges than Florida's Ridge. Transplanted New Englanders and mid-westerners expressed wonderment that the Ridge, with its sandy hills, could ever be a fertile crescent. An ancient shoreline and a modern watershed, the Ridge runs from Leesburg through Winter Haven to Sebring, a 120-mile stretch. Thirty thousand lakes buffered the Ridge from freeze and frost. Alas, nature (freezes and canker) and economics (land inflation and development) have diminished the legendary reputation of the Ridge.

If the Ridge was Florida's most prolific producer of oranges, the Indian River was its most famous trademark. Merritt Island, located between Cape Canaveral and the Indian River, seemed especially blessed for growing oranges. Spanish missionaries and British and American settlers had also planted groves along the Indian River. The freeze of 1835 damaged most of the groves but left untouched the Dummett plantation on Merritt Island, a place providentially situated between the Indian River (actually a tidal lagoon) and the Banana River. Dummett, a Seminole War veteran and judge, improved his sour orange trees by budding sweet orange stock from the ancient Turnbull groves of New Smyrna. Dummett grove budwood and seeds became the foundation for the acclaimed Indian River oranges. So renowned were Indian River oranges that locales 75 miles inland appropriated the brand name "Indian River." In 1930, the Federal Trade Commission ordered rivals to cease and desist. In 1931, growers organized the Indian River Citrus League. Here, too, rampant development has reduced Indian River's output but not its reputation.[39]

Urban growth has denuded the pine forest from Pinellas County, drained the lake out of Lake Apopka, and even squeezed the orange out of Orange County. In 1950, the St. Petersburg Chamber of Commerce produced a promotional film entitled *Sunny Days*. The film, intended to lure retirees to buy homes in St. Petersburg, was sent to civic clubs and television stations in the North. In an opening sequence, viewers accompany a retired New York couple to Florida. When their car reaches the northern edge of Pinellas County, the Sawyers gaze upon grove after grove of oranges. Pa Sawyer cannot resist. He pulls over to the side of the road and plucks an orange from a tree. Such an act would shock commuters negotiating bumper-to-bumper traffic along u.s. 19 today. But *Sunny Days* was no illusion. In 1950, farmers in Pinellas County still hung on to their agricultural roots, managing 769 farms, 16,816 acres of grove, and 341,000 citrus trees yielding 4 million boxes of fruit. A 1950 headline presciently speculated, "Some Day Apartments May Crowd Out Citrus." A half century later, one is as likely to encounter a Webb City mermaid as a packing-house in Pinellas County. By the turn of the century, the Pinellas citrus belt has shrunk to one working grove consisting of 37 acres.[40]

In 1950, Orange County was an agricultural powerhouse, its 1,780 farms settled along a half million acres. The number of farms and groves was actually increasing, not decreasing. Thousands of agricultural workers worked on a thousand groves cultivating 3.1 million orange trees, which produced nearly 10 million boxes of oranges. Orange County was synonymous with citrus. "Every time the citrus industry sneezed," wrote Henry Swanson, "a ripple went down Orange Avenue." But Orange County grove land became too valuable for mere oranges. As late as 1970, Orange County still managed 60,000 acres in citrus, but that quickly shrank to less than 8,000 acres in the 2002. "Our No. 1 crop is Yankees," quipped an Orange County agriculture extension agent in 1985. "We used to pick oranges. But now we pick Yankees. They don't freeze." Symbolically, the last orange grove on Orange Avenue was bulldozed in 1977 and replaced by a supermarket; more ominously, the last commercial groves on the Orange Blossom Trail sold in 2003.[41]

From the vantage point of the Citrus Tower in Clermont in Lake County, one can comprehend the parabola of orange fever, freeze, and fade out. Predictably, each spring travelers luxuriated in the intoxicating smells and hundreds of lakes alongside u.s. 27. Glorified as the Orange Blossom Trail, the road paid homage to Florida's fruit basket, the richest citrus lands in the world. In 1956, businessmen hoping to capitalize on the traffic rushing by Route 27 erected the Citrus Tower. Built atop a near-300-foot hill, the 226-foot tower allowed visitors to scan the vista and fathom the meaning of 17 million citrus trees. A belt along the Mount Dora Ridge boasted the world's most productive orange groves. The freezes of the 1980s, coupled with ever-increasing demands for Lake County real estate, changed the panorama. Between 1980 and 1988, Lake County grove owners surrendered 100,000 acres of prime citrus land to trailer parks and cul-de-sacs. Once Orange and Lake counties accounted for one-quarter of Florida's citrus. Today, they comprise less than 2 percent. Developments called Siena Ridge, the Savannas, and Kings Ridge line roads from Clermont to Interstate 4. Homes at the Ridge appeal to workers at Disney who cannot afford—or tolerate—Orlando, 15 miles away. Minneola groves had been sending oranges to northern markets since the Gilded Age; today its groves bloom single-family homes. Gone also are the juice plants, packinghouses, and unique sandhills environment, as well as the workers who had made this possible.[42]

The culture of agriculture measures time in freezes. The Great Freezes of 1835, 1886, 1895, 1957, and 1962 marked not only meteorological events but also watersheds in Florida history. In January 1981, Florida shivered as the "Alberta Clipper" plunged statewide temperatures well below freezing. Exactly one year later, another arctic cold front scoured the state. In December 1983, a devastating freeze recorded temperatures of 26 degrees in LaBelle. "I heard what sounded like rifle shots in all directions," recalled a Citra grove owner. "It was bark freezing and splitting." The event killed most of Lake County's citrus trees. In January 1985, still another terrible freeze left its mark on Florida. On 22 January 1985, temperatures reached 22 degrees at Lake Placid and 18 degrees in Fort Pierce. A decadal capstone freeze occurred on Christmas Day 1989, damaging fields and groves that had earlier been spared. The impact of the freezes can be starkly measured. In 1978–80, Florida groves produced 207 million boxes of oranges. A decade later, workers harvested 104 million boxes. The real beneficiaries of the 1980s freezes turned out to be Brazil and real estate developers.[43]

New forces, more destabilizing than frost, now threatened Florida's vaunted orange. The year 1981 marked a milestone in citrus history, a year as significant as 1944, when Florida succeeded California as America's premier orange state. In 1981, Brazil replaced Florida as the world's leading source of oranges. Brazil's assault upon Florida had actually begun in 1962, when a December freeze killed millions of Central Florida orange trees. At the time, José Cutrale Jr. was an insignificant fruit wholesaler in São Paulo. The son of a Sicilian immigrant, Cutrale had a vision: Brazil could penetrate American markets with cheap oranges. The vision must have struck many associates as blurred. In 1965, Brazil's orange juice concentrate exports to the United States amounted to a mere $84,000. Twenty-five years later, Brazil exported $1 billion worth of concentrate. Cutrale achieved the stupendous feat, ironically, by brokering a deal with Coca-Cola's Minute Maid—the company that pioneered frozen-juice sales in Florida. By the 1980s, Coca-Cola was purchasing nearly 100 percent of its Brazilian juice from Cutrale's firm, Sucocitrico. In the process, Cutrale became the world's greatest orange baron, owning in 1981 nearly 7 million orange trees. In 2000–2001, Brazilians harvested 325 million boxes of citrus, accounting for 53 percent of the world's orange juice. Brazil's citrus acreage (1.5 million) has doubled Florida's (665,000), while its labor cost per acre is one-fifth that of Florida. Mexico also poses a serious threat, having planted large groves. The passage of NAFTA (North American Free Trade Agreement) removed the thirty-five-cents-per-gallon tariff on imported Mexican and Brazilian orange concentrate. If anything, the interests of Florida, Mexico, and Brazil have been brought together by heavy investments by powerful agriconglomerates.[44]

A familiar litany of gloom and doom documents the history of Florida's citrus industry. In 1947, the chairman of Florida's Fruit and Vegetable Association complained that increased labor costs threatened the very future of Florida. "Before the war," testified Dixon Pearce, "field workers were paid from $1.75 to $2.00 per day; we had better workers than today, and they worked longer hours." The citrus industry has somehow resisted, adjusted to, and survived each new threat: menacing pests and diseases, the shortage of agricultural workers, rising land costs, new environmental regulations, falling prices, and foreign competition. Still the orange remains a powerful symbol of Florida.[45]

Quite simply, the greatest challenge to Florida's love affair with the orange may be society's changing tastes. Two huge shifts in taste appear to have taken hold in the last decades of the century. First, increasing numbers of consumers prefer ready-to-drink orange juice to frozen concentrate. Growers of Florida grapefruit would love such misery. In spite of decades of publicity and record harvests, Americans have never warmed up to the puckish-tasting fruit. In 1986, for the first time since the late 1940s, consumers bought more chilled juice than frozen concentrate. Tropicana's Pure Premium has become a favorite. More chilling to grove owners, increasing numbers of young Americans skip breakfast and prefer Coca-Cola or a café latte to a glass of O.J. Americans are too busy or too worried about carbohydrates to defrost frozen concentrate. To combat such heresy, corporate food divisions have offered young consumers new juice products. For decades, researchers have worked to transform plain orange juice from a prosaic breakfast drink into a "neutriceutical" beverage. Coca-Cola and Pepsi, acutely aware that carbonated soft-drink sales in the 1990s were as flat as a day-old soda, have launched massive advertising campaigns to promote New Age products: orange juice blended with teas, herbs, and vitamin and mineral supplements. Pepsi recently acquired South Beach Beverage Co., creators of the popular brand-name drinks Lizard Fuel and Tsunami. Meanwhile, Coca-Cola has introduced its own line of juice drinks, Fruitopia. Ironically, the plainest of drinks, water, has become a hot commodity in Florida. Sales of bottled water have become a $3 billion industry. Multiconglomerates, such as Perrier, have purchased the rights to several natural springs.[46]

Winter Vegetable State

Vegetables, no less than oranges, linked Florida with consumers. If, in 1950, the orange was king (28.6 million boxes worth $182 million), beans, tomatoes, and peppers were princely (103,961 railcars of Florida vegetables fetched $115 million). Since the late nineteenth century, Central and South Florida had carved reputations as the winter fruit and vegetable capital for the East Coast. Florida's farmers and agricultural workers contributed greatly to the diversification and richness of the American diet. Florida produced 104 different commercial crops—beans, tomatoes, peppers, cabbage, carrots, celery, lettuce, potatoes, squash, sweet corn, okra—supplying greengrocer carts in Brooklyn, family grocery stores, A & P, and Piggy Wiggly with an abundance of fruits and vegetables for the world to envy.[47]

Historically, the race to rush fruits and vegetables to market was a race against time. The appearance of the refrigerated tank car in the late nineteenth century opened new markets. While interstate highways and refrigerated trucks have reduced the dependence upon rail, the process of rushing crops to central rail shipping points has continued. In the 1950s, Winter Haven and Winter Garden—even the names suggest their destiny—touted themselves as the world's largest shippers of fruits and vegetables. Throughout the night from December through April, workers nimbly hooked 300-pound blocks of ice onto rollers headed into railcars brimming with Minneola oranges, Oviedo celery, Plant City strawberries, Venice cucumbers, Belle Glade tomatoes, Zellwood sweet corn, Homestead avocados, Indiantown onions, Immokalee watermelons, and South Bay beans.

New technologies that made possible frozen orange juice also helped revolutionize the vegetable business. Beginning in the late 1940s, corporations moved processing plants into Florida to capitalize upon this new and growing market. As early as 1950, one-seventh of the state's bean crop was being processed and frozen by Southland Frozen Foods.[48]

Vegetable farmers have survived a half century of devastating freezes, pesticide scares, worker shortages, and foreign competition. By the late 1990s, Florida's vegetable growers harvested crops annually worth $1.5 billion. Historically,

FIGURE 24. Belle Glade beans, much like Sanford celery, Plant City strawberries, and Indian River citrus, connected place and product in consumers' minds. Library of Congress, Washington, D.C.

winter tomatoes dominated Florida's vegetable cash crops, generating income of $610 million in 1997 alone.[49]

America's appetite for fruits and vegetables opened new sections of Florida to intensive cultivation. None was more remote than Immokalee. When Floridians first read the early 1950s headline, "Glades Farmers Strike It Rich in Immokalee," many learned that Immokalee was located on rich, high hammock land in north-central Collier County. Surrounded by swamp, forest, and Seminole reservation, Immokalee was a primitive place that acquired adequate roads only in the late 1940s. When farmers complained of panthers' depredations against livestock, the state sanctioned panther hunts. In the early 1950s, Dewey Garguilo founded Immokalee Tomato Growers. By the 1990s, Immokalee housed two of Florida's largest vegetable empires—Garguilo, Inc., and Six L's Packing Company.[50]

Since the 1920s, the size and scale of Florida farms have been growing. On the eve of Pearl Harbor, over 100 Florida farms sprawled over 10,000 acres, a doubling of such operations in just two decades. By the late 1980s, Florida claimed 30 of the nation's 400 largest farms. In the fiercely competitive agricultural business, the most successful farms survived and prospered by becoming giants. Fortunes rose and fell on the outcome of a freeze, price fluctuations, or strike, but modern Florida agribusiness has been very profitable for the survivors. Few contemporaries could have imagined that Andrew Duda's 40-acre Seminole County farm would grow to become the cornerstone of a 100,000-acre land empire. In the 1920s, Duda helped found Slavia, a religious community for Slovak immigrants, many of whom had first settled in Cleveland, Ohio. Duda and his sons pioneered the cultivation of celery in Oviedo, each year acquiring more acreage. By the 1980s, A. Duda and Sons had emerged as a conglomerate, with fruit, vegetable, cattle, and housing operations. In 2000, A. Duda and Sons had become Florida's largest marketer of vegetables, producing annual sales of $240 million in its collective operations. In the 1960s, stung by accusations of migrant worker abuse, the Duda family was among Florida's first agribusinesses to provide workers permanent housing.[51]

No Florida family has soared higher or farther than the Lykeses. In antebellum Hernando County, Frederick and Margaret Lykes purchased 500 acres of land, dabbling in citrus, timber, and cotton. Howell Tyson Lykes, only fifteen years old when the Civil War began, enlisted in a local Confederate company, was captured and later released. Following the war, he studied medicine and returned to practice in Brooksville. His passion, however, was business. A timely marriage with the daughter of Captain James McKay brought Lykes seven gifted sons and cemented his political and business alliances. During the Cuban Wars of Independence, Lykes made a fortune supplying the island with Florida beef. The Lykes family solidified its position in Cuba after the Spanish-American War, investing heavily in ranch lands, meat-packing plants, and shipping. Incorporated in Florida in 1910, the firm expanded its operations in shipping, citrus, and cattle. War contracts enriched the corporate coffers. By the 1970s, the Lykes Corporation became Florida's first billion-dollar company, ranking among the top 150 in the *Fortune* 500. A tightly run concern, the Lykes

Corporation was nothing short of imperial in its reach: steel mills, a fleet of ships and shipbuilding interests, huge citrus holdings with processing plants, Tampa Bay's biggest bank (First Florida), vast cattle ranches, and meatpacking operations. Peaking in the 1970s, the corporation has weathered misfortune (seizure of assets in Cuba; an ugly legal battle with the State of Florida involving the rights to Fisheating Creek; and bad investments), but the Lykes family still exerts a powerful influence.[52]

The Zellwood saga illustrates the extreme swings of Florida agriculture. Settled and named by Elwood Zell, a prominent Philadelphia publisher, Zellwood seemed like an unlikely place for one of Florida's great booms. Nature had endowed the northern shores of Lake Apopka with rich and rewarding soils, but the saw grass and muck hindered settlement. In 1940, only a few hundred winter residents called Zellwood home. Promise stirred, as scientists believed the local peat, once cut into bricks and sun-dried, might become a fuel source. Others had different designs for the mucklands. During the Second World War, the Florida legislature established the Zellwood Drainage and Water Control District, authorizing the diking and drainage of 200,000 acres of the northern shore of Lake Apopka. The boom was on. The Duda family, the National Ramie Corporation, and the New York Stock Exchange's Richard Whitney purchased large tracts of Zellwood property, convinced that capital and machines would make the land dry and bountiful. By 1950, the press trumpeted the Zellwood miracle. From geographic obscurity, Zellwood had become the number-one shipping point for perishable crops on the Seaboard Air Line Railway. A newspaper heralded Zellwood as a "wealthy new frontier of truck crop production."[53]

Zellwood corn was born of this marriage of geology and capital, Madison Avenue and the University of Florida School of Agriculture. The jet-black fields along Lake Apopka, framed by a perfect climate, sometimes yielded three harvests of Zellwood corn and celery a year. The Zellwood Sweet Corn Festival paid homage to the local delicacy. By the late 1980s, Florida farmers sent to market 11.5 million crates of sweet corn valued at $71.4 million. No other state and no other place produced so much sweet corn for fresh-market consumption. Ralston Purina also built a huge complex near the lake to grow mushrooms. Success followed, but not without costs. Bass and bream soon disappeared, and by 1981 all the fish camps had closed. Lake Apopka, once Florida's second-largest lake, became the fourth-largest as the bottom silted up. Still more muckland was drained. Environmentalists discovered alarming levels of DDT, dicofol, and toxic minerals. Workers fell ill; alligators were deformed. Federal officials stepped in, and after complicated negotiations, the government, in an effort to save Lake Apopka and the health of residents, bought the farms and shut down lake agriculture. Zellwood corn is now a memory. In 1999, the public watched in horror the near-biblical plagues of dead birds and live mice left over in the toxic residue. Millions of mice fled the abandoned fields and invaded the homes of area residents. Newspaper columnists debated the most humane method of disposing of trapped mice (breaking their necks versus flushing them down the toilets). Poison bait resulted in the deaths of hawks and owls, further disrupting any semblance of natural balance. The plight of the displaced workers evoked less public outrage. The same poisons and residues haunt many of the laborers who spent years in the tainted fields.[54]

"Big Lake Okeechobee, big beans, big cane, big weeds, big everything." The drift to massive agricultural operations was already apparent to Zora Neale Hurston when she set her 1930s novel *Their Eyes Were Watching God* in Belle Glade. "Dis game ain't no game fuh pennies," says her character Tea Cake, surveying the scale of the Okeechobee farms. Marjory Stoneman Douglas always contended that to understand the Everglades, one must first understand the geography. Today, one might add an appreciation of corporate greed, political influence peddling, human ingenuity, hubris on a colossal scale, a public's unquenchable appetite for winter vegetables, cheap sugar, and yes, even good intentions. How did the Everglades become home to America's winter vegetables and Big Sugar? In the 1880s, Hamilton Disston first surveyed a future agricultural empire. At the turn of the century, a "progressive" governor called for the drainage of the Everglades to open up South Florida to settlers and small farmers. In one of Florida's cruelest ironies, the dream of an Everglades populated by yeoman farmers yielded to the reality of a land dominated by corporate conglomerates. Following two devastating hurricanes in the 1920s, Congress built a levee around Lake Okeechobee. In the 1920s, the Pennsylvania Sugar Company vowed to tame the Everglades with the transforming wands of technology and capital. The Everglades resisted; bankruptcy dashed corporate dreams. Fatefully, nature, politics, and profits conspired against the Everglades in the late 1940s. Following a year of relentless rain and flooding, a coalition of South Florida officials, farmers, and citizens appealed to Congress to fix the problem. The engineers, complained Douglas, "wanted to 'correct' the flood plain system, as opposed to understanding it." She added, "A political body, the Central and South Florida Flood Control District, was established to work with the engineers. They dug canals to drain more water off the land. They did it to please the big agricultural interests." Ironically, Congress saw no contradiction between opening the Everglades to massive agricultural development and the dedication of the Everglades National Park (1947).[55]

Big Sugar

Big Sugar was not always so big, chiefly because the Everglades used to be much larger. At the end of the twentieth century, the Everglades is about half the size it was at the beginning of the century. As late as 1928, the south shore of Lake Okeechobee had hardly been touched by plows. In the 1930s, farm operators could rely upon a large, compliant labor force of African Americans. World War II changed the calculus of agricultural work and workers. West Indian workers soon displaced blacks. In the 1940s, Congress "sweetened" legislation to encourage the domestic production of sugar. U.S. Sugar Corporation seized advantage of strategic opportunities. The U.S. government helped Florida sugar growers obtain offshore laborers, even paying the workers' transportation costs. The Immigration and Nationality Act of 1952 ensured the importation of Caribbean laborers. Researchers also discovered new varieties of cane and proper cultivation techniques to produce fabulous yields of sugarcane. Castro's seizure of power in 1959 and his expropriation of foreign-owned sugar mills and plantations provided powerful economic and political reasons to showcase free-enterprise farming. To protect American farmers and punish Fidel's transgressions, the United States imposed a ban on Cuban sugar. At the time, Cuba was supplying one-third of America's sugar. One of the wealthy families to flee Cuba was the Fanjuls, who lost their 400,000 acres of sugarcane. The family established Flo-Sun (Florida Crystals), an agricultural company headquartered in Palm Beach. The price of Everglades land rose sharply in the early 1960s. In 1970, U.S. Sugar and other firms were planting 180,000 acres in Everglades sugarcane; by 1990, the acreage had ballooned to 400,000, climaxing to 440,768 acres in 2002. In 1975, Florida surpassed Louisiana and Hawaii to claim the title of America's sugar bowl. Large numbers of Jamaicans, Barbadians, Dominicans, and Haitians called Clewiston, "America's Sweetest City," home, where they cut and burned the area's cane fields. The land south of Lake Okeechobee had become so integrated with sugar, writes Paul Roberts, that "depending on the time of year, a visitor will find not only the U.S. Sugar Corporation and the Sugarland Highway, but also Sugar Industry Appreciation

FIGURE 25. Towering over the flat landscape of Hendry County like a colossus, U.S. Sugar Corporation's refinery dominated Clewiston. State of Florida Photographic Archives, Tallahassee.

Week, . . . and even, in the small black town of Harlem, a Miss Brown Sugar Contest."[56]

U.S. Sugar became Florida's leading agricultural corporation, ranked tenth nationally in 1988 with $365 million in sales. In 1960, the year the U.S. banned Cuban sugar, Florida processed 1.35 million tons of cane, less than one-tenth the amount it would produce forty years later. By 2002, the average sugar operation in Florida comprised 3,723 acres. With adroit subtlety, hardball lobbying, and masterful public relations, the sugar industry has prospered. *Time* called the Fanjuls the "First Family of Corporate Welfare" for having received in 1997 over $60 million in governmental subsidies and price supports. Skewered by *60 Minutes* and journalists, the Fanjuls (Spanish citizens) smugly rule Florida Crystals from Palm Beach, comforted by a $500 million family fortune. Columnist Carl Hiaasen writes, they "have gotten grossly wealthy because the U.S. government lets them charge eight cents per pound above the world price for sugar, and imposes strict import quotas on foreign competitors." U.S. Sugar embodied that contradictory trait that guided the development of American agriculture—a curious mix of rugged individualism and dependency upon public welfare. "In grateful recognition of such blessings," observed the _Nation_ magazine, "the sugar industry gives more money to candidates for federal office than Ford and General Motors combined. Disbursements in 1990 by the sugar barons ran at twice those of the National Rifle Association." No other agricultural commodity so lavishly supports politicians as the sugar industry. In the 1990s, the sugar industry contributed $18 million to political candidates and parties. Nat Reed, Florida environmentalist, jokes that Fidel Castro no longer fears assassins—American sugar interests guard him twenty-four hours a day! Through carefully crafted advertisements and strategically placed donations, Big Sugar has withstood its many critics who blame the industry for destroying wetlands and endangering South Florida's water supply. Pointedly and poignantly, no other industry stands so indicted for having exploited its workforce.[57]

A profound irony permeates the production of sugar: that a crop bringing so much sweetness and joy has resulted in so much pain and suffering. "Sugar is made with blood," an old Spanish proverb holds. Compared to cotton, corn, wheat, and other crops, sugar has resisted labor-saving technologies. Through the late decades of the twentieth century, sugar harvests required relentless effort, for fear of losing the crop or lessening its value. The day before the cane cutting, workers burn fields to rid the crop of trash and leaves, which allows crews to walk down the rows. Enduring the acrid smell of burned fields, workers wield sharp machetes to cut the thick stalks. In 1975, cane workers earned $3.03 an hour for doing what a Labor Department official called the "most arduous and unpleasant task in agriculture." By 2000, the era of the legendary cane cutters had ended. New machines capable of withstanding the fields' soft soil had finally been perfected.[58]

Big Phosphate

Big Sugar is hardly alone in deserving criticism. In 1950, Florida's highest land point was neither Hernando County's Chinsegut Hill (280 feet) nor Walton County's Lakewood (345 feet) but rather a phosphate dump heap atop Sand Mountain in Polk County. Rising to 350 feet, the "mountain" of phosphate waste was the brainchild of an official at the Swift and Company mine at Fort

Meade. The Chamber of Commerce at Fort Meade studied the idea of converting the mountain into a park. Lacking Big Sugar's public relations skills, Big Phosphate has somehow survived environmental calamities, economic dislocation, and scathing political criticism. Following World War II, Florida phosphate interests enjoyed record yields, the result of worldwide demands for fertilizers and a free hand to ignore pollution and environmental concerns. When it came to regulating phosphate, the federal government had little power and even less interest; the State of Florida placed few burdens upon its wood-pulp mills and extractive industries.[59]

In 1960, a confident, profitable phosphate industry looked back at a decade of soaring production and the construction of new plants. The "green revolution" augured good times in an industry that had experienced more bad times than boom times. The United States dominated world markets, and Florida was the heart of the American phosphate belt. As late as 1968, the *Wall Street Journal* described phosphate as "Florida's 'Good Guy' Industry." But the 1960s brought new anxieties. A number of powerful multinational companies gained control of the industry. International Minerals and Chemical Corporation (IMC), an industry pioneer, controlled seven phosphate rock mines. W. R. Grace and Co., Occidental Petroleum Corp., Continental Oil Co., Kerr-McGee Oil Co., and Socony Mobile Co. invested heavily in the future of phosphate, with the added hope of controlling offshore oil, a prospect at which environmentalists recoiled. Oil companies, supported by their tremendous assets and new technologies to produce and market phosphate, changed the face of the industry. By 1966, energy conglomerates controlled vast acreage across Polk-Hillsborough-Manatee-DeSoto-Hardee counties. Moreover, new processing techniques alarmed not only local farmers and ranchers but now also environmentalists and residents. The extraction, crushing, and drying of phosphate had always exacted a cruel price upon the land and workers. But at least most firms shipped Florida phosphate elsewhere for chemical refining. New technologies, however, allowed refining to take place in Florida, a process that required huge amounts of sulfuric acid and chemicals. Such methods released poisons in the air, fouling the skies and polluting the region's water on a scale never before seen. Cattlemen complained of sickened herds while grove owners noted decreased yields and stunted trees. Since the 1960s, environmental disasters have become alarmingly commonplace. Dam breaks released slime ponds into the Alafia and the Peace rivers. Spoil banks and radioactive, 150-foot-high gypsum stacks dot the Florida landscape. Parts of Polk County resemble a

FIGURE 26. Bone Valley in Polk County richly deserved its reputation as the capital of phosphate mining in America. Dredges and steam shovels left a scarred landscape. State of Florida Photographic Archives, Tallahassee.

moonscape. Phosphate profits peaked in 1980, when Florida firms mined a record 43 million tons of rock (one-third of the world's production). Employment also peaked, at nearly 15,000 workers. Since then, prices, production, and jobs have plummeted. Bankruptcies multiplied. Mounting environmental concerns at the local, state, and national levels excoriate the industry's egregious violations. Apologists argue that phosphate is more victim than violator, more a good neighbor than evil corporation, forced to adjust to new regulations, practices, and guidelines.[60]

Still, phosphate's ugly scars pockmark the riverbeds and pastures of Southwest Florida. No county has borne more of phosphates' successes and failures than Polk. For a century, Polk County has rested uneasily with the title "Phosphate Mining Capital of the United States." Like a sulphuric acid cloud, a pall hung over Polk County in the 1990s. Seven phosphate mines closed while output dropped by nearly half and 2,000 workers lost jobs. "What was once a mosaic of thick forests and pristine marshes," wrote one journalist, "has been reduced to a mostly treeless landscape of pasture, artificial ponds and pine plantations." Places like Mulberry, victimized by a century of too many busts and too few booms, struggle with the economic and environmental consequences of phosphate.[61]

To naysayers and optimists, Boca Grande and Piney Point provide examples of phosphate's future. For over seventy years, Boca Grande on Gasparilla Island provided the phosphate industry a critical link to markets. In 1909, engineers and laborers finished a Herculean project, building a railroad, trestle, and 1,000-foot dock onto the Charlotte Harbor island. There, over 2 million tons of phosphate sailed to markets in barges and ships. The last train rumbled across Boca Grande in 1981. Boca Grande now boasts some of Florida's most expensive beach homes. In Tampa, a similar transformation occurred, as Seddon Island was converted from a gritty memory where phosphate railcars unloaded their cargo to Harbour Island, now an exclusive residential and commercial complex. Piney Point, located in Manatee County, has become the poster child for phosphate's insoluble problems. Following a wave of bankruptcies in the 1990s, Piney Point and Mulberry Corp. became wards of the state. Polluted ponds and radioactive stacks of phosphogypsum sit while officials debate expensive remedies (shipping the remnants into the Gulf of Mexico or treating the waste at the site).[62]

Floridians in the new century will have to weigh the benefits of jobs and the heritage accrued by Big Sugar and Big Phosphate with their compatibility in an urban state. The debate is acrimonious, conducted not only at the local level but fashioned nationally by lobbyists and public relations firms. In 1996, the sugar industry spent $23 million to defeat a proposal to tax sugar growers for Everglades restoration. Agribusiness remains today, as it has always been, politically charged.

From the extraordinary thirty-six-year tenure of Commissioner of Agriculture Nathan Mayo (1923–60) to Big Sugar's deft defense against environmental attacks, Florida agriculture has been highly politicized. Florida planters, ranchers, grove owners, and corporations have exerted political pressure and exercised political clout disproportionate to their numbers. A vast network of federal, state, and local agricultural bureaucrats presided over Florida's farms and farmers. In 1935, the Florida legislature established the Florida Citrus Commission to set industry goals and advertise Florida fruit. Since World War II, the USDA, immigration officials, and Congress have championed the importation of cheap foreign agricultural laborers. In 1950, U.S. Senator Claude

Pepper reminded farmers that he had campaigned for free school lunches, providing "a better market to growers of citrus fruits, fresh vegetables, and to dairymen." In Bonifay, Pepper scoffed at his opponent's urban background. George Smathers "lives on Sunset Island at Miami Beach. They don't grow cotton and tobacco on Sunset Island. They don't have livestock over there, except poodle dogs." Pepper won the political affections of North Florida voters but lost the election. Florida's leaders trumpeted their lobbying triumphs. In 1967, U.S. Senator Spessard Holland announced that the USDA had purchased $8.7 million worth of frozen juice concentrate. Until Supreme Court decisions forced reapportionment, Florida's legislatures—creatures of the state constitution of 1885—allowed North Florida legislators to control power and dispense favors. The Commission of Agriculture maintained an extensive patronage network and held considerable power. In the late 1990s, Mediterranean fruit flies were discovered along the Gulf coast. Against the protests of urban politicians, the commissioner of agriculture sprayed infected areas with malathion. The future promises even more political conflict. Water rights, environmental policies, and trade policies will pit agriculture against urban and international interests. For decades, Florida's biggest agricultural interests have derided big government, but the USDA generously rewards America's wealthiest farms. Between 1996 and 2000, the forty largest Florida farms received a staggering sum of federal subsidies, ranging from the Melton brothers in Altha ($1 million) to James C. Hilliard in Highland Beach ($339,000). In 2002, Florida farmers received $22 million from the federal government.[63]

Urban Agriculture

In the late twentieth century, Florida's agricultural past and present fit uneasily with the state's urban and metropolitan future. A green revolution (technological and chemical) allowed farmers to reap harvests previously unimaginable, but the other green revolution (economic and class) continued to expose some of America's most exploited workers. Belle Glade, Clewiston, Pahokee, South Bay, Ruskin, Immokalee, and Hastings represent some of America's richest lands but poorest residents. Hastings, located south of St. Augustine, has seen better times. The community once grew many of the premium vegetables served in the fashionable dining rooms of the Flagler hotels. Potatoes and cabbages grew exceptionally well in Hastings. The soil's fertility and the profits generated from the harvests attracted as many as 17,000 Caribbean migrant

FIGURE 27. In 1941, photographers from the Farm Security Administration came to Florida to document the lives of migrant workers. Marion Post Wolcott's photograph captures a general store and juke joint at Canal Point in Palm Beach County. Library of Congress, Washington, D.C.

workers from December to June. A 1950 reporter described "box cars lined up on railroad sidings and fleets of large trucks on hand to take the crop to northern markets." Four packinghouses operated twenty-four hours a day to process the spuds. The profits, however, did not guarantee Hastings's future. By the late 1950s, mechanical harvesters had largely replaced workers. By 1990, Hastings had been reduced to a skeletal community with no doctors, no high school, but still the prized potato fields. Developers covet the open fields.[64]

Each winter a mass of migrant laborers prepared South Florida's field for vegetables destined for American tables. In the early 1950s, officials estimated the migrant labor force at 16,000. Increasing numbers of Caribbeans replaced black workers. Profits enriched investors who gambled against freeze and storm, but workers lived under dismal conditions. In the early 1950s, the "boomtown" of Immokalee still had no bank, no drugstore, no resident doctor or dentist, in what one reporter described as the "meagerest facilities," a collection of "tiny, filthy shacks." In some quarters, blacks and Puerto Ricans were

housed seven to a room. Rev. Frank Ramirez confessed, "I've served in mission-
ary work in many parts of the country, but I've never seen anything like this."[65]

On Thanksgiving evening, 1960, CBS television aired Edward R. Murrow's
exposé, "Harvest of Shame." From Belle Glade, the stern-faced Murrow nar-
rated its chilling opening: "This scene is not taking place in the Congo. It has
nothing to do with Cape Town or Johannesburg. No, this is Florida. These are
citizens of the U.S. This is the way humans hired to harvest the food for the best
fed people in the world get hired." Murrow's hard-hitting documentary reached
a national audience, moved in part because the depicted migrant workers were
mostly white. Agribusiness reacted angrily but did little to improve conditions.
In 1970, an NBC documentary, "Migrant," concluded that little had changed in
Florida field and grove. Minute Maid officials reacted angrily to criticism, but
corporate officials seemed more concerned with public relations than the lives
of the 6,000 migrant workers hired during picking season. Most Floridians
today show little concern for Murrow's parting words: "The question posed by
thoughtful men is, must the two to three million migrants who help feed their
fellow Americans, work, travel, and live under conditions that wrong the dignity of men?"[66]

When Zora Neale Hurston wrote that she had "licked all the pots in sorrow's
kitchen," she might have had in mind her experiences in Belle Glade. Other
Florida novelists have also chosen Belle Glade to expose the harsh conditions.
Lois Lenski, whose best-selling *Strawberry Girl* (1945) introduced "strawberry
schools" to readers, wrote *Judy's Journey* (1947), an indictment of living conditions in Palm Beach County labor camps. In *Angel City* (1974), Patrick Smith set
the scene in a squalid camp in Dade County. Workers there had always suffered
from poor sanitation, substandard housing, and dangerous conditions. Agricultural workers endured the residual effects of pesticide poisoning and the
everyday dangers of cutting cane, picking crops, and traveling up the coast. The
children of migrant workers struggled desperately to acquire an education, few
of whom start and finish the school year at the same place. Migrant children
faced a grim future, confronting barriers of language, education, and poverty.
In 1963, Poor Boy Slim's Labor Bus plunged into a Belle Glade canal, drowning
twenty-seven farm laborers. But the 1980s introduced a new horror. In 1990,
documentary journalists returned to Belle Glade. Little had changed. "New
Harvest, Old Shame" revealed that Belle Glade suffered from America's highest
AIDS rates. Locals suffered from AIDS at a rate four times higher than that of
residents of New York City; two of every one hundred Belle Glade residents

were afflicted with AIDS. Women accounted for one-third of the AIDS cases, a much higher rate than in other areas.[67]

Belle Glade's notoriety brought journalists. Some found a glimmer of hope. "Hunger still exists," wrote the *New York Times*' Jon Nordheimer in 1985, "but it is not the belly-swelling scourge of the past." Almost everyone noted the incredible string of All-American football players produced by Glades Central High. Truly, South Florida's sugar and vegetable fields have replaced Pennsylvania's coal mines as the lodestar for football recruiters. Others found the public housing, albeit modest, an improvement. No longer does law or custom require that "all negroes, except those employed with the town, be off the streets by 10:30 p.m.," as was the case in the 1930s. But overall, life remains bleak for workers and residents in what one reporter called "Belle Glade's 'Colored Town.'" Residents report that when they shop out of town, clerks sometimes spray their checks with Lysol.[68]

For more than a century, Florida has served as the winter home for a floating mass of migrant laborers who worked their way up the East Coast, schedules subject to ripening crops. In the 1960s, most of Florida's orange pickers were African American. "The decision to import workers during the Second World War," wrote historian Cindy Hahamovitch, "shaped the course of farm labor history over the next fifty years." By the 1970s, most of the fruit harvesters were foreign born. "Home" was elusive, given the peripatetic workplace and the fact that most workers were foreign born and desperately poor. Beginning in the 1970s and 1980s, migrant farmworkers began to settle in year-round residences. Following Hurricane Andrew's 1992 devastation of Homestead, many Mexican farmworkers moved to the depressed south Dade locale. Large numbers of Mexican laborers also have moved into areas such as Pierson, a fern-growing town in Volusia County.[69]

Florida agriculture invites contrasts: prosperity and depression, bountiful harvests and killer freezes, corporate farms, yeoman farmers, and impoverished farm laborers. Perhaps more than any other Florida story, it is a tale of winners and losers. The victors receive garlands of tax breaks and leave behind monuments in the form of football stadiums, philanthropic foundations, and restored reputations. Few public monuments honor the agricultural workers, the men and women who cleared the fields, picked the crops, and shipped the fruits of Florida to market. No statue honors the cane cutter. One could make a compelling case that no one has left more sweat and tears on Florida soil than

FIGURE 28. West Indian cane cutters wield machetes in the sugar plantations of South Florida. State of Florida Photographic Archives, Tallahassee.

those who cut sugarcane. For centuries, African slaves, southern farmers, Italian immigrants working under the "padrone," Japanese immigrants in work gangs, Jamaicans, Haitians, and West Indians cut sugarcane from North Florida to the shores of Lake Okeechobee. Since World War II, almost no native-born Americans have engaged willingly in this dangerous, backbreaking labor. Large numbers of West Indians worked Florida's cane fields. In 1980, an official of Gulf and Western, operating out of South Bay, defended the practice: "I am saying that no American will cut cane anywhere in the United States at any price." In the towns of Moore Haven, Clewiston, and Belle Glade, Jamaicans endured appalling conditions because, as one told a reporter, "It is better to be exploited then to lose the opportunity to come back next year."[70]

Among Florida's urban counties, Palm Beach, Dade, and Hillsborough have managed to retain a significant agricultural presence into the early twenty-first century. Palm Beach is huge enough to contain two Rhode Islands. A journey along S.R. 80 whisks the traveler from the urbane glitter of Worth Avenue and

Rolls-Royce dealerships to agricultural ghettos, where as late as the 1970s, a quarter of the homes lacked plumbing. Palm Beach's agricultural riches are centered around Belle Glade, Pahokee, and South Bay, the hinterland's lucrative truck farms and cane fields. In 2000, Pahokee's movie theater and hospital closed. Palm Beach County remained an agricultural superpower into the new century: its 1990–91 harvest exceeding $1 billion; its 2002 crops brought in $750 million, tops in the state. In 1999, no county in Florida devoted more sheer acreage (650,000) to farmland, and only a few counties in California surpassed Palm Beach County's cornucopia.[71]

To most Americans at midcentury, Dade County was synonymous with the urbanity of Miami Beach and Coral Gables; to New York City greengrocers and fruit wholesalers, Homestead and Florida City were rich sources for tropical fruits and early vegetables. Since 1903, African Americans have grown watermelons and tomatoes in Goulds, an agricultural community along the S. Dixie Highway. In 1950, Dade County ranked among Florida's top agricultural counties. Frenzied development has gobbled up thousands of acres of farms and dairies, but agriculture endures. In 2002, over 90,000 acres of farmland and 2,244 farms still existed in Dade, which ranked second in the state in total agricultural sales ($578 million). South Dade County remained the center of Florida's tropical fruit industry. Homestead was heartland to groves of avocados, mameys, and limes, but the mango was Dade County's signature fruit. Until the 1970s, Homestead supplied U.S. markets—especially New York—with truckloads of luscious Kents, Keitts, and Tommy Adkins. Foreign competition, Hurricane Andrew, and rising land values have taken a toll on Dade's tropical fruits, but the region's burgeoning Latin American population has an unquenchable appetite for the prized mango, sapodilla, and mamey.[72]

With almost 3,000 farmsteads still operating in 2002 and crops valued at $392 million, Hillsborough County remained one of the state's leading agricultural units, with 285,000 acres devoted to farming. In the 1980s, it was ranked one of America's top-fifty agricultural counties; it remains so. For more than a century, Hillsborough County farmers produced more strawberries than any county in America; the county also ranked in the top-five tomato-producing counties. But rich agricultural lands are being gobbled up by developers. In Plant City, the polo (yes, polo!) grounds of Walden Lake sprout upon land once reserved for strawberry fields. Plant City's access to Interstate 4 has also made it a popular distribution center.[73]

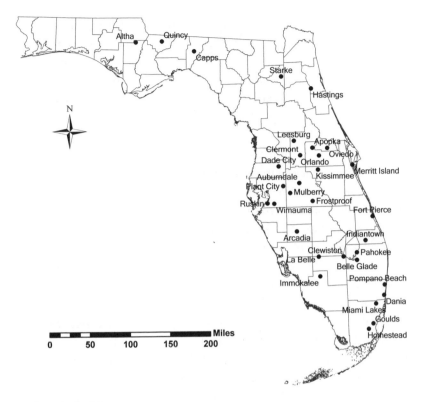

Agricultural Florida

The perfections and imperfections of American capitalism can be tracked in rural Hillsborough County. Land-use patterns, social stratification, and dreams failed and found stand out as templates of opportunism. Pioneering farmers discovered rich hammocks interspersed among the sandy palmetto scrubland. In 1908, the disciples of the English socialist John Ruskin established a college and cooperative colony in Ruskin. Leaders purchased 12,000 acres along the Little Manatee River and Little Cockroach Bay. Idealistic settlers belonged to the Ruskin Commongood Society. Members discouraged businesses that peddled tobacco. The utopian colony collapsed, but the Florida dream endured, pursued by succeeding waves of southern migrants, Italian immigrants, and, more recently, Mexican laborers and Mormons. In 2000, Deseret Farms, owned by the Church of Jesus Christ of Latter-Day Saints, owned 5,500 acres in the Ruskin area.[74]

But for fateful detours, Wimauma and Sun City Center might today resemble Hollywood, California. The Florida boom in the 1920s echoed even in southern Hillsborough County, promising glamour and prosperity. In 1925, a Miami realtor announced the creation of Sun City, "Florida's Moving Picture Development Just a Whisper South of Tampa." Promoters laid out a city with streets named Gish Drive, Pathé Place, and Vidor Avenue, but the real estate collapse and lure of Hollywood West doomed Sun City. A small agricultural community took hold, proclaiming itself as the "Chrysanthemum Capital of America." Mums replaced movie moguls. Everything changed when Del Webb planted a new crop, retirees, in nearby Sun City Center. Today the accoutrements of individual and group success are everywhere: national banks, golf courses, and medical complexes. Golf carts are ubiquitous; the community boasts half as many golf carts as residents.

Just two miles away, trailer parks and migrant labor housing mark the hardscrabble reality of Wimauma. It was not always so. In 1925, a Miami syndicate purchased the lands surrounding Wimauma, vowing to create an agricultural paradise. The Seaboard Air Line built a passenger and freight station, investors erected a sawmill and a fruit packinghouse, and the county dedicated a high school, but prosperity never materialized. The railroad closed the station, the mill shut down when lumbermen cut the virgin pine, and freezes shuttered the packinghouse. The Church of God established a campground, but mostly Wimauma attracted the working poor. Large numbers of Mexican farm laborers reside year-round. In 2000, Sun City Center households (median age 75) each earned almost $50,000 from investments and entitlements; Wimauma households (median age 23.5) are entitled to little but hope. Over one-third of the community's 8,000 residents lived below the poverty line.[75]

The transformation of an agricultural county into an urban megacounty is nowhere better illustrated than in Broward County. In the twentieth century, thriving agricultural communities took hold in Dania, "Tomato Capital of the World," and Pompano, "Bean Capital of the World." As late as 1950, Broward County claimed 423 farms and 140,000 acres of farmland. In 2002, on 23,741 acres, survivors were making farming's last stand. Broward verges on the brink of agricultural extinction. Pompano Beach athletic teams not long ago called themselves the "Beanpickers." They now wear the uniforms of the "Golden Tornado." The 1950s saw the end of Dania's Tomato Days Festival and Pompano Beach's Bean and Pepper Jamboree. In Dania, saltwater intrusion made farming impractical and real estate sales inevitable. Once famous for Danish immigrants and winter tomatoes, Dania reinvented itself in the 1960s as the "Antique Capital of the South." Not far away, Bud Lyons was building his own agricultural empire. From the 1920s until his death in 1952, Lyons steadfastly accumulated parcels of land in west Broward County, eventually becoming the largest bean farmer in the United States. Between 1961 and 1965, Lena Lyons sold 9,000 acres of Beanpatch to Coral Ridge Properties. The city of Coral Springs sprang from the bean fields, publicized by celebrity salesman Johnny Carson. In the 1990s, Coral Springs became one of America's fastest growing communities, its population surpassing 100,000.[76]

In a state hurtling toward the twenty-first century at breakneck speed, rural Florida has been paved, bulldozed, and urbanized. In 1964, Florida claimed 10 million acres of pastureland; by the end of the century, pastureland had been reduced by half. Each new Florida resident requires about one-half acre of land. Modern Jeremiahs wail at the fate of the family farm, but it is a tale oft-told. In Florida, the metaphor "vanishing Florida" has been repeated so often it could be the official state blues song, a dirge. Few Floridians wrote about the subject with more passion and purpose than Nixon Smiley. From the unlikely vantage point of Miami, Smiley reflected upon his beloved South Georgia and North Florida. In 1960, he took his readers for a tour of Bradford County. "I hardly recognized the countryside I had seen as a boy, when it was checkered by cultivated fields," reminisced Smiley. "Every farm then was partly self-sufficient; on each farm was a sugar cane patch, a sweet potato patch, and a vegetable garden." He also longed for the family mule. "Those farmers who could raise the cash to buy flour ate biscuits and syrup. But the poorer ate cornbread and syrup."[77]

At the dawn of a new millennium, Florida retained its premier agricultural status. Florida still produced more oranges, tomatoes, sugarcane, grapefruit, ferns, green peppers, sweet corn, gladiolas, cucumbers, watermelons, tangerines, snap beans, radishes, limes, and tangelos than any other state in the union. Ever resourceful and productive, Floridians cultivate new crops (bok chow, winter melons, and jicama) for new markets (Asians, Hispanics, and Indians) utilizing new and old methods (organic, hydroponic, and genetically altered). Extraordinarily efficient, the modern Florida farm produces far more on less land and with fewer workers. The number of Floridians employed in agriculture (125,000) has not changed much since 1950; meanwhile, the number of con-

struction workers has trebled, the number involved in manufacturing has quadrupled, and the number of those working in the service industry has grown
more than twentyfold.[78]

Indian River oranges and Ruskin tomatoes, as much as the beach and postcard, helped shape Florida's image as a winter paradise and bountiful dream
state. Dreams change, as do economies. One study suggested that Florida's or-
namental plant industry, which supplied palms and sod to the red-hot housing
and construction industry, was worth more than citrus. Foreign pests, fierce
foreign competition, the North American Free Trade Agreement (NAFTA), rocketing land values, and a changing workforce cloud Florida's agricultural future.

Machines in Paradise

Techno Florida

7

I N 1940, the Walt Disney Studios gambled on a new genre of film. *Fantasia* brilliantly combined classical music, German literature, and Hollywood dazzle. In one of the most memorable scenes, Mickey Mouse portrays Michael, the Sorcerer's Apprentice. Sorcerer Yen Sid demonstrates his mysterious powers by turning bats into multicolored butterflies and glittering dust. He then instructs Michael to fill pail upon pail of water. Michael then dons the Sorcerer's tall, pointed hat and commands a broomstick to follow him. The incantation works. But after the broomstick completes the task of filling buckets of water from the well, it refuses to stop. Soon the room is flooded with water. In desperation, Michael seizes an axe and breaks the broom into a thousand pieces. The splinters morph into broom disciples, each carrying a pail of water. Eventually, the wise Yen Sid (Disney spelled backward) intervenes and halts the chaos.[1]

Fantasia provides a cautionary parable for Florida. Like the out-of-control broomsticks loosed upon the castle, Florida's great conundrum challenges wizards and mortals: how to balance a dreamscape that drew so many tourists and residents to pristine beaches and an unhurried lifestyle with everyday necessities to sustain millions of people? Can a state possibly reject or alter a consumer culture that created prosperity and abundance and still maintain the aesthetics that attracted people to it in the first place? Real-life answers, unlike those

Every valley shall be exalted, and every Mountain and Hill made low, the crooked straight, and the rough places plain.

Isaiah 40:4

FIGURE 29. One of Broward County's drainage canals in 1959. The drainage of the Everglades, a dream in 1900, became a reality after World War II. State of Florida Photographic Archives, Tallahassee.

provided by sorcerers, are found in no book or spell. Yen Sid, however, would have appreciated the technological wizardry that changed the way we lived, that transformed swamp and forest into shopping plaza and mobile home park.

The struggle for paradise largely entailed the mastery of the environment. Modern technology aided in this conquest—marshaling tools, weapons, and capital to drain marshes, eradicate pests, and conquer distance. Millions of Faustian bargains made this conquest possible. The promise was irresistible: climate control, dignity in old age, the pursuit of happiness, affordable living, and sustained prosperity, all amid tropical paradise. A century later, such technological mastery has fulfilled Isaiah's prophecy, making the hot cool, the wet dry, and the crooked straight. It has also fouled the air, cluttered the highways, polluted the waters, and raised the standard of living to unsustainable levels.

The 1950s ushered in a decade buoyantly confident of its capacity to impose the machine upon the garden; indeed, technology would improve paradise.

World War II had unleashed terrifying weapons. Peace promised plowshares and the fruits of the technological war: DDT and penicillin, jet planes and television, freezers and frozen concentrate, transistors and computers. At the dawn of the nuclear age, technology seemed both terrifying and liberating. Just minutes after the *Enola Gay*—piloted by Miami native Col. Paul Tibbets—dropped the first atomic bomb, Bradenton Mayor Herbert Frink urged President Truman to hurl the weapon against nature itself to deflect an approaching hurricane. The Lee County Commission promptly offered the U.S. government a 7,500-acre tract to be used as a base for the "atomic bombing of hurricanes." For years, Floridians pressured the U.S. Weather Bureau to use nuclear weapons as a "hurricane stopper." Poised menacingly on launching pads in Cape Canaveral, Cuba, and the Soviet Union, modern missiles, the offspring of German V-2 rockets that terrified Londoners, symbolized Cold War bravado.[2]

Technology revolutionized the way Floridians lived, worked, and played, as well as the way they slept, shopped, and traveled. If the railroad modernized nineteenth-century Florida, air conditioning, television, malls, and the automobile permeated almost every phase of late-twentieth-century Florida, transforming and crisscrossing the state in breathtaking fashion. In 1950, it was hard to guess which future phenomenon would most astonish Floridians: a professional hockey team in South Florida, baseball played inside an air-conditioned dome, a nonstop superhighway from Miami to Pensacola, or evenings free of mosquitoes.

Technology made modern Florida accessible and livable. Commercial jet service linked Florida with distant places. DDT had seemingly tamed Cape Canaveral's ferocious mosquitoes, allowing rapid development along the Space Coast. Intercontinental missiles and scrub jays seemed to coexist in greater harmony than the United States and the Soviet Union. Soon, television antennae cluttered rooftops from Matacumbe Key to Niceville. Technological change, however, evolved unevenly. Motorists who sped along Melbourne Beach's first asphalt road noticed an eerie sight: Bumper 8 rockets lifting skyward from the salt marshes.

Swamp Angels

From the vantage point of the new millennium, a pre–World War II Florida lends itself to syrupy nostalgia, a land of unstraightened rivers and authentic relationships with nature. Few tears, however, are shed for the hordes of mosquitoes known to suffocate cattle and wreak havoc in cities and the hinterland. As late as 1888, mosquito-borne disease killed 400 Jacksonville residents. In a state where nature was both vision and barrier, no dream seemed more elusive than a paradise without itching and slapping.

Florida's fresh- and saltwater mosquitoes earned a well-deserved reputation for ferocity and single-mindedness. Pioneers battled the enemy with resourcefulness and imagination. Palmetto branches called "skeeter beaters" dislodged but did not eliminate the pests. A popular legend endures among the residents of the old pineries along the banks of the Indian River south of Fort Pierce. When armies of saltwater mosquitoes skimmed across the river, they were so thick you could grasp dozens at a time with your fist. The embattled farmers peeled pineapples and impaled them on posts. Attracted by the sugary fruit, the mosquitoes gorged themselves on the juice and then, too heavy to fly, fell to the ground to be carried off by ants. Mostly, people simply coped. In the 1920s, Floridians declared war on mosquitoes. The digging of drainage ditches and spraying and drizzling of oil onto waterways ameliorated the problem, but still the critters came. "Aside from tax-dodgers and constant knockers," complained the *St. Augustine Record* in July 1945, "the mosquito is [Florida's] worst enemy." Few Floridians would disagree, but relief was on the way.[3]

Like an avenging angel, DDT burst upon the Florida scene in 1945. First synthesized in 1874 by a Swiss chemist, DDT—dichlorodiphenyltrichloroethane—became the miracle pesticide of World War II. Deadly effective in the South Pacific jungles, DDT became the focus of intensive research by USDA scientists at Orlando's North Parramore Avenue Experimental Station. Researchers sought to test DDT's effectiveness against cockroaches, cattle ticks, and mosquitoes. In the spring of 1945, a cattle ranch near Lake Jessup became Ground Zero. A *Sanford Herald* reporter gushed, "Uncounted swarms of horn flies, [and] small blood-thirsty insects . . . met their doom at the ranch." Scientists discovered astonishingly successful results. Rancher Ralph Wright predicted, "It'll revolutionize the cattle industry." U.S. Senator Claude Pepper, recognizing the political capital of the issue, announced, "Today Orlando is the scene of a series of experiments which may eventually develop a method for the complete extermination of some of man's most ancient plagues."[4]

Quickly, DDT's fame spread, forcing municipalities and counties to lobby for release of the miracle pesticide. Homosassa, a quaint fishing village in Citrus County made famous by a Winslow Homer watercolor, became one of the first towns to be drenched by DDT. Housewives, anxious to rid homes of the annoy-

FIGURE 30. When it was first applied to ranches in 1945, Floridians proclaimed DDT a miracle; by the 1960s, reformers branded the chemical an "elixir of death." Dade County, 1948. State of Florida Photographic Archives, Tallahassee.

ing presence of ants and roaches, piled the furniture into the middle of rooms so walls could be sprayed. Impatient with a room-by-room approach, Floridians requested saturation bombing. B-25 bombers literally drenched 9 square miles of Orlando while specially fitted C-47 transport planes targeted Tampa. The Brevard County Mosquito Control District employed four surplus Stearman biplanes. An official described a "lovely cloud of DDT" left over Fort Lauderdale by Flying Avengers from the Naval Air Station.[5]

By the summer of 1945, DDT aerial assaults became as predictable as afternoon thunderstorms. A *Cocoa Tribune* headline eased newcomers' fears: "Don't Get Excited—It's a DDT Spray Plane." The *Titusville Star-Advocate* took to task naysayers, editorializing, "Some careless statements have recently been made about the alleged harmful effect of DDT upon honey bees." DDT's miraculous effectiveness against mosquitoes led some leaders to believe that it could combat another ancient plague, infantile paralysis. Amid a polio epidemic in Flor-

MACHINES IN PARADISE

ida, the State of Georgia imposed a brief quarantine on travelers passing from Florida to the Peach State.[6]

Alas, the miracle pesticide turned out to be a witches' brew. In October 1945, *Time* magazine cautioned readers: "Not much is known yet about the full effect of DDT on large areas." In an eerie warning, *Time* noted, "Thus far, wholesale sprayings have had some surprising—and bad—effects on birds, fish, and desirable insects." A state attuned to the gospel of growth held little tolerance for Cassandras or Jeremiahs. By the 1950s, DDT had become as commonplace in Florida as beach balls and tract houses.[7]

Brevard County, home to legendary swarms of insects, had established one of the state's first mosquito-control boards. Cape Canaveral's lagoons and wetlands had long provided a perfect sanctuary for mosquitoes. DDT arrived simultaneously with liquid oxygen and booster rockets. Early tests of DDT seemed magical. But the mosquitoes adapted to the poison, evolving resistant strains. As more and more poison was dumped upon the land, environmentalists observed a frightening decline in Florida's birdlife. The bird sanctuary at Pelican Island—one of Florida's earliest environmental victories—suffered grievous losses. Scientists estimated that early DDT spraying had devastated 70 percent of Merritt Island's dusky seaside sparrow population, one of the last known concentrations of the species. The road to its extinction was paved with crop dusters, fogging machines, dikes, draglines, and expressways.[8]

Reform sprang from a simple but powerful message. In 1962, the biologist Rachel Carson electrified the public and energized an emerging environmental movement with a timely book, *Silent Spring*. Research in Florida and elsewhere convinced Carson that we were poisoning the earth and waters, humans and animals, with a flood of pesticides and toxins. In a famous turn of phrase, she described DDT and insecticides as "elixirs of death." More than anyone else, Carson articulated and simplified the problem, pointing out the interconnectedness among chemicals, the earth, and humans. In 1969, the federal government banned the sale of DDT in the United States.[9]

Climate Control

The Sunshine State's vaunted year-round temperatures created alternating seasons of heaven and hell. For centuries, humans successfully assaulted the bay, forest, and savannah, but until recently, the region's unrelenting heat and humidity resisted the most ingenious efforts to control climate. From the pal-

FIGURE 31. Marjorie Kinnan Rawlings's home at Cross Creek, 1950. In the era before air conditioning, the time-honored cracker cottage effectively combined comfort and utility, form and function. State of Florida Photographic Archives, Tallahassee.

metto chickee to the Mediterranean-revival home, from the Gulf Coast cottage to the craftsman bungalow, climate dictated architectural guidelines. Coconut Grove homeowners learned to take advantage of prevailing southeast breezes; Jefferson County farmers knew to plant fast-growing chinaberry trees alongside dogtrot cabins. Floridians adapted their lives to the heat, making rituals of early evening walks, conversations on front porches, and soft breezes generated by paper fans. It was commonplace to close the windows and pull the blinds at mid-morning to keep the cool air inside. Then in the evenings when the heat broke, windows were opened again. In seersucker suits and Bermuda shorts, sleeveless and strapless sunbacks, Floridians adjusted fashionably to seasons. In Key West, shiny tin roofs reflected the sun's rays. The first principle of passive cooling passed from generation to generation: hot air rises and water may rise. The Deep South environment inspired dormers, screened windows, wide verandahs, high ceilings, sleeping porches, paddle fans, louvered jalousies, terra-cotta tile, classical porticoes, dogtrot breezeways, canvas awnings, shade trees, mid-day meals, and iced tea brewed in gallon pickle jars. Twilight, wrote Zora Neale Hurston, "was the time for sitting on porches."[10]

Air conditioning ushered in "quiet comfort," but the technology's impact was neither quiet nor always comfortable. Providing relief to suffering yellow fever patients had inspired John Gorrie, an Apalachicola physician, to patent a "Machine for the Artificial Production of Ice" in 1851, but a century later, precious few residents enjoyed air-cooled comfort. In 1902, Willis Haviland Carrier perfected the first mechanical air-conditioning system. For the next half century, air conditioning remained very costly and affordable only to movie theaters, select commercial establishments, and elite residences. If stores had it, they often flaunted it. In 1950, air conditioning was a luxury enjoyed by thankful customers who frequented Miami's Biltmore Theatre, Orlando's San Juan Pharmacy, Sanford's Yowell Building, St. Augustine's Alhambra Coffee Shop, and the cocktail lounge of the Sylvan Shores Hotel in Mount Dora. Such establishments acquired legendary status, a reputation enhanced by signs adorned with icicles and polar bears announcing, "It's Kool Inside." If the clickety-clack of the railroad inspired the fiddling tune "Orange Blossom Special," passengers aboard the Palm City lounge never heard the rhythm of rail and wheel, for the Atlantic Coast Line and Seaboard Air Line offered air-conditioned cars in the 1930s. Motels and hotels charged an extra dollar for the cool luxury. "The return on this investment has proven to be quite phenomenal," admitted the owner of the Raleigh Hotel in Miami. "Our summer trade has increased considerably." Another satisfied customer included Clare S. Brush, a Tarpon Springs poultry farmer who, in 1941, experimented with climate control at her chicken farm. Not everyone welcomed cool relief. The technology had first been tested in the Senate north wing of the State Capitol in the 1940s. In 1951, legislators authorized contractors to air condition the House wing. Two years later, the House launched an investigating committee to examine cost overruns, but critics suggested that the real issue was not money but the fact that as long as politicians lounged around Tallahassee they spent the peoples' money.[11]

The end of World War II augured relief. Industries that produced implements of war turned to peacetime appliances. Richards Department Store waited only hours after crowds in Miami had finished celebrating VJ Day in 1945 to announce that the firm would soon begin selling air conditioners. In June 1947, the Philco Company selected Russ and Dorothy Gray's Appliance Store in Miami for a demonstration of the first window air-conditioning units. For all of the promise, however, climate control awaited the 1960s.[12]

Why did Floridians and Southerners put off climate control, when the technology was available in the early 1950s? The answer is complicated. "Air conditioning," argues historian Marsha E. Ackerman, "had much less to do with hot weather than it did with prosperity, efficiency, and status, none of which the South could lay claim to during much of the twentieth century." When the median price of most Florida homes was less than ten thousand dollars, budgeting several hundred dollars and more on air conditioning seemed an extravagance. A simple $250 window unit in the early 1950s equaled a month's salary for a retail clerk. The annual cost of operating such a unit was $132, a stiff price. But economic determinism, whether explaining the motivations of Founding Fathers or the acceptance of new technologies, is almost always too simplistic. Many chose not to purchase window units because they simply enjoyed Florida as it was.[13]

But cheaper and more efficient units (especially heat pumps and central cooling) and rising levels of prosperity made air conditioning difficult to resist. "You'd go to someone's house with air conditioning, and you'd walk away knowing you just had to have it," remembered Tampa's Lester Olson, an industry pioneer. Working-class families could now afford window units—Webb's City in St. Petersburg advertised a Philco model in 1958 for $169. By 1962, the price of comparable models had fallen to $139 at the Western Way Shopping Center in Orlando.[14]

Businesses sprang up everywhere to install, repair, and sell the new appliances. In the early 1950s, Dade County friends gambled to launch the Miami Beach Air Conditioning Company with a $1,000 investment. By the end of the decade, the business was generating more than a million dollars and became the largest Westinghouse distributor in the South. Charles Buchanan, as much as the early astronauts, possessed the right stuff. A native of Mississippi, he moved his family to Delray after World War II. With a $5,000 loan, he opened a GE dealership. In 1957, he shifted operations to fast-growing Melbourne. His Tropic Air installed central air conditioning in new tract homes for $1,000. To promote the new product, "we would go door to door once a week." By the 1960s, Tropic Air was selling $4 million of heating and cooling equipment a year.[15]

Native Floridians who had left the state during World War II and not returned until the 1950s must have been startled at the odd sight of rectangular-shaped, metal-plated, water-dripping coiled boxes hanging from windows. Along with the television antenna, the room air conditioner reconfigured the landscape. The Carrier Corporation's introduction of the popular window unit in 1951 opened new markets and closed ice factories. Steadily if not quietly, the whir and rattle of the window air conditioner competed with frogs and crickets on sultry evenings. In July 1953, *Consumer Reports* first tested room model units. Nowhere in Florida was the rush of cold air more noteworthy than in South Florida. By 1955, every major hotel on Miami Beach had installed air conditioning. By 1960, the local chamber of commerce announced that Greater Miami was the "coolest spot in the U.S.," home to the greatest concentration of air-conditioned motel and hotel rooms in the world.[16]

Floridians may have admired, approved, and even coveted air conditioning, but the reality was that the majority of the state's households chose not to invest in any form of climate control until the 1960s. According to the 1960 census, fewer than one in five Florida households reported having air conditioning. By 1970, a majority of Florida households had converted to air conditioning, and only Texas (64.2 percent) boasted a greater proportion of air-conditioned homes among southern states than Florida (60.5 percent). But drastic distinctions and inequities remained. Even in homes listed as "air conditioned," acceptance took place over time and in increments. Historian Chris Warren asks, "Does one big window unit in the living room, which may only be turned on for half the day in much of the year, qualify the house as 'air conditioned'"? While only half the homes in Jacksonville, Orlando, and Tampa had installed air conditioning by 1970, the more affluent communities had eagerly installed cooling units: Hollywood (80 percent), Fort Lauderdale (77 percent), Coral Gables (87 percent), and Miami Beach (85 percent). When the Mackle brothers began development of Marco Island in the early 1960s, every new home included air conditioning. Upscale builders typically installed central air conditioning in new homes.[17]

Air conditioning exposed class distinctions. Large numbers of Floridians simply endured the heat and humidity, as southerners always had. Reasons varied—"snowbirds" migrating northward each May who preferred to have their air cooled in Buffalo or Green Bay; inhabitants of older homes who did not wish to install air ducts or lower ceilings; rural Crackers who thought the invention was pure nonsense; officials who branded the notion of air conditioning in public housing ludicrous—but mostly it was about money, or the lack of it. In 1980, while over 90 percent of the homes in Fort Lauderdale, Hollywood, Palm Beach, Cocoa, Sarasota, Naples, and St. Petersburg had air conditioning, only about half of the dwellings in Apalachicola, Avon Park, Bonifay, Blountstown,

Chipley, Fort Meade, Haines City, Moore Haven, and Okeechobee boasted the newest "necessity."[18]

Climate control also cut especially hard across racial lines. The 1960 census recorded the sobering reality that a scant one in fifty black homes was equipped with the luxury of air conditioning. Improvements came disproportionately. In 1970, when more than two in three white households had air-cooled comfort, only about one in ten black homes shared the amenity. It would not be until the early 1980s that a majority of African Americans homes had air conditioning.[19]

Making hot cold became one of the Sunshine State's most dynamic growth industries. From a rare domestic luxury in 1950, air conditioning had become near universal by 2000. Change could be measured not only by the mounting numbers of air-conditioned homes but also in society's expectations of change. In 1960, the U.S. Census Bureau first asked Americans if their homes had air conditioning; by 1980, census takers asked about homes "lacking air conditioning." Floridians have become so accustomed, so acculturated to climate control—in cars, trucks, malls, offices, and schools—that few consider how recently it has all come about; rather, we ask how in the world Floridians ever managed without it. The tourist season, which in 1950 began in December, has become a year-round industry. Baseball, enjoyed for a century and a quarter in the Florida sunshine, has a new home inside a domed stadium chilled to 72 degrees. In 1950, the very idea of a professional hockey team in Florida was so ludicrous as to be laughable. By the 1990s, the Sunshine State boasted two National Hockey League franchises. Skating rinks, once as rare as ice on Lake Okeechobee, appeared in numerous shopping malls.[20]

Air conditioning, more than any other technology, accounts for the greatest single source of energy expended by Floridians. In 1997, Florida households spent $1.8 billion for air conditioning. Climate control was the principal reason Floridians' consumption of electricity trebled between 1962 and 1982. Strikingly for a state associated with sunshine, solar energy plays a negligible role.[21]

In just one generation, air conditioning profoundly altered humans' routines and lifestyles, while also disassociating Floridians from nature. Historically, residents had adjusted to the rhythms of nature—sea breezes, afternoon thundershowers, southeasters—but climate control altered those relationships. Sleep was once joyously and annoyingly filtered through the sounds of nature, but the din of the air conditioners and closed windows drowned the noises of croaking frogs, hoot owls, and quarreling couples. The city governments of

Coral Gables and Hollywood even attempted to outlaw noisy units. When Hollywood neighbors protested to a city judge that a neighbor's air conditioner "blasts us out of bed every night," the defendant's lawyer explained that people will have to learn to live with the new technology, as they did with cars. A.C. also altered our landscape and cityscape, as structures took on new shapes, materials, and functions. Concrete block largely displaced wooden exterior walls, drop ceilings replaced loftier ones, carpet replaced wood floors and cool terrazzo, and TV rooms succeeded front porches. The doorway transom is as obsolete as the cistern. The porchless ranch house became the rage of the 1950s and 1960s. The single-lot, low-profile, low-ceiling, small-window, California-imported, suburbia-driven, rambling ranch homes adapted to forced air and heat with ease. The vaunted "Florida room," originally envisioned as a (screened) window to paradise, now became enclosed and cooled. The rectangular ranch home had little need for a front porch. The front porch had long functioned as more than an ornament. Families sat on verandahs and talked about cold fronts along storefronts. Air conditioning and television have nearly extinguished this evening recreation, taking with it the afternoon newspaper, mosquito nets, and the family excursion with the car windows rolled down. "General Electric has proved a more devastating invader than General Sherman," quipped historian Raymond Arsenault.[22]

Cooling Florida's schools ignited a hot debate. Many old-time residents and transplanted seniors argued that sweating (along with shivering and walking long distances) bred character, and besides, taxpayers could not afford the luxury. A Manatee County school board member pontificated that air conditioning instilled weakness. Curiously, court-ordered integration may have sped the popularity of climate control; leaders argued that air conditioning might cool down racial tensions. "The modern Florida school," noted a journalist in 1955, "closely resembles the rambling, open-styled Florida home, planned with Florida's climate in mind as a pleasant architectural fact of life." Here, too, the new technology mandated changes. Before air-conditioned schools, educational buildings featured spacious, open windows; climate control and efficiency dictated that functioning windows and style be sacrificed. School bells that once rang in September began to summon students in early August. If making students comfortable aroused debate, one can imagine the furor surrounding the cooling of prisons. As of 2004, only 10 of the state's 56 correctional facilities are air conditioned.[23]

Air conditioning represented only a down payment on what has been called America's Second Consumer Revolution. The first phenomenon occurred in the 1920s, as assembly lines produced waves of automobiles and durable appliances. Pent-up demands, abundant credit, parents wishing their children to have lives better than theirs, and grandparents wishing to live better as seniors than they had as juniors ignited a purchasing binge after World War II. Old wants became new needs. Deep freezers, dishwashers, and golf carts filled "all-electric homes" and garages.

Increasingly, lives were reoriented into places that never had existed: television rooms and entertainment centers. The interior of the home replaced the front porch as social focus and locus, marking a profound change in Floridians' relationship with neighbors and nature. Ironically, eternal sunshine had drawn so many people to Florida; prosperity and technology created cocoons of comfort, insulating residents from the place that had once tantalized them. Symbolically, the Sunday afternoon country excursion evolved from a ritual that had introduced Floridians to new places, smells, and sounds to an insulated, air-conditioned trip to the mall.

Automobility

Air conditioning offers welcome comfort to millions of Floridians who sit idly gridlocked in automobile traffic; indeed, conspiracy theorists insist there is a connection between bad road design and universal A.C. The year 1950 saw 6 million tourists and residents traveling Florida highways; by the late 1990s that figure had steamrolled to over 80 million. How did we get here?

Modern Florida and the automobile came of age together. In 1950, the automobile was as institutionalized and ubiquitous in Florida as the air conditioner was rare and luxurious. The car went unchallenged in a golden decade of power, affluence, and speed. The 1950s may have epitomized conformity, but more and more Americans sought individuality on the roadways. Investment in public mass transportation declined. Fewer and fewer Americans rode trains; an airplane ticket was a luxury. In Florida, rubber tires had always been preferable to steel wheels; streetcars named "Extinction" ended operations in Jacksonville (1936), Miami (1940), Tampa (1946), and St. Petersburg (1949). Within a decade after the demise of streetcars in Hillsborough and Pinellas counties, the number of automobiles had doubled. A 1946 headline summarized the feelings of many Floridians: "Parking in Miami Is a Chronic Year-Round Headache." The automobile seemed an American birthright. From courtship to vacations, from drive-in movies to vocations, Fords and Chevrolets helped create the American road story and Florida lifestyle. To millions of Americans, the meaning of Florida is associated with moving vans, convertible tans, and traffic jams. In a "wish you were here" state, getting there typically depended upon four wheels. By the 1980s, a technological and demographic convergence occurred: motor vehicles outnumbered residents in Florida.[24]

A recurring crisis bedevils Florida. To funnel millions of motor-bound tourists to and residents around the Sunshine State, Florida has devoted increasing amounts of federal, state, and local funds to transportation infrastructure. New bridges, roads, and airports quickly become obsolete because so many more people want to visit and live in Florida. Converts to the gospel of good roads and prosperity, Florida's cities embarked on a series of expensive, disruptive, and frustrating highway construction projects in the decades after 1950.

Jacksonville led the way. Begun April 10, 1950, the Jacksonville Expressway—originally estimated at $50 million but ultimately costing $100 million—bypassed downtown with bridges east and west of the city center. The system played a major role in opening the Arlington suburb and led to the construction of Regency Square Mall, the area's first enclosed mall in the 1960s. Jacksonville completed three bridges in the 1950s: the John E. Matthews Bridge ("the bridge to nowhere"), the Fuller Warren Bridge, and the Gilmore Bridge. By the mid-1960s, a total of five bridges crossed the St. Johns.[25]

Environmental concerns notwithstanding, bridge building in postwar Florida leapt across rivers and bays. For decades, ferries had carried passengers and cars across rivers and bays. The day of the ferry was closing. The new bridges also incorporated new materials and techniques. As late as the 1940s, a wooden bridge crossed the Halifax River in Daytona Beach. A sign warned motorists, "No driving faster than a walk on this draw." A new reinforced-concrete bridge replaced it, one of four such structures built in 1950s Volusia County. An antiquated Federal Highway drawbridge over the New River led to Fort Lauderdale being stigmatized as home to u.s. 1's "worst bottleneck." In 1956, voters approved the construction of a tunnel but only after a bitter bridge-versus-tunnel debate. Opened in 1960, New River Tunnel remains Florida's only public tunnel. In 1954, officials dedicated the Sunshine Skyway Bridge, a 15-mile, $20-million structure spanning Lower Tampa Bay and connecting Pinellas and Manatee counties. Construction began on the original Sunshine Skyway Bridge in

FIGURE 32. New bridges boosted tourism but often wreaked environmental havoc. In 1959, U.S. 98 connected the isolated cities of Fort Walton Beach and Destin through a series of causeways and bridges. State of Florida Photographic Archives, Tallahassee.

1950; on May 9, 1980, the vessel *Summit Venture* struck a southbound piling, plunging a span of the bridge and its traffic into the bay. The new Sunshine Skyway, completed in 1987, has garnered applause by architectural critics, but the bridge has also achieved ignominy as a popular site for suicide jumpers. The bridge to Gasparilla Island opened in 1958. The Howard Frankland Bridge, dedicated in 1960, became the third structure to cross Tampa Bay. Before the completion of the Choctawhatchee Mid-Bay Bridge, the journey from Niceville to Destin required a 30-mile, one-hour drive. The newly constructed bridge cut the distance to 17 miles.[26]

Bridges and roads comfortable by the standards of the Tin Can Tourists and 1920s could not handle new demands of modern travel. The Caterpillar road-grader, wooden barricade, and orange plastic cone became so familiar that they could qualify as state mascots. A road-building frenzy followed World War II. In the 1960s, the state authorized construction of the Sunshine State Parkway (known since as the Florida Turnpike and now the Ronald Reagan Turnpike), a toll road from Wildwood to Miami. The toll road has since made the isolated outposts of Wildwood and Yeehaw Junction familiar names to millions of travelers. In 1939, a writer described Yeehaw, population eight persons, as a "trading center for cattlemen and naval-stores workers." As Yeehaw Junction, the place has gained notoriety as a cultural crossroads for divorced parents to exchange children. Engineers also completed the Everglades Turnpike from Naples to Fort Lauderdale. Because so many reptiles and wild animals died on the dangerous thoroughfare, writer Hampton Dunn dubbed it Alligator Alley. The name stuck.[27]

In American history, the Federal-Aid Highway Act of 1956 represents a stupendous achievement, launching the most expensive and far-reaching public works project in history. Never had a major transportation program aimed so high and delivered so much, with so little thought as to its consequences. President Dwight Eisenhower understood the importance of the national transportation system: as a young army captain in 1917, he had led a motor convoy across America to call attention to the country's pitiful roads; as a general, he had observed the fast-moving, nonstop German Autobahn in the 1940s. In fact, planners rationalized that an American Autobahn would serve the purposes of rapid military mobilization, always a consideration during the Cold War. Politicians promoted the peacetime benefits: the construction of 44,764 miles of interstate highways (1,457 miles planned for Florida), expenditures of $25 billion over a dozen years, and the promise of no tolls. The Highway Trust Fund, brimming with federal gasoline taxes, promised Florida an initial outlay of $110 million and a pledge that federal share of construction costs would be 90 percent. Officials expected the system to be completed in thirteen years; it required forty.[28]

Floridians did not need to be sold on the benefits of Uncle Sam's largesse. Washington had lavished money on roads during World Wars I and II, evidenced by the construction of Dixie Highway and the completion and extension of u.s. 1 to Key West after the 1935 hurricane had derailed Flagler's legacy. Designed in the 1950s, Florida's first four-lane expressways appeared in the 1960s. Interstate 95 ran up the eastern rim of the coastal ridge, paralleling A1A and linking Southeast Florida with the population centers of the American Northeast (although the West Palm Beach–Fort Pierce link was not completed until the 1980s). Interstate 75 connected Tampa and later Sarasota, Fort Myers, Naples, Fort Lauderdale, and Miami with the Midsouth and the Midwest, 1,775 miles in

FIGURE 33. Eerily unoccupied, the newly completed junction of Interstates 4 and 75 awaits Tampa commuters in 1963. Traffic reporters would soon anoint the troubled interchange "malfunction junction." Author's collection.

all. Interstate 10 resurrected the dream of the Old Spanish Highway, bridging East and West Florida and linking Jacksonville to Tallahassee and Pensacola, beyond to New Orleans and Santa Monica, California. It spans 2,460 miles. As late as 1977, Interstate 10 connecting Pensacola to Jacksonville was incomplete, making the 370-mile drive seem even longer. Interstate 4 cleaved the state's peninsula, delivering expressway, nonstop comfort from Tampa to Orlando to Daytona Beach. The funds may have derived from Washington, but the politically charged decisions as to where to locate the highways were made at the local and state levels. The southern extension of I-75 from Tampa to Miami illustrates the politically charged process of route selection. Congressman William Cramer (R–St. Petersburg), ranking minority member on the House Public Works Committee, thwarted the State Turnpike Authority, which had long wanted a toll road along the Tampa-Miami route. The election of President Nixon in 1968 ensured Cramer's dream of a loop through Pinellas County, and

FIGURE 34. Multilaned Interstate 95 cutting a huge swath of land along NW Seventy-first Street in 1960 Miami. State of Florida Photographic Archives, Tallahassee.

Congress subsequently awarded Florida one-sixth of the nation's 1,500 miles of new interstate highway.[29]

While no one could fathom the sheer magnitude of change generated by concrete and asphalt, there was no shortage of soothsayers. The *Tampa Tribune*'s Paul Wilder observed in 1961 that the "expressways" [I-4 and I-75] will completely change the city and the living habits of everyone who lives in Tampa." Another journalist, also writing in 1961, predicted boldly that "Miami could lose its ranking as Florida's biggest metropolis." The reporter predicted a "moon boom" between Orlando and Melbourne, with Titusville its epicenter. Governor Farris Bryant foresaw "the day when there will be one solid city from Cape Canaveral to St. Petersburg." When Walt Disney first flew over Central Florida in November 1963, he surveyed the confluence of the Florida Turnpike, two interstate highways, and McCoy Jet Airport and gesticulated, "That's it." He envisioned the harmonic convergence of transportation and tourism. A half century earlier, Napoleon Bonaparte Broward had surveyed the land south of Orlando, proclaiming, "Water *will* flow downhill." Disney, surveying the same landscape, with visions of new expressways, could have uttered, "Tourists *will* come." He might have added that fast-food franchises, motels, warehouses, and semiconductor factories would also follow. So many people came that politicians and demographers now refer to an "I-4 corridor," a 142-mile concentration of people and businesses stretching from Tampa to Daytona Beach, a mirror not only of Florida but of America.[30]

The law of unintended consequences brought changes Orlando (and other state) civic leaders never imagined. Interstate 4, so it was believed, would save downtown Orlando, already hurt by suburban sprawl and shopping malls. But I-4 never revived downtown Orlando; instead, it encouraged sprawl and accelerated commercial development in unincorporated areas.

Superhighways bore superhuman costs. In Miami, Tampa, St. Petersburg, Jacksonville, and Orlando, planners and businessmen targeted racial and ethnic neighborhoods for extinction, the *intended* consequence of deliberate actions. African American leaders were powerless as I-95 cut through Overtown, the heart of Miami's black community. "Expressway building," contends historian Raymond Mohl, "initiated a vast racial restructuring of Miami's residential space." The destruction of 87 acres of Overtown "triggered a dramatic increase in the growth of the second ghetto," a dispersal of blacks to other African American neighborhoods. Parramore, Orlando's historic black community, was devastated by the construction of the East-West Expressway in the 1970s. In Tampa, planners erased the Central Avenue business district, a historic black neighborhood. In Ybor City and West Tampa, I-4 and I-275 devoured large swaths of the Latin quarters. "Ybor City has never been so divided," wrote a *Tampa Tribune* reporter in June 1962. "The colorful Latin section of Tampa is practically bisected by a two-block strip of desolation, site of future spans making up Interstate Hwy. I-4." José Vega Díaz and his wife, Blanca, had survived the rigors of revolution, immigration, and labor strife, but when bureaucrats made them move, she wailed, "I can't! I can't!" She was dead by sunset. Altogether, interstate highways in Hillsborough County alone razed over 3,300 homes and many family stores and businesses. Rural hamlets, too, were powerless in the face of highway planners. Interstate 75 bisected Long Hammock, isolating Sumter County farmers and shopkeepers from one another. Road building impacted not only the lives of the living; it also disrupted the graves of the dead, slicing through historic cemeteries and Indian mounds.[31]

FIGURE 35. In 1940, Franklin Street in downtown Tampa could be counted as one of the most desirable addresses in the state. The trolley and the city's most prestigious department stores, banks, and movie theaters lined the bustling street. Author's collection.

Planners and bureaucrats built urban expressways to speed motorists in and out of cities; few imagined that people would want to live *under* the interstates. In part because of the opening sequence of the 1983 film *Scarface,* in part because of the specter of homelessness in the 1980s, I-395 in Miami became a notorious address. Thousands of the Marielitos—the Cubans who had arrived as part of the 1980 Mariel boatlift—were detained under an interstate overpass. A decade later, reporter Rick Bragg described the site: "Shantytown is a society all its own, the homeless colony of makeshift huts and mattresses shielded from heat and rain by the Interstate 395 overpass to Miami Beach one block from scenic Biscayne Boulevard."[32]

Land was a commodity, and one price Floridians paid for the freeways was land, lots of it. Governments, employing the power of eminent domain, seized property that once supported farms or fostered neighborhoods. Land speculation rewarded Floridians who by chance or political influence sold property suddenly made valuable by new roadways. Interstate highways cut huge swaths through groves, neighborhoods, and cities—80 acres alone for each interchange. The construction of the I-95 and I-395 interchange in Overtown destroyed 20 square blocks, leaving 10,000 Miamians homeless.[33]

When offered federal incentives and aesthetic opportunities to beautify the interstate landscape, Florida legislators turned a deaf ear. Not even Lady Bird Johnson's blandishments could convince the legislature to plant wildflowers and eliminate billboards on Florida freeways. Once off the interchanges, motorists encounter a familiar clustering of motels, gas stations, and fast-food franchises. Ray Kroc and Edward DeBartolo, the driving geniuses behind McDonald's and DeBartolo Malls, often selected sites for their empires from the cockpits of Lear jets while surveying traffic patterns.[34]

A triumph of technology and engineering, the Federal Interstate Highway System stands as a monument to the best and worst of American society. Floridians' lives have become hopelessly and hopefully intertwined with the superhighway. An emblem to American freedom and mobility, the superhighway also reveals hubris and flaws. Before the 1960s, Florida cities had been virtually untouched by urban freeways; afterward, it was impossible to understand urban life without the monster highways. Aerial views of modern Miami, Orlando, Tampa, and Jacksonville reveal yawning stretches of double-decked freeways, looping cloverleafs, downtown parking lots, overpasses, underpasses, and eight-lane roadways, a treadmill serving the insatiable demands of commuters, tourists, and truckers. An urban parable depicts President Eisenhower studying a map of a proposed interstate dissecting Chicago. The president complained that this was not what he had envisioned. Eisenhower saw the interstate system as a link *between* cities, not as a path *through* cities. True, Interstate 4 made it easier to drive from Orlando to Daytona Beach, but it also made it possible to live in Ormond-by-the-Sea and work in Orlando. Suburban residents depend upon interstates as commuter highways and live farther and farther away from their workplaces, making downtowns irrelevant to many Floridians. A modern traveler pausing at an interchange in South Florida might mistake the packaged, interchangeable motels and fast-food outlets for somewhere in South Dakota.[35]

Interstate highways enabled families to travel faster and longer, opening new markets and spurring construction in the rapidly growing service industry. National chains welcomed the new travelers. Such franchises, notes writer Phil Patton, mirrored the blueprints of America's interstate highways: "a partnership of national standards and know-how with local capital and control." Interstates encouraged speed, efficiency, and homogeneity. Increasingly, families ignore the treasured roads of the 1930s and 1940s, speeding past fading and once-revered tourist attractions for interstate-friendly Walt Disney World and Busch Gardens.[36]

The completion of a national highway network encouraged long-distance trucking, further eroding the railroad. Warehouses that once lined city wharves and downtown districts have relocated near interstates, industrial parks, and airports. Modern travelers whisking along nonstop expressways bypass small tourist establishments located along older highways. Interstates undermined downtowns, spurring suburban development and threatening the central business district. Office parks, suburban shopping malls, and industrial parks rely upon the modern expressways. The capacity of superhighways to move large numbers of cars was hailed for its potential as an evacuation artery during emergencies. Yet in September 1999 and 2004, as millions of Americans fled Hurricanes Floyd and Frances, the motorists turned six-lane expressways into slowly moving parking lots.[37]

In a state where motor traffic can determine economic prosperity, location is paramount. The city of Starke's boom-and-bust fortunes illustrate the relationship between location and transportation. Located in Northeast Florida, the seat of Bradford County, Starke benefited from its nexus with early railroads and highways. The completion of Camp Blanding in the late 1930s brought thousands of workers, families, and soldiers to the bustling crossroads town. The

FIGURE 36. Neither billboards nor nostalgia kept Americans from abandoning Florida's historic roads in favor of the fast-paced, nonstop, direct-line interstate highway in the 1960s and 1970s. State of Florida Photographic Archives, Tallahassee.

New York Sun's Ward Morehouse pronounced Starke as "gauche, neoned and streamlined." The town's population doubled during the 1940s. The completion of Highway 301 running from Baltimore to Sarasota seemed to seal Starke's future. Or so it seemed. Almost 7,000 cars whisked by on a typical summer's day in 1959. New motels welcomed the hordes of tourists headed southward. The city even boasted a powerful patron, native son Charley Johns, who wielded power in the Florida Senate and served briefly as governor from 1953 to 1955. But Starke's future turned as bleak as its name. The new superhighways bypassed Starke. Interstates 10 and 95 isolated Starke, sending the city into decline.[38]

The automobile serves as grim reaper. Three thousand persons died as the result of traffic crashes in Florida in 2000. But the car erodes the quality of life in other measurable ways. In a nation of polls and lists, Florida ranked high in every study correlating the automobile and negativity. When several studies indicated that four of the nation's "most dangerous" traffic spots existed in Florida, residents expressed astonishment that the state got off so lightly. Broward County leads the state in traffic bottlenecks. Lists simply reminded residents what they already knew: Florida motorists face aggravating and costly commutes; pedestrians (especially seniors) in Fort Lauderdale, Miami, Tampa, Clearwater, Orlando, Hialeah, St. Petersburg, Jacksonville, Cape Coral, Coral Springs, Tallahassee, and Pembroke Pines were as likely to be killed by cars as almost any place in the United States. The Sunshine State also led the nation in traffic deaths involving drivers older than seventy (268 in 2000). The 1990s introduced the latest motorist hazards: road rage, ram-and-rob murders, attacks at visitor centers, and impalement caused by debris and junk left on roadways.[39]

The automobile has exacted a grievous price upon the Florida landscape. An automobile-driven society has required architects to adapt; the three-car garage is now standard in new subdivisions. Suburbia's rapacious appetite for and reliance upon the automobile have turned rush hour into gridlock. Earlier generations prided themselves on picturesque highways that brought country and city together. Today, Floridians regard the grid of expressways and roads as barrier, not as an escape. In Tallahassee, the legendary oak-canopied roads once radiated like spokes from the Capitol. "In slicing S.R. 50 through the middle of Orlando," writes Robert Foglesong, "magnificent trees were uprooted to howls of protest, part of two lakes were filled, and once attractive Colonial Avenue was transformed into a major commercial strip." U.S. 192 connecting Kissimmee with I-4 also ranks as one of the state's most unattractive roadways. Miami activist Elizabeth Virrick complained that Miami was afflicted with "bulldozitis followed rapidly by asphaltitis." Urban critic James Kunstler flails the Florida roadside as "violent and tawdry." He adds, "There is little sense of having arrived anywhere, because everyplace looks like no place in particular."[40]

How will cities and counties move increasing numbers of commuters without building more and more lanes of expressways? The 2000 census revealed that fewer than two in one hundred Floridians used public transportation to commute to work (responses ranged from a high of 11.4 percent of Miami commuters to a low of 1.4 percent of Hillsborough County workers). As early as the 1950s, Miami leaders searched for an answer to the city's transportation headaches. Miami remains Florida's best example of a city at least partly committed to a collective solution to urban transportation. During the late 1970s, the Carter administration lavished federal dollars to construct a mass transit system. Opening in 1984, Miami Metrorail ran from Dadeland Mall in the south to downtown, a 21-mile elevated and groundrail system costing a staggering $1 billion ($50 million per mile). In 2000, 14 million persons utilized the Metrorail; in contrast, that same year 35 million, 82 million, and 97 million passengers boarded subway/rail systems in Los Angeles, Atlanta, and San Francisco. Jacksonville has also attempted, on a more modest scale, an elevated transit system to relieve urban congestion. The Automatic Skyway Express (ASE) originally extended only seven-tenths of a mile, connecting downtown with the Prime Osborne Convention Center. Opened in 1989, the ASE cost as much but delivered only about a thousand passengers a day (one-tenth the estimate). In spite of determined opposition, Congress funded a $184 million two-and-one-half-mile extension. Thus far, few residents have surrendered their cars for the people mover. In 2000, only 2 percent of Duval County commuters used buses or rail. Critics argue that mass transit solutions are doomed because of Florida's low levels of population density and dependence upon the automobile. Most commuters travel not between the suburbs and downtown but between suburbs, where most of the new jobs are now located. Defenders contend that mass transit must be made to work, since paving over paradise with sixteen-lane expressways offers no solution.[41]

Art imitates life. The automobile and cinema trace their roots to the dynamic milieu of the late nineteenth century and grew to become major disseminators of American culture. Whether cast as vehicles of escape, romance, or danger, the automobile and Hollywood served one another well. John Schlesinger's *Honky Tonk Freeway* (1981) offered a parable for small-town Florida victimized by the car. In spite of a well-placed bribe, the citizens of Ticlaw (Mount Dora) learn that the new superhighway would bypass their city. Locals blow up an overpass and build an exit ramp into town. Alas, the low life headed toward Orlando instead descended upon Ticlaw. Cars and tourists—can't live with them, can't live without them. The cinema and automobile came together in still another way: the drive-in.

The Drive-In

The drive-in is pure Americana, with a generous slice of Florida. Starkly designed with a flat lot, earthen berms to accommodate parked cars, rows of crudely built speakers, and a concrete-block screen, the drive-in's daylight form changed hues and roles at dusk, acquiring its iconic and legendary status. The drive-in theater resulted from the harmonic convergence of three great national themes: Americans' love for cars, movies, and personal freedom. Invented in 1933 in Camden, New Jersey, the drive-in spread to Miami in 1938 and to Jacksonville (The Atlantic) the following year. At their peak in the late 1950s, 4,000 drive-ins graced American cities and towns, including 158 in Florida. Curiously for a state known for its sunshine, it was Florida's starry nights and year-round weather that made the drive-in a perfect match. The DDT fogger, citronella mosquito coils, and (rare) underground air-conditioning system that piped chilled air through tubes and out the window speaker made evenings synonymous with the outdoor big screen.[42]

The drive-in offered a generous slice of Floridiana. The Federal Highway paralleling the East coast was a favorite destination for drive-in devotees. The Swap-Shop in Delray Beach was so popular on Sunday evenings that traffic backed up. For a society enthralled with the "moon boom" in Brevard County, the Island Beach Theater on the Cocoa Causeway allowed workers and teenagers to enjoy the moon and spoon. To lure customers from as far away as Belle Glade, Thursday nights featured Spanish-language films. The Ocala Drive-In on U.S. 441/27 was built in the 1950s in the classical style: straight, terraced rows with a rooftop projector and mounted window speakers for each car. Fort Lauderdale's Thunderbird Drive-In, America's largest, doubles as a flea market. The Naples Drive-In was built on the edge of a swamp. The Ponce DeLeon Drive-In, still operating in the Panhandle, is one of the smallest venues, with room for just sixty cars. Florida's most celebrated drive-in may be the Flamingo, the fictional creation of novelist Larry Baker. In *The Flamingo Rising* (1997), Baker located the structure between Jacksonville and St. Augustine: "Facing AIA was the world's largest neon marquee, a glaring pink flamingo whose head continually dipped and whose body rested on one leg while the other extended and retracted."[43]

Drive-ins appealed to Floridians wishing to defy conventions. In the privacy of one's car, one could smoke, drink beer, and neck. If popcorn and soda were standard fare at the downtown Bijou, the North Side Drive-In in North Fort Myers offered patrons biscuits and gravy. Jacksonville's Playtime Family Drive-In specialized in navy bean soup, proper cuisine in a navy town.[44]

The drive-in's demise sounds a familiar lament in modern Florida. When the owner of Florida's first drive-in attempted to place an advertisement in the *Times-Union*, the salesman asked, "You put a screen up to show movies outdoors?" In 1972, Publix purchased Jacksonville's Atlantic Drive-In. By the 1980s, rocketing land values made spacious, treeless lots valuable commodities. What had seemed like cutting-edge technology in the 1950s (window speakers and images flickered on concrete-block screens) seemed obsolete in an age of digital images, DVDs, cable TV, and megaplex theaters. Even the drive-ins' romantic allure—preachers called them "passion pits"—dimmed as sex saturated every crevice of society. One by one, DeLand's Boulevard Drive-In, the Pasco Drive-In Theater, the Clervue at Clermont, Winter Garden's Star-Lite, and

FIGURE 37. The drive-in combined the most irresistible elements of Floridiana: cinema, sex, the automobile, and warm summer nights. Tallahassee's Four Points Drive-In, 1954. State of Florida Photographic Archives, Tallahassee.

others closed. In 2000, twenty-nine drive-ins still operated in Florida (down to nine in 2003). Drive-ins have morphed into flea markets and car lots, but mostly they have been gobbled up as real estate.[45]

Entrepreneurial ingenuity, Americans' love affair with their cars, and year-round sunshine popularized another form of drive-in—the fast-food eatery. Just blink the car lights for curb service. First popularized in the 1920s, the carhop drive-in reached its apogee in the 1950s. *Saturday Evening Post* paid homage to the Hut in West Palm Beach in a 22 June 1946 story. To appreciate the breadth of Florida's home-grown, drive-in teenage culture, one need only look at high-school yearbooks in the 1950s and 1960s. National chains rushed to emulate the success of the Smack in Sarasota, Tampa's Goody-Goody, or Miami's Royal Castle. The franchising of Florida has come in an astonishingly brief period of time, made possible by affluence, mobility, changing tastes, the changing American family, suburbia, and the interstate highway system. Today's Burger King traces its origins to the early 1950s and the first self-service drive-ins in Jacksonville and Miami. Giant signs boldly announced in neon, "Broiled Burgers, Thick Shakes, 19¢." Atop the sign sat a king astride a hamburger throne and holding aloft a milkshake. Orlando acquired its first Burger King in 1958 (and its first McDonald's in 1960). In 1975, Burger King inaugurated the concept of the drive-thru. From those beginnings, Burger King has grown to over

400 franchises in Florida. In 1957, Florida had 44 McDonald's; by 2000, Hillsborough County alone claimed 50.[46]

Subway, the state's leader in fast-food franchises, opened its first Florida store in Fort Lauderdale in 1976. In 1954, 7-Eleven opened a convenience store in Florida, its first operation outside Texas. Starbucks came relatively late to Florida, an understandable time lag considering the caffeinated state of Miami's and Tampa's Cuban communities. On February 22, 1997, Starbucks opened its first three stores in South Florida, the beginning of an expansion binge that brought 254 establishments statewide by 2004. The popular for-profit coffee shop chain now operates in nonprofit college and public libraries. Unerringly familiar, McDonald's, 7-Eleven, and Burger King offer travelers a reassuring experience. Fast food, writes Eric Schlosser, "is now served at not only restaurants and drive-thrus, but also at stadiums, airports, college campuses and elementary schools, on cruise ships, at Kmarts and Wal-Marts." The formula works, at least for the franchises. In 2000, consumers spent over $100 billion on fast food, up from $6 billion in 1970. Boca Grande, Sanibel, and a handful of other discriminating locales have voted to ban fast-food franchises.[47]

The Malling of Florida

Midcentury Florida offered shoppers a smorgasbord of choices. The large downtown department store reached its apogee in the 1950s, for decades luring customers with upscale brands and impeccable taste, making window shopping synonymous with urbanity. Burdines and Maas Brothers, once privileged sanctuaries of Miami and Tampa, expanded to downtown Fort Lauderdale, West Palm Beach, St. Petersburg, Lakeland, and Sarasota. The expansive interiors of Orlando's Dickson and Ives and Jacksonville's Cohen Brothers contrasted sharply with hundreds of wood-framed country stores across the state. In small towns and big cities, family-run grocery and hardware stores still predominated.

Throughout the 1950s, downtowns functioned as places of consumption, sociability, and glamour. African Americans, too, wished to participate in the consumers' paradise but were denied full citizenship. Signs of the Jim Crow society were everywhere: "colored" water fountains, separate waiting rooms, and black and white sections at movie theaters, ballparks, and courthouses. More striking than the "colored" and "white" signs of segregation was the code of conduct expected and demanded. Racial etiquette demanded that black cus-

FIGURE 38. Beginning in Greensboro, North Carolina, the civil rights movement spread across the South and Florida. On 13 March 1960, students from FAMU and Florida State conduct a sit-in at Woolworth's lunch counter in Tallahassee. State of Florida Photographic Archives, Tallahassee.

tomers not try on bathing suits or dresses, sit at downtown luncheon counters, or use public restrooms. While over half of Jacksonville's African American teachers held charge accounts at Cohen Brothers, the store refused black professionals a place at its lunchroom. In Fort Lauderdale, the Greyhound bus station was the only downtown establishment to allow blacks access to its restroom. In Fort Myers, while white patrons walked through the front doors of the Snack House restaurant, blacks picked up their orders in the alley.[48]

When in March 1960, the civil rights revolution spread across Florida, black leaders chose their targets deliberately. In Jacksonville, African Americans demanded service at Cohen's lunchroom. In Tampa and Miami, black students and ministers launched sit-ins at Woolworth and Kress stores. Civil disobedience and passive resistance worked. The Civil Rights Act of 1964 outlawed racial segregation in public accommodations. Ironically, the civil right triumphs occurred precisely at the moment Floridians began abandoning their downtowns. Suburban malls lured customers not only with free parking but with the implicit promise of a largely white clientele.[49]

Shopping strips paved the path between downtown and suburbia. The strip plaza blossomed in the 1950s, a perfect fit in a state oriented toward low-density development and low-rise roadside commerce. The era of the four-story, downtown department store was fading; the era of the retail strip was dawning. In late-twentieth-century Florida, the motorist triumphed over the pedestrian. The large department stores, with their revolving doors, tea rooms, and escalators, became victims of their location. Design followed strip-mall function. One-story stores set back from the highway allowed motorists to park, shop, and drive away with speed and efficiency. Cheap land encouraged businesses to expand horizontally. Above all, free parking and accessibility determined the shopping strips' future. In 1954, the *Miami Herald* presciently announced that a revolution in shopping was soon to come to South Florida. The strip plaza was passé; a new wave of shopping centers awaited ribbon cutting. "None of the centers [will] look alike," the *Herald* assured its readers.[50]

Capitalism continually reinvents itself. More sophisticated than the strip mall, the shopping center represented a triumph of individualism, affluence, and consumption in an automobile-driven, consumer-oriented, mobile society. The shopping center appealed to Floridians' growing distaste for parking meters, downtowns, and the inner city. The formula, first perfected in the 1950s and endlessly repeated in big towns and instant cities, was simple: obtain inexpensive land along a busy road, level the site, build a large parking lot and an open-air walkway, string together an L- or U-shaped assortment of small shops, lure a magnet—a Winn-Dixie, Eckerd, and a small department store—secure a catchy name (Gateway Center or The Groves), and announce a ribbon cutting. By the late 1970s, almost 20,000 such centers blanketed the United States.[51]

Large-scale retailing quickly advanced from the strip mall to shopping center to suburban mall. The first indoor, climate-controlled complex, Southdale Center, opened near Minneapolis in 1956. What heating accomplished for an indoor mall in a Minnesota January, air conditioning achieved in a Florida July. During the next four decades, over 1,500 such enclosed malls opened in the United States, with hundreds appearing in Florida. Indeed, by the early 1970s, Florida claimed the fourth-largest number of shopping centers in the United States. Malls, as distinguished from shopping centers, bring an interior orientation, dramatized by a showy entrance. Shopping centers are often anchored by grocery stores; malls need large department stores. Shopping centers em-

FIGURE 39. Shopping patterns quickly changed in the 1950s and 1960s from downtown to shopping centers to suburban malls. In 1958, Brevard County residents patronized Patrick Plaza. Note the sprawling new development of Patrick Shores in the background. State of Florida Photographic Archives, Tallahaseee.

phasize efficiency, time savings, and no-frills accessibility; malls encourage, indeed instill, the notion of leisure, timelessness, and glamour. Both establishments draw heavily upon female consumers. By 2000, over 45,000 malls blanketed the United States, generating $46.6 billion in sales taxes.[52]

In Dade County, shopping centers came earlier and in greater number than in any other place in Florida. Astonishingly, Dade County counted over fifty commercial plazas by 1960. A mercantile arms race was underway. The first shopping center, by which all others would be measured, was the 163rd Street Center. When it opened in 1956, the complex—which included a Burdines— was the largest in the South. The names of the first-generation malls—Northside, Central Shopping Plaza, Cutler Ridge, Flamingo Plaza, and Coral Gate Center—became landmarks but failed to sustain commercial dynamism. Competition and second-generation malls generating new levels of excitement and design undercut the pioneering shopping centers. Anchor stores added an allure. By 1962, the *Herald* promised that "the average housewife in Greater Miami will be little more than a coin's throw from a major shopping center."[53]

The history of retail shopping in modern Manatee County incorporates a familiar arc. Manatee County's first "covered shopping center" opened in 1959. Built upon a fruit stand and grapefruit grove on the busy corner of u.s. 41 and Cortez Road, Cortez Plaza opened to great fanfare. Florida's third-largest Belk-Lindsey store delighted shoppers who no longer had to travel to downtown Sarasota or Bradenton. To take advantage of the sprawling populations of Sarasota and Manatee counties, Bayshore Gardens Shopping Center also opened in 1959. It included the Cinema, "equipped with the largest screen in the South." The new development drew upon Trailer Estates, the state's largest mobile home park. In 1971, the DeBartolo Corp. purchased 100 acres of land on u.s. 301 and Cortez Road (uprooting an orange grove and trailer park). In August 1973, Manatee County's first enclosed, under-one-roof mall, De Soto Square, was born. Offering shoppers new and improved amenities—a six-foot statue of De Soto, a fountain, a Maas Brothers department store, a Sears, twelve shoe stores, and a four-screen theater—De Soto Square was chic. So popular was the attraction that bus service connected retirement communities and the mall. The opening of Brandon Town Center and the Ellenton Prime Outlets Mall in the 1990s drew away customers, but De Soto Square has managed better than most, in part because of shifting demographics in fast-growing east Manatee County. Revamped but dowdy Bayshore Gardens and Cortez Plaza struggle to remain relevant. In Southwest Florida or the American Southwest, malls must reinvent, adapt, or die.[54]

New shopping centers quickly appeared on Orlando's urban periphery. In rapid succession, the Western Way Shopping Center, the Azalea Shopping Center, the Colonial Plaza Mall, and the Orange Blossom Shopping Center drained shoppers away from downtown Orlando. Over 150,000 Central Floridians jammed the roads to participate in the opening of the Colonial Plaza Mall on 31 January 1956. Thomas Gilbert Lee sold 20 acres of his dairy to a New York investment group for $200,000. The $3.5 million Colonial Plaza, then the largest commercial development in Orange County history, sprang up at Colonial Drive and Bumby Avenue. Each successive mall offered new amenities for shoppers. Old businesses—some revered as institutions—followed the crowds. Walgreen's, J. C. Penney, and Ivey's left their downtown locations for the newer malls. Downtown Orlando reeled from the closures, none more painful than the loss of the beloved Dickson and Ives Department Store. Newer, more celebrated shrines to shopping appeared. The arrival of Jordan Marsh in 1962 heralded the first department store to be built outside downtown Orlando. Anchoring the new Colonial Plaza mall, Jordan Marsh—with its famed escalators, also a first—signaled Orlando's coming of age.[55]

Upon completion in 1974, Altamonte Mall, located on pastureland near I-4 in Altamonte Springs, was hailed as the largest shopping center in the American Southeast. Touted as Central Florida's second-greatest tourist attraction, the Altamonte Mall offered four "magnet" department stores along with 140 smaller establishments. So many traffic jams paralyzed S.R. 436 that locals cursed the road as the "world's largest parking lot."[56]

Ballyhooed as the South's most glorious suburban shopping center, Dadeland opened in Kendall in October 1962. Executives had chosen the site from a blimp. Critics derided the location as "Deadland." But Dadeland dazzled shoppers and statisticians: the mall boasted 1.5 million square feet of space needed to house its 175 stores, 9,000 employees, and 8,000 parking spaces. By the late 1980s, Dadeland was drawing 30 million shoppers a year, one of America's most successful malls. Dadeland endures, successful because of timing, place, and demographics.[57]

By the 1990s, megamalls vied for commercial and spatial supremacy, each bringing new elements in space, aesthetics, and function. Since its 1989 opening, Sawgrass Mills Mall, located in Sunrise, has emerged as one of the most popular tourist spots in Florida. Located ten minutes from I-495 and the Florida Turnpike, Sawgrass Mills combined elements of the modern theme park and a designer outlet mall. Its 200 stores included Saks Fifth Avenue and Waccamaw. In 1998, more than 24 million people visited the 2-million-square-foot, alligator-shaped institution, the largest mall in Florida. The Broward County mall also added a $50 million entertainment center, the Oasis, a menagerie of popular restaurants, a GameWorks Arcade, and colorful fountains.[58]

Just at the moment suburbia and the shopping center seemed perfectly aligned, the urban mall returned. Inspired by the success of Baltimore's revitalized waterfront and James Rouse's vision, politicians and financiers sought to duplicate the "festive marketplace," which combined shopping, entertainment, and atmosphere. The dedication of CoCoWalk in 1990 marked a spectacular beginning. French investors had gambled that Coconut Grove, a historic Miami neighborhood, was ideal for an open-air entertainment center. The opening of CoCoWalk profoundly changed the neighborhood's rhythms. The young and the beautiful crowded streets and cafes. Not everyone cheered CoCoWalk's success. Many neighbors despaired at the attraction's crowds, likening weekend traffic to "Dante's ninth circle of Hell." When sold to Chicago investors in 1998,

CoCoWalk's $429-per-square-foot price set a South Florida real estate record. The urban theme has been exported to Beach Place in Fort Lauderdale, Riverwalk in Jacksonville, and BayWalk in St. Petersburg. Centro Ybor, the latest Yaromir Steiner design, opened in 2000 in Tampa's historic Ybor City. The City of Tampa has invested hundreds of millions of dollars (tax benefits, parking garages, cruise terminals, and even a retro trolley) to reinvent Ybor City. Centro Ybor opened to disappointing crowds, in part because of a rival entertainment complex, Channelside. In West Palm Beach, the mid-1990s redevelopment of Clematis Street brought shoppers and residents back to the city's decaying urban core. The opening of CityPlace, a mixed-use, $550 million development only three blocks away, emptied the shops and restaurant along the earlier project. Ironically, the appearance of the glitzy, urban entertainment-shopping complexes comes at a time when the downtown department store—once the acme of glamour, urbanity, and consumption—is now extinct in Florida (except in Miami).[59]

Wal-Mart, Target, and other megastores have combined elements of the old department store and former retail giants (Montgomery Ward and Sears). Since its first store opened in 1962, Wal-Mart has offered shoppers low prices through ruthless economies of scale and efficiency. After opening its first Florida store in Quincy in 1982, Wal-Mart's Florida empire in 2003 included 182 stores and 68,000 employees. Wal-Mart has begun to lure high-income shoppers who find, under one roof, designer jeans and brand-name appliances. In Miami and Tampa, but also in Clewiston and Apopka, Kmarts as well as family-owned stores succumb to Wal-Mart.[60]

Scores of first-generation shopping centers and ill-placed, ill-designed malls have become dead zones; hundreds of others struggle to readapt. Some abandoned shopping centers have recruited churches and schools as tenants. The latest retail reincarnation involves the retro, open-air "power center," essentially a reinvented, decentralized, unenclosed mall. The concept first took hold in Palm Beach County, a commercial bellwether. Once popular, the Twin City and Delray Beach Malls lost their luster in the 1990s. Developers tore them down and replaced them with outdoor centers. Palm Beach Mall is also slated for a retro look. In 1973, shoppers cheered the opening of the 75-acre Clearwater Mall. Demolished in 2000, it has become an outdoor mall. Opened in the 1960s to large crowds, the Winter Park Mall, with its centerpiece champagne-glass fountain, was shuttered by the early 1990s. Reopened as a trendy plaza, it draws people to its outdoor cafes, movie theaters, and apartments.[61]

Malls have become more than simply big shopping centers; they now assume the roles of downtown, town square, and community center. In a morning ritual, senior citizens flock to malls to use the long walkways as exercise centers and social hubs. The suburban mall served as a comfortable refuge, an idealized downtown for Florida's middle classes. Attracting customers who are both pulled by suburbia's amenities (employment, housing, and safety) and repelled by inner-city fears (racial minorities, poverty, and slums), the mall became a potent symbol of what historian Lizabeth Cohen calls a "Consumers' Republic." Psychologist Robert Coles noted that by the 1970s the Saturday visit to the mall, meeting friends to walk from store to store, had become a new communal ritual in America. Malls defined and divided Floridians, offering citizens a new sense of community without the commitments. Advertisements touting property as being close to an upscale mall reassured buyers that the neighborhood was safe. Malls contributed to a new quality of life desired by Floridians. Where once work or ethnicity determined one's residence, increasingly, amenities govern such choices.[62]

Malls carefully cultivate reputations, subtly practicing politics of exclusion. "But shopping centers did not inadvertently exclude simply by virtue of their suburban location," notes Cohen. "Rather, developers deliberately defined their communities through a combination of careful site selection, marketing, and policing." African American leaders have charged that malls have discouraged public transportation access. Middle-class African Americans exercise the same consumer freedoms as whites, further eroding historic black business districts and limiting choices of inner-city residents.[63]

Malls and shopping centers helped a generation read and understand a shifting social gyroscope. Pam Gibson, today a librarian, came of age in Bradenton when Cortez Plaza and Bayshore Gardens became town centers, places for youth to socialize. Growing up in Pic-Town, a trailer park along U.S. 41, she recalls coming home one day as a young girl to see a huge fire. "Oh," said Mom, "they're just burning off the trees to build a new shopping center." The burned-out grove became Cortez Plaza. Her world soon revolved around Cortez Plaza: her parent's mixed-league bowling on Friday nights, the bookstore, Kresge's. "In other words, people sort of lived at these shopping centers." Not surprisingly, the mall has become a popular place for American teenagers to gather and hang out, even the site for senior proms.[64]

Shopping centers and department stores, so perfectly attuned to the values of the postwar era, seem oddly misaligned at the end of the century. In a Wal-

Mart, Internet-driven, exhaust-choked world, the enclosed mall seems obsolete. The department store, once the literal and figurative anchor of the mall, struggles to rediscover its magic and purpose. The demise of Maas Brothers, Cohen Brothers, and Jordan Marsh devastated and confused faithful customers. Once the department store moved from its downtown locations, it lost its iconic status; Burdines and Maas Brothers never carried the same cachet in suburbia.[65]

Homes on Wheels

While the automobile made possible the shopping mall, the trailer seemed at home in a state where most neighbors are from somewhere else, where roots are as shallow as the Australian pine's, where any vehicle can function not only as transportation but also as housing. A transient state, inexpensive land, lax zoning restrictions, and the inevitable law of supply and demand created a climate where today one in eight homes is a trailer, and nearly one in five Florida public school students attends class in a "portable."[66] The presence of the portable classroom has been especially noticeable in Orange County. From only 45 portables in 1984, the number of mobile classrooms has grown to over 4,200 portables in 2004.[67]

The first trailer campers—really wooden boxes mounted on trucks or a flatbed pulled by a Model T—appeared in the 1920s. Tin Can Tourists left their worries in the North and camped in Florida. Capitalizing upon Florida's inexpensive land values, some of the earliest trailer camps were situated on dreamy locations. Sunny South, located on NW Seventy-ninth Street in Miami, dates from 1925. Describing one such park on Miami's Biscayne Boulevard, *Fortune* magazine described the invasion of "expensive rigs." While devastating automobile manufacturers, the Great Depression boosted the fledgling trailer industry, giving birth to icons such as the Traveleze, Schult Aristocrat, Wally Byam Airstream, Aloja Sportsman, and Silver Streak Clipper. A veritable invasion of trailers headed for Florida, prompting such reactions as: "We are facing a movement of population besides which even the crusades will seem like Sunday school picnics." To be sure, trailer camps had appeared alongside military bases, shipyards, and migrant labor quarters, but the "motor bungalows" were considered respectably middle class until the 1950s stigmatized the mobile home as working class.[68]

FIGURE 40. To millions of retirees, trailer parks such as this 1962 complex in Leesburg offered an inexpensive slice of paradise. State of Florida Photographic Archives, Tallahassee.

The 1950 U.S. Census was the first to ask Americans about mobile homes. Enumerators took notice of 19,595 "houses on wheels." Within a decade, Pinellas County alone had almost as many as the entire state in 1950.[69] Once a curiosity, the mobile home found a niche in Florida's economy and Americans' lifestyle. By 1970, the statewide mobile home count had grown to 200,000. The 2000 Census identified 850,000 mobile homes: some rested on concrete blocks in crowded trailer parks; for others, the famed 16-foot double-wide, anchored down and immobile, became unrecognizable from the street as a house on wheels; while a few cruised the state as genuine *mobile* homes. The only time most mobile homes are on wheels is when they are being rolled from factory to lot. After four decades at the top, Pinellas County has surrendered the title of mobile home capital to Polk County. In 2000, Polk's 84,141 mobile homes led the state, followed by Hillsborough, Pinellas, Pasco, Lee, and Manatee counties. Over half of America's mobile homes can be found south of Orlando.[70]

Capitalism constantly reenergizes Florida, and it has broadened the possibilities of the Florida dream. From a trailer to a mobile home to a manufactured home, industry has responded to the needs of all classes. From the beginning, senior citizens on modest budgets comprised the biggest market in Florida, an exception to national sales. America's first mobile-home subdivision appeared in Bradenton. Opened and run by the Kiwanis Club since 1936, the Bradenton Trailer Park appealed to retirees on meager monthly pensions. By the 1950s, 3,000 residents called Bradenton Trailer Park home. The 1950s also introduced the 10-foot-wide mobile home, which more closely resembled a "real" home and dominated the market. By the 1960s, 12-foot-wide mobile homes had become the norm. The nation's first all-modular home development, St. Augustine Shores, attracted buyers who wished to move up from their mobile homes. In 1976, industry officials promoted the more semantically pleasing, euphemistic term *manufactured home*. Politicians know all too well that mobile home residents vote and attend city council meetings. In 1965, lobbyists helped pass legislation that taxed mobile homes as vehicles rather than property. In 1984, Congress directed the Veterans Administration to allow mobile homes to receive the same mortgage financial benefits as conventional housing.[71]

Sydney Adler keenly understood market forces and Florida dreams. A World War II veteran, he moved to Miami in 1946. Following law school, he convinced several friends to invest in a daring scheme. In 1955, trailer parks were popping up like strip malls in Florida. Adler added a new wrinkle to the landscape. He would sell, rather than rent, lots to the mobile home folk, in effect, creating a more cohesive residential community. He would offer amenities to attract middle-class retirees. Adler purchased 160 acres of land in Manatee County between u.s. 41 and Sarasota Bay. "I knew nothing about the trailer business," he confessed. At the time, Manatee County had no restrictions on subdivisions, so Adler implemented his ideas: $898 for the lot and monthly fees not to exceed fifteen dollars. Adler erected a display at the Michigan State Fair featuring a mobile home flanked by a palm tree and a TV. A sign read, "Put yourself in this pix." Another advertisement depicted fashionable beachcombers strolling next to a trailer. "Now, own your own Trailer Estate," read the ad.[72]

Trailer Estates opened in 1955. By 1958, its newsletter claimed status as the "world's largest trailer community." Trailer Estates also boasted a "master TV antenna system," a marina, and a grocery store. Adler eventually sold the park, and Trailer Estates became an age-restricted community. In 1998, one waterfront lot sold for $200,000. Once the largest trailer park in the world, by the 1990s it was only the thirtieth-largest in Manatee County. Today, Florida boasts over 3,500 mobile home communities.[73]

Mobile home living reinforced Florida's transient character. In the winter season, trailer parks and camping sites fill to capacity. In some counties, mobile homes have become a familiar part of the new residential fabric. In Citrus, Pasco, Hendry, Manatee, and Lee counties, one in four households owns or lives in a mobile home, anchored trailer, or recreational utility vehicle. In Lake and Highlands counties, one-third of the households own such mobile housing, and in Glades and Dixie counties, an astonishing one-half of housing units are mobile homes. On and around military bases, the trailer has become as familiar as the barracks.[74]

From their humble beginnings, the mobile home and trailer park became synonymous with low-brow culture and the working classes. The 1990s flooded the landscape with pricey recreational vehicles (RVs) and upscale parks to harbor palaces on wheels. Not long ago, the brand names Winnebago and Airstream elicited nods of approval from cognoscenti. In Naples, pastel driveways, lakes stocked with koi fish, and an 8,000-square-foot clubhouse beckon 40-foot motor coaches, some costing over a million dollars. An anchorage for Canadian-made Prevosts and Newell motor coaches, Pelican Lake may be America's most exclusive "trailer park." Other glamorous addresses define upscale. Six Lakes Country Club of North Fort Myers contains about 600 motor home lots surrounding a private eighteen-hole golf course.[75]

Class biases continue to stigmatize trailer parks. Witness a joke circulating among FSU alums: "What do tornadoes and University of Florida graduates have in common? They both end up at trailer parks." The Middle River Trailer Park in Wilton Manors (Broward Co.) served as the tawdry setting for producers of *Strip Tease*, the Carl Hiaasen novel adapted to film. Cities that once welcomed trailer parks as economic stimuli now scorn them as social pariahs. Hurricanes Andrew, Charley, and Frances, and rising land prices accomplished what zoning officials would not or could not, the destruction of 20,000 mobile homes. Delray Beach may have been the first city to prohibit mobile homes, when its 1960 ordinance forbade trailers that were used as "living quarters." Cents and sensibilities made Key West a favored destination for Volkswagen vans and trailers in the 1970s and 1980s. Key West land values, it seems, are more in tune with Warren Buffett than Jimmy Buffett. Key West also has lost its only drive-in, the Islander. Skyrocketing land values elsewhere have put the brake on trailer parks. For the first time in a half century, the state's percentage of mobile homes in 2000 declined. The number of mobile home parks in Miami-Dade plunged in the 1990s. For all of the mean-spirited, patronizing slurs, trailer parks allowed millions of Americans to enjoy a slice of the good life. The wealthy should not have a monopoly on dreams or paradise. And for all of its class distinctions, the mobile home provided millions of Americans fair-weather housing in a warm-weather state.[76]

Wings over Florida

New highways and powerful v-8 engines helped alleviate the dictates of Florida geography, but in a postwar world obsessed with speed and time, other technologies conquered the tyranny of distance. Florida's beaches and resorts were alluring, but Chicago was still 1,000 miles from Panama City, and Fort Lauderdale 1,250 miles from New York. World War II had generously endowed Florida with paved runways, modern hangars, and air bases. Cities quickly converted deactivated airports into municipal assets. "There will be a new world, of course, after the war," the *Tallahassee Daily Democrat* had boldly predicted in 1942. "It will be the era of air." Perhaps most important, the war had welded a bond of trust and faith between Americans and the unnatural act of flying at 20,000 feet inside a fuselage held together by thin layers of aluminum. The pre-1960s Pan Am Sikorsky Clippers and Stratocruisers glamorized flight, combining elegance and air travel, symbolized by the stylish pill-box-hat-wearing stewardesses. The trustworthy Douglas DC-3, the "Gooney Bird," convinced Americans that air travel was safe. First airborne in 1935, the DC-3 was also the first passenger plane to make money for the airlines. In 1948, Pan Am introduced a new type of service—economy class. Flying, once a privilege of the wealthy, was becoming democratized. In the 1950s, National Airlines advertised, "A Millionaire's Vacation on a Piggy Bank Budget." Cities celebrated the coming of jets and air service as they once threw parades for the arrival of railroads. In 1956, National's inaugural New York–Sarasota flight brought out Bradenton's DeSoto Queen, the Sunshine Springs Aquabelles, and long lines of public officials.[77]

If the slow but reliable DC-3 symbolized early commercial aviation, the DC-7 and DC-8 were emblems of early jet travel. In 1957, a prescient journalist predicted that Florida "is on the threshold of the jet age and its tourist business may see great change." As early as 1950, officials predicted the imminent arrival of jet service in Miami. Predictions came true in 1958. Soon, National Airlines DC-8s were whisking New York passengers to the Magic City in little more than two hours, ninety minutes faster than the old prop planes. The era of the courtly transatlantic cruise nearly ended when Pam Am inaugurated nonstop service on its jet-powered Boeing 707s. A new language followed: jetport, jet lag, and jet set. Cities faced immense challenges in building modern airports to handle new generations of planes and passengers.[78]

Miami understood the potential of air traffic decades before the 1950s. The city had been a major air hub since the 1930s, the headquarters for three leading carriers: Eastern, Pan American, and National. The *Miami Herald* promoted aviation with its column "Wings over Miami." Aggressively taking advantage of its location and facilities, South Florida became a gateway for international air travel. As late as 1990, Miami and New York City offered the only regularly scheduled flights to Buenos Aires, Caracas, and Bogota. The Dallas–Fort Worth metroplex, for instance, did not even offer international flight service until 1978.[79]

Called Dade County's number-one "economic engine," Miami International Airport (MIA) is largely responsible for 300,000 jobs (airport, trucking, tourism, and aviation). In 2000, almost 35 million passengers passed through MIA, making it Florida's busiest facility, ranking first among U.S. airports in international cargo and second in international passengers. Critics—and they are legion—lampoon MIA for its aging facilities, poor service, lax security, cost overruns, and political corruption. In recent years, MIA has lost passengers to the newer and more efficient Fort Lauderdale–Hollywood International Airport, which in 2000 attracted 14 million passengers.[80]

In 1959, World War I ace Capt. Eddie Rickenbacker urged Florida airports to expand "Now!" Such urgency may have seemed misplaced in Orlando; after all, only 53,025 passengers had emplaned at the local airport in 1950. But Orlando's civic and business leaders were hell-bent to transform the "City Beautiful" into the "Action City of Florida." Herndon Airport, formerly the Municipal Airport, had to go. Civic leaders looked to the federal government for help. The air force—after prodding by publisher Martin Andersen and powerful friends—agreed to share McCoy Air Field (formerly Pinecastle), which had been modernized to handle jet planes and commercial landings. In 1961, the first commercial jet landed in Orlando, a Delta flight from California. Shortly thereafter, a California businessman flew over Orlando with big dreams.[81]

When Walt Disney first surveyed the Central Florida landscape, the visionary was struck by the abundance of modern highways and cheap land. Ironically, Disney first saw Orlando from the air, and appropriately, air passenger traffic became a critical link to the success of Disney World. In 1971, the Orlando Municipal Airport enjoyed a successful year, emplaning 1.5 million passengers. The first year of Disney World, 1972, witnessed an 85 percent spike in air traffic. Two years later, the Department of Defense deactivated McCoy Air Force Base, handing the runways and buildings to the city for one dollar. A decade later, 7 million passengers flew into Orlando. Construction crews and turnstiles could hardly keep pace in the 1980s and 1990s. In 2000, Orlando International Airport (OIA) hosted 30.8 million passengers, including millions of foreign travelers. A thousand planes fly in and out of OIA on a typical day. Sod farms and cattle ranches once surrounding OIA were converted into engines of economic growth, spinning off warehouses, catering companies, and mixed-use developments. In 2004 OIA passed MIA as the state's busiest airport.[82]

Tampa's rise as an aviation hub on Florida's Gulf coast had more to do with timing than planning. In 1930, a feuding Board of Representatives spurned Pan American's plans to build a new airport on an island in Hillsborough Bay. Pan American moved on to Miami. Tampa's airfields consisted of a stump-littered runway at Drew Park and a small facility on Davis Island. World War II salvaged Tampa's rocky economy and laid an aviation foundation. The establishment of MacDill and Drew Army Air fields brought thousands of aviators to fly B-17s, B-24s, and Superfortresses. The air bases were huge and located advantageously. Whereas Jacksonville and Pensacola's fortunes of flight were tied to the navy, Tampa was wed to the army. In 1947, decommissioned Drew Army Air Field became Tampa International Airport (TIA). Tampa inherited a $20 million windfall and moved quickly to become a leader in aviation.[83]

"Tampa Rapidly Gaining Spot in Nation's Aviation Picture," announced a 1950 headline. In the 1940s, the newspaper reported, Tampa was served by only six flights a day; by 1950, TIA welcomed forty flights daily. In 1952, TIA dedicated an $800,000 terminal. Tampa developed an early niche with Trans-Canada and wintering Canadians. Tampa also offered several flights a day to Cuba, capitalizing upon the historic relationship between the "Cigar City" and the "Pearl of the Antilles." In 1960, Delta jets began service between Chicago and Tampa, followed by an Eastern route to New York. In the late 1960s, construction crews demolished the old terminal and the Aviation Authority dedicated a dazzling $80 million TIA in 1971.[84]

Airports and interstate highways are to the late twentieth century what railroad stations and harbors were to the nineteenth century: glamorous entry points. Atlanta, Orlando, Charlotte, and Dallas–Fort Worth—"hub cities"—emerged as Sunbelt powers in part because of linkages with airlines, airports, and highways. Miami, Orlando, and Tampa rank as three of America's thirty busiest airports. Airports have become dynamic centers of activity in a world economy reliant upon global goods and services. The modern airport has become an "aerotropolis," a high-tech hub of commerce and transportation. Airports have also become a favorite subject for students of popular culture. "Airports sacrifice a sense of place for a sense of occasion," states Karal Ann Marling. Pico Iyer contends airports "represent an image of the way more and more cities are going. It's a culture of nonculture."[85]

Commercial success has eluded a handful of Florida airports determined to lure large numbers of passengers. In 1945, Jacksonville's aviation future seemed assured. Its navy bases and airfields had trained thousands of aviators; its businessmen and politicians exercised clout at the capital and statewide. But Ed Ball and others held back commercial aviation in favor of rail, freight, and port connections. For decades, Jacksonville Municipal Airport achieved modest gains, but its ambition was overshadowed by successes in Miami, Orlando, and Tampa. A new facility, Jacksonville International Airport (JIA), opened to hurrahs in 1968. Deregulation and the rise of Atlanta as a regional air hub deflated Jacksonville's hopes. In 2000, JIA ranked seventh among the state's leading airports, behind upstart Fort Myers.[86]

The 1983 opening of the $68 million Southwest International Airport (SIA) in Fort Myers signaled a new era of aviation for the region. A *Miami Herald* correspondent had predicted in 1945 that "Fort Myers has a big future in the flying world," but success came slowly. As late as 1983, passengers embarked at Page Field, a cramped, converted World War II–era Army Air Force facility. New airports at Sarasota-Bradenton and Naples created intense competition, but Fort Myers has prevailed, devastating the dreams of its rivals. In 2000, SIA (5.2 million passengers) dwarfed Sarasota-Bradenton (1.5 million) and Naples (118,000).

In 1977, *Florida Trend* pronounced air service from Pensacola as "still relatively primitive." Eglin Field boasted as many daily commercial flights as Pensacola. "Pensacola will soon have a direct flight somewhere," local businessmen joked. If air service from Pensacola in 1977 was primitive, in 2000 it remained expensive and limited. For a half century, politicians and lobbyists have cursed Tallahassee's limited flight connections. Tallahassee and Pensacola are scarcely alone when complaining about air service to small and mid-sized cities.[87]

Television

At the end of World War II, Floridians still relied upon radio and newspapers for their news. In a state where large numbers of poor families still lacked electric refrigerators and indoor plumbing, a radio was considered indispensable. Over 90 percent of Florida households owned a radio in 1950. The debut in 1947 of static-free FM and the portability of the transistor only enhanced radio's hold. In pre-air-conditioned neighborhoods of bungalows, cottages, and Mediterranean revivals, radio was both intensely private and public. When Joe Louis fought, one could walk through any African American neighborhood and hear every word from announcer Clem McCarthy. Daily, newsboys delivered a morning and an afternoon paper. Evening rituals included chatting with neighbors and reading the day's papers on the front porch.[88]

A revolution began at precisely 7 p.m. on 21 March 1949. Miami Avenue was then an unlikely place for upheaval, but it was at the venerable Capitol Theatre that the big screen got smaller. The Capitol, a dream factory in stucco and statuary, epitomized boom-time downtown Miami. Customers paid $1.25 admission to enjoy a double feature, including a new Frank Capra movie, but the Capitol *was* the feature attraction. Few patrons realized that in a cramped back room, technicians were broadcasting the first television signals Floridians had ever seen. A 306-foot tower atop the Everglades Hotel broadcast signals to the few thousand South Floridians who owned a television set. What happened outside Miami Avenue was more revealing than what happened inside. Historian Arva Parks, then living in Miami Shores, vividly recalled standing outside an appliance store to watch WTVJ, the first TV station south of Atlanta and South Florida's only station until 1956. The new medium may have been crude—the airing of national shows was erratic at best, and WTVJ broadcast only four hours nightly and none at all on Tuesdays—but the public adored it. Ironically, the medium that piped signals to 12-inch screens doomed the movie palace. The Capitol soon closed its doors as more and more Miamians preferred to watch Frank Capra movies free on television. Today, an Arquitectonica-designed courthouse stands on the hallowed site.[89]

FIGURE 41. On 21 March 1949, a revolution occurred at Miami's venerable Capitol Theatre. While moviegoers watched *The Life of Riley,* technicians inside a utility room broadcast Florida's very first televised signals to a few thousand households. Historical Association of Southern Florida, Miami.

The new medium, television, upset the social equilibrium. Patented in 1907 and a sensation at the 1939 New York World's Fair, television's grand possibilities awaited the end of World War II. Timing is everything; 1949 also saw the first television sets in Sears Roebuck catalogues. The audience was estimated at between 30,000 and 35,000. "If TV proved anything last night in Miami," deadpanned the *Miami Daily News,* "it proved a commercial can be entertaining." In time, the new medium stratified and segmented audiences through programming and commercials, but the early days of television brought Floridians together. Neighbors with a Stromberg-Carlson or Emerson invited neighbors less fortunate; sons and daughters sat next to fathers and mothers.[90]

Television bewitched Americans, who crowded department and appliance stores to watch test patterns flickering black-and-white images on tiny screens. Though thousands of Miami households and bar-goers viewed the 1949 World Series, the first nationally televised games, not everyone was convinced of the

The "Talbot" . . . new 1954   only

21-Inch CONSOLE $299.⁹⁵

Budget-priced 21-inch RCA Victor console with
powerful, accurate "Rotomatic" Tuning! Fashion-smart
Contemporary styling with luxurious grained
mahogany.

(Smart modern grained blond finish slightly higher)

$30 Down   • Automatic Picture and Sound Intensifier
                      • Built in UHF - VHF Antena
$3 A Week   • "Magic Monitor" Circuit System
                      • The "Golden Throat" Tone System

Orlando's Oldest-Largest TV-Radio Dealer

FREE
PARKING   **ASSOCIATED** RADIO &
REAR OF   TELEVISION
STORE   *Inc.*
      143 N. ORANGE · ORLANDO · PHONE 5-1561

FIGURE 42. In 1954,
the selling *of* televi-
sions was as important
as the selling *on* television. Orange County
Regional History
Center, Orlando.

new gadget's potential. When asked to invest in Miami's first TV station, Ed Ball dismissed such folly. "We don't spend money on these foolish ideas," he scoffed. Ball also chose not to invest in WMBR-TV, Jacksonville, which aired in October 1949. "Television Is Here!" announced the *Florida Times-Union*. While an astonishing two-thirds of American households owned television sets in 1953, fewer than 10 percent of Floridians had joined the consumer stampede. The reason was not lack of interest but timing and politics. The Federal Communications Commission (FCC), the agency responsible for the politically sensitive task of awarding broadcast licenses, announced in 1948 after granting 108 licenses (including two in Florida) that it was freezing new stations. Further frustrating Floridians, the Korean War (1950–53) continued the freeze. While millions of New Yorkers, Californians, and even Cubans howled at the theatrics of "rassler" Gorgeous George, comedian Uncle Miltie, and the bejeweled Liberace, the entire West Coast, Panhandle, and interior of Florida was blacked out. Finally, on Easter Sunday 1952, the FCC lifted the freeze. Much of Florida had missed television's "Golden Age."[91]

Once Floridians saw the *Milton Berle Show* or the Friday-night fights, they had to buy their own set. Television sets preceded television stations. Orlando's first TV store opened in February 1951, three years before the city's first broadcast. The 1950 U.S. Census—the first to ask Americans if they owned a television—revealed that only 17,180 Florida households owned this new appliance. In contrast, 742,845 households reported having a radio.[92]

When new stations appeared—often after bitter partisan battles over ownership—newspapers touted their debut as a sign of urbanity. "Oh Happy Day. TV Today" crowed the *St. Petersburg Times* in 1953. Across the bay, the *Tampa Tribune*, owner of the popular radio station WDAE, barely acknowledged WSUN's existence. When viewers attempted to adjust their sets to the Channel 38 UHF (ultra high frequency) signals from St. Pete on 3 May 1953, complaints poured in about "snow." TV-starved Tampa Bay—the largest media market without a major television station—preferred to endure bad reception rather than curse no reception. By the end of WSUN's first year of operation, a quarter million viewers tuned in to Channel 38 each day. Many medium-sized cities lost out in the coveted bids for VHF (very high frequency) stations numbered two to thirteen but found a niche on the UHF band, numbered fourteen to eighty-three. Still, audiences welcomed the "Gala Debut." In 1954, WINK-TV began in Fort Myers; the following year WCTV in Tallahassee and Tampa's WFLA-TV debuted. Orlando's WDBO-TV (today's WCPX) also opened in 1954. A beaming

Mrs. Edward Kirkland told the *Sentinel*, "We're seeing an ad for prune juice now and it's real clear." Another happy viewer gushed, "The children have gone just hog-wild about it." Residents from as far away as Brevard County received pictures from WDBO—the letters stood for "Way Down By Orlando." The newspaper carried hints as to how to adjust the antenna to tune in to Miami and Jacksonville stations ("use a yagi antenna cut for channel 6 'stacked' on the same pole with one cut for channel 4 and switches which can be used to 'cut in' the antenna you wish to use"). Underpopulated and isolated areas waited impatiently for television. Naples did not receive transmission until 1960. Sarasota's first television station, WXLT, arrived in 1971. As late as 1977, Pensacola had only one station.[93]

Floridians paid dearly to be the first on their block to own a television set. Appliance shops, department stores, and even tire companies sold the latest marvel, but so did new establishments with names such as Allied Television, TV Center, and Tell-a-Ville. One firm promised deliveries "within the hour" of purchase! Shelley's Appliance Store in Jacksonville advertised a 12-inch Admiral for $400 in 1949. Associated Radio and Television in Orlando advertised a 21-inch Zenith Cinébeam in 1954 for $369.95 (although customers received a "fifty-dollar allowance for turning in their old radio"). In 1954, RCA introduced the first color televisions, with an eye-popping $1,000 price tag. Mount Dora's Rehbaum's Hardware sold 19-inch models in 1956 for $240 to $310. But prices fell dramatically as millions of customers rushed to appliance stores. By 1959, the cost of televisions had dropped to $99 at Sears.

Television profoundly altered the rhythms of Floridians' lives. The medium's informality and intensity made Ralph Rennick, Skipper Chuck, Bob Weaver, "Salty Sol" Fleischman, and Dr. Paul Bearer household friends and legends. Rennick, just weeks shy of his twenty-second birthday, developed a formula for local TV news in Miami when he first went on the air in July 1950. Perceptibly, television's global village replaced Florida's front-porch society. The ritual of across-the-fence gossip declined, as did attendance at downtown movie houses, nighttime dining, minor-league baseball, and the afternoon newspaper. The popularity of TV, coupled with another new technology, air conditioning, "privatized" Americans' leisure time, as we tuned a new world in and tuned the real world out. Americans, quipped a sociologist, would rather watch *Friends* than be friends. Critics blame TV for the decline of community and the falling numbers of Americans active in civic voluntary associations.[94]

Television rearranged our public lives and private spaces. Just months after Tampans had watched their first television show, the *Tribune*'s real estate editor began to notice interior home changes. "Home furnishers are stocking up with chairs that are designed principally for comfort," he wrote, adding, "the 'Florida Room'—which is no more than the screened porch gone modern and enclosed with jalousies—appears to be the likeliest candidate for the television viewing center. The most important home design innovation with television in mind is to locate the jalousied porch adjacent to and merging with the living room." The journalist concluded, in historic understatement, "Television, as many Tampans have found . . . is not something that just slips quietly in and makes itself at home." Home was fast becoming the place where Floridians and Americans gathered to watch TV.[95]

Nowhere was television's impact more disorienting or reorienting than St. Petersburg. Channel 38, broadcasting from the top of the Million Dollar Pier, may have been one of the state's most erratic signals, but the citizenry dearly loved it, especially because so many seasonal residents had already been exposed to the medium in places like Toledo and Albany. The debut of WSUN-TV coincided with a spike in St. Petersburg's elderly population. Retirees—many from the Midwest—brought their pastimes and habits with them. Part hypnotic, part addictive, television rattled St. Petersburg's habitually early-to-bed retirees. Soon the police chief was complaining of crowds of seniors congregating in front of Central Avenue appliance stores simply to watch the pictures. After the first three months of broadcasts in 1953, the *St. Petersburg Times* conducted a "State of the Viewnion," concluding that the typical "home watcher is still sufficiently engrossed to ignore friends, skip bedtime, forget his newspaper and inadvertently devour a bowlful of caloried snacks at a single sitting." Soon television antennae festooned St. Petersburg's growth industry: trailer parks. One such park, Ranchmobile, advertised "central television."[96]

Years before St. Petersburg obtained a television station, city publicists realized the selling power of the new medium. Beginning in the late 1940s, city officials developed a series of short films that touted the area's abundant sunshine and rejuvenating qualities. *Green Benches* (1951) and *Sunny Days* (1951) were shown in television markets in the Northeast and Midwest. Other cities and real-estate developers also pounced upon the new medium's potential.[97]

Televisions accompanied the moving vans and delivery trucks into and around Florida. Politicians took notice. Before the 1950s, statewide campaigns for political office imposed great logistical and physical challenges. Radio helped, but it remained for television to fill boundaries and saturate the airwaves. Historically, candidates had relied upon supporters to turn out crowds at county fairs and barbecues. Face-to-face communication still mattered. Television dictated new strategies. Candidates need not travel to every isolated hamlet to reach voters. In 1954, Bill Cramer shocked Florida's political establishment by becoming the state's first Republican to be elected to Congress since Reconstruction. "You've got to have a television personality to win in politics these days," a Democrat grumbled, who proceeded to blame the party's defeat on impressionable female voters who liked Cramer's "face and manner." In the 1955 gubernatorial campaign between challenger LeRoy Collins and Charley Johns, the former demonstrated the medium's effectiveness by besting the acting governor in the state's first televised debate. Television also dramatically escalated the costs of modern campaigning. Candidates must now purchase air time in each of Florida's ten media markets, comprised of 329 broadcast and cable television stations. Veteran poll watchers gasped at the $17.5 million price tag of the 1994 gubernatorial race between Lawton Chiles and Jeb Bush, topping the 1986 U.S. senatorial battle between Paula Hawkins and Bob Graham that cost $13.2 million. The 2000 elections set a new bar for campaign fundraising and media expenditures. Federal candidates, political parties, and political action committees (PACs) raised a staggering $83 million in Florida, much of it spent on television.[98]

Fifty years after the home invasion of television, we are still trying to understand its multiple meanings. From its beginnings, TV exposed and amplified America's virtues and flaws: affluence and vitality, discrimination and stratification, creativity and conformity. Statistics do not lie. Television in midcentury Florida was as exotic as it was remote—one set for every 170 residents; five decades later, television has evolved from the 12-inch black-and-white Zenith Cinébeam to wall-sized entertainment centers with Plasma screens and satellite dishes receiving 250 cable stations, with a TV for every other resident.

Modern political and popular culture cannot be understood without the unblinking eye of television. Ironically, for a state so image conscious, one of Florida's first televised moments was the 1950 Kefauver hearings on organized crime, an event indicting Miami, Tampa, and Broward County as underworld havens. The medium arrived like a deus ex machina, and soon Arthur Godfrey and Jackie Gleason refocused America's image of Florida as exotic and glamorous. *Sea Hunt, Flipper, Gentle Ben,* and clips of tourists in love with Cypress Gardens and Marineland eased Cold War anxieties.

Early on, the media's penchant to embellish Florida's most attractive qualities contrasted sharply with the portrayal of the state's underside in the 1980s and 1990s. Television united Floridians in its early days. Families sat around the "electronic hearth" to enjoy the medium. Viewers had, until the 1980s, only three or four stations. Perhaps it is coincidence, but the arrival of cable coincided with a barrage of negative images with Florida. Television reminded Americans that sunburn was the least of the Sunshine State's problems. Print defines; images magnify. Florida's manifold woes and blemishes went prime time: anthrax in Boca Raton, race riots in Miami and St. Petersburg, Hurricane Andrew, alien exotics, global warming, red tide, right-wing commandoes, the Mariel boatlift, Ted Bundy, the *Challenger* disaster, Aileen Wuornos, Versace, pregnant chads, and ballot-chasing lawyers. A backstage, sleazy Florida found its electronic muse. Nightly, millions of Americans tuned in to witness dateline Florida on *Hard Copy, A Current Affair,* and *Girls Gone Wild.* Television, once a unifying medium, had become a divisive one. Cable fragmented audiences, but it also sought out the coarse and bizarre. The phenomenon is not restricted to Florida; Alaska and Hawaii are connected by cable and wireless. But Florida's historic character and range of characters make it an irresistible subject for television exposés.

Techno Florida

In the 1940s, some imposing obstacles clouded Florida's future. Bloodthirsty mosquitoes and suffocating humidity discouraged summer tourism and year-round residence. Roads were primitive, distances were vast, and free-range cattle roamed highways with legal right.

The half century after 1950 introduced the most resourceful machines and technological innovations Floridians had ever known or even dreamed. Station wagons, superhighways, and jet planes made Florida accessible; air conditioning and DDT made Florida livable. Air conditioning allowed Floridians to keep their sunshine and "cool it" twelve months a year. Scientists have begun to question the impact of enclosed homes upon children's health and immunities. In bursts of creativity, automobiles, DDT, and mobile homes revolutionized living in the tropics, but they also resulted in doubt, confusion, and danger. Television, interstate highways, and airports allowed more Americans and citizens of the world to visit and live in the Sunshine State, but they also made features of Florida indistinguishable from other regions and nations. The shopping mall and fast-food chains offered Florida consumers a dazzling array of goods, services, and choices. But malls and franchises have contributed to the demise of downtowns and suburban sprawl and to the sense that the vast sections of developed Florida resemble other states and places.

Technology liberates and revolutionizes, but it also complicates and confounds. Fifty years after the massive invasion by motorists, mobile homes, and air conditioners, we are still trying to understand the consequences (intended and unintended). Clearly, Floridians' sense of place and community has suffered, as the air-conditioned TV room displaced the front porch, the mall replaced the Main Street five-and-dime, and the automobile promoted suburbia, strip malls, and sprawl. Machines have made Florida more inhabitable and are one of the chief reasons the Sunshine State has evolved from the least-populated state in the South (1.9 million residents in 1940) to the fourth-most-populous state in the nation (17.4 million in 2004).

The sheer sweep of technological advance in the twentieth century was nothing short of revolutionary. Consider Floridians who reached their one-hundredth birthday in 2000. All were born before the Wright Brothers achieved flight for the first time—gliding across sand dunes not quite the length of the wingspan of a Boeing 747. Most of the centenarians came into a world heated by coal, cooled by paper fans, and illuminated by kerosene. Their lifetimes witnessed the revolutions wrought by electrification, automobility, flight, radio, television, air conditioning, and health care.

Modernity's sweep and swath can be clearly seen in the Everglades. Technology's abilities to improve lives can also destroy an ecosystem. By the 1830s, long after Tequesta, Calusa, and Glades Indians had died as the result of Toledo steel and Old World diseases, new residents—Seminole Indians—took up lives in South Florida. They survived war and disease.

Twentieth-century Seminoles could neither totally ignore nor accept outside influences. The Seminole economy depended upon the fluctuations of capitalism, the prices of plumes and hides, and the tourist trade. The completion of the Tamiami Trail in 1928 and the incessant drainage of the Everglades resulted in a catastrophic decline in game animals and ecosystem. The Tamiami Trail, however, also accelerated the number of travelers who rushed past Seminole and Miccosukee villages. By 1950, alligator wrestling pits, gift shops, and air-boat rides were commonplace.[99]

The airboat perfectly encapsulated technology's possibilities, replacing dug-out canoes and dramatically advancing gladesmen's abilities to traverse the sea of grass. Twelve-foot flat-bottomed boats, equipped with 75-horsepowered auto engines, aircraft propellers, and wooden rudders, "whooshed" across saw-grass marshes. The airboat also enhanced frog hunting, cypress-pole gathering, and tourism. On land, Seminoles preferred automobiles, which they had been driv-ing since the teens.[100]

In 1946, a *Miami Herald* headline announced, "White Man's Ways Lure Seminoles." The *Herald* praised "progress" in diet and new economic opportu-nities. An agent confessed, however: "The Seminole's housing is crude. For the most part he lives in thatched-roof habitation, completely open at the sides." Beginning in 1956, the Rev. Bill Osceola and his wife, Charlotte, constructed the first concrete-block home on the Dania (now Hollywood) Reservation. At the same time, Friends of the Seminoles began moving scores of unwanted beach cottages and bungalows to the reservation.[101]

In 2000, Florida's Native Americans represented one of the state's most affluent and technologically wired groups. James Billie embodied the modern Seminole leader, with one foot in the old ways, and the other comfortable in corporate board rooms and jet planes. Born on the grounds of the Dania Chimp Farm in 1944, Billie wrestled gators, experienced combat in Vietnam, and in 1979 became tribal chairman. Wanting to know the ways of the tribal medicine man, Billie killed and ate an endangered Florida panther. Charged with a fed-eral crime, he was exonerated. On the steps of the courthouse, the press asked him what panther tasted like. He deadpanned, "Kind of a cross between bald eagle and manatee!" As leader, he ushered in the computer age and brought new–found wealth to the tribe. Gaming revenues have lifted the Seminoles out of grinding poverty: in 1983, each Seminole received $300 a year; in 2000, the state's 2,850 registered members received $3,000 each month. Seminoles and Miccosukees live in suburban-style homes, drive SUVs, and receive cable TV from satellite dishes. However, not all Seminoles have accepted this new life-style. Near some reservations live "Traditional Seminoles," who forgo monthly revenue checks and live in chickee huts.[102]

The Internationalization of Florida

8

F LORIDA'S historic trajectory is complete. How fitting and symmetrical that a place first called *La Florida* in 1513—a colony, territory, and state shaped by Spanish-speaking *floridanos*–has become a burgeoning center for Hispanic life at the beginning of the new millennium. Cuba and Florida share historic "ties of intimacy." The pulsating Cuban sound swept Florida and the United States long before 1960. Implicitly, Florida had always challenged American boundaries of propriety and decorum; explicitly, Cuban culture criss-crossed those boundaries. From the rumba, mamba, and cha-cha-cha, to Desi Arnaz, Xavier Cugat, and Tito Puente, Cuban rhythms crossed into mainstream American culture. A new Cuba was emerging in Florida that was distinct from its historic roots in St. Augustine, Tampa, and Key West.

In 1950 Ybor City and Key West, many of the immigrant cigarworkers had died, and the symbols of immigrant vitality—the San Carlos Club, El Círculo Cubano, and cigar factories—were in decline. In July 1955, Ybor City leaders called an emergency meeting to condemn the influx of African Americans into the historic Latin neighborhood. In November 1955, a twenty-eight-year-old Cuban lawyer toured Florida hoping to raise consciousness and funds for his cause: the overthrow of the corrupt Batista regime. "The republic of Cuba is the daughter of the cigarmakers of Tampa," he reminded Tampeños. But Ybor City, the seedbed of Cuban wars of independence and

"I know how men in exile feed on dreams of hope."
Aeschylus, *Agamemnon*

FIGURE 43. In 1945, an *ambiente* born of both culture and climate characterized Key West. In no other American city could one find daily flights to Havana, the rhythms of Duval Street, and the delicacies of turtleburger and conch fritters. Author's collection.

champion of José Martí, no longer comforted revolutionaries. Fidel Castro, the lawyer-turned-revolutionary, left Tampa disillusioned and empty-handed.[1]

By the 1950s, Florida's ethnic pressure center had shifted to Miami. Since the 1920s, large numbers of Cubans had been coming to Miami for vacations, while nervous Cuban officials and businessmen invested heavily in South Florida real estate. Florida welcomed overthrown dictators Porfirio Díaz, Gerardo Machado, and Fulgencio Batista, who made their homes along the east coast. Large numbers of Floridians traveled to Cuba, enjoying the island's sensual hospitality. On New Year's Day 1950, the *Herald* noted that Miami Mayor William M. Wolfarth and two hundred officials were headed to Cuba for a "good will junket." Throughout the 1950s, travelers could with ease fly and cruise to Cuba. Cuba's middle classes fell in love with South Florida, enjoying American culture and summer's off-season bargains. In September 1950, Miami Beach stores sponsored "Cuba Day" for the visitors.[2]

FIGURE 44. In 1940, the famed Tarpon Springs sponge fleet anchored on the Anclote River. Fishermen christened their boats with special names, such as *Eleni* and *Bozzaris,* the latter honoring a Greek patriot who "slew a thousand Turks before breakfast." Tampa-Hillsborough Public Library, Tampa.

On New Year's Eve, 1958, Cuban leader Fulgencio Batista abdicated power, turning over the government to a young rebel—the leader of the *barbudos* (bearded guerrillas) and 26th of July Brigade—Fidel Castro. In Florida newspapers, the event registered few tremors; to Americans, this was another "banana republic" coup. Mass executions of political opponents prompted the *Miami Herald* to warn Fidel Castro "and his summary executioners." It was not the 15 January 1959 editorial that shocked Floridians; rather, it was a set of photographs graphically showing José Rodríguez, a Batista supporter, kneeling, asking for priestly absolution before a firing squad. The events that followed—the expropriation of foreign-owned capital, the proclamations of a Communist state, and the exodus of hundreds of thousands of émigrés—were part of the unfolding revolution. Forty-six years later, Fidel is still in power, but other revolutions and revolutionaries, more cultural than political, more economic than ideological, have taken hold across the Straits of Florida.

In 1959, Miami was glitzy, gauche, and a city on the edge of crisis. Miami was home to large numbers of aging Jews and young blacks. African American leaders expressed anger at Miami's insensitivities toward poverty, education, and a Jim Crow color line. Precisely at the moment the civil rights revolution unfolded, Miami experienced its own upheaval. Miami was on the threshold of change so immense that words such as "profound" and "dislocation" seem inadequate.

The first wave of Cubans arrived in 1959. Defiantly insisting that they were exiles, not emigrants, émigrés were welcomed by civic and humanitarian groups. This vanguard represented Cuba's elites—governmental officers, propertied classes, and groups who had the most to lose in fortunes and lives. Confident that a restoration of the old homeland was only a military coup away, especially when Castro committed Cuba to revolutionary socialism, the exile community of Miami waited patiently, then impatiently, day by day creating a "Havana USA."

Miami, quipped a pundit, is the only city in the United States with a foreign policy. Miamians realized quickly that crises 90 miles away echoed across the Florida Straits and Biscayne Bay. In staccato bursts, the Bay of Pigs and the Cuban Missile Crisis, the Mariel boatlift and the controversy over whether to offer asylum to a Cuban boy named Elián marked not only new chapters in the Cold War but also new chapters in Miami and Florida history. As if in a chess match, Cuban, Soviet, and U.S. leaders maneuvered to maximize position. In July 1960, President Eisenhower cut imports of Cuban sugar by 700,000 tons, a move resulting in drastic increases in Florida-grown sugar. In January 1961, the U.S. government severed diplomatic relations with Cuba, a move precipitating riots in Tampa and Miami. Since the Bay of Pigs debacle in 1961, a politics of resentment and resolve has characterized Cuban-American foreign policy, an outlook reinforced by unity, passion, and economic resources. From Dwight Eisenhower to George W. Bush, every American president has denounced Castro and courted Cuban Americans. Long after American diplomats broke bread with former adversaries in China, Russia, and Vietnam, the Cuban embargo defiantly speaks to the power of the Cuba lobby and the lure of Dade county votes.

The first great wave of émigrés, 1959–62, brought well-educated, upper-middle managerial, professional, and propertied classes to Miami. They were received, welcomed, and assisted by the U.S. government. While the United States had maintained one of the most liberal immigration policies in history, the huddled masses at Ellis Island received, at most, a delousing and a meal. The Cuban Refugee Program, however, provided the most generous benefits ever offered in American immigration history. Such generosity reflected more than egalitarianism; the United States was anxious to embarrass and defeat Castro—militarily, economically, and diplomatically. Possessing middle-class, urban values and surrounded by strong families and a tight-knit network of kinfolk, entrepreneurial-minded Cubans excelled and thrived. As each day brought new arrivals, Miami's Cuban community generated new markets for labor, capital, and consumers.[3]

Operation Pedro Pan, a secret program coordinated by the Catholic Church in the United States with the aid of the State Department, smuggled 14,000 children out of Cuba. Miami International Airport became the emotional lodestar for this modern children's crusade. Children, some as young as five, arrived with only a printed name tag and the clothes on their back, destined for new families. Some never saw their parents again. For her efforts to spirit thousands of children out of Cuba, including her own daughter and son, Polita Grau was jailed for nearly fourteen years, accused of being a CIA conspirator. Revered as the godmother of Pedro Pan, Grau dedicated a lifetime of activism that spanned both sides of the Florida Straits, including four separate periods of exile in Miami. Monsignor Bryan O. Walsh, pastor of several South Florida Catholic churches, also worked tirelessly to relocate children to America. One of the émigrés was Carlos Eire, whose touching memoir, *Waiting for Snow in Havana*, relates his experiences in Cuba and Miami.[4]

On September 28, 1965, Castro shocked Cubans home and abroad by announcing that anyone with relatives in the United States who wished to emigrate would be free to go. The "Freedom Flights" from 1965 to 1973 marked the second great wave of Cuban migration to Miami. Almost 300,000 Cubans arrived in the United States. Only about 10 percent of the new émigrés were professionals or managers; rather, the Freedom Flights brought artisans, blue-collar, service, and agricultural workers. Women and the elderly were overrepresented; Afro Cubans were drastically underrepresented.

One of the most active spots in Florida during the period 1962–74 was Miami's Freedom Tower. Built in the 1920s to realize the architectural dream of publisher James Cox, the Giralda Tower became the home of the *Miami Daily News*. Renamed the Freedom Tower, it served as the Cuban Refugee Center for processing and registering Cuban exiles. From 1962 to 1974, nearly a half million Cubans passed through "Florida's Ellis Island." Jorge Mas Canosa, the fiery

FIGURE 45. Establishments like Café Al Minuto along Calle Ocho (Eighth Street) symbolized the energy and resourcefulness of Cuban settlers in 1960s Miami. State of Florida Photographic Archives, Tallahassee.

leader of the powerful Cuban American National Foundation, spearheaded a movement to restore the Freedom Tower and build a museum chronicling the Cuban-American experience.[5]

If the Freedom Tower symbolized the new Miami, Little Havana was its heart. Originating in the then Jewish neighborhood of Riverside in southwest Miami, the 4-square-mile area was reborn as "Little Havana." Bungalows, Mediterranean revivals, and concrete ranch homes were converted into multi-family dwellings. Eighth Street became Calle Ocho, a pulsating tropical presence: market stalls with sugarcane and hanging coconuts, aromas of *lechon y yuca*, and religious idols venerating La Virgen de la Caridad del Cobre. Soon, Little Havana expanded beyond its 4-square-mile borders, and new colonies took hold in the county. Not all Miamians, or even Cubans, welcomed the new symbols of *cubanidad*. Santería, an ancient Afro-Cuban religious cult, took hold, embarrassing elites because of the stigma of animal sacrifice.[6]

To fathom the upheaval that Miami underwent after 1960, one would have to compare the Miami experience with Boston in the 1840s or New York City in the 1890s. But in Boston and New York, immigrants and children required many decades, sometimes centuries to achieve wide-scale success. Miami represents one of the great, if not greatest, immigrant success stories in American history. Six-seat Cuban cafés appeared everywhere, but so did Cuban banks, construction companies, and television stations.

Cuban immigrants achieved an economic miracle, succeeding wildly and widely. Capitalizing upon family and group associations and taking advantage of generous financial assistance, Cuban businessmen penetrated almost every sector of South Florida's economy. As early as 1977, Cubans owned 8,000 businesses in Dade County; quickly, Cubans dominated the area's burgeoning financial and construction industries. In 1987, Cubans owned 34,771 Dade County firms, a stunning economic achievement when compared to African American–owned companies (6,747). Hispanic-owned enterprises in Miami then accounted for aggregate sales of $4 billion, a sum dwarfing such sales in the far larger Latino populations of New York and Los Angeles. Among Hispanics in the United States, no nationality has demonstrated the same entrepreneurial bent as Cubans. Dominicans in South Florida have also achieved remarkable successes.[7]

The events of the year 1980 fundamentally changed Miami and Florida, neatly cleaving history into a distinct "before" and "after." Once again, the impulse for change came from abroad. In April 1980, Castro again confounded Cubans and foreign policy experts by announcing that *gusanos* (critics of Castro, or worms) could leave. The Cuban port city of Mariel became the focal point and namesake of the tumultuous events. Little Havana erupted in glee; even Cuban Americans in Tampa chartered "freedom boats" to ferry countrymen. The decision caught President Carter, already ensnarled in the Iranian hostage crisis, by surprise. Soon American officials realized that this was emigration and diplomacy on Castro's terms. The 124,000 émigrés, called Marielitos, included several thousand criminals and mental patients. The Marielitos also spoke to the bankruptcy of the Cuban revolution. In contrast to the previous migrations, the Marielitos were blacker, poorer, and younger.

A public furor nationally and locally castigated President Carter for his inability to control American borders, and Castro for his crass motives. The Marielitos, unlike the passengers stepping off the Freedom Flights, received a rude reception. Strikingly, Miami's Cuban community repudiated the new undesirables, much as German Jews of the 1840s looked down upon the "green-horns," the Russian Jews of the 1880s.[8]

Images and memories of the Marielitos are now rooted in American popular and political culture: a tent city under I-95; the burning of an Arkansas prison, Fort Chafe, by Cuban detainees, an incident that caused Governor Bill Clinton to lose reelection; incessant evening news stories chronicling the latest crime attributed to the newest residents; and Hollywood's favorite Marielito, Tony Montana, played in an over-the-top performance by Al Pacino in *Scarface*. In reality, most Marielitos became hard-working, law-abiding citizens. The Mariel boatlift set in motion a tumbleweed chain of reactions that made 1980 a year of reckoning. Miamians were furious over the city's "decline": the crime rate rose 66 percent in 1980, while "cocaine cowboys," *balseros* (boat people), and drug money gave South Florida more negative publicity. Turmoil and revolutions in the Americas brought thousands of Sandinista Contras, Argentinians, and Co-lombians to Miami.

Ominously, African American voices were becoming more strident and an-grier. The government was winning the Cold War but losing the War on Pov-erty. African Americans watched in anger as 124,000 more Cubans arrived, then in disbelief when black Haitians loaded on tramp steamers were turned back by the Coast Guard. Images of bloated Haitians washed ashore on Miami Beach made the evening news. Conditions in Liberty City and other black neighborhoods approached Third World levels. In Liberty City, seven out of ten families lived in poverty in 1980. A jury verdict ignited the tinderbox. Four Miami police officers had been charged with beating to death a black man, Arthur McDuffie. So politically charged was the trial that the venue was moved to Tampa. When the jury found the police officers innocent, Miami erupted. The May 1980 riots lasted four days, resulted in eighteen deaths, 417 injuries, and $100 million in property losses, marking the most violent event in Miami history.[9]

In the bonfires of cultural and social change, citizens often look for scape-goats. In 1980, Dade County voters approved a referendum requiring that county business be conducted exclusively in English. In spite of public percep-tion, the great majority of the city's Cubans—and virtually all of their chil-dren—speak English. In South Florida, however, language became currency in the culture wars of everyday life. It was one thing for Cuban *tabaqueros* to con-verse in Spanish in cigar factories; it was quite another for Spanish to become the lingua franca among contractors, teachers, and, soon, mayors. "What was unusual about Spanish in Florida," wrote Joan Didion, "was not that it was so often spoken, but it was so often heard.[10]

The politics of anger and resentment boiled over in Miami's ethnic and racial cauldron. In 1973, Miami voters had elected Maurice Ferré mayor. Of Puerto Rican descent, Ferré won reelection as mayor four times, but he lost to Cuban-born Xavier Suarez in 1985. Ferré, a revolutionary in pinstripes, was devoured by a series of revolutions. In frustration, Ferré branded Miami as the "Beirut of the West." By the mid-1980s, Hispanics constituted half of Miami's registered voters and had control of the city commission. In 1989, Cuban Americans helped elect Ileana Ros-Lehtinen to Congress. Born in Cuba in 1952, Ileana Ros fled the island with her parents at age eight. Elected to the Florida House of Representatives in 1982 and the Florida Senate in 1986, she became the first Hispanic woman to win such posts. In Congress, she replaced liberal Democrat Claude Pepper, a symbolic shift in South Florida politics.[11]

The turbulence that whiplashed Miami was part of a tidal wave of change. The 1980s brought to America waves of immigrants not seen since the decades before World War I. In 1990, Dade County educational officials identified 120 countries represented in the student body. But immigration was no longer isolated to Miami, as more established Cubans and new arrivals moved beyond Dade County. The Latinization of Florida is a story of triumphs and tragedies, of "white flight" and a reconfigured dream state, of spatial conflicts and new coalitions. Interpreting Miami and Florida has become a cottage industry.

For a generation, Cuban exiles plotted revolutions, assured that Little Havana would soon be a memory when counter-revolutionaries swept into Fidel's Havana. A new generation, however, weaned on American culture and dazzled by consumer capitalism, regards Florida, not Cuba, as home. So piercing has been the process of Americanization that probably few Cuban Americans will leave Florida when Fidel falls from power.

Miami, Los Angeles, and New York are great American cities, but they are also *the* great immigrant cities. Miami, even more than New York or Los Angeles, has the highest proportion of its city's residents (60 percent) born abroad. Miami-Dade County has the highest percentage of foreign-born (51.4 percent) in the country. More than half of the population of Miami speaks a language other than English at home. More than half of all the Cubans residing in the United States live within commuting distance of Little Havana. But Miami is no longer exclusively a Cuban immigrant city. Miami has become the capital of Latin America. Revolutions in Nicaragua and Haiti, crises in Honduras and El

TABLE 6. Population Origins Miami-Dade County, 2000

Country of Origin	Number	Percent of Total Hispanic Population	Percent of Total Miami-Dade Population
Cuban	650,601	50.40%	
Puerto Rican	80,327	6.20%	
Nicaraguan	69,257	5.40%	
Mexican	38,095	2.90%	
Dominican	36,454	2.80%	
Honduran	26,829	2.10%	
Guatemalan	9,676	0.70%	
Salvadoran	9,115	0.70%	
Panamanian	5,863	0.50%	
Costa Rican	4,706	0.40%	
Other Central American	3,457	0.30%	
Colombian	70,066	5.40%	
Peruvian	23,327	1.80%	
Venezuelan	21,593	1.70%	
Argentinian	13,341	1.00%	
Ecuadorian	10,560	0.80%	
Chilean	7,910	0.60%	
Bolivian	2,418	0.20%	
Other Hispanics and Latinos	124,020	9.60%	
Hispanic and Latino Total	1,207,615	100%	56.00%
Caucasians (Non-Hispanic White)	465,772	21.70%	
Black or African American	427,140	19.00%	
Haitian	71,054	5.50%	
Two or More Races	31,636	1.40%	
Asian	30,537	1.40%	
Brazilian	13,078	1.00%	
Some Other Race	4,026	0.20%	
American Indian and Alaska Native	1,990	0.10%	
Native Hawaiian and Other Pacific Islander	524	0.00%	
Non-Hispanic and Latino Total	1,045,757	100%	44.00%
Total Population for Miami-Dade County	2,253,372	100%	

Sources: U.S Census Bureau, *Census 2000 Summary File, Miami-Dade County*; Department of Planning and Zoning, Research Section, 2002; *Miami Herald*, 2 January 2000; *St. Petersburg Times*, 29 March 2001.

Salvador, and instability everywhere brought hundreds of thousands of Caribbeans and South and Central Americans to Florida. The capital of Latin America also brought capitalists—bankers, businessmen, and elites—to South Florida.[12]

Understanding Miami has become a growth industry, attracting the energies of demographers, futurologists, and postmodern scholars. Veteran reporters chart the city's fluctuating population with an unerring gauge: listening to the accents of waitresses. For two decades following Castro's revolution, Cubans flooded the service industry, and such accents dominated restaurants. However, revolution and unrest in Central America in the 1980s and early 1990s brought large numbers of Nicaraguans and Hondurans. Little Havana would be more accurately called Little Central America. The inflections of waitresses and vendors changed accordingly. Cuban accents, however, have returned, confirming a re-Cubanization of Miami. The rafter or *balsero* crisis of the 1990s bolstered the Cuban population of Miami, resulting in another 230,000 Cuban emigrants.[13]

During the 1980s, Florida's Hispanic population surged 83.4 percent. The most dramatic changes occurred in Central Florida. The fastest-growing Hispanic county in the nation was Osceola County, with Kissimmee the chief destination. From barely 1,000 Hispanics in 1980, Osceola's Hispanic population increased twelvefold in a decade. Nearly one in five of the county's schoolchildren is Hispanic. In Orlando, residents now call Azalea Park "Little San Juan." Over half of Central Florida's Hispanics are Puerto Ricans. Beginning in the 1980s, home builders and realtors pitched Florida homes to Puerto Ricans living in San Juan, New York, and Chicago. *El Nuevo Día*, the largest daily in San Juan, contains pages of ads extolling work and life in Central Florida. "You don't have to be a millionaire to live like one," touted an advertisement. The 1998 election of Tony Suarez (D–Winter Park) to the Florida legislature exemplified the growing clout of Hispanic voters in Central Florida, and the point that Hispanic voters are not a monolithic bloc. By the late 1990s, Orlando's Sun Trust established Grupo Bancario Latino, a branch Hispanic bank with ten bilingual officers. Hispanics bring to Orlando skills relevant to a global economy but also cultural practices comforting to people in a strange land. A *botanica* on South Orange Avenue sells statues of St. Lazarus and Santa Barbara, icons of Santería.[14]

The Hispanic diaspora intensified in the 1990s. No urban county in America matched Miami-Dade County's magnetism for immigrants during

FIGURE 46. Bahamian immigrants, some sporting fashionable zoot suits, arrive for work in South Florida fields in 1943. Library of Congress, Washington, D.C.

the 1990s, outdistancing even New York and Los Angeles. Miami's reputation as the greatest Cuban center outside Havana endures. In 2004, 1.2 million of Miami-Dade's population of 2.3 million was Hispanic. Throughout the 1990s, immigrants arrived at a rate of 167 per day. Were it not for Hispanic immigration, Miami-Dade County would have lost population. Since 1990, over 236,000 persons moved out of Dade County, but immigration added 336,000 new residents. In other words, Miami-Dade County is becoming *more*, not less, ethnic and multicultural. Curiously, the most likely residents to move *away* from Dade County in the 1990s were not elderly Jews or Anglos; rather, they were the second- and third-generation Hispanics who sought new homes outside Miami for precisely the same reasons as WASPs who fled South Florida in the 1970s and 1980s. Adult Anglos also continue to leave Miami-Dade.[15]

At the dawn of the millennium, Florida's Hispanic profile is broadening. No county has been untouched. Florida's population rolls grew by over 700,000 Hispanics during the 1990s. Counties as diverse as Wakulla and Sumter witnessed increases in Hispanics during the decade of 434 percent and 340 percent respectively. Gadsden County became the unlikely center for Florida's Salvadoran refugees. Broward County alone added almost 200,000 Hispanics during the 1990s, but the most significant trend was the flow of Hispanics into

Central and Southwest Florida. Locales that historically attracted few Hispanics—Polk, Citrus, Pasco, and Hernando counties—claimed 83,000 Latinos by 2000. Martin and St. Lucie counties now contain large numbers of Mexicans. Martin County also reflects the diversity of immigrant settings and occupations. In 1981, the first Mayans from Guatemala settled in Indiantown, working the fields and groves. Other Mayans have settled near Jupiter where they maintain the lush lawns and golf courses. Significantly, Hispanic numbers surged statewide; in *no* county in Florida was Hispanic growth in the 1990s less than 30 percent. In DeSoto County, for instance, Mexicans constituted 21 percent of the population. The county's Hispanic residents increased by 251 percent in the 1990s. Ironically, Monroe County, once the center of Florida's nineteenth-century Cuban population, was the county with the slowest-growing Hispanic population in the 1990s (31 percent). In Hillsborough County, a place associated with Ybor City, café cubano, and José Martí, Puerto Ricans have displaced Cubans as the county's largest Hispanic group. Osceola County's already considerable Hispanic population quadrupled during the 1990s. Remarkably, 2.5 million Floridians—almost one in five Floridians—speak Spanish at home.[16]

To appreciate the impact of immigration, one should look at Hardee County. In 1945, Hardee County's 8,588 residents were overwhelmingly white and native-born. Over 90 percent of the whites were born in states of the Old Confederacy and only one African American was born outside the South. Locals proudly boasted of Hardee's status as the "cucumber capital of America." When the first migrant workers began picking area fields in the 1940s and 1950s, school officials puzzled over whether to assign the Mexican children to white or black schools. By 1971, enough Hispanics had clustered in Zolfo Springs, Bowling Green, and Wauchula that locals dubbed the quarters "Little Mexico." The Hispanic population doubled in the 1990s; Hispanics now constitute more than a third of Hardee County's residents.[17]

Haitians and Jamaicans represent a fast-growing segment of non-Spanish-speaking Caribbean immigrants. For over a hundred years, West Indians have contributed mightily to South Florida's economy. By 2000, about 160,000 Jamaicans had settled in Dade and Broward counties. Miramar, a booming city in southwest Broward County, reflects the Jamaican influx: in 2003, a majority of the Miramar city commission was Jamaican-born. Between 1977 and 1982, at least 50,000 Haitians arrived in South Florida, many of them dramatically appearing as part of the "boat people" exodus. Stigmatized by poverty and race, the quarter million Haitians have nonetheless adjusted to the challenges of

TABLE 7. Florida's Hispanic Population

Year	Population	Percentage of population
1970	299,217	4.4
1980	580,025	5.9
1990	949,700	12.2
2000	1,291,737	16.8

Source: U.S. Census Bureau.

America. Many speak four languages. They make up a majority of the population of El Portal in Miami-Dade County.

The real story behind the dizzying numbers of immigrants may be how the new residents are redefining the meaning and accounting of race and ethnicity. Ironically, precisely at the point Hispanics have edged ahead of African Americans in Florida in terms of population, more and more Floridians wish to redefine the terms of race. Mayan newcomers challenge the meaning of Hispanic. When Floridians filled out their 2000 census forms, almost half a million checked "some other race," when asked to identify themselves. Another 376,315 persons considered themselves "mixed race." Many foreign-born blacks feel uncomfortable being classified or lumped together as "African American." In 2000, over 100,000 blacks born outside the United States resided in Miami-Dade County. One in four blacks in metro Orlando is foreign-born. New and more fluid notions of race and identity ironically echo *floridano* attitudes of eighteenth-century Pensacola and St. Augustine.[18]

Streams of Cubans, Nicaraguans, and Mexicans created a critical mass of Latin consumers and talent; streams of pesos, gold, and dollars financed and underwrote a media empire, with Miami as its new capital; and streams of new technologies and entertainment revolutions connected Little Havana with Caracas, London, and Los Angeles. The result of creative synergy—social, economic, and global—Miami has emerged as the Pan American media center. It began modestly. In 1958, while Miamians listened to Perry Como's "Papa Loves Mambo," the city's Latin population depended upon *Diario las Americas*, a Nicaraguan-owned newspaper, as the only Spanish-language source of information. The Cuban diaspora of 1959 brought intellectuals, journalists, and ideologues to Miami, soon a hotbed for broadsides, pamphlets, magazines, books, and newspapers. Highly literate and politically active writers, propagandists, and poets attempted to define and maintain a sense of *cubanidad* (Cubanness), of what it meant to be a Cuban exile in Florida. On crude mimeograph machines and on modern presses, _Cuba Libre_ was once again redefined.

The trials, tribulations, and fortunes of the _Miami Herald, El Herald,_ and _Mira!_ illustrate the dynamics of exile politics played out on front porches and corporate boardrooms. No institution cast as wide a shadow over Dade County as the _Miami Herald._ Published by the Knight-Ridder Company, the _Herald_ exemplified corporate responsibility and philanthropic commitment. Socially liberal and anticommunist, the _Herald_ sympathized with the plight of the Cuban emigrants but maintained a social and political distance. Cuban leaders complained to the _Herald,_ criticizing its insensitivity and coverage of events within and outside Little Havana. Few Anglo reporters spoke Spanish in the 1960s. In 1965, the _Herald_ considered but dropped the idea of a daily news column in Spanish. Alarmed at the indifference most Cubans displayed toward the _Herald,_ publishers understood Miami's demographic destiny. In 1976, the _Herald_ reached out to Hispanic readers with an insert in Spanish, the first such effort by a major American paper. _El Herald_ began modestly, as essentially a Spanish translation of the _Herald_'s stories. The response disappointed the _Herald_'s publishers. By 1984, _El Herald_ reached 72,000 households. In 1987, Knight-Ridder launched _El Nuevo Herald,_ an independent publication. _El Nuevo Herald_ brought the resources necessary to compete in the competitive market. By the early 1990s, circulation surpassed 100,000. America's lucrative market of Hispanic consumers has attracted competing print media, aware that English-language newspaper sales in South Florida have been declining for decades. The popular Spanish-language tabloid _Mira!_ has invaded the United States after achieving success in Spain and Latin America. Located in Lantana and owned by American Empire—the company that also owns _National Inquirer_ and _Star—Mira!_ hopes to attract Florida's Hispanics with its alluring mix of flesh and gossip. Across Florida, the Spanish-language press is a growth industry. Spanish readers in the Tampa Bay area have ten publications from which to choose. _Latino Internacional_ in Orlando has 12,000 readers. In South Florida, more than seventy-five newspapers inform, entertain, and infuriate a polyglot readership. If one wishes to find the soccer scores from Brazil, readers have eight Portuguese-language papers alone. A survey of South Florida newspaper stands will reward linguists with newspapers in Spanish, Hebrew, Yiddish, Korean, Vietnamese, Thai, Hindi, Urdu, Gujarati, Chinese, French, Iranian, Japanese, and Russian.[19]

An influx of Latin American artists has meant that Miami also serves as a gateway of American culture. A Spanish-English-Spanglish cultural and media revolution has taken place in South Florida, evidence that globalization should not be confused with Americanization. Since the 1920s, radio waves connected Cuba and Florida. In post-1959 Miami, radio reached great numbers of Cubans on the mainland and island. Beginning with a few hours of Spanish on local stations, Cuban businessmen invested heavily in the medium of radio. By the 1970s, Cuban-owned radio stations transmitted in Spanish twenty-four hours a day. "*La Radio* is an institution in Miami," observed Herberto Padillo, "something that Cubans in Miami cannot live without." But it was television that profoundly changed the way tens of millions of Hispanics in Florida and the southern hemisphere viewed their world. Entrepreneurs like Joaquin Blaya, a native of Chile, launched Telemundo and Univision, the most watched Spanish-language networks. Univision and Telemundo, headquartered in Miami and Hialeah, tape such popular shows as *Sabado Gigante* in South Florida. The Venezuelan conglomerate Cisneros Group invested heavily in Miami. The Cisneros Company moved its operational headquarters from Caracas to Coral Gables, where corporate officials oversee thousands of employees in forty countries. Miami has become an incubator for media ventures. Cristina Saralegui Enterprises, headquartered in Miami, produces Saralegui's talk show, seen by an estimated 100 million viewers worldwide.[20]

In South Florida, cyberspace and living space have created a dynamic, multicultural environment, a techno-culture some have called "Silicon Beach." In the 1990s, businesses invested more than $1 billion to bolster Miami's position as telecommunications gateway to and for Latin America. At least seventy-five dot-com companies established firms in South Florida. The most promising, Yupi.com, founded for Spanish-language surfers, served 4.1 million users at the end of the century.[21]

South Florida's eclectic mix and media synergy have given rise to a dynamic musical scene. Miami once looked to Cuba for the conga, mambo, and rumba; now Cubans and Latin Americans look to South Florida for the "Miami sound." Latin salsa, pop, Jamaican reggae, Dominican merengue, *bachata*, hip-hop, and Afro-Cuban jazz thrive in Florida's creole setting. Fiesta Calle Ocho is the largest street fair of Latin music outside Brazil's Carnaval. Originating as a block party in 1978, Fiesta Calle Ocho has expanded into *Carnaval Miami*, a ten-day, 23-block event that draws 1.5 million people. Emilio and Gloria Estéfan, Celia

Cruz, Willie Chirino, Raul Malo, Israel Kantor, Juan Luis Guerra, Albita Rodríguez, Lisa M, Debbie Bennett, Cachao, and Luther Campbell of 2 Live Crew
have melded various sounds and cultures into the transnational "Miami
sound." The Latin Grammy Awards, scheduled for Miami in 2000, were
moved because of Cuban-American protests. Miami hosted the 2004 Video
Music Awards, a first for the city. Corporate America has recognized Miami's
emerging cultural role, and major companies have opened offices in South
Florida. Such flowering of talent has influenced other arts. Since 1996, the
Miami Latin Film Festival has drawn large crowds and movie buffs.[22]

The Latinization of Florida dominates the headlines, but even without the
Cuban diaspora, the profile of Florida has been and continues to be profoundly
changed by immigration. Florida's fastest-growing foreign-born group since
the 1970s was not Hispanic but Asian. Historically, relatively few Asians had
ever settled in Florida. A Japanese colony, Yamato, existed briefly near Boca
Raton in the 1920s. A few cities had attracted small numbers of Chinese—
chiefly employed in laundries—but most of the Chinese had disappeared by the
1950s. Nativist hostility made Florida an unattractive place. In the 1930s, the
Florida legislature even passed a law banning Asian immigrants from inherit-
ing property. Seven decades later, the law has not been repealed. But the Florida
of the 1920s was not the Sunshine State of opportunity and multiculturalism.
The number of Asians residing in Florida tripled during the 1960s, tripling
again during the 1970s, and doubled in the 1980s. Over 200,000 Asians (principally Filipinos, Chinese, Vietnamese, and Koreans) resided in Florida in
2000.[23]

Asians have settled across Florida, migrating especially to the state's dynamic, urban areas. Many Asian immigrants settle and work in the suburbs,
evidence of new urban and economic opportunities. Over 50,000 Filipinos
have settled in communities in Pensacola and Jacksonville, while 33,000 Vietnamese have clustered in Orlando, Hialeah, and St. Petersburg. Orlando has
a Vietnamtown. Pensacola has a Buddhist temple and Vietnamese churches.
Cambodians have settled in Pinellas County in large numbers. Asian Indians
are Florida's fastest-growing group, over a third of whom reside in Dade and
Broward counties. Over 1,100 Asian Indians have settled in Lee and Collier
counties. "The joke here among our circles is when someone comes to Fort
Myers in the summer months, they see the mango trees and became absolute
suckers," explained Kumar Nandur. "They won't look at any other place." Southwest Florida will soon have its first Hindu temple. Thai Buddhist monks have

dedicated a temple in Miami to serve the 1,000 faithful in South Florida. When the Thai monks first arrived, neighbors mistook the monks for Hare Krishnas. The number of Asian Indians in Florida, especially South Florida, nearly tripled during the 1990s (29,117 to 84,527). The generally well-educated, English-speaking Indians and Asians are attracted to Florida's climate, the high-tech corridors, and certain trades, such as operating convenience stores and managing motels. Many newly arriving Asians came from the Caribbean and Latin America. Asian immigrants are changing the face of Florida religion. Hindu temples, Islamic mosques, and Buddhist shrines, rare before the 1970s, attract the faithful. Anyone shopping at the fruit and vegetable stalls of a modern supermarket understands the ethnic changes sweeping the state. Almost 700 Asians operated farms in 2002, evidence of the demand for such as bok choy, Chinese cabbage, Thai basil, and oriental eggplant. On weekends at college campuses and urban parks, a spirited but proper game of cricket is as likely as baseball.[24]

Florida's Arab population is also surging. Jacksonville had supported a small Christian Syrian and Lebanese community early in the century, but for the most part, Arabs were rare in the state. The 2000 census counted 77,461 Arabs, ranking Florida fifth among the states in Arab population. Most of the new Arab residents are Muslim; and Miami, Orlando, Tampa, and Fort Lauderdale are home to the greatest concentration of Arabs. Central Florida Muslims had built ten mosques by 2002.[25]

Muslims also represent a fast-growing religious group in Florida. Dozens of mosques have appeared in Opa-locka, Pompano Beach, Orlando, and Tampa. As many as 20,000 Muslims reside in Broward and Miami-Dade counties. Schools are adjusting to the state's newest students.[26]

Change is guaranteed. A graphic indicator of change is Florida's schools. If one were to scrutinize a classroom photograph in 1950, images were strictly—and legally—etched in black and white. A portrait of a 2003 Florida classroom offers a striking contrast. Multicultural, multi-ethnic, and racial hues accentuate the photograph. At some unannounced moment during the fall of 2003, Florida's minority students became a majority. Hispanic, African American, Asian, and multiracial students outnumbered whites. Demographic change can occur in the flash of a war or revolution. The Balkan crises of the 1990s resulted in the resettlement of several thousand Bosnians in Jacksonville. Duval County officials suddenly needed Serbo-Croatian- and Bosnian-speaking teachers.

In Orange County, the reverberations of multiculturalism have come suddenly. In 1950, Orange County was relatively homogeneous, with 80 percent of the inhabitants white. Moreover, almost no Hispanics or Asians resided in Central Florida. In the late 1990s, experts tabbed the number of Asian Americans living in Central Florida at 45,000, many of them Vietnamese. Orange County school officials announced in the spring of 1997 that blacks, Hispanics, Asians, and other minorities had so tipped the demographic scales that slightly more than half of the county's students were "minority." The U.S. Census announced in 2004 that Hispanics now outnumbered blacks in Central Florida. Almost 100,000 new Hispanics, chiefly Puerto Ricans, moved to Greater Orlando between 2000 and 2003.[27]

Writing from the vantage point of Miami in the 1980s—a time and place of wrack and riot—author David Rieff postulated, "Cubans are probably the only people who really feel comfortable in Dade County these days." Could anyone in 1980s Miami have imagined that McDonald's would introduce dulche de leche McFlurries? On the ledge of the twenty-first century, predicting the future of immigration and assimilation in Florida remains a risky business. Policy planning and seminars held to discuss Cuba after Fidel have the shelf life of one revolution in Latin America or a presidential campaign in the United States. If the first years of the twenty-first century are an indication, the rush to Florida has not dampened. Between 2000 and 2003, almost a half-million new immigrants entered Florida, including almost 200,000 Puerto Ricans. But for all of Floridians' apprehensions about immigration and assimilation, Florida has changed Cubans, Hispanics, and Asians as much as they have changed the Sunshine State.[28]

The Beach

9

S ERENE and sensuous, bewildering and bewitching, the beach evokes allusions both sacred and profane. It is our Babylon, a Garden of Earthly Delights and a heaven on earth, a Paradise Lost and Sodom and Gomorrah. Buried cities of pleasure and faded frescoes attest to the ancients' fondness for luxuriant islands and seaside villas. Living too well and too close to the sea posed problems, then and now. "A foolish man," the Apostle Matthew cautioned, "built his house upon the sand, and the rain fell, and the floods came, and the winds blew and beat against that house, and it fell." Land salesmen, however, preferred the passage from Acts 8:26, "Arise and go toward the south."[1]

From the beginning, the simplicity and harmony of earth, sun, wind, and sky came together at the water's edge. "Florida was born out of the sea like Venus," write Wallace Kaufman and Orrin Pilkey. The cooling and warming of the climate constantly altered the shape of the Florida shoreline; only within the last several thousand years has the peninsula assumed today's distinctive identity. The Lake Wales Ridge formed one of Florida's earliest coastlines.[2]

The most recurring image of Florida is that of a beach. Nearly all representations—the palm tree, lighthouse, chaise lounge, sea oats, gin-clear waters, and sugar-white sand—connect Florida with the beach. The sum is greater than the parts. Without the beach, Florida is Arkansas with palm trees; with-

Pale invaders and
tanned crusaders
Are worshipping the sun
On the corner of "walk"
and "don't walk"
Somewhere on U.S. 1.

Jimmy Buffett, *Floridays*

out sea spray, Miami Beach is Hot Springs with pretensions. The beach, like Florida, is for living and forgetting. Humans have raced cars, fought for freedom, and engaged in high-jinks on Florida beaches. The beach is a story of relationships, how people connect with sand and water.

Among the states, only Alaska boasts more miles of coastline. The sheer breadth of Florida (almost 2,000 miles of tidal shoreline, including 650 miles of beach and 4,500 islands) ensures that no resident lives more than 60 miles from saltwater and sea foam. The beach results from wave action and wind energy constantly eroding and accreting the shore. The natural elements, write Lena Lenček and Gideon Bosker, "produce a staggering range of beaches, each subject to constant change, sometimes rhythmical and cyclical, sometimes linear and catastrophic." They surround Florida with a stunning choice of barrier islands and beaches: Topsail Hill and Seaside, South Beach and St. Armand's Key, Cayo Costa and Destin. Subtle and dramatic turns of color paint the shore, from the pinkish coquina beaches of Amelia Island to the white, hard-packed sands of Daytona, from the golden-brown textures of South Florida to the sugar-white quartz sand of West Florida.[3]

Not all beaches are created or judged alike. In a nation obsessed with measuring and commodifying almost everything, we publish lists of the most desirable beaches (based upon criteria ranging from sand quality to restrooms). *National Geographic Traveler* and Professor Stephen P. Leatherman (better known as "Dr. Beach") consistently rank Pensacola Beach, the Santa Rosa Seashore, St. Joseph Peninsula State Park, Grayton Beach, Fort DeSoto State Park, Sanibel Island, Caladesi Island State Park, Amelia Island, Cape Canaveral, and Cape Florida as among America's finest.[4]

Because of magical relationships created by sand and water, smells and sounds, the beach is pure nature, or so it seems. But in the language of academic discourse, the beach is "socially constructed," meaning that our associations with it constantly change our definitions. We construct our own beaches, as man has physically constructed and reconstructed Florida's dunes and shore. At times as becalming as a picture postcard, at other moments resembling a Hieronymus Bosch descent into Hell, the beach is an arena for creative and destructive tension: nature versus technology, personal freedoms versus communal control, and democracy versus plutocracy.

The Evolution of the Modern Beach

The first encounter between Europeans and Native Americans—perhaps the single most significant event in American history—occurred on a Florida beach. "The beach itself was a savage place," argues anthropologist Greg Denig, "made so by the mutual contempt of those who stood across it from one another." Sometime in the early sixteenth century, a soldier, slaver, or ship's carpenter waded ashore. A breath of air, the smells of rancid palm oil and fetid sailors, the clasping of hands, and the drawing of blood set into motion a series of revolutions still unfolding. The Columbian exchange brought together continents and people that had been separated for millennia; the interchange of plants, animals, and microbes helped create a New World. And a new beach.[5]

The Spanish cared little for Florida's panoramic sunsets over pristine beaches. A succession of dons and governors regarded the coast dispassionately, nervously watching for marauding Protestants. Alternately terrifying and transcendent, the beach served as a meeting place and battleground. On Gulf beaches, Ponce de León received his mortal wound and Father Luis Cáncer met his martyrdom. On Atlantic beaches, Tequesta and Ais Indians dove frantically into the surf, desperate to slacken raging fevers brought about by smallpox and measles.

For most of Florida's recorded history, the beach was as remote as it was mysterious. Sea monsters lurked offshore—witness the occasional stranded leviathan. To reach the coastal dunes, travelers had to navigate marshes, lagoons, and mangrove swamps. Barrier islands were aptly named. Hurricanes, unannounced and unnamed, pummeled everyone and everything. Predatory salt marsh mosquitoes and voracious pests devoured intruders. For good reasons, almost no one lived *on* the beach. Things Floridians needed did not grow on the beach. An odd collection of hermits and adventurers pioneered beach settlements—barefoot mailmen, bruised Civil War veterans, New England consumptives. Life was hard and lonely on the beach.

"The beach was as remote and forbidding as the vast Everglades," remembered Charles Pierce. Describing his 1870s childhood on the shores of Lake Worth, Pierce reminisced: "No one thought of building much near the ocean, because it would eventually sweep any structure away. Beach land was cheap, particularly compared to the good farmland behind it."[6]

To a nation drawing deeply from the well of the Protestant work ethic, the beach tested the values of an older America that equated and rhymed leisure with pleasure. Physicians prescribed the saltwater cure for upper-class, over-stressed patients suffering from catarrh and neurasthenia. Shrewd entrepreneurs opened amusement parks for the working classes. Before Florida got into the business of amusing the millions, Coney Island functioned as a social safety valve, allowing immigrants and their families to frolic on sand and boardwalk while testing social norms and sampling American culture.[7]

Florida's first beach resorts appeared in the late nineteenth century. Jacksonville capitalized upon the national beach craze by building a narrow-gauge rail track to the ocean town of Ruby, better known by its later names, Pablo Beach and Jacksonville Beach. Murray Hall, a magnificent six-story wooden building highlighted by a curved veranda and an enormous tower, welcomed revelers. The *Florida Times-Union* estimated that a quarter of Jacksonville's residents celebrated Independence Day 1901 at the beach.[8]

Railroad magnates Henry Plant and Henry Flagler ushered in the era of Florida's luxury resorts. Elegant and stately, but built far from the ocean, the Ponce de León and Tampa Bay hotels neither turned profits nor transformed St. Augustine and Tampa into glamorous resort towns. Plant and Flagler quickly appreciated Americans' love affair with the beach, constructing ornate hotels along the Atlantic and Gulf coasts that defined seaside architecture. From Ormond Beach to Key West, Flagler extended his railroad and left behind some of the era's grandest structures. Above all, the robber baron made Palm Beach "Queen of Winter Resorts." The Royal Poinciana opened in 1894. Standing six stories and built of wood painted lemon yellow, the Royal Poinciana stood as the world's largest hotel. Nearby, Flagler constructed the even more renowned Breakers, an immediate success among America's most conspicuous consumers. The patrician Henry James depicted Palm Beach as "Vanity Fair in full blast."[9]

By rowboat and side-wheel steamer, by bicycle and wagon, ordinary Floridians escaped to enjoy the simple pleasures of the beach. As America was fast becoming a nation of cities, and as more and more inhabitants lived and worked in urban settings, a back-to-nature movement swept the country. In Gilded Age Florida, tourists and city dwellers discovered the peninsula's mysterious rivers and beaches. The seaside holiday became an American institution. In 1886, the *Halifax Journal* reported the latest pastime, "surf bathing, a perfectly safe gigantic bathing trough provided by nature." Santa Rosa Island, described by an American official in 1821 as "little more than a sand bar, with scattered shrubs," became a favorite destination for locals. In 1887, the

Pensacolian announced, "It is only within the last few weeks that bathing on the outer beach has become popular, and we predict that the day is not far distant when this part of Santa Rosa Island will become the Coney Island of the South." Apalachicola oystermen and cotton merchants took their families on excursions to picturesque St. George Island, where they picnicked by day and gigged for flounder at night. In her 1880s travel guide, Sylvia Sunshine marveled at Daytona's beach, "so firm that a pair of horses and a carriage scarcely make an indentation on the surface in passing over it." In St. Johns County, the horse-drawn St. Augustine and South Beach Railway plied locals and tourists across the marshes and dunes to Anastasia Island.[10]

Everything about the beach—the refreshing waters, cooling breezes, open-air dance pavilions, wooden bathhouses, and smells of fried fish and hush puppies, boiled crabs and roasting oysters, smoked mullet and sea salt—evoked pleasure. The beach oozed sensuality and hedonism, which moral guardians strictly confined in bathing attire. Highly ornamented and fashionable, women's earliest bathing outfits consisted of dark stockings, knee-length skirts, and serge bloomers with elaborate bodices designed to de-accentuate the feminine figure. The sight of a man's bare chest also scandalized moral gatekeepers, and, accordingly, men wore jersey tops.

As a beach culture emerged, a nervous society attempted to regulate youthful passions and enforce a code of conduct. In 1917, the American Association of Park Superintendents issued its infamous "Bathing Suit Regulations," which stipulated that women could wear knit suits *if* the bottom of the skirt was not "shorter than two inches above the bottom of the trunks." But Victorian America succumbed to an emerging Jazz Age. In a dress rehearsal for the Roaring Twenties and boom-time Florida, women abandoned bathing bloomers and flannel smocks for snug-fitting swimsuits. Jane Fisher, the irrepressible wife of Miami Beach mogul Carl Fisher, claimed credit for liberating South Florida beaches of Victorian reserve. A swimmer and flapper, Fisher's "form-fitting" beachwear prompted Dade County preachers to denounce her as a "symbol of brazenness of the modern woman." In her autobiography, *Fabulous Hoosier,* she noted wryly that "within a few weeks of my public pillorying, not a black cotton stocking was to be seen on the beach." Nonetheless, Florida police arrested scores of bathers for violating decency codes. A 1920 *Miami Herald* headline heralded the future: "Nymphs Want Bare Knees."[11]

There was nothing inevitable about a barrier island becoming Miami Beach. Geography was not destiny. Before glitterati and paparazzi, before South Beach and art deco, there existed an untamed island. With equal parts Olympian ambition and Barnumesque cunning, Carl Fisher imagined Miami Beach. First, the island entangled in strangler figs and populated by crocodiles would have to be transformed. Work crews blasted away, drained, and filled in the mangrove swamp. Instruments of his ambition, giant steam shovels dredged the bay bottom, dumping shell and muck into dikes. Carl Fisher, contended Marjory Stoneman Douglas, "was the first to realize you could create land by pumping it from the bay bottom." The humorist Will Rogers put it differently: "Carl rowed the customers out into the ocean and let them pick out some nice smooth water where they would like to build, and then he would replace the water with an island, and today the dredge is the national symbol of Florida."[12]

The founder of the Indianapolis Motor Speedway, Fisher was endowed with genius in both imagining and promoting his tropical paradise. Miami Beach became America's most exotic dream factory. Fisher sponsored bathing beauty pageants, popularized polo and sport fishing, and persuaded the "smart set" to build pleasure palaces on Biscayne Bay.[13]

Miami Beach was a harbinger, ushering in a revolution in leisure and lifestyles. The beach bedazzled American popular culture in the 1920s, epitomizing everything that made Florida, Florida: ballyhoo, pleasure, and captivation. Surging numbers of tourists, made possible by Republican prosperity and democratic impulses, flocked to Florida beaches. Mobsters and celebrities shared the good life on the beach. Resort hotels and the Gold Coast bespoke Florida dreams.

Beach and water became interchangeable metaphors for the Florida boom. In Boca Raton and Hollywood, St. Petersburg and Sarasota, Mediterranean revival was the rage, as the New World looked to the old for a suitable architecture. "Waterfront living" became an essential element in the selling of Florida. "The water is the thing," declared a 1916 St. Petersburg real estate advertisement. "Keep close to the water." Terra-cotta tile and serpentine columns suggested a patina of elegance and whispers of the Côte d'Azur, Málaga, and Portofino, even in Orlando or Ocala.

The dream of a Carl Fisher, John Ringling, and David P. Davis crashed but endured during the Land Bust and Great Depression. Economic misery reduced the flow of northern tourists, but the idea of the beach as a place of escape and romance intensified during the 1930s. To capitalize upon the national beach craze, New Smyrna, Deerfield, and Delray added the word to their names in the 1930s. A 1930s building frenzy redecorated Miami Beach in a stream-

Venice-Nokomis

White City Supreme On the Gulf

The Next *Logical* Water-front City

RIGHT IN THE LINE OF DEVELOPMENT

FAMOUS for its beauty and its THIRTY MILES OF SUPERB SHORE-FRONT, is VENICE-NOKOMIS. Here, south of Sarasota, is being designed and laid out by John Nolen, noted City Planner, the ideal city of semi-tropical loveliness. With every superior advantage of unrivaled scenic location, fronting on the Gulf, four bays and river—directly on the Tamiami Trail—with active development program now under way—the property-wise investor cannot fail to see that here is the next logical development of the lower West Coast.

Write for Beautiful Booklet

The Roger C. Rice Company, Inc.

Exclusive Sales Agents

SARASOTA, FLORIDA

FIGURE 47. During the 1920s, the architectural style known as Mediterranean revival swept Florida, the American Riviera. Borrowing elements of southern Spain and Renaissance Italy, such homes featured terra-cotta tiles, stucco walls, and patios. Author's collection.

lined style known as art deco, or Depression moderne. Celebrities as diverse as Al Capone and Eleanor Roosevelt sought refuge on Florida beaches.[14]

December opened the high tourist season. Resort hotels shuttered between May and November came alive the first Sunday in December. Hotel managers beamed at the growing stacks of reservations the morning of 7 December 1941, the day the Japanese would bomb Pearl Harbor. By sunset, the specter of oil-covered beaches, total blackouts, and curfews cast shadows across the Sunshine State. Soon, resort cupolas turned into redoubts and watchtowers.

The war came terrifyingly close to St. Augustine Beach, Jupiter, and Miami. The stench of burning oil tankers replaced the smell of suntan lotion in the winter of 1942, as German U-boats unleashed a terrifying assault on Allied shipping off the Atlantic Coast, sinking twenty-four ships in just four months. Floridians prepared for an invasion. Mounted patrols and armed sentries guarded beaches from Perdido Key to Biscayne Bay throughout the war.[15]

In the predawn hours of June 17, 1942, not far from where Spanish Catholics had massacred French Protestants in 1565, U-boat 584 deposited its top-secret cargo, four German saboteurs. The infiltrators wore their marine caps with swastika insignia (so that, if captured, they would be tried as prisoners of war). German agents had selected Ponte Vedra as their point of infiltration, a sparsely populated resort south of Jacksonville Beach. The FBI eventually captured and executed the invaders as spies.[16]

The War Department became an unlikely beach tenant, requisitioning hundreds of resort hotels from St. Augustine to St. Petersburg for basic training. By the fall of 1942, almost 350 Miami and Miami Beach hotels had been converted to military barracks and hospitals, housing hundreds of thousands of soldiers. "Baby pink and egg-shell furniture," quipped a reporter, had been replaced by bunk beds and spartan furnishings. The grand experiment to turn resort hotels into military barracks had the effect of a massive publicity campaign for the Sunshine State. "Mother," wrote one GI from Miami Beach's Blackstone Hotel, "This is the most beautiful place I have ever seen. Green palm trees, green grass, blue ocean and sky. . . . I really think when the war is over, I'll move down here."[17]

Armored landing craft and dynamite disrupted paradise on the beach. The invasions of Tarawa, Iwo Jima, and Normandy were rehearsed on Caladesi, Hutchinson, and Dog islands. To "hit the beach" acquired an eerie new meaning. Underwater demolition teams set off explosives on the beaches of Fort Pierce, while recruits perfected amphibious assaults at Carrabelle's Camp Gordon Johnston, aka "Hell-by-the-Sea." A veteran later sighed that nearby Dog Island was "the most 'fought over' piece of land in Florida."[18]

Freedom and the Beach

The beach has always captured the imagination of artists. In the 1950s, one of Florida's most accomplished landscape artists, A. E. "Bean" Backus, began giving painting lessons to a group of young African Americans in Fort Pierce. Harold Newton, George Buckner, Alfred Hair, Mary Ann Carroll, and others—later anointed the "Highwaymen" because they sold their cheap, mass-produced, formulaic oil paintings along u.s. 1—became the best-selling artists in Florida history. Such colorful landscapes, contended Mark Derr, "shaped the state's popular image as much as oranges and alligators." The landscapes, painted on Upson board, rarely included humans. Highwaymen paintings portrayed billowing clouds, wind-bent palm trees, azure-colored waters, a beating surf, and spectacular sunsets. People would have complicated the beach. As the Highwaymen painted and peddled serene images of the Sunshine State, the civil rights movement was unfolding.[19]

In 1950s Florida, there was a beach for everyone: working-class white southerners frequented Gulf Breeze and Seagrove; midwesterners adored Fort Myers Beach and Clearwater Beach; working-class New Yorkers escaped to Pompano Beach and Stuart; Jews called Miami Beach home; Cubans adopted Miami as a favorite summertime destination; and college students made Fort Lauderdale and Daytona Beach synonymous with spring break. The beach defined Florida, but it also divided Floridians. Race mattered, and the resulting divisions defined Florida as a southern state. In city codes and social custom, Florida had long dictated that boardwalks and sand dunes existed for the pleasure of white patrons. Blacks worked as bellhops and dishwashers; they neither strutted nor played on "whites-only" beaches. In many seaside communities, blacks were permitted on the beach only if they carried an ID indicating they worked there.

The beach was forbidden land to African Americans, whose back-breaking labor made many resort towns possible. Northern whites, while occasionally questioning and even challenging Jim Crow, typically accepted the tenets of beach segregation. Planning a 1950 vacation to Casa Glamaretta in Fort Lauderdale, Mrs. Robert C. Clark of Michigan wrote the manager to inquire about rates and maid service. The manager dutifully informed Mrs. Clark that a deck-front apartment would cost $1,700 for six months. "In regards to your colored maid," he explained, "I am sorry it would be quite impossible here in the south for her to live in the same building with white people. There is a city ordinance that prohibits it and they are not allowed on the beach after 9 p.m." If Mrs. Clark acceded to the white watermark, others did not. In 1958, an Alabama visitor asked to be driven along the ocean at Daytona Beach. The Rev. Rogers P. Fair, pastor at Bethune-Cookman College, explained to his fellow clergyman that blacks were not allowed on the beach. "Isn't this a shame," the visitor responded. "This is God's ocean and these people want to restrict people from enjoying it. But that won't last long." The visitor, Rev. Martin Luther King Jr., was also a prophet.[20]

Moved by profit and altruism, African American businessmen opened a number of black beaches. Since Pablo Beach (later known as Jacksonville Beach) allowed African Americans admission on Mondays only, Duval County blacks welcomed the opening of Manhattan Beach in 1907, "an all-colored beach." The navy purchased Manhattan Beach during World War II. About the same time, the State of Florida purchased Big Talbot and Little Talbot islands, designating a pier and pavilion for blacks on the latter and a park for whites on the former. Farther south, Mary McLeod Bethune, the imperious founder and president of Bethune-Cookman College, frustrated when all-white Daytona Beach refused black students access to the beach, persuaded a group of black businessmen to purchase two and one-half miles of oceanfront from the Atlantic to the Mosquito Lagoon. Bethune-Volusia Beach was born. After World War II, African American families purchased lots, and vacationers flocked to the Welricha Motel and the Beach Casino. Crowds heartily cheered "colored" race-car drivers. In the 1950s, black businessmen from Tallahassee purchased property and opened Money Bayou Beach at Port St. Joe.[21]

American Beach—portrayed as Lincoln Beach in John Sayles's *Sunshine State*—became Florida's most celebrated black beach. American Beach—the name rings with bittersweet irony—welcomed blacks from forty-eight states. In the 1930s, Jacksonville's Afro-American Life Insurance Company purchased the property, located on the south end of Amelia Island. Eager to capitalize upon his investment, insurance magnate Abraham Lincoln Lewis began selling $150 lots for vacation homes. In the words of the founders, American Beach offered African Americans "recreation and relaxation without humiliation." Generations of visitors fondly recall the legendary establishments: Honey Dripper and Duck's Ocean-Vu-Inn.[22]

FIGURE 48. In South Florida, Virginia Beach was the area's most famous and revered black beach. State of Florida Photographic Archives, Tallahassee.

Empowered and emboldened by the dreams and realities of World War II, African Americans envisioned a new day at the beach. Miami boomed during the war, attracting large numbers of soldiers to its military bases and training facilities. Black soldiers from the North chafed at Jim Crow practices, especially the existence of whites-only public beaches. The war rattled social convention. In May 1944, Dade County designated Virginia Key as a temporary black beach. In the waning days of the war, Miami's civil rights movement sprang forward with a powerful statement. In May 1945, Miami's Colored Ministerial Alliance orchestrated a "swim-in." The target was Baker's Haulover Beach, the county's white beach. Chagrined city and county leaders responded by offering blacks a separate beach at Virginia Key, until 1947 accessible only by a seventy-five-cent ferry ride. Banned from Miami's white hotels, celebrities Nat King Cole, Lena Horne, and Jackie Robinson stayed on the storied island, which became a unifying symbol for South Florida blacks.[23]

African American leaders and civil rights activists selected their targets carefully: schools, Woolworth's five-and-ten stores, and the whites-only beaches. In a state where image mattered dearly, businessmen and politicians realized the only thing more unsettling than blacks and whites swimming together on pub-

lic beaches were newsflashes of empty Florida resorts, the result of costly boycotts and protests.

In the early 1950s, most African Americans were perfectly willing to accept
the tenets of segregation—if white society was willing to provide decent accommodations. The opening of black public beaches may have irritated some
whites, but the policy maintained the racial status quo. Just weeks after the
Brown decision in May 1954, the Associated Press circulated a story titled, "Segregation Still Rules on Beaches of Florida." A handful of separate, public black
beaches existed in Pensacola, Miami, St. Petersburg, Fort Myers, West Palm
Beach, and Palm Beach. All Florida cities prohibited "race mixing" at the beach.
The AP story hinted that Negro leaders were prepared to "use public beaches" if
demands for adequate recreational facilities were not met.[24]

Florida civil rights leaders chose the Fourth of July 1956 to challenge the
sanctity of the all-white beach. At precisely the moment that Dr. Martin Luther
King Jr. and Reverend C. K. Steele were leading bus boycotts in Montgomery,
Alabama, and Tallahassee, African Americans roiled the waters of Florida. Rumors swirled from Pensacola to Key West that the NAACP planned to invade
white beaches. "Will they come or won't they?" speculated officials at Jacksonville. "Rumors upon rumors" that busloads of Negroes from Tampa (Hillsborough County) would invade Pinellas County prompted Clearwater Beach city
commissioners to pass an "emergency measure" empowering the police to
regulate "the time, manner, and number of persons using Memorial Causeway
to the beach." White leaders resisted, but time was on the side of the scorned.[25]

In Miami, the local NAACP delegation confronted the Dade County Commission with evidence that the county operated twenty-eight public beaches but
only one restricted black beach, Virginia Key. Led by Garth Reeves, the Baha-
mas-born publisher of the *Miami Times*, the group told the commissioners that
they would integrate Crandon Beach that afternoon. "We slipped on our trunks
under our clothes, and we walked down to the beach," remembered Reeves.
"The police didn't stop us . . . [we] kicked off our sandals, took off our slacks, and
went into the water. Nobody said a word. No police officer came up. . . . From
that day [7 November 1957] the beaches of the county became integrated."[26]

Sarasota seemed an unlikely place to be condemned as racist. A city known
for its cultured gentility, Sarasota had attracted artists, authors, and wealthy
northerners eager to enjoy the comforts of sun and sand. The city motto, "You
can't stop progress," was challenged in 1955 when the Sarasota NAACP demanded the integration of white beaches. Long frustrated at unsuccessful

efforts to secure a black beach, African American leaders selected Lido Beach as a site for protest. Officials closed the beach. On Independence Day 1956, four African Americans "invaded" Siesta Key. Sarasota county commissioners passed a bill allowing the sale of public recreational facilities to private parties. In August 1956, the Sarasota City Council enacted an "emergency ordinance" authorizing police to remove African Americans from Gulf beaches. A companion bill banned boats with Negro passengers from cruising too close to shore. The protests shattered the image of the progressive city. Sarasota resident and author Mary Freeman bristled at the city's hypocrisy and foot-dragging. She charged in a series of 1957 articles in the *Nation* that the deception deployed by citizens and politicians "has been worthy of this home of three circuses." Pulitzer Prize–winning author MacKinlay Kantor threatened to write an article titled "Sarasota Cheats Its Colored Children," but no black beach was ever secured. Each time the county selected a potential site, angry residents and business interests challenged the choice. The president of the Longboat Key Civic Club in neighboring Manatee County also implored Sarasota officials to consider the "disastrous results of the establishment of such a beach."[27]

Delray Beach became a flashpoint in the struggle for justice. In 1954, the city had purchased a separate tract for local blacks, a 500-foot strip of beach at Ocean Ridge. Black leaders complained that the facility was dangerous, inadequate, and inconvenient, pointing out the mile-long stretch of public beach for whites. In February 1955, nine local African Americans sued the city, demanding the right to use white beaches. White leaders responded by passing specific measures prohibiting the mixing of races on the beaches, calling the action an "emergency ordinance to prevent interracial riots." City commissioners permitted police to set up roadblocks to halt and search motorists headed for the beach. Furthermore, the city commission asked the Florida legislature to remove the "entire Negro area" from Delray Beach. Threatened with Fourth of July protests in 1956, Delray Beach officials agreed to find a more suitable black beach.[28]

Broward County blacks once claimed a beach of their own, a stunning and undeveloped tract of land called the Galt Ocean Mile. The owners allowed African Americans to use the beach. In 1953, a developer purchased the Galt tract, which included a mile of ocean frontage, for $19.4 million. The developer's plans did not include a black beach. Exasperated, black leaders badgered Broward County officials that the recreational needs of African Americans mattered. Fort Lauderdale stonewalled. A delegation marched at the county courthouse, to no avail. In 1957, commissioners voted to sell the city golf course at a greatly reduced price to private owners, lest Negroes integrate the facility. Mayor John V. Russell explained, "A handful of Negroes can put us out of the recreation business entirely." Broward county commissioners finally purchased a tract of beachfront south of Port Everglades in Dania. But the site was so isolated that it took residents hours to reach. The county dragged its feet over a new road to the black beach. Frustrated and mad, Eula Mae Gandy Johnson, president of the local NAACP chapter simply decided, "we were going to integrate our beaches." Johnson and Dr. Von D. Mizelle, a Fort Lauderdale physician, chose the Fourth of July 1961 to integrate the Fort Lauderdale Beach. When the small party entered the water, every white swimmer departed. Some spat on Mrs. Johnson. A radio bulletin announced, "Negroes are lounging on the municipal beach." The publisher of the *Fort Lauderdale News* offered black leaders money if they would call off the wade-ins. City officials called Mrs. Johnson a "public nuisance." The city sued Mrs. Johnson for "inciting a riot," but a judge ruled in her favor, striking down the statute segregating the beaches.[29]

Then there was the case of St. Augustine. In 1960, St. Augustine was a small tourist city of about 18,000 residents. Behind the carriage rides and colonial architecture stood a southern white community resistant to integration. As the "Ancient City" prepared for its four-hundredth anniversary, civil rights leaders pressed for change. White leaders in Fort Lauderdale, St. Petersburg, and Miami also opposed integration, but they understood that a protracted civil rights siege would be costly and ruinous. Beach communities depended entirely upon reputations. The leadership and populations of South Florida beach communities were increasingly composed of northern-born residents who were more willing to accommodate racial change. St. Augustine whites bitterly opposed black boycotts and protests; "outside agitators" from both sides poured into the city to press their causes. On June 23, 1964, an Associated Press photograph appeared on the front pages of hundreds of U.S. newspapers. The subject and message mortified Florida tourist officials. The *New York Times* blared, "Segregationists Break up Wade-Ins at St. Augustine." The photograph depicted a white mob attacking blacks who had dared wade into the water on the all-white beach.[30]

St. Augustine dashed any die-hard segregationist hopes that the movement could be stopped on the beach. Governor LeRoy Collins had voiced the hopes of many Floridians when, in a 1956 address, he argued that the state could "pre-

FIGURE 49. The struggle for freedom also took place at the water's edge. In one of Florida's most famous civil rights demonstrations, blacks and whites confront one another at St. Augustine Beach, 25 June 1964. State of Florida Photographic Archives, Tallahassee.

serve segregation without furor." Collins, at heart a moderate, emphasized that Florida "cannot afford an orgy of race conflict and discord." By the time the governor left office in 1961, he spoke openly against the immorality of segregation, but his worst fears had been realized. While many Florida communities had begun the process of desegregation, other cities and towns resolved to fight it. St. Augustine demonstrated the cost of resistance. Tourism plunged between 1963 and 1964; local officials estimated economic losses at over $5 million.[31]

What is most striking about the St. Augustine affair is neither the heightened rhetoric nor the ugly violence—Florida experienced many such acts of incivility and brutality. Indeed, in the first three decades of the twentieth century, Florida, not Mississippi or Alabama, led the South in lynchings per capita. What is striking about St. Augustine in 1964 was timing. Considered unthinkable in 1956, the integration of beaches in Ft. Lauderdale and Sarasota was accomplished by 1961. The crisis symbolized the growing differences between the two Floridas—North Florida and South Florida—but also between rural and urban Florida, and between the beach and interior communities. In 1953, Miami Beach hotels welcomed 20,000 members of the Negro Baptist Convention. Such a reception was unthinkable in any other Deep South city. St. Petersburg desegregated its public beaches in 1958; Miami accomplished the same in

1960. Virtually every South Florida beach community between Volusia County and Pinellas County had resolved this issue by the early 1960s. The Civil Rights Act of 1964 mandated the integration of Panhandle beaches.[32]

The relative peaceful integration of Florida's beaches also illustrates the social and political distance separating Florida from its Deep South neighbors, and the gap between cities and towns *within* the state. Florida presents a puzzling dichotomy to social scientists. In many ways, Florida was the most moderate and least southern of the Deep South states. Between 1947 and 1960, the percentage of African Americans registered to vote increased from 13 percent to 39 percent. Among southern states, only Tennessee had registered a greater proportion of its black residents. In contrast, only 6 percent and 14 percent of Mississippi's and Alabama's black citizens had registered to vote by 1960. When blacks attempted to integrate the beaches of the lower gulf in 1959, legislators and townfolk resisted forcefully, employing the draconian Mississippi State Sovereignty Commission to investigate and persecute suspects. No southern state had more Yankee transplants than Florida. Yet in many ways, the relatively peaceful integration of Florida's beaches was illusory. Florida had its Sovereignty Commission to investigate suspected civil rights leaders (as well as homosexuals and communists), the Johns Committee. School integration was painfully slow in the Sunshine State, by the standards of any southern state. In 1967, the University of Florida had no black faculty and only 67 African American students. The Florida legislature passed an Interposition resolution, only to have Governor LeRoy Collins veto it. The Tallahassee Bus Boycott and the Florida sit-ins represent massive examples of civil obedience and white incivility.[33]

Youth and the Beach

Sand dunes and salt water also encapsulated youthful dreams. Tested, contested, and negotiated, the beach became part of the vocabulary of American youth: beach music, beach movies, beach week, bikinis, beachniks, surfing, the Beach Boys, and spring break. Part harmonic convergence, the result of millions of teenagers coming of age in a time of rebellion and affluence, and part hormonic convergence, a coming of age in a society saturated with sexual images, the Florida beach perfectly matched generation and lifestyles. Fort Lauderdale, Daytona Beach, and Panama City Beach were reinvented to fit an American rite of passage.

FIGURE 50. Sitting atop a Fort Myers Beach sand dune, four youths embody 1940s beach culture. Fort Myers Historical Museum.

The genesis of spring break dates from the Great Depression. Fort Lauderdale, like many cities buffeted by a decline in tourism and the collapse of the real estate market, sought new sources of revenue. In 1935, the city's first Collegiate Aquatic Forum was held at the casino pool on the beach. A resident persuaded his fellow Colgate University swim team members to train in his hometown over Christmas break. When the swimmers returned to frigid New York, the image of sunny Fort Lauderdale had been imprinted upon the student body. The following year, many Colgate students chose to explore the reputed charms of the city. In time, the migration shifted from Christmas to Easter vacation. Following the war, more and more students returned. Familiar landmarks became cherished institutions. The Elbo Room on the ground floor of the Sea-breeze Hotel acquired a legendary status. But mostly it was the spacious beach that lured young people from Hamilton, New York.[34]

In 1953, Fort Lauderdale's Hospitality Committee mailed invitations to hundreds of college student councils, fraternities, and sororities. The publicity paid off. Spring break 1953 drew almost 15,000 collegians. "Although generally well behaved," observed the *Fort Lauderdale Daily News* in 1956, "the college students have caused past concern over pranks like stocking swank hotel pools with an occasional alligator and in one instance a dead shark." In the lexicon of the fifties, the beach welcomed both "beachniks" and "I like Ike" Republicans.[35]

The 1960s changed the trajectory of spring break. A 1959 *Time* magazine article, "Beer and the Beach," chronicled 20,000 collegians who "grilled themselves medium-rare all day [and] beach-boozed all night." A journalist naively asked a coed why she came to Fort Lauderdale. "This is where the boys are," she cooed. A risqué novel by Glendon Swarthout and an immensely successful MGM movie immortalized the student's comments. *Where the Boys Are* made Fort Lauderdale synonymous with spring break. Premiering at Fort Lauderdale's Gateway Theatre on December 21, 1960, *Where the Boys Are* showcased the sultry voice of Connie Francis and the suntanned charm of George Hamilton. The film spawned a cinema genre—the drive-in beach movie: *Beach Blanket Bingo, How to Stuff a Wild Bikini, Beach Party,* and *Spring Break.* Hollywood produced over a hundred beach movies. In *Follow That Dream* (1961), Elvis starred as a dutiful son of rural folk who find paradise along a deserted Citrus County beach.[36]

Where the Boys Are delivered a jolt of testosterone to spring break. The movie coincided with the New Frontier and a dashing, youthful president. Just three months after the release of the film, 50,000 young people descended upon Fort Lauderdale beaches. *American Bandstand* impresario Dick Clark blessed the crowds from his hotel balcony. Pandemonium followed. Headlines told the story: "Scores of Unkempt College Youths Jailed or Fined at Ft. Lauderdale," "Unruly Students Whoop It Up in Ft. Lauderdale," and "Lauderdale Jail Bulging."[37]

Neither personal appearances by the Rev. Billy Graham nor "public decency" and "open container" laws could halt the April migration to Fort Lauderdale. The Button, Jolly Roger, and the Elbo Room became hallowed hangouts. At one point in the 1970s, the Button—said to have been the place that made the wet T-shirt contest an art form—sold more Miller's draft beer than any other place in America. In 1973, the mayor of Fort Lauderdale vowed to change the city's image from "where the boys are" to "where the bums aren't." As late as 1980, over 250,000 students still flocked to Broward County, but Fort Lauderdale's time in the youthful sun soon passed.[38]

By the time Fort Lauderdale had filed for divorce, college youth had fallen in love with a new suitor, Daytona Beach. From the beginning, it was a star-crossed affair. The home of the state's most famous boardwalk and 27 miles of beaches that doubled as racetracks, Daytona Beach was fading in the 1960s. The city invited artist Norman Rockwell in hopes of refurbishing its image. The opening of Disney World in 1971 and the energy crises further devastated local businesses. Daytona Beach aggressively romanced college students, hoping to lure them to Volusia County. At one point, the city hired helicopters to drop thousands of ping pong balls on Fort Lauderdale Beach. The balls contained messages encouraging the crowds to migrate to Daytona Beach.[39]

It worked, and few could deny the bottom line: spring break spurred an economic bonanza for Volusia County. Spring break 1973 attracted a quarter million students. By the late 1980s, over 400,000 young people were strolling the city's expansive beaches, leaving behind annually $120 million in sales and accounting for half of the city's revenues. Residents soon discovered that the readers of *Saturday Evening Post* and those of the *Rolling Stone* did not share the same manners or morals. Prosperity came with a price tag. Crime soared. The president of the local motel association complained that spring break was "destroying the family concept so carefully built up over the years." In 1979, *Penthouse* magazine dubbed the city, "Sleaze Summit, U.S.A." Then came 1989, the mother of all spring breaks. Daytona Beach police received 10,000 complaint calls and arrested almost 2,000 revelers. Main Street became known as the "Boulevard of the Busted." Revolted at the excesses, residents demanded that officials take back their city, preferring less possessive bikers and racing fans to students.[40]

Obeying the most elementary law of physics, displaced college students moved to a new destination. Panama City Beach became the most popular spring break destination in the late 1990s, drawing as many as a half million students, and anointed by MTV as the capital of debauchery. Fame came late but furiously for this Bay County community described by a 1939 writer as a "fishing resort" with "gay-colored summer cottages lining the dunes." A reporter recently described Front Beach Road as "twelve miles of motels, liquor stores, fast-food restaurants, bars, arcades, miniature golf courses and adult tattoo and body-piercing shops." Again, it was time to conclude, "Spring Break is to Florida beach cities what Mephistopheles was to Faust: a great deal, if you don't mind the downside." Panama City Beach, too, is resisting youthful excesses. The local tourist council, hoping to recast the city's image, has launched a new slogan: "White Sand, White Wine, White Necks." Officials have even made overtures to host a World Temperance League convention! But spring break is also worth a staggering $220 million to the town annually.[41]

The modern beach also pulsates with money—witness the billion-dollar business named spring break. As its capitals have shifted from Fort Lauderdale to Daytona Beach to Panama City Beach, investors follow the March money trail to Negril, Jamaica; Cancún, Mexico; and South Padre Island, Texas.

"What began twenty-five years ago as a pleasant interlude for a few hundred students during the Easter vacation," wrote a 1961 observer, "has turned into a folk ritual that could be better described by anthropologist Margaret Mead." Yet for all of the youthful passion and seaside reveling, for all of the exposure (media and flesh), Florida's spring break is more fizz than substance. Why has such revelry not produced or sustained a Florida beach culture?[42]

California and Florida were America's most touted dream states. But California, not Florida, nurtured and exported a youth-defined beach culture. "Other places had 'the shore,' or 'the coast,' or they had 'beaches,'" insists essayist Robert A. Jones, "but no place had The Beach until we [southern California] invented it." In the decades preceding the 1950s, Californians expressed great passion for their beaches. A cult of physicality, athleticism, and pleasure followed. Beginning in the 1950s, southern California caught the imagination of youth and the media. Dick Dale, the father of surf music, philosophized that California youth, bent upon claiming a culture of their own, invented and reinvented the beach. Home to Hollywood and Los Angeles, Malibu and Venice Beach, California became a cultural incubator, center of a media and popular entertainment industry. The Golden State drew upon the creative energies of large numbers of young people attracted to alternative lifestyles and the lure of the beach. Some of America's most prestigious universities—UCLA, UC Santa Barbara, and UC San Diego—were hothouses of intellectual ferment and student activism but were also located only short distances from great beaches. From St. Petersburg to Miami Beach to Boca Raton, Florida's beaches were more likely teeming with retirees than teenagers.[43]

Music targeted youth and popularized an emerging beach culture. The 1950s introduced mass-produced, transistor-powered radios, which blanketed beaches with the new sounds of FM stations and rock and roll. "The California

Sound became famous," writes cultural historian Stephen Whitfield, contending that "a Florida Sound never developed." A succession of hit songs in the early 1960s glamorized the Golden State, but not even the Honeys' 1963 song "Surfin' down the Swanee River" made the Sunshine State a musical magnet. If an era and place had an acoustical beat, California's was the driving guitar of Dick Dale. Singing hits about hot rods and cool girls, Jan and Dean and the Beach Boys had no rivals in Florida. Myrtle Beach (South Carolina) and the Jersey shore—not Florida—developed distinctive beach sounds. Jimmy Buffett, more than any other singer, incorporated the "flip-flops" lifestyle of the Florida Keys in his records, and in spite of a faithful, if aging, Parrot Head following, he has achieved more commercial success than cultural influence. A native of the Deep South, Buffett moved to Key West in 1970. Legend claims that the Cabbage Key Fishing Lodge—which has no beach—inspired Buffett's song "Cheeseburger in Paradise." His 1977 hit "Margaritaville" became an unofficial anthem for the Conch Republic.[44]

Surfin' USA exemplified and popularized California's and Hawaii's beach culture, but for most of the Florida peninsula, the surfboard was more an item of curiosity than cultural symbol. In Hawaii, tourists (especially women) fell in love with native "beach boys" who combined sexuality and athleticism to glamorize surfing. One need not surf to rhapsodize about surfer girls. Jim Morrison was born in Melbourne, but nearby Cocoa Beach and Melbourne Beach were more famous for astronauts and early-bird specials than what was arguably the finest waves in Florida. Brevard County may have been home for the men with the "right stuff," but its leaders and attitudes reflected small-town conservatism. Florida's first surfboard enterprise, the Daytona Beach Surf Shop, opened in 1961, long after the sport had become a big business on the Pacific Coast. Precisely at the moment California youth popularized riding the waves off Corona Del Mar, Doheny, and Malibu Beach, Miami Beach, St. Petersburg, and Stuart had become destinations for waves of retirees. A Palm Beach County law prohibits surfboards within 500 feet of fishing piers. In Hawaii, the name Duke Paoa Kahanamoku is synonymous with the history of surfing; in California, three museums pay homage to the Pacific Coast sport. In Florida, no such shrines exist, despite the fact that the 120-mile span of waves between Amelia Island and the Sebastian Inlet is home to many world-class surfers. Few Floridians could identify Kelly Slater or Frieda Zamba, in spite of the fact that the Cocoa Beach and Flagler Beach residents have won the world surfing championships several times. Since 1964, dudes have gathered at the Cocoa Beach

Pier to participate in the Easter Surfing Festival; Jimmy Lane's Surfing Academy has operated out of New Smyrna Beach, home to the Florida State Surf Championships, since the 1970s. Florida's Gulf coast, long derided by world-class surfers for its genteel breakers, has attracted attention because of Treasure Island's Suncoast Surf Shop and the exploits of Indian Rocks Beach athletes Cory and Shea Lopez. Opened in 1963, the Ron Jon Surf Shop on AIA in Cocoa Beach is the largest surfing chain store in the world. Ron Jon's paraphernalia, clothing, and marketing has expanded to malls, where one can buy sunglasses, surfboards, or one of the sixteen million T-shirts the company has sold. Underappreciated and underestimated, Florida surfing is on the rise.[45]

The beach is theater and spectacle. As intercontinental ballistic missiles (ICBMs) blasted heavenward at Cape Canaveral, youthful eyes gazed the water's edge, measuring the social change in swimwear. From the bikini to the thong, from wet T-shirt to topless, beach fashion is part youthful exuberance, part corporate America, part generational rebellion.

Development of the Modern Beach

For all of our fascination with the beach, astonishingly little of it had been developed at midcentury. Destin and Carrabelle were fishing villages; occasional clapboard cottages and fishing piers interrupted long stretches of pristine Panhandle beaches. One could walk for hours along Atlantic and Gulf beaches and not see any signs of habitation. In 1950, Flagler Beach counted a population of 374, Fernandina Beach claimed 445, and Boca Raton 992. Jupiter, Hillsboro Beach, and Lauderdale-by-the-Sea accounted for a scant 313, 84, and 234 residents respectively.[46]

Like a time-delayed fuse, Florida exploded after V-J Day, 1945, unleashing powerful forces that shaped and reshaped the state's physical and social landscapes. Once a society organized around production and privation, America was increasingly concerned with consumption and abundance. Americans had been forced to give up weekend excursions and beach vacations during the war, and they were eager to catch up. To citizens discomforted by hot and cold wars, Florida once again served as refuge and escape. Millions spent time simply swimming, sunbathing, and beach strolling. In an era before theme parks, the beach *was* Florida's grandest theme, a glittering combination of allurement and escape. Free of belching smokestacks and gritty foundries, Florida's major industry was the selling of itself.

In his much-discussed book *The Affluent Society*, economist John Kenneth Galbraith contended that prosperity had become a template for 1950s America. Nowhere was prosperity rearranging America with more force and speed than along Florida's beaches. It was free enterprise at its best and worst.[47]

Lashing Florida's coasts with the force of a hurricane, the development of the beach has been relentless and omnipresent, leaving in its wake high-rise condominiums, time-share resorts, and luxury vacation homes. Wave after wave of migrants settled along Florida's coasts: successful retirees, the first generation of Americans to take advantage of Social Security benefits and generous pensions; businessmen who shrewdly speculated in beachfront property; others who struck it rich through inheritance or dot-com ventures; South American exiles and Asian millionaires who wished to invest their fortunes in a safe place; bankrupt venture capitalists and bankruptcy lawyers guarding the formers' homesteaded waterfront estates from angry creditors; the wealthy and healthy who can now live *and* work on the beach because of new technologies and customs.

America's beach story contains an epic quality, as today one in six Americans lives along the Atlantic and Gulf coasts, part of a celebrated series of migrations. The 2000 census recorded the effects: fully 45 million Americans massed along the east and Gulf coasts from Maine to Florida to Texas. Over 800,000 Floridians registered "pleasure boats," more than the number of state residents in 1910. Fort Lauderdale basks in its reputation as the yacht capital of the world. When asked recently why she moved to Bonita Shores, a new Floridian pointed to the waters of Estero Bay. "Otherwise, what's the point?" she shrugged. Millions have been drawn to the water for a quality of life revolution. Life appears easier, the scenery exotic, and people more beautiful at the beach.[48]

Florida's population has shifted spectacularly in the twentieth century. In 1900, most Floridians lived within a day's wagon ride of the Alabama and Georgia borders; today, most Floridians reside within an hour's drive of the beach. Profound shifts in where Floridians chose to live accompanied the waves of newcomers. Demographers typically point out the shift in population from North Florida to South Florida that began in the 1920s. But another pattern, even more conspicuous, was the concentration of new residents after 1950 along coastal counties.

In 1950, Florida's 35 coastal counties contained a population of 2 million inhabitants, while 750,000 other residents were scattered among the state's 32 noncoastal counties. Fifty years later, the results have dramatically altered the

TABLE 8. Population of Florida's Coastal Areas, 1950 and 2000

County	1950	2000	Relative Growth (%)	Absolute Growth
Bay	42,689	148,217	247	105,528
Brevard	23,653	476,230	1,913	452,577
Broward	83,933	1,623,018	1,833	1,539,085
Charlotte	4,286	141,627	3,204	137,341
Citrus	6,111	118,085	1,832	111,974
Collier	6,488	251,377	3,774	244,889
Dixie	3,928	13,827	252	9,899
Duval	304,029	778,879	156	474,850
Escambia	112,706	294,410	161	181,704
Flagler	3,367	49,832	1,380	46,465
Franklin	5,814	11,057	90	5,243
Gulf	7,460	13,332	79	5,827
Hernando	6,693	130,802	1,854	124,109
Hillsborough	249,894	998,948	300	749,054
Indian River	11,872	112,947	851	101,075
Jefferson	10,413	12,902	24	2,489
Lee	23,404	440,888	1,784	417,484
Levy	10,637	34,450	224	28,813
Manatee	34,704	264,002	661	229,298
Martin	7,807	126,731	1,523	118,924
Miami-Dade	495,084	2,253,362	355	1,758,278
Monroe	29,957	79,589	166	49,632
Nassau	12,811	57,663	350	44,852
Okaloosa	27,533	170,498	519	142,965
Palm Beach	114,688	1,131,184	886	1,016,496
Pasco	20,529	344,765	1,579	324,236
Pinellas	150,249	921,482	478	762,233
St. Johns	24,998	123,135	393	98,137
St. Lucie	20,180	192,695	855	172,515
Santa Rosa	18,544	117,743	535	99,189
Sarasota	28,827	325,957	1,031	297,130
Taylor	10,416	19,256	85	8,840
Volusia	74,229	443,343	497	369,114
Wakulla	5,258	22,863	335	17,605
Walton	14,725	40,601	176	25,876
Total	2,016,926	12,285,697	609	10,268,771

Sources: *Census of Population: 1950*, vol. 2, *Characteristics of the Population*, pt. 10, *Florida*, table 12; *www.census.gov/census2000/states/fl.html*

TABLE 9. Population of Florida's Noncoastal Area, 1950 and 2000

County	1950	2000	Relative Growth (%)	Absolute Growth
Alachua	57,025	217,955	282	160,929
Baker	6,313	22,259	253	15,946
Bradford	11,457	26,088	128	14,631
Calhoun	7,922	13,017	64	5,095
Clay	14,323	140,814	883	126,491
Columbia	18,216	56,513	210	38,297
DeSoto	9,242	32,209	249	22,967
Gadsden	36,457	45,087	24	8,630
Gilchrist	3,499	14,437	313	10,938
Glades	2,199	10,576	381	8,377
Hamilton	3,981	13,327	234	9,346
Hardee	10,073	26,938	167	16,865
Hendry	6,051	36,210	498	30,159
Highlands	13,636	87,366	541	73,730
Holmes	13,988	18,564	33	4,576
Jackson	34,645	46,755	35	12,110
Lafayette	3,440	7,022	104	3,582
Lake	36,340	210,528	479	174,188
Leon	51,590	239,452	364	187,862
Liberty	3,182	7,021	121	3,839
Madison	14,197	18,733	32	4,536
Marion	38,187	258, 916	578	220,729
Okeechobee	3,454	35,910	940	32,456
Orange	114,950	896,344	680	781,394
Osceola	11,406	172,493	1,412	161,087
Polk	123,997	483,924	290	359,927
Putnam	23,615	70,423	198	46,808
Seminole	26,883	365,196	1,258	338,313
Sumter	11,330	53,345	371	42,015
Suwannee	16,986	34,844	105	17,858
Union	8,906	13,442	51	4,536
Washington	11,888	20,973	76	9,085
Total	749,379	3,696,681	493	2,643,273

Sources: Census of Population: 1950, vol. 2, *Characteristics of the Population,* pt. 10, *Florida,* table 12; *www.census.gov/census2000/states/fl.html*

geo-demographic balance. Between 1950 and 2000, Florida's coastal counties added 10 million new residents, while the noncoastal counties increased by slightly less than 3 million. The 2000 census listed six coastal counties with populations of 750,000 and greater. Among the noncoastal counties, only Orange County claimed such status (see table 9). To accentuate the distinctions further, the slowest-growing "coastal" counties (Wakulla, Jefferson, Taylor, Dixie, and Levy) lack classic beaches and are areas with more wetlands and salt marshes than sand dunes and sea oats. Strikingly, much of Florida's post-1950 development occurred in regions relatively untouched by earlier migrations. Naples and Sanibel, Destin and Jupiter Island, Lido Key and Cape Canaveral—places endowed with magical names and blessed beaches—became some of the best-recognized places in America.[49]

An elbow of pristine beach and jungle in 1950, Cape Canaveral carried one of America's oldest place-names. In 1949, Congress authorized Cape Canaveral as America's Long Range Proving Ground. On 24 July 1950, beach strollers witnessed a new sight: the first successful rocket launch from a spit of land Ponce de León had first noted in 1513. Rocket fever swept Brevard County's sleepy beach communities, renowned for their tranquility. *Florida: A Guide to the Southernmost State*, published in 1939, described Cocoa Beach as "a small ocean resort built on a dune ridge along the shore." By 1950, Cocoa Beach numbered a scant 246 residents. Neighboring Melbourne Beach counted only 230 inhabitants.[50]

The lower Gulf Coast was especially inviting to promoters and developers. Sprawling over 2,100 square miles of land and water, Collier County holds the distinction of being Florida's largest landmass. Dominated by the baronial Collier family, growth came slowly to the southwest coast. The Colliers were determined to bolster their domain; in 1956 the family purchased 3 miles of additional beachfront for $2 million. In the 1950s, as sawyers, oil riggers, and orchid thieves harvested the Fakahatchee Strand and Big Cypress Swamp, few investors took notice of Collier's 50 miles of pristine beach—more than any other Florida county. One could walk miles and not see another person or dwelling on the beach.[51]

If Naples had barely been touched by modernity in 1950, nearby Marco Island deserved the epithets "pristine" and "paradise." Six miles long and four miles wide, it was the northernmost jewel and largest of the Ten Thousand Islands. Owned by the Colliers, Marco Island offered the occasional visitor a natural wonder of stunning dunes and the site of some of Florida's most significant archaeological treasures. In the 1950s, the Colliers offered Marco Island to the State of Florida for $1 million, but officials expressed little interest. In 1961, only one home existed on the island.[52]

Instead of a nature reserve, Marco Island became reserved for the wealthy. Sold to the Mackle brothers, the Miami developers of Key Biscayne, Port Charlotte, and Spring Hill, Marco Island became one of the state's most contested and controversial developments. The Mackles and the Deltona Corporation divided the island into 11,000 homesites, carving 91 miles of canals to maximize the number of "waterfront homes," as well as creating dikes to rid the island of mosquitoes. Construction began in 1964. Brochures touted homes ranging from the Martinique ($41,500) to the Samoa ($19,900). Charged by the U.S. Army Corps of Engineers with dredge-and-fill violations, the development and developers eventually prevailed and triumphed. Today, 13,000 residents inhabit Marco Island. Forty years after bulldozers first scraped away historic Indian middens and sand dunes and erected mosquito dikes, realtors hail Marco Island as one of America's great success stories. Environmentalists grieve.[53]

Strategically situated at the mouth of San Carlos Bay and the Gulf of Mexico, crescent-shaped Sanibel Island has been described as a "sandspit of Eden" and the "Tahiti of America." For thousands of years, humans have beach-combed for heart cockles, angel wings, and lion's paws. At times, shells were piled in huge mounds along the beach. Only since the 1960s, however, have travelers found easy access to Sanibel, one of the three greatest shelling beaches in the world. One of the largest Gulf barrier islands, Sanibel offers a remarkable setting: ancient beach ridges, undulating swales, shell mounds, haunting bayous, mangrove jungles, and a freshwater river. For over a century, naturalists have marveled at the island's bird rookeries and biodiversity. The island's salt marsh mosquitoes were legendary; a scientist once collected 366,000 in one trap in a single night. Longtime resident Clarence O. Rutland, when recalling the island's voracious critters, swore, "You could just swing a bucket around in the yard and get a bucket of 'em." One entomologist called Sanibel the "world's greatest pest hell-hole."

Sanibel prided itself on its colorful collection of Thoreauvian characters. At the turn of the twentieth century, tomato farmers, lighthouse keepers, and fishermen populated the place. Increasingly, the island's solitude and beauty attracted nature lovers and writers. Edna St. Vincent Millay, Rachel Carson, and Jay "Ding" Darling took up residence or settled on neighboring Captiva Island. The contemplative morning stroll on the beach became part of the island ritual.

Millay meandered Sanibel's beaches at low tide, collecting shells and shipping them to Steepletop, her New York farm where she displayed the specimens in handsome cabinets.[54]

Sanibel Island inspired Anne Morrow Lindbergh to write *Gift from the Sea*. In her 1955 book, Lindbergh addressed the powerful hold Sanibel exercised upon her life and those of her neighbors: "How wonderful are islands! Islands in space, like this one I have come to, ringed about by miles of water, linked by no bridges . . . no telephones. . . . People, too, become like islands in such an atmosphere, self-contained, whole and serene; respecting other people's solitude, not intruding on their shores, standing back in reverence before the miracle of the individual."[55]

Good farmland on Sanibel sold for ten to twenty-five dollars an acre early in 1900. Beach property was cheaper. But hurricanes and competition ruined the once-legendary tomato farms. By the 1920s, Sanibel was capitalizing upon its image as a shelling paradise and the "last frontier of rustic simplicity." The first ferry brought mainlanders and vacationers to the island. As late as 1946, Sanibel claimed about 100 residents and two small hotels but no telephones. Mosquitoes helped curb the human population, serving as a kind of "tax put on by nature."[56]

Not everyone cherished Sanibel's quaint charm and remoteness. Planners imagined a freeway to paradise, proposing a series of roads and bridges to connect Gulf barrier islands, a west coast version of AIA. Draglines and dredges began transforming saltwater lagoons and mangrove forests, but nothing threatened serenity like the 1963 bridge to the mainland. The causeway destroyed the vaunted scallop beds but opened Sanibel to mass tourism. The numbers of new arrivals appalled longtime residents and rewarded developers. The ferry, in its last year of operation, brought about 2,000 visitors across San Carlos Bay to the island. In 1968, about 160,000 motorists paid the three-dollar fee to cross the causeway; by 1978, almost 1.2 million had done so. Apartments and condominiums named Sanibel Siesta, Sunset South, and Mariner Pointe began to crowd the beach. The year 1973 was one of reckoning. In one single week, the value of building permits on Sanibel exceeded all of 1972; population trebled in one year.[57]

Lee County commissioners had little time to listen to naysayers. The county was booming and the numbers convinced investors and planners that Sanibel could grow to 90,000 tax-paying condominium owners. In the midst of thunderous growth along Southwest Florida, Sanibel Islanders revolted. In 1974, residents voted to incorporate Sanibel Island and exert home rule. Strict new zoning rules were implemented, sectioning the island into ecological zones and drastically limiting development. Protected wetlands and a wildlife preserve now occupy more than half of the island. Sanibel remains an island without traffic lights, four-lane highways, and towering condominiums. A single Dairy Queen—the community's only fast-food establishment—exists only because city fathers "grandfathered" it in. City statutes also forbid any new seawalls and jetties.[58]

The struggle to save Sanibel, many believe, largely succeeded. Today's permanent population rests at about 6,000, although the numbers rise during winter. Not everyone, however, exults over Sanibel's fortunes. "The island that would not compromise has been compromised," reflects Al Burt, a veteran observer. "The wetlands have been chopped up, the beaches sprout condominiums little more than the arm's length from sea level, the wildlife had been reduced and the serenity modified." Burt confesses, "However altered Sanibel may be, it still looks better than almost any other place, still an Eden by comparison."[59]

There was nothing inevitable about Marco, Sanibel, or Captiva becoming island paradises. Pioneers had struggled valiantly to make a living on these mosquito-infested, isolated outposts. Abandoned clam and shark processing plants, a copra plantation, and tomato packinghouses document graveyards of dreams. Sand dunes and coves became waterfront estates, but also nature preserves.

A certain cachet threads together Naples, Sanibel, and Sarasota. Since the 1920s, Sarasota has carefully cultivated an image of a place imbued with arts and culture, a paradise bejeweled with some of Florida's most seductive-sounding islands: Longboat Key, Bird Key, Lido Key, Siesta Key, and St. Armand's Key. They were not always so privileged and exclusive.

Early civic leaders expressed disappointment with Sarasota. Its harbor welcomed pelicans and herons, not deep-water tankers. The islands seemed more a barrier to Sarasota's greatness than an asset. But Sarasota's destiny was tied to circus impresarios and philanthropists, not to harbormasters and industrialists.[60]

Sarasota owes its modern identity to the vision and deeds of John Ringling. A circus magnate with a larger-than-life appetite for art and landscaping, Ringling and his vivacious wife, Mable, arrived in Sarasota in 1912. On Shell Beach they constructed Cà d'Zan, a palace fit for a Venetian doge. A wave of monument building followed. With dredges and buckets of cash, Ringling embarked on a grandiose plan to transform 6,000 acres of waterfront property into an empire befitting an American aristocrat. He built bridges and causeways to connect the isolated islands, constructed an eighteen-hole golf course, and began a $3 million Ritz-Carlton Hotel. Longboat Key housed his lavish nurseries and greenhouses. Financial misfortunes derailed Ringling's grand designs, but he laid the foundation for Sarasota's future.[61]

Blessed with 37 miles of Gulf shoreline and 28 miles of classic beaches, Pinellas County had for decades fashioned its beaches as a summer playground for Tampa Bay residents and a winter resort for midwesterners. From Pass-a-Grille to Clearwater Beach to Anclote Key, development along Gulf Boulevard had touched the narrow strip of islands, but population growth did not take off until after World War II. The value of beach property increased seventeenfold in the 1940s, and population burgeoned exponentially. A wave of postwar prosperity incorporated the towns of Madeira Beach, Redington Beach, Indian Rocks Beach, Boca Ciega, Belleair Shores, Belleair Beach, Treasure Island, Long Key, and St. Petersburg Beach. Prime beachscape that cost $300 per frontage foot in 1950 soared to $1,600 twenty years later.[62]

Two great forces, free enterprise and nature, decided the fate of Honeymoon Island. For centuries, Indians, pirates, and fishermen populated this barrier island off the coast from Dunedin in Pinellas County. The earliest maps identified the boomerang-shaped place as Hog Island. The 1921 hurricane split the body of land into two separate islands divided by Hurricane Pass. In 1938, Tampa promoter Clinton M. Washburn paid $25,000 for the property. The 434-acre spit of land deserved a better name for dreamers. He christened the place Honeymoon Island. While construction crews erected palmetto-thatched huts, Washburn began recruiting newlyweds to spend their first days and nights of marital bliss on his mosquito-infested love island. He even promised a free cottage to the first honeymooners to conceive a child on his island. A massive publicity campaign followed; Ripley's "Believe It or Not" and *Life* magazine touted Honeymoon Island. A handful of couples actually endured the island's privations until World War II disrupted the honeymoon. Across Hurricane Pass, Marines assaulted Caladesi Beach on amphibious vehicles called Roebling Alligators. In 1966, the State of Florida purchased Caladesi Island for $3 million. In 1934, the Betz family had offered to sell the property for $15,000.[63]

Developers had more lucrative designs for Honeymoon Island. In 1956, Washburn sold the land to Arthur Vining Davis for $600,000. Islands were becoming a luxury, even for millionaires. Following Davis's death, Honeymoon Island became a chip in a very expensive poker game. In 1963, the City of Dunedin completed a causeway to the island, about the same time Hyman Green announced plans to build a massive city. Green, a shady associate of Jimmy Hoffa, borrowed $40 million from the Teamsters union to finance several controversial Florida developments. Ensnarled by the recession of 1973 and environmental challenges, Green sold Honeymoon Island to the State of Florida for $25.5 million. It is now a state park.[64]

That affluence and publicity shaped the course of Sarasota and St. Petersburg beaches came as no surprise. Since the 1920s, their identities as watery Edens had been promoted and validated. Such was not the case with Destin. Named for a New England sea captain, Destin lies nestled on Choctawhatchee Bay, 45 miles east of Pensacola. Nicknamed the "World's Luckiest Fishing Village," Destin rests close to the continental shelf, allowing anglers easy access to deep-water fishing.[65]

The term *village* aptly described old Destin. Not until 1936, with the construction of the bridge spanning East Pass and the paving of u.s. 98, could motorists reach Destin. A 1939 guide characterized the community as a "fishing resort" with a year-round population of 25. For decades, Destin was a favorite summertime destination of white southerners who appreciated the legendary fishing and small-town hospitality. Locals affectionately called the area "L.A.—Lower Alabama." In the 1950s, remembered a visitor, Destin "was mostly charter boat wharves, a handful of motels, the usual tacky souvenir shops, and a few seafood restaurants."[66]

Growth came slowly to Destin. As late as the 1960s, the population hovered around 1,000, but most were seasonal residents. Americans discovered Destin in their search for the perfect beach. And what beaches! "The beach along Destin is full of beauty and contrast and illusion," observed Al Burt. "A breeze stirs powdery white sand into tiny land waves that gather and break. . . . These are Florida's most spectacular beaches: a scene of almost immaculate perception." Historian Jack E. Davis resided at Fort Walton Beach in the 1960s, where he recalled fondly the sport of sand skiing the local dunes. The *New York Times'* Rick Bragg rhapsodized, "The sand dunes of Okaloosa County, like snowbanks, line both sides of U.S. Highway 98 between Fort Walton and Destin, and they are so pretty that people weave off the road, looking at them." The dunes between Destin and Cape San Blas can soar 40 feet high. Bragg likened the waters of the Gulf of Mexico to "an emerald green when the sun is out and a deep, deep blue on cloudy days."[67]

The word *village* scarcely describes Destin today. "Concrete condominiums," notes Bragg, "as imposing as anything in Miami or Fort Lauderdale line the beachfront on both ends of the paradise, blocking views of the Gulf." A development frenzy has now seized this section of the Panhandle. Congressman Robert Sikes, Florida's original "He-Coon," ensured a free hand for developers when, in the early 1960s, he shepherded a bill through Congress banning any growth restrictions for Destin and the "Miracle Strip." The construction of the high-rise condominiums started in 1971. In the 1990s, condominium sales increased tenfold. Destin is no longer a poor man's paradise; condominium units with a Gulf view begin at $300,000 and have surpassed the $1.3 million plateau. No longer the "Redneck Riviera," Destin and environs have been repackaged as the "Emerald Coast" and "Florida's Great Northwest."[68]

The Privileged Beach

The beach is privilege. In Florida it is a very big business. Sand dunes and submerged lands, once so devalued that owners allowed the property to be sold for back taxes, now account for some of the most valuable real estate in the world. Communities blessed by nature with thin rinds of beach suddenly became exclusive and desirable.

Once affordable to public school teachers, retired pharmacists, and working fishermen, the family beach cottage has become a luxury, the result of a scarce resource (a finite beach), prosperity (more Americans seeking vacation homes), demand (investors wishing to replace single-family dwellings with motels or megamansions), and an amenities revolution (life *is* better on the beach). Location, location, location has determined the inexorable inflation of living in paradise. Ray Hester, a New Smyrna Beach realtor, recalled that in 1945 he had the opportunity to purchase 3,600 feet of undeveloped beachfront for ten dollars a foot. "I turned it down," he sighed. "I thought the price was too high." In 1945, fresh from the war, Frank T. Hurley Jr. moved to Pass-a-Grille, where his mother encouraged him to purchase a home, telling him prophetically, "This sand is not white, it's gold." In 1947, Hurley purchased a gulf-front lot for $5,000. Many such properties are valued at more than $1 million today. Wistful

Beaches of Florida

journalists love to write about the once inexpensive but now vanishing beach cottage.[69]

A 1950s headline encapsulated the dreams of many Americans: "Waterfront Homes for the Common Man." But beach fever has spiked the cost and prestige of living on the water. When newspaperman Ben Funk settled in Miami in 1931, he recalled Key Biscayne as a "wild coconut plantation inhabited by raccoons and a small colony of humans." By 1955, Arthur Krock, the venerable *New York Times* journalist, wrote of his astonishment that oceanfront property in Key Biscayne was selling for $18,000 an acre—double that of land on the northern shore of Long Island. In the benchmark year of 1956, prices ranged from a few hundred dollars for lots on the Panhandle gulf to $25,000 and more for properties along the Gold Coast. An advertisement offered 320 waterfront acres in the "missile base area" for $800 an acre. A 1956 lot on Amelia Island sold for

$3,750; two-bedroom homes on the Gulf of Mexico sold for between $14,000 and $20,000. Waterfront homes in Stuart and Sarasota ranged from $15,000 to $30,000; similar homes in Fort Myers and Venice sold for less than $10,000. As the waterfront and residences in Miami Beach, Boca Raton, and Sarasota became more precious, investors gobbled up cheap, undeveloped properties. A writer lamented in 1973 that "a little Florida hideaway on a surf-washed beach" had become so expensive that families earning less than $15,000 a year should shelve their home ownership dreams. In 2000, the average price of a Palm Beach one-acre estate on the oceanfront averaged $12 to $15 million. In Stuart, a similar home brought $2 million.[70]

Rising land values and the shrinking supply of beach posed a dilemma to a state bent upon growth: How could Florida lure more and more new residents and tourists if there was less and less beach? Would the beach become an exclusive haven for the super-rich and their single-family dwellings? The answer shaped and reconfigured the beach skyline and introduced two new buzzwords: condominium and time-share. Instead of five single families inhabiting five lots, a high-rise condominium could in the same space concentrate hundreds of families onto the precious beachfront, allowing more Americans, Europeans, and Asians a slice of the Florida dream. The time-share concept multiplied the numbers by fifty-two, allowing the middle classes who could never afford a house or condominium on the beach an opportunity to own the place for one week a year. So many co-operative dwellings had been built along the Palm Beach, Broward, and Dade County beaches that a 1970 commentator suggested that the "Gold Coast be renamed the Condominium Coast." By the 1990s, "supertowers" rising over 500 feet dwarfed Sunny Isles Beach and Miami Beach.[71]

A booming national economy and low mortgage rates created fabulous opportunities for investors who wished to purchase a second home on the water. Almost a quarter million second-home purchases fueled the Sunshine State's robust real-estate market in the 1990s.[72]

Beaches have helped transform some of Florida's historically poorest places into boomtowns. The Big Bend (Wakulla, Franklin, Gulf, and Bay counties) had not shared in the Sunbelt prosperity enjoyed by South and Central Florida. In 1950, the combined populations of the Big Bend counties had not surpassed 62,000 inhabitants. Harvey Jackson III recalls fondly the stretch of beach communities between Destin and Panama City. "I never heard the term 'Redneck Riviera' back then [1950s]," confessed Jackson, now a historian, "though it

FIGURE 51. Technological advances allowed developers to create more coastline and waterfront living for the masses. Punta Gorda Isles, with its finger canals, typified 1950s and 1960s developments. State of Florida Photographic Archives, Tallahassee.

could have been applied without insult. Visitors were mostly from Alabama (like us) or southwest Georgia, with a few from Mississippi. The lower south demographic was easily recognized and exploited by enterprising entrepreneurs like the one who named his bar the 'Little B'ham.' Natives, influenced by similar post-war circumstances, weren't that much different from the tourists." Wealth and exploding land values have changed the character and composition of the Big Bend and Panhandle coast. If Miami has become "Havana USA," Panama City Beach and St. George Island have become Atlanta South. In the late 1990s, Georgians bought one of every four condos sold in Panama City Beach. A longtime St. George resident, when asked to explain the recent land rush, replied simply, "One word: Atlanta." On nearby upscale Rosemary Beach, nearly three of every four SUVs feature a Fulton County, Georgia, license plate.[73]

In the 1920s, Ed Ball, the manager of the powerful du Pont estate, obtained hundreds of thousands of acres of Big Bend forest and shoreline. The irascible Ball despised South Florida manners and morals, preferring the security of North Florida land. Ball's St. Joe Company, with its paper mills and timberlands, prospered, while surrounding communities languished. Gulf and Franklin counties gained only 11,000 inhabitants between 1950 and 2000. But

THE BEACH

the St. Joe Company held on to one asset no other Florida business could match: 1.1 million acres, including 40 miles of privately owned, snowy-white, undeveloped beaches. Arvida, a St. Joe's development partner, has unveiled River Camps, Carillion Beach, SummerCamp, WaterColor, WaterSound Beach, and WindMark Beach, all luxury developments. Single-family lots start at $230,000 and top the million-dollar mark. Their designs have been called "cracker chic." Journalist Chris Sherman writes, "They draw from rickety Old Florida, New Urbanism—and plenty of New South money."[74]

Changing Tastes

For eons, Florida's beaches shifted according to the laws of nature. Until recently, motorists driving along Highway 98, and A1A gazed upon long stretches of unbroken seascape. The prevalence of sand dunes, sea oats, and beaches dwarfed homes and piers. Roads built to bring tourists to Florida beaches worked so well that, within a brief span of time, views of the Gulf and Atlantic were blotted out by walls of condominiums and private estates.

Supply (beach frontage), supplies (wood, concrete block, and structural steel), and demands (more people and better amenities) altered the skyline. In 1950, the most popular building material was lumber; the most common structure was the simple cottage. Built of wooden clapboard and shingles, and rarely more than two stories high, the beach cottage harmonized form and function. The cottage was to the beach what the wood-frame, dogtrot Cracker home was to the hinterland. It was a simple building for a simpler time. Screen doors, clusters of windows, and front porches took advantage of the cooling ocean breezes.

Each year succeeding 1950 changed the character and composition of the beach more than had the preceding five hundred years. Considering the breathtaking setting, the state of beach architecture in Florida is uniformly disappointing. The problem, argues the writer James H. Kunstler, is not that so many hotels and motels look alike, "but that they are of uniformly miserable quality." Architectural critic Beth Dunlop has written extensively about Floridians and their relationship to the land and built environment. "Year by year, we did our share to alter it all, house by house, building by building," Dunlop reflected. "As the decades rolled by, we seemed to respect our setting less and less. Pavement rolled. Condos rose. We began walling off the bay, blocking visual and actual access to the ocean." Concrete block began to dominate the beachscape in the

1950s. Two-story structures adorned with flashy neon signs announced the beach motel. Cinder block adapted to air conditioning with ease. In the 1970s, high-rise apartments began their march across the state's beaches. As late as 1973, motorists still enjoyed an open vista on the Gulf of Mexico. But not for long. "If this condominium isn't an asset to the beach and better looking than a vacant lot full of sandspurs and sea oats," insisted one developer, "then I'm crazy." He added, "Indian Rocks Beach could use a little more Miami or Fort Lauderdale." National prosperity, a free-market frenzy coupled with loose or nonexistent governmental controls, and the popularity of time-share resorts and condominiums intensified high-rise developments on Florida's three coasts.[75]

Facing the very real prospect of supertowers shadowing the shore from Brevard to Monroe counties, a citizen rebellion has challenged the rights of developers to erect supersized structures along the beach. On four separate occasions, Cocoa Beach residents have voted to control growth and restrict the heights of new buildings and density. Martin County exemplifies the anti–beach growth sentiment spreading from coast to coast. In contrast to its neighbors St. Lucie and Palm Beach counties, Martin County has no high-rise structures blocking ocean views. For good reason, the beachfront lining Broward County's Galt Ocean Mile—a space largely untouched until the 1950s—is now known as the "Galt Wall." Critics decry the soulless "McMansions" and "condo towers" that block the vistas of bay and sky. Beth Dunlop labels such architecture "egotecture."[76]

Rebelling against the uninspired uniformity sweeping Florida, Robert Davis reached back to his boyhood memories of summers on Panhandle beaches and sought an alternative to the high-rise blandness and Lower South blight that had enveloped Florida. Eighty acres of Walton County dunes and pines held special meaning for Davis. Occasional naturalists and picnickers visited the spot abutting the Gulf of Mexico, but the area was isolated until the late 1930s, when modern highways encouraged summer day-trippers from Birmingham and Atlanta. Davis's grandfather purchased the property in 1946, but his dream of a beach retreat for his Alabama employees never materialized. Davis conceived the idea of an alternative development in the early 1980s. He hired two extraordinary architects, Andres Duany and Elizabeth Plater-Zyberk, then associated with Miami-based firm Arquitectonica, to implement his dream. First, the team forbade any building upon the beach or dunes. Second, they dictated strict design and zoning guidelines. Codes forbade fast-food restaurants, strip malls, and asphalt parking lots. Drawing from ideas of "new urbanism," the architects of Seaside designed a place where home, work, and shopping come together in a single community. In the early 1980s, lots sold started at $15,000. The resulting community of Seaside became an instant success. Journalist Peter Applebome described Seaside as an "instant Dixie Cape Cod of cobblestone streets [and] white picket fences." Another writer dubbed Seaside a "Utopia-by-the-Sea." Retro homes featuring crowning cupolas, tin roofs, front porches, and scalloped shingles generally impressed critics and delighted consumers. So wholesome was Seaside's ambience that filmmakers chose the new town as the backdrop for the seamlessly idyllic setting of director Peter Weir's *The Truman Show* (1998). In keeping with the principles of new urbanism, Seaside was envisioned as an "old" new alternative for the middle classes. Ironically, Seaside's phenomenal commercial success has largely made this coveted lifestyle unaffordable to middle-class, year-round residents, and the community has become a collection of second homes for the affluent. Seaside homes that cost $100,000 in the 1980s have zoomed past a million dollars. City planner Tom Martinson found Seaside's gulf gazebos and pastel-painted cottages "charming" on his first trip in 1987. Returning in 1994, he discovered a place "almost unrecognizable . . . the architectural norm had transmogrified into elaborate if not outright-baroque villas." While some critics satirized Seaside's coerced conformity, developers at SouthWood (Tallahassee), St. Croix (Lauderdale Lakes), and University Heights (Gainesville) pay Davis, Duany, and Plater-Zyberk the ultimate compliment: imitation.[77]

Yesterday's Redneck Riviera is today Florida's Great Northwest. Within a half hour's drive of Seaside, one encounters upscale WaterSound Beach, Rosemary Beach, Sandestin, and the Village of Baytowne Wharf. Brochures tout "pan-Caribbean" and Gulf-vernacular building. Writer Diane Roberts finds such places "as fake and inorganic and history-less as Disney World." At least the glorified beach cottages look as though they belong. Consider Disney's Grand Floridian Hotel. Disney corporate officials so admired the look of San Diego's Hotel del Coronado that they erected a copy of the sprawling seaside Victorian structure in landlocked Orange County.[78]

Beachfront living, once a reasonable dream, has become an exclusive privilege. On St. George Island, which for decades basked in obscurity in Apalachicola Bay, the price tags of some homes have broken the million-dollar barrier. Houses on Atlantic Beach, Jacksonville Beach, Ponte Vedra, and Neptune Beach have likewise skyrocketed in price. Collier County, home to chic waterfront neighborhoods in Naples and Marco Island, has evolved in just decades from frontier to the color pages of *Coastal Living, Gulfshore Life,* and *Latitudes and Attitudes.* Eleven Florida cities share exclusive membership in *Worth* magazine's list of America's wealthiest communities. These places—Jupiter Island, Palm Beach, Highland Beach, Boca Grande, Golden Beach, Sea Ranch Lakes, Bal Harbour, Indian River Shores, Captiva, Key Biscayne, and Ocean Ridge—all possess one unifying feature: waterfront.[79]

The beach is boundary and sanctuary, frontier and *frontera* to the world's most comfortable and most desperate. Higgs Beach in Key West is a final resting place for hundreds of African slaves. In 1860, the U.S. Navy captured three slave ships. The Africans were taken to Key West. Those who died were buried at Higgs Beach. To modern residents of Palm Beach, Ocean Ridge, and Key Biscayne, life on the water fulfills the American dream; to refugees from Cuba, a raft on the water holds promise of the immigrant dream. A peculiar American foreign policy coldly calculates freedom measured from the water's edge. Popularly and derisively called "wet foot/dry foot," the 1990s law allows Cuban refugees to remain in the United States permanently if they reach the beach, but denies asylum to Haitians, Dominicans, and others who make it past the surf. If you are Cuban and reach the beach, you're in. On Florida sand and water, extremes of wealth and freedom exist side by side.[80]

The Technological Beach

America's infatuation with the beach depended upon changing aesthetics and tastes: the collective urge to live and play near the ocean and the lure of water. But the modern beach also represents a triumph of shoreline engineering. Technological revolutions—air and ground travel, bridge construction, air conditioning, bay and channel dredging, and the erection of walls and jetties—made possible modern beach life and year-round tourism.

The "natural" beach was flawed. Nature imposed obstacles to the perfect beach: mangroves blocked views of sunsets and harbored the dreaded no-see-ums, lagoons bred mosquitoes, and the surf eroded valuable real estate. The beach, like hammock and lake, is pliable and can be anything humans will it to be—provided one has sufficient capital and tools. What private enterprise would not and could not finance, federal and state governments have obliged, renourishing beaches and insuring endangered property from storms.

American land law enshrined the principle of individualism. In no other country could a person acquire property so easily and with so few restrictions. The Homestead Acts exalted individualism and the American dream of land ownership, even if the results were not always egalitarian. Land was and is a commodity. In nineteenth-century Florida, a state with too much land, too much water, and too few people, lawmakers granted individuals and corporations liberal rights of development. The legislature imposed few restrictions on homesteaders and businesses. Twentieth-century land developers inherited this generous legacy of freedom and audacious spirit. Willa Cather wrote in *My Ántonia* that the people of the Great Plains were "bridled with caution." Reservation was never a Florida virtue.[81]

Beachfront is valuable, as the saying goes, because God isn't making any more of it. But people do. Investors, lawyers, and engineers utilize Florida land laws to exploit the waterfront. Submerged lands belonged to the State of Florida; rights and title rested with the Internal Improvement Fund. The Trustees of the Internal Improvement Fund, a state commission chaired by the governor and comprised of the cabinet, routinely sold the submerged lands for little recompense. The Riparian Rights acts of 1856 and 1921—originally intended to grant landowners the right to fill in adjoining freshwater and tidal land and build wharves and warehouses out to the navigable channel—became even more valuable in the hands of visionaries. In 1921, legislators urged "waterfront property to be improved and developed." Not only a legal principle, dredge-and-fill now became a public service, a populist impulse evidenced by a 1959 advertisement: "'Island Living' Costs No More! $390 Down."[82]

Headlines document the great land rush of the 1950s: "Lowly Mangrove Swamp Is Turned into 'Paradise Island,'" "Bay-Bottom Sand Turns into Florida's Silver Coast," "Largo Wants a Beach, So Largo Builds a Beach!," "How to Make a Brand New Island," and "Beach Project Ready for Dredging." The phrase "waterfront living" pleased homeowners who could boast to astonished friends and fellow workers in Michigan and Ohio that they were living on the water in Florida, even if it meant a mobile home on a finger canal. A 1958 real estate advertisement touting the opening of the McCormick Mile exemplified what technology had wrought. Located six miles north of Delray Beach, McCormick Mile featured "an island of all waterfront homesites." Lots began at $8,750, "seawall included."[83]

Land and water parted. In 1953, dredges began construction on canals connecting to the New River in Fort Lauderdale. Two-bedroom homes in South New River Isles, seawall included, cost $12,000–$14,000. Appropriately, the concept of finger canals originated here in 1921 when developer Charles G. Rodes anointed Fort Lauderdale as the "Venice of America." Other cities watched carefully. "Look at Miami and Miami Beach today—in fact, almost the entire East Coast," asked an envious Tampa real estate developer in 1953. "They started developing their bayfronts years ago. Now look what they have. A real Gold Coast. Their mangrove swamps and bayfronts were just as mean as ours, but they got busy early. We're just now catching on here."[84]

Pinellas County is Florida's most dredged-up and built-out county. Beginning in the late 1940s, developers purchased large tracts of waterfront property, some of which included the rights to submerged lands. Prices of pre-fill island land averaged about two dollars per front foot. Realizing the potential for profit in turning submerged baymuck into waterfront lots, developers assaulted the Pinellas coastline, waterways, and bays with a vengeance. Like medieval alchemists, they produced gold by turning water into land. By 1956, new bayfront subdivisions had literally added 37 miles of new shoreline.[85]

John D. and Dorothy MacDonald took part in America's great postwar migration to Pinellas County. The young couple discovered a "clean and sparkling and bright" Clearwater. A few years later they moved to Sarasota, where they built their dream beach house on Siesta Key. MacDonald, a graduate of the Harvard School of Business, was especially fascinated by the scramble for prize real estate. In *Dead Low Tide*, one of his first books, he described riparian rights as "turning water into land and putting houses on it." In 1983, the novelist returned to Clearwater to see what progress had wrought: "It had always been especially restful and refreshing . . . to drive back home, out across the causeway and the bridge to Clearwater Beach, to look over the rail at the broad glassy bay. It was shocking to discover . . . that one could [now] go halfway to the beach and turn right! There was a bay-fill development down there, white roofs, tidy yards, boat docks, and flower beds."[86]

Boca Ciega Bay deserved its legendary reputation as a prolific marine ecosystem. In 1950, only a few hundred people lived in homes built on the islands speckled between Boca Ciega and Lower Tampa Bay. In rapid succession, the Pinellas County Commission approved a series of ambitious development projects. Within a decade, Boca Ciega Bay had been wholly altered "into a channelized cesspool."[87]

Barely peeking above Boca Ciega Bay at high tide, Mud Key provided turtles and gulls a sanctuary. But the deed to Mud Key contained two magical words: "riparian rights." Albert Furen shrewdly purchased the rights to dredge-and-fill

504 acres of Boca Ciega Bay. Although the plan was opposed by Governor LeRoy Collins, Furen triumphed. By 1957, Mud Key had become Vina Del Mar, a 225-acre development requiring 2.8 million cubic yards of fill. A 1957 newspaper proclaimed, "Mosquito-Ridden Key Now Beach Beauty Spot."[88]

The writer John Rothchild's family moved to a "fresh section" on Boca Ciega Bay in the 1950s. There, "dredges were as routine as seagulls." He described how "local manufacturer" Jack Holton developed his subdivision, the 163rd Street finger fill: "The dredging equipment was floated over from Tampa on two huge barges. Sections of concrete seawall were lowered into the water with a crane. . . . The seawall defined the territorial boundaries of the new property. From the other barge, a large pipe was extended into the water, like a hose on a vacuum, to suck up the bay bottom. . . . The silt and muck was drawn through a cutter and into the pipe, then pumped along the full length of the barge and spilled out of a discharge line and into the seawall mold."[89]

Tierra Verde marked still another high-stakes dredge-and-fill on Boca Ciega Bay. In 1959, the *New York Times* trumpeted plans to build a new city on fifteen uninhabited keys. The 1,800 acres and the rights to their submerged lands fetched a stunning $12 million. Clint Murchison, the Texas oilman, helped finance the project. Once one of the most isolated places in Florida, Tierra Verde benefited from a wave of 1950s transportation projects, most notably the completion of the Sunshine Skyway Bridge, a 15-mile structure spanning Lower Tampa Bay and connecting Pinellas and Manatee counties.[90]

Construction crews, barges, and steam shovels dredged the bay to consolidate the original fifteen islands into six. Laborers poured, dug, and sectioned 42 miles of seawall, 17 miles of canals and waterways, and five bridges. The newly constructed Bayway allowed motorists to drive to Fort De Soto, 900 acres of incomparable beaches and islands. Today, Tierra Verde basks on its 8 miles of gulf front. The 2000 census acknowledges the community's reputation as a wealthy retreat; one in five households, the highest proportion in Pinellas County, earned incomes of $150,000 or more. Skeptics wonder what will happen when a hurricane-generated storm surge engulfs the community that rests only a few feet above sea level.[91]

Wanton destruction of Florida wetlands and damage to estuaries and bays galvanized environmentalists and concerned citizens. An emerging environmental movement coincided with a court-ordered reapportionment of the Florida legislature. The 1967 Florida legislature passed the Randell Act, requiring the State Board of Conservation to conduct a biological survey before a state permit was issued. Nathaniel Reed, Governor Claude Kirk's environmental lawyer, urged a halt to the ruinous dredge-and-fill practices. Help also came from Washington. The National Estuary Protection Act (1968) recognized the critical importance of America's estuaries. The collision between Americans' right to develop their property and the states' right to protect environmentally threatened lands occurred on Boca Ciega Bay. *Zabel v. Tabb* (1970) represented a landmark court case. The 1969 Aquatic Preserve Law prohibited dredge-and-fill development in designated areas. Alfred Zabel wished to expand his trailer park and fill in an additional 12 acres of the bay. The U.S. Army Corps of Engineers, an organization with a disappointing record of protecting Florida's environment, rejected Zabel's request. For the first time, the corps denied a landowner the right of development because of potential environmental damage. The U.S. Supreme Court concurred with the corps' decision. Dredge-and-fill requests, routinely granted by the state cabinet before 1967, suddenly became suspect. Still, the trustees continue to allow sales of submerged lands if such actions are in the "public interest."[92]

In the 1970s and 1980s, sweeping federal and state environmental legislation addressed problems of past abuse and future growth. In 1970, state legislators enacted the Florida Coastal Coordinating Council. Mounds of documents mapped the state's most endangered areas. Reports cautioned that more than half of Florida's coastal areas were unsuitable for development. However noble in its efforts to preserve and protect Florida's coastline, the legislation was toothless and ineffectual. The passage of the Coastal Resources Act (1982) was designed to control rapidly eroding beaches and dunes. Influential lobbyists and the construction industry mediated and mitigated the law's intent to permit further development. In reality, the law permitted rampant development on some of Florida's most sensitive beaches and dunes. Since 1978, only 52 coastal building permits have been denied while 5,000 new structures have been approved. In the struggle between the right to build and the need to protect, power resides with the powerful. Beach guru Orrin Pilkey despairs, "It's probably too late in Florida because you already have a shoreline of high-rises." No other state, the professor argues, has so mismanaged its beaches. Charles Lee, an official with Audubon of Florida, laments: "Any notion of keeping beaches pristine is lost. . . . there's no environmental protection."[93]

The U.S. Army Corps of Engineers is charged with the responsibility of protecting America's beaches and waterways. Originally founded for the purposes of mapping and building military roads and fortifications, the corps has become the most forceful advocate in the reconstruction and armoring of Florida's beaches. In *The Corps and the Shore*, Orrin Pilkey and Katharine Dixon describe the agency's mission: "This organization of engineers builds seawalls, pumps up beaches, dredges inlets, stabilizes inlets with long rock jetties, gives permission to others to do any of these activities, and more." The engineers' checkered record with Everglades drainage, the Kissimmee River debacle, and the infamous cross-state barge canal makes environmentalists justifiably nervous. But the corps ultimately responds to the wishes of Congress and presidents.[94]

The beach, even an engineered beach, could be Eden and paradise, but it could also be a sewer and garbage dump. If quartz-white beach and emerald waters symbolized the Florida dream state, the septic tank and drainage canal haunt the dystopian state. Historically, the state's cities, counties, and legislature worried more about tourism and promotion than environment and infrastructure. Growth, boosters argued, would pay for the future. For decades, coastal communities simply dumped their raw sewage into estuaries, bays, and rivers. In 1953, Miami journalist Helen Muir observed, "Out of sight, out of mind would be Miami's treatment of sewage through the years until the day would come when she fouled up her clean, sweet river and shining blue bay to such an extent that it was no longer out of sight and fish would die . . . and the beautiful Biscayne Bay would lie, a pollution between man and God." Not until 1952 did Miami begin construction of its first sewage treatment plant. *Look* magazine, in an article entitled "Polluted Paradise," called Miami's problems "shocking." Two decades after Muir's warnings, Miami's problems had worsened. In 1973, only four in ten Dade County homes had been hooked up to sewers. Fourteen of the county's seventeen waterways were labeled unfit for swimming. As late as 1950 on a 15-mile strip of Pinellas gulf communities from Pass-a-Grille to Belleair Beach, only one municipality had invested in a modern sewage system. Millions of gallons of raw sewage emptied daily into Tampa Bay. Sarasota's wealthy beach communities relied upon septic tanks to treat its sewage throughout the 1950s. Cocoa Beach completed its first sewage treatment plant in 1959. Since 1987, thousands of citizens have volunteered for Florida Coastal Cleanup. Every September thousands walk beaches and coastline where they haul away millions of cigarette butts and tons of trash (including appliances, syringes, automobiles, and bales of marijuana).[95]

Lax restrictions and pell-mell growth have produced frightening levels of pollution and toxic runoff. In spite of local, state, and federal efforts to protect the environment, Florida is awash in toxic poisons. Beachgoers must battle not only traffic and insects but also alarming bacteria counts. Health departments routinely close beaches because of filth and disease. In the 1990s, only California closed its beaches more often than did Florida on account of pollution. Between 1970 and 2000, Floridians constructed 1.4 million additional septic tanks, bringing the total to more than 2.35 million. In 2000, the Environmental Protection Agency identified 286 toxic waste-dump sites and over 22,000 contaminated underground fuel-storage tanks in Florida. Millions of well-manicured lawns—the pride of American homes and golf courses—dump tons of pesticides and fertilizers into storm sewers and streams that run into rivers that flow into the Gulf and Atlantic. Good intentions also pave the road to and from the beach. In the 1970s, Florida boaters, with the blessings of state officials, came upon a popular way to rid the state of unwanted tires. In one experiment, teams dumped 2 million tires off the coast of Hugh Taylor Birch State Park in Broward County. The tires, bundled together, were designed to attract and support marine life. Alas, masses of tires have broken loose and become a dangerous source of pollution, killing the coral reefs and spoiling the beaches. In a very costly operation, all tires will have to be retrieved and disposed of elsewhere.[96]

The cruise-ship industry reveals the hidden—and not so hidden—costs of doing business in Florida. Once a luxury reserved for conspicuous consumers, the cruise has become a middle-class comfort and a $3 billion business, helping make Carnival Cruise's Ted Arison the wealthiest person in Florida. In 2000, over 13 million passengers embarked on voyages from Florida's six busiest seaports. Miami alone is home to three of the world's largest lines: Norwegian, Carnival, and Royal Caribbean. Walt Disney World's landed empire now extends to the seas; Port Canaveral lured over 3 million cruise-ship customers. In sharp contrast to the industry's giddy commercials extolling fun on the deck and galley, cruise ships have been fined repeatedly for dumping raw sewage, oily bilge water, dry-cleaning fluids, and food waste off the state's shores. Commercial shipping has also polluted some of Florida's most ecologically sensitive zones. In 1973, Coast Guard officials warned Florida residents that almost 400 barrels of deadly toxic cyanide might wash ashore on west coast beaches following a ship collision in the Gulf of Mexico. Since 1984, officials point to twenty-seven coral-killing ship groundings and anchor damage from freighters in the Straits of Florida. The damage to sensitive coral reefs between Key Biscayne and the Dry Tortugas has been devastating.[97]

Hope stirs. Tampa Bay, a cesspool in the 1970s, is cleaner today than a half century ago, in spite of the fact that a half million passengers embarked on a cruise from Tampa in 2000. The shellfish industry—the bay's canary in the coal mine—has made a comeback after decades of bans. Today Cedar Key fishermen out of work because of the net ban, cultivate clams. Once abundant between Charlotte Harbor and Steinhatchee, scallops made a dramatic return in the late 1990s. Critics concede that state-mandated programs have improved the water quality of Miami's Biscayne Bay, an accomplishment achieved in part by dumping sewage farther offshore.[98]

Instead of an irresistible force meeting an immovable object, the surf meets—and moves—the beach. There is nothing new under the sun and on the beach. In 1690, Spanish engineers completed the first seawall in St. Augustine. The battle to preserve moving and eroding beaches is now fought with an arsenal of shoreline armor: seawalls, jetties, bulkheads, riprap revetments, and groins. The war is expensive and controversial.[99]

Obeying elementary laws of physics and geology, impermanent beaches and islands constantly migrate and reform as the result of relentless waves and winds, storms and hurricanes. Nature had a design. Beaches function as nature's perfect shock absorbers; sea oats and beach grass hold together sand dunes. Geologists have long advocated that beaches should be permitted to form and change shape freely. However, the irrefutable facts remain: Florida's beaches have eroded and are eroding at the frightful rate of one to six feet per year. Poets and geologists lament the retreating beach. The Florida Department of Environmental Protection has classified significant portions of the state's coastline as "critically eroding."[100]

The natural laws of the beach collide violently with elementary laws of economics and politics. Anyone who can afford a million-dollar waterfront estate *will* fight to preserve it. Furthermore, people who live on beaches enlist influential friends and allies. A phalanx of forces champion beach development: the construction industry, real estate boards, and tourist interests. Seawalls attract lobbyists.

Critics lampoon seawall proponents as flat-earth thinkers. The "Newjerseyization" of Florida beaches, they argue, represents a metaphor for failed practices and flawed policies. Building a modern "Atlantic Wall" by dumping additional sand on beaches and building more seawalls address the symptom, not the cause of erosion. To protect houses, we destroy the beach, generously subsi-

FIGURE 52. From an untamed, crocodile-infested barrier island, Miami Beach has become the best-known place in Florida. The Miami Beach skyline in the 1970s. State of Florida Photographic Archives, Tallahassee.

dizing seashore property with flood insurance and federal disaster aid, new forms of welfare for the rich.[101]

Powerful coalitions have succeeded in persuading Washington to spend billions of dollars replacing the sand that nature washed away. The practice, euphemistically called "beach renourishment," has become so commonplace that both conservatives who denounce big government and liberals who preach environmental responsibility eagerly lobby for more sand and seawalls. "There are no party lines in the sand," quipped one journalist. In 1950, Congress authorized $5 million to rebuild beaches; in 1999, the figure had grown to $100 million. During the 1990s, Congress allocated $1.69 billion for beach renourishment. Supporters of the federal program defend the practice, arguing that beaches protect the mainland from storm surges. Beaches are also economic engines, generating more than $17 billion a year in direct tourist spending. In 2000, almost 40 million tourists visited Florida beaches. Attempting to calculate the worth of Florida's coastline, an economist estimated that in 2002, state beaches generated $16 billion in property values, accounting for 250,000 jobs and $4.7 billion in payrolls. "It's pretty hard to have a beach resort," sighed one motel owner, "without the beach." Since 1969, Florida has received $1 billion to pump sand on more than forty rapidly eroding beaches inhabited by some of the world's wealthiest citizens. No other community in the United States can match the $60 million in subsidized sand that has benefited Miami Beach. Beach renourishment takes millions of dollars of taxpayers' money to refurbish beaches that are virtually closed to the public. The federal government has generously appropriated millions of dollars to beautify Lee County beaches, including several miles along Captiva Island's South Seas Resort, a gated retreat. The *Sarasota Herald-Tribune* predicts that another $5.5 billion will be necessary to maintain America's endangered beaches in the next half century.[102]

Beach renourishment has generated its own set of problems. New beaches threaten ancient habits. For millennia, sea turtles have returned to Florida beaches to lay eggs. Endangered loggerhead and leatherback turtle eggs sell for thirty-six dollars a dozen on the streets of Miami, as poachers supply Asian apothecaries and Caribbean kitchens. Annually, hundreds of endangered sea turtles are sucked up and pulverized by dredging machinery, and many hatchling sea turtles are run over by cars as they crawl toward the lights of houses and roads instead of following the beacon of moonlight that has long directed their forebears from egg to ocean. Indian River County officials discovered that while the newly refurbished beaches pleased humans, the alien sand confused turtles. Temperature-sensitive sea turtles find some sand too fine and some beaches too tightly compacted. A journalist recently concluded, "The massive dredge-and-fill operations that create a new beach can bury shallow reefs, sea grass and other habitats known to nurture more than 190 species of fish and 325 species of invertebrates at the base of the food chain."[103]

Humans, too, can be extremely sensitive about their new beaches. Not everyone, it appears, appreciates the generosity of the federal government. Critics find fault with both the process and product of rebuilding beaches. The problem is not sand—of which there is much—but locating cheap, readily accessible, and aesthetically pleasing sand. Quarry-washed sand pleases the most demanding beach connoisseur, but coastal residents object to long, noisy lines of dump trucks. Thus, the U.S. Army Corps of Engineers allows private companies to dredge up sand offshore. To beachfolk accustomed to pure white sand, the color, composition, and texture of the darker, coarser, dredged sand is unacceptable. Pensacola Beach takes pardonable pride in its alabaster-colored, quartz-particled dunes and shore, whereas devotees of Alligator Point in Franklin County have an affinity for their beach's grainy dark sand. Sand patrols report scofflaws utilizing red clay for building foundations and developers who import inferior sand.[104]

In ancient Hawaii, the beach and surf were sacred. Queens and kings claimed the most spectacular breaks and waves as a royal prerogative; ordinary surfers straying off Waikiki Beach violated the natural order. So, too, Florida denies the public some of its most spectacular beaches. In Florida, the beach up to the high-water line may be public, but access to it is more problematic. As early as 1950, newspapers editorialized about Florida's vanishing public beaches. Five decades later, the problem is far more acute. In a state of gated communities and private police, restricted access to some of Florida's most coveted beaches heightens the tension between community rights and Americans' fierce attachment to property rights. In 1972, Californians voted to guarantee "access" to the beach, declaring that "Development shall not interfere with the public right to access to the sea." The beach is both democratic and elitist. On any Sunday afternoon at Naples's Tigertail Beach, one might encounter European royalty, American nouveau riches, and Caribbean migrant laborers. There may be no class distinctions on nude beaches, but the battle for access to public beaches has been contentious and class conscious. In the 1960s, Clearwater Beach contemplated restricting parking to local residents and tourists, in effect discouraging working-class Tampans from day visits. Whether the discrimination they perceive is motivated by race or class, African Americans complain that they feel unwelcome at Florida's most prestigious beaches. The scarcity of black homeowners on the dunes and shore is glaring. In 2004, Sanibel doubled the price to $6 for motorists who visit the island. Developers have been known to erect barbed-wire fences to keep the public away from exclusive retreats. Beach communities are legally obligated to provide public access and parking if they accept federal or state dollars for beach improvements. Palm Beach boasts 12 miles of oceanfront but offers only two municipal beaches with few parking places. Jupiter Island's 9 miles of beach include only three points of public access. Hillsboro Beach's 3 miles of beachfront have no public beach, park, or access. Bellaire Beach discourages public gawking along its exclusive shore by providing a single public parking lot that is unpaved and unlined. Real estate owners contend that public mandated walkways to the beach amount to a "taking of property without compensation."[105]

Foreign observers are often struck by the privatism of American beaches. In many European and Latin American countries, private ownership of beachfront property is forbidden. Mexico, for instance, opened the beaches to the masses after the revolution of 1910. Since all of Mexico's beaches are public, anyone has the right to use the beach by walking through the lobby of any hotel to the sands. But all American beaches are only technically public, meaning anyone can walk seaward of mean high tide. In other words, wet sand belongs to the public; dry sand is/may be private.[106]

Eternal summers required seemingly endless beaches. Who could imagine a beach shortage? Floridians awakened in the 1960s to confront the reality: public beaches were disappearing. In 1961, the New York Times addressed Florida's "beach problem." In a state with 1,016 miles of suitable beaches, only 310 miles were publicly owned, and over half of those beaches were located in Northwest Florida. The problem was especially acute in the state's most populous areas, precisely those places with the most expensive beachfront. The prestigious Gold Coast (Palm Beach, Broward, and Dade counties) possessed only 17.5 miles of public beach (versus 72 miles of privately owned beach). In Martin County, where only 7 percent of the seaside was public, schoolchildren raised money to purchase several public beaches on Hutchinson Island. By the early 1970s, local and state officials discovered that the cost of acquiring public beachfront had soared to over $1 million a mile.[107]

Preservation 2000 (started under the Save Our Coast program of Governor Bob Graham) addressed the problem of Florida's vanishing ecosystems. Created by the 1990 Florida legislature and endowed with $3 billion to acquire endangered lands, Preservation 2000 has purchased miles of threatened beach. The acquisition of Topsail Hill represents one of Florida's stirring conservation triumphs. A 3-mile stretch of 40-foot sand dunes between Fort Walton Beach and Panama City, Topsail awed spectators. When nature writer Julie Hauserman first encountered the place, she exclaimed, "I had never seen such a wild Florida beach." In the early 1990s, Topsail wound up in the hands of the Federal Resolution Trust Corporation, after the savings and loan collapse. The Nature Conservancy purchased the property at auction and promptly sold it to the state. Today, Topsail Hill belongs to all Floridians.[108]

Never in modern history have places like Sunny Isles and Boca Grande been so seductive and bewitching, yet demons lurking deep in our collective past haunt the beach. Today, the doomsday prophecies of global warming hang over the Sunshine State like storm clouds. Floridians, alarmed by daily reports of calamity, must wonder whether they can survive a weekend at the beach, let alone a century of melting ice caps. Summer bathers expose their toes to E. coli bacteria and hypodermic needles, stingrays and jellyfish. Ominous-sounding and -smelling red tides and black zones contaminate the Gulf of Mexico. Elkhorn Coral—"the redwoods of the Keys barrier reef"—is dying at an alarming rate. Swimmers battle riptide, undertow, and jet skis, while overstretched municipalities are forced to lay off lifeguards. Even the suntan, once a beauty mark of beach worshipers, now evokes images of wrinkles and, worse, melanoma. More than a natural resource, the sun was Florida's civic and state emblem. St. Petersburg crowned itself the Sunshine City of the Sunshine State. Miami claimed it was the "nearest major U.S. city to the sun." Sun protection has become a $3 billion business. A twenty-four-hour-a-day Weather Channel caters to a public obsessed with ozone levels and "skindex" bulletins.[109]

Once the beach suggested sexual innocence and innocent pleasure. Ever since Mack Sennett introduced his bathing beauties to early moviegoers, the beach has served as the setting for passion (*the* kiss on the surf in *From Here to Eternity*), entertainment (Esther Williams and her aquabelles), and youthful frolic (the Frankie Avalon and Annette Funicello movies). *Jaws* (1975) changed the way Americans put their toes in the water. "Since *Jaws*," writes critic Stuart Klawans, "the beach has turned into a site of isolation, anxiety, and horror."[110]

Jaws awakened our primordial fears of great whites, and ever since, Floridians have been obsessed by the mere appearance of sharks off the coasts. The problem, of course, is not a new influx of sharks. In fact, the shark population has been plummeting because of humans' appetite for shark steaks and shark-fin soup and our sadistic delight in killing them. The problem is that more and more humans play in the sharks' habitat. Nor is the rate of shark attacks on the rise. Volusia County nervously wears the crown "Shark Attack Capital of the World" (138 attacks since 1882). County spokespersons impatiently point out that no one has ever been actually killed by a shark on a Volusia beach. The public hysteria generated by the so-called "Summer of the Shark," confesses Peter Benchley, the author of *Jaws*, has been media- and Internet-driven.[111]

In their vision of Florida hurricanes, novelists Zora Neale Hurston, Philip Wylie, Herman Wouk, and John D. MacDonald attempted to convey the pandemonium resulting "when the big one comes." Real-life developments—millions of Floridians living on or near the beach, billions of dollars of property built on low-lying barrier islands, and a transportation infrastructure exhausted during normal times—add up to an impending apocalypse. What earthquakes are to California, hurricanes are to Florida. Hurricanes mock the hubris of humans who impose their will on the beach. But the Sunshine State has been extraordinarily lucky in the last forty years. Since the 1950s, Hurricanes Donna (1960), Dora (1964), Agnes (1972), Eloise (1975), Andrew (1992), and the quadruplets of 2004 have demonstrated the wrath of nature, and even these storms spared Florida a worst-case scenario. But what a scenario! Consider Andrew's legacy: 690,000 persons left without electricity, 250,000 people left homeless, the destruction of 10,000 apartments and 9,000 mobile homes, and $25 billion to $35 billion in property damage. Hurricane Andrew may have been America's most costly natural disaster, but if a storm of the intensity and path of the 1926 hurricane were to strike South Florida today, the price tag would total $72 billion. The hurricane of 1926 smashed Miami and punctured the speculative balloon. "Picture Hurricane Andrew churning with devastating power," urged the *South Florida Sun-Sentinel*, "only this time it is aiming right down [Fort Lauderdale's] Broward Boulevard. With ferocious gusts up to 180 mph, it pounds Port Everglades, the Swap Shop and Sawgrass Mills Mall. . . . By the time this compact system departs the area, it has cut a 30-mile swath of destruction . . . causing up to $70 billion in damage." Tampa Bay and Sarasota Bay last took direct hits from hurricanes in the 1920s, when the population of the counties totaled 125,000 residents. The succeeding eighty years have witnessed spectacular population growth, especially along the coasts and the most vulnerable barrier islands. Pinellas and Hillsborough counties alone accounted for 100,000 mobile homes in 2000.[112]

In September 1999, Floridians nervously awaited the arrival of Hurricane Floyd. Like the menacing clouds in the movie *Independence Day*, Floyd rumbled across the Florida Straits, prompting displays of panic and pandemonium. Choosing caution over certainty, authorities ordered the largest peacetime evacuation in American history. Interstate highways resembled parking lots. For the first time in its history, Disney World shuttered its doors and castle windows. While Floyd narrowly missed Florida, a political hurricane hit the state squarely, as angry citizens demanded apologies and compensation.

Not everyone believes that hurricanes are "natural" disasters. People, after all, choose to live on barrier islands, purchase mobile homes, ignore shoddy building practices, and then pressure private businesses and governments to insure the property. "When I fly over the coast, I just shake my head," confesses Max Mayfield, director of the national Hurricane Center in Miami. "Too many people are crammed into coastal communities with too few evacuation routes, leaving too little a margin for error." Hurricanes punish human foibles, but optimists manage to find a silver lining in the storm clouds. Society can learn from nature's fury. "The logical, long-term remedy," writes journalist J. Earle Bowden, "means moving the buildings off the beaches . . . behind the primary dunes, not a thoughtless assault against the natural forces." History, however, has shown that after each hurricane, bigger and more expensive buildings, not fewer structures, occupy the beach. One person's hurricane is another's opportunity. Harvey Jackson III recalls how Hurricane Eloise in September 1975 smashed the Panhandle's Choctawhatchee Bay and the outlying barrier islands. "Surveying the wreckage, developers quickly realized that storms did not destroy so much as they cleared the way for new construction, and soon speculators were buying property, drawing plans, and laying foundations. . . . Soon there were more motels, restaurants, and amusement outlets than ever before."[113]

The specter of killer-force winds and storm surges unloosing toxic demons frighten scientists who fear the deadly combination of a natural disaster disturbing the human patchwork of containment ponds, sewage treatment works, landfills, and overflowing septic tanks. Had Hurricane Andrew veered 20 miles northward and smashed Liberty City and Little Havana, the Magic City might have descended into the Dystopian City, unleashing in Mike Davis's words, the explosive energy of "natural hazards and social contradictions."[114]

Condominium was John D. MacDonald's sixty-sixth book, but many readers believe it best exemplifies the author's code of ethics and best captures his adopted state's shortcomings. The novel connects all of the dots: sleazy county commissioners eager to approve Golden Sands, a doomed, eight-story "geriatric ghetto" on fictitious Fiddler Key; shady contractors performing shoddy work; fast-talking salesmen; and Hurricane Ella taking vengeance upon the innocent and guilty.[115]

Humans fear the beach for reasons real (hurricanes) and imagined (great white shark attacks). But if the beaches are creepy, contaminated, and imperfect, the American solution is to create a better beach. Corporate America has responded ingeniously to the challenge by constructing water theme parks. Wet 'n Wild, Adventure Island, Typhoon Lagoon, and Blizzard Beach offer landlubbers the amenities of the beach without the dangers. Since these parks exist miles from ocean or gulf, patrons are spared even the annoyances of salt water. Wave machines called Flow Riders pump 40,000 gallons of water per minute to simulate surfing conditions found not even off Cocoa Beach. Inside the biosphere at Kissimmee's Gaylord Palms, diners at the Key West–style restaurant experience not only a wave generator but a gentle misting of salty sea air.[116]

Nothing, it seems, can keep the world from wanting to live and play on Florida's beaches. Not even politicians or protestors can ruin this love affair. In 1972, the New Age Abbie Hoffman turned to an Old Age political tactic to disrupt the Republican National Convention at Miami Beach. Hoffman, the self-appointed leader of the nonexistent Youth International Party (whose followers were called Yippies), had summoned America's countercultural tribes to Florida. Even Hoffman, however, was required to secure a permit for the Yippies to sleep along the beach. Mockingly, he warned that if the permit were not granted, his father, John Hoffman of Worcester, Massachusetts, would remain in the Bay State for the winter. An exasperated councilman and acquaintance of the father called the ringleader's bluff, exclaiming that John Hoffman would not dare boycott Miami Beach. "He'll still come down. He loves the beach!"[117]

The beach changes but remains the same. At its worst, the beach terrifies and disappoints; at its best, it stirs our soul and softens a harsh world. In a state where civic bonds are as weak as Australian pines in a storm, sunrises and sunsets over Amelia Island and Mullet Key connect generations of Floridians. Coconut palm, sea hibiscus, and bougainvillea seem at home on today's beaches, but these residents, like so many Floridians, also came from somewhere else.

Epilogue

IN *Their Eyes Were Watching God*, Zora Neale Hurston writes, "There are years that ask questions and years that answer."[1] Oracles will be pondering the meaning of 2000 for many years. A centennial and millennial year, 2000 was also an election and census year. Like Norma Desmond in *Sunset Boulevard*, Florida was ready for its curtain call.

"The Sunshine State is a paradise of scandals . . ."

Carl Hiaasen, *Time*, 20 November 2000

If, in the words of publisher Henry Luce, the twentieth century was *the* American century, few soothsayers could have imagined that the backwater state of Florida would become a bellwether state. At the century's turn, barely half a million residents called Florida home. To put those numbers in perspective, South Carolina boasted a population of 1,340,000 in 1900. On maps and in people's minds, Florida was the most isolated state east of the Mississippi River. Most residents lived a wagon's drive from the Georgia and Alabama borders; residents of Tallahassee (population 2,981) could walk to Thomasville, Georgia, in one day.

In spasms of prosperity and promotion, Florida lurched forward. Not until 1920 did the state surpass a population of one million. More than any other single event, World War II served as a springboard for the meteoric ascendancy of the Sunshine State. Never had so many impressionable young adults visited Florida than in the years 1940–45. But Florida has always been more about tomorrow's possibilities than today's realities. Every recruit who spent time at Hendricks Field in Sebring, the Jacksonville Naval Air Station, the Sopchoppy Bombing Range, or Miami Beach's training facilities vowed to return some day.

Dreams and possibilities came together in the decades after 1940. In the war's aftermath, elements coalesced to make possible Everyman's Florida: uninterrupted prosperity, most notably the rising standard of living for the middling classes; a resurgent federal government determined to contain Communism abroad and expand the New Deal at home; revolutions in health care, leisure, and technology; the affordability and popularity of air conditioning and air travel; the selling and manufacture of dreams by a loosely connected group of businessmen, developers, and press corps; the realization that Florida was a place where workers, retirees, and pleasure seekers could enjoy and share paradise. Nothing—not the murders of civil rights leader Harry T. Moore or the Groveland boys, the nagging recessions of 1973 and 1990, or environmental calamities—could douse Americans' stampede to sunshine and water.

From an afterthought in 1900, Florida emerged as a megastate in 2000. Census takers counted 15,982,378 residents; millions more maintained homes in the Sunshine State part of the year or visited as tourists. Miami-Dade County alone accounted for two million Floridians, a stunning accomplishment when one considers that in 1900, Dade County (then constituting the future entities of Broward, Palm Beach, and Martin counties), claimed 4,955 inhabitants.[2]

Unremitting growth had not come without social consequences. In 1900, most residents had been born in Florida or had migrated from the Deep South, bound tightly by regional and sectional attitudes toward race, politics, and folkways. A century later, only about four in ten Floridians were native born. Only Nevada (28.2 percent) had a lower percentage of natives. When combined with the elongated shape of the state and the climate of individualism, so many newcomers contribute to a weak civic bond, what commentator Michael Barone calls "a feeble public sector that extends from universities to environmental protection to criminal justice." But Americans and Floridians, unlike Britons or the Chinese, have always been united by the prospects of a better future, not a shared past.[3]

Landmarks and signposts blur in a state of flux. In 1930, Dixie, Charlotte, and Martin counties were among the state's most sparsely settled places. Dixie County's 6,419 residents made a meager living from turpentining, lumbering, and hunting; Charlotte County's 4,013 citizens depended upon cattle ranches, tourism, and the Gulf of Mexico. Martin County's groves, fields, and beaches supported 5,111 inhabitants. Meanwhile, in Madison County—where cotton, cattle, and powerful state legislators were king—the population of 15,614 looked toward a bright future. Madison County had almost as many mules as there were people in some counties. Madison may have been home to Florida's greatest World War II hero—Colin P. Kelly Jr.—but the war brought no new industry and few recruits dreamed of returning to Greenville some day. The ghosts of the Old South haunted New South Dixie and Madison counties. Until the 1940s, more African Americans than whites lived in Madison, part of the once-rich cotton belt. In 1956, county commissioners fired the public health officer because she was seen dining with a black friend. In Dixie County, black "lifers" told tales of horror to Stetson Kennedy and Zora Neale Hurston when they interviewed turpentine workers in Cross City and Dixie's backwoods. Black residents of Madison and Dixie have largely migrated to the north while increasing numbers of white migrants preferred South Florida to North Florida. Seventy years later, the combined populations of Dixie and Madison counties (28,024) pale compared to the number of tourists headed to the beaches of Charlotte and Martin counties on a single March afternoon. Once sand poor, Charlotte and Martin counties glitter as Sunbelt jewels, their combined 2000 populations surpassing 268,000.[4]

In Madison and Cross City, and in the surrounding communities of Greenville, Graceville, Jacob, Midway, Monticello, Gretna, Bristol, and Port St. Joe, over three-quarters of the white inhabitants are self-identified crackers, native-born and bred. African-Americans who reside in North Florida are even more likely to be natives. Residents also care deeply about their neighbors and a landscape rich in steephead ravines, cypress swamps, and red clay hills. The rapid growth in Charlotte, Martin, and many South Florida counties has created places of strangers. Membership in the voluntary associations that once made America a nation of joiner—the Elks, Knights of Columbus, and Oddfellows—is plummeting. The erosion of community is hardly confined to South Florida, but because of the region's vast number of newcomers, the impact of sprawl, and the nature of retirement life, a sense of community is lacking and fleeting. A recent poll, however, suggested optimism for this place called Florida. When asked whether they considered themselves "Floridians," fully 71 percent of non-native residents and 85 percent of Cuban-Americans replied yes.[5]

Once, Seminoles and Miccosukees were also strangers in this land. Three wars, forced exile, and physical isolation forged among them a remarkable sense of identity and identification with place. How fitting—and improbable—that the most famous YK2 blowout in Florida was held at an Indian reservation.

On 31 December 1999, over 75,000 Floridians and visitors crowded the Big Cypress Indian Reservation to cheer the rock band Phish and usher in a new century and millennium.[6]

The Phish Bow concert welcomed in a year that many Floridians soon wished to forget. In Miami, the Elián González imbroglio transcended Miami and soon became an international symbol. The six-year-old Elián had survived a harrowing voyage by sea, a voyage that claimed his mother's life. Should he be reunited with his father in Cuba, or remain with his exiled compatriots in Miami? Camp Elián soon became shrine and symbol. Ultimately, U.S. Attorney General and Miami native Janet Reno ordered federal agents to seize the boy and return him to Cuba. Angry Cubans vowed vengeance in November. Carl Hiaasen joked that it would be poetic justice if "the presidential election shakes down to a single vote—an overseas ballot from Havana bearing the childlike signature of one E. González."[7]

The 2000 presidential election stigmatized Florida as more a collection of zany tribes, warring counties, and partisan groups than a state. In lasting frames, Americans tuned in to witness confused senior citizens, angry African-Americans, publicity-crazy lawyers, highly partisan politicians, besieged ballot counters, and hanging chads. Florida would decide the fate of the Free World. It had happened before.

The 2000 election had fascinating overtones—and undertow—to the 1876 election. In addition to accusations of massive political corruption, disputed vote counts, and the legitimacy of a Republican president and governor, the elections had also isolated Florida as a critical "battleground" state. In 1876, twelve companies of the U.S. Army still enforced a bitter peace in Tallahassee while hundreds of journalists and party officials—the latter politely called "visiting statesmen"—attempted to report and influence the fate of the republic and the future of Reconstruction. The election climaxed a decade marred by massive political and racial violence. Republican success in Washington came at the price of Democratic "redemption" in Florida and the South. It would be almost a century before Republicans triumphed again in Florida.[8]

Vestiges of Reconstruction resurfaced in 2000. A law remained on the books limiting citizens to five minutes in the voting booth, a measure originally intended to intimidate illiterate voters. Most dramatically, almost 700,000 Floridians were ineligible to vote, despite the fact they were adult citizens. They were disenfranchised because they were in prison or had been convicted of felonies. Over half of Florida's prison population is black. In black majority Gadsden County, officials disqualified 12 percent of the ballots.[9]

Whipsawed by political storms in 2000, Florida was whiplashed by real storms in 2004. In a span of 44 days, four powerful hurricanes slammed the state, leaving in their wake historic property losses and a weary population. The Sunshine State has become the Plywood State, the State of Fatigue, and the National Disaster State. A red state in the November presidential sweepstakes, Florida is more accurately a blue tarpaulin state, and September, not April, is the cruelest month of the year.

Hurricanes dashed the dreams of Spanish kings, Old South planters, and New South merchants. Now Charley, Frances, Ivan, and Jeanne join Andrew and the Nor'easter of 1871, taking their places alongside other great natural disasters in Florida history. Winds of change have again altered the course of Florida history. The hurricane of 1561 destroyed the de Luna colony that had settled on Pensacola Bay, thus allowing the upstart settlement of St. Augustine to claim the title of the nation's oldest city. Four years later, a hurricane scattered a French fleet dispatched to relieve Fort Caroline. The Spanish destroyed the French settlement, and then put to the sword the storm-tossed Huguenots. Hurricanes in the 1840s destroyed the promising towns of Port Leon and St. Joseph. Cedar Key's prosperity and promise were obliterated by a fierce hurricane in 1896. A 1926 hurricane punctured Miami's balloon, inspiring the nickname for the fledgling University of Miami football team. In 1928, a storm, so powerful that locals swore it "blowed a crooked road straight," killed thousands on the southern shore of Lake Okeechobee. "They seemed to be staring at the dark," wrote Zora Neale Hurston as she imagined the mass of workers running from the storm surge, "but their eyes were watching God." The year 1947 witnessed two hurricanes strike Broward County within thirty days, part of a deluge that saw Dania record 103 inches of rain for the year. Officials demanded and received authorization to drain new portions of the Everglades. Hurricane Donna—the Weather Bureau began assigning feminine names to the storms in 1953—roared through southwest Florida in 1960, leveling many old beach cottages, and paving the way for modern redevelopment. At the time, southwest Florida had a population of about 80,000 inhabitants.[10]

In *Anna Karenina*, Leo Tolstoy begins, "Happy families are all alike; every unhappy family is unhappy in its own way." Great hurricanes, too, bring their signature styles of approach and destruction: some loop and meander, while others follow unswerving paths; some wreak havoc across a tightly formed eye, while others spawn massive centers that hover over the entire state.

Floridians know the drill. In a media-saturated culture where the Weather Channel operates twenty-four hours a day, hurricanes signify geo-political-cultural markers. In the past, hurricanes came and went with little warning. When an 1848 'cane roared across Tampa Bay, engulfing Fort Brooke and the Pinellas peninsula, it took weeks for Floridians to learn about the calamity. Now reporting on hurricanes has become the domestic equivalent of covering wars. Each new threat necessitates a familiar cast of characters and actions: weather maps and sophisticated technology (VIPIR radar) predict and chart the storm's path; a marathon hurricane watch by TV meteorologists, many (The Weather Channel's Jim Cantore) who have become media celebrities; network anchors bent backward by the force of Category 3 winds and blinded by sheets of rain; live oaks uprooted and tidal surges hammering seawalls; and live camera shots from emergency shelters. Since schools now serve as emergency shelters, every single school in Florida was closed at least once during the 2004 storms.[11]

The hurricanes of 2004 scoured the coasts and soaked the interior, but the events left more than physical damage. Natural disasters shear the social and cultural, economic and ecological landscape. The tempests allow novelists, anthropologists, and historians to put events in perspective.

For millennia, tropical gales shaped and reshaped the place we call Florida. Before humans ever set foot on the finger of land jutting into the warm waters of the Gulf; indeed, before the peninsula assumed its present shape 10,000 years ago, late summer storms brought wind and waves pushing and pulling flora and fauna from distant continents and islands to Florida.

The Taíno Indians of the Caribbean called the destructive storms *hurrácan*. The Spanish quickly understood the demonic overtones of the native word and its associations. The New World awed the Europeans with its natural wonders, its exotic plants and animals. But compared to the most severe Mediterranean storms, *el hurrácan* combined a fury and power never before seen or felt. Creoles and natives learned to read the signs of an approaching storm: aching bones, severe headaches, premature births, insects and birds behaving strangely, the sawgrass blooming–all the result of plunging barometric pressure.[12]

The Taínos attributed a malevolent quality to the hurrácan. Modern society—and unreconstructed, yellow dog Democrats who chart the hurricanes' paths as divine retribution for the stolen election of 2000—share a similar outlook, depicting the disruptive quadruplets Charley, Frances, Ivan, and Jeanne as evil and aberrational. But a hurricane is a natural, not a moral phenomenon. What has changed is not nature, suddenly unleashed, but the fact that 17 million people now reside in Florida, most of them living on or near the coasts. To put this into perspective, consider that the last time four hurricanes struck a single state (Texas) in one season was 1886. At that time, the entire population of Florida numbered about 340,000 inhabitants. As with alligators devouring pet dogs and sharks biting exposed limbs, there is nothing unusual about such natural behavior. In William Shakespeare's *Julius Caesar,* Cassius—he of the "lean and hungry look"—understood this condition. "The fault, dear Brutus," states the Roman, "lies not in our stars, but in ourselves."

"War," so went a popular slogan in the 1940s, "is God's way of teaching Americans geography." A revised proverb holds that "hurricanes are nature's way of making Floridians learn geography." A state of vast distances and distant strangers, this special place that inspires dreams and hopes needs citizens who care about the welfare of Florida and its people. Millions of Floridians now know about Punta Gorda, Lake Wales, Sewall's Point, Barefoot Bay, Fort Pierce, Stuart, Jensen Beach, Perdido Key, Santa Rosa Island, and even the Grande Lagoon subdivision, the Ocean Breeze Trailer Park, and the Cracker Trails R. V. Park. In rare gestures of civic communion, strangers helped one another as national guardsmen, emergency workers, and volunteers assisted the young and old, rich and poor. New heroes emerged: utility linesmen, paramedics, and mechanics who knew how to operate gas-powered electric generators.

The hurricanes battered and bent, leveled and disheveled some of Florida's wealthiest neighborhoods and poorest places. Twin outposts of glamour and prestige, Sanibel and Captiva islands and Jupiter and Hutchinson islands faced the wrath of Charley, Frances, and Jeanne. Ivan left Pensacola Bay a "graveyard of yachts." On the evening news and front pages, Americans discovered a diverse, multicultural Florida. Separated by only a few miles, the million-dollar mansions lining the barrier islands of Charlotte Harbor are worlds apart from the modest mobile home parks of Punta Gorda and the retirement communities of Lehigh Acres and Port Charlotte. When the storms veered inland and exposed the migrant labor camps in Zolfo Springs, Bowling Green, Wachula, and Arcadia, the plight of Florida's invisible poor became painfully visible. Great storms respect neither the newest nor oldest parts of Florida. Hurricane

Charley ripped several sections away from the ancient Calusa mound on Pine Island.[13] Thrice struck, Volusia County's DeBary and Polk County's Lake Wales and Deltona became unlikely candidates for America's hurricane capital.[14]

Polk County, situated equidistant between the Gulf of Mexico and Atlantic Ocean, seemed blessed for much of the twentieth century. Powerful politicians—Park Trammell, Spessard Holland, and Lawton Chiles—burnished the legend of "Imperial Polk County." Endowed by nature with rich soil, abundant rivers and lakes, and rich deposits of phosphate, Polk County earned the title *fruit basket* of Florida. Frostpoof and Winter Haven, Loughman and Agricola—place names with magical and mundane attachments—spoke to the richness and promise of Central Florida. It was here, residents told folklorists in the 1920s, that water tasted like cherry wine. Alas, nature and history have left the population shaken and depressed. Historic freezes and environmental crises have displaced and devastated the local citrus and phosphate economies. Home to some of the richest communities in Florida (Iron Mountain), Polk County's half million residents also reside in some of the state's poorest places (Mulberry). No county in Florida suffered more sustained damage than Polk County, in the crosshairs of three hurricanes.[15]

Assessing the physical damage is the work of insurance agents; measuring the consequences of natural disasters is the challenge of social scientists. Newspapers offer the first drafts of history, and the early accountings of the fourth estate suggest a rich source of future scholarship. Once the reader gets past the inevitable "roofs peeled back like sardine cans" and "tall trees snapped like twigs," the reportage is revealing.[16]

Hurricanes may be natural disasters, but they also teach political lessons. For most of American history, hurricanes were local events. Victims relied not upon the generosity and kindness of strangers or faraway governments, but rather neighbors and local charities. The turning point was the Labor Day hurricane of 1935. Hundreds of World War I veterans working on a new highway in the Florida Keys drowned in the waters off Upper and Lower Matecumbe. When Ernest Hemingway arrived to inspect the damage he was appalled at the carnage. "Who murdered the vets?" he asked in *New Masses*, adding sardonically, "The writer of this article lives a long way from Washington and would not know the answers to these questions." Presidents and governors have become more responsive and sensitive to national disasters. The same impulses that empowered the Imperial presidency also created powerful federal agencies, such as the Weather Bureau and the Federal Emergency Management Administration. Today, the chief executive and governor also must play the role of national griever, healer, and provider. Witness the criticism in 1992 when President George H. W. Bush was accused of lacking sensitivity for the victims of Hurricane Andrew. Yet the hurricanes of 2004 seemed to have softened the image of the president's son Jeb, who spent weeks handing out bottles of water, hugging mobile home survivors, and giving bilingual press conferences. The governor's brother, President George W. Bush, swiftly signed a $7.1 billion hurricane aid package. Black Caucus Democrats criticized the chief executive for not providing enough relief for Haiti. Others accused Miami officials of gorging on public funds intended for more deserving areas. Even Fidel Castro used the disasters for political gain, pointing out that Communist Cuba suffered no human losses.[17]

Washington, D.C., once remote, is now inextricably linked to Floridians' lives on barrier islands and rural hamlets. Decisions involving flood insurance, beach renourishment, and building codes are preeminently political decisions. As bad as 2004 will be remembered, future hurricanes will almost certainly inflict greater pain and damage. Florida is about taking chances. Governments could, of course, prohibit mobile homes and construction along barrier islands and flood-prone areas, but powerful interests want the freedom to build, along with federally subsidized insurance as a hedge against catastrophes.

Environmentalists and reformers point to the success of Seaside, the much ballyhooed development in Okaloosa County that survived Ivan with minimal damage. Seaside's strict building codes mandate housing ("Think New Money Norman Rockwell," wrote one journalist) set back behind the dunes. Yet to its critics, Seaside is expensive, confining, and impractical.[18]

Debates over costs, blame, and responsibilities are already raging. But there is only one thing more certain than future hurricanes striking Florida: class, power, and political influence will triumph. Bigger will replace smaller; new will supplant old. The 22,000 mobile homes of Charlotte County (most of them underinsured) that lined lakes, rivers, and canals will likely be replaced by expensive condominiums and commercial development. It is the most elementary law of Florida physics. Where will the displaced residents go? Laws of physics do not help with such questions.

Whatever meanings scholars divine from 2004, one point is undeniable: the hurricanes' price tag ($21 billion in insured losses, and rising; 25,000 homes destroyed; 270,000 homes damaged) will add up to the most expensive—and disruptive—natural disaster in American history. The storms forced as many as ten million Floridians to evacuate. A new book of lamentations memorializes the individual stories of loss. Vero Beach's legendary Driftwood Inn had survived depressions, wars, and deaths, but hurricanes finally forced the historic structure designed by Waldo Emerson Sexton to close. Not far away, McKee Botanical Gardens registered severe damage to its grounds, most notably its state champion Toog tree. Miami's Fairchild Gardens, Lake Wale's Bok Tower, and Orlando's Leu Gardens also bore scars. Almost every household lost power for at least a day. In the short run, the storms will devastate local economies and state government: the loss of sales taxes, canceled holidays, and lost income. But in the long run, an avalanche of federal, state, and insurance money—2004 *was* an election year—descended upon the Sunshine State. Over 600,000 Floridians have already applied for assistance. The mother of all reconstruction booms followed. A sense of perspective is important. Florida suffered 117 deaths. Contrast that tragic statistic with Haiti's losses of over two thousand people or the Pacific tsunami.[19]

While roofers, landscapers, and contractors reap a bonanza, the outlook is less optimistic for grove owners, truck farmers, and migrant laborers. Predictions of crop losses have been grim: perhaps $3 billion, or a third of the state's agricultural economy. Most of the state's citrus crop wound up on the ground; the booming nursery and landscaping business is in shambles; migrant laborers fear accepting government assistance, lest they be detected as illegals. But powerful agribusiness will rebound.[20]

Tropical winds blow across political, class, and geographic boundaries. Million-dollar beach houses and double-wide mobile homes both disintegrated under a 16-foot storm surge and 120-mile-per-hour winds. But in hurricanes, as in life, class matters. From storm prep to evacuation routes to insurance claims, it helps to be rich. Poor Floridians have neither trucks nor SUVs to haul plywood to shutter homes, do not own generators, and have little disposable income for motels. Along the Gold Coast, some families escaped the danger by leasing private jets ($17,000 a flight). The residents of Florida's gated communities discovered that the very amenities that attracted them to such locales— private roads, lush landscaping, and restricted access—also kept out emergency crews. Moreover, officials at the state and national level have initially denied government aid to private homeowners' associations. The islands of the Florida Keys, long a refuge for Conchs and smugglers, became temporary home to hundreds of expensive craft, whose owners hoped to save the megayachts. Loren "Totch" Brown surely was smiling in his grave at such news. His father had taught him the ways of sea and land and how to ride out hurricanes by tethering boats amid the mangroves of the Ten Thousand Islands. In Totch's day, most of the residents of Chokoloskee Island were poor. The stakes are higher today.[21]

Environmentalists will be sorting out the meaning of 2004 for years. As in the past, hurricanes rearrange the landscape. Hurricane Charley sliced the island of North Captiva in half. The winds also blew down bald eagles' nests and pine trees inhabited by the red-cockaded woodpecker. Beaches and dunes took a severe hit, although scientists point out that one place's erosion is another's gain. While most of Volusia County's 49 miles of beach sustained severe beach erosion, Bethune Beach gained tons of new sand. The havoc has turned Charlotte Harbor, Pensacola Bay, and miles of canal into a vast dumping ground for sunken boats, plastic privies, mobile home parts, and navigational signs. Stone crab fishermen, however, report healthy yields of the tasty claws. The storms also hurt severely endangered sea grasses and loggerhead and green turtle nests. Perdido Key beach mice and land tortoises suffered large losses. The high winds ripped away thousands of acres of unwanted Australian pine (in addition to staggering amounts of deadwood) but the swaths of destroyed forest provide new opportunities for other invasive species. Species such as laurel oaks were especially vulnerable to the storms because of their brittle limbs. Frances overwhelmed a dike on a Hillsborough County gypsum stack, unleashing 60 million gallons of acid wastewater into the Alafia River and bay. Class action suits have already begun, as well as pointed discussions over the very existence of radioactive phosphate waste in the center of a metropolis. Across Florida, barometric pressure and torrential rain played havoc with septic tanks, sewers, and sewage treatment plants. From Pensacola to Broward County, raw sewage poured out of manhole covers. But ill winds can blow benefits to an environment (the Everglades and aquifer) that needed flushing and recharging.[22]

To be a Floridian is to be optimistic. Florida is open for business. Within days after the devastation, real estate speculators were ready to reinvest in Florida. Governor Bush and legislators have promised millions of dollars to tourist officials to promote the Sunshine State. The future seems as bright as the past. A hurricane afterall, in Shakespeare's *The Tempest*, inspired a "Brave New world," the "stuff of dreams. But the past is not always prologue. The period between 1965 and the 1990s was an era of remarkable prosperity and moderate weather. Not since 1964 has the Sunshine State been hammered by three hurricanes in a season. During the decade of the 1970s, a total of only three hurricanes struck the state. Between 1978 and 1985, not a single hurricane hit Florida. Like biblical plagues upon a wicked people and an ill-begotten land, the hurricanes of 2004 take their place beside global warming, melanoma, red tide, alien exotics, West Nile virus, and the predictions of new, even more ferocious storms. A popular bumper sticker provides a parable to the recent events: "Nature Bats Last." Yet the Florida Dream endures, if slightly mildewed, frayed, and stressed.[23]

Even in disaster, Florida brings elements of spectacle and theater to a world expecting nothing less of the Sunshine State. By October 2004, armies of roofers and insurance adjusters collided with battalions of news crews and political operatives. As hurricanes became yesterday's news, visits by presidential candidates dominated the front pages. President Bush and John Kerry visited Florida so often they began pronouncing Miami as "Miamah" and recommending the best Waffle Houses to the press corps. Journalists labored to pronounce the placenames Kissimmee, Boca Raton, and Alachua.

Reporters scanned dusty history books to find out when a sitting president last visited Alachua County. When President Grover Cleveland came by train to Gainesville in the late nineteenth century, Alachua County was the state's second largest county and an agricultural powerhouse. When President Bush flew into Gainesville and spoke at an airport rally, Alachua was no longer the center of the state's Sea Island cotton belt, but was home to bulging numbers of voters. More importantly, old Democratic-leaning Alachua is overwhelmined by new Republican-leaning Gilchrist, Lafayette, Suwannee, and Union counties.

The results of the 2004 election lay bare the Florida as neatly as the season's hurricanes. If Wellington's victory at Waterloo was won on the playing fields of Eton, President Bush's triumph can best be understood in places like Land O' Lakes, Floral City, Palm Coast, Tavares, St. Cloud, Haines City, and New Port Richey. It was here and not the great cities that demographics intersected with politics. For years the exurbs—places that blurred the suburbs and cities—had grown by strip malls and subdivisions. It was as if a giant centrifuge had spun American toward the edges of Florida. President Bush won Flagler, Osceola, Lake, Wakulla, Walton, Collier, Santa Rosa, and Pasco counties, which also happen to be included in the 100 fastest-growing counties in America.[24]

The election of 2004 reawakened the ghosts of race in Florida. In West Florida, three blue counties stuck out in a sea of red. Gadsden, Leon, and Jefferson counties, once the heart of Florida's Black Belt, staunchly supported the Democratic candidate. But the center no longer held. West Florida is now Republican country.

Hispanics, too, reflected the decentralizing tendencies of decades of migration and immigration. Hispanics in Polk County helped elect Melquadies Rafael Martínez the first Cuban-born U.S. Senator in Florida and American history. Martínez, a Pedro Pan alumnus, is an Orlando resident who helped the president with the now legendary I-4 corridor vote.

On the eve of the 2004 hurricane season, I traveled from Tampa to London. From the perspective of altocumulus clouds, the distinctive peninsula offers bold and subtle geographic tableaus. What a majestic setting. From this vantage point, one understands the question: "What are the two man-made features on earth that astronauts can see from Outer Space?" Answer: The Great Wall of China and the Broward County line. One might also add Metro Orlando, although that configuration is constantly changing. Cape Canaveral's glistening rocket pads melt and complexes blend into the graceful curves and colors of the Indian River, the Seminole Forest, the St. Johns chain of lakes, and the Green Swamp, only to encounter suddenly the vast series of grids and squares of Central Florida. Following the I-4 corridor, as the jet flies, one appreciates the loss of grove and forest and the newly minted words coined to explain Florida's growth: megalopolis, exurbs, microburbs, and boomburbs. But the sheer grandeur of Tampa Bay underscores why so many people wish to come to Florida. I wondered what Florida might have looked like from a plane in 1900. Of course, airplanes had not been invented yet, but neither had modern Florida. The dream endures.

Notes

Abbreviations Used in Notes

AJC	*Atlanta Journal Constitution*
AJYB	*American Jewish Year Book*
BH	*Bradenton Herald*
BW	*Business Week*
CCN	*Collier County News*
CHE	*Chronicle of Higher Education*
CS	*Clearwater Sun*
CSM	*Christian Science Monitor*
CT	*Chicago Tribune*
DBEN	*Daytona Beach Evening News*
DBNJ	*Daytona Beach News-Journal*
DSN	*DeLand Sun News*
FG	*Florida Grower*
FLDN	*Fort Lauderdale Daily News*
FLHS	Fort Lauderdale Historical Society
FLN	*Fort Lauderdale News*
FMNP	*Fort Myers News-Press*
FS	*Florida Sentinel*
FSA	*Florida Statistical Abstract*
FT	*Florida Trend*
FTU	*Florida Times-Union* (Jacksonville)
GCD	*Glades County Democrat*
GDS	*Gainesville Daily Sun*
GS	*Gainesville Sun*
HASF	Historical Association of South Florida
HCN	*Hendry County News*
HN	*Herald News* (Charlotte County)
JCF	*Jackson County Floridian*
JJ	*Jacksonville Journal*
KWC	*Key West Citizen*

LAT	*Los Angeles Times*
LL	*Lakeland Ledger*
MDN	*Miami Daily News*
MDPLSC	Miami-Dade Public Library Special Collection
MER	*Madison Enterprise-Recorder*
MH	*Miami Herald*
MN	*Miami News*
NASS	National Agricultural Statistics Service
NC	*News Chief* (Winter Haven)
NDN	*Naples Daily News*
NYT	*New York Times*
NYTM	*New York Times Magazine*
OCRHC	Orange County Regional History Center
ON	*Okeechobee News*
OS	*Orlando Sentinel*
OSB	*Ocala Star Banner*
OSS	*Orlando Star Sentinel*
PBDN	*Palm Beach Daily News*
PBP	*Palm Beach Post*
PCNH	*Panama City News-Herald*
PJ	*Pensacola Journal*
PNJ	*Pensacola News Journal*
SAR	*St. Augustine Record*
SDU	*San Diego Union*
SFBJ	*South Florida Business Journal*
SFC	*San Francisco Chronicle*
SFSS	*South Florida Sun-Sentinel*
SH	*Sanford Herald*
SHT	*Sarasota Herald Tribune*
SLT	*Salt Lake Tribune*
SN	*Stuart News*
SPT	*St. Petersburg Times*
TD	*Tallahassee Democrat*
TDD	*Tallahassee Daily Democrat*
TDT	*Tampa Daily Times*
TMT	*Tampa Morning Tribune*
TSA	*Titusville Star-Advocate*
TT	*Tampa Tribune*
USAT	*USA Today*
USNWR	*U.S. News and World Report*
USFSC	University of South Florida Special Collections
VBPJ	*Vero Beach Press-Journal*
WHA	*Wachula Hardee Advocate*
WP	*Washington Post*

Introduction

1. More than any other author, Kevin Starr's magisterial writings illuminate the field of "dream states." See Starr, *Americans and the California Dream; Inventing the Dream; Material Dreams; The Dream Endures; Embattled Dreams;* and his latest work, *Coast of Dreams*. In Florida, Raymond Arsenault has most fully explored that theme. See Arsenault, *St. Petersburg,* and "Is There a Florida Dream?"

2. Arsenault and Mormino, 168–69; 2000 Census.

3. *Florida: A Guide to the Southernmost State,* 3; Reed quoted in "Mouse In, South Out," *TT,* 7 December 1997.

4. See Applebome; Cobb; Egerton; Reed.

5. Gannon, "Columbus Quincentenary," 331–32.

6. Castro quoted in *Tampa Times,* 30 November 1955.

7. Hurston, *Mules and Men,* 1.

8. "Wish You Were Here—But Where Is Here?" *OS,* 14 August 1991.

9. Paterniti, 6.

10. Hiaasen quoted in Paterniti, 74.

11. "Fred Hoyle Dies," *NYT,* 22 August 2001.

Chapter 1. Look Away Dixieland: The Contours of Sunbelt Florida

1. Rieff, 218.

2. Phillips, 437; Sale, 6; Bernard and Rice, 1–26.

3. Newspaper quoted, *SPT,* 5 November 1950; "Florida Sixth in Census Gain," *TMT,* 11 April 1950; "Florida to Gain Two Congressmen," *SPT,* 3 November 1950; *NYT* quoted in "Redrawing Will Form Districts," 19 June 1981; *NYT,* 17 June and 16 November 1960; 12 July and 19 October 1970; 18 September 1972, 22 April 1973; "Florida Takes No. 3 Spot in Growth," *TT,* 4 June 2000; "15,982,378 and Counting," *OS,* 29 December 2000.

4. *SFSS,* 13 August 2000; "Staying Close to Home," *NYT,* 10 June 1982; "Florida Luring Jerseyans," *NYT,* 2 May 1982.

5. "Sunshine State Has 920,000 'Snowbirds,'" *TT,* 25 November 2004; "Census Shows Migration of 'Snowbirds,'" *NYT,* 11 June 1982; *WSJ,* 27 November 1984; "Mobile Population," *NYT,* 22 April 1973; "Guess Who's Leading the Great Migration?" *SPT,* 11 August 2003. Vance Packard coined the term *nation of strangers* in his 1950s book of that title.

6. "Now There Are Only 20 Vets," *TMT,* 27 May 1951; "Florida's Last Confederate Veteran Dies," *TMT,* 3 September 1957; "Fewer Say They Are Southerners," *SPT,* 7 October 2003. Professor Larry J. Griffin, Vanderbilt University, conducted the survey for the University of North Carolina's Center for the Study of the American South; e-mail, Griffin to author, 9 October 2003.

7. Kirby, "Southern Exodus," quoted 587; see 587–97.

8. Black and Black, 16–17; Cobb, 180; "Florida Only Southeastern State," *TMT,* 3 June 1956.

9. Dietrich, 117, 143, 212; "A Florida Isolated in Time," *FT,* May 1973, 27–28.

10. *Census of Population: 1950,* vol. 2, pt. 10, *Florida,* 39; pt. 11, *Georgia,* 47; pt. 2, *Alabama,* 38; Arsenault and Mormino, 166; Pérez, *On Becoming Cuban,* 433–36.

11. "Hispanics," *SPT*, 1 September 2000; "Hispanic Growth in '90s," *MH*, 3 September 2000; "Florida Has More Hispanics," *NYT*, 28 March 2001; U.S. Census Bureau Census 2000 Redistricting Data, tables PL 1–4.

12. "Orlando a New Magnet for Blacks," *OS*, 19 February 2002; "Sun Belt's Changing Face," *OS*, 29 December 2000; "Census: Blacks Moving Back," *SPT*, 31 October 2003; 2000 Census.

13. Arsenault and Mormino, 164; *Census of Population: 1950*, vol. 2, pt. 10, *Florida*, 6; pt. 11, *Georgia*, 6.

14. *FSA 1998*, 43; *FSA 1999*, 49; "As Cities Grow," *OS*, 29 November 1992; "Census Puts Orlando 28th," *OS*, 3 April 2001; "Census Will Combine Tampa and St. Pete," *TDT*, 22 May 1950. In 1950, recognizing the interdependence between cities and surrounding counties, the Census Bureau designated the Standard Metropolitan Statistical Area (SMSA) as a measurement and a new category for cities of 50,000 residents or surrounding areas of at least 100,000 inhabitants. In 1983, the Standard Metropolitan Statistical Area (SMSA) designation became the Statistical Metropolitan Area (SMA); Goldfield, 144–45.

15. *Census of Population: 1950*, vol. 2, *Characteristics of the Population*, pt. 10, *Florida*, 10–12; *WSJ*, 8 February 1991; *FSA 1999*, 49.

16. *USAT*, 19 November 1997, 3 July 2000.

17. Ward, 221–22; James Crooks's scholarship on modern Jacksonville represents the best study of that modern city.

18. Crooks, *Jacksonville: The Consolidation*, 1–37; Hewlett, 65–70; *FTU*, 5 March 2000; Keuchel, 137; "Fighting the Good Fight," 62–64, 69; Finotti, "River City,"48–50.

19. Crooks, *Jacksonville: The Consolidation*, 63–85; 124–202; "Downtown's Future," a three-part series in the *Florida Times-Union*, examines the history and future of downtown Jacksonville (*FTU*, 21–23 May 2000).

20. Crooks, *Jacksonville: The Consolidation*, 203–26; Morris and Morris, 626; *FTU*, 5 March 2000; "Making the Transition," *FTU*, 22 May 2000; "Fighting the Good Fight," 62–64, 69; Finotti, "River City," 48–50; "Jacksonville," *USAT*, 28–30, January 2005.

21. Dietrich, 88, 102, 176; Nathankane and Podell, 609; Morris and Morris, 625, 630–31; *MH*, 3 April 1960; *USAT*, 16 August 2000; Nordheimer, "Development Boom."

22. Dietrich, 88–89; *Eastward Ho!* 1–85; *MH*, 28 December 1997; *SFSS*, 6 June 1999; *NYT*, 21 May 1992; McIver, *Fort Lauderdale*, 138–57; *SFSS*, 19 March 2000; *MH*, 9 March 2000.

23. *Eastward Ho!*; Morris and Morris, 625.

24. "Communities of Choice," *SFSS*, 13 August 2000; Muller quoted in Dorschner, 9; "Terrorists," *TT*, 24 June 2002; "South Florida's Growing Population," *SFSS*, 28 March 2001.

25. Morris and Morris, 625; Dorschner; *SFSS*, 6 June 1999; "Whites Moving West," *SFSS*, 27 April 2001; "Broward's Population Center," *SFSS*, 29 March 2001; "Running Out of Room," *MH*, 16 December 2001.

26. Morris and Morris, 630; *SFSS*, 13 August 2000; *MH*, 3 April 1960, 20 December 1999, 2 January and 9 March 2000.

27. No city in Florida has benefited from such impressive scholarship and insight as Miami. See Didion; Allman; García; Rieff; M. Dunn; George; Parks; Bush; and especially Mohl; *MH*, 1 and 3 April 1960.

28. Painton, 52.

29. Bacon, 2:267; "Spreading from Disney World," 60–62; Dietrich, 173; Thomson, 492–516; Shofner, *Orlando*, 122–23, 138, 149, 152, 155, 165, 166–77; Foglesong, *Married*, 14–33.

30. Langford quoted in "Spreading from Disney World," 63; Corliss, 102–4; "Disney World Triggers Trouble," 60–61; Painton, 52–59.

31. Langford quoted in "Spreading from Disney World," 60, 62–63; Morris and Morris, 628, 631, 634; Painton, 52; "Booming Metro Economy," *OS*, 11 July 2001; Langford quoted in Painton, 58.

32. La Hurd, 14; *FMNP*, 21 November 1984; B. Green, 2; "Orlando Has It All, But," *WSJ*, 3 October 1991; Foglesong, *Married*, 67.

33. Kenneth Jackson's *Crabgrass Frontier*, a history of the relationship between American cities and suburbs, is the best study of this significant topic.

34. George, "Downtown Fort Lauderdale," 13, 16–18.

35. *SPT*, 29 April 1999; *MH*, 3 October 1999; Dunlop, "How Hialeah Happened"; Mohl, "Miami: The Ethnic Cauldron," 74–75.

36. Bacon, 2:299, 303, 306, 310.

37. *MH*, 4 July 1999; "Developers' Dilemma," *SPT*, 1 May 2000; *Population: A Comprehensive Analysis for the Tampa Bay Region*, 37–39; *FSA 1999*, 64, 743; 1990 Census, "City Population Density"; "Density Rates," Bureau of Economic and Business Research, University of Florida, 2000.

38. Colburn and deHaven-Smith, 126–28, 141–50; Longman, "Sprawl," 40–42; Eastman, 24; Blake, 228–29; Willson, "Coming Backlash," 54–58.

39. *TT*, 29 December 1989, 12 September, 14 December 1998, 6 June 1999; *SPT*, 16 February 1991; *NYT*, 21 May 1992; Colburn and deHaven-Smith, 119–34; Sierra Club quoted in "Sprawl Overview," http:www.sierraclub.org/sprawl/overview; Putnam, 407–8.

40. Siegal; George, "Kendall," 118–22; *MH*, 9 May 1965; "Now Florida Gets Ready Made Hills," 113–14; "Pasco Boom," *SPT*, 29 January 2005.

41. Garreau, *Edge*, 4–7, 429–37; *MH*, 10 November 1991; *SPT*, 18 December 1995; *TT*, 9 November 1992.

42. "Clearwater Booms," *TT*, 22 June 2001; *Eastward Ho!*; Dorschner.

43. George, "Downtown Fort Lauderdale," 13, 16–18; "Downtown Revivals," in "Mega-Stakes," *MH*, 19 November–10 December 2000.

44. O. White, "The Best-Run Town," 36–43.

45. Ziemba, 59, 280; *History of Martin County*, 131.

46. "Downtown's Future," *FTU*, 21–23 May 2000; Crooks, *Jacksonville: The Consolidation*, 124–203.

47. Ellsworth and Ellsworth, 131–35; Mormino, "Urban Rivals," *TT*, 4 April 2004; Crooks, *Jacksonville: The Consolidation*, 129–31.

48. Villano, "Solid Foundation," 78–80; Koenig, "Florida's Best," 46–49; Mahoney, 18; "Florida's Nonprofits," *SPT*, 3 November 2003; "Culture Climate Thrives without Fortune 500," *TT*, 13 April 1998; Hewlett, 53–54, 193–94, 285–86.

49. "Arts & Culture," 15–21; Buck, Corbino, and Dean, 1–118.

50. Janet Snyder Matthews, director, Division of Historical Resources, to author, 23 May 2000; Dunlop, *Vanishing Architecture*, 14; Dunlop, "Guardian of Historic Architecture," *MH*, 6 April 2003; "From Regal to Rumble," *MH*, 22 January 2005.

51. Dunlop, *Vanishing Architecture*, 17–21, 69–71; Burt, "Fernandina Beach," 10–15; Zimny, "Mainstreet," 19–21; Zimny, "Panhandle Surprise," 21–23; Embry, 26–33; "Bricks Come Back," *USAT*, 31 July 2003.

52. Whyte quoted in *Time*, 4 April 1983, 61; Gill, 396–402; Wright quoted in *MH*, 3 November 1955.

53. Coletti, "Victims," 32–36; Patricios, 238, 240; Hatton, 120–23; Scully.

54. Mormino and Pozzetta, 297–316; *TT*, 13–15 May 1979; "Guavaween Revelers Let Loose," *SPT*, 28 October 2001.

55. Mormino and Pozzetta, ix–xi; *TT*, 13 May 1979.

56. Dietrich, 112–13; Morris and Morris, 626; *SHT*, 13 September 1994; Wolf, 19, 22; "Florida's Expansion," *PNJ*, 28 March 2001; "Wakulla County," *TD*, 5 October 2003; "Some Complain, Others Happy at Palm Coast," *OS*, 1 July 1973; "Ecology Utopia or Flop?" *OS*, 1 July 1973; Kunerth, "Forgotten Towns"; "Through the Roof," *SPT*, 19 February 2005.

Chapter 2. Florida on the Installment Plan: The Third Great Land Boom

1. "Expanding Florida," 23–33; "A Playboy Grows Up," 90–91; "Florida: A Place in the Sun," 18–21; "The New Florida Land Rush," 55–81; "Big Rush to the Sun," 67–73; "The Boom That Space Built," 50–54; "Moon Boom," 88–90; "Fast-Growing Florida," 96–105.

2. Thomson, 492–96; Andersen quoted in Thomson, 497; Arsenault, *St. Petersburg*, 122, 138–39.

3. "Ponce de Leon Began State Publicity," *FTU*, 18 January 1950; Starr, *Material Dreams*, 70–71.

4. Lessing, 65; 2000 Census.

5. McIver, 140; Dodrill, 6, 25, 27; Fuller, 34–35; Darragh, "Danger," 12–13; "It's Miramar," *MH*, 23 July 1961.

6. "Father of the Westward Expansion," 169; McGoun, 168–69; "Lou Perini," *NYT*, 17 April 1972.

7. Parks, *Miami*, 178; Smith, 122–23; Nolan, 261–64; Darragh, "Danger in Florida Land Developments," 12; "Florida's Land Tycoons," *MH*, 1 May 1960; "What Happens?" *MH*, 22 July 1956.

8. *MH*, 7 November 1965, 4 March, 15 April 1973; *OS*, 3 October 1976; *SHT*, 14 March 1976; *TT*, 19 March 1972; *SPT*, 29 October 1972, 9 January 1978; MacArthur quoted in "The Other MacArthur," 64.

9. H. Dunn, 416; Hiaasen quoted in "Fanciful Names," *MH*, 9 September 1999; Dodrill, 6.

10. McIver, *Fort Lauderdale*, 140–41.

11. Rothchild, *Up for Grabs*, 83–84; Dodrill, 1–41.

12. Rothchild, *Up for Grabs*, 85–90; Dodrill, 1–134.

13. Dodrill, 35; M. Paulson, 14–29; Nolan, 255; Darragh, "Danger," 14; "Land-Use Tragedy,'" *SPT*, 5 March 1977; "Cape Coral Magnet for Korea Veterans," *FMNP*, 26 May 2002; *OS*, 15 April 1984.

14. "Mackle Plans 102 Homes," *MH*, 25 February 1940; Waitley, 1–3, 25; Nolan, 253–54; Smith, 121–24; Calonlus, 62–63; Mackle quoted in *FT*, August 1973; 72; Krock; "Biscayne Bay," *MH*, 18 March 1960; "Key Biscayne," *MH*, 11 December 1977; "Nixon Visits," *MH*, 10 November 1968; "Biscayne Bay," *MN*, 6 February 1971; "Biscayne Key Dream City," *MH*, 6 August 1950; "Nixon Presidential Retreat," *MH*, 22 July 2004.

15. M. Paulson, 14–29; Mackle quoted in Calonlus, 61–65; *Life*, 31 October 1955, 134; *Look*, 17 March 1959; Mackle quoted in "The New Florida Land Rush," 57.

16. "Big Sellers of Sunshine," 77–80; see also *Life*, 31 October 1959; Nolan, 253–54; Dietrich, 92–93; *FSA 1999*, 12; *TMT*, 1 September 1955; Smith, 121–24; Waitley, 1–3, 25; *SPT*, 1 January 1959; Derr, 343–44; Darragh, "Danger," 14; *TMT*, 1 September 1955; "Port Charlotte," *HN*, 18 March 1965; "Fast-Growing Florida," 105; "Florida Land Fever," *NYT*, 17 May 1959; "New Port Charlotte," *TT*, 8 February 1959; "Booming Port Charlotte," *TT*, 25 June 1960.

17. Dietrich, 189; "Bad Times?" *NYT*, 21 January 2002; "Cowtown," *SFSS*, 9 June 1991; Morris and Morris, 633; "St. Lucie Developer," *MH*, 30 December 1989.

18. *TT*, 27 August 1990; "Mackle Family Folder," *HASF*; "7-Year-Old Spring Hill," *SPT*, 23 June 1974; "Spring Hill," *SPT*, 14 September 1986; "Brooksville, Spring Hill," *TT*, 27 August 1990; http://www.co.hernando.fl.us/hcstat.htm. Deltona city manager quoted in "Development's Haphazard Approach," *OS*, 22 June 2003.

19. Lundstrom, 25; Douglas Waitley's *The Last Paradise* is the only full-length study of Marco Island.

20. Dodrill, 26, 56–58, 60, 77–78, 158–69, 171–73, 178; Rothchild, *Up for Grabs*, 94–98; *USAT*, 5 December 1997; Tebeau, *Last Frontier*; Waitley, 39–40; *CT*, 12 May 1991.

21. A sample of Trumbull's articles includes: "Volusia City," *MH*, 17 July 1956; "There's a 'Gold Mine,'" *MH*, 3 July 1956; "For Sale in St. Lucie," *MH*, 13 July 1956; "Paradise Made of Mist," *MH*, 22 June 1956.

22. "Florida Land Fever," *NYT*, 17 May 1959; M. Paulson, 109–16; Mieher, 73–76; Dennis, 79–80; "The New Florida Land Rush," 80; "Land of Lost Dreams," *OS*, 17 May 1987, 21 July 1992, 8 December 1996; "Lead Balloons," *MH*, 24 April 1970; "Developers' Legacy Costs Millions to Fix," *OS*, 22 June 2003; Shofner, *Brevard County*, 2:136; "Online Pitches Put New Spin on Old Swampland," *OS*, 6 April 2003.

23. Readers interested in black housing projects should consult the Agnew Welch scrapbooks, MDPLSC. See housing and race files, 1940s and 1950s. See also *TMT*, 16 May 1954; *PCNH*, 10 September 1947; *OS*, 30 July 2000; *Guide to Orlando's Afro-American Heritage*, 32–33; *SN*, 27 March 1947; *OS*, 30 July 2000; *SN*, 27 March 1947; M. Dunn, 169.

24. *TD*, 4 September 1955; Moscow, 1–200; "Tycoon Jim Walter," *TT*, 8 January 2000; "James Walter," *NYT*, 9 January 2000.

25. "Founder of Homebuilder Lennar," *MH*, 29 July 2002. See also "The Business That Rutenberg Built," *SPT*, 27 March 2004.

26. "Mashall Rinker Dies at 91," *PBDN*, 13 April 1996; Washam, 30–32.

27. Mormino, "Florida's Year of Reckoning," 18–20.

28. Ibid., headlines culled from the *Orlando Sentinel* and *Tampa Tribune*.

29. "Disney: Trouble in Dreamland"; "Disney World Triggers Trouble for Orlando"; "Florida: Biggest Fraud Yet?"; official quoted in "Orlando's Hotel Boom," *MH*, 16 September 1973; "Disney World Almost Pollution Casualty," *TT*, 17 July 1973; Billitteri, "No One," 58–62; Dietsch, 13–14.

30. Billitteri, "No One," 58–62; *OS* and *MH*, 1973–1975; "Ecology Utopia or Flop?" *OS*, 1 July 1973.

31. Mormino, "Reckoning," 19; Nordheimer, "Development Boom."

32. "Condominium Prices Cut in Florida," *NYT*, 1 December 1975; official quoted in "Florida Real Estate," *USNWR*, 8 August 1976, 63.

33. "South Florida Is Stirred by Study Indicating the Boom Has Ended," *NYT*, 19 September 1976.

34. *NYT*, 24 November 1990; "Miamians," *NYT*, 7 October 1984.

35. Godkin quoted in *FT*, April 1993, 36; Rimer, "Economists Predict," *NYT*, 24 November 1990.

36. Longman, "Why Florida Won't Bust," 52; Longman, "Enjoy It While It Lasts," 33–36; "Beached Like a Whale," 52–53.

37. Resnick, 62; developer quoted in Henwood, 359–60; "Bankruptcy Bill," *NYT*, 6 April 2001.

38. "Silver Lining," *WSJ*, 31 October 1992; "So Many People—and Nowhere Left to Run," *USAT*, 25 July 2000; "Donna Blew in Year-End Prosperity," *MH*, 1 January 1961, Naples edition.

39. M. Sullivan, 6:647; "Multiple Residences in Vogue," *TT*, 28 May 2002; Professor Edward Wolff e-mail to Travis Puterbaugh, 15 October 2003; Carroll, 35, 43–45; "Gated Communities," *USAT*, 16 December 2002; E. Blakely and Snyder, 5, 122–23.

40. "Happy Birthday Dear Condo," *MH*, 21 November 1982; Morris and Morris, 639, 653; "Broward in Lead of Co-op Parade," *FLDN*, 29 March 1958. "Condominiums—a New Life-style," *FT*, October 1970, 24; "Condomania," *FT*, October 1972, 35–36.

41. "Gated Communities," *USAT*, 16 December 2002; E. Blakely and Snyder, 5, 122–23; "Beauty Reigns Supreme in a Florida Enclave," *NYT*, 28 May 2000; "Fortune Sets Off Family Feud," *MH*, 2 March 1986.

42. "House an Emblem," *SPT*, 22 July 2002; "Where Wealthy Go," *TT*, 29 January 2001.

43. Mansfield, 23–29; Morris and Morris, 631–32; "Utopia on Earth," *MH*, 11 October 1959; "Trouble in Paradise," *SPT*, 19 October 2001; "Population Growth Limits," *OS*, 3 October 1976; "Florida's Flossiest," *MH*, 22 July 1973; Nordheimer, "Florida Seeks"; "Florida Finds a High-Tech Fountain of Youth," 58–59.

44. Bragg, "New Economy"; data obtained from Okaloosa County Property Appraisers Office, 10 September 2004.

45. "Growing Pains in the Grove," *MH*, 2 November 2003; "1 Million Home Barrier Tumbles," *SFSS*, 1 February 2002; realtor quoted in "Fort Lauderdale Rich with Million Dollar Homes," *SFSS*, 31 May 2003; Palm Beach County Property Appraisals, http://www.co.palm-beach.fl.us/propapp/parsdent.htm; "How Do We Heat Those Starter Castles," *WP* in *TT*, 23 February 2003; "Million-Dollar Homes," *USAT*, 6 December 2000; architect quoted in "Palm Beach's Ultraluxury Market," *NYT*, 5 August 2001.

46. "By Jupiter," *SFSS*, 11 May 2001; "Richest Towns," 88–104; *History of Martin County*, 15–16, 199–202, 497–98; Ziemba, 22–23; *SS*, 11 May 2000; "Jupiter Island," *MH*, 12 April 1959; "For Richer For Poorer," *MH*, 5 June 2002; "Fisher Island," *MH*, 5 June 2002; "The Fisher King," *MH*, 16 January 2005.

47. "Isleworth," *OS*, 25 March 2001; "No Neverland," *NYT*, 7 May 2004.

48. "High-Flying Celebrities," *TT*, 28 July 2002; "High-Flying," *SHT*, 2 November 2003.

49. Tebeau, *Last Frontier*, 178–91; *Census of Population: 1950, Florida*, 9, 14, 19; *MH*, 14 January 1959, Naples edition; *CCN*, 3 January 1960; "Land Rush," *SHT*, 9 January 2005.

50. Tebeau, *Last Frontier*, 188–91; "Naples," *FT*, June 1959, 27; "Once a Sleepy Town," *TMT*, 18 March 1951; "New Naples," *MH*, 30 April 2000; "Naples," *SPT*, 17 July 1989; "In Naples," *NYT*, 14 January 2001; "Putting on the Ritz," *WSJ*, 8 April 2002; "Building Tension," *SFSS*, 23 July 2000; "Naples Confronts Growth," *TT*, 8 June 1987; Booker, "Naples," 24; "Who"s the Toniest?" *FMNP*, 28 April 2002.

51. Poppe, 60; Dortch, 6–11; "Top of the Market," *Gulfshore Life*, April 2002, 86–90; Goodkin, "Lap of Luxury," 54–56; "Sticker Shock," *SHT*, 3 October,2004.

52. "Blaze Destroys Shell Factory," *MH*, 1 January 1953; "Census Illustrates Disparities," *SPT*, 24 May 2002; "The Keys," *SFSS*, 30 March 2001; *SPT*, 14 May 1999; *SHT*, 16 June 1991; "Sarasota," 30–32; *TT*, 21 May 2000; *FT*, April 2000, 74–78; Booker, "No Room," 24; *USAT*, 31 July 2000; "McDonalds," *AJC*, 22 March 1988; "Livin' Large," *SPT*, 2 June 2002; "Gap Burgeons between Haves, Have-Nots," *FMNP*, 22 September 2002; "Welcome to Sarasota," *SPT*, 16 September 2001; "Families in Poverty," *FMNP*, 7 December 2003.

53. "Southern Florida's Curious Economy," *NYT*, 6 March 1982; Dunlop, "'Egotecture'"; *SHT*, 25 March 2001; "Mansions Threaten This Quaint Community," *SPT*, 31 March 2001, Tampa edition; "Big Garages Now Standard," *FMNP*, 22 June 2003; "The Tear Down Trend," *MH*, 20 April 2003; "Houses of Style," *SPT*, 11 August 2000.

54. Mormino, review of *Sunshine State*, in *Forum* (Fall 2000): 34–35; Roberts, "Here Golf Courses Grow Like Weeds," *SPT*, 14 September 2003: "Building Tensions," *SFSS*, 23 July 2000; information supplied by the National Golf Foundation; "For Richer For Poorer," *MH*, 5 June 2002; "High-End Golf Community Coming to Manatee," *SPT*, 13 December 2003; "Going in Style," *MH*, 9 May 2003; Goodkin, "In the Rough," 80–84.

55. Rothstein, "Paradise Lost," *NYT*, 5 February 2000.

56. Jenkins, 6, 100–101, 174; "Keeping Up with the Joneses' Lawn," *SPT*, 11 September 2004; "The Perfect Lawn," *OS*, 16 June 2002.

57. *MH*, 20 March 1977; Ray, 14–15; "Pines in Peril," *TT*, 10 December 1990.

58. "Window to the Past," *TT*, 27 March 2004.

Chapter 3. Tourist Empires and the Invention of Florida: B.D. (Before Disney) to A.D. (After Disney)

1. Barrett, 170–71.

2. Kasson, 106–12.

3. "Florida and California Rated High," *SPT*, 20 January 1945; Belasco, 186; Aron, 204–5, 248–49.

4. The literature on tourism and leisure is impressive; see especially Aron, 3–11; D.

Brown; S. Davis; Desmond, xii–xxv, 2–9. Considering the importance of tourism to the state, the literature on tourism in Florida is sparse. For insights into Florida tourism, see Foglesong, *Married*, 104–5, 184–85; Bush, 153–72; George, "Passage to the New Eden," 440–63; Mormino, "Trouble in Tourist Heaven," 11–13; Braden, 48–54, 77–86, 279–80; poll results in "Is Sun Setting on Allure of the Sunshine State?" *SPT*, 22 September 2002.

5. Genovese, 150–97; Breslauer, 25; Hollis, 5–7; quotation in "Banana Port," *TMT*, 14 April 1946; "Chief Calls It Biggest," *TMT*, 7 February 1950; "350,000 Attendance Breaks All Records," *TMT*, 15 February 1959; "Top Tourist Boom Jams West Coast," *TMT*, 17 February 1952; "Thousands at Tarpon for Epiphany," *SPT*, 6 January 1956; "Greeks Who Dive after Cross Must Wear Clothes Now," *TMT*, 12 March 1921; "Highway Hospitality," *SPT*, 27 September 1953; "Sara-De-Soto Pageant," *SPT*, 19 March 1916; "Annual DeSoto Fete," *SPT*, 11 March 1953; "Thousands See Circus," *TMT*, 9 March 1952; "Sloshing Buggies," *MH*, 2 November 1959, Collier Co. edition; "Canadians May Flock Here," *SPT*, 6 October 1950; "Naples Swamp Buggy Races," *MDN*, 29 October 1950; "Queen Chasco," *New Port Richey Press*, 16 March 1922.

6. Arsenault, *St. Petersburg*, 186–87, 193–94, 202–5, 261–62, 312–13; "Historic Highway," *SHT*, 13 January 2002; "Highway into History," *SPT*, 28 April 2002; "Sports in Full Swing: Shuffleboarding Busy," *SPT*, 27 February 1956; "'No Vacancy' Signs Tell Tourist Season Story," *SPT*, 26 February 1956; "From Canada To Arkansas, They All Come," *SPT*, 19 February 1956.

7. "A Roadside History of the American Tourist," *SPT*, 24 August 1986; Breslauer, 27–28; Hatton, 175–77; Funk quoted in Carter, 146–47; Dow, 240–41; Weber, 348–49; "Ripley Brought His Bizarre Fare," *FTU*, 16 April 1997; "30,000 Attend Dania Tomato Festival," *FLDN*, 9 March 1956; Crooks, *Jacksonville: The Consolidation*, 2.

8. "1950 Standard Oil of Florida Road Map," Map Collection, General Drafting Archives, case 15, Newberry Library; Schulten, 197–203; Danzer, 77; Jakle and Sculle, *The Gas Station*, 56, 69, 106, 114, 122, 163–82, 186, 189; Belasco, 3–20, 170.

9. Jakle, Sculle, and Rogers, 23–89, 262–63; Jakle and Sculle, *Fast Food*, 133–45; Belasco, 141, 153, 156, 172; "Tampa's First Motel," *TT*, 14 April 2002; observer quoted in *Florida: A Guide*, 297–98; Dunlop, *Vanishing*, 33–40; K. Jackson, 253–55; "An Invitation for Recreation," *OS*, 26 December 1999; "Mileposts in Memory Landmarks," *OS*, 29 July 1986; Hatton, 177; "Highway Hospitality," *SPT*, 27 September 1953; "Kemmons Wilson, 90, Dies," *NYT*, 13 February 2003; "Wigwam Village," *OS*, 18 June 2000; "The Trail Offered Delights for Eye and Palate," *OS*, 25 June 2000; Kleinberg, *Miami Beach*, 176; "Builders of Luxury Motels," *TT*, 7 July 1961; "Goodbye, Sunny," *MH*, 15 February 2003; "Rural Gulf Coast Highway Fast Becoming Teeming City," *SPT*, 22 January 1956; "Abundance of Motels Along u.s. 1," *MH*, 3 June 1951; "Never Say Die," *OS*, 29 September 2003.

10. L. Brown, 85, 267; Viele, 91, 122; S. Kennedy, 241, 246–53; B. Green, 33, 74; Hepburn and Logan, 1–71; Bucuvalas, 34–37; *Seventy-Five Years of Sebring*, 75. My thanks to Michael Gannon for his culinary suggestions.

11. Hollis, 55–63; "800,000 See Beach Here during Year," *PNJ*, 1 January 1950; "Air-Conditioned Train," *FTU*, 1 August 1998; "Summertime Santa Claus," *MH*, 7 July 1950; "Record Summer Vacation Play," *TMT*, 11 July 1954; "Florida Ranked Third for Summer

Vacation," *MH*, 1 July 1950; "More Air Conditioning," *TMT*, 10 April 1935; "Tourists Now Big Business When Once Were Seasonal," *TDT*, 8 January 1952; "State Summer Tourist Business Now Equaling Winter Rush," *SPT*, 20 September 1953; "Florida Sees Big Summer Tourist Influx," *TMT*, 10 June 1951; "Summer Drawing the Tourists," *MH*, 5 July 1959; Kleinberg, *Miami Beach*, 153; Muir, 233–34; H. Jackson, "Florida Room," 317; "Last Ride at Miracle Strip," *OS*, 3 May 2004.

12. Breslauer, 69; Clark; "Florida's Oldest Tree," *TMT*, 25 February 1951; "Best Tourist Year in Decade," *OS*, 6 February 1950; journalist quoted in "County's Early Pitchmen," *OS*, 11 July 1999; "An Invitation for Recreation," *OS*, 26 December 1999; "Memory Landmarks," *OS*, 29 July 1986; "Tangerine Queen," *TMT*, 12 December 1955; "Record Throng Crowds Opening of Citrus Exposition," *TMT*, 19 February 1952; "Silver Spurs Rodeo," *OS*, 30 January 1956.

13. Breslauer, 53–54; OCRHC, Gatorland files; "Greetings from Gatorland," *OS*, 28 January 1993; "Survival of the Fittest," *SPT*, 4 May 2003; "The Class of '71," *OS*, 27 June 1988; "Gator Tales," *TT*, 20 September 1998.

14. "A 1930s Florida Attraction Booms Again," *NYT*, 10 February 2002; quotations from Herold, 27; "Natural Beauty," *SPT*, 5 July 1976; *Florida: A Guide*, 309; McGoun, 122–27.

15. Breslauer, 59–60, 75–76; "Sunken Gardens for Sale," *SPT*, 7 June 1989; "Sun Sets on Gardens," *TT*, 14 June 1999; "Ralph Turner," *SPT*, 17 January 1979.

16. Breslauer, 71–74; Crum, 52–73; "Silver Springs," *MH*, 4 April 1946.

17. Newton Perry to Edward Ball, 1 June 1947. The letter is from the private collection of Delee Perry, Ocala. My thanks to Elizabeth Bettendorf; Breslauer, 78; Dunlop, *Vanishing*, 33–34; "Even Mermaids," *SPT*, 9 November 2001; "Mermaid Memories," *SPT*, 30 September 1997; "Weeki Wachee," *TT*, 6 July 2003; "Sad Days for Mermaids," *NYT*, 12 August 2003; "Last Rites for the Springs?" *SPT*, 24 August 2003; "Gulf Coast Highway," *TMT*, 2 January 1949.

18. Dick Pope folder, USFSC; S. Branch, 487–89, 492; "Dick Pope," *FTU*, 28 January 1973; "He Promised a Rose Garden," *Orlando Star*, 18 July 1976.

19. S. Branch, 493; "Gardens' Dick Pope," *NC*, 1 November 1981; Pope quoted in "Dick Pope," *LL*, 1 March 1998.

20. S. Branch, 495–96; Carr, 41, 42–43; Nelson, *Lights!*, 57, 59–60; Newberry Library, Non-catalogued travel scrapbooks, box 6; "In Invitation for Recreation," *OS*, 26 December 1999; "Tourists' Eden," *TT*, 30 October 1994; "Florida's Human Buzz-Saw," *TMT*, 9 May 1954; "Dick Pope," *FTU*, 28 January 1973; "Announcement of Closing," *OS*, 11 April 2003.

21. Lears, xiii, 7; Kasson, 3–9; Akin, 146–47, 155–163; Dunlop, *Vanishing*, 41–48; Curl, 61–164; Braden, 40–77, 112–15, 118–21.

22. "Marineland Revisited," *OS*, 20 August 1989; "Nostalgia," *USAT*, 1 September 1998; "Marineland," *NYT*, 11 January 1999; "Sink or Swim, " *OS*, 12 April 1998; Newberry Library, Non-catalogued travel scrapbooks, box 5; see Susan Davis, *Spectacular Nature*, for a study of California's SeaWorld.

23. See *MH*, 1950s and early 1960s, especially "King Orange's Court, 455,000," *MH*, 1 January 1961; "Orange Dazzles 500,000," *MH*, 1 January 1960; Parks, 133–34.

24. "Tourism Brings 300 Million in '51," *MH*, 30 December 1951; Kleinberg, *Miami Beach*, 154–55, 159–66; Kleinberg, *Miami*, 165–67; *MH*, 1950, 1956, 1959; Muir, 234; Carter, 146–47; Colburn and Scher, 268; "21,591 See Tripoli Take Gulfstream," *MH*, 5 March 1952; "Hialeah Hits New Records," *MH*, 3 March 1956; "Gulfstream Opener Sets New Records," *FLDN*, 4 March 1956; Anderson, "Miami Beach: Mobsters' Playground," *TMT*, 3 September 1957; "Gamblers Head Back to Gold Coast," *SPT*, 16 November 1952; "Florida: Gansters' Hangout," *SPT*, 17 May 1950; "Cream Cheese," *Time*, 9 February 1948, 21.

25. Schwartz, 39–42, 85, 100–101, 139–46, 182–83; Pérez, *On Becoming Cuban*, 432–36; "More Latin Tourists," *MH*, 1 August 1950; "Four Cuban Airlines to Serve Florida," *MH*, 14 June 1950; "Miami Beach Stores Planning Cuba Day," *MH*, 1 September 1950; "Summer Visitors Include Cuban Families," *MH*, 6 August 1950; advertising, *MH*, 12 March 1950; Kleinberg, *Miami Beach*, 157, 173–75; Bretos, 119–22.

26. Kleinberg, *Miami Beach*, 170–73; D. Moore, "The Ta'am of Tourism," 193–212; D. Moore, *Golden Cities*, 21–32; Singer quoted in *My Love Affair*, viii; "Babylon, U.S.A.," *Life*, 29 December 1947, 31–42; "Hotels Jammed," *MH*, 19 February 1956; Bush, 166–69; Green and Zerivitz, 21.

27. D. Moore, *Golden Cities*, 34; Koenig, "Invasion," 75; Hine, 139–41; Patricios, 113–35; Hatton, 92–101, 110–14; Huxtable quoted in "Morris Lapidus," *NYT*, 19 January 2001; "Miami Beach," *NYT*, 17 March 1975; "When More Was More," *NYT*, 25 November 2001; Lessing, 212.

28. "Tourist Mecca of Entire World," *FTU*, 1 January 1950; "1951 Tourist Flow Greatest Since '45," *MDN*, 16 February 1957; "Record Tourist Year for Florida," *TDT*, 2 May 1950; "Tourism in Florida at All-Time High," *TMT*, 13 January 1952; "Field of Travel," *NYT*, 25 March 1962; "Tourism," *TT*, 13 December 1959; "Florida," *Time*, 9 February 1948, 21–22; "Destination of Auto Tourists in 1970," 43–44; "1955 Tourist Spending Is \$700 Million," *FTU*, 8 July 1956; "81.5 Per Cent of Florida Tourists Come in Cars," *TMT*, 30 January 1955; "Florida's Fattest Tourist Fling," 32–39; journalist quoted in "Florida Is Preparing for Jet Travel," *TT*, 1 September 1957; Jakle, 182–83; "Florida Flowers," *Time*, 9 December 1957, 96.

29. Ellinor Village brochure, Jewish Museum of Florida, *The Art of Hatred* exhibit; D. Moore, *Golden Cities*, 48, 253–54; D. Brown, 174.

30. D. Moore, *Golden Cities*, 21–52; Kleinberg, *Miami Beach*, 136–37, 167–70; "Religious Discrimination," *SPT*, 17 May 1953; "Number of 'Restricted' Hotels Drops, *MH*, 24 April 1960; "New Laws and Florida Tourists," *NYT*, 6 November 1955; Aron, 217–18.

31. Aron, 213–16, 218; Braden, 110–11, 125–132; Akin, 157–59, 163; Jakle, 58; brochure quoted in Breslauer, 55; "Quaint Little Carts Fading Fast from Palm Beach," *MH*, 7 April 1946; Kleinberg, *Miami Beach*, 134; "Color Line Drawn in West Palm Beach," *MH*, 17 January 1917.

32. "The Leading Negro of Florida," *FS*, 14 February 1953; "The Negro at the Florida State Fair," *FS*, 21 February 1953; "'Better Living' Is Theme of Negro Day," *TMT*, 12 February 1952; "State Fair Is Honoring Negro Achievement Today," *SPT*, 11 February 1955; "Ozepher B. Harris, Ran Restaurant," *TT*, 31 October 2003; Mason, 11, 72, 78.

33. Breslauer, 72–73; Rymer, 10, 95–96; Phelts, 1–2, 74; "An Era Nears Extinction," *OS*, 15 December 2003; *FTU*, 26 August 1998; "Blacks Enjoy a Better Day on Beach," *OS*,

10 April 2002; "Bethune Beach," *OS*, 31 March 1985; "Ghosts of Music Past," *NYT*, 22 July 1988; M. Dunn, 90–92; "Bidding a Fond Farewell," *MH*, 19 January 2003; Parks, 141–42; Mason, 9–18, 68–78; "Legend Hit the Road," *FTU*, 11 June 2004.

34. Patsy West has explored the evolution of tourism and its role in the Seminole-Miccosukee economy. For the early years, see West, 4–31.

35. West, 83–93; "Gator Grappling," *FMNP*, 3 December 2000; Kersey, *Buffalo Tiger*, 59–60, 63, 83, 116, 147.

36. West, 112, 116–19; "Seminoles Complete Arena for First Rodeo," *MH*, 21 February 1956; Kersey, *An Assumption*, 79–134; "Survival of the Fittest," *SPT*, 4 May 2003; "Seminoles Go Modern," *MH*, 22 May 1960.

37. Grizzard quoted in Hollis, 3; "Roadside Gyp Joints," *TMT*, 9 February 1950; "Operators of Roadside Gyp," *TMT*, 9 March 1952; Hoover quoted in Belasco, 168; Hatton, 177; Crispell, 6–7, 30; "West Florida Towns Boast More Slots," *TMT*, 15 July 1949.

38. Watts, 243–80; "Dick Pope Sr.," *OSS*, 22 April 1979; Disney quoted in "Gardens' Dick Pope," *NC*, 1 November 1981.

39. Ball quoted in "A Land Giant Stirs," *NYT*, 12 April 1998.

40. Watts, 7, 19.

41. Watts, 22–23, 363–403; Hine, 152; Taubman, 431.

42. Foglesong, *Married*, 14–33, 38–40; Watts, 421–22; "Magic Kingdom in Ocala?" *OS*, 16 December 2001; Robison and Andrews, 268–69; Peter, 12.

43. Foglesong, *Married*, 34–54; Watts, 422–24; "Disney Creates a Magic Kingdom," 75–79; Bacon, 2:265, 266–67, 275; "Disney World," 60–61.

44. Foglesong, 34–54; Watts, 422–24; "Disney Creates a Magic Kingdom," 75–79; Bacon, 2:265, 266–67, 275.

45. Foglesong, *Married*, 78–81; Watts, 434–35; S. Davis, 14; Derr, 378–79.

46. Disney quote on display in Orange County Regional Museum; Kissinger quoted in Foglesong, *Married*, 101; Derr, 382; Bacon, 2:281, 291; "Animal Kingdom," *SPT*, 22 April 1998; "Theme Parks' Wild Ride," *USAT*, 3 January 1997; "Tourism's Long Climb Is Over," *OS*, 22 September 2001; Adams, 156–60.

47. "Underdog Takes On Mouse," *USAT*, 13 March 1997; *TT*, 25 January 1988; "Attendance at Central Florida Attractions," *SPT*, 27 February 1995; "Most Popular Theme Parks," *SPT*, 31 December 1997; Foglesong, *Married*, 3; "Theme-Park Attendance," *OS*, 6 October 2002.

48. Rifkin, 7.

49. "Admission Fees," *USAT*, 11 June 1999; "SeaWorld," *SPT*, 15 April 1999; "Universal Matches SeaWorld," *OS*, 2 March 2002; "Theme Parks Break $50-a-Day Barrier," *MH*, 5 January 2001; "Disney Trip to Cost More," *SPT*, 3 December 2004.

50. Adams, 67.

51. Pope quoted in "Area Leaders See Solid Growth in Disney," *OS*, 29 October 1965; In *Roadside Paradise*, Ken Breslauer has compiled the most complete list of Florida tourist attractions (see 83–85). O'Connor, 75–77; R. Johnson, "If You've Seen One Gator," 56–58; Hatton, 183–88; "Rainbow Springs," *MH*, 8 March 1974; "Six Gun on Auction Block," *OS*, 8 December 1978; *SPT*, 4 May 2003; "Trouble's Blooming Amid Flowers," *TT*, 2 December 1984; "Four Big Attractions Close," *TMT*, 13 July 1958; "Mammoth Ringling

Tent Comes Down," *TDT*, 17 July 1956; West, 110–11; "Surviving in a Disney World," *TT*, 14 May 2000; "Strangulation of the Cotton Candy Kings," 54–57.

52. McKee's grandson quoted in "Natural Beauty," *SPT*, 5 July 1976; "Bidding Farewell to Kitsch," *MH*, 19 January 2003; "Last Rites for the Springs?" *SPT*, 24 August 2003; McGoun, 122–27.

53. "Faded Attractions," *SPT*, 5 July 2000; "Dinner Isn't the Attraction," *OS*, 14 December 2001; Foglesong, *Married*, 186–87.

54. Sherrill, "Can Miami Save Itself?" 18–24; "Tourism," *CT*, 27 September 1987; "Destinations of Auto Tourists in 1970"; "South Beach Revelers," *MH*, 26 May 2002; Villano, "SoBe Fashion Emergency," 60–64; Allman, 21–110; Didion, 23–29, 35–48; Rieff, 54–90; Bush, 168–71; "The 'American Riviera,'" *SPT*, 17 March 2002; Rothchild, *Up for Grabs*, 207–9, 218–19; Friedlander; "Miami Worries about Disney World," *TT*, 14 March 1976; "Success of Flashy 'Miami Vice,'" *WSJ*, 5 May 1985.

55. Hiaasen, *Team Rodent*, 11; Koenig, "Invasion," 74–75; Breslauer, 45–47, 71–75, 78; S. Branch, 498–501; "A 1930s Florida Attraction Blooms Again," *NYT*, 10 February 2002; "Developer Works on '3rd Strike,'" *TT*, 27 March 2002; "Disney Buys Fox Family," *TT*, 24 July 2001; "Disney to Purchase Fox Family For $3.2 Billion," *USAT*, 23 July 2001; "Japanese Park," *OS*, 13 December 2000; "Silver Springs Up for Sale," *SPT*, 25 November 1999; "Busch's Big Fish," *TT*, 28 February 2000; Adams, 115–16, 122–23.

56. "Roadside Distraction?" *SPT*, 15 September 2003; "Cypress Gardens Bows Out," *SPT*, 11 April 2003; "Trouble's Blooming Amid Flowers," *TT*, 2 December 1984; "Rainbow Springs," *MH*, 8 March 1974; "Parks' Sag," *OS*, 6 October 2002; "Cypress Gardens," *SPT*, 28 January 2004; "Sunken Gardens for Sale," *SPT*, 7 June 1989; "State's Purchase of Nature Park Raises Questions," *TT*, 21 August 1988; "Weeki Wachee," *TT*, 6 July 2003; "State to Save Cypress Gardens," *SPT*, 27 August 2003; writer quoted in Siano, "A Road Trip Back to the 50's," *NYT*, 21 September 2003, Travel section.

57. "Busch Gardens—New Tourist Gem," *TT*, 10 February 1964; reporter quoted, "Adolphus Busch Marker," *TMT*, 1 April 1959; Busch Gardens folder, USFSC; "How Did Busch Gardens Grow?" *TT*, 27 January 2002; "Vast Busch Gardens Expansion," *TT*, 6 June 1970; "Busch Adds Industrial Park Tract," *TT*, 4 November 1965; Adams, 115–18; R. Johnson, "Thrill Rides," 22–23.

58. "Busch Gardens," *TT*, 6 November 1983; "A Post-Panda Future," *TT*, 5 December 1988; "Busch Will Close Brewery," *TT*, 26 October 1995; billboard quoted in Adams, 105.

59. "Rising Ticket Prices," *OS*, 13 November 1994; "How Did Busch Gardens Grow?" *TT*, 27 January 2002; "Busch Gardens Coasts," *TT*, 22 December 1994; "Busch Hopes Folks Flip for Ride Name," *TT*, 28 December 1995; "So Long Splashes, Hello Shrieks," *SPT*, 14 August 2002; "Expansion Seeks Harvest of Visitors," *SPT*, 10 April 2000.

60. "Parks To Woo Gen X's Families," *OS*, 2 April 2002; "Booming Amusement Parks," 12; "No Mickey Mouse," *CT*, 29 July 1999; "Disney Coaster No Small Whirl," *TT*, 19 April 2002; "Cheer vs. Fear," *SPT*, 12 June 2001; "Sky's the Limit," *TT*, 26 May 2000; "SeaWorld Coaster to Be Bigger and Faster," *SPT*, 25 January 2000; "Scream Parks," 62–68.

61. Breslauer, 40–41, 52, 70, 83–85; "Rediscovering Roadside Florida," *AJC*, 14 May 2001; "Survival of the Fittest," *SPT*, 4 May 2003; "Seeking the Untrendy," *NYT*, 6 April

2003; Gittner, 5–40; "Parrot Jungle at 50," *MH*, 18 May 1986; R. Johnson, "If You've Seen One Gator," 56–60; "Parrot Jungle," *MH*, 19 August 2001; "Snakes Are the Stars," *MH*, 13 September 1968; HASF, Parrot Jungle files; "Francis Scheer, 83, Opened Parrot Jungle," *MH*, 18 December 1973; "Parrot Jungle Gets New Island Home," 23 June 2003; "Seminole Casino Plans," *NYT*, 29 December 2003.

62. "Seminoles Top Political Donors," *FMNP*, 9 October 2000; "Pueblo in California Aids Seminoles," *MH*, 27 April 1946; Kersey, *Assumption*, 79–134; "Princess Tells Seminoles' Needs," *MDN*, 5 October 1949; "High-Stakes Bingo Comes To Everglades," *NYT*, 23 March 1987; "Seminoles, Hard Rock Plan Casino Resort," *TT*, 9 January 2001; "Gator Grappling Holds Its Group," *FMNP*, 3 December 2000; "Seminoles Offer Others Fighting Chance," *TT*, 8 September 2000; "Election Marks New Era for Tribe," *SPT*, 14 May 2003; "Road To Riches," *MH*, 11 May 2003.

63. Hiaasen, *Tourist Season*, 103–66; Hiaasen, *Team Rodent*, 79; Rothchild, *Up for Grabs*, 50; Boorstin, 9, 79; O'Rourke, 42–43; Eco, 48, 57–58; Rifkin, 149; M. Davis, 396.

64. D. Brown, 206, 209–11; Jakle, Sculle, and Rogers, 4–5, 23–31; "Luxury Motels," *TT*, 7 July 1961.

65. MacCannell, 146; Ogle, 214, 218–19, 234, 236; "Mickey, Too," *NYT*, 24 May 2003; Hiaasen, *Team Rodent*, 12; "Gay Days," *OS*, 31 May 2002; "Gay Key West," *MH*, 15 September 2002; Vogel, "No. 1," 65; "Natural Success," *SPT*, 21 April 2002; "Nudists Get Well Tanned," *TMT*, 19 July 1954; "Nudist Resorts," *TT*, 18 January 2003; "Pasco Resort Styles Itself for Gay People," *TT*, 31 October 2002; "Where Skin Is Typically Bare," *NYT*, 18 June 2003; "Over the Rainbow," *SPT*, 9 July 2000; "Pitch for Gay Tourists," *MH*, 16 January 2002; "Miami Beach to Come Out," *MH*, 18 June 1998; Fort Lauderdale Convention and Visitors Bureau to author, 10 September 2004; "Gay-Friendly Ads," *MH*, 25 February 1999; "Sex, Drugs and Techno," *Tampa Weekly Planet*, 16–22 April 2003, 19–24; "Sailing the Seas Au Natural," *SPT*, 8 February 2002; "Dade Nudist Camp," *MH*, 9 July 1950; "No Shirt, No Pants," *TT*, 28 November 1997; "Nudists Fear for Their Rights," *TT*, 6 March 1997.

66. D. Moore, *Golden Cities*, 32; "Passovers at Hotels," *NYT*, 27 April 2000; "City of God and Mickey," *SPT*, 22 May 2003; "Black College Reunion," *SPT*, 3 March 2000; scholar quoted in Whitfield, "Florida's Fudged Identity," 432; Painton, 54–58; Green and Zerivitz, 22.

67. Rymer, 100–101, 111–13; Phelts, 176–78; Betsch quoted in Cohen, 327; "Guardian for the Beach," *TT*, 1 July 2003; "Change of Face," *DBNJ*, 4 October 2003; Barnes and Roberts, 42.

68. "Park Visitors," *OS*, 13 November 1994; "How Florida Relies on Tourism," *USAT*, 20 September 1993; Jarvis, 188–89, 197; Harney, 21–40; "Osceola Woos Hispanic Tourists," *OS*, 20 April 2002; "Canadian Tourism on Rebound," *SPT*, 13 September 2000; "Lure Snowbirds Back," *OS*, 29 September 2000; "Canadian Tourism," *SPT*, 6 November 1988; *Visit Florida: Annual Report, 2000–2001*; Koenig, "Invasion," 78; "Quebeckers Feel Chill in South Florida," *SPT*, 9 February 2001.

69. "Presenting the Past," *TT*, 24 September 2000; "Promoting the 'Other' Florida," *SPT*, 6 March 2000; "Marketing Shift at "Eco-Lodge," *WSJ*, 12 July 2000; Hiller, "The Real Florida," 22–27; Hiller, "How to Save Florida Tourism," 42–49; "Greenhouse De-

fect," *Lingua Franca* (October 2001): 10–11; "Tourists Seek Ecological Attractions," *SLT,* 14 January 1901; "Nature Awaits," *TT,* 3 January 2002; West, 115, 119; "Park Visitors Threaten Environment They Sought," *TT,* 18 April 2003; tour guide quoted in "On a Silent Landscape," *NYT,* 4 November 2003; Aron, 260–61.

70. Paterniti, 34; "Where the Jobs Are in Florida," *USAT,* 20 September 1993; *Visit Florida: Annual Report, 2000–2001*; Barnett, 78; "Record Tourist Year for Florida," *TDT,* 2 May 1950.

71. "Tourists Paid 18 Per Cent of All Florida Taxes," *SAR,* 15 June 1958; "Tourists Pay 17.7 Per Cent of State Taxes," *TT,* 3 February 1959; "Hotel Kings Build a Palace," *OS,* 19 December 2001; Judd and Swanstrom, 386; "Convention and Meeting Facilities," *FT,* March 2001, 88; "Convention Center," *TT,* 15 August 2003; "Fewer Conventions," *Denver Post* in *TT,* 6 December 2004.

72. Dietrich, 146, 172, 174, 194; "Tourism's Long Climb Is Over," *OS,* 22 September 2001

73. "Orlando," *NYT,* 23 March 2003; "Tourists Grab Thrills—Locals Ride Same Old Economy," *OS,* 16 December 2001; "One-Ticket Town: The Costs of a Tourism Economy," *OS,* 18 December 2001.

74. Whitfield, "Florida's Fudged Identity," 431; Rothchild, *Up for Grabs,* 49; Painton, 52.

75. Painton, 52–53; "Hotels and Resorts," 72; Foglesong, *Married,* 4, 104; "Area Prepared for Disney World?" *TT,* 7 April 1968; "Quality of Life Index," *SPT,* 3 December 2001; "Rooms at the Inns," *Newsweek,* 19 March 1973, 78; "Gaylord's Story," *OS,* 7–13 January 2002; "Mom-and-Pop Roots," *OS,* 16 October 1995; "Boom Times Hotel Growth," *OS,* 27 June 1988; "Tourist Facilities: Hotels and Motels," *FSA 2001,* table 19.60; "Disney World, Deluxe," *WSJ,* 18 July 2003; "Ranches Vanish East," *OS,* 17 March 2002.

76. "Locals Ride Same Old Economy," *OS,* 16 December 2001; "Tourism Tax Bounty," *OS,* 17 December 2001; "One-Ticket Town: The Costs of a Tourism Economy," *OS,* 18 December 2001; "All Roads Lead to Aggravation," *OS,* 18 December 2001; Foglesong, *Married,* 182.

77. Hiaasen quoted in *SPT,* 27 February 1995; Rothchild, *Up for Grabs,* 50; "Tacky Town," 51–53; Foglesong, *Married,* 93–98, 122–31.

78. Derr, 379; Carter, 5, 34–36, 176, 320; Blake, 241, 279, 289.

79. Dunlop, *Vanishing,* 23.

80. Cronon, 266–67; Hiaasen, *Team Rodent,* 18; Foglesong, *Married,* 60–61.

81. *Florida Trend: 2001 Annual TopRank Florida Book of Lists,* 100–101; Barnett, 77–78; Villano, "Paradise Paradox," 80–83; "Cruisers Crowd Port, Streets of Key West," *TT,* 6 January 2003; Ogle, 222; "Trouble in Paradise," *AJC,* 29 July 1979, Sunday magazine; "Condo Conflict," *NYT,* 22 November 2002; "Voice of Reason Muffled," *MH,* 31 January 1986; "Key West," *SPT,* 20 July 1998; Hiaasen, *Team Rodent,* 79; "Homeless Face Hard Times," *TT,* 8 March 2004; "Selling Key West," *SPT,* 13 June 2004.

82. Gibson, 3–4; "Florida," *CT,* 7 January 1988; "Calamity Calendar," *MH,* 2 December 1990.

83. "Parks Try to Woo Gen X Families," *OS,* 2 April 2002; "Ailing Turnstiles," *NYT,* 24

January 2002; "Disney's Eroding Attendance," *OS*, 13 November 1994; "Problems Plague the House That Mickey Built," *USAT*, 13 March 2002; "Parks' Sag Puts Disney on Roller Coaster," *OS*, 6 October 2002; Adams, 169–81; "Tourism's Long Climb Is Over," *OS*, 22 September 2001; "A New Theme Park Theme: Glut," *Time*, 31 May 1999, 84.

84. Kelly quoted in Tebeau and Marina, 253.

Chapter 4. Old Folks at Home: The Graying of Florida

1. Lanier, 131; Brooks, 44.

2. Arsenault and Mormino, 165–68.

3. Hopkins, 33, 44, 115–17; "Near-Riot," *TT*, 10 May 1965; "Beatles Set Off Teenage Riot," *MH*, 14 February 1964; "Rock Singer Posts Bond," *TT*, 18 November 1969; "Jack Kerouac at Road's End," *SPT*, 22 October 1969; "Jack Slept Here," *NYT*, 14 March 2004.

4. Whitfield, "Florida's Fudged Identity," 432; Irby, "Beat in St. Pete"; Steinbeck, 35, 36.

5. Rowles, 103–13; "Gone Fishing," *TT*, 21 April 1998; "The Mistress State," *SPT*, 10 February 1985; *SPT*, 16 July 1999, 3 January 2000; *FSA 1998*, 99; Colburn and deHaven-Smith, 33; Rothchild, "Everything under the Sunshine State," 7.

6. The literature on aging in America is rich and vast. See especially Cole, *The Journey of Life*; Fischer, *Growing Old in America*, 142; Achenbaum, *Old Age in the New Land*.

7. DeBeauvoir, 262; Graebner, 3–53. No consensus exists as to the number of working seniors before 1950. A syndicated story in the *Tampa Tribune* on 16 November 1997 noted that in 1950, three-quarters of men sixty-five and older worked. "Ex-Slave," *TMT*, 21 January 1946; "Clearwater Pioneer," *TDT*, 8 March 1950; "Auburndale Citrus Picker, 115," *TMT*, 23 September 1956; "How Our Work and Play Have Changed," *SPT*, 3 September 2001.

8. *NYT*, 2 January 2001.

9. Arsenault and Mormino, 169, 174; *Seventh Census of Florida: 1945*, 91–120; *A Report of the Seventeenth Decennial Census—1950*, vol. 2, *Population Characteristics of the Population*, pt. 10, *Florida*, 364–76.

10. "Pride of the Yankees," *TT*, 17 April 2003; "They Remembered," *TD*, 10 September 1967; "Yankee Memorial," *MER*, 27 February 1970.

11. Eleanor Roosevelt Papers, Old Age Pensions, box 966; Kennedy, "Ex-Slaves of Miami Organize," *Opportunity* 17 (1939): 271, 287; Putnam, 48.

12. "Old Age Payments," *TDT*, 2 January 1940; *SPT*, 20 September 1945; *TMT*, 1 July 1947, 20 September 1945; "Mass Migration Threatens Florida's Old Age Relief," *TMT*, 4 August 1947; *Seventh Census of 1945: Florida*, 70; *TT*, 15 December 1996; Lade; "America by the Numbers," *WSJ*, 3 January 2001.

13. Whitfield, "Blood and Sand," 73–96; D. Moore, *To the Golden Cities*, 1–52; Kleinberg, *Miami Beach*, 52, 69–76, 117–19; Green and Zerivitz, 18–20.

14. D. Moore, 39–41; Kleinberg, *Miami Beach*, 136–38, 153, 174–75; "Russian Emigres Remember Birthplace," *MH*, 5 February 1973; Mahoney, 18–19; Green and Zerivitz, 21; *1950 Census*, pt. 10, *Florida*, 27–29.

15. D. Moore, *To the Golden Cities*, 32, 48, 153–56; Mahoney; Kleinberg, *Miami Beach*, 132–34; *MH*, 3 July 1947, 3 March 1949; *NYT*, 19 April 1984; Stone became the first Jew

in the twentieth-century South to be elected to the U.S. Senate; "Liebermans Court Voters in South Florida," *MH*, 11 September 2000; "Gore and Company," *NYT*, 24 August 2000.

16. "New York City Milestone, Jews," *NYT*, 16 June 2003; *AJYB*, 1961, 57; *AJYB 1981*, 176; *AJYB 2001*, 259–60, 264, 345; Green and Zerivitz, 22; "Jews Choose Miami," *SPT*, 7 December 2004.

17. "Oldsters Like Florida," *MH*, 9 May 1954; *OS*, 21 April 1996; *SPT*, 24 March 1993; Longino, *Retirement*, 17, 19; "Englewood," *TMT*, 4 April 1954; "Sarasota's Population," *SPT*, 10 March 1973; "1972 U.S. Birth Rate Was Lowest in History," *TT*, 2 March 1973; "Florida Gains Most of Elderly Migrants," *MH*, 20 March 1951; "U.S. Tracks Interstate Migration of Americans," *NYT*, 6 August 2003; "Florida," *TT*, 6 August 2003; "Florida Slips," *SPT*, 13 August 2003.

18. Irby, "Razing Gerontopolis," 37; Dusenbury and Dusenbury; Dodrill, 15–29, 67–90.

19. "Huge 'City' for Retired Is Planned," *TT*, 6 July 1961; Fitzgerald, 203–43; McCally, "Sun City Center," 31–44; *USAT*, 1 November 1999; *SPT*, 6 November 1999; *TT*, 21 July 1963, 23 May 1966, 10 August 1981, 8 January 1986; "In Full Swing," *TT*, 21 April 2002.

20. Linsin, 3–4, 95–99, 113; Lade; "Condo Entertainers," *TT*, 31 September 1998; "Florida's Golden 'Borscht Belt,'" *TT*, 14 July 1974, Florida Accent.

21. Lade; Longino, *Retirement*, 117, 140; "Levy," *SPT*, 28 November 1999; "A Condo in Paradise," *SFSS*, 7 December 1986; "U.S. Tracks Interstate Migration of Americans," *NYT*, 6 August 2003.

22. *The Seventh Census of the State of Florida*, 1945, 70; *Census of Population: 1950, Florida*, 9–10, 28–30; *FSA 1999*, 36; "A Moving Experience," *TT*, 10 August 1991; "Florida," *NYT*, 7 August 1996; "Retirees Keep Safe Distance," *TT*, 4 October 1999; *OS*, 28 November 1989; *TT*, 10 August 1992; data in *FT*, April 2000, 76, 130, 140, 147, 154, 158; *SHT*, 16 June 1991 and 23 May 2001; Wolf, 22; "Exploring a Nation of Extremes," *WSJ*, 25 May 2001; "Booming Port Charlotte," *TT*, 26 June 1960.

23. "Miami Beach Leads in Aged," *TT*, 17 August 1973; "St. Petersburg Ranks No. 1," *FTU*, 24 May 1954; "City of Seniors," *TT*, 28 July 1998; "Elderly," *SHT*, 23 May 2001; "Pinellas City Still Old," *SPT*, 14 October 2001; "A Magnet for Korean Veterans," *FMNP*, 26 May 2003.

24. Data in *FT*, April 2000, 50, 51; "Retirement," *GS*, 13 July 2001; "5 Counties Buck State Trend," *SPT*, 8 April 2001; "UF to Build Retirement Community," *TT*, 13 August 2000; "A Chance to Relive College Days," *NYT*, 29 December 2003; "Gator Retirees," *FMNP*, 7 March 2004; Greene quoted in Pleasants, 168–69.

25. Vesperi, 30–48; *SPT*, 6 April 1925, 19 November 1950; Arsenault, *St. Petersburg*, 136–37; Irby, "Razing Gerontopolis," 13–49; *SPT*, 6 April 1925.

26. Lessing, 72; "St. Petersburg Oldsters Change Way of Life," *SPT*, 27 June 1953; "Green Bench TV," *SPT*, 7 September 1953; Thielen, 80; Irby, "Razing Gerontopolis," 49–54; "The Old Subscribers," 80; businessmen quoted in "St. Petersburg Image," *SPT*, 6 October 1960; "Gerontoville," *SPT*, 2 July 1965; Vesperi, 50.

27. Irby, "Razing Gerontopolis," 54–67; Irby, "Beat in St. Pete," 18–28; Vesperi, i–iii.

28. "Four-Square Miles of Dade," *MH*, 13 January 1984; D. Moore, *Golden Cities*, 41, 85; "Retirement Community," *MH*, 28 January 2002; "Inflation Hurts State's Elderly," *TT*, 27 July 1973; "Hispanics Are Dade's Fountain of Youth," *MH*, 15 September 1999;

"Changing Face of Florida," *SFSS*, 23 May 2001; "Afterlife of Synagogues," *MH*, 16 November 2003; "A Latin Generation," *MH*, 25 April 2004.

29. *SPT*, 20 January 1999; *MH*, 13 January 1984, 9 August 1991, 26 April 1998; *NYT*, 27 April 1989; "The Way We Ate"; "Council Studies Mosh Pits," *SPT*, 6 March 2000; Arsenault, *St. Petersburg*, 263–64; "St. Pete: Younger," *Philadelphia Inquirer*, 23 January 2000.

30. Golant quoted in Kunerth, "Retiree Dreams"; Kunerth, "Issue of Death"; Kunerth and Sargent; "Village Patriarch Dies," *OS*, 24 December 2003.

31. Rimer, "Retirement"; "Florida Burden," *NYT*, 14 July 1986; "More Centenarians," *OS*, 25 July 2001; Clendinen.

32. "Hispanics Are Dade's Fountain of Youth," *MH*, 15 September 1999; Frank V. Castellano, Grand Lodge of Florida, Order of the Sons of Italy in America, to author, 27 February 2000; Karol Belohlavek, interview by the author, 30 April 1979, Winter Park, Fla.; "Slovak Gardens," *OS*, 14 April 2002; "Slovaks," *OS*, 3 March 1988; "Florida Sees Huge Influx of Hispanics," *SFSS*, 28 March 2001; Longino, *Retirement*, 78; Census 2000, Census of Housing and Population Data; Calandra Institute to author, 3 October 2002; "Frankly Finnish," *SFSS*, 3 December 2000; Immigrants Now Embrace Homes for Elderly," *NYT*, 20 October 2003; "A Latin Generation," *MH*, 25 April 2004; "Cubans Returning to Retire," *MH*, 27 June 2004; "Cuban Exiles," *TT*, 30 January 2005.

33. Irby, "Razing," 33–51; "Negro Aged Provided for in Rickety Frame Shacks," *MH*, 2 January 1956, Broward edition; "Racial and Ethnic Gap," *SPT*, 10 August 2000; Vesperi, 76–80, 93–94; "America Then and Now," *NYT*, 31 December 2000; "Pinellas," *SPT*, 17 April 1961.

34. Harrington, 101–20; J. Patterson, 572–77; Sikes, 440; MacManus, "Aging in Florida and Its Implications," 8; "Old Age," *Life*, 13 July 1959, 14; Quadagno, 162–64; "Poverty in America," *Time*, 17 May 1968, 24–30; "Seniors Grimly Do Math of Living," *SPT*, 17 October 2003; "Medicaid Spending," *SPT*, 22 February 2004; official quoted in "State of Rage," 48; "Dollar Dilemma," 72.

35. Harrington, 108; information obtained from AARP, 2000 and 2004; Quadagno, 163–64, 168, 170; Holmes; A. Sullivan; Schulman, 86.

36. Pepper, 214, 258–70; "Claude Pepper," *NYT*, 31 May 1989.

37. Isenberg, "Senior Power," *Nation*, 14 May 1973, 627; Schulman, 85; "Older Americans," *WSJ*, 3 December 2000; Schulman, 84.

38. Peterson; Schulman, 84; Isenberg, "Senior Power," *Nation*, 14 May 1973, 627; Harris, "Old People Power," *New Republic*, 23 March 1974, 10; Samuelson, "Paying for Those in Retirement," *SPT*, 13 June 2000; "Age, Poverty Linked for Women," *TT*, 5 November 2000; journalist quoted in "The Ten Loneliest Places in Florida," *SPT*, 24 June, 2001; Bragg, "Aged Beefcake"; "Elderly Women," *SPT*, 11 June 1973; Harrington, 107–14.

39. *SPT*, 18 February 1996; *SHT*, 16 June 1991; Navarro; Matthews, *Venice*, 219–48; Fitzgerald, 207–8; "Penney Farms," *OS*, 1 May 1977; "Penney Farms," *TT*, 2 August 1989; *FTU*, 4, 6 November 1950; "Chicago School Retirees," *TT*, 2 May 1965; Smith, 121. Sun Valley ended up in bankruptcy court. Shofner, *Brevard County*, 2:136; "Lakeland Bid for Colony of Ex-Railroaders," *TMT*, 10 June 1938; "Booming Port Charlotte," *TT*, 26 June 1960; "Mail Carriers," *NDN*, 4 August 2004.

40. "Florida Copes with New Breed of Worker-Retiree," *TT*, 4 June 2000; Working

Overtime," *TT,* 20 May 2001; "Nation's Oldest Worker Dies," *TT,* 5 March 2001; "Retiree Rebels," *TT,* 12 October 2003.

41. *SPT,* 1 December 1997, Pasco edition; *SHT,* 19 November 1989; *SFSS,* 27 April 1997; Lade; "Life on the Wing," *OS,* 14 November 2003; "Annual Exodus Gains Steam," *FMNP,* 8 April 2001; Longino, *Retirement,* 75–78; "Churches Feel Seasonal Swing," *FMNP,* 24 March 2002; reporter quoted in "Snowbirds," *FMNP,* 2 November 2003.

42. Resident quoted in Hart, Rhodes, and Morgan, 116, see also 110–21; Longino, *Retirement,* 77–78; Kaplan and Longino, 389–98; "Sun Sets on Sunnydale," *TT,* 27 August 2000; "Florida's Mobile Homes," *NYT,* 22 June 2003.

43. "Senior Drivers Spotlighted," *SHT,* 18 July 2003, "Time to Turn in Car Keys?" *SPT,* 18 July 2003; "Florida Elderly Fatalities," *SPT,* 27 July 2003.

44. *SHT,* 16 June 1991; Kaplan and Longino, 389; "Florida," *NYT,* 7 August 1996, 4 December 1995; *OS,* 18 April, 4 October 1999; "A Flood of Floridians," *FTU,* 9 June 1996; "Sarasota's Population," *SPT,* 10 March 1973; "Entitlements," *TT,* 18 June 1995; *SPT,* 9 February 1984; *SHT,* 16 June 1991; R. Johnson, "Sarasota," 37–38; U.S. Veteran's Administration estimate of military retirees in Florida, *SPT,* 12 November 2001; "Cities Scramble," *WSJ,* 21 April 1999; "Englewood," *TMT,* 4 April 1954; "Inflation Fattens Social Security Checks," *TT,* 15 October 2003; Social Security Administration, 2000.

45. *OS,* 8–9 November 1950; *FTU,* 9 November 1950; *SPT,* 8–9 November 1950; "State GOP to Woo the Elderly Voter," *SPT,* 19 October 1969; Colburn and deHaven-Smith, *Florida since Statehood,* 4, 31, 51–52, 65, 69–74; Quadagno, 163; "Cramer, a GOP Pioneer Dies," *SPT,* 20 October 2003; Black and Black, 65.

46. Bragg, "A Political Era"; *TT,* 1 August 1987; *SFSS,* 27 April 1997; Quadagno, 163–65; "Retirement Community," *MH,* 28 January 2002; "Retirees Play Active Role in Politics," *ACJ,* 6 February 1988; "South Florida Retirement," *WSJ,* 27 November 1984.

47. MacManus, "Aging in Florida," 9; MacManus, *Senior Voters,* 1–20; *TT,* 1 August 1987; "A New Respect for Age in Florida," *NYT,* 21 October 2000; "Senior Vote," *FTU,* 15 October 2000; Sullivan, 6; "Trinchi Dead at 87," *SFSS,* 5 February 2005.

48. "Retirees Staying Put," *USAT,* 14 May 2002; "Retirees Seek Good Life," *WSJ,* 8 August 1994; *MH,* 17 June 1985; Sack, "Florida"; *TT,* 4 December 1995; "Romancing the Retiree," *SPT,* 11 April 1999; "State of Rage," 4; *TD,* 1 June 1997; Gardner quoted in Reed, *One South,* 156; "Branson Courts Veterans," *SPT,* 29 August 2000; Longino, *Retirement,* 117; "Florida in Battle for Retirees," *FMNP,* 3 November 2002; "States Pan for Gold," *NYT,* 18 March 2003; Kunerth, "Gray Gold."

49. "Retirees Seek Good Life," *WSJ,* 8 August 1994; "Fearing Isolation," *NYT,* 21 October 1999; "Gay Seniors," *SFSS,* 4 February 2002; Fletcher, "Retirees."

50. "Florida Slips," *SPT,* 13 August 2003; "Florida," *TT,* 6 August 2003; "U.S. Tracks Interstate Migration of Americans," *NYT,* 6 August 2003; *TT,* 31 May 1999; *SFSS,* 28 May 2000.

51. *TT,* 31 May 1999; *SFSS,* 28 May 2000.

52. "Caught in the Middle," *TT,* 5 March 2001; "Elderly Americans?" *USAT,* 23 October 2000; "Florida's Economy," *USNWR,* 11 October 1993, 52; *SFSS,* 15 June 2000; "Demographic Shifts," *TT,* 15 December 1996; "A Graying Europe," *NYT,* 10 July 1998; "An Aging Europe," *NYT,* 29 June 2003. In a stunning shift, the numbers of young

Floridians outpaced the growth of seniors in the 1990s. Navarro; "State's Population," *SHT*, 16 March 1997; "Known for Seniors, Booming in Juniors," *SPT*, 18 September 2003; A. Sullivan, 6; Wynne, "Will the Young Support the Old?" 40–47; "Florida Burden," *NYT*, 14 July 1986; "Florida's Generational Strife," *NYT*, 13 June 1981; Samuelson, "Paying for Retirement," *SPT*, 3 June 2000; MacManus, 146; Will quoted in "Social Security," *SPT*, 4 March 2004.

53. Sack; "Retirees' Influx," *OS*, 21 April 1996; "Retirement," *SPT*, 11 April 1999; Navarro; *2000 Census*, table DP-1. In 2005, Florida's 5th Congressional District had more social security beneficiaries than any other place in America. *USAT*, 10 February 2005.

54. *WSJ*, 24 May 2000, Florida edition; "Romancing the Retiree," *SPT*, 11 April 1999; Kunerth, "Old People"; "A Place for the Living," *MH*, 6 October 2002.

Chapter 5. Sunbelt Hues: Cold Wars, Hot Markets, and Nagging Doubts

1. *SPT*, 26 November 1950; *OS*, 10 November 1950; "Where There's Smoke," *SPT*, 15 December 1999.

2. "Florida's Governor Collins," *Time*, 19 December 1955; Cobb, 73, 123, 140; Colburn and Scher, 203–6; "The Florida Lure," 229–32; *MH*, 9 September 1959; Wagy, 54–57; *MH*, 1 May 1960; E. Bennett, 454; "Collins," *TDT*, 25 July 1955; "Collins Industry Council," *TMT*, 17 July 1955; "Howard Hughes Plans Vast Industrial Plant," *FTU*, 12 January 1956.

3. Colburn and Scher, 21–23, 194; *A Study of the Economic Impact of Project Apollo*, 92; Nash, 77–121; *OS*, 10 November 1950; Gelfand, viii–ix, 380–89; Nathankane and Podell, 97; Daniel, 39–87.

4. Armstrong quoted in "Paradise," *PBP*, 9 June 1942; Mormino, "World War II"; "War Touched Florida," *MH*, 8 May 1945.

5. "Pahokee Rally," *MH*, 8 August 1946; "Veterans to Get Free Lots," *SPT*, 18 October 1944; "DeLand," *DBEN*, 2 March 1946; "Tarpon Springs," *TMT*, 14 September 1947; *SH*, 22 August 1945; Cohen, 137–46.

6. Cohen, 133–40; Redding quoted in Papers of the NAACP, pt. 5, The Campaign Against Residential Segregation, reel 18, 410–15; M. Dunn, 206–9; Mormino, "G.I. Joe Meets Jim Crow," 38–42; 133–51; Crooks, *Jacksonville: The Consolidation*, 190–91; Mohl, "Elizabeth Virrick," 5–37.

7. *ONJ*, 5 May 1944; Sikes, 192.

8. "Riddle Field Closing," *GDC*, 24 August 1945; "Navy Closing Eleven Bases," *FTU*, 25 September 1945; "Army Barracks and Crowded Schools," *TMT*, 19 September 1947; "Girls' College," *TMT*, 28 April 1947; "U. of Florida Dedicates Veterans Housing," *TMT*, 12 February 1946; "Flavet Village," *MH*, 3 April 1946; "Palm Beach College Promised Morrison Field," *MH*, 8 October 1947; "Arcadia Named Location for Vet Facility," *Arcadian*, 9 May 1946; "German POWs Left Their Mark," *OS*, 23 January 1994, Lake Co. edition; "Two Army Air Fields Go to Waste," *MH*, 10 March 1946; "Vero Naval Base to Be Released," *VBPJ*, 23 September 1945; "Army Frees Last Beach Hotel," *MH*, 21 December 1945; Shofner, *Jackson County*, 523; "When a Bad Girl Feels Pretty," *TMT*, 2 May 1954; "Brooklyn Dodgers Select Vero Beach," *VBPJ*, 12 December 1947.

9. Sikes, 192; Pelt, 366–68; "Navy Will Open Research Station," *PCNH*, 22 August 1945; "Tyndall Field," *PCNH*, 27 September 1945; "Flavet Village," *MH*, 3 April 1946.

10. Crispell, 34; McGovern, 170.

11. *MH*, 19, 20, 25 July 1950; "Atomic Base," *MH*, 9 August 1945; *SAR*, 2 October 1945; G. Patterson, "Countdown," 163–64.

12. "Canaveral Site," *TMT*, 17 February 1946.

13. "Missile at Cocoa," *MH*, 25 July 1950; "Rocket Fails to Fire," *MH*, 20 July 1950; Eriksen, 106–7; G. Patterson, "A Special Place," 19; *NYT*, 27 October and 22 December 1957.

14. G. Patterson, "Countdown," 163–80; G. Patterson, "A Special Place," 19–21; Brunais, 14–18; "America's Race for Space," *FT*, June 1983, 51–57; Cobb, 164; *A Study of the Economic Impact*, 92; Sikes, 332–33; "Aerospace Is Great Florida Asset," *SPT*, 6 December 1959, 95–98; "'Moon' May Boost Industry," *SPT*, 8 October 1957.

15. *CHE*, 5 May 2000, A-32; "Did Politics Rob Florida of NASA's Space Program?" 47–49.

16. Wilford; Long and Merzer; *MH*, 1 August 1999; *A Study of the Economic Impact of Project Apollo*, 15–18; "Was NASA's Mission Control Stolen from Florida?" 46–49; "Space Shuttle," *OS*, 8 September 2000; "Florida's Space Coast," *NYT*, 2 February 2004; O. White, "The Big Bang," 78.

17. "A Military Marriage"; *SPT*, 16, 19 August 1981; Nash, 77–101; *TT*, 4 October 1981; Crispell, 113–36; Colburn and deHaven-Smith, 34, 103–4; "Southern Militarism," 69–71.

18. "Sikes: A New Political Dynasty," *PJ*, 9–10 May 1976; "Southern Militarism," 71; Sikes, 463, see also 342–43, 365–66, 503; "Sikes Is the Big Daddy in Crestview," *CS*, 25 April 1975; "'He-Coon' Sikes to Call It Quits," *NC*, 10 August 1978; "Sikes," *SPT*, 5 June 1978; Black and Black, 157.

19. "Southern Militarism," 60; Sikes, 342, 460–62, 503; Nash, 84. Under Young's generous tutelage, University of South Florida campuses in Tampa and St. Petersburg benefited from federal grants (see "Academic Pork," *CHE*, 26 September 2003, 18–20).

20. "Eglin's Missions," *SPT*, 17 August 1981; "Okaloosa," *FT*, December 1974, 49–52; "Top Florida Defense Sites," *SPT*, 23 May 1992; "America's Military Might," *FT*, July 1978, 31–39; "Special Operations," *FT*, August 2004, 36.

21. "Southern Militarism," 69–71; *WSJ*, 21 April 1999, Florida edition; *SPT*, 17 August 1981; *SPT*, 28 March 1988, 23 May 1992; "North Florida's New Era," 21; Bowden, *Pensacola*, 153–56; Green and Kromm, 15–18.

22. Shofner, *Orlando*, 106–13; Rotundo, 41–57.

23. *OS*, 10 April 2000; Foglesong, *Married*, 87; Thomson, 506–13; "Ready to Rise and Shine," *OS*, 6 June 2001.

24. Sikes, 342–43, 365–66, 463, 503; Bacon, 2:179, 211–16, 255, 269; "Southern Militarism," 69–71; O. White, "Big Bang," 75–80; Green and Kromm, 15–18.

25. *FTU*, 9 January 2000; Willson, "Trident's Hidden Treasure," 52–56; Ward, 244–45; "North Florida's New Era," 21–24; "Federal Pay Day," *FT*, July 2000, 29; "Top Florida Defense Sites," *SPT*, 23 May 1992.

26. "Making the Transition," *FTU*, 22 May 2000; *TMT*, 27 July 1950.

27. *MH*, 30 July 1950; Blakey, *Parade*, 231–32; *FT*, April 1999, 94, 96; Morris and Morris, 625.

28. "MacDill," *TMT*, 9 January 1950; "B-47 Stratojet," *TMT*, 13 January 1953; TMT, 16 April and 30 July 1950; *TT*, 28–29 November 1960, 28 June 1961, October 1962, 13

February 2000; *SPT*, 19 August 1981, 23 May 1992; O. White, "The Big Bang," 79; "What Would Peace Do to the Florida Economy?" 13–14; "When the Base Closes," *TT*, 2 July 1961; "U.S. Group to Study Impact of MacDill Closing," *TT*, 8 July 1961; "B-52, Biggest Bomber," *TMT*, 31 January 1957; "Supersonic Planes," *TT*, 10 February 1959; "War Commands Come from Tampa," *USAT*, 5 December 2001.

29. *MH*, 1 January 1960; *TT*, 17 October 1999; *TDT*, 5 December 1958; Tebeau, *Last Frontier*, 264–66; *SPT*, 12 October, 5 December 1958, 27 December 1959; "Brevard Feeling Cold War Chill," *MH*, 21 May 1960, Brevard edition; "13 Days," *OS*, 12 January 2001; "When the Cold War Burned Hot," *SFSS*, 2 January 1999.

30. "Southern Militarism," 71; *WSJ*, 21 April 1999, Florida edition; "Old Soldiers Fading Away," *SFSS*, 10 November 2002; Wassum quoted in "Military Matters in Florida," *OS*, 26 December 1999; *SPT*, 16, 17 August 1981, 28 March 1988, 24 October 1999; *TT*, 25 April 1993 and 30 December 1999; C. Bennett, "Too Little"; 2000 Census cited in *SPT*, 28 May 2001; "A National Challenge," *LL*, 28 May 2001.

31. *WSJ*, 21 April 1999, Florida edition; Green and Kromm, 15. Statistics vary. The *St. Petersburg Times* lists $6.5 million in state military contracts in 2000. See "Local Contractors," *SPT*, 21 October 2001; "Key West," *SPT*, 17 October 1973.

32. *FSA 2002, table 6.01*; *A Study of the Economic Impact of Project Apollo*, 92; *Census of Population: 1950*, vol. 2, pt. 10, *Florida*, 45–56.

33. Crooks, *Jacksonville: After*, 29–30; Funk quoted in *MH*, 22 December 1959; "Miami to Become Industrial Center," *SPT*, 19 May 1950; "Orlando," *NYT*, 22 October 1957; "Central Pinellas Gets Defense Plant," *TMT*, 25 July 1956; Cobb, 180; Bacon, 2:173, 207, 215, 219, 223, 298, 310; "The Florida Lure," 229–32; Mansfield, 27; Robison and Andrews, 257; *TT*, 10, 29 December 1959; *SPT*, 27 July 1959; Bowden, *Pensacola*, 171; "Florida to Have Two Mills," *TMT*, 16 November 1950; Keuchel, 109, 111–12; *A Study of the Economic Impact*, 92; In 1999, Pratt and Whitney announced the closing of its Palm Beach County defense plant (*SPT*, 13 August 1999); "The Pratt Pack," *SFSS*, 29 October 2000; "State Gets 441 New Plants," *TMT*, 20 March 1957; *MT*, 3 June 1950; *NYT*, 19 March 1956; "Panhandle Pace Quickens," *FT*, March 1960, 13–14; "North Florida's New Era," *FT*, August 1965, 18–24.

34. McLamore, 1–33; "The Burger That Would Be King," *SPT*, 16 October 2000; "Hooters: A Case Study," *Fortune*, September 1, 2003; Jakle and Sculle, *Fast Food*, 116–19, 227, 228, 252, 275; "Chain Reaction," *TT*, 5 April 2004; J. White, 75–78.

35. "Top Fifty Most Important Floridians of the 20th Century," *LL*, 1 March 1998, 22–24; Eckerd and Conn, 55–64; "Eckerd without Jack," *TT*, 1 May 1956; "Eckerd Sale," *SPT*, 7 January 2004; "Rise and Fall of Eckerd Empire," *SPT*, 11 April 2004; Hinder, 4–6.

36. "George Jenkins," *NYT*, 10 April 1996; "Publix," *MH*, 26 Oct. 1980; Hinder, 4–6; "They Parlayed $10,000 into Billions," *MH*, 25 June 1967; Mormino and Pozzetta, 29–30; "The Kash n' Karry Story," *TT*, 4 Oct. 1964; "Deconstructing Winn-Dixie," *TT*, 6 Mar. 2005.

37. "The Pizza King," 82–86; *OS*, 30 September 1995, 30 September 1999; "Kemmons Wilson," *OS*, 22 July 1985.

38. "A Tycoon," *MH*, 21 March 1999; "There's No Business Like Show Business, *MH*, 23 November 1981.

39. Tebeau and Marina, 519–20; "Forbes' Richest," *SPT*, 1 March 2002; Clary, "All Work," 28–33.

40. "Brownie Wise," *OS*, 25 September 1992; "Is the Party Over?" *OS*, 15 March 1987.

41. "Tupperware Ladies Dig for Treasures," *BW*, 17 April 1954, 54–62; Don Boyett quoted in "The Lady Who Built Tupperware," *OS*, 29 September 1992, Seminole edition.

42. Frazer and Guthrie, 139–63.

43. Hewlett, 61–69, 74, 99, 101, 169–70, 181–82, 196–97; Danese, 88–110, 137–56; *SPT*, 12 September 1999; "Giants of Florida," *TT*, 5 February 1950; "DuPont Sales Tax Fight," *TMT*, 4 February 1950.

44. R. Bennett, "Banking's Hottest Market"; Danese, 88–110, 219.

45. Crooks, "*Jacksonville: The Consolidation*," 6–7, 122, 142; *TMT*, 22 January 1950; *SPT*, 27 May 1991, 30 August 1997; *FTU*, 1 January 1950; "Prudential Building Opens," *TMT*, 8 May 1955; "Growth of Florida Banks Reflects Thriving State," *TMT*, 20 January 1957; "Bank Building Boom," *FT*, October 1961, 26; Tebeau and Marina, 456–57.

46. Berman, 41; R. Bennett.

47. Quotes in R. Bennett; McColl quoted in *SPT*, 2 October 1999; *SPT*, 30 August 1997, 23 August, 7 September 1999; "Is It Too Late to Save Southeast?" *FT*, October 1990, 36–37; economist quoted in *SPT*, 27 May 1991; Keuchel, 137; "Small Banks," 72–76; Vogel, "One," 34; Ginzl, 261–87.

48. Mohl, "Changing Economic Patterns," 65; Mohl, "Miami: The Ethnic Cauldron," 73; "Booming Aviation Industry," *MH*, 30 December 1951; J. Schwartz, 36; *NYT*, 19 January and 5 December 1991; *NYT*, 25 February 1986; "Frank Borman and 'The Wings of Man,'" *SPT*, 25 July 1976; "Eastern's $16 Million Jet Air Base," *MH*, 30 July 1961.

49. Pleasants, 9–10; R. Pierce, 183–205, 224–25, 349, 379–84; *Florida Trend: 1998, Top Rank Florida*, 78; "Selling the Sun," *GS*, 23 May 1999; *TT*, 4 March 1990; Bacon, 2:258–61; *NYT*, 25 November 1982; Thomson; Pleasants, 1–15; "Who Owns and Controls Florida Newspapers?" 34–38; "Newspaper Chains," *SPT*, 25 March 1973; "John Perry Dies," *SPT*, 5 December 1952.

50. "John S. Knight Dies," *NYT*, 17 June 1981; Pleasants, 41–58, 245–76, 319–39; Lawrence quoted in Pleasants, 56.

51. Clary, "Middle Man," 32–35.

52. R. Pierce, 264–66, 334–41; Orrick and Crumpacker, 304; Clary, "Middle Man," 35; "Circulation Gains," *SPT*, 1 May 2001; "Martin Andersen," *SPT*, 5 May 1986; Pleasants, 132.

53. *SPT*, 9 April 1997, 23 August 1997; "Florida Economy," 52; "Can Florida Compete?" *FT*, November 1996, 44; "Florida's Top 250 Public Companies," *FT*, July 1999, 68–76; "Unfortunate," *TT*, 13 April 1998; "The Florida Store No More," *SPT*, 17 September 2004.

54. "Loophole Inc.," *SPT*, 26 October 2003; Selz, "How Lucky Can You Get?" 30–39; "Updating Florida's Tax Structure," *SPT*, 20 January 2002.

55. "Jupiter Island," *SPT*, 14 May 1999; "It Takes Cash," *TT*, 27 June 1999; Martin County Property Appraisers Office to author, 14 September 2004.

56. "It Takes Cash," *TT*, 27 June 1999; data derived from *FT*, April 1999, 59, 101; April 2004, 30, 41.

57. "Patterns of Wealth," *SPT*, 17 May 1992; Kilborn, "Scraping By"; *USAT*, 1 October 1999; *MH*, 25 June, 12 August 1992; *NYT*, 1 August 1992; *FT*, April 2004, 74.

58. "Cattle Industry Booms in Florida," *SDU*, 2 May 1943; Painton, 58; *FSA 1999*, 15, 524; "Ranches Vanish Fast," *OS*, 17 March 2002; "Thriving Kissimmee," *TMT*, 11 July

1954; "Buggy Whip," *TMT*, 19 April 1953; "Development Plows over Farming," *OS*, 1 July 2002; *FT*, April 2004, 59.

59. "Tung Nuts and Milk Bring New Prosperity to Calhoun," *TMT*, 28 December 1949; Longman, "The Species," 34–39; "North Florida's New Era," 18; "Negroes Say Vote Denied," *TMT*, 8 November 1949; "No Negro Voters," *TT*, 3 November 1963; "Little Train," *MH*, 29 July 1977; "Line's Only Freight," *MH*, 9 September 1973; "Blountstown Finds a Dead End," *SPT*, 14 September 1969; "But Blountstown Hopes," *MH*, 14 September 1969; *FT*, April 2004, 86.

60. "'You Can Hear Anything Here,'" *SPT*, 4 March 1979; Dietrich, 91, 155; *FSA 2001*, table 1.14; "Backwoods Counties," 13–17; Sloan and Pardue.

61. "Pulp Plant," *TMT*, 1 December 1952; "Spoil a River," *SPT*, 6 October 1991; "'Industrial River,'" *SPT*, 1 December 1992; "Perry," *SPT*, 26 April 1992; "Poison Levels," *SPT*, 9 February 2001; "Race Allegations," *SPT*, 31 October 2003.

62. "3000 Jobless Cigar Workers," *TMT*, 30 April 1947; "Tampa Cigar Industry Faces Fight," *TMT*, 23 September 1951; "The Cigar Has Seen Much Better Days," *WSJ*, 4 November 1986; *NYT*, 28 May 1988; *TT*, 7, 8 May 2000; "Embargo's End," *TT*, 18 August 2000; "Conversations with Carlito," *TT*, 15 September 2003; Kennedy quoted in Goodwin, "President Kennedy's Plan, *NYT*, 5 July 2000; "Kennedy to Ban Cuban Tobacco," *TT*, 3 February 1962; "Embargo Jars Cigar Industry," *TT*, 4 February 1962; "Crisis in the Cigar Industry," *TT*, 11 February 1962.

63. "Orlando's Rat Race," *TT*, 24 July 2000; J. White, 75–78; "100 Biggest Employers," *OS*, 6–12 September 1999, Central Florida Business; "Numbers Reflect Florida's Problems," *SPT*, 8 August 2001; Foglesong, *Married*, 98–99; "Working Poor," *TT*, 10 December 2000.

64. "Orlando's Rat Race," *OS*, 24 July 2000.

65. Mohl, "Changing Economic Patterns," 63–74; "Aviation," 21; *WSJ*, 27 December 1995, Florida edition; Mohl, "Miami: The Ethnic Cauldron," 76–78; Garreau, *Nine Nations*, 172; *Forbes* quoted in Berman, 37; R. Bennett; *CT*, 3 January 1982; "As Florida Grows," *NYT*, 7 July 1982; "Southern Florida's Curious Economy Relies Heavily on the Underground," *NYT*, 6 March 1982; "Where Have All The Jobs Gone?" *MH*, 10 August 1997; journalist quoted in "Brazilian Beachhead," 56; "Home of Free Trade," *SPT*, 2 November 2003; "Miami Leads U.S. Poverty," *TT*, 15 September 2002; Lipsitz, 213–16; "Poverty Rate a Challenge for Miami," *MH*, 20 November 2001.

66. "Families," *FMNP*, 7 December 2003; "Numbers Say State Low in High Tech," *TT*, 4 June 2000; "State Standings in New Ecomomy," *USAT*, 22 July 1999; Cobb, 180; *USAT*, 1 October 1999; *WSJ*, 27 December 1995, Florida edition; "Last Dance," *NYT*, 3 September 2000; "Personal Income," in Morris, 393; official quoted in "The Welfare State," *FT*, December 1993, 46; "Boom Zooms Past Florida Workers," *SPT*, 30 August 1999; "Bay Area Not Fertile Ground for Growth," *TT*, 27 March 2000; "Miami Leads U.S. in Poverty," *TT*, 15 September 2002; "How Panhandle Ranks below Poverty Level," *MH*, 28 January 1973; Nissen and Cattan, 7, 14; Gall, 223–49; Vogel, "Made in Florida," 44–50.

Chapter 6. Wondrous Fruit, Bountiful Land: From Farms to Agribusiness

1. *MH*, 4 January 1950.

2. *JCF*, 12 May 1950.

3. Shofner, *Jackson County*, 443, 554–56; Shofner, *Jefferson County*, 485–86, 539, 542; *SPT*, 10 February 2000; *FSA 1999*, 336–37; *TT*, 1 October 1998; "Gadsden Shade Leaf," *TD*, 3 September 1950; "Florida's 'Tobacco Road,'" *TMT*, 8 October 1950.

4. Rivers, 16–33; *USAT*, 5 January 1999; *FSA 1999*, 332; Daniel, 41–42; NASS, *2002 Census of Agriculture*, tables 49, 52; *U.S. Census of Agriculture: 1945, Florida*, table 5.

5. *TDD*, 5 April 1940; *TD*, 8 September 1974, 26 April, 6 September 1976, 17 December 1991.

6. Akerman, 1–16, 209–56; Platt quoted in Otto, "An Oral History," 24; engineer quoted in Philips, *The Lowery Collection*, 270.

7. "Who Still Recalls the Cattle Wars?" *MH*, 18 January 1959; "Okeechobee Rancher, 100," *TMT*, 31 December 1948; "Thriving Kissimmee Claims It's Cow Capital of Florida," *TMT*, 11 July 1954; "Can a Cowtown Go Uptown?" *SFSS*, 9 June 1991.

8. *MH*, 19 November 1950; *FT*, July 1971, 171; Carlson, 14–21; *U.S. Census of Agriculture: 1950, Florida*, vol. 1, pt. 18, 10.

9. *FSA 1999*, 339; *Atlas of Florida*, 169.

10. "Can a Cowtown Go Uptown?" *SFSS*, 9 June 1991; "Florida Cracker," *GS*, 14 January 1979; "The Shrinking Range," *TT*, 2 April 1990; Akerman, 239; "The Starkey Legacy," *SPT*, 11 April 1988; "Subdivision Would Preserve Heritage," *SPT*, Pasco edition, 9 November 1997; "Noose Tightens around Paradise," *TT*, 9 January 2000.

11. *OS*, 21 February, 7 July, 27 September 1991, 3 April 1996, 19 July 1997; *TT*, 1 October 1950 and 8 March 1980; *SPT*, 12 December 1976; "The Church's Ranch," 56–61; Shofner, *Brevard County*, 2:137; "The Church Industry," 22; Lykes Family file, USFSC; *Glades County*, 34; "Ranchland," *TT*, 18 February 2005.

12. Bushnell, 118–38; Akerman, 2–20; Gray, 834; *The Travels of William Bartram*, 118, 119–20.

13. Proctor and Wright, 18–20, 27, 28, 80; "Memories of the Boston Santa Fé River Ranches as told by Melda Bassett," 6, 14. Kersey, *Florida Seminoles*, 66–67, 78–79, 86, 124; "Seminoles, Inc.," 15–17; Akerman, 244; "Seminoles Find Wealth in Cattle," *FMNP*, 1 February 1950.

15. "A Range War," 21; Mormino and Pozzetta, 273, 278–80; "Florida Dairy Hall of Fame," *TT*, 4 March 1979; McGoun, 83–88.

16. "Dairy Empire," *OS*, 13 November 1997; "Dairy Farms," *USAT*, 7 August 2003.

17. "Fifty People Who Changed South Florida Business," *MH*, 20 December 1999; *OS*, 13 November 1997; Halberstam, 158–66; "People in Cracker Politics," *JCF*, 27 January 1950; "Blessings," *SPT*, 13 July 2003.

18. *OS*, 6 October 1996, 13 November 1997, 4 October 1998, Lake Sentinel edition; *FT*, May 1998, 21; "Dairyman Ups Profit in Labor Pinch," 37; *FSA 1998*, 341; *Atlas of Florida*, 169; Jeff Klinkenberg, "And on This Farm There Was No Stink," *SPT*, 21 December 2000; McGoun, 83–88; NASS, *2002 Census of Agriculture, Florida*.

19. Song quoted from "Sunshine, Soil and Citrus," *OS*, 26 December 1999; Crosby, 151; McPhee, 6–7, 12, 62–66.

20. Hughes, 243–64; Starr, *Inventing*, 140–45, 163–64.

21. Lessing, 211; "Citrus Industry," *TMT*, 18 January and 4 February 1948; McPhee, 118; Bachus, 165; *BW*, 12 August 1944, 50; *TDT*, 1 July 1944; *NYT*, 19 September 1948; "Million-Box Record," *SPT*, 15 October 1950.

22. "Squeezing Gold from the Groves," *NYT*, 23 February 2000; McPhee, 8, 18–21.

23. "'Uncle Jeff First to Ship Citrus?" *MH*, 22 March 1946; Daniel, 61–87; "Machines," *NYT*, 22 March 2004.

24. Joy Dickinson, "The Doc Says It's Good," *OS*, 26 December 1999.

25. Ibid.

26. Davidson, 50–51, 107; Shofner, *Apopka*, 264.

27. MacDowell, 6, 15, 19; *NYT*, 8 June 2000; *LL*, 6 June 2000; "Orange Juice Pioneer," *OS*, 16 July 2000.

28. "American Housewife," *TMT*, 8 April 1950; "Citrus Peel," *TMT*, 17 September 1950; "Concentrate Sales Up Again," *TMT*, 6 October 1950; "Frozen Asset," *NYT*, 30 January 1954; "Cuts Frozen Food Sale," *NYT*, 4 March 1952.

29. *NYT*, 6 December 1949; *OS*, 27 January 1946; Morris and Morris, 554–55, 557.

30. *TDT*, 11 August 1950; McPhee, 12–13.

31. *Classic Crates from Florida*, 11, 22–27; official quoted in *TDT*, 20 April 1950; *TMT*, 11 June and 1 August 1950; "Growing Half a Billion," *FG*, January 1950, 30; *OS*, 5 July 1954; *NYT*, 8 November 1981; Miracle, "Family," 68–71; *FSA 1999*, 331; McPhee, 10; Bachus, 165.

32. Swanson, 155; Bacon, 2:232; *TMT*, 7 November 1950; "Citrus Prosperity Lures Many," *TMT*, 20 March 1957; "A Corporate Squeeze Turns the Citrus Business Sour," 65–70; *TT*, 7 March, 17 April, 23 June 1978, 23 July 1999; *OS*, 29 March 1998; *SPT*, 7 December 1981, 21 July, 26 August 1998; Pendergrast, 293; McPhee, 138–39, 144; Robison and Andrews, 136; Bacon, 2:191; "Minute Maid," *NYT*, 13 December 1949; "Minute Maid Planning $5,000,000 Grove Purchase," *TMT*, 13 November 1954, 9 September 1956; "Minute Maid Buys Out Dr. Phillips," "Minute Maid Buys Groves of Edwards at $2,400,000," *TMT*, 24 May 1953; "Miss America Pushes Florida Citrus on Television," *TMT*, 26 April 1953.

33. "Tropicana," *TT*, 7 March, 17 April, 23 June 1978; *SPT*, 7 December 1981; "PepsiCo Now Owns Tropicana," *SPT*, 26 August 1998; "Tropicana," 28–34; "Hall of Famer," *BH*, 10 January 1987. In 2003, Tropicana Products Inc. announced it was moving its Bradenton headquarters to Chicago. "Tropicana Relocates," *TT*, 3 December 2003.

34. McPhee, *TT*, 23 July 1999; Miracle, "Family," 68.

35. *TMT*, 10 February 1950; *TT*, 19 August 1981, 6 November 1994, 23 July 1999; Stavro, "Griffin," 52–54; *PBP*, 2 December 1989; *SPT*, 28 November 1977; McPhee, 140–49.

36. "Florida's Biggest Citrus Produced," *FG*, May 1999, 8–12.

37. *FSA 1999*, 331; *U.S. Census of Agriculture: 1950*, Florida, 111–13; O. White, "Frozen Out," 79–80; *NYT*, 19 January 2000; *TT*, 30 December 1989, 27 May 2000; *SPT*, 13 March and 19 June 2000; Adams, 17–23; Attaway, 151–301.

38. "From Florida Oranges," *NYT*, 8 November 1991; Miracle, "Family," 70.

39. McPhee, 90–108; Shofner, *Brevard County*, 1:35–36, 84, 136, 180.

40. Adams; *U.S. Census of Agriculture: 1950*, Florida, 111–13; Stephenson, 187; "Sunny Days," St. Petersburg History Museum; *SPT*, 12 March 1948, 7 December 1959; "Some Day," *SPT*, 19 October 1950; "Pinellas Citrus," *SPT*, 18 October 1950; "Multi-Million $$$ Citrus Season," *SPT*, 6 September 1953; "Pinellas County Ranks Seventh in State," *SPT*, 7 September 1953; "Sunny Florida," *SPT*, 1 February 2004.

41. *U.S. Census of Agriculture, 1950*, 112; O. White, "Frozen Out," 79–83; J. Jackson;

Shofner, *Orlando*, 165; Swanson, 33, 34–38, 159–68; Robison and Andrews, 127–28; *USAT*, 23 October 1989; Painton, 58; agriculture agent quoted in *WP*, 15 February 1985; "Citrus Tower Opens Today," *TMT*, 14 July 1956; "Orange Blossoms Fade," *OS*, 16 December 2002; NASS, *2002 Census of Agriculture, Florida*, Orange County.

42. *TT*, 30 December 1989, 12 September 1990; Hughes, 245–52; Klinkenberg; R. Moore.

43. Klinkenberg; Attaway; O. White, "Frozen Out."

44. LaVigne; O. White, "Frozen Out," 79–83; Willson, "Anita Bryant," 29–30; "Brazil's José Cutrale," *WSJ*, 22 January 1987.

45. Willson, "Anita Bryant," 29–32; "Orange Juice," *NYT*, 7 March 1975; "Squeezed Out?" *WSJ*, 12 March 1987; "A Squeeze on Citrus," *SFSS*, 10 November 2003.

46. "Grapefruit Outlook Dark," *TMT*, 10 November 1950; "Squeezed Out?" *WSJ*, 12 March 1987; "Non-Cola Combat," *SPT*, 7 November 2000; "Putting the Squeeze on Frozen O.J.," *TT*, 13 February 1999; "The Squeeze on O.J. Sales," *ACJ*, 2 July 1988; "Healthy Juice Line," *TT*, 17 January 2004; "Seeded Bliss," *SPT*, 29 January 2005.

47. Hahamovitch; "Growing Half a Billion," *FG*, January 1950, 30; *U.S. Census of Agriculture: 1950*, vol. 1, pt. 8, *Florida*, 12–21; "Carloads of Venice Cucumbers," *TMT*, 30 April 1950.

48. "Frozen Bean Demand," *FG*, March 1950, 10–27.

49. *FSA 1999*, 318; "Florida Tomato Growers," *TT*, 4 October 2000.

50. *TMT*, 14 May 1950; "Glades Farmers," "Immokalee Farm," *TMT*, 28 October 1951; Miracle, "Family," 72; "Top Ten Florida Vegetable Growers," *FG*, May 2000, 17; *TT*, 3 May 1989; "Immokalee," *NDN*, 6 March 1973; Tebeau, *Last Frontier*, 192–206, 258.

51. *MH*, 21 March 1946; Stavro, 63–69; *SPT*, 28 November 1977; Robison and Andrews, 154–55; *TT*, 12 June 1989, 3 May 1989; Miracle, "Family," 72; Morey, 14–15; Hahamovitch, 121; Wehr; NASS, *2002 Census of Agriculture, Florida*.

52. *SPT*, 5 December 1971, 23 July 1978, 4 June 2000; Selz, "How Lucky Can You Get?" 30–39; *TMT*, 29 September, 1 October 1950; Biographical Folder, Lykes Family, USFSC; *Glades County*.

53. "Zellwood Mucklands," *TT*, 18 June 1950; *Florida: A Guide*, 532.

54. *WSJ*, 20 October 1999, Florida edition; Shofner, *Apopka*, 262, 275, 282, 284–85; Robison and Andrews, 246; *TT*, 6 July 1998, 24 October 1999; "New Life for a Lake," *SPT*, 9 January 1994; *FT*, December 1988, 12; Maxwell, "Farm Workers Displaced, Then Forgotten," *SPT*, 8 October 2003; "Harvest of Pain," *OS*, 19 May 2002; Riley, 137–47.

55. Hurston, *Their Eyes*, 123–24; Douglas, 228; Hanna and Hanna, 302–26; Will, 282–90; *TT*, 28 October 1951; Heitmann, 45–53.

56. McCally, "Cane Cutters," 64–90; *OS*, 14 May 1995; P. Roberts, 56; *U.S. Census of Agriculture: 1950, Florida*, 103; "Glades Land Boom," *TT*, 19 March 1961; *MH* in *SPT*, 29 September 2000; McCally, *Everglades*, 169; Mormino, "World War II," 330–31.

57. P. Roberts, 54–68; McCally, *Everglades*, 170–74; Wilkinson, 1–52; Hiaasen, "Sugar Bosses," *MH*, 30 April 1995; "Taxpayers Foot Bill for Big Sugar," *MH*, 21 March 2002; "Sugar Program," *NYT*, 6 May 2001; *TT*, 3 May 1989; *MH*, 16 July 1999; McGoun, 160–65; "State Sugar Industry Booms," *TT*, 22 March 1961; *Time* quoted in Bartlett and Steele, 81; "Munich in the Canefields"; "Sugar Forfeitures," *SPT*, 29 September 2000; "Sweet

Contributions," *USAT,* 19 August 2002; "Big Sugar Seeks Bailout, Gives Money," *WSJ,* 27 April 2000; NASS, *2002 Census of Agriculture,* table 1.

58. Official quoted in Auerbach; Mintz, 19–74; *SPT,* 25 January 1979; Wilkinson, 23–28, 39–48; *TDT,* 13 June 1950; Petrow, 15–21.

59. Dewey, 565–603; Blakey, *Florida Phosphate,* 90–129; Selz, "Why," 68–74; *TT,* 20 September 1981, 29 March 1982, 12 August 1984; *SPT,* 25 August 1984; "Life in Bone Valley," *TT,* 16 August 1999; "Waste Water from Miners," *TMT,* 17 November 1954; "Pollution of Peace River," *TMT,* 20 March 1950; "Mining Is Mainstay," 110–112; Keuchel, 170–71; "Phosphate," *WSJ,* 21 October 1968; "Coronet Says Plant Closing Just Business," *SPT,* 31 January 2004.

60. Dewey, 565–603; Blakey, 99–144; Selz, 68–74.

61. Stokes, 104–5; "Twilight," "Boom and Bust," and "Planners Look to Future As Polk's Phosphate Dries Up," *LL,* 15, 16, 17 October 2000.

62. "A Least Worse Pollution Solution," editorial, *TT,* 1 July 2003; "Severance Tax," editorial, *TT,* 29 October 2003; "A $140 Million Mess," *SPT,* 6 July 2003; Reidy, 21–32; "See County's Deep Harbor," *FMNP,* 19 February 1950; "Phosphate Nightmare," editorial, *SPT,* 21 March 2003; "State May Dump in Gulf," *SPT,* 15 March 2003; "Mountains of Trouble," *TT,* 17 March 2001.

63. "Mayo Regime," *TMT,* 16 April 1950; "Commissioner Mayo Builds Political Machine," *TMT,* 27 January 1956; Pepper quoted in *TDT,* 22 and 24 April 1950; Colburn and Scher, 19–20; Colburn and deHaven-Smith, 126–28; Blake, 278–82; *CCN,* 5 December 1946; *WSJ,* 3 February 1967; "Texts of Talks by Governor Stevenson," *NYT,* 12 October 1952; Daniel, 39–87; "Florida's Farms under U.S. Thumb," *TMT,* 16 December 1952; "U.S. Farm Aid Mushrooms," *TMT,* 18 December 1953; Top Forty Subsidy Recipients in Florida, *www.ewg.org.* Environmental Working Group; "Failing Farmers Profit from U.S. Subsidies," *NYT,* 24 December 2000; "Florida's Farming Interests," *SPT,* 15 April 2001; NASS, *2002 Census of Agriculture, Florida.*

64. *SPT,* 21 July 1988; *SAR,* 4 June 1950, 4 June 1988, 25 September, 21 October 1989, 28 December 1990; *FTU,* 9 May 1954 and 20 June 1998.

65. *TMT,* 14 May 1950, 28 October 1951; "Glades Labor Migration," *TMT,* 17 May 1953; reporter quoted in "Tiny, Filthy Shacks," and "Meagerest Facilities," *TMT,* 19 November 1954 and 18 November 1954.

66. "Harvest of Shame" aired over the Columbia Broadcasting System Television Network on 25 November 1960.

67. Hahamovitch, 200–205; Jones, 167–204; Kirby, *Rural,* 283–85; *MH,* 19–22 May 1963, 25 November 1990, Palm Beach edition; "Seasonal Learning," *TT,* 14 May 2000; Pendergrast, 293; Rimer, "Spotlight"; Nordheimer, "Poverty-Scarred"; *CT,* 24 June 1991; "Migrants Ride on Risky Roads," *MH,* 8 January 2005.

68. Nordheimer, "Poverty-Scarred"; Rimer; "Spotlight"; *TT,* 7 December 2000; Riley, 169.

69. Hahamovitch, 200; "Life Is Worth Dollar a Day in the Fields," *MH,* 18 March 1973; Kilborn, "Immigrants," "Little Mexico," *WHA,* 11 February and 25 March 1971; McPhee, 54–58; "Puerto Rican Migrants," *TMT,* 22 July 1954; "Filthy Labor Camps," *TMT,* 18 April 1955; "Changing Face of Rural Florida," *FTU,* 11 March 2001.

70. Wilkinson, 167–200; McCally, *Everglades,* 164–74.

71. *FSA 1999*, 3–6, 314–20; Hahamovitch, 121–22; C. Johnson, "Palm Beach County," 46–50; *FLN*, 28 January 1973; Mansfield, 22–37; "Economy's Explosion Skips Town," *TT*, 8 October 2003; "Hanging Awakens Ghosts of Past," *SPT*, 28 August 2003; NASS, *2002 Census of Agriculture, Florida*, Palm Beach County.

72. "100 Years of Fortitude," *MH*, 15 November 2003; *MH*, 3 March 1949; *FSA 1999*, 305–6, 314–20; "South Florida: Backyard to the World," *NYT*, 7 June 2000; Crouch; NASS, *2002 Census of Agriculture, Florida*, Dade County.

73. *FSA 1999*, 305–6, 314–20; Andrews, 303–25; *SPT*, 20 September 1999 and 11 December 1959; *TT*, 28 June 1981, 8 March 1994, 4 October 2000; information provided by Chip Hilton, executive director of the Florida Strawberry Growers' Assoc., 2000; "New Crops Ahead for Plant City," *Florida Business*, October 1988, 40–45; NASS, *2002 Census of Agriculture, Florida*, Hillsborough County.

74. Mormino and Pozzetta, 146, 278; *SPT*, 19 May 1974, 4 September 1989; "Ruskin Turns 'Flop' into Success," *TDT*, 22 April 1948; "Labor Camp Owner Found Guilty in Servitude Case," *TT*, 23 July 1974; "Their Land," *SPT*, 2 February 2004.

75. Nelson, 47–49; Fitzgerald, 203–43; *TT*, 26 September 1974, 26 June 1975, 30 March, 24 June 1978, 4 October 1999; *TDT*, 10 April 1959; *Tampa Weekly Planet*, 21–27 October 1999; "Contrast and Connections," *TT*, 7 April 2001.

76. *SFSS*, 4 May 1999; McIver, *Fort Lauderdale*, 49–50, 99, 138, 146, 154; *FSA 1999*, 12; NASS, *2002 Census of Agriculture, Florida*, Broward County.

77. "Old Time Cracker Farms," *MH*, 2 April 1960, 27 March 1946; Morey, 14.

78. *A Study of the Economic Impact*, 92; *FSA, 1999*, 223; Vogel, "No. 1," 65; "Mexican Competition Bad News for Florida," *SLT*, 26 March 2003; "Producing Peril," *TT*, 17 March 2003; "Florida Feels NAFTA's Pinch," *TT*, 15 February 2003; "How Their Garden Grows," *SPT*, 27 July 2003; "Not Your Average Vegetable," *FG*, March 2000, 16–17; "Discovering Flower Power," *TT*, 25 May 2002; "The Big Squeeze," *MH*, 9 December 2002.

Chapter 7. Machines in Paradise: Techno Florida

1. D. Taylor, 46–69.

2. "Use of Atomic Bomb to Break Up Hurricanes," *FLDN*, 1 November 1953; "Hurricane Bombing Base Offered," *MH*, 9 August 1945; "Courthouse Square Strollers," *TMT*, 24 June 1947; "WW II Legacy Haunts Florida," *TT*, 14 September 2003.

3. Gordon Patterson's *The Mosquito Wars* is a definitive study of this important topic. See *SAR*, 16 July 1945; Michael Gannon to author, regarding the Indian River, 5 January 2004.

4. *CN*, 17 August 1945; *VBNJ*, 17 August 1945; *BH*, 6 August 1945; Wright quoted in *SH*, 26 April 1945; *MH*, 13 May 1945; *TDT*, 15 July 1945; Bacon, 2:126; Swanson, 237.

5. *FTU*, 19 September 1945; *FLDN*, 8 March, 28 August 1945; *FMNP*, 7 August 1945; *VBPJ*, 12 July 1946; *SN*, 8 March 1945; *TMT*, 5 April, 31 May 1945, 11 July 1946; *MH*, 13 May 1945.

6. "Don't," *Cocoa Tribune*, 26 July 1945; "Georgia Puts Quarantine on Floridians," *TMT*, 19 June 1946; "City Starts DDT Spraying," *TMT*, 15 July 1946; *BH*, 20 August 1945; *TSA*, 1 September 1945; *CN*, 20 July 1945; *TDT*, 21 April 1950.

7. "Careful with DDT," *Time*, 22 October 1945; see also *TMT*, 16 July 1947, 15 December 1948.

8. Walters, 20, 27, 44; Manning, 106–13.

9. Carson, 15; Patterson, *Mosquito Wars*, 713, 725; Derr, 341.

10. Raymond Arsenault's seminal article remains the best study of this topic, "The End of the Long Hot Summer," 616, 623–24; "Weather Influences," *FTU*, 4 August 1999; "What Did We Do without Air Conditioning?" *MH*, 15 May 1977; Dolan, 94–101, 174–79, 198–99.

11. Arsenault, "Long Hot Summer," 599–601, 603–10; "More Air Conditioning," *TMT*, 10 April 1935, 26 November 1999; "Millennium Moment: Nov. 26, 1933"; "Air-Conditioned Train," *FTU*, 1 August 1998; "Chrysler Airtemp Installed in Tampa Home," *TDT*, 18 April 1938; Owner of Raleigh Hotel, letter in Parks and Bush, 113; "Capital Cooling," *TMT*, 21 April 1953; "Air Conditioning for Three in Cabinet," *TMT*, 5 June 1953; "Florida Poultry," *TMT*, 11 August 1941; Robison and Andrews, 248.

12. "Philco One-Room Air-Conditioner Here," *MH*, 19 March 1946; "Local Stores Announce Plans for Miami's Postwar Future," *MH*, 15 August 1945.

13. Akerman, 3, 110; "100 Years of Cool," *TT*, 14 July 2002; "Air Conditioning," *SPT*, 20 August 1978; "Year-Round Air Conditioning," *SPT*, 15 March 1953; Laux, 51.

14. "Air Conditioner Sales Soar," *MH*, 10 July 1969; "Florida Now Fourth in Air-Conditioned Homes," *FLN*, 1 July 1961; "Sears," *OS*, 1 July 1954; "Webb's City," *SPT*, 19 July 1958; *OS*, 17 June 1962; Olson quoted in "100 Years of Cool."

15. MPLSC, "Air conditioning files," Agnew Welch Papers; "Can Miami Keep Its Cool without Air Conditioning," *MH*, 22 September 1974; *TT*, 14 July 2002; Charles Buchanan, interview, 29 April 2004.

16. Akerman, 158; "Sunny Dade Coolest Spot in U.S." *MH*, 28 May 1961; Kleinberg, *Miami Beach*, 153; "Credit Air Cooling for Summer Tourism," *MH*, 9 June 1957; "Dade County's the Coolest," *MH*, 12 June 1960.

17. Arsenault, 611; "Air Conditioning Now an Essential," *MH*, 4 June 1961; *Nineteenth Census of the United States, 1970: Census of Population and Housing*, vol. 1, *Housing*, pt. 11, Florida, Census Tracts, Jacksonville, Fort Lauderdale–Hollywood, Miami, table H-2; *Twentieth Census of the United States, 1980: Census of Housing*, pt. 11, *Florida*, tables 60, 64, 65, 77; vol. 1, *Housing Characteristics*, pt. 11, *Florida*, table 44; "Cooling Off," *TT*, 25 May 1975, Florida Accent; Chris Warren to author, 18 April 2004.

18. *1980 Census of Housing*, table 54.

19. Ibid., table 77.

20. Ibid., "Public Housing to Get Central Air," *FTU*, 16 September 1998; 2000 Census, "Overview: Most Populous States"; Nordheimer, "Development Boom"; Derr, 212.

21. Morris and Morris, 633–35; "Utility," *FTU*, 19 March 2002; 2000 Census, "Overview: Most Populous States"; "AC Leads Energy Use," *OS*, 21 June 2002.

22. Arsenault, "Long Hot Summer," 616, 622–23, quoted 628; Derr, 340; "Cooling Gables' Noise," *MH*, 23 March 1966; "Air Conditioning Men Boiling Over 'Hush' Law," *MH*, 8 July 1956; "Florida Switched on AC," *MH*, 17 May 1990; neighbor quoted in "They're Cool to Cooler," *MH*, 12 October 1959, Broward edition; Faragher, 149–71; "'Florida Room' Becoming Popular," *TMT*, 19 February 1956; Dolan, 205–6, 227–28.

23. "Program to Air Condition All Polk Schools Proposed," *TT*, 27 September 1973, Heartland edition; "Air Conditioning Plan Lambasted," *BH*, 21 February 1961; "Fifteen Schools to Get Air Conditioning," *MH*, 27 September 1973; "Should Florida Build Air Conditioned Schools?" *FT*, January 1961, 15; "Cooling Off on Air Conditioning," *TT*, 25 May 1975, Florida Accent; "Longest Days," *SPT*, 31 August 2003; journalist quoted in "Sunshine and Climate," *TMT*, 27 February 1955.

24. "Parking," *MH*, 24 March 1946; "Buses Wave of Future," *FTU*, 13 May 1999; "Florida and the Horseless Carriage," 12–20; 1988 Dept. of Highway statistics; "Old Miami Trolleys," *MN*, May 1984; "Hail and Farewell," *TMT*, 4 August 1946; Arsenault, *St. Petersburg*, 310–11; "Suncoast Has Over 100% Hike in Motor Vehicles," *SPT*, 1 March 1960; "Bob's Barricades," *SPT*, 25 April 1989.

25. "Work Progresses on Huge Jacksonville Expressway," *TMT*, 27 April 1952; "Gilmore Bridge," *FTU*, 6 June 1954; Ward, 243; "Big Expressway to Change Way of Life," *TT*, 3 July 1961; "Jacksonville Expressway," *TT*, 10 May 1959; "Collins Opens Link in Jacksonville Expressway," *TT*, 10 May 1959; Crooks, *Jacksonville: The Consolidation*, 5–6.

26. Http://www11.myflorida.com/publicinformationoffice/historicaldotphotos/bridges/halifax.hi; "Pinellas-Manatee Bridge," *TMT*, 24 May 1953; "Tampa Bay Skyway to Open Today," *TMT*, 6 September 1954; Ward, 243; "One of World's Most Unusual Bridges," *TMT*, 2 January 1953; "Skyway Pursuit," *SPT*, 4 February 1987; "Bridges Are Down-and-Out Relics," *OS*, 30 November 2003; Bragg, "On Florida Bridge"; "An Amazing Span," *TT*, 6 September 2004.

27. "Pike," *MH*, 26 January 1957; "Drive Pike to Believe It!" *MH*, 18 January 1957; McIver, "Alligator Alley," in *Dreamers*, 209–18.

28. Kendrick, 19; "Routes Set for Florida's 1,100 Miles of Interstate Roads, Costing $500 Million," *TMT*, 26 January 1957; "Interstate Roads Are Coming," *SPT*, 9 October 1958; Sikes, 320–21; "Plans for Big Tampa Expressway," *TMT*, 15 September 1956; Lewis, 156, 166.

29. "Routes Set for Florida's 1,100 Miles of Interstate," *TMT*, 26 January 1967; "New Section of I-75 to Open," *TT*, November 1967; Thomson, 503–4; *http://www.ihoz.com/I75.html*; interview with William Cramer, 2 September 2003; "Cramer Sees Quick Extension of I-75," *TT*, 20 December 1967; "Volpe Asked to Change Route," *SPT*, 8 January 1969; "I-75 Extension To Include Belt around St. Pete," *TT*, 24 November 1968; "Cramer Playing Politics?" *TT*, 25 August 1968.

30. Wilder, "Big Expressway to Change Way of Life," *TT*, 3 July 1961; "One Solid City," *OS*, 6 October 1961; Robison and Andrews, 259; "Campaign for the Corridor," *TT*, 25 January 2004.

31. "Building I-4," *TT*, 28 April 1996; "Interstate Roads," *TT*, 25 September 1994; "Many Ybor City Streets," *TT*, 3 June 1962; author's interview with Díaz, 3 May 1980; "What About Negroes Uprooted?" *MH*, 4 March 1957; Mohl, "Race and Space," 100–158; "A Place Called Parramore," *OS*, 15 December 2003; "Officials Hike through Wilds of Loxahatchee Hunting I-95 Route." *MH*, 17 May 1974, Palm Beach edition; "I-95's Rumble Disrupts Lives," *PBP*, 5 January 1976; "Country Hamlet," *OS*, 17 February 2004.

32. Bragg, "Living in Another World."

33. Mohl, "'Concrete Monsters,'" 29.

34. Kowinski, 42; Patton, 171–74, 204; Schlosser, 8; Langdon, 73–108; Lewis, 168–169, 282–85.

35. Patton, 188–89; "Survival of the Fittest," *SPT,* 4 May 2003.

36. K. Jackson, 248–50; Patton, 231–33; Kay 232.

37. "I-95, the East Coast's River of Commerce," *NYT,* 29 December 2000; "Interstates," *SLPD,* 4 August 1996; Patton, 177–78; K. Jackson, 248–50, 300; "Facing Mother Nature's Fury," *USAT,* 24 July 2000; Kay, 232–33.

38. E. Bennett, 451–67; *New York Sun,* 16 February 1942; "Old Soldier Trade," *MH,* 27 March 1946.

39. *http://www.hsmv.state.fl.us/reports/crash,* "Traffic Crash Facts 2000"; "All Roads Lead to Aggravation," *OS,* 18 December 2001; "Lauderdale, Miami Top in Pedestrian Fatalities," *SFSS,* 23 April 2003; "Average Commute in State Is 26 Minutes," *TT,* 27 May 2002; "Live in the Slow Lane," *TT,* 10 May 2001; "Drive to Work Grows Longer," *OS,* 19 June 2002; "South Florida Is L.A. East," *MH,* 24 April 2003; "Impalement South Florida's Special Highway Hazard," *NYT,* 12 October 1999; "Study of Nation's Worst Traffic," *NYT,* 9 May 2001; *USAT,* 9 March 1999; "Impalement," *NYT,* 12 October 1999; "Lauderdale, Miami Top the Nation," *SFSS,* 23 April 2003; "Florida's Busy Roads Deadly for Walkers," *USAT,* 3 December 2004.

40. Kunstler, 131; Virrick quoted in Mohl, "Race and Space," 124; "Parking in Miami Is a Chronic Year-Round Headache," *MH,* 24 March 1946; Kay, 238–39; Foglesong, *Married,* 21.

41. Billitteri and Selz, 51–56; *1990 Census of Population and Housing, Summary Population and Housing Characteristics, Florida,* table 15, 186; "2000 Metrorail Boardings"; "Busiest Urban Subway/Rail Systems," *USAT,* 15 March 2004; Crooks, *Jacksonville: The Consolidation,* 120, 196–98; 2000 Census, DP-3, Profile of Selected Economic Characteristics, Florida.

42. *http://www.driveinmovie.com/fl;* "Lake Worth Drive-In," *TT,* 26 May 2002; "Keeping the Trail Alive," *PBP,* 6 January 1993; K. Jackson, 255–56.

43. Roger Moore, "Twilight Time," *OS,* 20 October 2002; "Memories Vanish," *PBP,* 19 September 1991; Baker, 14.

44. "Twilight Time"; "Once-Endangered Drive-Ins Alive," *FMNP,* 19 November 2000.

45. "Not the Last Picture Show," *USAT,* 31 August 2001; "Pasco Drive-In," *TT,* 5 July 2003; "Memories by the Carload," *SPT,* 3 July 2000; salesman quoted in Johnson, "The Changing Picture," 35.

46. Langdon 35, 59–77, 94–97; McLamore; "Now in Tampa! Burger King," *TT,* 13 June 1955; Patton, 182, 188–204; Cohen, 402; "Background of Burger King Corp."; http://www.starbucks.com/retail; Jakle and Sculle, *Fast Food,* 116–17, 170–71, 176; "Golden Arches," *SPT,* 8 February 2005.

47. Schlosser, 3, 61; *http://www.burgerking.com;* Schlosser, 3; "Starbucks," *SPT,* 3 September 2002; "Fast Food Not Welcome Here," *OS,* 30 September 2003; J. White, 75–78.

48. "Vestiges of Separation," *FMNP,* 23 February 2004; "Blazing a Path," *SFSS,* 20 February 2004; Crooks, *Jacksonville: The Consolidation,* 21.

49. "Eight Negro Ministers 'Sit' at Lunch Counter," *MH,* 5 March 1960; "Negroes Stage Lunch Strikes over Florida," *MH,* 3 March 1960; "Negroes in Tampa Sit-Down," *TT,* 1 March 1960.

50. "South Florida Designer Abandoning Objectionable 'Strip Type Centers,'" *MH*, 5 September 1954; Cohen, 1050–81; K. Jackson, 259; Kowinski, 34.

51. Kowinski, 34; Cohen, 1050–81; "Britton Plaza," *TMT*, 16 August 1956; "Hollywood Gets Two Big Shopping Centers," *MH*, 14 May 1960, Broward edition.

52. Kowinski, 33–55; K. Jackson, 257–61; Cohen, 276–78; Farrell, International Council of Shopping Centers cited, xi–xii, "Florida Fourth in Shop Centers," *TT*, 20 May 1973.

53. *Herald* quoted in "Big New Shopping Areas," *MH*, 4 March 1962; "Two Shopping Centers Planned," *MH*, 27 November 1955; "Hialeah Shopping Center Opened," *MH*, 24 November 1956; "Coral Gate Center," *MH*, 5 September 1954; "Battle of the Shopping Centers," *MH*, 15 November 1959; "Richards Opens at 163rd Street," *MH*, 7 April 1957; "Davis Plans South's Largest Shopping Center," *TMT*, 5 May 1957.

54. "Bayshore: Mecca of Beauty," *BH*, 31 October 1962; "Cortez Plaza's Birthday," *BH*, 1 February 1961; "A Look Back at the Cortez Plaza," *SHT*, 11 February 1988; "DeSoto Square Ready," *BH*, 14 August 1973; "Million Dollar Land Buy," *BH*, 5 November 1971; "Mall Openings," *BH*, 13 August 1973; "Change the Mix," *BH*, 2 October 2000.

55. "Shoppers Say Goodbye to Jordan Marsh," *OS*, 2 October 1991; Shofner, *Orlando*, 122, 123–25; "Colonial Plaza Opens Today," *OS*, 31 January 1956; "All the Cows Are Gone," *OS*, 25 October 1992; "Orlando to Get South's Biggest Mall," *FT*, June 1968, 44; Bacon, 2:193, 197, 200, 224.

56. Shofner, *Altamonte Springs*, 210–11.

57. "Dadeland's Formula," *WSJ*, 13 April 1987; "Dadeland," *MH*, 29 October 1987.

58. With the opening of Millenia in 2003, Orlando will have seven "super-regional" malls within 24 square miles. "Millenia," *OS*, 13 October 2002; "Sawgrass Mills Opens," *SFBJ*, 22 October 1990; "More Than Malls," *SFBJ*, 24 September 1999; "An Enormous Landmark," *NYT*, 24 December 2003.

59. "Plazas Share Design, Not Success," *TT*, 11 January 2004; "Front and Centro," *TT*, 29 September 2000; "Ybor's New Holy Shrine," *Tampa Weekly Planet*, 5–11 October 2000; "Miami Developer Eyes Ybor City," *TT*, 15 July 1996; "Miami's CoCoWalk," *MH*, 20 July 1998; "CoCoWalk," *MH*, 3 May 1998; quotation from "Best Reason NOT to Go to CoCoWalk," *Miami New Times*, 15 May 2003; "City's Tale of Renewal," *CSM*, 12 February 2004; Patton, 212, Farrell, 182.

60. "Wal-Mart Soars As Mall Crashes," *SPT*, 28–31 January 2004, Neighborhood Times; Sharon Zukin, "We Are Where We Shop," *NYT*, 28 November 2003.

61. "An Enormous Landmark Joins Graveyard of Malls," *NYT*, 24 December 2003; "A Retail Resurrection," *SPT*, 6 October 2003; "Empty Boxes," *SPT*, 4 March 2002; "Competition," *PBP*, 26 September 1988; "Palm Beach Mall," *PBP*, 21 April 1996; "Whither Palm Coast Plaza?" *PBP*, 27 March 1983; "K-Mart and Schools," *TT*, 30 December 2003; "Religious Conversion," *TT*, 8 February 2004, Pinellas edition; "Makeovers," *USAT*, 23 April 2003; "What Can Save This Mall?" *PBP*, 27 February 2004.

62. Liz Cohen's *A Consumers' Republic* brilliantly analyzes the impact of mass consumption upon American society. See also "Malls," *SPT*, 11 April 1976; "Shopping Malls, Our New Hangouts," *TT*, 4 February 1973, Florida Accent; Coles paraphrased in "Malls," *SPT*, 11 April 1976.

63. Ibid., 236–53, 265.

64. Pam Gibson to author, 24 April 2002, 9 December 2003; Kowinski, 33–34.

65. Gopnik, 104; "Goodbye to Jordan Marsh," *OS*, 2 October 1991; "Burdines Macy's," *SPT*, 25 January 2004; "Wal-Mart Soars As Mall Crashes," *SPT*, 28–31 January 2004, Neighborhood Times; "Burdines," *SPT*, 14 February 2005.

66. "Law on Portables Raises Alarm." *SPT*, 8 June 1997; "Portables," *SPT*, 9 February 2001.

67. "Glut of Portables," *OS*, 22 October 2004.

68. K. Jackson, 261–63; Hurley, 198–204; "Time Travel in a Trailer," *NYT*, 26 December 2003; "The Changing Image," *TT*, 13 February 1977, Florida Accent; *Fortune* and critic quoted in Kay, 210.

69. "Census on Wheels," *SPT*, 6 March 1961; "The Factory Built Home," *FT*, August 1971, 20–26; O'Hare and O'Hare, 26–32.

70. "Polk Mobile-izing," *TT*, 6 May 2002; "Suncoast Is Mobile Home Mecca," *SPT*, 19 October 1969; "Census on Wheels," *SPT*, 6 March 1961; "A Formula for Disaster," *TT*, 5 December 2004.

71. "Factory Built Home," 20; "Census on Wheels,"*SPT*, 6 March 1961; "Trailers—Compact Houses or Fat Vehicles?" *SPT*, 19 October 1959; "Trailer Parks Get Tax Break," *MH*, 12 January 1959; "Mobile Homes," in *Encyclopedia of Southern Culture*, 510; Hart, Rhodes, and Morgan, 110–21; "Houses On Wheels," *OS*, 6 September 1998; Hurley, 258–64.

72. Sydney Adler, interview, 22 December 2003; Santiago, 76–85; Crouthamel, 1–40; *Trailer Estates News*, April 1958; advertisements, Eaton Room, Manatee County Public Library.

73. "Walter Knorr," *Manatee Times*, 23 May 1977; "Mobile Homes," *SHT*, 23 June 1998; "Mobile Home Parks," *BH*, 26 August 1991; "Manatee Trailer Project Grows," *SPT*, 6 August 1956.

74. "Mobile Paradise," *SFSS*, 26 April 1996; "No Parking Zone," *SPT*, 28 July 2003; "Migrant Work," *SFSS*, 8 September 1993; "Suncoast Is Mobile Home Mecca," *SPT*, 19 October 1969; O'Hare and O'Hare, 32.

75. "At Pelican Lake, Birds of a Feather," *NYT*, 8 April 1999; Hart, Rhodes, and Morgan, 117–19; Hurley, xv; Santiago, 76–85; "High Rollers Only," *SPT*, 23 January 2004.

76. "Sun Sets on Sunnydale," *TT*, 27 August 2000; "Florida's Mobile Homes," *NYT*, 22 June 2003; Irby, "Trailer Trash," 182–95; "Largo's Rebirth," *SPT*, 10 July 2003; "S. Florida Losing Mobile Homes," *SFSS*, 18 June 2002; "Delray," *SFSS*, 9 November 1994; "Trailer Parks," *SFSS*, 28 August 1992; "South Florida Trailer Parks," *MH*, 10 December 2000; "Add Murder, Mayhem to Trailer Park's Credits," *SFSS*, 8 October 1995; "Delray's Trailer Law Hit," *MH*, 20 December 1960, Palm Beach edition; "No Parking Zone," *SPT*, 28 July 2003; Provenzo and Provenzo, 94.

77. *TDD*, 16 July 1942; "When Flying Was Caviar," *NYT*, 10 October 2003; Parks, 129, 202; "Admirers Mourn Decline of DC-3," *SPT*, 28 November 2003; "Sarasota, Bradenton Hail Direct New York Air Service," *TT*, 8 January 1956; "National Heralds Its First Sarasota to New York Flight," *SPT*, 8 January 1956.

78. "First Jet Airliner May Serve Miami," *MH*, 17 October 1950; "Florida Airports: How High Is Up?" *FT*, February 1971, 21–26; "Arrival of Jet Engines," *TT*, 11 August 1995.

79. "Ready for the World," *Dallas Morning News*, 2 January 2000; "Foreign Travelers,"

MH, 5 November 1973; "Florida's Ten Largest Airports," *FT*, June 1980, 74–76; Danese, 151, 153, 167.

80. Clary, "Wind Shear," 32–34; "More Airports Are Latin American Gateways," *MH*, 19 October 1999; "Airport Expansion," *SFSS*, 27 July 2000; "Airport Mess," *MH*, 17 October 1999; "Unwelcome Mat," *MH*, 18 October 1999; "A Debt Pit," *MH*, 19 October 1999; "Big Project Having Big Trouble," *MH*, 20 October 1999.

81. "International Air Traffic Ahead for City," *Orlando City Cupboard*, 29 May 1958; "Rickenbacker... Now!" *MH*, 2 July 1959; Shofner, *Orlando*, 138; *Greater Orlando Chamber of Commerce Statistical Data* (1960), 42; Rotundo, 41–57.

82. Foglesong, *Married*, 88; Bacon, 2:299–300; "Airports," *SPT*, 14 Sept. 1998; "Orlando's Airport," *SPT*, 27 Feb. 1995; "Old Air Force Base," *OS*, 19 Dec. 2001; "Growth at Full Throttle," *OS*, 15 Dec. 1999; "OIA Passes MIA," *MH*, 15 Feb. 2005.

83. "Drew Field with 15 Square Miles," *TMT*, 27 May 1945; "Training B-29 Crewmen," *TDT*, 10 July 1945; "MacDill Shifts to Big Peace Asset," *TMT*, 23 September 1945; "City Prepares for Possession of Drew Field," 7 March 1946; "Tampa Rapidly Gaining," *TMT*, 29 October 1950; "Jet Planes Put Tampa on Air Map," *TT*, 28 June 1960; "Tampa Places $30 Million Bet," c. 1971 clipping; journalist quoted in "Florida Chamber Prepares for Jet Age," *TT*, 1 September 1957; Danese, 71–72.

84. "Drew Field's Name Changed to International Airport," *TMT*, 16 October 1947; "Tampa Gets Cuban Air Line," *TMT*, 7 December 1950; "Elaborate Ceremonies Officially Open $800,000 Air Depot," *TT*, 16 August 1952; "Tampa Airport Steps into Jet Age," *TT*, 14 February 1961; "Tampa International Whizzes into 21st Century," *TT*, 14 April 1963; "Tampa International," *TT*, 14 April 1963; "Year-Old Airport Handles 4 Million," *Tampa Times*, 16 April 1972.

85. "New 'Cities' Springing Up around Airports," *USAT*, 25 September 2003; "It's Orlando vs. Charlotte," *OS*, 29 November 1992; "Airport's Growth Soaring," *SPT*, 14 June 2000; "Airports and Their Growth," *SPT*, 1 January 2000; Marling and Iyer quoted in John Leland, "Our Airports, Ourselves," *NYT*, 11 July 2004.

86. Danese, 71–72; "Aviation: Jacksonville," *TMT*, 9 April 1961; Finotti, "Wings," 61.

87. Finotti, "Wings," 56–62; "Fort Myers Has Big Future," *MH*, 23 April 1946; "Page Field Returned to Lee County," *TMT*, 13 April 1947; R. White, 36–37; "Air Travelers Scorn Tallahassee," *TDD*, 1947 clipping; "Small Cities Wrestle to Land Airline," *TT*, 4 June 2000.

88. *Census of Housing: 1950*, vol.1, *General Characteristics*, pt. 2, table 13; "WDAE to Begin FM Broadcasts," *TDT*, 15 November 1947.

89. "The First Television," *MH*, 21 March 1999. The author thanks Paul George for information about the Capitol.

90. "Television Arrives, 1949," in Parks and Bush, 113; Cohen, 292–344; Barnouw, 13–14, 113; "2,000 Sets in Miami Awaiting Television," *MH*, 6 March 1949.

91. Barnouw, 110–14; "Television Comes to Jacksonville," *FTU*, 11 October 1949; Orrick and Crumpacker, 303; Cohen, 302; "Maas Bros. Demonstration Brings Television to Tampa," *TMT*, 1 August 1947.

92. Bacon, 2:168. On 24 January 1957, the House of Television Opened on North Mills in Orlando; *1950 Census of Housing*, vol. 1, pt. 2, tables 12, 20; Laux, 51.

93. "250,000 Now Are Regular Viewers of WSUN-TV," *TMT*, 9 May 1954; "Oh Happy

Day!" *SPT*, 31 May 1953; "Gala Debut," 1 June 1953; "TV Boom in Florida Seen," 1950 clipping; Bacon, 2:168; R. White, 37; "Orlando Viewers Hail Local TV Reception," *OS*, 2 July 1954; "WDBO-TV" *OS*, 5 July 1954. WDBO Stood for "Way Down by Orlando"; "Piped-In TV Starts Next Week," *CCN*, 7 January 1960; "A Look Back at 30 Years of Local Television," *Suncoast Lifestyle*, Fall 2001, 39–40; R. Pierce, 196–201; Orrick and Crumpaker; "WCTV Opens Today," *TD*, 15 September 1955.

94. J. Patterson, 348–55; R. Pierce, 196–201; "The Reign of Ralph," *MH*, 21 March 1999; Putnam, 209–13, 237; Barnouw, 114, 142.

95. Leonard Brown, "Tampa Homes Make Room for TV," *TMT*, 1 November 1953.

96. "Is Green Bench TV on the Way Out?" *SPT*, 7 September 1953; "St. Petersburg Oldsters Change Way of Life," *TMT*, 28 June 1955; "City TV Viewers Still Miss Meals, Skip Bedtime, Ignore Friends," *SPT*, 6 September 1953; "Pinellas Trailer City Has Central TV," *TT*, 5 October 1958; Irby, "Trailer Trash," 194–95.

97. Copies of these films may be found at the St. Petersburg Historical Society and the Poynter Library at USF, St. Petersburg.

98. "Governor Hopefuls Set New Pattern," *MH*, 3 April 1960; Colburn and deHaven-Smith, 70; Wagy, 36–39; "Hillsborough Demos Blame TV," *TMT*, 7 November 1954; Center for Responsive Politics, *www.opensecrets.org/states/county*.

99. West, 1–69; Kersey, *Florida Seminoles*, 116–17; "First Airboat," *PBT*, 4 August 1955.

100. Kersey, *Florida Seminoles*; West, 92–116; McIver, *Dreamers*, 1:205–10.

101. "White Man's Ways Lure Seminoles," *MH*, 13 January 1946; Patsy West to author, 2 March 2004; "Road to Riches," *MH*, 11 May 2003.

102. "Road," *MH*, 11 May 2003; "Seminole Gambling," *SPT*, 19–21 December 1997.

Chapter 8. The Internationalization of Florida

1. *TT*, 28 November 1955; Bretos, 97–114; "Castro Promised Victory," *TT*, 2 January 1959; "Preserve Latin Culture," *TDT*, 29 July 1955; Watson, 4–68.

2. *MH*, 1 January 1950; *TMT*, 5 February 1950; Pérez, *On Becoming Cuban*, 432–44; "Four Cuban Airlines to Serve Florida," *MH*, 14 June 1950; Bretos, 110–23; "Cuba Day," *MH*, 1 September 1950; Garreau, *Nine Nations*, 171–72; Didion, 11–13; Rieff, 153–55; Sicius, 5–46.

3. Garreau, *Nine Nations*, 172–74; García, 13, 16–23; Didion, 13–14; Rieff, 144.

4. García, 23–26; *SPT*, 18 January 2000; *NYT*, 25 March and 2 April 2000; "'Pedro Pan' Priest Dies," *MH*, 23 March 2000; Eire, 341–73.

5. García, 37–45; *MH*, 20 November 1988, 23–24 November 1997, 23 December 1999; *SPT*, 28 November 1999; "Freedom Fights," *MH*, 7 April 1973.

6. García, 86–99; Canizares, 1–22; "Cubans Flock to Dedication of Shrine," *MH*, 3 December 1973.

7. Garreau, *Nine Nations*, 176–77; Portes and Stepick, 126–49; "Hispanics Lead New Boom," *OS*, 23 March 2001; García, 86–93; "How the Immigrants Made It in Miami," 88; "Havana, Fla.," *WSJ*, 11 December 1969.

8. Portes and Stepick, 18–37; García, 46–82; Didion, 36–48; Fabricio, 140–45; "The Legacy of Mariel," *MH*, 18 April 2000; "The Faces of Mariel," *MH*, 21 April 2000.

9. Rieff, 130–34; M. Dunn, 267–98; "Roots of a Riot," *WSJ*, 22 May 1980; "Cubans and Blacks in Miami," *WSJ*, 29 May 1980.

10. Portes and Stepick, 161; García, 74, 89, 114, 210–11; Didion, 63–64; Rieff, 130–35.

11. García, 70, 77, 147, 156; Portes and Stepick, 23, 24, 177, 183, 201, 314; Mohl, "Maurice Ferré," 302–27; Mohl, "Miami: The Ethnic Cauldron," 83–84; "Cuban Émigré Wins Election to U.S. House," *NYT,* 31 August 1989.

12. *MH,* 20 December 1999; "New Immigrant Majority," *MH,* 20 November 2001; Lipsitz, 213–16; "Born in U.S.A.? Not in Miami," *SPT,* 3 September 2003.

13. *MH,* 2 January, 9 March 2000; "Cup of Culture," *MH,* 23 June 2002; García, ix–x, "Rafters," *TT,* 5 September 2004.

14. *NYT,* 6 June, 13 July 1993, 31 January 1994; *OS,* 6 March 1991; *SPT,* 3 May 1982, 16 September 1999; *FT,* May 1998, 67; "Orlando Area Is Magnet for Puerto Ricans," *SPT,* 19 June 2003; "Mexican Migrants," *OS,* 5 November 2003; "Mexican Migrants Pass Cubans," *MH,* 27 November 2002.

15. "Hispanic Boom Reshapes Florida," *SPT,* 28 March 2001; "Census: Migrants Lead Dade Growth," *MH,* 9 March 2000; "Highest Immigration Rate Belongs to Dade," *MH,* 21 May 2003; U.S. Census Bureau, 2001 American Community Survey.

16. "Hispanic Population Surges North of Miami," *SPT,* 18 September 2003; *MH,* 6, 7, 17 March 1991, 9 March 2000; *NYT,* 20 August 1994; "How We've Changed," *MH,* 28 March 2000; "Census Illustrates Disparities," *SPT,* 24 May 2002; "Puerto Ricans," *TT,* 30 November 2003; Rohter; Burns, 152–71.

17. *WHA,* 11 February, 18 March, 25 March 1971; "Hispanic Boom," *SPT,* 28 March 2001; *Seventh Census of the State of Florida, 1945,* tables 2.5, 23, 24.

18. "State Growth Brings Hispanics," *SFSS,* 28 March 2001; 2000 Census; "Race Choices," *SFSS,* 28 March 2001; "Going Beyond Black and White," *NYT,* 9 November 2003; Swarns; Lipsitz, 15–16; "Diversity for Blacks" *OS,* 23 March 2003.

19. García, 105–6; Soruco, 34–35, 74–98; *NYT,* 24 April 2000; Fabricio, 141; *MH,* 15 June 2000; "Hispanic Newspapers Multiply," *TT,* 31 July 2003; "A World of News in South Florida," *MH,* 13 August 2001; "The Herald Is Wooing Cuban Readers, *WSJ,* 5 March 1987.

20. Soruco, 99–124; García, 106–8; Padilla quoted in García, 106; *MH,* 20 December 1999, 5, 19 March 2000; *WSJ,* 22 March 2000, Florida edition.

21. "La vida loca.com," *SPT,* 14 May 2000.

22. *Music City,* 141–45; Pérez, *On Becoming Cuban,* 198–210; "Calle Ocho a Global Draw," *MH,* 9 March 2000; García, 119; *MH,* 9 March 2000; "Hip-Hop Honcho," *MH,* 19 August 2001; "Latin Film Fests," *MH,* 6 April 2003; Cepeda, 32–34.

23. Mohl, "Asian Immigration," 261–86; "Florida's Alien Law," *TT,* 27 May 2002; "Asian Numbers Surge," *SFSS,* 24 May 2001.

24. Mogelonsky, 32–39; "Caribbean Surge Adds Blacks, Asians," *SFSS,* 28 May 2001; "Ancient God, New Country," *TT,* 27 October 2003; "Asian Concentration," *SPT,* 9 April 2001; "The Deities of Lynn Road," *SPT,* 24 October 2003; "Diversity Deepening: Asian Americans," *FMNP,* 27 July 2003; "Vietnamese," *SFSS,* 3 September 2000; "Thai Buddhist Monks," *MH,* 15 June 2003; Eck, 294; NASS, *2002 Census of Agriculture, Florida.*

25. "Arab Immigrants," *TT,* 25 November 2001; "Muslims Grow in Numbers," *OS,* 3 March 2002; Crooks, *Jacksonville After,* 84, 119; "Florida," Arab American Institute, 2003.

26. Eck, 226, 263; "New Faith," *OS*, 22 October 2003; "A Community of Faith," *SFSS*, 10 October 1999.

27. "Minorities Reach Majority in State Schools," *SPT*, 27 February 2004; "Hispanics Emerge," *OS*, 1 October 2004.

28. *OS*, 18 May 1997, 28 February 2000; "Hispanics Emerge," *OS*, 1 October 2004; "Hispanic Vote in Florida," *NYT*, 17 October 2004; Rieff, 224.

Chapter 9. The Beach

1. Matthew 7:26–27; Lenček and Bosker, 25–51.

2. Kaufman and Pilkey, 42; *NYT*, 18 June 1991; "Vanishing Habitat," *SPT*, 20 May 1990.

3. *Atlas of Florida*, 38–39, 213; Morris and Morris, 549, 600–601. The beach, of course, is not interchangeable with the coast and shore. The authors of *The Atlas of Florida* note, "Florida has approximately 2,000 miles of tidal shoreline, about 650 miles of which are true, high-energy beaches." According to another source, Florida possesses 825 miles of sandy beach. "Shrinking Shoreline," *Paradise at Risk*, 1; Tebeau and Marina, 4; Lenček and Bosker, 4–5.

4. "Beaches," *SPT*, 21 June 2002; "Life at the Water's Edge," *SHT*, 28 July 2002; drbeach.org.; "Beauty and the Beach," *SPT*, 14 July 2002.

5. Crosby, 18–19, 140; Denig, 271.

6. C. Pierce quoted in "Beach Development," *SFSS*, 14 November 1999.

7. Kasson, 37–54; Lenček and Bosker, 113–71; Aron, 15–45; Rowe, 26–43.

8. Crooks, *Jacksonville after the Fire*, 27, 106–7; "Big-City Rat Race," *FTU*, 19 August 1997.

9. C. Pierce, 249–50; Lenček and Bosker, 204–7; Akin, 145–46, 154–56; Derr, 42–45; James quoted in Rowe, 61.

10. American official quoted in Brackenridge, 14; *TMT*, 31 July 1911; *Pensacolian*, 16 July 1887; *Halifax Journal*, 30 September 1886; Graham, 202; Rogers, 134–35; Rogers and Ellis, 80, 92; Brooks, 26.

11. Lenček and Bosker, 136, 193–94; Fisher, 148; *SPT*, 4 June 1918, 18, 30, and 31 July 1918; *MH*, 18 November 1918; "Nymphs," *MH*, 9 July 1920; J. Davis, 101–2.

12. Douglas, 197; Foster, 200–222, Rogers quoted in Foster, 206; Kleinberg, *Miami Beach*, 22–24; Rothchild, *Up for Grabs*, 36–42.

13. Foster, 206–7.

14. Kleinberg, *Miami Beach*, 117–34; Hatton, 92–100; Patricios, 96–97, 112–13, 116–20; "Miami Beach," *NYT*, 17 March 1975; Luther, 106–7; "Garish Tourist Spot? Not Prim Delray," *MH*, 13 October 1950; "First Lady," *SPT*, 22 February 1940.

15. Gannon, *Operation Drumbeat*, 347–48; "German Subs," *MH*, 3 August 1945; Lenček and Bosker trace the development of sunscreens and tanning lotions in *The Beach*, 213–15.

16. Prior, 129–30.

17. Mormino, "Miami Goes To War," 10–15; "Miami Greatly Changed," *SDU*, 11 April 1943; GI quoted in Mormino, "World War II."

18. Mormino, "World War II," 334–35; Taylor, "Frogmen in Florida," 289–302; Lenček and Bosker, 196–97.

19. See Gary Monroe, *The Highwaymen*; Derr quoted in *NYT*, 27 November 2001; "A Street Named Desire," *MH*, 14 April 2002.

20. Sam Summers to Mrs. Robert Clark, 6 December 1949, FLHS. "Holiday Stirs Memories of King's Daytona Visit," *DBNJ*, 21 January 2003.

21. Manhattan Beach was located between Atlantic Beach and Mayport. Crooks, *Jacksonville after the Fire*, 107, 168; Crooks to author, 28 June 2002, 14 July 2002; Phelts, 1–7; Rogers, 105; "Photo May Unlock Secrets," *FTU*, 26 August 1998; "Negroes Want Bathing Beach," *TMT*, 14 October 1916; "Bethune Beach," *OS*, 31 March 1985; "Change of Face," *DBNJ*, 4 October 2003; Mason, 85–88; Barnes and Roberts, 42, Seay, 1–11.

22. Rymer, 10, 95–96; "Blacks Enjoy a Better Day on Beach," *OS*, 10 April 2002; "Bethune Beach," *OS*, 31 March 1985.

23. "Negroes Test Beach," *MH*, 10 May 1945; "Overtown," *MH*, 25 February 1985; Bragg, "Alliance"; M. Dunn, 160–61; "Negroes Ask for Own Beach at Palm Beach," *FS*, 21 June 1947.

24. "Segregation Still Rules," *BH*, 20 June 1954.

25. *Southern School News*, August 1958, 15; "Clearwater to Keep Negroes Off Beach," *TMT*, 3 July 1956; "Plan for Negro Recreation," *MH*, 4 July 1956, Key West edition; "Sarasota County Commission Rejects Siesta Key Site, Delays Negro Beach," *TMT*, 25 September 1956; "Sarasota Recommends Negro Beach," *TMT*, 15 September 1956; "Shoreline Reminiscent of Racism," *FMNP*, 22 February 2004.

26. Reeves interviewed in Pleasants, 204–5.

27. "Sarasota Acts to Ban Beach Integration," *TMT*, 21 August 1956; "House Passes Bill," *TMT*, 21 July 1956; "Sarasota Closes Beach," *TMT*, 23 October 1955; "Negroes Told: 'Find Beach, We'll Buy,'" *SPT*, 1 June 1955; Freeman, "Florida's Pure White Sands," 77–80; Freeman, "You Can't Stop Progress," 521–24; "Venice Moves to Block Canal If Negro Beach Put in Area," *TMT*, 5 October 1956; "Sarasota NAACP Leader Says Group Will Continue Drive for Integration of Beaches," *TMT*, 28 October 1955; "New Negro Invasion," *TMT*, 31 July 1956; "Sarasota Novelist," *TMT*, 26 September 1956.

28. "Negroes Drop Suit," *TMT*, 16 May 1956; "Delray Closes Negro Beach," *MH*, 5 July 1961, Broward edition; "Racial Tensions in Delray," *MH*, 4 July 1956, Broward edition; "Delray Gives Beach Outing to Tots," *FLDN*, 5 July 1956; "Anti-Riot Move," *NYT*, 29 May 1956; "Delray Asks Negro Area Cut Off," *TMT*, 6 June 1956; "Top Negroes Vetoed Deal," *MH*, 29 June 1956, Broward edition; "Delray Beach," *TMT*, 24 May 1956; "Delray Bans Gun Carrying," *TMT*, 26 May 1956.

29. Work, 23, 144–47; McIver, *Fort Lauderdale*, 150; "2,466–Acre Galt Tract Sold," *FLDN*, 23 October 1953; "Galt Property Sale Kills Plan of Negro Beach," *FLDN*, 27 October 1953. "Negroes Get Ocean Beach," *OS*, 4 July 1954; "Negroes to Get 1–Day Use," *TMT*, 4 July 1954; "Race Relations," *MH*, 21 June 1956, Broward edition; "Backward Step," *Time*, 22 July 1957, 16; "Seven Negroes Stage Wade-In," *MH*, 5 July 1961, Broward edition; "100 Negroes Stage Wade-In," *MH*, 24 July 1961; "Beach Development," *SFSS*, 14 November 1998.

30. Colburn, *Racial Change*, 82, 96–115, 322–25, T. Branch, 33–40, 141–43, 236–38, 281–82, 350–51, 392, 395–96, 446–47; Goodwyn, 74–81; "New Violence Erupts at St.

Augustine," *TT*, 19 June 1964; "Whites Attack Integrationists," *TT*, 23 June 1964; "Wade-In at St. Augustine," *NYT*, 23 June 1964.

31. Colburn, *Racial Change*, 148; "Collins Says State Can't Afford 'Orgy of Racial Conflict,'" *TMT*, 8 February 1956; Wagy, 132–43.

32. "Miami Welcomes Negro Baptists," *SPT*, 13 September 1953; Johnson, *Statistical Atlas*, 43, 73; Raper, 483; *Thirty Years of Lynching*, 53–56; Paulson, 6–19; "Collins Orders Probe," *TMT*, 14 February 1956; "End Miami Segregation," *NYT*, 26 November 1959; "City Pools and Parks Integrated," *MH*, 28 October 1959; "St. Petersburg May Drop Swim Segregation Fight," *TT*, 2 April 1957.

33. "Miami Welcomes Negro Baptists," *SPT*, 13 September 1953; Johnson, *Statistical Atlas*, 43, 73; Raper, 483; *Thirty Years of Lynching*, 53–56; Paulson, 6–19; "Collins Orders Probe," *TMT*, 14 February 1956; "End Miami Segregation," *NYT*, 26 November 1959; "City Pools and Parks Integrated," *MH*, 28 October 1959; "St. Petersburg May Drop Swim Segregation Fight," *TT*, 2 April 1957.

34. "A Spring Break History," *SLT*, 1 April 1994; "Beer and the Beach," *Time*, 13 April 1959, 54; "Spring Break's Shifting Sands," *NYT*, 28 January 2001; "Beach Class of '65," *MH*, 21 March 1965.

35. George, "Where the Boys Were," 1–5.

36. Ibid., 6; "When Elvis Came to Yankeetown," *OS*, 14 August 1987; May, 119–29; "Beer and the Beach," *Time*, 13 April 1959, 54; Lenček and Bosker, 260–63.

37. McIver, *Fort Lauderdale*, 151; "Dick Clark," *FLDN*, 21 March 1960; "Collegians Begin Invasion," *FLDN*, 13 March 1960; "Where the Bores Are," *Time*, 7 April 1961, 25; "Cavorting Collegians," *FLDN*, 20 March 1960; "Lauderdale Jail Bulging," 29 March 1961; "Lauderdale Officials Map Anti-Riot Plans," *SPT*, 30 March 1961; "Collegians Get Curfew," *MH*, 28 March 1961; "Unruly Students Whoop It Up," *BH*, 28 March 1961.

38. George, "Where the Boys Were," 7–8; "Mayor Reigned Over Sun, Suds," *MH*, 15 September 2002; "Where the Bores Are," *Time*, 7 April 1961, 25; "Students Invade Lauderdale," *MH*, 19 March 1961; "Where the Bums Aren't," *TT*, 1 April 1973; "Bidding a Fond Farewell," *MH*, 19 January 2003.

39. "Easter Invasion," *NYT*, 15 March 1964; "Florida's Spring Break," *MH*, 25 March 1964; "Spring Break's Shifting Sands," *NYT*, 28 January 2001.

40. "Students Overflow Beaches," *MH*, 22 April 1973; Willson, "Who's Sorry Now?" 36–38; "The Community Speaks Out," *DBNJ*, 7 April 2002; "Law Outlaws Driving on the Beach," *NYT*, 6 October 1985; "Spring Break's Shifting Sands," *NYT*, 28 January 2001; Burt, *Becalmed*, 115–17; "Know Thyself," *WP*, 20 December 1981; Tucker, "Daytona Beach," 46–55.

41. Reporter quoted in *DBNJ*, 22 March 1998; *USAT*, 14 May 2002; "Spring Break Mecca," *TD*, 22 March 1998; "Where the Teens Are," *AJC*, 6 April 1988; "Spring Break '00," *USAT*, 5 April 2000; "White Sand, White Necks," *PCNH*, 9 May 2002; "The Teeming Beaches of Florida," *WP*, 31 March 1985.

42. "On—and Off—The Beach," *Newsweek*, 10 April 1961, 40.

43. The most perceptive study of California youth remains Kirse Granat May's *Golden Gate State, Golden Youth* (see 9–26, 95–168); Starr, *The Dream Endures*, 10–16; Hopkins,

33, 44, 115–17; Jones, "Sands of Time," *LAT*, 28 June 1995; Whitfield, "Florida's Fudged Identity," 425; Young, 85–86.

44. Reed, 15–17; Gaines, 59–62, 98; Whitfield, "Florida's Fudged Identity," 416–17; "What Makes Jimmy Fun?" *MH*, 30 March 1997, *Tropic Magazine*; May, 95–115; "New Tribune FM Station," *TMT*, 9 May 1948.

45. Whitfield, "Florida's Fudged Identity," 417; Young, 82–87, 225; May, 95–99, 111–15; Desmond, 124–29; "Surf's Up," *NYT*, 4 August 2002; Starr, *The Dream Endures*, 10–11; "Homage to a Hero," *SPT*, 30 August 2002; "Surf's Up," *SN*, 12 August 2002; "Surfing for Business," *DBNJ*, 21 April 2002; "Soul Surfers," *DBNJ*, 7 November 1999; "Surfing School," *OS*, 1 August 2002; "Searching for a Champ," *OS*, 10 October 2003; "Boards and Bunnies," *OS*, 18 April 2003; Stone, 29; "An X-treme Outing," *SPT*, 8 August 2003; "Surfers Make Waves," *PBP*, 31 August 1999; "Surfers," *PBP*, 7 June 1999; "Catch the Wave," *TT*, 15 August 2003; Barnett, "Surf's Up," 72–74.

46. *Census of Population: 1950*, vol. 2, *Characteristics of the Population*, pt. 10, *Florida*, 14–15; Funk, "Miami," *TD*, 21 March 1971.

47. J. Patterson, 61–81, 311–42.

48. Resident quoted in "Growth," *FMNP*, 26 May 2002; "Coastal Growth," *TT*, 6 August 2002; "Beach Prepares for Influx," *FMNP*, 3 November 2003; Florida Department of Highway Safety and Motor Vehicles; "Big Boat Boom," *MH*, 22 October 2000.

49. *Census of Population: 1950*, vol. 2, *Characteristics of the Population*, pt. 10, *Florida*, 29–30; *www.census.gov/census2000/states/fl.html*; "Growth Reshapes Coasts," *USAT*, 21–23 July 2000.

50. *Florida: A Guide*, 345; *Census of Population: 1950*, vol. 2, *Characteristics of the Population*, pt. 10, *Florida*, 14; Shofner, *Brevard County*, 2:76, 82, 84, 97, 99–138.

51. Tebeau, *Last Frontier*, 252–56; "Plundering Nature's Treasure," *TT*, 12 June 1994; Orlean; "Syndicate Pays $2 million for Beachfront at Naples," *TMT*, 8 June 1956.

52. Lundstrom, 25; Tebeau, 139; *TT*, 27 August 1990; "Largest of Ten Thousand Islands," *NYT*, 9 July 1961; "Florida's 'Last Frontier,'" *NYT*, 7 November 1965.

53. "U.S. Denies Permits," *SPT*, 17 April 1976; "Naples Confronts Growth," *TT*, 8 June 1987; "Progress," *MH*, 9 August 1970, *Tropic Magazine*; "Marco Island," *SPT*, 28 July 1975; "Marco Island," *SPT*, 18 June 1972.

54. Betty Jean Steinshower to author, 10 July 2002, regarding the Millay Shell Collection; "Civilization Moves on Sanibel," *TT*, 26 October 1952; "Mosquitoes on Lovely Sanibel," *MH*, 23 April 1961, Gulf Coast edition; Burt, *Becalmed*, 222–25; "Darling," *FMNP*, 16 February 1955; Anholt, 96.

55. Lindbergh, 40.

56. Anholt, 35, 62, 87–88, 115, 116; "Captiva Island," *MH*, 24 April 1946; Quotation from Burt, *Becalmed*, 222.

57. "Sea Shells," *SPT*, 7 August 1979; "Big Change at Sanibel," *TT*, 2 September 1962; Anholt, 138; "Remote Island Gets $140,000 State Road Link," *TMT*, 21 October 1952; Burt, *Becalmed*, 172–74.

58. "Fighting Development," *MH*, 28 July 1974, *Floridian Magazine*; "Will Sanibel Dreams Thwart Get-Rich Schemes?" 114–17; "Where Nature Is an Immovable Object," *USAT*, 28 July 2000; Kennedy, "Eden Fights Back," 28–35; Anholt, 156–57.

59. Burt, "The Saving of Sanibel," *MH*, 27 November 1983; Burt, "Another Paradise Lost?" *MH*, 5 August 1979; "Sanibel," *SPT*, 1 April 1979.

60. For histories of early Sarasota, see Grismer, *The Story of Sarasota*, and Matthews, *Edge of Wilderness*.

61. Matthews, *Sarasota*, 91, 105, 107, 108, 111, 113–14, 124–25, 129–31, 132–33, 150; Grismer, 182–84, 210–11; Weeks, 90–97.

62. Hurley, vii–x, 158–204, 210; "Population of Pinellas Beaches Up 700 Per Cent," *TMT*, 20 July 1947; Frank T. Hurley Jr., interview, 25 May 2002.

63. "200 Couples Get Free Honeymoons," *TMT*, 24 November 1940; "Honeymoon Island," *SPT*, 9 September 1973; "Return to Honeymoon Island," *TT*, 3 December 1991; "Promoter Lured Newlyweds," *TT*, 27 September 1986; "Honeymoon Island," *TT*, 2 August 1980; "Honeymoon," *TDT*, 30 December 1940.

64. "Teamster Money," *TT*, 12 October 1978; "Enough Is Enough," *SPT*, 16 February 1980; "Value of Honeymoon," *TT*, 18 May 1977; "Honeymoon Island," *SPT*, 11 October 1978.

65. Burt, *Becalmed*, 94–96.

66. Quotation from *Florida: A Guide*, 494; 1950s quote, H. Jackson, "Florida Room," 317.

67. Bragg, "New Economy"; Jack Davis to author, 18 October 2002.

68. Bragg; "Destin," *SPT*, 25 December 1981; "Town's New Identity," *TT*, 23 September 1984; "Cracker Chic," *SPT*, 6 April 2003; Burt, *Becalmed*, 94–96.

69. "Prices Pushing Florida Hideaways Out of Reach," *TT*, 2 January 1973; "Beach Dream Cottage," *TDT*, 9 June 1950; Frank T. Hurley Jr., interview, 25 May 2002; Hester quoted in "Beaches Scarce," *TT*, 12 March 1973; "Waterfront As Good As Gold," *FMNP*, 22 June 2003.

70. Frank quoted in Carter, 146; Krock, *NYT*, "Explosive Growth," 29 March 1955; Classified Ads: "Waterfront Homes For Common Man," *TT*, 1 March 1959; *FTU*, 1 July 1956; "Summer Beach Cottage," *TT*, 26 June 1960; "High-Priced Units," *FTU*, 12 December 1998; "Island Living," *SPT*, 1 March 1959; "Gilt By Association," *NYT*, 2 August 2002; *FMNP*, January 1950; *SPT*, 1950, 1956; *FLDN*, 5 July 1956; "Missile Base Area," *FLDN*, 1 July 1956; Writer quoted in "Prices Pushing Florida Hideaways," *TT*, 2 January 1973; "Beaches Scarce Even at $1,000 a Foot," *TT*, 18 March 1973; "Biscayne Bay," *MH*, 18 March 1960.

71. Commentator quoted in "Condominiums—A New Lifestyle," 24, 30; "Soaring Condominium Sales," *PCNH*, 9 May 2002; "Last of the Super Towers," *MH*, 29 August 2002; "Happy Birthday Dear Condo," *MH*, 21 November 1982; "Condominium," *SPT*, 5 March 1973, Suncoast Times; "Where Have All the Beaches Gone?" *MH*, 22 April 1973.

72. Carroll, 43–45.

73. "Tide of Atlantans," *AJC*, 17 June 2002; resident quoted in "Cracker Chic," *SPT*, 6 April 2003; "Little Atlanta," 42; H. Jackson, "Florida Room," 317.

74. Danese, 9, 58, 80, 101–2; "Vast Change Looms," *NYT*, 22 June 2002; "'New Urbanism' Sweeps Panhandle," *TD*, 19 November 2001; "St. Joe Is Selling," *TD*, 2 March 1999; "Ed Ball," *TMT*, 5 June 1956; "Distinctive Properties & Estates," *WSJ*, 16 August 2002; Sherman, "Cracker Chic," *SPT*, 6 April 2003.

75. "Last of the Super Towers," *MH*, 29 August 2002; "Town Fights Development War," *MH*, 3 September 2002; "Beach Looks to Further Cap Building Size," *FMNP*, 10 November 2002; "Going Against the Tide," *SPT*, 6 October 2002; "Demolition Sends Builders Message," *TT*, 23 September 2002; Dunnigan, 28; "High Rises, High Tempers," *SPT*, 27 October 2002; "Cocoa Beach Growth Pains," *TT*, 26 December 2002; "Space Coast City Says No," *NYT*, 21 March 2003.

76. "Cocoa Beach Growth," *TT*, 26 December 2002; Kunstler quoted in editorial "Harsh Edges," *TT*, 19 June 2002; Dunlop, "'Egotecture'"; "Condominium," *SPT*, 5 March 1973, *Suncoast Times*; "Our Ugly Beach," *SPT*, 17 February 1983; Kaufman and Pilkey, 225; "Beach Development," *SFSS*, 14 November 1999; "High-Rises, High Tempers," *SPT*, 27 October 2002.

77. Rob Walker, "Utopia-by-the-Sea," *NYT*, 3 May 2002; H. Jackson, "Seaside," 41–51; Applebome, 21; "Down Home Goes Uptown," *MH*, 18 August 2002; Sexton, 97–104; Martinson, 148–49; D. Roberts; Whitfield, "Florida's Fudged Identity," 426; Dunlop, "In Florida."

78. D. Roberts; Whitfield, "Florida's Fudged Identity," 426; "Down Home," *MH*, 18 August 2002.

79. "Richest Towns," 88–104; "Beaches a 'Gold Mine,'" *FTU*, 14 July 1997; "Newcomers Hit Shores," *FTU*, 23 October 1999; "Growth Pains Move North," *TD*, 5 January 1998; "Neptune Beach Growing," *FTU*, 20 April 2002; "A Beachfront Boom," *NYT*, 12 March 2002; "Posh Pads on St. George Island," *TD*, 4 April 1999.

80. Portes and Stepick, 150–51; "Fair Play for Haitian Refugees," *SFC*, 11 November 2002; "Cubans Landing Draws Criticism," *SFSS*, 12 November 2002; "U.S., Cuba Discuss Immigration Pact," *WP*, 13 December 1999; "Graves," *TT*, 9 February 2004.

81. Cronon, 32–34, 61, 101–2; K. Jackson, 53; Jasper, 103–5, 108.

82. "'Island Living,'" *SPT*, 1 March 1959; Shofner, *Nor Is It Over Yet*, 109; Carter, 74.

83. "Three Dredged Subdivisions," *TT*, 28 September 1958; "What Man Hath Wrought," *TMT*, 9 March 1958; "Dredges Spout New Subdivisions," *TDT*, 24 June 1950; "Lowly Mangrove Swamp Is Turned into 'Paradise' Island," *TMT*, 17 February 1952; "Florida's Silver Coast," *TMT*, 13 January 1952; "How to Make a New Island," *TT*, 18 January 1959; "Dredger Break Hudson's Quiet," *TT*, 22 February 1959; "Largo Wants a Beach," 10 February 1959; "Opening of McCormick Mile," *FLDN*, 29 March 1958; "New Coastline," *TMT*, 18 October 1952.

84. McIver, 78–79; Derr, 191; *FLDN*, 1 November 1953; "Developer Has Faith in Tampa Bayfronts," *TMT*, 25 January 1953.

85. "New Waterfront Property," *TMT*, 7 February 1956; Stephenson, vii, 5–9; Rothchild, *Up for Grabs*, 17–18, 32–34.

86. MacDonald, "Quarter Century of Growth," 34; Yardley, 9.

87. Stephenson, 139; see also 126–42.

88. Stephenson, 128–33; *SPT*, 1 November 1953; "Bayway Adds New Fills to Bay," *SPT*, 1 January 1961; "Mosquito-Ridden Key Now Beach Beauty Spot," *TT*, 13 November 1957; "Canals Cut," *TT*, 1 March 1959.

89. Rothchild, *Up for Grabs*, 33–34.

90. "New York Builder Plans City," *NYT*, 3 June 1959; editorial, "A Boon across the Bay," *TT*, 1 July 1960.

91. "Full-Scale City Rises on Islands," *TT*, 9 April 1961; "Percentage of Wealthy Folks," *SPT*, 2–4 June 2002, Seminole edition.

92. Blake, 195–97; Stephenson, 138–42; Kallina, 66, 68, 155, 160.

93. "Coastal Protectors Poor and Powerless," *SPT*, 12 March 1973; "Curb State's Coastal Growth, Study Warns," *MH*, 4 February 1973; "Coastal Overdevelopment," *TT*, 3 August 2002; "Development Goes As Beaches Deteriorate," *USAT*, 29 July 2002; Pilkey quoted in "Shrinking Shore," *Paradise at Risk*, 2, 4, 5; Dean, 192–95; J. Patterson, 725–29.

94. Pilkey and Dixon, quoted ix, 1–12, 219–44; Blake, 203–7, 260–61; Carter, 275–77; Dean, 96–105.

95. Lenček and Bosker, 273–74, 283–84; Blake, 293–97; Carter, 147–48; "Florida Bay Is Sick," *NYT*, 15 April 1997; Freeman, "You Can't Stop Progress," 523; "City's Sewer Problem," *SPT*, 10 July 1950; "Biscayne Bay Now 99 Pct Pure," *MH*, 15 May 1960; "Biscayne Bay," *MH*, 18 March 1960; "Biscayne Bay," *MN*, 6 February 1971; "Booming Pinellas Beaches Worried by Sewer Problem," *TMT*, 26 September 1952; "Sewer Benefits Hampered," *TMT*, 27 September 1952; *TMT*, 21 July 1947; "Beach Revelers Trash the Beach," *FTU*, 7 July 1999; Muir, 58, 218–19; Montague and Wiegert, 512; "Progress Marker," *MH*, 14 October 1959, Brevard edition; "Dade Growth Pains Hurt Environment," *MH*, 28 January 1973; "Paradise Lost," *MH*, 29 March 1970, *Tropic Magazine*; "They Won't Leave," *SPT*, 16 September 1992; "Coastal Cleanup," *Hernando Times*, 18 September 2000.

96. "Buried Poison," *OS*, 7 July 2002; "The Perfect Lawn," *OS*, 16 June 2002; Derr, 365; "Test the Waters," *CSM*, 15 July 1997; "Summer Fun Dampened by Trash and Pollution," *CSM*, 24 July 1997; "'Venice of America' Faces Pollution Risk," *FLDN*, 29 October 1958; "Blooms Signal Ocean Pollution," *DBNJ*, 1 September 2002; "Sewage Pouring into Lakes, Streams," *USAT*, 20 August 2002; "Raw Sewage Reaches Gulf," *SPT*, 23 March 1973; "The Reef Plan Goes Adrift," *SFSS*, 13 July 2003.

97. "Cruise-Ship Dumping Poisons," *USAT*, 8–10 November 2002; "Pollution Taking Toll on Coral Reefs," *TT*, 30 November 2002; *Florida Trend: 2002 Annual TopRank*, 98; "Cruise Ships' Trash," *SPT*, 9 June 2002; "Dumping Oil off Florida," *WSJ*, 20 May 1994; "Cruise Ships," *WSJ*, 9 April 2001; "Danger Floats toward Gulf Beaches," *SPT*, 15 September 1973; "Waiting for the Ship to Come In," *SPT*, 20 November 2000; Selz, "How Lucky Can You Get?" 30–39.

98. "Mussel Bound," *SPT*, 1 July 2002; Derr, 365; "A Return to Pristine," *TT*, 8 October 2003; "Channeling Business," *TT*, 13 October 2003; "Scallops," *FMNP*, 29 October 2003.

99. Pilkey, 6; Kaufman and Pilkey, 188–222.

100. Kaufman and Pilkey, 12–17, 164–87; Pilkey, *Living*, 32–52; Dean, 36–69, 120–34; *Paradise at Risk*, 1; Ricciuti, 48–53; "Sandy Science," 2–3.

101. Collier, "Crusader," 64–79; Dean, 36–69; Pilkey and Dixon, 1–2.

102. "Sandy Shore," in *Paradise at Risk*, 29 July 2002; "Development Goes on As Beaches Deteriorate," *USAT*, 29 July 2002; "The Beach Builders," *SHT*, 3 July 2000;

"Sandmen," *SPT*, 13 May 2002; "You Bought This Beach," *SPT*, 12 May 2002; "Miami Beach's Shoreline under Siege," *LAT*, 17 December 1996; "Wanted: Tons of Sand," *CSM*, 7 January 1997; Pilkey and Dixon, 8–9. The earliest use of the term *renourishment* that I have discovered dates to a newspaper article, "Artificial Renourishment," *TMT*, 14 December 1956.

103. "A License to Kill," *SHT*, 4 July 2000; "Environmental Toll of Rebuilding," *SHT*, 4 July 2000; "Eggs of Endangered Turtles," *NYT*, 2 August 2002; "Turtles Die in Record Numbers," *SPT*, 3 January 2003.

104. "Gray Area," *WSJ*, 24 July 2001; "Perfect Sand," in *Paradise at Risk*, 14–15; "Sandy Science," 2–3.

105. Mormino and Pozzetta, 239–42; Rothchild, *Up for Grabs*, 144; "Pinellas Beach Towns," *SPT*, 21 March 2001; "Access," *FTU*, 17 October 1998; "Tampa Still Lacks a Public Beach," *TT*, 3 July 1960; "A Beachfront Boon for South Florida," *NYT*, 12 March 2002; "Sanibel Raises Beach Parking Fees," *FMNP*, 24 July 2002; California quotes in "Owners of Malibu Mansions," *NYT*, 25 August 2002; "Access Denied," *SHT*, 1 December 2002; editorial, "County Parks and Our Future Prosperity," *SPT*, 16 April 1950; "Where Have All the Beaches Gone?" *MH*, 22 April 1973; "Off-Limits."

106. http://historicaltextarchive.com/Mexico/1917const.html Article 27; http://www.frommers.com/destinations/cancun/0037020389.html.

107. "Beach Problem in Florida," *NYT*, 1 October 1961; "Beauty and the Beach," *MH*, 23 May 1982; "Malibu's Rich and Famous Fight to Keep Beach Private," *USAT*, 3–5 May 2002; Carter, 322; "Tri-County Beach Losses 'Critical,'" *MH*, 21 July 1961; "Where Have All the Beaches Gone?" *MH*, 22 April 1973; "Beach Access," *NYT*, 21 January 2005.

108. Hauserman, 86–91.

109. Batten, 1–9; "Tans Turn Deadly," *SPT*, 10 September 2002; "Beach Safety" *SHT*, 16 August 1999; "Made in the Shade," *WSJ*, 2 August 2002; "Sentinels for Beach Safety," *FTU*, 30 June 1999; "Pesky Men O' War," *MH*, 27 October 1951; "Beaches Open; Apply Caution," *FTU*, 23 April 1999; "Life at the Water's Edge," *SHT*, 28 July 2002; "Apocalypse Now or Never?" *SHT*, 4 August 2002; Sun quote in *SPT*, 21 March 1926, in Arsenault, *St. Petersburg*, 191; Revkin, "Forecast for a Warmer World," *NYT*, 28 August 2002; "Miami," *Time*, 19 December 1938, 37; Barnett, "Distress Syndrome," 74–79.

110. Lenček and Bosker, 186–90, 260–63; Klawans, "What Ever Happened to Fun in the Sand?" *NYT*, 12 May 2002.

111. Benchley; "Shark Maulings," *SPT*, 13 May 2002; "Experts," *SPT*, 14 June 2002.

112. Provenzo and Provenzo, 1, 56, 65, 91, 93, 94; Gore, 2–38; "Coastal Growth Can Mean More Hurricane Liability," *TT*, 6 August 2002; Steinberg, 54; Kaufman and Pilkey, 178–79; "It Could Happen Here," *SPT*, 24 August 2002; "After the Storm," *SPT*, 18 August 2002; Yardley, 9; "What If Andrew Hit Us Today?" *SFSS*, 24 August 2002; Derr, 211; Arsenault, "Public Storm," 262–93.

113. Mayfield quoted in "Coastal Growth," *TT*, 6 August 2002; Bowden, "Mother Nature Rules," in *Paradise at Risk*, 29 July 2002; Steinberg, 92–95; Dean, 189–90; "Facing Mother Nature's Fury," *USAT*, 24 July 2000; H. Jackson, "Florida Room," 318–19; Pérez, *Winds*.

114. "After the Storm: An Ecological Bomb," *NYT*, 30 November 1999; M. Davis, 54; Steinberg, 82, 90–93; "When Aliens Attack," *SPT*, 13 August 2002.

115. MacDonald, *Condominium*; Yardley, 9–14.

116. "If The Power's On, The Surf's Up," *NYTM*, 16 June 2002, 18–19.

117. I am indebted to scholar Stephen J. Whitfield for the story.

Epilogue

1. Hurston, 20.

2. Dietrich, 102–3.

3. "Staying Close to Home," *NYT*, 10 June 1982; Barone, 53; "Most Live in Their State of Birth," *USAT*, 4 September 2001.

4. Dietrich, 92–93, 154–69.

5. Putnam, 48–64, 117–18; "Dwindling Herd Downsizes," *SHT*, 27 January 2002. "New Floridians Loyal to State," *MH*, 15 July 1999; "Feeling at Home," *SPT*, 15 July 1999; Klinkenberg, "Florida's Deepest Roots," *SPT*, 30 June 2002; "Terrorists," *TT*, 24 June 2002.

6. "And the Band Plays On," *SFSS*, 31 December 1999; "Fans, Band Groove in Phish Bowl," *MH*, 1 January 2000.

7. "Little Havana," *USAT*, 25 January 2000; "Legacy of a Cuban Boy," *NYT*, 10 May 2000; "In Two Countries," *NYT*, 9 January 2000.

8. Shofner, *Nor Is It Over Yet*, 300–384; "The Florida Scene Is 1876 All Over Again," *WSJ* 11 December 2000.

9. Carl Hiaasen, "When the Going Gets Weird," *Time*, 20 November 2000, 20; "Ex-Felons," *NYT*, 20 February 2005; "Disenfranchised Florida Felons," *NYT*, 28 March 2004; "Reassurance for Florida Voters," *NYT*, 24 May 2004; "Electors," Florida State Statutes, 101.51.

10. Hurston, *Their Eyes*, 151; Scott Huler, "The Perfect Storm Name," *NYT*, 4 September 2004.

11. Arsenault, "Public Storm," 262–63; Batten, 156–57, 251–53; Weathermen with Fatigue," *MH*, 26 September 2004; "The Storm Chaser," *SPT*, 20 September 2004.

12. Pérez, *Winds of Change*, 13.

13. "Charley Puts Calusa Site in Hole," *FMNP*, 29 October 2004.

14. "Town . . . a Magnet," *MH*, 26 September 2004; "On Jupiter Island," *NYT*, 9 September 2004; "Town Struggles," *SPT*, 16 August 2004; "Mobile Home Owners," *SPT*, 3 September 2004; "Upended Lives," *USAT*, 20 August 2004; "Will Mobile Home Culture Survive?" *SPT*, 21 August 2004; "A Formula for Disaster," *TT*, 5 December 2004; "A Second Wind," *SPT*, 5 December 2004; "In Florida," *NYT*, 1 January 2005.

15. "Faith, Humor, Charity," *TT*, 3 October 2004.

16. Sam Efling, "Like a Hurricane," *New Times*, 27 September 2004; "A Tempest Over Aid," *SFSS*, 10 October 2004.

17. Arsenault, "Public Storm," 272–75; Ernest Hemingway, "Who Killed the Vets?" *New Masses*, 17 September 1935; *KWC*, 5 September 1935; "Black Caucus," *SFSS*, 23 September 2004; "In English and Spanish," *SPT*, 29 September 2004.

18. "Seaside's Mystique," *SPT*, 24 September 2004; "Town's Construction Prevents Destruction," *MH*, 18 September 2004.

19. "Haiti Buries Storm Victims," *SFSS*, 23 September 2004; "Gated Communities," *SFSS*, 23 September 2004; "Famed Resort," *SFSS*, 30 September 2004; "Downed Trees," *MH*, 19 September 2004; "Paradise Pounded," *SPT*, 4 September 2004; "Wind-blown," *SPT*, 1 December 2004; "Battered and Bruised," *SHT*, 28 November 2004.

20. "Storms Took Toll," *TT*, 19 September 2004; "Officials," *NYT*, 29 September 2004; "More Fruit on Ground," *NYT*, 10 September 2004; "Citrus Endures," *SPT*, 5 February 2005.

21. L. Brown, 174; "Leased Jets Evacuate Moneyed Residents," *MH*, 11 September 2004; "Where the Boats Are," *MH*, 11 September 2004.

22. "Destruction Brings Renewal," *TT*, 6 September 2004; "Marine Cleanup," *SHT*, 4 October 2004; "Florida's Boats and Marinas Battered," *NYT*, 7 September 2004; "Beaches Bank on Hurricanes," *TT*, 14 October 2004; "Federal Help for Beaches," *TT*, 9 October 2004; "Frances Ruins Sea Turtle Nests," *SPT*, 11 September 2004; "Beaches Take Beating," *OS*, 3 October 2004; "Spill Corrodes," *SPT*, 8 September 2004; "Ill Winds," *NYT*, 23 September 2004; "Hurricanes Took a Toll, *SHT*, 27 November 2004.

23. "Paradise Lost?" *SPT*, 14 September 2004; "Even in Stormy Weather, Florida's Appeal Endures," *NYT*, 4 September 2004; "Climate and Bad Luck," *NYT*, 5 September 2004.

24. "Plowing Ahead," *OS*, 23 January 2005.

Bibliography

Archives and Collections

Charlton Tebeau Library. Archives. Historical Association of Southern Florida. Miami.

Dunn, Hampton, Papers. Special Collections. University of South Florida Library, Tampa.

Florida State Archives. Tallahassee.

Manatee Public Library–Eaton Room. Bradenton, Fla.

NAACP. Papers. pt. 5. *The Campaign Against Residential Discrimination, 1914–1945.* Frederick, Md.: University Publications of America, 1982.

Newberry Library Travel Collection. Chicago.

Orange County Regional History Center. Archives. Orlando.

Pepper, Claude, Papers. Florida State University, Tallahassee.

Pizzo, Tony, Papers. Special Collections. University of South Florida Library, Tampa.

Roosevelt, Eleanor, Papers. Franklin D. Roosevelt Library, Hyde Park, N.Y.

Roosevelt, Franklin Delano, Political correspondence. Franklin D. Roosevelt Library. Hyde Park, N.Y.

Southern Collection. University of North Carolina, Chapel Hill.

State of Florida Photographic Archives. Tallahassee.

Welch, Agnew, Papers. Florida Collection. Miami-Dade Public Library.

Yonge, P. K., Library of Florida History. University of Florida, Gainesville.

Government Documents

Sixth Census of the State of Florida, 1935. Tallahassee: Orange Press, 1936.

Seventh Census of the State of Florida, 1945. Tallahassee: Department of Agriculture, 1946.

U.S. Bureau of the Census. *Sixteenth Census of the United States, 1940: Population.* Washington, D.C.: U.S. Government Printing Office, 1942.

———. *Seventeenth Census of the United States, 1950: Population.* Washington, D.C.: U.S. Government Printing Office, 1952.

———. *Eighteenth Census of the United States, 1960: Population.* Washington, D.C.: U.S. Government Printing Office, 1962.

———. *Nineteenth Census of the United States, 1970: Population.* Washington, D.C.: U.S. Government Printing Office, 1972.

———. *Twentieth Census of the United States, 1980: Population.* Washington, D.C.: U.S. Government Printing Office, 1982.

———. *Twenty-first Census of the United States, 1990: Population.* Washington, D.C.: U.S. Government Printing Office, 1992.

———. *Seventeenth Census of the United States, 1950.* Vol. 2, *Characteristics of the Population,* pt. 10, *Florida.* Washington, D.C.: U.S. Government Printing Office, 1952.

———. *Nineteenth Census of the United States, 1970: Census of Population and Housing.* Vol. 1, *Housing Characteristics for States, Cities, and Counties,* pt. 11, *Florida.* Washington, D.C.: U.S. Government Printing Office, 1972.

———. *Twentieth Census of the United States, 1980: Census of Housing: Detailed Housing Characteristics,* pt. 11, *Florida.* Washington, D.C.: U.S. Government Printing Office, 1992.

———. *Twenty-first Census of the United States, 1990: Census of Population and Housing, Summary Population and Housing Characteristics, Florida.* Washington, D.C.: U.S. Government Printing Office, 1992.

———. *1950 Census of Housing.* Vol. 1, *Housing Characteristics for States, Cities, and Counties,* pt. 2, *Alabama-Georgia.* Washington, D.C.: U.S. Government Printing Office, 1953.

———. *1960 Census of Housing.* Vol. 1, *Housing Characteristics for States, Cities, and Counties,* pt. 11, *Florida.* Washington, D.C.: U.S. Government Printing Office, 1962.

———. *1970 Census of Housing.* Vol. 1, *Housing Characteristics for States, Cities, and Counties,* pt. 11, *Florida.* Washington, D.C.: U.S. Government Printing Office, 1972.

U.S. Department of Commerce. *United States Census of Agriculture: 1950.* Vol. 1, pt. 18, *Florida.* Washington, D.C.: U.S. Government Printing Office, 1952.

———. *United States Census of Agriculture: 1945.* Vol. 1, pt. 18, *Florida.* Washington,, D.C.: U.S. Government Printing Office, 1946.

———. *United States Census of Agriculture: 1959. Florida: Counties.* Washington, D.C.: U.S. Government Printing Office, 1961.

Books and Articles

Achenbaum, W. Andrew. *Old Age in the New Land: The American Experience Since 1790.* Baltimore: Johns Hopkins University Press, 1978.

Adams, Frank. "Citrus Freezes and Developers Keep Citrus Belt Heading South." *Florida Business* 22 (September 1990): 17–22.

"Aerospace Is Great Florida Asset." *Florida Trend* 10 (April 1968): 95–98.

Akerman, Joe A., Jr. *Florida Cowman: A History of Florida Cattle Raising.* Kissimmee, Fla.: Florida Cattlemen's Assoc., 1976.

Akerman, Marsha E. *Cool Comfort: America's Romance with Air Conditioning.* Washington, D.C.: Smithsonian Press, 2002.

Akin, Edward N. *Flagler, Rockefeller Partner and Florida Baron.* Kent, Ohio: Kent State University Press, 1988.

Allman, T. D. *Miami: City of the Future*. New York: Atlantic Monthly Press, 1987.

Andrews, Stephen D. "'Brasshats' and 'Babyfingers': The Battle over Rural Education." *Florida Historical Quarterly* 75 (Winter 1997): 303–25.

Anholt, Betty. *Sanibel's Story: Voice and Images*. Virginia Beach: Donning Co., 1998.

Applebome, Peter. *Dixie Rising: How the South Is Shaping American Values, Politics, and Culture*. New York: Times Books, 1996.

Aron, Cindy S. *Working at Play: A History of Vacations in the United States*. New York: Oxford University Press, 1999.

Arsenault, Raymond. "The End of the Long Hot Summer: The Air Conditioner and Southern Culture." *Journal of Southern History* 50 (November 1984): 597–628.

———."Is There a Florida Dream?" *Forum: The Magazine of the Florida Humanities Council* 17 (Summer 1994): 22–27.

———. "The Public Storm and the State in Twentieth-Century America." In *American Public Life and the Historical Imagination*, edited by Wendy Gamber, Michael Grossberg, and Wendrik Hartog, 262–93. Notre Dame: University of Notre Dame Press, 2004.

———. *St. Petersburg and the Florida Dream, 1880–1950*. Norfolk: Donning Co., 1988.

Arsenault, Raymond, and Gary Mormino. "From Dixie to Dreamland: Demographic and Cultural Change in Florida, 1880–1930." In *Shades of the Sunbelt*, edited by George Pozzetta and Randall Miller, 161–92. Westport, Conn.: Greenwood Press, 1988.

"Arts and Culture: Helping Florida Build a Diversified Economy." *History and the Arts* 12 (Spring 2004): 15–21.

Atlas of Florida. Edited by Edward A. Fernald and Elizabeth D. Perdum. Gainesville: University Press of Florida, 1996.

Attaway, John A. *A History of Florida Citrus Freezes*. Lake Alfred: Florida Science Source, 1987.

Auerbach, Stuart. "Cane Cutters: Are Their Jobs Agriculture's Worst?" *St. Petersburg Times*, 28 December 1975.

Bachus, Edward J. "Who Took the Orange Out of Orange County? The Southern California Citrus Industry." *Southern California History* 63 (Summer 1981): 157–73.

"Backwoods Counties." *Florida Trend* 2 (March 1961): 13–17.

Bacon, Eve. *Orlando: A Centennial History*. 2 vols. Chulota, Fla.: Mickler House Publishers, 1977.

Baker, Larry. *The Flamingo Rising*. New York: Knopf, 1997.

Barnes, Althemese, and Ann Roberts. *Tallahassee, Florida*. Black America Series. Charleston, S.C.: Arcadia, 2000.

Barnett, Cynthia. "Distress Syndrome." *Florida Trend* 46 (June 2003): 74–79.

———. "Surf's Up." *Florida Trend* 43 (February 2000): 72–74.

Barnouw, Eric. *Tube of Plenty: The Evolution of American Television*. New York: Oxford University Press, 1990.

Barone, Michael. "Snares of a Lost Paradise." *U.S. News and World Report*, 11 October 1993, 53.

Barrett, James R. "Americanization from the Bottom Up: Immigration and the Remaking of the Working Class." In *Discovering America,* edited by David Thelen and Frederick Hoxie, 162–86. Urbana: University of Illinois Press, 1994.

Bartlett, D. L., and J. B. Steele. "Sweet Deal." *Time,* 23 November 1998, 81–82.

Batten, Frank. *The Weather Channel: The Improbable Rise of a Media Phenomenon.* Boston: Harvard Business School Press, 2002.

"Beached Like a Whale." *U.S. News and World Report,* 11 October 1993, 51–52.

"Behind the Bankruptcy Boom." *The Nation,* 5 October 1992, 359–60.

Belasco, Warren James. *Americans on the Road: From Autocamp to Motel.* Cambridge: MIT Press, 1979.

Benchley, Peter. *Shark Trouble: True Stories About Sharks.* New York: Random House, 2002.

Bennett, Cynthia. "Too Little, Too Late." *Florida Trend* 46 (November 2003): 60–61.

Bennett, Evan. "Highways to Heaven or Roads to Ruin? The Interstate Highway System and the Fate of Starke, Florida." *Florida Historical Quarterly* 78 (Spring 2000): 451–67.

Bennett, Robert A. "A Guide to Banking's Hottest Market." *New York Times,* 23 May 1982.

Berman, Phyllis. "Miami Saved Again." *Forbes,* 1 November 1977, 37–41.

Bernard, Richard. "Sunbelt," in *Encyclopedia of Southern Culture,* 1126. Chapel Hill: University of North Carolina Press, 1989.

Bernard, Richard, and Bradley R. Rice, eds. *Sunbelt Cities: Politics and Growth Since World War II.* Austin: University of Texas Press, 1983.

"Big Rush to the Sun." *Newsweek,* 17 January 1955, 67–73.

"Big Sellers of Sunshine." *Life,* 9 February 1959, 77–80.

Billitteri, Thomas J. "No One Was Invincible." *Florida Trend* 35 (January 1993): 58–62.

Billitteri, Thomas J., and Michael Selz. "Is Mass Transit a Quick Trip to Nowhere?" *Florida Trend* 26 (January 1984): 51–56.

Black, Earl, and Merle Black. *The Rise of Southern Republicans.* Cambridge: Harvard University Press, 2002.

Blake, Nelson Manfred. *Land into Water—Water into Land.* Tallahassee: University Presses of Florida, 1980.

Blakey, Arch Frederic. *The Florida Phosphate Industry: A History of the Development of a Vital Mineral.* Cambridge: Harvard University Press, 1973.

———. *Parade of Memories: A History of Clay County.* Jacksonville: Drummond Press, 1976.

Blakey, Edward J., and Mary Gail Snyder. *Fortress America: Gated Communities in the United States.* Washington, D.C.: Brookings Institute Press, 1997.

Booker, Stacie Kress. "Naples: A City in Transition." *Florida Trend* 42 (September 1999): 24.

———. "No Room at the Inn." *Florida Trend* 43 (July 2000): 24.

"The Boom That Space Built." *U.S. News and World Report,* 26 March 1962, 50–54.

Boorstin, Daniel. *The Image: A Guide to Pseudo-Events in America.* New York: Harper and Row, 1961.

Bowden, J. Earle. *Pensacola: Florida's First Place City.* Norfolk: Donning Co., 1989.

Braden, Susan. *Architecture of Leisure: The Florida Resort Hotels of Henry Flagler and Henry Plant*. Gainesville: University Press of Florida, 2002.

Bragg, Rick. "Aged Beefcake Calendar Turns Heads." *New York Times*, 1 July 2001.

———. "Alliance Fights a Plan to Develop a Florida Gateway Born of Racism." *New York Times*, 28 March 1998.

———. "Living in Another World." *St. Petersburg Times*, 16 June 1991.

———. "New Economy Eclipses a Sliver of Old Florida." *New York Times*, 14 August 2000.

———. "On Florida Bridge Troopers Are Also Suicide Counselors." *New York Times*, 9 May 1999.

———. "A Political Era Fades in Florida's Condos." *New York Times*, 8 April 1999.

Branch, Stephen E. "The Salesman and His Swamp: Dick Pope's Cypress Gardens." *Florida Historical Quarterly* 80 (Spring 2002): 483–503.

Branch, Taylor. *Pillar of Fire: America in the King Years, 1963–65*. New York: Simon and Schuster, 1998.

"Brazilian Beachhead." *Florida Trend* 36 (October 1993): 56–59.

Breckenridge, Henry M. *Topographical Description of Pensacola and Vicinity in 1821*, edited by Brian B. Rucker. Bagdad, Fla.: Patagonia Press, 1991.

Breslauer, Ken. *Roadside Attractions: The Golden Era of Florida's Tourist Attractions, 1929–1971*. St. Petersburg: Type House, 2000.

Bretos, Miguel. *Cuba and Florida: Exploration of a Hispanic Connection, 1539–1991*. Miami: Historical Association of Southern Florida, 1991.

Brooks, Abbie M. *Petals Plucked from Sunny Climes*. Nashville: Southern Methodist Publishing House, 1879.

Brown, Dona. *Inventing New England: Regional Tourism in the Nineteenth Century*. Washington, D.C.: Smithsonian Press, 1995.

Brown, Loren G. *Totch: A Life in the Everglades*. Gainesville: University Press of Florida, 1993.

Brunais, Andrea. "Memories of a Child of the Space Program." *Forum* 20 (Winter 1997/98): 14–18.

Buck, Pat Ringling, Marsha Corbino, and Kevin Dean. *A History of Visual Art in Sarasota*. Gainesville: University Press of Florida, 2003.

Bucuvalas, Tina. "Cuisine: Food with Attitude." *Forum* 27 (Fall 2003): 34–37.

Burns, Allan F. "Indiantown, Florida: The Maya Diaspora." In *The Maya Diaspora: Guatemala Roots, New American Lives*, edited by James Loucky and Marilyn Moors, 152–71. Philadelphia: Temple University Press, 2000.

Burt, Al. *Becalmed in the Mullet Latitudes*. Port Salerno, Fla.: Florida Classics Library, 1983.

———. "Fernandina Beach: Blessed and Burdened." *Forum* 23 (Winter 2000): 10–15, 22–28.

Bush, Gregory. "'Playground of the U.S.A.': Miami and the Promotion of Spectacle." *Pacific Historical Review* 68 (May 1999): 153–72.

Bushnell, Amy Turner. "Tomás Menéndez Márquez: Criollo, Cattleman, and Contador."

In *Spanish Pathways in Florida,* edited by Ann Henderson and Gary Mormino, 118–32. Sarasota: Pineapple Press, 1992.

Butler, J. Michael. "Mississippi State Sovereign Commission and Beach Integration, 1959–1963: A Cotton Patch Gestapo?" *Journal of Southern History* 68 (February 2002): 107–48.

Calonlus, Erik. "Deltona Says It's Back—Stronger Than Ever." *Florida Trend* 23 (March 1981): 61–65.

Canizares, Raul. *Walking with the Night: The Afro-Cuban World of Santería.* Rochester, Vt.: Destiny Books, 1993.

Carlson, James A. "Florida's Stake in Steak." *Florida Trend* 12 (September 1969): 14–21.

Carr, Patrick. *Sunshine States: Wild Times and Extraordinary Lives in the Land of Gators, Guns, and Grapefruit.* New York: Doubleday, 1990.

Carroll, John. "My (Other) House." *American Demographics* 24 (June 2002): 43–45.

Carson, Rachel. *Silent Spring.* Boston: Houghton Mifflin, 1962.

Carter, Luther. *The Florida Experience: Land and Water Policy in a Growth State.* Baltimore: Johns Hopkins University Press, 1975.

Cepeda, María Elena. "Miami Dances at Center of Today's Latin Music Scene." *Forum* 28 (Winter 2004): 32–34.

"The Church Industry." *Florida Trend* 11 (June 1968): 22–34.

"The Church's Ranch." *U.S. News and World Report,* 24 December 1979, 62–63.

Clark, James. "Orlando Is Swell, Elegant." *Orlando Sentinel,* 24 August 1986.

Clary, Mike. "All Work, No Play Make Wayne . . ." *Florida Trend* 32 (April 1990): 28–33.

———. "The Middle Man." *Florida Trend* 33 (November 1990): 32–35.

———. "Wind Shear at Miami's Airport." *Florida Trend* 34 (July 1991): 32–34.

Classic Crates from Florida. Edited by Marilyn C. Russel. Winter Haven, Fla.: Citrus Showcase, 1985.

Clendinen, Dudley. "What to Call People Who Used to be Old." *New York Times,* 2 July 2000.

Cobb, James C. *The Selling of the South: The Southern Crusade for Industrial Development, 1936–1980.* Baton Rouge: Louisiana State University Press, 1982.

Cohen, Lizabeth. *A Consumers' Republic: The Politics of Mass Consumption in Postwar America.* New York: Knopf, 2003.

Colburn, David. *Racial Change and Community Crisis: St. Augustine, Florida, 1877–1980.* Gainesville: University Presses of Florida, 1991.

Colburn, David R., and Lance deHaven-Smith. *Government in the Sunshine: Florida Since Statehood.* Gainesville: University Press of Florida, 1999.

Colburn, David R., and Richard K. Scher. *Florida's Gubernatorial Politics in the Twentieth Century.* Gainesville: University Presses of Florida, 1980.

Cole, Thomas R. *The Journey of Life: A Cultural History of Aging in America.* Cambridge: Cambridge University Press, 1992.

Coletti, Richard J. "Recovery Brings the Bite, Jaguars Bring the Roar." *Florida Trend* 36 (April 1994): 89–92.

———. "Victims of Success." *Florida Trend* 35 (July 1992): 32–36.

Conboy, Vince. *Exposé: Florida's Billion Dollar Land Fraud*. Naples: n.p., 1972.

Corliss, Richard. *"You're Under Arrest."* Time, 8 May 1989, 102–4.

Crispell, Brian Lewis. *Testing the Limits: George Armistead Smathers and Cold War America*. Athens: University of Georgia Press, 1999.

Cronon, William. *Nature's Metropolis and the Great West*. New York: W. W. Norton, 1991.

Crooks, James B. *Jacksonville after the Fire, 1901–1919*. Gainesville: University Presses of Florida, 1991.

———. *Jacksonville: The Consolidation Story from Civil Rights to the Jaguars*. Gainesville: University Press of Florida, 2004.

Crosby, Alfred W. *Ecological Imperialism: The Biological Expansion of Europe, 900–1900*. Cambridge: Cambridge University Press, 1986.

Crouch, Lori. *"The Final Fields."* South Florida Sun-Sentinel, 4 May 1999.

Crouthamel, Thomas G., Sr. *A History of Trailer Estates*. Laneloth, Penn.: Keystone Press, 1987.

Crum, Lou Jean. *"The Oklawaha River."* Master's thesis, Florida State University, 1954.

Curl, Donald. *Mizner's Florida: American Resort Architecture*. Cambridge, Mass.: MIT Press, 1984.

Danese, Tracy E. *Claude Pepper and Ed Ball: Politics, Purpose, and Power*. Gainesville: University Press of Florida, 2000.

Daniel, Pete. *Lost Revolutions: The South in the 1950s*. Chapel Hill: University of North Carolina Press, 2000.

Danzer, Gerald A., with James Akerman. *Paper Trails: Geographic Literacy via American Highway Maps*. Chicago: Newberry Library, 1996.

Darragh, Charles. *"Danger in Florida Land Developments."* Florida Trend 2 (September 1959): 12–16.

———. *"Shakeout in Land Development."* Florida Trend 5 (April 1963): 21–24.

Davidson, William L. *Dunedin thru the Years, 1850–1978*. Charlotte, N.C.: Delmar Printing, 1978.

Davis, Jack E. *The Wide Brim: Early Poems and Ponderings of Marjory Stoneman Douglas*. Gainesville: University Press of Florida, 2002.

Davis, Mike. *Ecology of Fear: Los Angeles and the Imagination of Disaster*. New York: Vintage, 1998.

Davis, Susan. *Spectacular Nature: Corporate Culture and the Sea World Experience*. Berkeley and Los Angeles: University of California Press, 1997.

Dean, Susan. *Against the Tide: The Battle for America's Beaches*. New York: Columbia University Press, 1999.

DeBeauvoir, Simone. *The Coming of Age*. Translated by Patrick O'Brian. New York: G. P. Putnam's Sons, 1972.

DeGrove, John M. *Land Growth and Politics*. Washington, D.C.: Planners Press, 1984.

Denig, Greg. *Islands and Beaches: Discourse on a Silent Island, Marquesas, 1774–1880*. Honolulu: University Press of Hawaii, 1980.

Dennis, Richard P. *"Land Fraud: The Investigation Spreads—and Spreads."* Florida Trend 18 (January 1976): 79–80.

Derr, Mark. *Some Kind of Paradise: A Chronicle of Man and Land in Florida.* New York: William Morrow and Co., 1989.

Desmond, James C. *Staging Tourism: Bodies on Display from Waikiki to Sea World.* Chicago: University of Chicago Press, 1999.

"Destinations of Auto Tourists in 1970." *Florida Trend* 13 (May 1971): 43–44.

Dewey, Scott H. "The Fickle Finger of Phosphate: Central Florida Air Pollution and the Failure of Environmental Policy, 1957–1970." *Journal of Southern History* 65 (August 1999): 565–603.

Didion, Joan. *Miami.* New York: Simon and Schuster, 1987.

"Did Politics Rob Florida of NASA's Space Program?" *Florida Trend* 23 (November 1990): 47–49.

Dietrich, T. Stanton. *The Urbanization of Florida's Population: An Historical Perspective of County Growth, 1830–1970.* Gainesville: Bureau of Economic and Business Research, 1978.

Dietsch, Robert W. "Trouble in Fantasyland." *New Republic,* 17 July 1971, 13–14.

"Disney Creates a Magic Kingdom," *Florida Trend* 26 (June 1978): 75–79.

"Disney: Trouble in Dreamland." *Duns* 101 (June 1973): 54–57, 112.

"Disney World Triggers Trouble for Orlando." *Business Week,* 1 April 1972, 60–61.

Dodrill, David E. *Selling the Dream: The Gulf American Corporation and the Building of Cape Coral, Florida.* Tuscaloosa: University of Alabama Press, 1993.

Dolan, Michael. *The American Porch: An Informal History of an Informal Place.* Guilford, Conn.: Lyons Press, 2002.

"The Dollar Dilemma of Florida's Aged." *Florida Trend* 15 (January 1973): 72.

Dorschner, John. "Life inside the Blob: Searching for the Soul of Broward County." *Miami Herald, Tropic Magazine,* 2 November 1986.

Dortch, Shannon. "Metros with Moola." *American Demographics* 19 (December 1977): 6–11.

Douglas, Marjory Stoneman. *Voice of the River: An Autobiography with John Rothchild.* Sarasota: Pineapple Press, 1987.

Dow, Robert N. "Yesterday and the Day Before: 1913 to the Present." In *The Oldest City,* edited by Jean Parker Waterbury, 211–42. St. Augustine: St. Augustine Historical Society, 1983.

Dunlop, Beth. "'Egotecture' Is Stealing our Big Views." *Miami Herald,* 7 July 2002.

———. *Florida's Vanishing Architecture.* Englewood: Pineapple Press, 1987.

———. "How Hialeah Happened." *Miami Herald,* 28 April 1991.

———. "In Florida, A New Emphasis on Design." *New York Times,* 9 December 2001.

Dunn, Hampton. *Back Home: A History of Citrus County, Florida.* Clearwater: Artcraft Printing, 1976.

Dunn, Marvin. *Black Miami in the Twentieth Century.* Gainesville: University Press of Florida, 1997.

Dunnigan, Pat. "How Big Is Too Big?" *Florida Trend* 45 (October 2002): 28.

Duryea, Bill. "The Tradeoff." *St. Petersburg Times,* 12 September 2004.

Dusenbury, George, and Jane Dusenbury. *How to Retire to Florida*. New York: Harper, 1947.

Eastman, Susan. "The Big Drain." *Tampa Weekly Planet*, 13–19 April 2000, 19–24.

Eastward Ho! Development Futures: Paths to More Efficient Growth in Southeast Florida. Fort Lauderdale: Florida Department of Community Affairs, 1999.

Eck, Diana L. *A New Religious America: How a Christian Country Has Become the World's Most Religiously Diverse Nation*. San Francisco: Harper, 2001.

Eckerd, Jack, and Charles Paul Conn. *Eckerd*. Clearwater: JME, 1987.

Eco, Umberto. *Travels in Upper Reality*. Translated by William Weaver. New York: Harcourt Brace Jovanovich, 1986.

Egan, Jack. "A New Battle for the Sultans of Sugar." *U.S. News and World Report*, 17 July 1995, 22.

Egerton, John. *The Americanization of Dixie: The Southernization of America*. New York: Harper's, 1974.

Eire, Carlos. *Waiting for Snow in Havana: Confessions of a Cuban Boy*. New York: Free Press, 2003.

Ellsworth, Lucius, and Linda Ellsworth. *Pensacola: The Deep Water City*. Tulsa: Continental Heritage Press, 1982.

Embry, Joel. "The Appeal of Small Town Living in North Florida Endures." *Forum* 20 (Summer 1997): 26–33.

Encyclopedia of Southern Culture. Edited by Charles Reagan Wilson and William Ferris. Chapel Hill: University of North Carolina Press, 1989.

Eriksen, John M. *Brevard County: A History to 1955*. Tampa: Florida Historical Society Press, 1984.

"Expanding Florida." *Look*, 14 April 1959, 23–33.

Fabricio, Roberto. "Miami Goes Latin and Likes It." *Florida Trend* 18 (April 1976): 140–45.

Faragher, John Mark. "Bungalow and Ranch House: The Architectural Backwash of California." *Western Historical Quarterly* 32 (Summer 2000): 149–75.

Farrell, James J. *One Nation under Goods: Malls and the Seductions of American Shopping*. Washington, D.C.: Smithsonian Books, 2003.

"Fast-Growing Florida: A State That Can Hardly Wait." *Time*, 14 April 1961, 96–105.

"Father of Westward Expansion." In *Our Century: The Palm Beach County 100*, 169. West Palm Beach: *Palm Beach Post*, 2000.

"Fighting the Good Fight Pays Off." *Florida Trend* 14 (July 1971): 62, 64, 69.

Finotti, John. "The River City Gang." *Florida Trend* 41 (February 1999): 48–50.

———. "Wings." *Florida Trend* 44 (October 2001): 56–62.

Fischer, David Hackett. *Growing Old in America*. New York: Oxford University Press, 1977.

Fisher, Jane. *Fabulous Hoosier*. New York: R. M. McBride and Co., 1947.

Fitzgerald, Frances. *Cities on a Hill: A Journey through Contemporary American Cultures*. New York: Simon and Schuster, 1986.

Fjellman, Stephen M. *Vinyl Leaves: Walt Disney World and America*. Boulder, Colo.: Westview Press, 1982.

Fletcher, June. "Retirees Say No to Parents' Communities." *Wall Street Journal*, 14 November 1997.

Florida: A Guide to the Southernmost State. American Guide Series. New York: Oxford University Press, 1939.

"Florida: A Place in the Sun." *Time*, 19 December 1955, 18–21.

Florida Department of Highway Safety and Motor Vehicles, "Big Boat Boom," *Miami Herald*, 22 October 2000.

"Florida: Biggest Fraud Yet?" *Newsweek*, 26 May 1975, 69–70.

"Florida and the Horseless Carriage." *Florida Trend* 10 (June 1967): 12–20.

"Florida Finds High-Tech Fountain of Youth." *U.S. News and World Report*, 25 April 1983, 58–59.

"The Florida Lure." *Fortune*, February 1958, 229–30, 232.

"Florida's Fattest Tourist Fling: Millions Seek a New Place in the Sun." *Life*, 23 January 1956, 32–39.

Florida Statistical Abstract 1999. Gainesville: Bureau of Economic and Business Research, 1999.

Florida Statistical Abstract 2002. Gainesville: Bureau of Economic and Business Research, 2002.

Florida Trend: Economic Yearbook 2000. 41 (April 2000).

Foglesong, Richard E. *Married to the Mouse: Walt Disney World and Orlando.* New Haven: Yale University Press, 2001.

———. "When Disney Came to Town." *Washington Post Magazine*, 14 May 1994.

Foster, Mark S. *Castles in the Sand: The Life and Times of Carl Graham Fisher.* Gainesville: University Press of Florida, 2000.

Frazer, William, and John J. Guthrie Jr. *The Florida Land Boom: Speculation, Money and the Banks.* Westport, Conn.: Quorum Books, 1995.

Freeman, Mary. "Florida's Pure White Sands." *Nation*, 26 January 1957, 77–80.

———. "You Can't Stop Progress." *Nation*, 15 June 1957, 521–24.

Friedlander, Paul J. C. "Miami Worries about Disney World." *New York Times*, 4 April 1971.

Fuller, Walter P. "Barons, Promoters, Visionaries—Is the Past the Pattern for the Future?" *Florida Trend* 10 (April 1968): 31–32, 35, 129–31.

Gaines, Steven. *Heroes and Villains: The True Story of the Beach Boys.* New York: New American Library, 1986.

Gall, Gilbert J. "Southern Industrial Workers and Anti-Union Sentiment: Arkansas and Florida in 1944." In *Organized Labor in the Twentieth-Century South*, edited by Robert H. Zieger, 223–49. Knoxville: University of Tennessee Press, 1991.

Gannon, Michael. "The Columbus Quincentenary." In *Spanish Pathways in Florida*, edited by Ann Henderson and Gary Mormino, 328–45. Sarasota: Pineapple Press, 1991.

———. *Operation Drumboat: The Dramatic True Story of Germany's First U-Boat Attacks along the American Coast in World War II.* New York: Harper and Row, 1990.

———, ed. *The New History of Florida.* Gainesville: University Press of Florida, 1996.

García, María Cristina. *Havana USA: Cuban Exiles and Cuban Americans in South Florida, 1959–1994.* Berkeley and Los Angeles: University of California Press, 1996.

Garreau, Joel. *Edge City: Life on the New Frontier.* New York: Doubleday, 1991.

———. *The Nine Nations of North America.* Boston: Houghton Mifflin, 1981.

Gelfand, Mark I. *A Nation of Cities: The Federal Government and Urban America, 1933–1965.* New York: Oxford University Press.

Genovese, Peter. *The Great American Road Trip: U.S. 1, Maine to Florida.* New Brunswick, N.J.: Rutgers University Press, 1999.

George, Paul. "Downtown Fort Lauderdale: Its Demise and Renaissance in the Post-War Era." *Broward Legacy* 14 (Summer-Fall 1991): 9–20.

———. "Kendall." In *Miami's Historic Neighborhoods,* edited by Becky Roper Matkov, 118–22. San Antonio: Publishing Historical Network, 1992.

———. "Passage to the New Eden: Tourism in Miami." *Florida Historical Quarterly* 59 (April 1981): 440–63.

———. "Where the Boys Were." *South Florida History Magazine* 19 (Winter 1991): 5–8.

Gibson, Linda. "Selling Florida." *Creative Loafing* 6, 10 June–16 June 1993, 3–5.

Gill, Brendan. *Many Masks: The Life of Frank Lloyd Wright.* New York: G. P. Putnam's Sons, 1987.

Ginzl, David I. *Barnett: The Story of Florida's Bank.* Tampa: University of Tampa Press, 2001.

Gittner, Cory H. *Miami's Parrot Jungle and Gardens.* Gainesville: University Press of Florida, 2000.

Glades County, Florida. Moore Haven: Rainbow Books, 1985.

Goldfield, David. *Cotton Fields and Skyscrapers: Southern City and Region, 1607–1980.* Baton Rouge: Louisiana State University Press, 1982.

Goodkin, Lewis M. "In the Rough." *Florida Trend* 39 (March 1997): 80–84.

———. "The Lap of Luxury." *Florida Trend* 44 (February 2002): 54–56.

Goodwyn, Larry. "Anarchy in St. Augustine." *Harper's,* January 1965, 74–81.

Gopnik, Adam. "Under One Roof: The Death and Life of the New York Department Store." *New Yorker,* 22 September 2003, 92–103.

Gore, Rick. "Andrew Aftermath." *National Geographic* (April 1993): 2–38.

Graebner, William. *A History of Retirement: The Meaning and Function of an American Institution, 1885–1978.* New Haven: Yale University Press, 1980.

Graham, Thomas. "The Flagler Era." In *The Oldest City,* edited by Jean Parker Waterbury, 181–210. St. Augustine: St. Augustine Historical Society, 1983.

Gray, Lewis Cecil. *History of Agriculture in the Southern United States to 1860.* New York: Peter Smith, 1941.

Green, Ben. *Finest Kind: A Celebration of a Florida Fishing Village.* Macon, Ga.: Mercer University Press, 1985.

Green, Henry Alan, and Marcia Zerivitz. *Mosaic: Jewish Life in Florida.* Coral Gables: Mosaic, 1991.

Green, Jordan, and Chris Kromm. "Missiles and Magnolias: The South at War." *Southern Exposure* 30 (Spring/Summer 2002): 15–18.

Grismer, Karl H. *The Story of Sarasota.* Sarasota: M. E. Russell, 1946.

Gross, Eric L. "'Somebody Got Drowned, Lord': Florida and the Great Okeechobee Hurricane Disaster of 1928." PhD diss., Florida State University, 1995.

Guide to Orlando's Afro-American Heritage. Orlando: Central Florida Society of Afro-American Heritage, Inc., 1991.

Hahamovitch, Cindy. *The Fruits of Their Labor: Atlantic Coast Farmworkers and the Making of Migrant Poverty, 1870–1945.* Chapel Hill: University of North Carolina Press, 1997.

Halberstam, David. *The Powers That Be.* New York: Knopf, 1979.

Hanna, Alfred Jackson, and Kathryn Abbey Hanna. *Lake Okeechobee: Wellspring of the Everglades.* New York: Bobbs-Merrill, 1948.

Harney, Robert. "The Palmetto and the Maple Leaf: Patterns of Canadian Migration to Florida." In *Shades of the Sunbelt,* edited by Randall Miller and George Pozzetta, 21–40. Westport, Conn.: Greenwood Press, 1988.

Harrington, Michael. *The Other America: Poverty in the United States.* New York: Macmillan, 1962.

Hart, John Fraser, Michelle J. Rhodes, and John T. Morgan. *The Unknown World of the Mobile Home.* Baltimore: Johns Hopkins University Press, 2002.

Hatton, Hap. *Tropical Splendor.* New York: Knopf, 1987.

Hauserman, Julie. "The Ugliest Beach in Florida." In *The Wild Heart of Florida,* edited by Jeff Ripple and Susan Cerulean, 86–90. Gainesville: University Press of Florida, 2001.

Heitmann, John A. "The Beginnings of Big Sugar in Florida, 1920–1945." *Florida Historical Quarterly* 77 (Summer 1998): 39–61.

Henderson, Ann L., and Gary R. Mormino, eds. *Spanish Pathways in Florida, 1492–1992.* Sarasota: Pineapple Press, 1991.

Henwood, Doug. "Behind the Bankruptcy Boom." *Nation,* 5 October 1992: 345, 359–60.

Hepburn, Andrew, and Harlan Long. *Florida: A Complete Guide.* New York: Simon and Schuster, 1949.

Hewlett, Richard Greening. *Jesse Ball duPont.* Gainesville: University Press of Florida, 1992.

Hiaasen, Carl. *Team Rodent: How Disney Devours the World.* New York: Ballantine Publishing Group, 1998.

———. *Tourist Season: A Novel.* New York: Warner Books, 1986.

Hiller, Herbert L. "How to Save Florida Tourism." *Florida Trend* 38 (March 1996): 42–49.

———. "The Real Florida." *Forum* 24 (Spring 2001): 22–27.

Hinder, Kimberly. "Publix—Where Shopping Was a Pleasure." *Society for Commercial Archaeology Journal* 19 (Fall 2001): 4–13.

Hine, Thomas. *Populuxe.* New York: Knopf, 1986.

Hines, Christopher Needham. *The Truth about Florida.* North Miami: Florida Research Press, 1962.

History of Martin County. Stuart: Historical Society of Martin County, 1988.

Hollis, Tim. *Dixie before Disney: 100 Years of Roadside Fun.* Jackson: University of Mississippi Press, 1999.

Holmes, Steven. "The World According to AARP," *New York Times,* 21 March 2001.

Hopkins, Jerry. *The Lizard King: The Essential Jim Morrison.* New York: Charles Scribner's Sons, 1992.

"Hotels and Resorts." *Florida Trend* 44 (February 2002): 72.

"How the Immigrants Made It in Miami." *Business Week*, 1 May 1971, 88.

Hughes, Melvin Edward, Jr. "William J. Howey and His Florida Dreams." *Florida Historical Quarterly* 66 (January 1988): 243–64.

Hurley, Frank T., Jr. *Surf, Sand, and Post Card Sunsets: A History of Pass-a-Grille and the Gulf Beaches*. St. Petersburg: 1977.

Hurston, Zora Neale. *Mules and Men*. Philadelphia: J. B. Lippincott, 1935.

———. *Their Eyes Were Watching God*. New York: Harper and Row, 1937.

Irby, Lee. "Beat in St. Pete." *Tampa Weekly Planet*, 13–21 October 1999, 18–28.

———. "Razing Gerontopolis: Green Benches, Trailer Trash, and Old People in St. Petersburg, Florida: 1910–1970." Master's thesis, University of South Florida, 1999.

———. "Taking Out the Trailer Trash: The Battle over Mobile Homes in St. Petersburg, Florida." *Florida Historical Quarterly* 79 (Fall 2000): 181–200.

Jackson, Harvey H., III. "The Florida Room: From 'Redneck Riviera' to 'Emerald Coast': A Personal History of a Piece of the Florida Panhandle." *Florida Historical Quarterly* 81 (Winter 2003): 316–22.

———. "Seaside, Florida: Robert Davis and the Quest for Community." *Atlanta History* 42 (Fall 1998): 41–51.

Jackson, Jerry. "Citrus Cashes in on Growth." *Orlando Sentinel*, 29 March 1998.

Jackson, Kenneth T. *Crabgrass Frontier: The Suburbanization of the United States*. New York: Oxford University Press, 1985.

Jakle, John. *The Tourist: Travel in Twentieth-Century America*. Lincoln: University of Nebraska Press, 1985.

Jakle, John A., and Keith Sculle. *Fast Food: Roadside Restaurants in the Automobile Age*. Baltimore: Johns Hopkins University Press, 1999.

———. *The Gas Station in America*. Baltimore: Johns Hopkins University Press, 1994.

Jakle, John A., Keith A. Sculle, and Jefferson S. Rogers. *The Motel in America*. Baltimore: Johns Hopkins University Press, 1996.

Jarvis, Eric. "Florida's Forgotten Ethnic Culture: Patterns of Canadian Immigration, Tourism and Investment since 1920." *Florida Historical Quarterly* 81 (Fall 2002): 186–97.

Jasper, James M. *Restless Nation: Starting Over in America*. Chicago: University of Chicago Press, 2000.

Jenkins, Virginia Scott. *The Lawn: A History*. Washington, D.C.: Smithsonian Institution Press, 1994.

Johnson, Charles S. *Statistical Atlas of Southern Counties*. Chapel Hill: University of North Carolina Press, 1941.

Johnson, Robert. "America's Military Might Is Also Bastion of the Florida Economy." *Florida Trend* 21 (July 1978): 30–39.

———. "The Changing Picture of the Drive-In Movie." *Florida Trend* 20 (March 1978): 35–41.

———. "If You've Seen One Gator, You've Seen 'Em All." *Florida Trend* 23 (September 1980): 56–58.

————."Palm Beach County: Florida's Land of Contrast." *Florida Trend* 18 (February 1976): 46–51.

————. "Sarasota: A Strong Economy Influenced Heavily by Retirement." *Florida Trend* 21 (August 1978): 30–38.

————. "Thrill Rides Draw the Crowds." *Florida Trend* 21 (May 1978): 22–23.

Jones, Jacqueline. *The Dispossessed: America's Underclass from the Civil War to the Present.* New York: Basic Books, 1992.

Judd, Dennis R., and Todd Swanstrom. *City Politics: Private Power and Public Policy.* 3rd ed. New York: Longman, 2002.

Kallina, Edmund F., Jr. *Claude Kirk and the Politics of Confrontation.* Gainesville: University Press of Florida, 1993.

Kaplan, Kenneth M., and Charles F. Longino Jr. "Gray in Gold: A Public-Private Conundrum." In *Growing Old in America,* edited by Elizabeth W. Markson, 389–98. New Brunswick, N.J.: Rutgers University Press, 1991.

Kasson, John F. *Amusing the Millions: Coney Island at the Turn of the Century.* New York: Hill and Wang, 1978.

Kaufman, Wallace, and Orrin H. Pilkey Jr. *The Beaches Are Moving: The Drowning of America's Shoreline.* Durham, N.C.: Duke University Press, 1983.

Kay, Jean Holtz. *Asphalt Nation: How the Automobile Took Over America.* New York: Crown, 1997.

Kendrick, Bayard. *Florida Trails to Turnpikes, 1914–1964.* Gainesville: University of Florida Press, 1964.

Kennedy, Ray. "Eden Fights Back." *Sports Illustrated,* 3 February 1975, 28–35.

Kennedy, Stetson. *Palmetto Country.* New York: Duell, Sloan and Pearce, 1942.

Kersey, Harry A. *An Assumption of Sovereignty: Social and Political Transformation among the Florida Seminoles, 1953–1979.* Lincoln: University of Nebraska Press, 1996.

————. *Buffalo Tiger: A Life in the Everglades.* Lincoln: University of Nebraska Press, 2002.

————. *The Florida Seminoles and the New Deal, 1933–1942.* Gainesville: University Presses of Florida, 1989.

————. *Pelts, Plumes, and Hides: White Traders among the Seminole Indians, 1870–1930.* Gainesville: University Presses of Florida, 1975.

Keuchel, Edward F. *Florida: Enterprise under the Sun.* Chatsworth, Calif.: Windsor Publications, 1990.

Kilborn, Peter. "Economists Predict Florida Can Keep Recession at Bay." *New York Times,* 24 November 1990.

————. "Immigrants Rebuilding City after Storm." *New York Times,* 21 February 2000.

————. "Scraping By." *New York Times,* 27 November 1990.

Kirby, Jack Temple. *Rural Worlds Lost: The American South, 1920–1960.* Baton Rouge: Louisiana State University Press, 1987.

————. "The Southern Exodus, 1910–1960: A Primer for Historians." *Journal of Southern History* 49 (November 1983): 587–97.

Kleinberg, Howard. *Miami Beach: A History.* Miami: Centennial Press, 1994.

————. *Miami: The Way We Were.* Miami: Vanderbilt Printing, 1985.

Klinkenberg, Jeff. "The Citrus Tower." *St. Petersburg Times,* 16 February 1997.

Koenig, John. "Florida's Best Fund-Raisers." *Florida Trend* 30 (May 1987): 46–49.

———. "The Invasion Continues." *Florida Trend* 36 (March 1993): 74–78.

Kowinski, William S. "The Malling of America." *New York Times*, 10 May 1978, 30–55.

Krock, Arthur. "In the Nation: Key Biscayne." *New York Times*, 29 March 1955.

Kunerth, Jess. "Developers Skate around Issue of Death." *Orlando Sentinel*, 26 November 2002.

———. "Forgotten Towns Fade Away." *Orlando Sentinel*, 10 December 2001.

———. "Old People." *Orlando Sentinel*, 16 July 2000.

———. "Retiree Dreams Come True." *Orlando Sentinel*, 24 November 2002.

———. "Southern Towns Are Digging for Gray Gold." *Orlando Sentinel*, 27 April 2003.

Kunerth, Jess, and Robert Sargent Jr. "Towns See Villages as Mixed Blessing." *Orlando Sentinel*, 25 November 2002.

Kunstler, James Howard. *The Geography of Nowhere: The Rise and Decline of America's Man-made Landscape*. New York: Simon and Schuster, 1993.

Lade, Diane. "Gray Wave." *South Florida Sun-Sentinel*, 27 April 1997.

La Hurd, Jeff. *Quintessential Sarasota*. Sarasota: Clubhouse Publishing, 1990.

Langdon, Philip. *Orange Roofs, Golden Arches: The Architecture of American Chain Restaurants*. New York: Knopf, 1986.

Lanier, Sidney. *Florida: Its Scenery, Climate and History*. Philadelphia: J. B. Lippincott and Co., 1875.

Laux, James M. *Mount Dora, Florida, A Short History*. Orlando: FirstPublish, 2001.

LaVigne, Andrew W. "Tariffs on Citrus Imports Help Level the Field." *Tampa Tribune*, 27 May 2000.

Lears, T. J. Jackson. *No Place of Grace: Antimodernism and the Transformation of American Culture, 1880–1920*. New York: Pantheon, 1981.

Lenček, Lena, and Gideon Baker. *The Beach: The History of Paradise on Earth*. New York: Viking, 1998.

Lessing, Lawrence P. "State of Florida." *Fortune*, February 1948, 65–72, 211–13.

Lewandowski, Monica. "Formulating Frozen Concentrate." In *History of Florida Citrus*, 44–48. Willoughby, Ohio: Meister Publishing Co., 2000.

Lewis, Tom. *Divided Highways: Building the Interstate Highways*. New York: Viking, 1997.

Lindbergh, Anne Morrow. *Gift from the Sea*. New York: Pantheon, 1955.

Linsin, Christopher. "More Than an Amenity Alone: A Social History of Retirement in the Century Villages, 1968–1992." PhD diss., Florida State University, 1997.

Lipsitz, George. "World Cities and World Beat: Low-Wage Labor and Transnational Culture." *Pacific Historical Review* 68 (May 1999): 213–32.

"Little Atlanta." *Florida Trend* 42 (September 1999): 42.

Long, Phil, and Martin Merzer. "Will Florida Lose Its Space Program?" *Miami Herald*, 1 August 1999.

Longino, Charles F., Jr. "From Sunbelt to Sunspots." *American Demographics* 22 (November 1994): 22–31.

———. *Retirement Migration in America, 1970–1990*. Houston: Vacation Publications, 1994.

Longman, Philip. "Enjoy It While It Lasts." *Florida Trend* 36 (April 1994): 34–38.

———. "The Species Comes First." *Florida Trend* 36 (May 1993): 34–39.

———. "Sprawl." *Florida Trend* 37 (December 1994): 40–49.

———. "Why Florida Won't Bust after the Boom." *Florida Trend* 34 (April 1992): 50, 52–54.

Lundstrom, Mary S. "I Remember Marco." *The Miamian* (August 1971): 25–27, 48.

Luther, Gary. *History of New Smyrna, East Florida.* N. Smyrna Beach: Luther's Publishing, 2001.

MacCannell, Dean. *The Tourist: A New Theory of the Leisure Class.* New York: Schocken, 1976.

MacDonald, John D. *Condominium.* New York: Ballantine, 1985.

———. "Why a Quarter Century of Growth May Not Have Been Progress." *Florida Trend* 25 (June 1983): 34–40.

MacDowell, Liz. "Research Adding Citrus Wealth." *Florida Grower* 58 (March 1950): 6, 15, 19.

MacManus, Susan A. "Aging in Florida and Its Implications." *The Graying of Florida, Report of the Reubin O'D. Askew Institute, 1999,* 8, 9, 18. Gainesville: Askew Institute, 1999.

———. *Targeting Senior Voters.* New York: Rowman and Littlefield, 2000.

MacManus, Susan A., with Patricia Turner. *Young vs. Old: Generational Combat in the Twenty-First Century.* Boulder, Colo.: Westview Press, 1996.

Mahoney, Lawrence. "Is Miami the Nation's Number Two Jewish City?" *Florida Trend* 20 (September 1977): 18–24.

Manning, Phillip. *Orange Blosson Trails.* Winston-Salem, N.C.: John F. Blair, 1997.

Mansfield, Bill. "Palm Beach County." *Florida Trend* 5 (July 1962): 22–37.

Martinson, Tom. *American Dreamscape: The Pursuit of Happiness in Postwar Suburbia.* New York: Carroll and Graf, 2000.

Mason, Herman, Jr. *African-American Life in Jacksonville.* Charleston, S.C.: Arcadia Publishing, 1997.

Matthews, Janet Snyder. *Edge of Wilderness: A Settlement History of Manatee River and Sarasota Bay.* Tulsa: Caprine Press, 1983.

———. *Sarasota: Journey to Centennial.* Tulsa: Continental Heritage Press, 1985.

———. *Venice, Journey from Horse and Chaise.* Sarasota: Pine Level Press, 1989.

May, Kirse Granat. *Golden Gate State, Golden Youth: The California Image in Popular Culture, 1955–1966.* Chapel Hill: University of North Carolina Press, 2002.

McCally, David P. "Cane Cutters in the Everglades." Master's thesis, University of South Florida, 1991.

———. *The Everglades: An Environmental History.* Gainesville: University Press of Florida, 1999.

———. "Sun City Center." *Tampa Bay History* (Spring/Summer 1992): 31–44.

McGoun, William E. *Southeast Florida Pioneers: The Palm and Treasure Coasts.* Sarasota: Pineapple Press, 1998.

McGovern, James R. *The Emergence of a City in the Modern South: Pensacola, 1900–1945.* DeLeon Springs, Fla.: Painter, 1976.

McIver, Stuart B. *Dreamers, Schemers and Scalawags: The Florida Chronicles.* 2 vols. Sarasota: Pineapple Press, 1994.

———. *Fort Lauderdale and Broward County: An Illustrated History.* Woodland Hills, Calif.: Windsor, 1983.

———. *Glimpses of South Florida History.* Miami: Florida Fair Books, 1988.

McLamore, James W. *The Burger King: Jim McLamore and the Building of an Empire.* New York: McGraw-Hill, 1998.

McPhee, John. *Oranges.* New York: Farrar, Straus, and Giroux, 1966.

"Memories of the Boston Santa Fé River Ranches as told by Melda Bassett." Gainesville: Institute of Food and Agricultural Services, 1999.

Mieher, Stuart. "Ghost Subdivisions: Living Legacy of the Land Scam." *Florida Trend* 28 (May 1985): 73–76.

"A Military Marriage Has Embraceable Compensations." *Florida Trend* 26 (June 1983): 93–96.

Miller, Annetta. "Cashing in on Florida's Wealth of Elderly." *Florida Trend* 28 (October 1985): 118–24.

"Mining Is Mainstay." *Florida Trend* 10 (April 1968): 68–74.

Mintz, Sidney. *Sweetness and Power: The Place of Sugar in Modern History.* New York: Viking, 1985.

Miracle, Barbara. "Family Comes First." *Florida Trend* 35 (February 1993): 68–74.

———. "Get There Early." *Florida Trend* 36 (November 1993): 62–65.

Mogelonsky, Marcia. "Asian-Indian Americans." *American Demographics* 11 (August 1995): 32–39.

Mohl, Raymond. "Asian Immigration to Florida." *Florida Historical Quarterly* 74 (Winter 1996): 261–86.

———. "Changing Economic Patterns in the Miami Metropolitan Area, 1940–1980." *Tequesta* 42 (1982): 63–74.

———. "Elizabeth Virrick and the 'Concrete Monsters': Housing Reform in Postwar Miami." *Tequesta* 61 (2001): 5–38.

———. "Maurice Ferré, Xavier Suarez, and the Ethnic Factor in Miami Politics. In *Spanish Pathways in Florida,* edited by Ann L. Henderson and Gary R. Mormino, 302–27. Sarasota: Pineapple Press, 1991.

———. "Miami: The Ethnic Cauldron." In *Sunbelt Cities,* edited by Richard Bernard and Bradley R. Rice, 58–99. Austin: University of Texas Press, 1983.

———. "Race and Space in the Modern City: Interstate 95 and the Black Community in Miami." In *Urban Policy in Twentieth-Century America,* edited by Arnold R. Hirsch and Raymond Mohl, 100–58. New Brunswick, N.J.: Rutgers University Press, 1993.

Monroe, Gary. *The Highwaymen: Florida's African-American Landscape Painters.* Gainesville: University Press of Florida, 2001.

Montague, Clay L., and Richard G. Wiegert. "Salt Marshes," in *Ecosystems of Florida,* eds. Ronald L. Meyers and John J. Jewell. Orlando: University of Central Florida Press, 1990: 481–512.

"Moon Boom." *Newsweek,* 16 October 1961, 88–90.

Moore, Deborah Dash. "The Ta'am of Tourism." *Pacific Historical Quarterly* 68 (May 1999): 193–212.

———. *To the Golden Cities: Pursuing the American Jewish Dream in Miami and Los Angeles.* New York: Free Press, 1994.

Moore, Roger. "The New View from Citrus Tower." *Orlando Sentinel,* 28 May 2000.

Morey, Lesa. "A. Duda & Sons: Bigger Is Better." *Florida Grower* 93 (May 2000): 14–15.

Mormino, Gary. "Florida's Year of Reckoning, 1973." *Forum* 27 (Winter 2003): 18–19.

———. "G. I. Joe Meets Jim Crow: Racial Violence and Reform in World War II Florida." *Florida Historical Quarterly* 74 (July 1994): 23–42.

———. "Miami Goes to War, 1941–1945," *Tequesta* 57 (1997): 5–52.

———. "Trouble in Tourist Heaven." *Forum* 17 (Summer 1994): 11–13.

———. "World War II." In *The New History of Florida,* edited by Michael Gannon, 344–72. Gainesville: University Press of Florida, 1996.

Mormino, Gary, and George E. Pozzetta. *The Immigrant World of Ybor City: Italians and Their Latin Neighbors in Tampa, 1885–1985.* Gainesville: University Press of Florida, 1998.

Morris, Allen. *The Florida Handbook, 1953.* 4th ed. Tallahassee: Peninsular, 1953.

Morris, Allen, and Joan Perry Morris. *The Florida Handbook, 2003–2004.* Tallahassee: Peninsular, 2003.

Moscow, Alvin. *Building a Business: The Jim Walter Story.* Sarasota: Pineapple Press, 1995.

Muir, Helen. *Miami, U.S.A.* 1953. Gainesville: University Press of Florida, 2000.

"Munich in the Canefields." *Nation,* 13 September 1993.

"Naples, Hideaway for Top U.S. Executives." *Florida Trend* 2 (June 1959): 27–29.

Nash, Gerald D. *The Federal Landscape: An Economic History of the Twentieth-Century West.* Tucson: University of Arizona Press, 1999.

Nathankane, Joseph, and Janet Podell. *Facts about the States.* 2d ed. New York: H. W. Wilson Co., 1993.

Navarro, Mireya. "In Florida, the Young Are Gaining On the Old." *New York Times,* 25 June 1997.

Nelson, Richard Alan. *Lights! Camera! Florida! Ninety Years of Moviemaking and Television Production in the Sunshine State.* Tampa: Florida Endowment for the Humanities, 1987.

"A New Battle for the Sultans of Sugar." *U.S. News and World Report,* 17 July 1995, 22–23.

"The New Florida Land Rush: $10 Down for a Dream." *Newsweek,* 5 January 1959, 55–81.

Nissen, Bruce, and Peter Cattan. *Labor Report on the State of Florida Labor Day 1999.* Miami: Center for Labor Research and Studies, Florida International University, 1999.

Nolan, David. *Fifty Feet in Paradise: The Booming of Florida.* New York: Harcourt Brace Jovanovich, 1984.

Nordheimer, Jon. "Development Boom in Southeast Florida Megalopolis Creates a Host of Urban Ills." *New York Times,* 22 April 1973.

———. "Florida Seeks To Curb Runaway Growth." *New York Times,* 9 February 1973.

———. "Miamians Sense the Advent of Another Season and See Their City Change." *New York Times,* 7 October 1984.

———. "Miami Beach Sees Signs of Revival." *New York Times,* 3 November 1985.

———. "Poverty-Scarred Town Now Stricken by AIDS." *New York Times,* 2 May 1985.

"North Florida's New Era." *Florida Trend* 8 (August 1965): 18–24.

"Now Florida Gets Ready-Made Hills." *Florida Trend* 10 (April 1968): 113–14.

O'Connor, Rory. "It's Grow or Die For Small Tourist Attractions." *Florida Trend* 20 (November 1977): 75–77.

"Off-Limits." *Florida Trend* 46 (June 2003): 80.

Ogle, Maureen. *Key West: History of an Island of Dreams.* Gainesville: University Press of Florida, 2003.

O'Hare, William, and Barbara Clark O'Hare. "Upward Mobility." *American Demographics* 15 (January 1993): 26–32.

"The Old Subscribers." *Time,* 26 October 1959, 80.

Orlean, Susan. *The Orchid Thief.* New York: Random House, 1998.

O'Rouke, P. J. "Inside Epcot Center." *Harper's,* August 1983, 42–43.

Orrick, Bentley, and Harry L. Crumpacker. *The Tampa Tribune: A Century of Florida Journalism.* Tampa: University of Tampa Press, 1998.

"The Other MacArthur." *Florida Trend* 14 (October 1971): 54–55, 57–60, 64.

Otto, John S. "Open-Range Cattle Ranching in South Florida: An Oral History." *Tampa Bay History* 8 (Fall/Winter 1986): 23–35.

Painton, Priscilla. "Fantasy's Reality." *Time,* 27 May 1991, 52–59.

Paradise at Risk. Special statewide report in *Pensacola News Journal, USA Today,* and *Florida Today,* 29 July 2002.

Parks, Arva. *Miami: The Magic City.* Tulsa: Continental Heritage Press, 1981.

Parks, Arva, and Gregory Bush. *Miami: The American Crossroad.* Needham Heights, Mass.: Simon and Schuster, 1996.

Paterniti, Michael. "America in Extremis." *New York Times Magazine,* 21 April 2002.

Patricios, Nicholas N. *Building Marvelous Miami.* Gainesville: University Press of Florida, 1994.

Patterson, Gordon. "Countdown to College: Launching Florida Institute of Technology." *Florida Historical Quarterly* 67 (Fall 1998): 163–80.

———. *The Mosquito Wars: A History of Mosquito Control in Florida.* Gainesville: University Press of Florida, 2004.

———. "A Special Place." *Forum* 20 (Winter 1997/1998): 19–21.

Patterson, James T. *Grand Expectations: The United States, 1945–1974.* New York: Oxford University Press, 1996.

Patton, Phil. *Open Road: A Celebration of the American Highway.* New York: Simon and Schuster, 1986.

Paulson, Darryl. "Stay Out, The Water's Fine: Desegregating Municipal Swimming Facilities in St. Petersburg, Florida." *Tampa Bay History* 4 (Fall/Winter 1982): 6–19.

Paulson, Morton C. *The Great Land Hustle.* Chicago: Henry Regnery Co., 1972.

Pelt, Peggy Dorton. "Wainwright Shipyard: The Impact of a World War II War Industry on Panama City, Florida." PhD diss., Florida State University, 1994.

Pendergrast, Mark. *For God, Country, and Coca-Cola*. New York: Basic Books, 1993.

Pepper, Claude Denson, with Hays Gory. *Pepper: Eyewitness to a Century*. New York: Harcourt Brace Jovanovich, 1987.

Pérez, Louis A. *On Becoming Cuban: Identity, Nationality and Culture*. Chapel Hill: University of North Carolina Press, 1999.

———. *Winds of Change: Hurricanes and the Transformation of Nineteenth-Century Cuba*. Chapel Hill: University of North Carolina Press, 2001.

Peter, Emmett, Jr. *Lake County: A Pictorial History*. Virginia Beach: Donning Co., 1998.

Peterson, Peter G. "Our Graying Budget Priorities." *New York Times*, 18 September 2000.

Petrow, Steven. "The Men Who Bring You Sugar." *St. Petersburg Times, Floridian Magazine*, 7 December 1980, 15–21.

Phelts, Marsha Dean. *An American Beach for African Americans*. Gainesville: University Press of Florida, 1997.

Philips, Philip Lee, ed. *The Lowery Collection, a Descriptive List of Maps of the Spanish Possessions, 1502–1820*. Washington, D.C.: U.S. Government Printing Office, 1912.

Phillips, Kevin P. *The Emerging Republican Majority*. New York: Arlington Place, 1969.

Pierce, Charles W. *Pioneer Life in Southeast Florida*. Coral Gables: University of Miami Press, 1970.

Pierce, Robert N. *A Sacred Trust: Nelson Poynter and the St. Petersburg Times*. Gainesville: University Press of Florida, 1993.

Pilkey, Orrin. *Living with the East Florida Shore*. Durham, N.C.: Duke University Press, 1984.

Pilkey, Orrin, and Katherine L. Dixon, *The Corps and the Shore*. Washington, D.C.: Island Press, 1996.

"The Pizza King Finds a New Home in Central Florida." *Florida Trend* 26 (December 1983): 82–86.

"A Playboy Grows Up." *Time*, 8 March 1954, 90–91.

Pleasants, Julian M. *Orange Journalism: Voices from Florida Newspapers*. Gainesville: University Press of Florida, 2003.

Poppe, David. "The Two-Class Economy." *Florida Trend* 38 (April 1996): 60–67.

Population: A Comprehensive Analysis for the Tampa Bay Region. St. Petersburg: Tampa Bay Regional Planning Council, 1973.

Portes, Alejandro, and Alex Stepick. *City on the Edge: The Transformation of Miami*. Berkeley and Los Angeles: University of California Press, 1993.

Prior, Leon O. "Nazi Invasion of Florida!" *Florida Historical Quarterly* 49 (October 1970): 129–39.

Proctor, Samuel, and Wright Langley. *Gator History: A Pictorial History of the University of Florida*. Gainesville: South Star Pub. Co., 1986.

Provenzo, Eugene F., Jr., and Asterle Baker Provenzo. *In the Eye of Hurricane Andrew*. Gainesville: University Press of Florida, 2002.

Putnam, Robert. *Bowling Alone: The Collapse and Revival of American Community.* New York: Simon and Schuster, 2000.

Quadagno, Jill. *The Color of Welfare: How Racism Undermined the War on Poverty.* New York: Oxford University Press, 1994.

"A Range War." *Florida Trend* 41 (May 1998): 21.

Raper, Arthur Franklin. *The Tragedy of Lynching.* Montclair, N.J.: Patterson Smith, 1969.

Ray, Janisse. *Ecology of a Cracker Childhood.* Minneapolis: Milkweed Editions, 1999.

Reed, John Shelton. *One South: An Ethnic Approach to Regional Culture.* Baton Rouge: Louisiana State University Press, 1982.

Reidy, Jeanne P. "Boca Grande: The Town the Railroad Built." *Tampa Bay History* 4 (Spring/Summer 1982): 21–33.

Resnick, Rosalind. "The Deadbeat State." *Forbes* 148 (8 July 1991): 62.

Ricciuti, Edward R. "Elegant Builder of Southern Dunes." *Audubon* 86 (September 1984): 48–53.

"Richest Towns." *Worth* 9 (June 2000): 88–104.

Rieff, David. *Going to Miami: Exiles, Tourists, and Refugees in the New America.* Boston: Little, Brown, and Co., 1987.

Rifkin, Jeremy. *The Age of Access.* New York: Putnam, 2000.

Riley, Nano. *Florida's Farmworkers in the Twenty-first Century.* Gainesville: University Press of Florida, 2002.

Rimer, Sara. "New Needs for Retirement Complexes Oldest." *New York Times,* 23 March 1998.

———. "Spotlight Fades on Aids in Town." *New York Times,* 14 November 1990.

Roberts, Diane. "Old Florida Is Falling to the Developers." *St. Petersburg Times,* 12 August 2002.

Roberts, Paul. "The Sweet Hereafter." *Harper's,* November 1999, 54–68.

Robison, Jim, and Mark Andrews. *Flashbacks: The Story of Central Florida's Past.* Orlando: Orange County Historical Society and the *Orlando Sentinel,* 1995.

Rogers, William Warren. *Outposts on the Gulf: Saint George Island and Apalachicola from Early Exploration to World War II.* Pensacola: University of West Florida Press, 1986.

Rogers, William Warren, and Mary Louise Ellis. *Favored Land: Tallahassee.* Norfolk: Donning Co., 1988.

Rohter, Larry. "A Puerto Rican Boom for Florida." *New York Times,* 31 January 1994.

Rothchild, John. "Everything under the Sunshine State." *Forum* 18 (Fall/Winter 1993): 4–7.

———. *Up For Grabs: A Trip through Time and Space in the Sunshine State.* Gainesville: University Press of Florida, 2002.

Rotundo, Louis. *Into the Unknown: The x-1 Story.* Washington, D.C.: Smithsonian Press, 1994.

Rowe, Anne E. *The Idea of Florida in the American Literary Imagination.* Baton Rouge: Louisiana State University Press, 1986.

Rowles, Graham D. "Returning Home: The Interstate Transportation of Human Remains." *Omega* 17 (1986–87): 103–13.

Rymer, Russ. *American Beach: A Saga of Race, Wealth and Memory.* New York: Harper Collins, 1998.

Sack, Kevin. "Florida, Long Identified with Old People, Is Struggling with Surge Of Young People." *New York Times,* 25 June 1997.

Sale, Kirkpatrick. *Power Shift: The Rise of the Southern Rim and Its Challenge to the Eastern Establishment.* New York: Random House, 1975.

Samuelson, Robert J. "Paying for Those in Retirement Places Too Heavy a Burden on Young." *St. Petersburg Times,* 13 June 2000.

"Sandy Science." *Florida State University Research in Review* 12 (Fall 2002): 2–3.

Santiago, Chiori. "House Trailers Have Come a Long Way, Baby." *Smithsonian,* June 1998, 76–85.

"Sarasota: A Strong Economy Influenced Heavily by Retirement." *Florida Trend* 21 (August 1978): 30–38.

Schlosser, Eric. *Fast Food Nation.* New York: Perennial, 2002.

Schulman, Bruce J. *The Seventies: The Great Shift in American Culture, Society, and Politics.* New York: Free Press, 2001.

Schulten, Susan. *The Geographical Imagination in America, 1880–1950.* Chicago: University of Chicago Press, 2001.

Scully, Vincent. "Back to the Future." *New York Times,* 27 January 1991.

Schwartz, John. "Pan American World Airways: 1927–1991." *Newsweek,* 22 July 1991, 36.

Schwartz, Rosalie. *Pleasure Island: Tourism and Temptation in Cuba.* Lincoln: University of Nebraska Press, 1997.

"Scream Parks." *U.S. News and World Report,* 10 May 1999, 62–68.

Seay, Geraldine. "Money Bayou." Unpublished. Florida Humanities Council.

Selz, Michael, "How Lucky Can You Get?" *Florida Trend* 32 (August 1989): 30–39.

———. "Why the Phosphate Industry May Soon Scrape Bottom." *Florida Trend* 29 (September 1986): 68–74.

"Seminoles, Inc." *Florida Trend* 3 (December 1960): 15–17.

Seventy-five Years of Sebring, 1912–1987. Sebring: Sebring Historical Society, 1987.

Sexton, Richard. *Parallel Utopias: The Quest for Utopia.* San Francisco: Chronicle Books, 1995.

Sherrill, Robert. "Can Miami Save Itself?" *New York Times Magazine,* 19 July 1987, 18–24.

Shofner, Jerrell H. *History of Apopka and Northwest Orange County, Florida.* Tallahassee: Rose Printing Co., 1982.

———. *History of Brevard County.* 2 vols. Stuart: Brevard County Historic Commission, 1996.

———. *History of Jefferson County.* Tallahassee: Sentry Press, 1976.

———. *Jackson County, Florida: A History.* Greenwood, Fla.: Penkevill Publishing, 1983.

———. *Nor Is It Over Yet. Florida in the Era of Reconstruction, 1863–1877.* Gainesville: University Presses of Florida, 1974.

———. *Orlando: The City Beautiful.* Tulsa: Continental Heritage Press, 1984.

Sicius, Francis. "The Miami-Havana Connection: The First Seventy-five Years." *Tequesta* 58 (1998): 5–46.

Siegal, Fred. "Sprawl a Byproduct of Nation's Prosperity?" *Orlando Sentinel, Insight Magazine*, 11 July 1999.

Sikes, Bob. *He-Coon: The Bob Sikes Story.* Pensacola: Perdido Bay Press, 1984.

Singer, Isaac Bashevis. "My Love Affair with Miami Beach." In *My Love Affair with Miami Beach*, edited by Richard Nagler, i–vii. New York: Simon and Schuster, 1991.

Sloan, Jim, and Douglas Pardue. "Loggers' Lament." *Tampa Tribune*, 19 March 2000.

"Small Banks Next on the Food Chain." *Florida Trend* 36 (October 1993): 72–76.

Smith, Richard Austin. "Florida: O.K., If the Brakes Work." *Fortune* 61 (January 1960): 121–26, 208, 210.

Soruco, Gonzalo R. *Cubans and Mass Media in South Florida.* Gainesville: University Press of Florida, 1996.

"Southern Militarism." *Southern Exposure* 1 (Spring 1973): 60–93.

"Spreading from Disney World: A Spectacular Boom in Florida." *U.S. News and World Report*, 12 June 1972, 60–63.

Starkey, Jay. *Things I Remember, 1899–1979.* Brooksville: Southwest Florida Management District, 1980.

Starr, Kevin. *Americans and the California Dream, 1850–1915.* New York: Oxford University Press, 1973.

———. *The Dream Endures: California Enters the 1940s.* New York: Oxford University Press, 1997.

———. *Inventing the Dream: California through the Progressive Era.* New York: Oxford University Press, 1985.

———. *Material Dreams: Southern California through the 1920s.* New York: Oxford University Press, 1990.

"State of Rage." *U.S. News and World Report*, 11 October 1993, 41–50.

The Statistical History of the United States from Colonial Times to the Present. Stamford, Conn.: Fairfield Publishers, 1965.

Stavro, Barry. "Ben Hill Griffin." *Florida Trend* 24 (June 1981): 52–55.

———. "How a New Crop of Managers Took Root at A. Duda & Sons." *Florida Trend* 25 (January 1982): 63–69.

Steinbeck, John. *Travels with Charley: In Search of America.* New York: Viking Press, 1962.

Steinberg, Ted. *Acts of God: The Unnatural History of Natural Disaster in America.* New York: Oxford University Press, 2000.

Stephenson, Bruce R. *Visions of Eden: Environmentalism, Urban Planning, and City Building in St. Petersburg, Florida, 1900–1995.* Columbus: Ohio University Press, 1997.

Sterngold, James. "Is This Tomorrow? Yesterday." *New York Times*, 10 May 1998.

Stokes, Sherwood L. "Waiting for the Last Train." *Florida Trend* 23 (July 1981): 104–5.

Stone, Robert. "Skating the Surf in Style." *Forum* 27 (Summer 2004): 29–30.

"Strangulation of the Cotton Candy Kings." *Florida Trend* 19 (June 1976): 54–57.

A Study of the Economic Impact of Project Apollo On Florida and Selected Counties. New Orleans: First Research Corporation, 1962.

Sullivan, Andrew. "Old Guard." *New Republic*, 9 October 2000, 6.

Sullivan, Mark. *Our Times: The United States, 1920–1925*. 6 vols. New York: Charles Scribner's Sons, 1935.

"Swamp Plan Mired in Dream." *USA Today*, 5 December 1997.

Swanson, Henry F. *Countdown for Agriculture*. Orlando: Designers Press, 1975.

Swarns, Rachel. "African American Becomes a Term for Debate." *New York Times*, 26 August 2004.

"Tacky Town." *Florida Trend* 24 (January 1981): 51–54.

Taubman, William. *Khruschev: The Man and His Era*. New York: W. W. Norton, 2003.

Taylor, Deems. *Walt Disney's Fantasia*. New York: Simon and Schuster, 1940.

Taylor, Robert A. "The Frogmen in Florida: U.S. Navy Combat Demolition Training in Fort Pierce, 1943–1946." *Florida Historical Quarterly* 75 (Winter 1997): 289–302.

Tebeau, Charlton W. *Florida's Last Frontier: The History of Collier County*. Coral Gables: University of Miami Press, 1957.

Tebeau, Charlton W., and William Marina. *A History of Florida*. 3rd ed. Coral Gables: University of Miami Press, 1999.

Thielen, Benedict. "St. Pete, Florida." *Holiday* 24 (November 1958): 79–82, 96.

Thirty Years of Lynching in the United States, 1889–1918. New York: NAACP, 1919.

Thomson, Bailey H. "Orlando's Martin Andersen: Power behind the Boom." *Florida Historical Quarterly* 79 (Spring 2001): 492–516.

The Travels of William Bartram, edited by Francis Harper. Athens, Ga.: University of Georgia Press, 1998.

"Tropicana—The Investor's Dream." *Florida Trend* 15 (November 1972): 28–34.

Tucker, Jeffrey. "It's Daytona Beach vs. the Fickle Tourist." *Florida Trend* 20 (June 1977): 46–55.

———. "Strangulation of the Cotton Candy Kings." *Florida Trend* 19 (June 1976): 54–57.

Vesperi, Maria D. *City of Green Benches: Growing Old in a New Downtown*. Ithaca, N.Y.: Cornell University Press, 1985.

Viele, John. *The Florida Keys: A History of the Pioneers*. Sarasota: Pineapple Press, 1996.

Villano, David. "The Paradise Paradox." *Florida Trend* 43 (February 2000): 80–83.

———. "SoBe Fashion Emergency." *Florida Trend* 45 (May 2002): 60–64.

———. "A Solid Foundation." *Florida Trend* 46 (December 2003): 78–80.

Vogel, Mike. "And Then There Was One." *Florida Trend* 43 (May 2000): 34.

———. "Made in Florida." *Florida Trend* 47 (September 2004): 44–50.

———. "No 1 (Or So They Say)." *Florida Trend* 46 (October 2003): 64–65.

Wagy, Tom. *Governor LeRoy Collins of Florida: Spokesman of the New South*. Tuscaloosa: University of Alabama Press, 1985.

Waitley, Douglas. *The Last Paradise: The Building of Marco Island*. Coconut Grove, Fla.: Pickering Press, 1993.

Walters, Mark Jerome. *A Shadow and a Song: The Struggle to Save an Endangered Species*. Post Mills, Vt.: Chelsea Green Publishing Co., 1992.

Ward, James Robertson. *Old Hickory's Town: An Illustrated History of Jacksonville*. Jacksonville: Florida Publishing Co., 1982.

Washam, Cynthia. "Material Man." *Palm Beach Life* 12 (September 1992): 30–32.

"Watch Out for Florida Condominiums!" *Duns* 101 (June 1973): 58, 61–62.

Waterbury, Jean Parker. *The Oldest City: St. Augustine, Saga of Survival.* St. Augustine: St. Augustine Historical Society, 1983.

Watson, William R., Jr., "Fidel Castro's Ybor City Underground." Master's thesis, University of South Florida, 1999.

Watts, Stephen. *The Magic Kingdom: Walt Disney and the American Way of Life.* Boston: Houghton Mifflin, 1997.

"The Way We Ate." *St. Petersburg Times*, 2 November 1989.

Weber, David J. *The Spanish Frontier in North America.* New Haven: Yale University Press, 1992.

Weeks, David. *Ringling: The Florida Years, 1911–1936.* Gainesville: University Press of Florida, 1993.

Wehr, Paul. *Like a Mustard Seed: The Slavia Settlement.* Chulota, Fl.: Mickler House, 1982.

Weidling, Philip, and August Burghard. *Checkered Sunshine: The Story of Fort Lauderdale, 1793–1955.* Gainesville: University of Florida Press, 1966.

West, Patsy. *The Enduring Seminoles: From Alligator Wrestling to Ecotourism.* Gainesville: University Press of Florida, 1998.

"What Would Peace Do to the Florida Economy?" *Florida Trend* 10 (March 1968): 12–14.

White, Jodi. "Too Many Burgers and Fries: Time for a Shakeout." *Florida Trend* 29 (February 1987): 75–78.

White, Otis. "The Best-Run Town in Florida." *Florida Trend* 37 (February 1995): 36–43.

———. "The Big Bang from Defense Blues." *Florida Trend* 24 (October 1981): 75–80.

———. "Frozen Out: Cold Weather and Imports Killed the Citrus King." *Florida Trend* 26 (September 1984): 79–83.

White, Rich. "On the Edge of Florida: Pensacola Does Its Own Thing." *Florida Trend* 19 (January 1977): 35–37.

Whitfield, Stephen. "Blood and Sand: The Jewish Community of South Florida." *American Jewish History* (1982): 73–96.

———. "Florida's Fudged Identity." *Florida Historical Quarterly* 71 (April 1993): 413–35.

"Who Owns and Controls Florida's Newspapers?" *Florida Trend* 15 (March 1973): 34–48.

Wilford, John Noble. "25 Years Later, Moon Race in Eclipse." *New York Times*, 17 July 1994.

Wilkinson, Alec. *Big Sugar: Seasons in the Cane Fields of Florida.* New York: Knopf, 1989.

Will, Lawrence. *Cracker History of Lake Okeechobee.* St. Petersburg: Great Outdoors, 1964.

"Will Sanibel Dreams Thwart Get-Rich Schemes?" *Audubon* 78 (March 1976): 114–17.

Willson, Elizabeth. "Anita Bryant, Where Are You Now?" *Florida Trend* 34 (June 1991): 29–32.

———. "The Coming Backlash." *Florida Trend* 31 (January 1989): 54–58.

———. "Finding Trident's Hidden Treasure." *Florida Trend* 29 (December 1986): 52–56.

———. "North Central Florida Is Brimming with Growth." *Florida Trend* 28 (Spring 1986): 97–100.

———. "Who's Sorry Now?" *Florida Trend* 32 (March 1990): 36–38.

Wolf, Peter. *Hot Towns: The Future of the Fastest Growing Communities in America.* New Brunswick, N.J.: Rutgers University Press, 1999.

Work, Deborah. *My Soul Is Rested: A History of Black Fort Lauderdale.* Norfolk: Donning Co., 2001.

Wynne, E. A. "Will the Young Support the Old?" *Society* 23 (September/October 1986): 40–47.

Yardley, Jonathan. "'Condominium': MacDonald's Dreadful Lemon Skyline." *Miami Herald, Tropic Magazine,* 6 March 1977.

Young, Nat. *The History of Surfing.* Tucson: Body Press, 1987.

Ziemba, Caroline Pomeroy. *Martin County: Our Heritage.* Stuart: Stuart Heritage Inc., 1997.

Zimny, Michael. "Main Street: On the Rebound in Florida." *Florida Heritage* 2 (Fall 1994): 19–21.

———. "Panhandle Surprise." *Florida Heritage* 2 (Winter 1994): 21–23.

Index

Page numbers in *italics* indicate photographs and tables.

Gary R. Mormino is Frank E. Duckwall Professor of Florida Studies at the University of South Florida, St. Petersburg.

Land of Sunshine, State of Dreams: A Social History of Modern Florida

Titles of Related Interest from the University Press of Florida

Cracker
The Cracker Culture in Florida History
Dana Ste. Claire

Florida: A Short History, revised edition
Michael Gannon

Florida's Megatrends
Critical Issues in Florida
David R. Colburn and Lance deHaven-Smith

Florida's Space Coast
The Impact of NASA on the Sunshine State
William Barnaby Faherty

From the Swamp to the Keys
A Paddle through Florida History
Johnny Molloy

Highway A1A
Florida at the Edge
Herb Hiller

Key West
History of an Island of Dreams
Maureen Ogle

Miami, U.S.A., expanded edition
Helen Muir

The New History of Florida
Michael Gannon

Paradise Lost?
The Environmental History of Florida
Jack E. Davis and Raymond Arsenault

Some Kind of Paradise
A Chronicle of Man and Land in Florida
Mark Derr

St. Petersburg and the Florida Dream, 1888-1950
Raymond Arsenault

For more information on these and other books, visit our website at www.upf.com.